David Frost – An Autobiography
Volume One:
From Congregations to Audiences

Sir David Frost is currently represented on television in Britain by 'Breakfast with Frost' (BBC Television), 'The Frost Programme' (Carlton) and 'Through the Keyhole' (Yorkshire Television), and in the United States by 'Talking with David Frost' on the PBS network, which is seen in the UK on Sky News.

Among the many world figures he has interviewed are the five most recent presidents of the United States. His 'Nixon Interviews' achieved 'the largest audience for a news interview in history' (*New York Times*).

David Frost has been awarded all the major television prizes – the Emmy Award (for 'The David Frost Show' – twice); the Royal Television Society Silver Medal and the Richard Dimbleby Award in the UK; and, internationally, the Golden Rose of Montreux. He was knighted by the Queen in the New Year's Honours List of January 1993.

He is married to the former Lady Carina Fitzalan Howard. They have three sons: Miles, Wilfred and George.

DAVID FROST

An Autobiography

PART ONE
From Congregations to Audiences

HarperCollins*Publishers*

HarperCollins*Publishers*
77–85 Fulham Palace Road,
Hammersmith, London W6 8JB

This paperback edition 1994
1 3 5 7 9 8 6 4 2

First published in Great Britain by
HarperCollins*Publishers* 1993

ISBN 0 00 638082 4

Set in Linotron Meridien
by Rowland Phototypesetting Ltd
Bury St Edmunds, Suffolk

Printed in Great Britain by
HarperCollinsManufacturing Glasgow

TO CARINA,

who is far too young to
remember much of what follows!

CONTENTS

	List of Illustrations	ix
	Preface	xiii
1	Early Days	3
2	The Road to TW3	19
3	'That Was The Week That Was'	51
4	First-Time Commuter	112
5	'The Frost Report'	161
6	'The Frost Programme'	188
7	1967	254
8	'The Next President'	328
9	On the Air with LWT	362
10	A New Show in New York	440
	Index	533

ILLUSTRATIONS

1939, Tenterden, with Jean and Margaret.
1948, aged nine, in the back garden at Gillingham.
July 1955. In the front garden of the Raunds manse with Father, Mother and Jean.
1961, at a Cambridge Union debate.
Graduation, 1961.
With Peter Cook and Peter Bellwood in a Footlights cabaret gig at a Cambridge pub.
The 1960 Footlights Review, 'Pop Goes Mrs Jessop'.
The first 'That Was The Week That Was'. *(BBC)*
Roy Kinnear as Baz in conversation with Jim and Nige in 'Jim's Inn' on the first TW3. *(BBC)*
On a day trip to Tangier with Jan.
Mounting a satirical assault on the Mother of Parliaments. *(Howard Grey/Camera Press)*
Accepting the prestigious Christine Keeler Chair of Applied Gymnosophy, 1963. *(Lewis Morley/National Portrait Gallery)*
On set in New York with Mike Nichols and Elaine May for 'A Degree of Frost'. *(Henry Grossman)*
With Paul McCartney for our interview on 'A Degree of Frost'. *(Hulton Deutsch)*
'I know my place'. Ronnie Corbett looking up at John Cleese and Ronnie Barker in one of John Law's classic 'Three Classes' sketches. *(BBC)*
'HP on everything,' 1964. *(Ron Cohen)*
The surprise party at Egerton Crescent to celebrate winning the Golden Rose of Montreux. *(Ben Jones/Rex)*
With the 'Frost Report team outside the BBC Television Centre. *(BBC)*
'Not a "workaholic". If, however, you were to ask me if I was a telephonaholic, I would have no defence at all.' *(Hulton Deutsch; Terence Spencer/Life/Katz;Terry O'Neill/Camera Press)*

Brainstorming for 'The Frost Programme'. *(Terence Spencer/Life/Katz)*
'The use of a studio audience not simply as a responsive backdrop, but as a key ingredient in the actual programme mix.' *(Terence Spencer/Life/Katz)*
Robert Morley on the first 'Frost Programme'. *(LWT)*
George Brown. 'The Frost Programme', February 1967. *(LWT)*
Seeking enlightenment from George Harrison and John Lennon. *(Production Design Company)*
Dr Savundra, 'The Frost Programme', February 1967. *(Production Design Company)*
Monday 12 June 1967. With Michael Peacock and Aidan Crawley twenty-four hours after hearing the good news about our bid for the London weekend franchise. *(Times Newspapers Ltd)*
'Bihar: the emergency feeding was saving millions of lives.' *(Oxfam)*
Charity cricket in Kent. *(Kentish Times)*
Saved! Charity football in Essex. *(Allan Ballard/Scope)*
Governor George Wallace. *(Group W)*
Senator Robert Kennedy. *(Group W)*
Senator Eugene McCarthy. *(Group W)*
Vice-President Hubert Humphrey. *(Group W)*
Ross McWhirter and Mr Albert Cornelius, the 'Strongest Head in the World'. 'Frost on Saturday, September 1968. *(LWT)*
Mick Jagger. 'Frost on Saturday', October 1968. *(LWT)*
Cardinal Heenan. 'Frost on Friday', December 1968. *(LWT)*
Muhammad Ali. 'Frost on Friday', December 1968.
Noël Coward. 'Frost on Saturday', December 1968. *(Group W)*
Enoch Powell. 'Frost on Friday', January 1969. *(LWT)*
HRH Prince Charles on the eve of his investiture as Prince of Wales, May 1969.
Rupert Murdoch. 'Frost on Friday', October 1969. *(LWT)*
Peter Ustinov. 'The David Frost Show', December 1969. *(BBC)*
The first television tour of Downing Street. Harold Wilson, July 1969. *(Group W/Crispian Woodgate)*

CARTOONS

pp. 72, 243 Emmwood (*Associated Newspapers/Solo*); p. 86 Aston (*Punch*); pp. 101, 250 Cummings (*Express Newspapers*); p. 149 Franklin (*Mirror Group Newspapers*); p. 173 Francis Minet (*Associated Newspapers*); p. 215 Jon (*Associated Newspapers/Solo*); p. 221 Jak (*Express Newspapers*); p. 245 Osbert Lancaster (*Express Newspapers*); p. 386 Mike Williams (*Punch*); p. 489 Cookson; p. 517 Jim Berry (*NEA*)

PREFACE

WHILE THIS BOOK IS INDEED, as its title indicates, the first part of my autobiography, it is also an autobiography of the Sixties. I hope, therefore, that I have managed to go easy on the extraneous personal detail, and where there was a choice between a Sixties anecdote and a personal anecdote with equal claims to inclusion, I have always tried to choose the former.

This book would not have been possible without the work of Ben Ramos, who not only organised all the research that was required, but focused my thoughts by the questions he asked, the points he raised and the gaps he spotted. Brainstorming with Sir Antony Jay, a one-man think-tank, has been as helpful and instructive in the Nineties as it was in the Sixties. Michael Shaw of Curtis Brown and Clive Irving have also made invaluable contributions.

At HarperCollins, Eddie Bell and my editor, Stuart Proffitt, have both been indispensable. To have their joint support is a formidable boost to the morale of any author, and certainly was to mine.

Back at my own offices I owe a long-term debt to Tricia Pombo, my secretary for fourteen years until her return to Florida earlier this year, and a more recent debt to Vanessa Bullen, who transferred her wizardry at Sunday television transcripts to book manuscripts on an as-needed basis.

I also want to place on record my thanks to all the writers quoted here, who were such an inspiration to work with, and to all the reporters and critics who provided a running commentary on our activities during the Sixties and whose role is repeated here. An interviewer is nothing without his interviewees, and I also owe a huge debt to all of them.

Most heartfelt of all is my gratitude to the friends and colleagues who people this book, and whose contributions to my life have, I fear, far outweighed mine to theirs.

DAVID FROST
London, 1993

FROM CONGREGATIONS TO AUDIENCES

ONE

Early Days

MINE WAS A HAPPY AND, I suppose, relatively sheltered childhood. Sheltered from Sunday newspapers and alcohol by my parents' principles; sheltered from meals in restaurants, overseas trips and aeroplanes by my parents' budget; and sheltered from the contemplation – or, very nearly, the awareness – of disturbing words like 'divorce' by the strength and constancy of my parents' love for each other.

I was born at 10.30 in the morning on 7 April 1939 in Tenterden, Kent – an event which Mussolini celebrated by marching into Albania a few hours later – and it was very much a case of P.S. David Frost. My two sisters, Jean and Margaret, were respectively sixteen and fourteen years older than me. I was very much an afterthought. Not even that – I was quite simply an accident. As my mother always told people, 'We'd sold the pram and everything . . .' It was probably not a good start to my relationship with my sisters that I was the only one of the three of us to be born with blue eyes and curly blond hair, but over the intervening fifty years we have managed to come to terms with that.

Since my father, the Reverend W.J. Paradine Frost, was a Methodist minister, and the Methodist ministry is a peripatetic one, we were soon on the move to Kempston in Bedfordshire. Whenever we revisited Tenterden people would always remark to me, 'Oh my, you've grown,' which was reassuring.

My earliest childhood memory is of Brinklow's, a small general store in Kempston. At approximately the age of two, I was sitting in a pushchair outside the said Brinklow's when I spotted a container of mustard in Mother's basket, which was hanging from the pushchair. I managed to get it open while Mother was inside the shop, and tried to swallow all the mustard down in one giant swig. The taste was horrendous, and to this day I have never been able to touch even a smidgen of mustard. (Thank God it wasn't caviar or *crême brulée* in that basket.)

As children we were little aware of the war. There was brief excitement about the possibility of an unexploded bomb having fallen in the allotments in the park at the end of our road, but the moment passed, and the war remained a somewhat distant rumble. I was not old enough to absorb either the consequences of defeat or the absolute necessity of victory.

At the age of four, my parents sent me to the Crescent and Froebel House School in Bedford. The teachers were passionate devotees of 'free discipline', and when a boy called Thorne would leap up while the teacher, Miss Cowan, was speaking and yell, 'Dick Barton, Special Agent!' Miss Cowan would continue blithely on, not wishing to damage his tender psyche with a reproof. At the age of five I made my dramatic debut, as the back legs of the dragon in *St George and the Dragon*.

It wasn't the Beacon Readers at the Froebel School that got me to read; it was wanting to know the football results and the latest cricket scores. In the garden at Kempston I would assemble imaginary cricket teams, and my luckless sisters, their boyfriends and my father would bowl to me. When I was out, I would retire to the woodshed and emerge as the next batsman. 'Who are you now?' the bowlers would ask wearily. As often as possible my reply would be either 'Bill Edrich' or 'Denis Compton'. I will never forget my first visit to Lord's, which my father somehow arranged. It was the glorious summer of 1947, when Edrich and Compton were clouting the South African bowlers to kingdom come. On the balmy June day that we went to the Test, they put on 370 for the third wicket. It was Bill Edrich who particularly captured my imagination, with four successive fours off the South African spin bowler V.I. Smith.

In 1947 my father's ministry moved to Gillingham, Kent, where – fortunately for me – I was sent to Barnsole Road School, which used the good old-fashioned technique of corporal punishment if you disobeyed badly enough or made too much of a racket. There would be no shouting 'Dick Barton, Special Agent!'

here, although he remained a wireless favourite with me every night, Monday to Friday at 6.45.

Sundays meant simply church. So much church that we had to have our Sunday lunch on Saturdays, because Mother was too busy on Sundays supporting Father. There was always a service to attend in the morning at 10.30 or 11, Sunday School in the afternoon, and another service in the evening at 6.30. It never occurred to me that there was any other way to spend Sunday.

My earliest memories of Sunday School are of missionaries, arriving from years devoted to dangerous and noble self-sacrifice, confronted with a rowdy group of small children, and falling back on descriptions of leprosy in order to hush the room. Leprosy, they would explain, meant that you couldn't tell the difference between hot and cold water. It began with a tiny speck, but it was the inability to differentiate between hot and cold water that meant the disease had really caught hold. We would rush home petrified and thrust our hands under the hottest water we could find, while searching for the tell-tale speck. Some years later, when my brother-in-law Andrew, who has had a long and distinguished career as a missionary doctor, was setting out on a tour of Britain to talk to children and adults, I said to him, remembering my own experience, 'Spare them the leprosy spiel. Please, spare them the leprosy spiel.' He was able to reassure me that he was planning nothing of the kind.

Some hymns bewildered us, as I am sure they did children everywhere. 'Hark, my Soul, it is the Lord', for instance, which had the baffling lines: 'Can a woman's tender care/Cease toward the child she bare.' None of us could work out what a child she-bear was doing in the middle of a hymn. 'Abide With Me' will always be the dentist's hymn to me because of the line, 'Change and decay in all around I see.'

My golden moment at Sunday School was entirely undeserved. One Sunday a visiting speaker took as her theme the letters 'SW', and told a story. 'Jesus Christ, the Saviour of the World (SW), met a Samaritan woman (SW) at Sychar's Well (SW). He gave her satisfying water (SW). And what, children, did she become? It's an SW . . .'

This seemed like a very silly game to me, so since she had just mentioned satisfying water, I suggested 'Satisfied woman,' in an attempt to be done with the whole thing. The preacher's eyes lit up. 'Sanctified woman! Sanctified woman! That is the most brilliant answer I have ever heard from a child in the whole of my life.' She was so wrong (SW), but it seemed a shame to let her down, so I happily accepted her plaudits and waited for the tea break.

My father was a marvellous pastor of his flock, always trying to hit on new ruses to get people's attention. One poster outside the church read: 'Who's missing from this CH—CH?' Underneath was written: 'UR' (not SW). My favourite was a poster he put up one September: 'Come to church next Sunday and avoid the Christmas rush.'

Life at home was always interesting. On one occasion an escaped convict knocked on the front door and stayed talking to Father in the front room for half an hour. This was a cause of great excitement, though the drama was not quite as great as we thought, since the man turned out not to be a local Crippen who had made a daring escape, but simply someone who had strolled out of an open prison.

Around that time my sister Jean and I had certain deep-seated cultural disputes. Jean was back home before going to China to join Andrew, and get married there. She had what seemed to me a bizarre taste for listening to broadcasts of Henry Wood's Promenade Concerts when 'Ignorance is Bliss' with Gladys Hay, Harold Berens and Avril Angers was on a different wavelength. It was a debate that was never satisfactorily resolved. In addition to Dick Barton and 'Ignorance is Bliss', radio in general, and the Light Programme in particular, had a great impact on me. 'Educating Archie' ('Oh, what a job for anyone'); Charlie Chester ('The Char-lee Chester Show'); Al Read ('I thought, "Right, monkey"'). Then there was 'Variety Bandbox' with guest stars like Robert Moreton and Frankie Howerd; 'Henry Hall's Guest Night' ('My name is Henry Hall, and tonight is my guest night'). Not to mention Wilfred Pickles' 'Have a Go'. I still have an aged clipping from the *Radio Times* which announces: 'This week "Have a Go" visits Crowndale Farm where Sir Francis

Drake was born with Mabel at the table and Harry Hudson at the piano.' And – joy of joys – there was of course 'The Goon Show'.

If you lived in a small town in England in the Forties and Fifties, the radio was really important. It was our only passport to the world of entertainment: comedy, quizzes, plays (and, indeed, in Jean's case, Promenade Concerts). In that sense, even as a child, broadcasting was an indispensable ingredient of my life, although of course I knew it only as 'the wireless'.

Looking back on it later, I could see that it was important for another reason too – as a unifying force. There was in all conscience not much sense of identity between people in different parts of the country outside London, and what there was stemmed in large measure from radio. Any sense of togetherness or community was more a function of radio than of, say, newspapers, because even the individual listener alone in a room knows that he or she is part of a shared experience.

It also taught me a valuable lesson for when I got to London later: never to forget that the viewers in the Kempstons, Gillinghams and further afield were as intrinsic a part of our audience as those close by in the metropolis, and often a good deal hungrier.

My boyhood absorption with soccer and cricket continued, and 3 June 1950, the day that Gillingham – The Gills – were re-elected to the Football League from the Southern League, was one of the happiest days of my young life. As was the day when we got lead pencils that were painted in different colours. For a few weeks writing with a pencil became positively luxurious (an early lesson perhaps in the power of packaging).

At the age of eleven I became an uncle when Jean and Andrew had their first child, Michael. Everybody at school thought I was frightfully clever, and I was enough of an innocent to believe that the birth had something to do with me, too – guiding the stork towards the gooseberry bush, or something.

I successfully navigated the 11-Plus and moved on to Gillingham Grammar School, which had the great distinction of having a Latin motto that nobody could explain. The motto was 'Valet Virtus Ancora', but whether it meant that virtue is a good anchor, or that an anchor is a good virtue, or something else altogether, nobody could tell us.

The four years I spent at Gillingham Grammar School were carefree years. The only bane of my life was physics problems, which I found tiresome and incomprehensible. When presented with a question like: 'What would the weight of a tin can be without the oxygen?' I neither knew nor cared. The ordeal was made the greater in that I could not turn up and simply say that I was unable to do my physics homework, as my being top, or near-top, in maths would have created something of a credibility gap. So I had to sit at home trying to solve idiotic problems like those of the aforementioned tin can.

We had no television in those days, and there were no Sunday newspapers in our house, though my parents turned a blind eye to my weekly strolls across the road to the Stewarts', where I was able to catch up with the football results from the *Sunday Pic.*, as well as the latest pronouncements of Jack Peart, 'The Loudest Voice in Sunday Soccer'.

At the age of fifteen I wrote my first humorous sketches. They were for 'The Grand Sunday School Scholars' and Teachers' Jubilee Concert', to celebrate the fiftieth anniversary of Byron Road Methodist Church. One was called 'In Matrimony', and another 'The Annual General Teachers' Meeting' – clearly the early stirrings of local satire!

It was at that time, in 1954, that Billy Graham made his first visit to Britain. Prior to his arrival he was usually depicted as an unwelcome hot gospeller in an electric blue suit. The general newspaper attitude was one of 'Go back where you came from. Sort out what's wrong in your own country first, Mr So-called Graham.' My father, a keen evangelical himself, had invited a member of the Billy Graham team to address a meeting in his own church in Gillingham, and Billy's number two, Dr Grady Wilson, came to Father's church for a very well-received service.

But it was the Youth Club's coach trip to Harringay Arena, where Graham was conducting services every night, that had the greatest impact on me. I was at a watershed in my schoolboy life: getting in with what my parents would have called 'bad company'; unsure about the existence of God, and about whether it mattered one way or the other anyway. Even though it differed little from my father's, Billy Graham's message made a real impression on me that night. I did not actually 'go forward', but I think that was probably because of self-consciousness as much as lack of conviction (together with a nagging fear that the bus home might not wait for me). I do not want to be melodramatic, to portray Harringay as a Damascus experience. But it was certainly a Harringay experience. I remained happy to be a mischief-maker when it looked like being fun, but somehow there was never any danger any more of my really going off the rails. And religion now engaged me intellectually in a way it had never done before.

My parents and I also attended the Wembley Stadium rally with which Billy Graham concluded his visit. The prayers that day were led by the Archbishop of Canterbury, who had been one of the main doubters when Graham first announced his Crusade. His was a 'conversion' as remarkable as any in the whole three months of the campaign.

In September 1954 Father's preaching took us to Raunds (pronounced 'Rahrnce' by the older locals), near Wellingborough in Northamptonshire. I was lucky enough to go to Wellingborough Grammar School, which was a first-class school. Because the 'A' stream at Wellingborough sat their O-Levels after four years rather than the usual five, I had to go straight into the Lower Sixth and take the more essential O-Levels in December. More important, I had to make the choice between science and the arts. My interest in the arts and in language was not yet fully awakened, and the fact that I made the right decision for me and chose the arts was mainly due to those wretched physics problems at Gillingham.

Grammar school education in those days was very much exam-oriented. A grammar school's success was measured in terms of the number of pupils who got into university and the professions. The unspoken aim was to turn out good employees rather than good employers, leaders or creators. This was in a sense a subsidiary role to that of the public schools, which educated the people who actually ran the country.

The grammar schools, and the whole post-1944 Education Act

system, gave opportunities to children of my generation that our predecessors never had. At the same time, the priorities of the system meant that anything over and above the preparation for examinations depended more than ever on individual teachers' calibre and enthusiasm. And that is where we were particularly blessed.

There was one teacher at Wellingborough who really ignited my interest in words, and the use of words. He was my English teacher, Mr Cooksey, and he managed to transmit his passion for the written word in a way that was irresistible. He was also concerned to see that we could discern the difference between an accurate report in a newspaper and a loaded one. He urged us to read two newspapers rather than one. During its courageous opposition to the Suez invasion, he urged us to make the *Observer* one of those two papers. He made us more aware of the outside world. He introduced us to John Osborne and explained the significance of Jimmy Porter.

Even at the time I think I sensed that I was fortunate to have Mr Cooksey as a teacher: it was only later that I realised that I was also very fortunate to have reached my late teens at the precise moment that the new order was beginning to make itself heard, and the old order was beginning its accelerated slide into desuetude.

In addition to English, my other Sixth Form subjects were Latin and history. When it came to writing history essays at home I was very grateful for my father's treasured set of encyclopedias, until one day when I was writing an essay on Gladstone. The encyclopedia's profile of the great man concluded with the words: 'W.E. Gladstone retired from politics in 1892 and is now living at Hawarden Castle near Chester.' It dawned on me that perhaps I was not receiving the full benefit of the latest scholarship on the subject. When in need of a rousing climax to a history essay, I used to take great joy in trying to dream up the most impressive-sounding and yet meaningless sentence that I could. I remember one that read: '1857' – 1857 being a year when nothing happened anywhere in Europe – ' witnessed the *Res Culmina* of dictatorial collectivism inevitable in all but an archeo-Benthamite society.' Words to live by.

There was plenty of opportunity at Wellingborough to indulge my taste for performing. I won the Public Reading Competition two years running, and appeared regularly in the school play, usually wearing a beard and meeting an untimely end early in the proceedings, as in the case of Banquo and Sir Roger Ackroyd.

Out of school hours, we were pretty busy too. The *Daily Express* at that time was running a passionate (and over the top) campaign against the Common Market. To the zealots among their readers they promised to send copies of their twenty-page colour brochure 'Your Future'. This was too good to miss; we all sent off for thirty or fifty copies of this masterpiece, which revealed among other things that the price of tea was higher in France than in England – scarcely surprising considering how popular tea was in Britain and how relatively unpopular in France. 'Your Future' was full of rousing material:

> Ask yourself: what good has Europe ever done you? . . . The Empire is the world's greatest market with 640 million customers. That is, four times as many customers as the European Common Market offers . . . If we link ourselves with Europe our living standards will shrink to theirs over a period of years . . . Consider Italy – and you will realise why the Italians are so keen on the plan . . . In Britain, two in every nine homes have their own fridge. But the Continental housewife is not so well off, is she? . . . The Empire is an expanding market. Europe can never replace the Empire.

The young Norman Tebbit was clearly already at work.

We managed to accumulate thousands of copies of 'Your Future' – and tried to work out how much we had cost the *Daily Express*. One of our best moments prior to the great bonfire which we staged at the back of the school was when one of our number from Rushden had a note included with his supply of fifty copies. It read: 'You will be encouraged to learn that your area of Northamptonshire is proving to be more receptive to the message of "Your Future" than any other part of the country.'

When Bill Haley fever was at its peak, we got some soapy water, put it in small bottles and sold it at the corner of the street in Wellingborough as 'Bill Haley's Bath Water'. Four or five people snapped up this bargain at threepence a time.

The local evening paper, the *Northamptonshire Evening Telegraph*, was based in Kettering, and I managed to infiltrate their columns under the name of J. Howard Grainger. J. Howard Grainger had a theory – which I hoped would provoke a response, preferably indignant – that all parks should be abolished. The *Evening Telegraph* headlined J. Howard's letter: 'Why Waste Space on Pleasure?' J. Howard sought 'the forcible acquisition of all such wasted land for building purposes'. He wanted to begin with a park in Wellingborough, the Swanspool, which was 'disfigured by a statue of a semi-naked woman in an extremely prominent position' (it was the most harmless half-draped statue of Euterpe that you could imagine).

All of this caused a gratifying little fuss in the columns of the *Evening Telegraph*. It was clearly time to choose another yet more public-curdling topic – and for safety's sake, a new *nom de plume*. The name was Lawrence E. Walgrave, and the campaign – that all dogs should be shot – seemed suitably provocative. The *Evening Telegraph*, rather helpfully, gave Mr Walgrave's letter the headline 'Dogs: Shoot or Gas Them All'.

Mr Walgrave wrote:

> How many readers have had their walks defiled – and I use that word advisedly – by the excrement of dogs, encouraged by their owners? These animals, so falsely called our four-legged 'friends', are a positive menace.
>
> My young daughter alone has been bitten five times during her short life, once having to spend a night in hospital. I would like to see all dogs shot or gassed. How can workers today press for more pay when many of them waste so much of their wages and food on these obnoxious vermin?
>
> Lawrence E. Walgrave
> Bedford Road
> Rushden

The replies took over an entire page of the *Evening Telegraph*. This was highly satisfactory. I had expected a considerable response – though what I had certainly not expected was that four of the first seven correspondents would be on Mr Walgrave's side!

'Anti-Fido' wrote: 'Mr Walgrave has probably gone a little too far in suggesting that all dogs should be shot or gassed. But I agree with him that too many are being kept in towns in this area . . .'

'A *little* too far'?

A Mr S. Lawrence put forward what he clearly felt was a statesman-like amendment: 'I agree with Mr Walgrave's idea that all dogs should be done away with, but not, I hope, by shooting as he suggests. Gas is a far more humanitarian way. Perhaps councils should set up a gassing chamber for this purpose, and thus avoid any danger of shooting. This compromise could then be acceptable to both parties. Those who wish for the disappearance of all dogs, and those who do not want them to suffer unnecessarily.'

As I re-read the correspondence now, I find myself racking my brains. I know I was Lawrence E. Walgrave – but could I have been Mr S. Lawrence as well?

I was trying to manage a difficult juggling act at the time. Wellingborough Grammar School was a rugby-playing school, but I disliked rugby intensely, and wanted to play soccer on Saturdays for the local team, Raunds Town. That meant I had to avoid getting selected for the school first or second fifteen, while at the same time doing my patriotic duty for my house, 'The Stags', in matches against other houses during the week. Luckily the system worked (or maybe I was just no good at rugby), and I was able to turn out for Raunds on Saturdays.

On one memorable – and, it must be said, somewhat atypical – occasion, I had eight shots at goal and scored eight goals. A Nottingham Forest scout was at the match and afterwards asked me to sign on with Forest. For a soccer-mad youngster like myself, it was a thrilling accolade, but I found it very easy to say, 'Thanks, but no thanks,' for two reasons. First and foremost, I had my heart set on going to Cambridge; and secondly, there was no particular financial incentive. Footballers in those days were paid about as badly as Methodist ministers. If, for instance, a great player like Stanley Matthews had ever tried to be paid a pound more than the maximum wage of £15 a week, he would have been suspended for life. This iniquitous and Victorian system was eventually breached by Jimmy Hill and the Players' Union in the early Sixties.

Years later, when Jimmy Tarbuck and I led out the two Lord's Taverners teams to play an eight-a-side game immediately before the 1987 FA Cup Final, I thought to myself that I had chosen a far safer way to get to Wembley – through television rather than through the sweat of my brow and Nottingham Forest. Particularly since, as I write this, I would have had to 'hang up my boots' more than two decades ago.

I was old enough by the end of 1956 to take my first paid job – as a part-time postman helping out with the Christmas mail. The salary was all of 1/6½*d* an hour, and there was no danger money, although I thought there should be. There was at least one house in every street where the postman would be greeted by a fearsome barking dog seemingly poised to sink his teeth into the first available piece of flesh. 'Don't worry about the dogs,' the head postman, Mr George Cheese, would say. 'You'll soon have them eating out of your hand.' I was more concerned about having them eating out of my leg, but I did my best. On the doorstep the lady of the house would be smiling indulgently and saying, 'It's all right. It's just his way of being friendly,' but the temptation was always to drop the letters and run. (Of course, it may just have been the canine community's revenge on Lawrence E. Walgrave.)

Mr Cheese was a real character. He took great pleasure in his job, particularly in reading any postcard messages he could lay his eyes on. ('You'll never guess what the Simpsons' girl has done. She went off to France without telling her parents. Now she's asking them to forgive her.') One day Mr Cheese came back to the sorting office full of righteous indignation. 'How dare he? How dare he?' he said. 'Just look at this.' We all looked at the offending postcard. An enterprising young man had begun his message home, 'Dear Mum, Dad and Mr Cheese.'

That was the winter that I went up to Gonville and Caius

College, Cambridge, to take the entrance exams to read English. I was not aware of ever having met anyone who had been to Oxford or Cambridge, and this was the first night I had spent away from my parents, but I was not daunted – only excited. In fact I had to take care not to get *too* excited as I gazed at King's College and walked along the Backs. I loved everything I saw, and yet I knew I must not get too fond of Cambridge yet – after all, I might not be coming back. A few weeks later I was able to let my feelings have full expression when I got the news that I had won a place at Caius for the Michaelmas Term of 1959, after National Service. As it turned out, it was later ruled that undergraduates would do their National Service after their time at university and not before, and then while I was at Cambridge National Service was abolished altogether. I have often wondered whether National Service would have changed the direction of my career. I would probably have plunged into the only area of army life that had any appeal for me – the soccer and the cricket – and who knows, I might have been tempted again into essaying a sporting career.

Caius College was only able to move my entrance forward by one year, to 1958, so I had a free year after I left school. I decided to fill it by spending a year as a temporary teacher in the area's secondary modern schools. After short spells at other schools, I actually had my own class to look after at Irthlingborough Secondary Modern School. Watching other teachers at work had convinced me that discipline, indeed authority, was very much in the mind of the teacher, and had to be conveyed to the pupils. Looked at on a purely numerical basis, I and my fellow teachers were outnumbered forty-eight to one by children, many of whom were as big as us. Still, I managed to bring off the disciplinary confidence trick, and once you know you have a class under control, it is possible to relax more than if you are in a continual battle for supremacy or even survival with your forty-eight pupils. Real communication can then take place.

I remember two particular aspects of that time at Irthlingborough. One was forming the school's first-ever athletics team. One of the best runners in the school turned out to be a boy who was considered, in a disciplinary and an academic sense, quite impossible. But finding something in life that he could do as well as or better than other people really transformed him as a pupil.

The other part of the experience I remember was persuading a couple of very bright pupils to go on to a technical school and then on to the grammar school. That particular year had been a good one for Northamptonshire brains, and there were children at the secondary modern school who ought really to have been at a grammar school. The only way they could catch up was if at the age of fifteen, after four years at the secondary modern school, they went to a tech for two years, took O-Levels, and then joined the sixth form in Wellingborough, a year older than the other pupils. Managing to persuade those two pupils to take that course and to reject the instant money that their former classmates would be earning from the boot and shoe factories was one of the most rewarding experiences of my life. The others went off to the local factories, and even if they got £5 a week on day one, they wouldn't be getting much more in real terms thirty years later. There was not just a lack of opportunity for those pupils, there were positive barriers to their progress. At the time this seemed to me to be an inequity in the English school system that was in urgent need of reform: but quite soon, as my perspectives widened, I started to see that it was symptomatic of a wider need for reform across society – of attitudes as much as structures.

In addition to teaching for that year, I also wrote, produced and appeared in a revue at the Methodist Youth Club in Raunds. This was a rather more ambitious affair than the concert in Gillingham – we actually had a printed programme, and the show 'ran' for all of two nights – though Busby Berkeley it was not.

The three main sketches were all parodies of radio or television programmes. The targets were 'Have a Go', 'Take Your Pick' and 'This is Your Life'. The victim in the 'This is Your Life' sketch was played by one of the youth club members, Kenneth Holmes, who fifteen years later was tracked down by an enterprising producer at Thames and asked to appear in the 'This is Your Life' they were planning to do for real about me.

During 1958 I also became a lay preacher on the local Methodist Circuit. I had started by reading the Lessons, but now I was doing the sermons as well. One of these sermons, I remember, was based on a line from 'Ol' Man River': 'I'm tired of livin', and scared of dyin'.' Having dealt with the condition of people who were tired of living and scared of dying, I then went on to people who were tired of dying and scared of living, taking 'dying' to mean the little deaths people suffer as days pass by, the rejection and killing off of their better instincts. 'Scared of living' was all about those people whose lives were unnecessarily blinkered, or whose growth was unnecessarily stunted, emotionally, intellectually or spiritually, either by their own mindset, or by factors beyond their control. If I were to preach from the same text today, my examples might be different, but the underlying message would scarcely have changed at all.

We still didn't have a television set, and on Saturday evenings I used to go across the road to Mr and Mrs O.D. Hall in order to watch Benny Hill or Dave King. On my father's salary of fifteen pounds a week or less, our holidays were never abroad. I can still recall the delight with which I first saw the sea at the age of eight at Llandudno. Several holidays during my teens took place at Methodist Guild holiday homes. These were presided over by my parents, thus giving us all two weeks' free holiday. The thought of flying in an aeroplane was totally unheard of – much less commuting to New York. When my sister Jean and Andrew came back from China and went to Nigeria, it all just seemed amazingly exotic to me.

Sex was never discussed at home. It was not forbidden in any way, it just didn't win a mention. In fact, the only remark I can ever remember my parents making to me on the subject of sex was once when I was home from Cambridge for the vacation, and told them about a girl called Marion who I was very keen on. As Mother was seeing me off she said, 'Have a wonderful term, dear. And remember it could ruin your career. Now you mustn't be late.' I doubt that anyone listening to that conversation would have realised that we had just talked about the dangers of getting a girl pregnant.

If, to a sophisticated eye today, mine looks like an austere childhood full of deprivations and denial, nothing could be further from the truth. It was an incredibly happy time. I will never understand how my mother managed to arrange for us to eat so plentifully on what I now know was such a small budget. Mother was the more outgoing, the more extrovert of my parents; Father had a quiet strength and wisdom. His preaching was that of a pastor caring for his flock, not a dogmatist seeking to merchandise his dogma. It was the same at home. Father never engaged in preachiness. He probably qualified as a puritan, but he was never puritanical. He believed in the hymn which went, 'The only gospel that some men will read is the gospel according to you.' He was probably unaware of C.P. Scott's dictum 'Never underestimate the public's intelligence; never overestimate their knowledge,' but his sermons always bore that imprint. It was impossible to talk to my father for any length of time without being conscious of the emphasis he placed on the innate worth of the individual. He would quote the old Turkish proverb: 'Even a stopped clock is right twice a day.' It was the most wondrously stable childhood that anybody could have.

At the same time, my desire to write revues, my passion for all the radio and television I could lay my eyes and ears on, indicated that I was ready for something fresh. I knew I wanted to be involved in writing and appearing and producing in some way – Cambridge would show me how. The university can rarely have had a more eager or willing freshman. I was ready for the wider world that beckoned to me from Cambridge, and I was determined to fill each day with as much activity as I could, and not to waste a moment on marginal activities such as lectures, essays and the like. Of which more anon . . .

TWO

The Road to TW3

THE FIRST NIGHT I SPENT at Gonville and Caius College, on Saturday 27 September 1958, was only the second night I had ever spent away from my parents. I had arrived at five that afternoon, driven by my father from Beccles, our new home in Suffolk, in his 1935 Singer, and by six I felt as if I had lived there for years.

'Oxford has a university, Cambridge is a university,' ran the old partisan rubric, and to a freshman life on the banks of the Cam certainly felt that way. Everything was so *old*. You felt surrounded by history, and the atmosphere of cloisters and spires gave a sense of the medieval. As for the building next door to us at Caius – King's College Chapel – well, it certainly bore very little resemblance to any chapel that I had ever clapped eyes on.

Although I carried on playing soccer for Caius long enough to win a six-a-side Cuppers' medal, the die was basically cast. Writing, producing and appearing had already become a greater priority than the sporting life. Thus the Societies Fair at the beginning of that Michaelmas Term could not have been better timed. The Fair was basically designed to keep as many undergraduate societies as possible in funds, luring unwary freshmen to pay annual subscriptions to a multitude of societies before they realised that they would never have the time to attend even a fraction of them. Two of the larger stalls were for *Granta*, the university's general arts magazine, and the Footlights, the revue and cabaret society which dated back to 1882. I remember thinking, 'God, I'd love to edit that, and I'd love to run that.'

The Footlights smoking concerts, called 'Smokers', presided over by Adrian Slade at the Oak Room of The Dorothy seemed almost impossibly grand. For a start, you needed a dinner jacket.

And then you had to pass an audition. I suppose the greatest thrill for me of that first term was to receive a note from The Footlights' secretary, David Monico, after the second of the term's two Smokers informing me that I had been elected a member of the Club. 'If you wish to take up your election,' the card went on, 'you should notify me to the effect and send the subscription of two guineas plus ten and sixpence election fee to the Junior Treasurer, David Howell (Kings), as soon as possible.' (Yes, *that* David Howell, the one who became a Cabinet Minister. Cambridge at that time was peopled by as many future Conservative Cabinet Ministers as embryonic satirists.)

That second Smoker was the first time that Peter Cook and I performed together. The occasion was a piece I had written dedicated to scarlet prose, called 'Novel Reactions', which Peter read and I attempted to play out: 'He turned away, clenching and unclenching his hands rapidly. He clenched them tight until his knuckles showed white. He bit his lips until the blood came.' Reluctant pause by D.F. '*Until the blood came.*' That sort of thing. After a first year at Pembroke in which Peter had not been involved in The Footlights, his comic genius was really beginning to flower. In that same Smoker he wrote and performed 'Astounding Facts' and 'Mr Boylett Speaks Again', Mr Boylett being an early manifestation of E.L. Wisty.

On Poppy Day, the Cambridge equivalent of Rag Week, I went over to the Pembroke festivities where Peter staged his own 'tribute' to Ingmar Bergman entitled 'The Seventh Deadly Seal', and sold 'miniature flagels' to his audience as souvenirs: each lucky purchaser received one safety match. Peter was already becoming a Cambridge cult figure based on an extraordinary ability to improvise a brilliant stream-of-consciousness monologue in even the most unpromising circumstances.

It was the Lent Term before I really got going with the writing. *Granta* and *Varsity*, the undergraduate newspaper, each accepted a piece, and as it turned out both were published on the same day. My *Granta* article was inspired by a World's Press News contest for the writer of the best published article 'showing the beneficial contributions made by Free Enterprise Trade and Industry to the National Life and Economy'. The ruthless fictional self-made millionaire about whom I wrote has a curiously Thatcherite ring about him:

> 'You will never equate life and justice,' he told me simply on one occasion. 'With the world as imperfect as it is, wealth will always be concentrated in a few hands. And what will happen to our freedom if anyone starts trying to make changes? Freedom is all too precious a gift for us to imagine it will cost us nothing. We must expect to suffer a little injustice and a little inequality, a little hardship and a little misery as the price of our freedom. For,' he warned, 'if we lose our freedom, we lose our soul.'

The piece for *Varsity* was a four-page pull-out called 'Non-Reader's Digest', which you could transform into a sixteen-page pull-out by tearing along assorted dotted lines if you had the patience. It was inspired by the style of all those generic *Reader's Digest* titles we had come to know and love: 'The Most Unforgivable Character I Have Ever Met', 'Your Pets Can Make You Rich' and 'New Towns For Old: The Miracle of Nagasaki'. Also on offer was a Non-Reader's Digest Condensed Bible which included 'The Four Gospels: The Story of One Man's Fight Against Communism. By the Men Who Knew Him Best'; 'Pontius Pilate: The Father of Modern Hygiene'; 'Obesity Can Kill: I Gained a Stone and Lost the Will to Live, A First Person Story by Goliath'; and 'Your Child May Be More Gifted Than You Think: The Story of Joseph and Mary'. (The Non-Reader's Digest produced a card which I cherished then – and cherish even more now – from one of Cambridge's artistic giants, Timothy Birdsall. Timothy also wrote for a Footlights Smoker a memorable little ditty entitled 'I Like it too, Mother, but Take Your Boots off First'.)

My first summer vacation from Cambridge was by no means as blissful as summer vacations are supposed to be. It started out fine, but by the end of July there was a real crisis. In the preliminary examinations, of which I'd scarcely been aware until the last moment, I had only achieved a 'special'. That is not a fail, but it is certainly not a pass either. When the college compared my performance in the prelims with my entrance examinations they were – to put it mildly – hopping mad. At the beginning of August I received a letter from my old headmaster, H.A. Wrenn. It read:

> Dear Frost,
> I have now had a full report from Caius, and frankly I am disgusted. We did everything we could for you here, and you repay the school by doing your best to queer the pitch for us at a college to which we normally send a number of boys. I chose Caius for you in order to improve your chances, and it now looks as though you will be the first boy of ours to be sent down from Oxford or Cambridge.
>
> I gather that there is a temporary reprieve. As it is not lack of brains which is your trouble, but lack of common sense, I hope that you will pull yourself out of the mess. If you don't, you will regret it for the rest of your life.

We were on holiday at my sister Margaret's home in Whitby, Yorkshire. My father was under treatment for a chronically inflamed coccyx, which made any form of travel almost unbearably painful, but the mere hint of a reprieve was enough. I will never forget the way he drove immediately to Cambridge to plead my cause. Every mile of the journey there and back was agony for him, the interview itself probably even more so. But a few days later the temporary reprieve became permanent. I knew already that I could never repay the debt that I owed my parents, but this was yet one more entry in that ledger.

When the poet and critic Donald Davie took over as my tutor the next term, I did spend a little more time on my studies. Dr Davie was always preaching the virtues of form in poetry, in an age when content was taking over. At one tutorial I asked him why he always reiterated this view to the exclusion of all others. 'Surely it's a bit like mixing two colours to make green,' I ventured. 'You need both blue and yellow. Content is not the whole truth.'

'No,' said Davie, 'but it's the half of the truth needed at the moment.'

In the heat of various controversies over the years, I have

often remembered Donald Davie's words, and thought that I should have spent more time attending his classes at Cambridge. But other priorities were increasingly taking over. At the beginning of my second year (and Peter Cook's third) The Footlights led directly to television. We were asked to produce a special edition of the Anglia series 'Town and Gown' which was normally hosted by Dr Glyn Daniel. It was Anglia's weekly acknowledgement of an important part of their region, namely Cambridge. Michael Jeans, the producer, wanted the post-Christmas edition to be a special send-up edition, and Peter and I wrote most of the show for him.

Chronicling the activities of their local lad, the *Beccles and Bungay Journal* gave a wondrously literal and po-faced report of what was planned:

> The programme will consist of a satire written by David and a friend, Peter Cook, who lives in Dorset and is the author of sketches for Pieces of Eight, a revue now running at the Apollo Theatre, London. Among the topics they have satirised are travel, letters from viewers, new discoveries, Birk, burning issues, men in the street, modern drama, provocative young writers, sports, slow motion films and worldwide link-ups. The show is to be introduced by Peter Cook who also appears as F. Nidgcombe. David has five roles – an explorer, Professor Nain, Lionel Sope, Goalie Finn and Ron Plindell. Peter Bellwood undertakes the three parts of an explorer, Colonel Mountebank Fowler and Larry Splutt. Peter Foster figures as interviewing Lionel Sope in Vienna and as Mr Saffron. The cast is completed by Tim Mathias in charge of an international telephone call and as Colonel Nagger and by Ray Mitchell as W. Rupp, P.L. Wedge and Arthur Frad.

What the luckless readers of the *Beccles and Bungay Journal* made of this list of unknown and indeed meaningless roles is not recorded. 'International Phone Call' was an Ed Murrow parody, a link-up of people allegedly in various distant countries, but who in fact appeared in front of transparently false travel posters.

'Burning Issue', introduced by the aforementioned Mr Şaffron, was 'a weekly feature in which topics of importance are brought up and passed over by a team of people. Are British missiles more effective than birds? Is there a life after birth? And who should receive priority on our buses – the cripples or the old folk? Or should they be allowed to fight it out for themselves? These are some of the issues we shall be avoiding this week.'

'Science: Fact or Fiction?' featured a marvellously hectoring performance by Peter Cook as the interviewer:

Peter: Cambridge Professor Arthur Nain has this week perfected what is believed by Nain and his mother to be the world's smallest cell, and I'm just going over to have a word with him about this pretty remarkable British achievement. Now Professor, this cell of yours – can I see it please? Can I see it?

Nain: Hardly.

Peter: Well, proof positive that this is indeed a very small cell. But what exactly are all these tubes and retorts, wax effigies of Professor Lovell and so on? Part of some great atomic project, is it?

Nain: No, that's where I percolate my coffee.

Peter: Well, coffee too has an important role to play in the modern world . . . and if the nations of the world were to spend more time dropping coffee on one another and less on hydrogen bombs, then the Dalai Lama might still be walking hand in hand with Princess Grace in a free Israel. I hope that you and men like you will continue to work behind locked doors for many years to come. Thank you on behalf of all those who, like me, like me. Goodnight.

'Tales from Afar' was inspired by the Armand and Michaela Denis genre of genteel travel programmes.

Peter Bellwood: We also managed to capture many wild animals of the greatest interest to all naturalists . . . In this soundproof box I'm holding close to the microphone we have a genuine specimen of the elusive Gumbaran cave mouse. I'm afraid I daren't open the box for fear the cool English climate might prove fatal to this sensitive creature.

DF: The Gumbaran cave mouse hibernates for eleven months of the year . . . and is actually asleep at the moment . . .

PB: In fact, for all we know, it may be dead . . .

DF: These creatures make faithful if somewhat undemonstrative pets.

That special edition of 'Town and Gown' was the first time I had ever ventured inside a television studio, and I loved the whole process immediately. The show itself was a television programme parodying other television programmes, but send-ups of that kind were very much a staple of what we were doing at the time. The joy was no longer to be doing it alone – rather to be finding others with a similar sense of humour, a similar inclination towards poking fun at whatever we happened to find ludicrous. Having had that experience of sharing and cross-pollination, it was easy to understand later why so many comedy writers in London chose to write in pairs.

At the same time we were starting to move further afield in our choice of subject matter. John Bird had produced the June 1959 Footlights Revue 'Last Laugh', and its political – even polemical – commitment had been a revelation to me. You could not be alive in an environment like that without wanting to broaden your own horizons.

On 13 January 1960 I was summoned to appear before the Magistrates Court 'at the hour of 10.30 in the forenoon' to answer to the following statement of offence: 'Causing a bicycle to be on a certain road during the hours of darkness without carrying thereon front and rear lights contrary to the Road Transport Lighting Act, 1957, Sections 1, 6 and 12.' Peter Cook gallantly volunteered to appear as my Defence Counsel with the classic legal tactic of alternative defence.

'My client was not in Cambridge on the day in question. Or, if he was in Cambridge, he does not possess a bicycle. Or, if he does possess a bicycle, it has got lights. Or, if it hasn't got lights . . .' Peter was then going to launch into a rousing peroration, getting somewhat carried away en route, and end by demanding the death penalty. Fortunately, wiser counsels prevailed and we were saved both from ourselves and from a citation for Contempt of Court, which, as we all know, is the one offence that the legal profession really cares about.

Peter and I also did a cabaret at the Corn Exchange the night after the Friar House, a local hostelry, had been found guilty in the same court of insanitary conditions – they had only one toilet. 'I have good news for you – the Friar House does now have two toilets,' Peter told a cheering audience. 'But they do the cooking in one of them . . .'

At the end of that Lent Term, I was made editor of *Granta*. Part of the credit for that should go to the publisher Anthony Blond, who had given me a rattling good interview for *Granta* which had been published in February 1960, a month before I was appointed. It caught the attention of Whitefriar in *Smith's Trade News*, who wrote:

> From Cambridge last week came a surprising piece on book publishing. That undergraduate-written and -edited sheet, *Granta*, carried the story of Anthony Blond, a very personal investigation by someone called David Frost.
>
> When I read it, I asked publisher Blond what he thought of it; did he really say these things? 'Well, I suppose I did. But you know what it's like – you don't always expect everything to be printed . . .' *Granta* couldn't have agreed less. Quizzed by the *Granta* reporter, Blond admitted, 'We don't have ideals, we have standards. And we're constantly capitulating on them. I am. I have to.' For why, says Blond, 'I publish books that I think are interesting. And that will sell. I have to publish a lot of stuff I'm not proud of.' Books about Jews did badly: 'I am a Jew myself,' Blond told *Granta*, 'but I'm very annoyed with the Jews. They just don't buy books. Particularly about Jews . . .
>
> Asked about *Eros*, an anthology of homo-erotic love poems he's readying for publication, Blond said, 'Yes, I think it's finished now, but I've lost the author again; I lost him once before, advertised for him in *The Times* and got him back. Now I've lost him again. I suppose I shall have

> to advertise for him again.' He thought he'd make a lot of money from the book when it was finished. 'There's always a market for a homosexual book. Not a large one, but a sure one.'

I have always admired Anthony Blond for not trying to disown any of his quotes in that piece. Indeed, writing to me on 22 February, after commenting on my 'embarrassingly good memory', he added, 'I think some of my burblings may have been influenced by Frascati, and there were two or three things which, while true, were a little indiscreet of both of us. Nevertheless, it was rare to see such honesty in print. I look forward to meeting you when you're editor of the *Guardian*.'

Alas, I was to disappoint him, but I did make a number of changes at *Granta*. I kept up the level of original short stories and poems, but cut back on the pure literary criticism, and gave more space to humour and to film, which was becoming a major preoccupation of my contemporaries. The French magazine *Cahiers du Cinema* was a cult item, and British cinema seemed, at last, to be responding to change. Charles Barr, my Associate Editor, began his article on *Saturday Night and Sunday Morning* by quoting the rebellious hero Arthur Seaton, played in the film by Albert Finney: 'I'd like to see anybody try to grind me down. That'd be the day . . . What I want is a good time. All the rest is propaganda.' The speech – and the film – struck a chord with younger audiences all over the country.

Charles himself was a worried man at the time. In praise of one of his *Cahiers du Cinema* heroes, the director Samuel Fuller, he had written a panegyric to the popular weekly *Picturegoer*, and signed it 'Charles Barr, Kings College, Cambridge'. In order to try and ensure that his somewhat highbrow letter was published, he had added: 'P.S. I think *Picturegoer* is the best fourpence-halfpenny worth money can buy.' Charles's letter was indeed published, albeit in a somewhat abbreviated form. It read, in full: 'Dear Sir, I think *Picturegoer* is the best fourpence-halfpenny worth money can buy. Charles Barr, Kings College, Cambridge.' However hard I tried to reassure him that his exalted role-models at *Cahiers du Cinema* had probably never even heard of *Picturegoer*, it was little solace to our doubting *cinéaste*.

I wanted to increase the size of the magazine, which we did – by doubling the advertising revenue and by means of special issues, one on 'Film', and another, a joint issue with *Oxford Opinion*, which featured a short story by a promising Oxford lad called Alan Coren.

I turned the editorial page over to a mythical character called P.L. Wedge, which allowed me to use every month the madder of the columnists' slogans from Fleet Street, e.g. 'The Loudest Voice in Sunday Soccer' (of course), 'who knows and tells in his unmistakable way'; 'Britain's Voice in the Sixties'; 'the cut-it-out-and-keep-it-page'; and 'For girls with marriage in mind'. My particular preoccupations in those days were issues like South Africa, the death penalty, and the standards of veracity in television and the press. This, for instance, was a comparison of two different approaches to a story that P.L. Wedge made in his second column:

> 'I don't for a minute question the propriety of the British Government's actions in Nyasaland,' said Mr Louw. 'They probably had very good reasons for shooting forty or fifty natives.' *News Chronicle*
>
> 'He was not questioning the propriety of the British Government's action. Probably they had very good reason for shooting in the maintenance of law and order.' *Daily Telegraph*

Another early *Granta* contained 'Dateline: Rome', Peter's and my homage to the way the press had been covering the Rome Olympics.

> On the red-shale track, it was another black, black day of gloom, despair and despondency for the British lads and lasses who ran their hearts into the ground in the sizzling cauldron that is Rome.
>
> *Rome? I prefer to call it the Muddle City of All Time.*

> 'If British girls are men, then I'm a Dutchman,' declared prominent Amsterdam businessman Hugo van der Huyst.

The spirit of Desmond Hackett was alive and well in Cambridge, and indeed lives on in the diaspora of Fleet Street to this day.

The first of the two Footlights Revues at the Arts Theatre, Cambridge, in which I took part, in June 1960, was called, somewhat oddly, 'Pop Goes Mrs Jessop'. Originally we had wanted to call it 'Coming Shortly', which was intended as a challenge to Mr Norman Higgins of the Arts Cinema, Cambridge. Mr Higgins always used to use the words 'Coming Shortly at the Arts Theatre' in a rather portentous style in his announcements, so we wanted to give him the creative challenge of having to say, 'Coming Shortly at the Arts Theatre, Coming Shortly.' This was, however, vetoed by the proctors, the university's own regulators, on grounds that had never even occurred to us – namely the title's sexual connotations. It was Peter's last May Week revue and he was in magnificent form, writing no fewer than sixteen of the twenty-nine numbers, as well as collaborating on others. My contributions included the return of the angry young playwright, Lionel Sope, who by now had produced four epic works: 'The Withered Spoon', 'The Bowels of the Earth', 'The Death of Water' and 'A Day of Air'.

The other character that I introduced to 'Pop Goes Mrs Jessop' was, somewhat ironically, Mr Art Prelman, the Head of Adulterated Rediffusion. Mr Prelman waxed eloquent about the wonders of ITV in general, and Adulterated Rediffusion's plans in particular:

> At ten o'clock we've got a programme of old films. Now we were going to call this programme 'Old Films', but we have just renamed it 'Outstanding Motion Pictures of Our Day and Era'.
>
> Now there have been those who have said that we at Adulteration House cater only for entertainment and not for serious music, talks, poems and that. While we admit we don't have them on *all* the while – I don't think we'd want them on *all* the while – but we certainly do not ignore

> them. And at 11.46 every night, we shall have 'Culture Dip' with Hughie Green as your compere, and until he takes the slip of paper out of the hat – provided by the British Hat Association – no one will know what sort of culture we're going to get tonight, not even the audience. They'll all be blindfolded, of course . . . You may get anyone from Mantovani to Nancy Spain.

During my last summer vacation, the relationship with Anglia Television reasserted itself. Michael Jeans was masterminding a new magazine programme called 'About Anglia', hosted by Dick Joice. He invited me to do some interviews for the programme, and I was delighted to accept. Most of them took place in the studio, but I will never forget one that took place on location. I was interviewing one of the new breed of scientific farmers who was pointing proudly to some new insecticide that was being sprayed onto his vegetables. 'Look at that spray,' he said. 'Do you realise it's never been used before but it will prove absolutely fatal to every bird, insect or animal who comes into contact with those vegetables.' 'That's wonderful,' I said, 'but if it's never been used before, isn't it possible that it might prove absolutely fatal to every human being who comes into contact with the vegetables?' The farmer looked amazed. 'We'll cross that bridge when we come to it,' he said.

The interviews went pretty well, but the relationship with Anglia Television suffered something of a hiccup when *Time and Tide* published an article of mine about Anglia called 'Profile of a Programme Company' on 24 September 1960. Michael Norman, then the Senior Controller, was said to be somewhat miffed. Quite what the cause for concern was, I was never quite sure. Was it the sentence: 'Ever since a commercial depicting a man successfully swallowing a glass of local beer was followed by a haggard professional boxer vomiting into a bucket in his corner, Anglia executives have scrutinised each day's advertisements with particular care'? I don't know. Perhaps it was a later paragraph: 'They have not hesitated to sign up the big names – Laurence Harvey, Richard Todd, Margaret Leighton, Louis Jourdan and Dawn Addams have all had leading roles to date. Soon afterwards, Miss Addams was in fact invited to dinner by one of Anglia's board. "I'm awfully sorry," she told him regretfully, "but I'm afraid I'm busy shooting at Elstree." "Oh," said the director. "Who owns the shooting at Elstree?"' Whatever it was, suffice to say that I was soon busy again at Cambridge, and Anglia Television were too busy to call! I moved on to do some modest freelancing for the BBC's East Anglian Television News, and received my first ever cheque from the BBC – for two pounds twelve shillings and sixpence.

The 5 November issue of *Granta* brought us all fireworks. In August, Tom Rayfield of Queen's College had written a powerful short story called 'Highwaymen 474', and in September I accepted it for publication in the November *Granta*, which happened to coincide with the fascination of the press in the effects and aftermath of the *Lady Chatterley* trial in October.

The story described the life of a road gang, and in particular that of the elderly foreman, Bill, who was stirred to recall his past by the arrival of a new apprentice. The emotions aroused in this previously inarticulate man become uncontrollable, and then the object of his fury, the Highway Superintendent, arrives on the scene. 'One syllable escaped the foreman, an incommunicable yell of rage as the ball of anger burst in his throat. Then the only way he could give vent to his emotions . . .' There followed what Fleet Street called 'that word', repeated more than once. I agreed with the author that the words were necessary on grounds of authenticity, and even more as an emotional climax to what had gone before.

Three days before publication, Foister and Jagg, the printers of *Granta*, decided that they needed a police go-ahead and an assurance of no action from the Proctors. However, despite the *Chatterley* verdict and a legal all-clear, the police advised the printers against using the word. The Proctors decided they must await public reaction before pronouncing their verdict. That had the same effect as a refusal. The printers felt they could not possibly risk a ban on all their printing for the university. So the four-letter word became a three-letter one – 'sod'! As I wrote to the *Cambridge Review*:

> The position is clouded with ambiguities. What is meant by 'decorum'? How does a publication give 'offence'? As *Varsity* enquired: 'Does a magazine "bring the University into disrepute" by printing details of an incident where the University has done something disreputable?' . . . Surely the most logical advance would be a statement that the Authorities will in future regard as libellous and obscene only what the law regards as libellous and obscene.

'That word' had come to Cambridge . . . and left again pretty smartly, though not before a bright young local reporter for the *Daily Mail* called Charles Wilson had managed to report the tale, and get his first lead story in the Charles Greville column.

I was by now secretary of The Footlights, and the launch of the new Clubroom in Falcon Yard off Petty Cury was a cause of celebration for all of us. It was The Footlights' first home of its own since 1939. Depending on which way the wind was blowing, the air was full not so much of sacred cows being roasted as of discarded fish fillets waiting for the dustmen, since the Clubroom was strategically placed above the local branch of MacFisheries. The Clubroom had two major assets – a permanent stage, and a permanent bar. Both had a formative role in our script sessions.

As the year wore on, *Granta*'s circulation doubled and The Footlights prepared for another revue. Leon Brittan took his turn as President of the Union. I had the opportunity of debating with a rising young star from London, one Bernard Levin, during Tony Firth's Presidential Debate. Trevor Nunn started building his reputation as a director. Ian McKellen and Derek Jacobi strode the boards. John Cleese, Graham Chapman, Tim Brooke-Taylor, Humphrey Barclay, Colin Renfrew and Ian McKellen were all elected to The Footlights; but for those of us in our third year, other, more prosaic considerations started to intrude.

The first was simple housekeeping: paying for our newly discovered tastes in restaurants and at Miller's Wine Parlour. Here I found the *Sunday Express* an invaluable aid. It was possible to read an item in *Varsity* on the Saturday – say, the result of a Girton–Newnham hockey match – and phone it through to

Fleet Street. The *Express* news desk would note it down politely, together with one's address. Needless to say they would then find the item to be totally unusable, but would send a note of apology together with a cheque for three glorious guineas the following week.

Then there was the sudden realisation that examinations were imminent, and that a degree was required. Mine was achieved by a judicious combination of purple hearts and a stop-press reading of essays generously loaned by Corin Redgrave, David Reid and Ian McKellen.

Finally there was the delicate matter of a job after Cambridge. For the BBC's annual drinks party to trawl for candidates for a General Traineeship – the previous year had produced John Tusa – they sent a strong team led by Kenneth Adam, Leonard Miall (then Head of Talks), Lionel Salter (Head of Music Productions), David Attenborough (in charge of BBC Expeditions – though this must have seemed a pretty tame one), and Eric Maschwitz (Head of Light Entertainment), author of the lyrics for *Goodnight Vienna* and already a legend for his famous exchange with a theatre manager in Lewisham: 'How's the show doing, my good man?' 'Well, Mr Maschwitz,' the good man had replied, 'I'd say *Goodnight Vienna* is doing about as well in Lewisham as *Goodnight Lewisham* would do in Vienna.'

The General Traineeship sounded a bit too much like a training programme for a life in management for my taste, so I decided not to apply. One of the biggest ITV companies announced that for the first time they were going to take on one man and one woman from the universities as one year trainees, and that attracted me much more. The job as described sounded a bit closer to the programming side and, since it was a first, I thought it would be less structured in advance, with a correspondingly greater chance to make your own way in the organisation once you got through the door. Sue Turner from Reading University (who went on to become Head of Children's Programmes at Thames) was the chosen woman, and I got the men's slot. The name of the ITV company was Associated-Rediffusion!

The second Footlights Revue in which I took part, in June

1961, was called 'I Thought I Saw it Move'. The title was a parting gift to The Footlights from Peter. The aforementioned Mr Boylett had been based on a real-life member of the staff at Radley with a lively interest in matters financial. On one occasion he had said to Peter, 'I was sitting watching a stone and I thought I saw it move. Do you think there's money in it?' The show was splendidly directed by David Reid, and John Wood (now John Fortune) was in brilliant form. *Broadsheet* commented, 'David Frost is an existentialist, of course.' I was not quite sure what that meant, but I liked the 'of course'.

We also had the benefit of the first bit of vintage John Cleese in a Footlights Revue: his 'Mine Disaster' piece, written with Alan Hutchison:

> This evening, prospects of a successful rescue are rapidly diminishing. Nevertheless, whilst any hope remains, operations are still being continued by floodlight. Betsy, the eight-year-old collie belonging to the Clarke family of Mabshurst in Cornwall, who's been trapped on a ledge 120 feet down a disused tin mine, is weakening despite quantities of brandy and rabbit lowered to her. Earlier, Mr Clarke and his son Ronald tragically fell to their death during the descent, when within barking distance of the dog. Julia, Mr Clarke's teenage daughter, then descended and actually reached the ledge, but fell to her death when bitten by Betsy. Mrs Clarke, thirty-nine, the one surviving member of the family, said before attempting the perilous descent this evening, 'Inhumane people will say this is madness, but I know it is what my husband would have wished.'

However, the supreme award for 'I Thought I Saw it Move' should go to Bill Drysdale. We had actually appointed a professional choreographer to try and whip us into shape for the musical numbers. Knackered after five nights of all-night revision for the tripos, and never accused, even by my best friends, of a vestige of a sense of rhythm, I must have provided Bill with what is euphemistically called a 'challenge', when the word that is really being sought is 'nightmare'.

It was an extraordinary plus to have been to Cambridge at that time. It had continued the process begun by Mr Cooksey: becoming more aware of the outside world. And indeed becoming increasingly addicted to the *Observer* into the bargain. It was almost an undergraduate bible of the time – a loyalty still grounded in its editorial independence over Suez, with Kenneth Tynan as its John the Baptist figure crying in an increasingly receptive wilderness.

Not that we all felt that we were entering a Brave New trouble-free, problem-free World. I wrote a piece for *The Caian* called 'Where Death Thy Sting?', allegedly from the pen of Dr Robert Fritsch, Head of the New World Laboratories, Cheshire, which was profoundly dubious about some of the 'advances' of science:

> Child euthanasia is in fact the first step in what may well turn out to be a long and arduous process of enlightenment. We may find that there are other lives which are equally unproductive, and there too science must lead the way towards a more humane and realistic approach. Of course we must respect human life – no one would dispute that – but it is our duty to see that that respect is not abused and so cheapened.
>
> At present we are still experimenting. There will be errors, mistakes and paroxysms for some, of course, but for most of us the march of progress will continue. Death will no longer be the prerogative of the dying . . .

It was not so much that we expected our generation to take over the world and suddenly turn it into paradise. It was just that we were being forced to the conclusion that we could scarcely make a worse job of things than the current crew. In the meantime, as we read – and indeed wrote – about everything from Supermac to Blue Streak and the Aldermaston marches, the frame of reference for our jokes was growing.

But how to explain the amount of talent that flowered in that place at that time, with others like Bill Oddie, David Hatch, Jonathan Lynn and Eric Idle all about to bloom? The number of Conservative Cabinet Ministers (and indeed *ex*-Cabinet Ministers) who were at Cambridge then seems to grow with every passing year. In addition to Leon Brittan and David Howell, there was Kenneth Clarke, Norman Fowler, John Gummer, Michael Howard, Norman Lamont, Ian Lang and John Nott. But why *then*? There can't be a single explanation for the profusion of embryonic figures of authority and embryonic mockers of authority. Perhaps there was an atmosphere that valued extra-curricular involvement as more important than narrow academic success, or that was particularly conducive to creative endeavour. Maybe talent does have a knock-on effect, inspiring and creating more talent. Or perhaps much of this talent was simply fortunate to have the Sixties as a receptive audience for its wares. I recently asked Peter Cook: 'How on earth can I explain the extraordinary cross-section of people who were up at Cambridge with us at one and the same time?' Peter leaned forward conspiratorially. 'Rationing,' he said sagely. 'Put it all down to rationing.'

My decision to make television my 'day job' had been part instinctive and part influenced by how much I had enjoyed my experiences at Anglia and with the BBC in Norwich. It has often been said that my generation was the first to have the opportunity to go direct from university into television, rather than via Fleet Street. Looking back, this clearly was true, but it was not something I was conscious of then. At the same time, I was determined to continue with the other strands that I had developed at Cambridge – writing and cabaret. There was also the little matter of an outstanding bill at Miller's Wine Parlour to consider . . .

In all of this I was greatly assisted by the fact that, by the time I arrived on my first day at Associated Rediffusion at the beginning of August, I had already taken on an agent. Richard Armitage of Noel Gay Artists had travelled down to see The Footlights Revue in June with his close friend and secretary, Diana Crawfurd. After the revue he wrote and asked me to come and see him. Richard seemed very grand to me – a powerful agent who had been to *Eton*! – but he was witty and enthusiastic. The decision was a relatively easy one, though I did have a choice. Donald Langdon of MCA, in the days before it had to divest itself of its agency activities, had approached me in Cambridge to join him, but he was already Peter's agent, and I thought that his loyalty would naturally be to Peter, *Beyond the Fringe* and his existing clients. He might be more interested in understudies than new directions. So, with no disrespect to Donald, it had to be Richard.

Not that the early days at Noel Gay went entirely smoothly. Richard first put me in the care of Jack Adams, a delightful old-time variety agent. After Jack had organised an audition for me at the Windmill Theatre, I began to feel that the new wave of satirical comedy might not be entirely for him. (I did actually go to the audition, but South Africa, the death penalty and Harold Macmillan's press conferences were not at the top of that theatre's agenda at the time.) Everyone was very polite, but afterwards Richard agreed that some new thinking was required. He promoted Diana to the rank of agent, and put more and more of my activities in her care. I could not have been luckier. Within the next few months she placed a short story of mine with *Strand* magazine and articles with *Queen* and the *Daily Mail*. But what about cabaret? We decided that our two prime targets were the Royal Court Theatre Club, run by Clement Freud, and the Blue Angel in Berkeley Street. The Royal Court Theatre Club came first. I will never forget arriving late for one rehearsal and explaining apologetically that there had been no tubes from Regent's Park to Sloane Square for more than half an hour. Immediately Clement looked intrigued. 'Do tell me,' he said, 'what is it like down there?' What elegance, I thought. Perhaps one day I would be able to make 'Let them eat cake' remarks like that!

It was, however, the Blue Angel that led to 'the big break'. The week's cabaret engagement there went well and was extended. It was not the most promising venue for satire – slipping there into a word which we all tried to use as little as possible. Since the London opening of *Beyond the Fringe* in May 1961, it was already becoming a buzz-word – a catch-all Fleet Street phrase for almost anything young or new. The Blue Angel was a sort of cross between the Windmill and the Royal Court Theatre Club. The club was full of Guards Officer types worrying if they had given *her* enough to drink, and then worrying if maybe they had perhaps had a little too much themselves. (This was in the days when seduction was still an art rather than a matter of course, though that was changing fast.) Hutch, a stalwart of the post-war London cabaret scene, or a Spanish group called Los Valdemosas would often top the bill, and Peter Maxwell, the piano playboy, was a regular favourite. His speciality was the single entendre: 'I've got you under my skin. One-skin, two-skin, three-skin, five-skin. Yes, I've got you under my skin . . .'

Soon reviews started appearing in *The Stage*: 'David Frost is the latest Cambridge University type (the town is full of 'em nowadays) to bring a refreshing wind of change to the cabaret business. I wonder what some of the old music hall comics would make of these newcomers with their satirical shafts at revered figures of the Establishment.' A not wildly photogenic study of yours truly followed with the caption, 'David Frost, satirical comedian, booked for one week at the Blue Angel, now retained for two months.' Noel Gay Artists took an ad to celebrate the fact.

One or other of these mentions caught the eye of Ned Sherrin, at the time one of the producers of the BBC's ground-breaking daily topical programme 'Tonight', who had been charged by his bosses, Donald Baverstock and Alasdair Milne, with developing a new late-night Saturday entertainment. He visited the Blue Angel, and what happened on his arrival constitutes one of our few disagreements over the years. Ned swears that I was about to be 'rested' that evening by the owner, Max Setty. Beatrice Braham, the booking agent, intervened, according to Ned, with the memorable words, 'Come on, Max, give the boy a chance.' My version is that I had certainly never been told that I was getting the night off – it would have been a first – and that Max Setty was far too budget-conscious a businessman to pay somebody and then not use him. But Ned and I have agreed to disagree on this story for thirty-one years, and no doubt we will continue to disagree on it for the next thirty-one, God willing.

It was the ad-lib Macmillan press conference that was of the most interest to Ned. 'Ask me about any subject,' I invited the audience. 'What about the Queen?' someone shouted. 'The Queen is not a subject,' I replied. Ned's memo to Donald Baverstock apparently commented: 'Ex Footlights (Cambridge) looks promising. Have seen him conducting press conference as cabaret turn at a nightclub where he was limited by the stupidity of the customers.'

Anyway, enough had happened for Ned to invite me to lunch the next day, 9 January 1962, at Lime Grove. I arrived late, limping from a soccer injury, drenched to the skin and wearing a quite hideous turquoise floral plastimac purchased from the shop on the corner for 2/11*d*. We went on to lunch at Bertorelli's on Shepherds Bush Green with another 'Tonight' producer, Tony Jay. Having the chance to talk to two of the producers of a programme that, since it had first gone on air in 1957, had captured my imagination as a new sort of television, was exciting enough. Talking to them about what role I might have in the new show was positively exhilarating. That first get-together was purely exploratory, but meetings like it continued regularly over the next few months.

Meanwhile, back at Television House, Kingsway, Sue Turner and I had been taken on a tour of Rediffusion. A bubbling character called Cyril Bennett – no Art Prelman, he – explained features programmes to us; someone called Guy Paine explained advertising. I was anxious to get on with some programmes, and escape from the traineeship as soon as possible. First of all I joined Neal Bramson in Presentation, who was about to launch a new five-minute preview of the weekend. It was the first programme I had worked on at Rediffusion, and was called, somewhat prophetically, 'London Weekend': 'Two sporting events that take place tomorrow: the British Karting Championship at Brands Hatch racing circuit, starting at two. And also on wheels – or more or less – the last stock car racing of the season at 7.45 at Harringay.'

Nothing very earth-shattering, but it was a start. After a spell on 'London Weekend' I joined 'This Week', the company's flagship current affairs programme, as a researcher. 'This Week' was produced by Cyril Bennett and Peter Morley, with the patrician figure of Brian Connell as the host and Desmond Wilcox as the ace reporter. Before the weekly transmissions at 9.15 every Thursday, to my admiration, nay amazement, Brian Connell used to stroll across from Television House to the Waldorf and partake of half a dozen oysters. What style, what glamour! (Even more than Clement Freud!)

At first my duties were purely confined to research. The most imaginative writing I got the chance to do was on my expenses. The year's traineeship carried a salary of £750, so the petty cash vouchers were vital. I still have copies of some of them: 'Taxi to Black Star, Keystone, Planet News to select photos, 8/6d.' Where Black Star, Keystone and Planet News were actually located, I couldn't tell you. Looking back at those life-giving vouchers, I am not too sure about the 'Taxi to Anglo-Chilean Society and return' for 9 shillings either, though I certainly did entertain a Mr George Martin of EMI for an LP records item that was never aired. That, in retrospect, was a bargain at £1 1*s*.6*d*.

Eventually I graduated to doing some off-camera interviews. One item on smoking among children even caught the eye of the respected *Daily Mail* television critic, Peter Black: '"This Week" has steadily improved since it was moved to its new day and time. Its interviews in particular have found increased vitality. Last night it had a terrific sequence of filmed interviews with young proletarian smokers (aged thirteen to fifteen) who testified to their addiction in language that lost none of its horror through being drawn, as far as one could judge, from a total vocabulary of about two hundred words.' However, this was all off-screen stuff. In the years that followed, and particularly when we worked so closely together, Cyril Bennett took great delight in reporting how he'd decided that I was 'totally unsuitable' to appear on the box. 'I was the man who wouldn't put Frost on the screen,' he would announce gleefully. I was impatient, however, and moved over to the Light Entertainment Department headed by Elkan Allan, and by April, glory be, I had a show to introduce.

There was a fifteen-minute gap in the schedules on Monday

9 April and Tuesday 10 April at 9.15 p.m., so, with the twist at its height as a dance craze, Elkan decided to produce a contest called 'Let's Twist to Win'. I was to supply some tongue-in-cheek linking, but the letter to the contestants was appropriately serious. They all had to sign a form stating: 'I agree to attend and to dance in the contest at my own risk and expense', followed by a traditional contest clause that I've never understood: 'I am not an employee or relation of any employee of any television programme company.' Quite how the second cousin of a lighting man at Scottish Television would exert undue influence on a panel of independent judges was never explained. And the judges *were* independent. They included the owner of the Saddle Room, Helene Cordet, and the model Caterine Milinaire, who brought with her two actors who were currently 'resting' between jobs, a Mr Michael Caine and a Mr Terence Stamp. 'We only came for the cucumber sandwiches,' Michael told me in hospitality.

The programme was an instant ratings success, and a follow-up was immediately planned by Elkan – 'Let's Twist in Paris'. 'Time is short,' he said. Would I mind going over in advance to select the most beautiful girls from the twist clubs of Paris for the show? *Would I mind?* Pausing only to learn the French for 'Would you like me to make you a star?' I headed for Paris.

Associated Rediffusion prepared another letter. 'Je ne suis ni employé(e) ni parent d'un(e) associaté de télévision en Grand Bretagne.'

Needless to say, I had no complaints about the assignment. When the programme was aired, a memo from an executive at Rediffusion pronounced that the commentary had been highly successful, but that perhaps the 'strain' of pre-producing the programme as well had been a bit much as David Frost was looking a little 'tired' on the broadcast!

By now Elkan and I were beginning to see the twist as our passport to world travel, and next we chose the Riviera. Our efforts were blessed by the *Sunday Times*:

> The neatest job of the week was AR's 'Let's Twist on the Riviera'. This was the third and best of a series of

> programmes using a tenuous twisting competition as a device to fill the screen with exciting rhythms and shapes. Wednesday's was entirely, and rightly, French and delivered a sensuous kick like a superb firework, leaving nothing after it but memory of pleasure and adrenalin in the bloodstream.
>
> David Frost introduced the programme well in quick throw-away sentences and quoted a stricture of Khrushchev's: 'The twist arouses the passions, inflames the lusts and is an enemy of the State.' Too right: who would bother to vote if they could achieve that mindless ecstasy?

Before the programme went out we had one problem. We had quoted someone who had said that the twist had turned everything upside down or back to front, and we decided to do the same with the credits. The Associated Rediffusion star could hardly be turned back to front, but their name could be. But was the designation 'A Noisuffider Detaicossa Production' *lèse majesté*? It took many internal memos before such unspeakable corporate irreverence was finally sanctioned.

Throughout the year Ned Sherrin and I had been keeping in touch, and I had also been keeping up with old friends from Cambridge by guest appearances at Peter Cook's new nightclub, The Establishment, in Greek Street, often on my way to a gig at the Blue Angel or the Royal Court Theatre Club. Sometimes back at Television House the next day, I would encounter astonishment – or indeed outright disapproval – that I had chosen to be out appearing in a nightclub until one o'clock in the morning. 'You can't do both,' someone would say. It was not a philosophy that appealed to me, either then or since. Provided that the will is there, there is almost no limit to how many different things you can do at the same time if the adrenalin is flowing. And there is no greater adrenalin than the laughter of an audience. I have never been surfing – my swimming ability, or lack of it, has always made the thought highly academic – but I imagine that riding the crest of a wave of laughter is the landlubber's equivalent.

John Bird and I had discovered a mutual love of football in

general, and Tottenham Hotspur in particular. At one Spurs–Fulham game, we had even been fortunate enough to discover a Desmond Hackett clone in the seat in front. When Johnny Haynes hit the post he turned to his companion and said, 'Oh, luckless Haynes.' With the forthcoming World Cup in mind, when Haynes performed a brilliant dribble, he commented, 'He *must* be on the boat for Chile.'

At the time I did not know that John had thought of the title 'That Was The Week That Was', or that he was Ned's first choice as the programme's link-man – a tribute to John's discretion, and indeed Ned's. By the time the pilot for TW3 was moving towards serious pre-production, John had opted for The Establishment's new venture in America and my role had been defined as joint link-man with Brian Redhead. The underlying philosophy of the programme was very much Donald Baverstock's. As he explained it in one memo: 'Late on Saturday night people are more aware of being persons and less of being citizens than at any other time of the week. It is, therefore, the best time to hang contemporary philosophy on the hook in the hall, to relieve the pressure of earnest concern and goodwill which presses down on us throughout the rest of the week. To abandon what Mary McCarthy calls "The Slow Drip of Cant".'

Putting the philosophy into practice was our responsibility.

As the pilot drew closer, and my involvement grew, TW3 was still highly experimental – not only in terms of its future in the eyes of the BBC hierarchy, but in our eyes too. The first pilot was going to be a real potpourri of items that looked as if they would work, and a few that even then looked as if they might not. After the pilot the make-or-break decisions would have to be made.

One point of style seemed to be settled – the casual let-it-all-hang-out style of Ned's camera work, with the cameras in shot. This was important for two reasons. It was right for the feel of the show, and it helped the performers. In a situation where you can see the back walls of the studio, the cameras and the sound boom, the performer can suggest the essence of Harold Macmillan two minutes after another quite different sketch, without having to be made up for twenty. Instinctively, with his already well-established West End theatrical background, Ned tended to gravitate towards the musical and artistic items, while I tended to concentrate on the political ones, and started to enlist my Cambridge – and, with admirable ecumenicalism, Oxford – contemporaries.

Back at Rediffusion, while Elkan pored over a map to decide where we next wanted to go with the twist, I was working on Rae Knight's film magazine 'Close Up'. I conducted interviews with Robert Preston about *The Music Man*, James Mason and Jane Fonda. On 10 July lunch with Jane Fonda (in London to promote *Tall Story*), her travelling companion Andreas Voutsinas – whom I envied considerably – and agent cost £3.19, with a tip of eleven shillings.

Five days later, the pilot of TW3 lasted two and a half hours, and by the end the audience of seventy or eighty were on the edge of their seats, not so much with excitement as with the sheer pressing inconvenience of having to sit for so long waiting for an interval with which none of us had thought to provide them.

The opening song was sung by Millicent Martin, who then leaped on to a plane to Spain and was probably basking in the Andalusian moonlight before our audience were released from the studio. The show began with a topical piece on the main news of the week, a calypso from Lance Percival and some longish looks at the press and the political issues of the week.

We had spent Monday to Thursday wondering what they would be, and then on Friday the Prime Minister – God bless him – announced the biggest-yet Government reshuffle. Little wonder that our patron saint became Selwyn Lloyd, the sacked Chancellor. 'Selwyn Lloyd is a man after my own job,' we quoted Macmillan as saying. We attempted various forms of conversation. Peter Bull came along and answered splendidly a set of those lunatic stock-interview-questions-for-actors: Does the make-up hurt your face? How do you know when to speak? What job do you do during the day? and, When you kiss in a play or a film, is it the real thing? ('If it's a girl, yes; if it's a man, no.') We also tried a lengthier conversation piece with George Melly, Seth Holt and Harold Lang on the rather unpromising theme of human unhappiness. Perhaps not surprisingly, it didn't work. There were items on the Telstar satellite station, the neo-Fascist Colin Jordan, the *Daily Express* and abortion. However, as it turned out, the most important item was the Bernard Levin confrontation. His first adversaries were an invited group of Conservative ladies who rose splendidly to the occasion.

First Lady: Mr Macmillan has always satisfied *me* . . .
Second Lady: It seems to me, Mr Levin, that anyone is rational if they agree with you . . .
Levin: That's one definition of rationality certainly . . .
First Lady: Mr Macmillan has always satisfied us . . .
Third Lady: Mr Levin, how would you like your daughter to be walking along a dark street at night . . . and nothing done about it?

By the end of fifteen minutes, the ladies were saying anything that sounded even vaguely like a reply, so that when Bernard concluded, 'Because of the letters you write to them, the Conservative Party's Central Office has bigger waste-paper baskets than anywhere else in the world,' one of them leapt authoritatively to her feet shouting, 'And they need them, Mr Levin! And they need them!'

The confrontation made splendid entertainment, but the reason for its importance was political. When the formidable Grace Wyndham Goldie, the Head of Talks Television, watched the pilot with Donald Baverstock and Alasdair Milne, she was unenthusiastic, to put it mildly. Despite Donald's and Alasdair's confidence – or at least intuition – that there was 'something there', the project might have proceeded no further. However, the Conservative ladies complained to Central Office, who then complained to the BBC that they had 'been made a laughing stock of'. (In fact, of course, they had needed no outside assistance.) It was decided that Kenneth Adam, as Director of Television, and Joanna Spicer, the Head of Programme Planning, must view the offending article. They found the complaints nonsensical, but decided that the project was indeed worth proceeding with, and another pilot was duly scheduled for 29 September –

all thanks to the Conservative ladies. Ned, of course, was to be the producer and I was to be the host.

However, almost immediately I had another problem. When Associated Rediffusion heard about the BBC pilot, they offered me a two- or three-year contract to stay, which soon became a four-year contract. The sums were, in my terms, astronomical. £3000 was the figure they reached for the first year, £4000 for the second, £5000 for the third and £6000 for the fourth. A guaranteed sum of £18,000 plus performance fees for all the programmes in which I appeared. They even offered me a satire programme at Rediffusion – later to be called 'What the Public Wants' – into the bargain. I telephoned Ned and explained my predicament.

The BBC acted quickly and he was able to come back with an offer, authorised by Donald Baverstock, of £50 per week for thirteen weeks of preparing the programme, plus £135 per week for hosting it if it got on the air. At that stage it was a big 'if'. So the guarantee was £18,000 versus £650. I had always believed in the slogan 'Never resist a challenge', and now was the chance to prove to myself whether I was prepared to practise what I preached. I was, because I was convinced that TW3 had a future, albeit currently undefined. The conviction was ultimately an instinctive one. TW3 was the sort of show I would have wanted to watch. Later in the Sixties the new pre-Murdoch *Sun*, a remodelled *Daily Herald*, was to describe itself as 'Born of the age we live in'. As it turned out, it wasn't, but TW3 certainly was.

Once I had made my decision, the meeting with John McMillan, Rediffusion's Controller of Programmes, was not an easy one. John said that Rediffusion had increased their offer as far as they possibly could. What was my response? I said I was deeply grateful for their generous proposals, but had decided that I believed in TW3 and that consequently I would like to leave when my year's contract expired, 'two weeks from tomorrow'. 'Is that your final word?' asked McMillan. 'Yes, I'm afraid it is.' 'In that case, you're fired as from *next* Friday.' 'In that case, I resign *tomorrow*.'

They were the last words we exchanged on the subject.

Indeed, when, two or three years later, Elkan Allan took me to lunch to discuss a proposal for returning to Rediffusion, that particular item in his expenses was specifically disallowed. (If he'd put 'Taxi to Black Star, Keystone and Planet News', he might have got away with it.)

From then on, I was full-time at Lime Grove, sharing an office with Ned as we worked on the second pilot. By now we had become *de facto* joint editors of the programme, and we spent much of the time between July and the end of September lunching writers – usually at the Café Royal – and trying to boil down the ingredients that we thought had worked on 15 July. On those taxi journeys to the Café Royal, I never ceased to marvel at Ned's Churchillian ability with catnaps. We would read two or three sketches together, and then when we had finished Ned would say, 'I think I'll take a nap,' and doze off immediately, awaking again with almost psychic intuitiveness when we were about fifty yards from our destination.

That period was really the making of TW3. By September we thought we knew what the shape of the show would be. Although Donald had talked of trying to 'recreate the qualities of witty, informed, irreverent conversation late at night', conversation was, ironically, one of the casualties. We had discovered in the first pilot that the literal transfer of late-night conversation to television in a format as fast-paced as TW3 did not really work. To recreate it you had to dramatise it either by fast-paced dialogue with intercutting, or by sketches and music.

We did not come to TW3 with a specific agenda or political programme. We were not further examples of what the newspapers called 'the Angry Young Men'. We were the Exasperated Young Men – exasperated by Britain's recurring failures, by hypocrisy and complacency and by the shabbiness of its politics. When asked, I said in one interview that we were 'against everything that makes life less than it can be for people'. That category alone meant that there was no danger of running short of material.

TW3 began from the then revolutionary starting point that public men were in fact the same as private men – though with more power to cause havoc – and should be measured by the same criteria, without the traditional *cordon sanitaire* of sanctimony that still surrounded them. We kept coming back to the way that audiences in Britain were underestimated by so much of television, and by so many of the newspapers and advertisers. These themes were to recur again and again in TW3.

There were two immediate comparisons between life at the BBC and at Rediffusion. The sexual temperature at The Club at Lime Grove did not match that of the Rediffusion Club at Television House in Kingsway – it was positively tame by comparison. However, the inspirational quality of Donald Baverstock was a revelation. I was already interested in television, I was already excited by television, but I had never been inspired by the potential of television in the way that I was by Donald. He truly was the original author of 'the mission to explain'. After a day of labouring on the as-yet-unseen Saturday night epic, Ned and I would often join Ned's old colleagues in the 'Tonight' hospitality room. Though by now promoted to Assistant Controller, Donald would be there as often as he could. If seventeen people all said, 'That was a great item,' but the most junior person in the group had added, 'I didn't quite understand the point about . . .' Donald would just block out the rest of the room and focus on that one person to find out not only how the other seventeen people could have continued to enjoy the item, but how that person could have understood and appreciated it too.

As 29 September approached, Ned and I began to feel cautiously that we might have the format licked. The cast was almost all in place. Roy Kinnear and Kenneth Cope had joined the company – no Timothy Birdsall as yet – and the Café Royal luncheons were paying off in terms of writers. On the twenty-ninth the opening song, with lyrics by Ned and Caryl Brahms, and music by Ron Grainer, worked a treat. Christopher Booker and I followed it with a couple of topicals about Hugh Gaitskell and the new Liberal defector to Labour, Colonel Patrick Lort-Phillips. Then a lead into a sketch: 'The attention of the world was focused on the week's two fights – that of Floyd Patterson and Sonny Liston, and that of James Meredith to get into the all-white University of Mississippi. With Patterson's performance so weak and Meredith's opposition so strong, in the return fights Patterson will fight Meredith and ex-convict Liston, always eager to improve himself, will actually be hammering his way into the mighty portals of Mississippi University.' Lance Percival and I then did a piece about the Liston–Patterson fight.

There was an item on the Common Market and a mock tribute to Norrie Paramor, for ten years Artists and Repertoire Manager of Columbia Records, which had been inspired by a comment made to me some months earlier by George Martin. Then an item on the latest controversy about Berlin. 'What statesman,' I asked, 'could ever afford to say what he thinks about Berlin?' Then the statesmen's quotes and what they really meant followed: 'Adenauer: Germany must be reunited.' Which meant, 'Germany was never united. But if I say this I lose the next election and the next and the next maybe, and as an eighty-nine-year-old Prime Minister I must think of my political future.'

Bernard Levin then took on a group of lawyers, preceded by a series of quotes like Baxter Holyday's 'A man may as well open an oyster without a knife as a lawyer's mouth without a fee.' The lawyers, it has to be said, provided somewhat doughtier opposition than the Conservative ladies. David Kernan's song 'Teenage Nun' was followed by a Henry Brooke sketch. Steven Vinaver provided a brilliant 'jazzer' for Millicent Martin. We also experimented with a debate between Norman St John Stevas and Colin Renfrew on the motion 'That this studio considers that Madame Dubarry was more useful than Mrs Pankhurst.' Both of them did well but somehow the formalised quality of a debate did not seem to fit.

We then had some fun with a parody of 'Jim's Inn', the leading exemplar of one of television's more bewildering gifts to the world, the advertising magazine, in which advertisers paid for one or two minutes of allegedly real dialogue devoted to their product, allegedly without the seam showing. One of Lance's calypsos rounded off the evening. Ned and I made a verbal note that the Norrie Paramor item, the Steven Vinaver 'jazzer' and 'Jim's Inn' were worthy of retention for the series, if there was one, and we went home reasonably content with the proceedings.

All was, however, not yet plain sailing. After the pilot, as far as Ned and I could tell, an attack of schizophrenia seemed to descend on the BBC. Donald and Alasdair Milne gave us the green light, but Stuart Hood, who was Donald's boss and certainly ought to have known what was going on, contented himself with quotes like, '*If* the show does go ahead, of one thing you can be sure, it will *not* have a ridiculous title like "That Was The Week That Was".' Angus Wilson in *Queen* later reported a similar sense of bewilderment. 'I had supposed from vague press releases that TW3 was to appear three weeks earlier, but when I rang Broadcasting House Information, I was told that nothing was known of any such project.'

Eventually Ned and I got our advance copies of the *Radio Times* for the week beginning Saturday 24 November, and we finally knew for sure that we had a show and that it *was* going to be called 'That Was The Week That Was'.

THREE

'That Was The Week That Was'

HARDLY SURPRISINGLY, I woke early on the morning of Saturday the twenty-fourth; by then I had moved from a flat in Regent's Park to one in Churton Place, Pimlico. I set off for the BBC and arrived early. That was probably more of a surprise, since punctuality was not exactly my strong suit in those days.

Ned and I went over the script, and camera rehearsals in Studio 2 began at noon. In the afternoon we pre-taped the Norrie Paramor item, because it was fairly complicated, and then went back to rehearsing. We had a dinner break during band call between seven and eight and a run-through afterwards. There was no time to get nervous, even if we wanted to. The audience arrived at 10.15 and we were on the air at 10.50.

After the first chorus of 'That Was The Week That Was' from Millie, the first words I uttered on TW3 were:

There's a one-eyed yellow idol to the north of Kathmandu,
With a little Chinese rifle in 'is 'and.

Scarcely the stuff of which revolutions are made, but in its reference to current Chinese designs on India it was topical and got a respectable laugh.

Christopher Booker's and my first political opener was a parody of the week's by-election coverage. William Rushton was making the best of it for the Conservatives in the studio:

DF: Well, Mr Rushton, you must be extremely disappointed with this result.

WR: Far from it. Everyone expected us to lose this seat. I think the only people who will be disappointed by this result are the Labour Party. A majority of seven hundred . . . I mean, really, what's seven hundred people in a population of some fifty million?

Lance Percival reported from the constituency: 'If the trend in North Suffolk is followed in the rest of the country then the result here may be a guide to the way the trend is going. But if the result here is not going to be repeated in other constituencies, then it's no use, no use at all, taking it as any sort of guide.'

Roy Kinnear followed with a Party Political Broadcast on behalf of the Army:

> Our Shadow Secretary for Commonwealth Affairs is Provost-Sergeant McMichael, J., MACM, who has done extensive tours of the Commonwealth and is in fact married to a wog bint. So what Jock doesn't know about these hot countries is not worth knowing: Get your knees brown, Lord Home.
>
> I would like to introduce you tonight to our European expert, Fusilier George Woolerton . . . He outlines our Common Market policy quite simply and succinctly: You cannot trust the Krautheads. Also, if the price of a bottle of lager at Helga's Bar, Windelstrasse, is indicative of Common Market trading, you can stuff it . . . As my late-meal chitty expires very shortly indeed, I have no time to go into detail about our other policies as, for example, get the nancy boys out of security jobs, smarten up the young troops, and stop the guards working as servants in lords' houses, why should they? It's a man's life in the British Government today: I thank you.

Next followed the tribute to Norrie Paramor. It was tough, in a way the clearest declaration in the whole of the show that TW3 intended to be different. As Britain's most powerful recording manager, Paramor had the power to decide what song went on the 'B' side of potential hit records.

> It's very easy to pick holes in Norrie. All too easy – for example, Helen Shapiro had had four enormous hits –

several with a Paramor song on the 'B' side of the record. Then genial Norrie promoted himself to the 'A' side and wrote 'Let's Talk About Love' and Helen failed to get into the Top Ten for the only time in her career.

LPs too are in Norrie's power. With his LP 'The Wonderful Waltz', he had quite a problem. Where amongst twelve of the most famous waltzes of all time could the author Paramor appear? On the sleeve we read, 'The opening track of Irving Berlin's "Always" and the last waltz on the second side, Romberg's "Will You Remember", are both separated by a charming melodic fragment of Norrie's own composition.'

We played it: 'I think that you'll agree that you certainly don't get melody much more fragmented than that.' We played some more examples and I added: 'It's simple, isn't it? Something we can all respond to, automatically. Very Russian in a sense. Many of our best English composers have been influenced by Russians, and Norrie's no exception. Edward Elgar by Tchaikovsky, Benjamin Britten by Stravinsky. Norrie, too – by Pavlov.'

Bernard Levin's victims on the first show were a group of PR men. David Kernan and Millicent Martin sang 'Sixty-One Ways'.

The Empire Games gave us a chance to update the Desmond Hackett piece that Peter Cook and I had written at Cambridge. There was another echo of Cambridge later when Timothy Birdsall, who had joined us just the day before, made his welcome arrival. By now a rising cartoonist in London, he had appeared in our office on the Friday with some sketches about Identikit. As we talked, the sketches grew into a dialogue which we scripted together on the spot. This became our regular way of working.

Michael Gwynn led us through an anthology of 'Abroad'; Millicent Martin sang the 'jazzer' – Steven Vinaver's new words to a Wardell Grey jazz instrumental, 'Take a Little Time'. Willie Rushton and Kenneth Cope had a conversation piece about the bomb, and then there was just time for 'Jim's Inn' with its unique brand of 'natural' advertising magazine dialogue.

Nige: Excuse me noticing it, but I didn't know you could run to a tie like that, Baz. It must have set you back all of fifteen guineas.

Baz: No, I'm rather pleased to see your eye lighting on this my tie because, in fact, it wasn't altogether as costly as that.

Nige: How much was it?

Baz: Three and sixpence, as a matter of fact. I got it at Arthur Purvis, Marine Parade, Gorleston. It's a dacron tetralax masturpene in the new non-iron histamine luxipac.

Jim: Oh my, oh my.

Nige: Suddenly my eyes light upon your trousers . . .

And so on.

I ended the show with a reference to Dr Adenauer turning to one of his critics and saying, 'Young man, I'm old enough to be your Führer,' and then it was into the titles. They rolled across the bottom of the screen, with a casual studio shot above them, ending with the words 'That Was BBC TV That Was'. Well, not quite ending with that. There was still one more vital fact to convey. In those early days, it too rolled across the bottom of the screen. 'Of the 3,500 tennis balls exported by the United Kingdom to Austria Hungary in 1913, ten were unsuitable for tournament play.' And that was it.

We went off to The Casserole in the Kings Road to celebrate. Quite what, we didn't know, except that it was over. We had sent out the best show we could and we did not yet know what would be coming back.

When Ned and I met for coffee the following morning in the Kenya Coffee House, again in the Kings Road, we still did not know. Then a moment of pure joy. I found a review by Pat Williams on the back page of the *Sunday Telegraph*. It was headed: 'Late Night TV Satire Hits Target'. It said everything that, on behalf of everyone involved, we could have prayed for.

> Without reservations 'That Was The Week That Was', the BBC's first late-night satirical show, is brilliant. It based itself securely on the week's events, repeating and expanding on its idiocies, invectives and near-libels also . . .

> Bernard Levin in unarmed combat took on and wonderfully insulted a crew of public relations representatives . . . Targets were defined precisely. There was an incisive ambush on Norrie Paramor, pop song writer, which could only have been an inside job . . . There was a chat-up from one of the army candidates at Wednesday's by-election . . . Best of all was a manic sketch of 'Jim's Inn' . . . If the pattern does not ossify into a formula, then for the first time it seems reasonable that one should need a licence for a television set – it can be as lethal as a gun. And the cast was as good as the rest of it.

Ned has never been one to wear his heart on his sleeve, but I swear that at that moment he was as excited – and relieved – as I was. Then we were off to our respective flats to burn up the telephone wires, in a two-man attempt to boost the circulation of the *Sunday Telegraph* amongst as many of our group as we could find. That night I relaxed by attending a pop concert in Bromley with my flatmate, Bryant Marriott (later Head of Radio 2) and his girlfriend Alison. The star of the show was Helen Shapiro. It was a good concert but I did not go backstage afterwards, perhaps because I did not know Miss Shapiro and was not yet into that particular show business convention. On the other hand, perhaps it was because I did not at that particular moment relish the prospect of meeting her recording manager. (In fact, during that same month, the 'pop' torch was already passing from the more traditional artist like Helen to a new group with new ideas. That November the Beatles went into the charts for the first time with 'Love Me Do'.)

Monday's newspapers were also welcoming, with different papers picking their own particular favourite parts of the show. Dennis Potter's review in the *Daily Herald* was headlined: 'This TV Newcomer Smiles as she Bites', and Peter Black in the *Daily Mail* added: 'David Frost, the anchor man, established himself as what you could call the first anti-personality on TV.' 'Do you think that's good?' I asked Bryant. The *Daily Sketch*'s report was headlined: 'Helen's Chief Calls his Lawyer', and went on to inaugurate the score-card that was to become a weekly feature of TW3 coverage: 'Only five viewers phoned the BBC to complain about the programme and eighty-three phoned in congratulations.'

By early Tuesday morning we were back at Lime Grove trying to work out a) what we had done right and b) how we could do it again. Alasdair Milne has said that he thought that TW3 really took off with a piece featuring 'The Consumers' Guide to Religion' in January. I do not agree. I believe that TW3 confirmed its initial impact in week two, and really 'went critical' with the third edition on 8 December and the compound effect of editions one, two and three.

The second show, on 1 December, did not ignite the switchboards or trigger off the newspapers' score-cards, but it was full of strong material. Peter Lewis and Peter Dobereiner provided one of my favourite 'quickies':

DF: I think Harold's sincere, don't you?

Roy Kinnear: No doubt of it. And you know I believe Hugh's sincere, too.

Lance Percival: And you've only got to look at Jo to see that he's sincere.

Kenneth Cope: Utterly. For that matter, there's no questioning that Jack Kennedy's sincere.

Lance: Oh yes. Come to that, so is Khrushchev. Give him his due, whatever else he may be, he's sincere.

Roy: True, true. Thank God there aren't any Machiavellis in world politics today.
(Pause)

DF: You knew where you were with Machiavelli.

'Dixon of Dock Green' was no longer the sole public image of the police:

(Lance enters in policeman's uniform)

Roy: Good evening.

Lance: Evening, sir. (He beats Roy up) Just a routine enquiry, sir.

The Cambridge connection again asserted itself. John Cleese made two contributions, 'TV Episode 6', and 'Regella' which had begun life as a sketch called 'Startistics' at Cambridge. It was the popularisation of science gone wrong: 'And to give you some idea of how large 528 million is: fifty people dotting continuously at three and a half dots per second for four and a half months . . . would fill two warehouses with exercise books . . .'

Tim Birdsall's illustrated dialogue with me explained the daily life of a cartoonist: 'Occasionally I have to go and ask the boss for a rise – he can never give me one, of course, because the line on the sales graph slumps so sharply that it goes through the floor and into the office below.'

That show held and built our audience, and prepared for what was to come. Donald Baverstock had waxed eloquent after the first show. He had predicted a starting audience of two to three million, and now he was predicting an eventual audience of eight to nine million. Neither Ned nor I could possibly believe a figure like that. However, Donald was that sort of visionary. And eventually his ludicrously optimistic prediction turned out to be an underestimate.

In the third show, on 8 December, Millie's TW3 song contained one of its best inserts. In response to the Churches' restated desire to update their Mass, we had an updated hymn from Lewis and Dobereiner.

Oh God our help in ages past
Remember, we implore
If we poor humans are the last
You'll have to make some more.

Teach thou our neighbours us to love
As we do love ourselves
And make the fall-out up above
Fall out on someone else.

Television had dealt with that week's fog crisis almost like a sports event, so we did the same at 'Death Desk': 'Tottenham Court Road 2, Hammersmith Flyover nil; Sheffield Wednesday

2, Thursday 5.' I commented bitterly on the Barbara Fell case, in which a fifty-four-year-old senior official at the Central Office of Information had been sentenced to two years' imprisonment under the Official Secrets Act for passing what were generally agreed to be harmless documents to her lover, a Press Attaché at the Yugoslav Embassy who was generally acknowledged to be both pro-Western and anti-Russian. It all fitted in with one of the security patterns of the early Sixties – the system was missing out on catching the big fish, while simultaneously venting its vindictiveness on the little fish who happened to swim into the net.

Roy Kinnear performed a splendid parody of John Grierson's film series 'Our Wonderful World', and the new Lord Chamberlain, Lord Cobbold, was profiled in the spirit of Norrie Paramor. That weekend the Cardinals were leaving Rome after the Cardinals' Conference: portrayed by our cast, their swaying performance of 'Arrivederci Roma' was a mini-classic.

Timothy Birdsall took on the political cartoonists and Bernard Levin took on Charles Forte on the subject of British catering. Bernard began: 'If there is one word to describe British catering – and there is – it is "disgusting".' After that he got somewhat more critical. 'Why is the restaurant food in Glasgow served cold? And what about the hotel guest who asked for breakfast at 8.15 and was told, "You're not on the Continent now, sir"?' When Charles Forte attempted a response, his listeners laughed. 'Is the audience briefed?' he asked. 'No,' said Bernard, 'but their stomachs may be.' Mr Forte had come along to discuss British catering in general. 'You're not attacking me, of course,' he said at one stage. 'Not personally,' said Bernard, reassuringly. 'I have no doubt you're guilty of some of these crimes.'

Charles Forte was brave and remarkably good-humoured, but Bernard was quite unstoppable. 'You're either a sanguine man or you're something I would not sully my lips with,' he said at one point. The audience held its breath: 'I think you are probably a sanguine man.'

The encounter had all the atmosphere of the bullring. At the end I felt compelled to thank Mr Forte for subjecting himself to 'Mr Levin's own form of grill and griddle'.

There was an item where we showed some footage of Harold Macmillan, then said how appalling it would be if such a piece of film were to be tampered with, 'Like this . . .' (Actually the original needed very little enhancement.)

After a sketch on carcinogens, it was the turn of Lionel Bart. Caryl Brahms and I had tried to demonstrate how great the debts were that Lionel owed to the past. 'Shall we Dance' by Rodgers and Hammerstein was compared with Bart's 'I Shall Scream'; 'I've Got a Handful of Songs' was compared with 'Margaretta'; 'Food, Glorious Food' with Jerome Kern's 'Whose Baby are You?'; 'Fings Ain't What They Used to be' was compared with 'In Our Mountain Greenery'. What a lot all these composers had 'in common'. After medleys like that, the message was simple (and cleared by the lawyers!): namely, 'Next time you hear a Lionel Bart song, remember – there's plenty more *where that came from.*'

There was plenty more to come in the show, too, notably Steven Vinaver's famous fly-buttons sketch, set in a café where an embarrassed Millicent Martin has to tell her boyfriend, Roy Kinnear, that his fly is open. He is not immediately cooperative.

Roy: Now I'm very curious about your motivation for telling me my fly is open.
Millie: Well . . .
Roy: It strikes me as an aggressive, hostile action.
Millie: Hostile?
Roy: Obviously. I am very embarrassed now.
Millie: Well, button it up.
Roy: That's what you want, isn't it? Don't eat the ketchup; button your fly. You want to stamp out any individuality I've got, don't you? I wouldn't button that fly if it was open all the way.
Millie: It is now.

Lance Percival sang one of his rousing calypsos and I rounded off the programme with a review of the following day's Sunday newspapers, a feature we had tried out the week before. When the papers arrived, the show was under way, and Christopher

Booker conducted a first look at the assorted journals. During other people's sketches in the second half of the show, we would whisper frantically as we tried to select the most quotable pieces. That particular week the tabloids were full of uplifting material: 'EIGHT WIDOWS WANT TO WED THE THIEF WITH MUSCLES', said one. 'DID MRS GRIMES SEE THE VIRGIN MARY THROUGH HER KITCHEN WINDOW?' asked another.

I ended the programme with a news item: 'During the week Mr Maudling, the Chancellor of the Exchequer, held a meeting with the unemployed at the end of which he got up and said, "Well, I don't know about you, but I've got work to do."'

That night the BBC's telephone switchboard lit up as never before. The *Daily Telegraph* reported that 987 people had telephoned the BBC and that the lines were kept busy until 12.45 a.m.: 'More than half the calls, 544, were complimentary, the other 443 were complaints. A BBC spokesman said yesterday, "We were very much gratified at the interest shown."' (Whoever he was, the nameless spokesman deserved instant promotion.)

The complaints made the reviewer in the *Listener* complain in turn:

> I really begin to despair of my fellow countrymen . . . We mustn't make fun of Mr Macmillan or we mustn't be rude about British catering – and the terrifying thing is that the views of these witless subtopian boot-lickers command attention. *Why* in heaven's name, why do newspapers take their crackpot correspondence so seriously? Why is the Postmaster General calling for this programme script? Is free speech in this country to be nannified out of existence by official vanity and the servile urge to worship and placate the powers-that-be?

'Not for another year or so,' was probably the correct answer to that, although we did not know it at the time.

The decibel level of the response to that third programme took us all by surprise. Looking back now, the volume of outrage may seem surprising, but the mythical Disgusteds of Tunbridge

Wells had never before seen authority, the established Church and the Tory Party treated as subjects for humour or mockery. Least of all on the BBC, at a time when the growing number of television news bulletins were able to ensure that even 'wives and servants' understood all the jokes. The whole thing was disruptive in the extreme.

Fortunately for us, the majority of viewers shared our belief that these were appropriate subjects for ridicule. Occasionally, perhaps, they too were shocked by some of the earlier programmes, but shocked more by the realisation that at last somebody was saying publicly what they had been thinking privately.

The Postmaster General, Reginald Bevins, had indeed called for the script – and had then suddenly gone quiet, which seemed a bit odd, although we thought little of it at the time. We only found out the reason for that about-turn thirty years later, on 1 January 1993, when the Government papers for 1962 were released under the Thirty-Year Rule.

Mr Bevins had received a personal note from Prime Minister Harold Macmillan: 'I hope you will not, repeat not, take any action about "That Was The Week That Was" without consulting me. It is a good thing to be laughed over – it is better than to be ignored.'

How many politicians could save themselves heartburn by adopting the same approach!

We of course carried on, blithely unaware of the fact that, within only three weeks, the Prime Minister had become involved in the fallout from TW3. But we knew enough to feel that by now TW3 was definitely in orbit. The following week I even stumbled upon a catch-phrase by accident. Keith Waterhouse and Willis Hall had written a piece for Roy Kinnear entitled 'The Safe Comedian', a portrait of a comedian *à la* Max Miller, Charlie Chester or Arthur English, trying desperately to catch up with the new satire boom and yet copping out in the traditional manner whenever he could.

Right! David Frost, eh? 'Though the frost was cruel.' I know his brother, Jack Frost. Oh, he's vicious, is David. I'm not saying he's got a cutting tongue but he's the only man I know who doesn't have to slice his bread before he eats it. (SMARMILY) No, but seriously, David, you're doing a grand job and it's a great pleasure and privilege to be working on your show tonight. Work, eh? Half a million unemployed. My brother's unemployed. He is! Unemployed, my brother. Still, he's lazy. Well, I won't say he's lazy, but he's the only man I know with elbow patches on his pyjamas. Unemployment! Still, we don't want to get maudlin' about it, do we? Maudling? Get it? Maudlin', Mr Maudling. No, but seriously, boys and girls, he's doing a grand job.

A couple of times later in the same programme it was irresistible to add the words, 'Seriously though, he's doing a grand job' to political jokes that were already in the script. I probably only used the phrase half a dozen more times in the rest of the series, but it stuck.

TW3 was clearly having an impact. I was writing out a cheque the following week in Harrods when the assistant said, 'We never miss your programme, Mr Frost.'

'Thank you very much,' I replied, and continued writing the cheque.

'If we're at home, we always make sure we've finished eating before the programme begins.' he said.

'That's very kind of you.'

'And if we're out, we always make sure we're home in good time for the programme.'

'Thank you,' I said, and handed over the cheque.

He looked down at the cheque and then looked up at me. 'Do you have any means of identification?' he asked.

In the programme after Christmas, Gerald Kaufman made his first contribution to TW3 as a writer and researcher. His subject: the accuracy of Cross-Bencher's predictions in the *Sunday Express*. 1962 had been a bumper year:

Willie: At Lincoln, the Liberal intervention could easily have the effect of putting Labour out and the Tories in.

Ken: Labour wins at Lincoln – majority up three thousand.

Events of the summer were particularly fruitful.

Willie: 1 July. Cluster round now, all you hopeful Tory Backbenchers. I bring the news you so anxiously await. It concerns the big Government reshuffle which everyone has been expecting this month. And what is my news? There won't be one.

Ken: 13 July. Macmillan carries out biggest-ever Government reshuffle.

There were many more examples, leading to the simple summation: 'Don't miss tomorrow's *Sunday Express* for the latest glimpse into Cross-Bencher's amazing crystal balls.'

It was undoubtedly one of the best-researched pieces in the series, though there was an unfortunate, indeed tragic, postscript. When it came to the round-up of the Sunday papers at the end of the programme, naturally the first feature that Christopher Booker and I turned to was Cross-Bencher. What predictions had he made this week? One stood out: 'Despite his mysterious minor illness, Hugh Gaitskell is on the way to recovery. In no time at all he will be fit and back at work again.' It thus seemed a good throwaway to quote Cross-Bencher's prediction and then turn back to the camera again and say, 'Sorry, Hugh.' That is to say, it seemed a good throwaway for a few days – until Hugh Gaitskell's sudden death. Needless to say we were all mortified, Chris and I more than anyone. It was almost worse that there were no lessons to draw from the incident. We just wished it had never happened.

Early in the New Year, we broadcast 'The Consumers' Guide to Religion', and all Heaven broke loose. Written by Charles Lewsen and Robert Gillespie, it was one of the longest pieces that I performed in the entire series. The thrust of the piece was that as religion became more and more determinedly earthly in its value judgements and its appeals to the public, it would be judged more and more by earthly standards – by consumer magazines like *Which?* (The piece was in fact called 'Why?')

As I explained:

Of the dozens of products on the market, we investigated the following sects: Judaism, the Roman Catholic Church, the Church of England, Islam, Buddhism and Communism. We ruled out Hinduism. It embodies a caste system which we felt was alien to the British consumer. However, the Hindu does believe that animals have souls, every bit as good as human ones. In this sense it could be said that every Englishman is a Hindu at heart. But we felt that this still did not outweigh the main objection.

We began by applying three basic tests: a) What do you put into it? b) What do you get out of it? c) How much does it cost?

We started with Judaism.

You are one of the chosen people – this gives confidence, and we particularly like the guarantee of eternal life through the Messiah or Saviour who will take responsibility for all your guilt – when He arrives.

What does it cost? In crockery alone the expense is fantastic, plus the wages of a reliable gentile to run the business between sunset on Friday and sunset on Saturday. Infertility is the only grounds for divorce. We did not try to obtain one.

Next we tested the Roman Catholic Church.

We must stress here that the idea that the Head (or Pope, as he is called) claims infallibility in all matters is a fallacy. The Pope cannot tell you which television set is the best. His infallibility is strictly limited to matters of faith. He can only tell you which television programme you cannot watch. An interesting survival from classical prototypes is virgin birth. Most groups have dropped this labour-saving accessory, but the testers found it refreshing and it gave no difficulty . . . The confessional mechanism is standard: it operates as an added safety factor to correct running mistakes, making salvation almost foolproof. The rule here is

'Don't' – but if you must, confess as soon as possible afterwards. We found this very useful. We found it impossible to obtain a divorce.

We found that all the better religions offered perfect happiness in heaven as a reward for a good life. We decided to test these claims. Unfortunately we were unable to find anyone who would undertake this. Contact with the deceased also appeared to be difficult. We apologise for our failure to verify this important aspect.

After analysing all the various religions we came back to the Church of England.

The attraction of the Church of England is its democratic spirit. If you want transubstantiation, you can have transubstantiation. If you don't want transubstantiation, well, you don't have to have it. You can just walk down the road into another church, and not have it. And it's a jolly friendly faith. If you are one, there's no onus on you to make everyone else join. In fact no one need ever know. It doesn't interfere with essentials. And it's pretty fair on the whole. With some of these productions – Roman Catholicism and Judaism, for instance – you start guilty from the off, but with the C of E, on the whole you start pretty well innocent, and they've got to prove you're guilty.

You get eternal life – of course you get eternal life – but there's none of this toffee-nosed nonsense about the *only true faith* and the *chosen people* and so on.

All in all we think you get a jolly good little faith for a very moderate outlay, and we have no hesitation in proclaiming it the Best Buy.

The reaction was immediate. Canon John Duffield, preaching at St Peter's Church, Onchan, Isle of Man, said, 'If we were 100 per cent Christian we would storm the BBC building and make it drop this horrible programme.'

Fleet Street suddenly registered the fact that my father was a Methodist minister, and spent that Sunday on the phone to

Beccles. My father was used to genteel calls from the *Beccles and Bungay Journal* with questions like, 'What would you like us to put in the paper this week, Reverend Frost?' or 'When should people bring their produce to the Harvest Festival?' Having a pack of Fleet Street tigers on the phone, all trying to put words into his mouth, then printing them if he so much as paused for a second before denying them, was a new experience. As a result, the *Daily Mail* had the headline: 'David Frost was Wrong, Says his Clergyman Father'. According to the *Sketch*, however, he approved of my performance: 'The sketch caused me no embarrassment,' he was alleged to have said. In one paper he was quoted as saying that the sketch may have done some good, 'if it wakes people up and makes them alive to the church and religion'. But according to the *Daily Telegraph*, my father was not among that number: 'I had a busy day and was rather tired. I dozed off during it.'

After the weekend, the *Eastern Daily Press* asked my father about the number of calls he had received, and what he had really said. 'I told them all that I would not discuss anything relating to the programme because I was not in possession of the facts,' he replied.

A vicar in Surrey telephoned wanting to know how many viewers had written in or telephoned in favour of the humorous reference to religion. He told me he was giving a sermon in favour of TW3, and he wanted to give his parishioners 'the latest score'!

On the following Friday morning Douglas Marlborough of the *Daily Mail* called Ned Sherrin with the innocent-sounding question, 'Are you going to church on Sunday, Ned?' Ned could foresee the headline that Dougie was going for – 'TW3 Producer Repents' – and deflected the question.

It was certainly all a far cry from the Fifties and the days of the 'BBC Variety Programmes Policy Guide for Writers and Producers', which decreed: 'references to and jokes about different religions or religious denominations are banned. The following also are inadmissible: jokes about A.D. or B.C. (e.g. "Before Crosby").' The same document had also noted: 'The Corporation's policy is against broadcasting impersonations of leading political figures.' And it had added: 'There is an absolute ban upon suggestive references to: honeymoon couples, chamber maids, fig leaves, prostitution, ladies' underwear, e.g. "winter draws on", animal habits, e.g. rabbits, lodgers and commercial travellers. Extreme care should be taken in dealing with references to or jokes about prenatal influences (e.g. "His mother was frightened by a donkey"). The vulgar use of such words as "basket" must also be avoided . . . 'When in doubt, take it out,' is the wisest maxim.'

The following week the show made news again for two separate reasons. One was Herbert Kretzmer's 'Lullaby for an Illegitimate Child', commemorating the latest birth statistics.

Papa was no bridegroom and your mama was no bride,
Yet sleep in peace, my angel baby, time is on your side.

In its skilfully crafted journey from comedy to pathos, 'Lullaby' was one of the two or three best songs in the entire series. But it was the return of Gerald Kaufman that really caught the press's attention. Gerald had been working for us for some time on a piece called 'The Thirteen Silent MPs', a mock-salute to the thirteen Members of Parliament who had been in the House of Commons for ten years or more and not yet made a speech. One of the thirteen who was definitely not amused was Sir Norman Hulbert (Conservative, Stockport North). And he – rather unwisely, as it turned out – decided to raise the matter in the House of Commons itself.

The *Daily Mail* headlined its report of his speech 'That Was the Week has MPs Laughing'; and the *Daily Sketch*'s headline was 'MPs Roar at TWTWTW Protest THAT'S A JOKE THAT IS'. The report in *The Times* caught the mood of hilarity:

> Finally, Sir Norman said, there had been a striking reference to the Speaker – that the BBC would be very pleased to supply him with photographs of the members referred to. The inference was, Sir Norman argued, that the Speaker was unable to recognise them. This remark, to coin a phrase, almost brought the House down; and the Chancellor of the Exchequer, rumoured to have a weakness for

> the modern vogue for satire, did not bother to conceal his amusement . . . Mr Sidney Silverman had the last word, 'Would it be a breach of privilege,' he asked innocently, 'if this admirable programme included this incident in its programme next week?'

A day later the Speaker ruled that there was no *prima facie* case of any breach of privilege. Norman Shrapnel in the *Guardian* commented, 'All may now be considered to have ended happily. Mr David Frost and his men should be happy, since they succeeded in getting at least one of the rare speakers to speak. Sir Norman Hulbert should be happy, since in speaking he proved his own implicit point – that making speeches in the Chamber may not be the best service an MP performs.'

Sir Norman's intervention certainly made an impact. Some nine years later, a viewer sent me a copy of his obituary from a local paper. The simple headline, after more than thirty years of public service? 'Silent MP Dies'.

On the following Sunday, in the *Sunday Pictorial*, James Pettigrew invited readers to send him their opinion on what the headline described as 'The Show Business Rage of 1963'. Under the larger headline 'Clever or Sick? Disgusting or Brilliant?' Mr Pettigrew gave examples of the latest satirical jokes of TW3 and elsewhere. He made it all as emotive as possible and certainly, if anything, encouraged a nay-saying result: 'Well, that's just some of the new satire. Does it offend you? Annoy you? Disgust you? Do you mind jokes about the Queen and religion?'

The following week Mr Pettigrew had to report – albeit in small print in the body of his article – that more than six hundred people had said 'yes' to the new humour, and only 160 had said 'no'. The readers' letters revealed the strength of feeling about 'pompous overblown officialdom', though one of my favourites was a slightly confused negative one from a reader in Pinner, who asked: 'How a so-called lady can sing about babies as bastards and the flies of men's trousers being open is beyond my ken.' Even Herbert Kretzmer would have had problems making a lullaby out of the latter.

We had confirmation ourselves, almost simultaneously, about

people's attitudes. On the night before the *Sunday Pictorial* revealed its findings, we had broadcast 'The Sinking of the Royal Barge', a piece by Ian Lang. As I write, Ian is the Secretary of State for Scotland, thus making him perhaps the only example of somebody whose career has combined the two Cambridge trends of the time – satire and membership of Conservative Cabinets. The sketch was Ian's tribute to the fact that royal commentators would carry on regardless in the same old way, *whatever* happened:

> And now the Queen, smiling radiantly, is swimming for her life . . . Her Majesty is wearing a pale blue taffeta dress with matching lace . . . And now the Duke of Gloucester and Mr Angus Ogilvy have rushed forward to the edge of the quay. To get a better view. And Lord Snowdon has just taken a colour photograph. And what a gesture – the Band of the Royal Marines have just struck up 'God *Save* The Queen'.

Not yet having had the benefit of reading Mr Pettigrew's findings, we expected a stronger negative response than in fact we received. There were only forty-seven calls of complaint that week, only thirty-six of which were about the Royal Barge. There were also 113 calls in favour of that particular show.

At the same time, we were putting the finishing touches to an album produced by George Martin, who was taking some time off from the Beatles, and the following week I had agreed to make a sentimental return to the Blue Angel. It was thus perhaps not the ideal week for the *Daily Express* to publish my ex-directory phone number ('You might try VIC 2861') as part of a Saturday-morning profile. The first unsought wake-up call came from Manchester at 5 a.m. I thanked the caller for telephoning, murmured a brief tribute to the editor of the *Daily Express*, took the phone off the hook and tried to get back to sleep. In fact, when the *Daily Express* finally arrived, it was quite a jolly read. Max Setty of the Blue Angel was quoted as commenting: 'He was one of those new vague comics. But we liked him. His act never interfered with the waiters serving dinner.

And they didn't mind sharing their changing rooms with him.'

Bernard Levin's confrontation on the show that evening was with George Elvin, of the Association of Cinematographic and Television Technicians. Bewildered beyond belief by the varying explanations of how and why the Boulting brothers were or were not members of his union, or non-union, in a rash moment I suggested that any children watching might like to try to précis the situation. We looked forward to a few replies. By Monday there were thousands. And they were a revelation. Not only because of the age of some of the entrants – the runner-up was nine years old – but simply because of their hipness and intelligence.

In that same programme Lance Percival and David Kernan had performed a sketch by Peter Shaffer about the after-effects of the Vassall case. William Vassall, an Admiralty clerk and as it happens a homosexual, had been found guilty of spying. From a number of innocuous letters between Vassall and his superior, Thomas Galbraith, alarming and unjustified inferences were drawn about their so-called 'relationship'. Galbraith had resigned and said that he would never start a letter with 'Dear' or 'My dear' again. As a romp, it was great material: 'Mr Vladimir Chedamorokovsky, an Admiralty spokesman, has appealed to all Civil Servants . . . at one time or another.' When Galbraith's resignation letter was published, we tried to subject Macmillan's reply to the same treatment that Galbraith's own letters had received. Macmillan had written: 'I would like to thank you for all your services.' TW3: 'What services, we may ask . . .'

Now we were taking the matter a stage further, as Peter Shaffer's senior civil servant tried to acquaint a junior civil servant with the new rules for safe letter-writing in Whitehall.

Senior officer: Now, let's see what you've done. (reading) 'Yours faithfully' . . . I don't believe it.

Junior officer: That's normal, sir.

Senior officer: Normal? In the context of a man writing to a man it's nothing less than disgusting. It implies you can be unfaithful.

Junior officer: I never thought of that, sir.

Senior officer: You think of very little, don't you? Even the word 'Yours' at the end of a letter is dangerous. It suggests a willingness for surrender.

Junior officer: Then what can I say, sir?

Senior officer: What do the Pensions Department use? They're about as unemotional as you can get, without actually being dead.

Junior officer: 'Your obedient servant' I think.

Senior officer: Are you mad?

Junior officer: Sir?

Senior officer: 'Your obedient servant' . . . That's just plain perverted. People who want to be other people's obedient servants are the sort who answer those advertisements: 'Miss Lash, ex-governess of striking appearance.' To sign yourself an obedient servant is an *ipso facto* confession of sexual deviation. And that, as we all know, is an *ipso facto* confession of treason . . .

Back to the children's letters: at least 60 per cent of them began 'To Mr Frost', or 'Frost', with postscripts to say they would have liked to have begun 'Dear David', but they feared that would be misunderstood.

Any satirical programme is inevitably accused of being anti-Government, but the following week gave us a chance to put the record straight, because Harold Wilson had just been elected Leader of the Labour Party.

Chris Booker and I prepared an advertising campaign for New Instant Wilson:

> 'I cannot tell New Instant Wilson from Old Pipe-Smoking Attlee. P.S. I can't tell New Instant Wilson from Old Stab-in-the-back Wilson.'
>
> 'I was a floating voter until they discovered Wilson – now I'm sunk.'
>
> 'Remember, 144 out of every 249 Labour MPs prefer Wilson.'

'Want to know something, Dorothy? For the first time, I think I'm really *going to enjoy this programme!'*

That was based on a washing-powder advertisement, and we also used a current Pearl Assurance one: 'At twenty-five I was only a don – what did I need with a policy? At thirty-five I was in the Cabinet – I was sure that a policy would only tie me down. At forty-five I began to worry about the future Labour offered – but I knew that a policy would be the biggest disadvantage of all. But today at forty-six at last I can afford a policy. Any ideas?' And it was irresistible to include: 'You'll look a little lovelier each day, with fabulous Douglas Jay.'

Ploughing through a mass of over-the-top ads for 'fabulous Pink Camay' and myriads of washing powders made that a particularly light-hearted session for Chris and me. We would meet on a Friday morning to hammer out the main political/topical sketch of the week which would open the show following the TW3 song. We started as early in the morning as we could, and tried to be finished by the end of lunchtime so that I could get in to Lime Grove with our piece – or, occasionally, pieces – to complete the programme's script which, ad-libs apart, we usually had pretty well complete by then. Although I wrote other pieces for the show, and worked with other writers, I could not have wished for a better weekly collaborator than Chris. The sessions were invariably enjoyable as well. We were reminded again why there is such a plethora of writing teams. There is no logical explanation, but when you refine a line between two people rather than on your own, the polishing happens much more than twice as quickly. The effect is geometrical rather than arithmetical. That was certainly our experience.

On the Monday morning following the Wilson show, I drove to Pinewood for a week on the movie *The VIPs*, appearing in a featured cameo role as a reporter with Elizabeth Taylor, Richard Burton and Orson Welles – and getting paid into the bargain. For a twenty-three-year-old it was a particularly delicious example of the by-products of TW3. It was an enjoyable week, and the beginning of three friendships that I cherished, though I do not think that the large screen did a great deal for the Frost haircut, or indeed vice versa.

I did not know a great deal about the conventions of movie-making, and just went about things as I would in a television studio. Years later, on 'The David Frost Show' in New York, Orson Welles suddenly told me out of the blue, 'When I first met you on *The VIPs*, I always knew you would make it.'

I gazed at him somewhat blankly. After all, my role had scarcely been a demanding one. 'Why?' I asked.

'Well, your first scene was with Elizabeth Taylor and Richard Burton and me. And at the end of the scene when Anthony Asquith called "Cut," you said, "I'd just like to do that scene one more time, if I may," and Anthony Asquith went along with it. That was something none of the three of us would have dared to say!'

Fools rush in . . .

On the Friday of that week Parlophone released a 'Best of TW3' record, and rather enterprisingly Jack Bell in the *Daily Mirror* managed to get BBC Radio to admit that two of the items on it had been placed on its 'restricted list'. A BBC official explained: 'The playing of these items will depend on the context of the programme. The fly-button sketch would not be suitable for a programme like "Housewives' Choice".'

'That Was The Week That Was' caused a considerable number of behind-the-scenes headaches at the BBC – some more serious than others. When the series began, we had realised that 10.30 at night was fairly late to be inviting audiences to the BBC Television Centre, so we had developed the idea of serving mulled claret to those loyalists who turned up. One day I was in Donald Baverstock's office and he pointed to two large piles of filed correspondence. He pointed to the smaller of the two piles: 'That is the correspondence from members of the public, the Tory Party and so on complaining about individual items in the show,' he said. Then he pointed to the larger pile: 'And that is the correspondence from within the BBC and from S.G. Williams (Head of Administration) about the questionable precedent of serving mulled wine on BBC premises.' It was a poetic reminder of all the BBC managers who felt that their lives could be made much easier and much tidier if only the one random ingredient – the programmes – could be got rid of.

Our audience was by now approaching ten million, compared to the starting figure of three and a half million. This was announced by Mr Robert Silvey, head of the BBC's Research Department, who added, 'Some enjoy it even though its barbs threaten their own ego-involved concepts.' One could imagine the dialogue in homes all over Britain: 'Come to bed, Grannie, those barbs are threatening your ego-involved concepts again.'

Research was in fact an important ingredient of the show itself. Joe Haines and Andrew Roth of 'Parliamentary Profiles' produced a splendid piece called 'Hardly Hansard', demonstrating that noble journal's editorial techniques. For example, the Conservative Member for Putney, Sir Hugh Linstead, had remarked in the House of Commons: 'One has only to look round this Chamber to see all the Honourable Members who are not here.' That was 'reconstructed' by Hansard to read: 'It is obvious from looking round the House that Honourable

Members who are considerably concerned with the details of the Bill, and who would have liked to have been here today, have not found it possible to come.'

That was one technique; another was simple deletion. Sir Barnett Janner (Labour, Leicester Northwest) had said: 'The boy shot one bird, and had to be destroyed.' Mr Robert Woolf (Labour, Blaydon) had said: 'The future is yet to come.' And Mr Donald Wade (Liberal, Huddersfield) had remarked: 'Although I refer to widows, it does not mean I am not interested in spinsters.' All of these remarks simply never happened, according to the printed edition of Hansard.

Officialdom was proving a better and better source of material. On Ned's and my desks there landed an Endorsement of Licence number 3133, dated 31 January 1963, which contained the Lord Chamberlain's comments on Spike Milligan's 'The Bed-Sitting Room'. The Lord Chamberlain had already banned 'The Sinking of the Royal Barge' sketch, after we had done it on television, from a revue at the Duchess Theatre called 'See You Inside'. Charles Ross, the revue's director, had commented, 'It seems strange to me that millions of people can see it on television, but hundreds are forbidden to see it in the theatre.'

His feelings were understandable, and we were delighted to get hold of Spike's particular licence because it not only cited required deletions, but also acceptable alterations. For example:

> Act I, page 21, The Daz song: Omit 'you get all the dirt off the tail of your shirt'. Substitute 'you get all the dirt off the front of your shirt'.

How was that any better? Indeed, wasn't it marginally worse? The licence went on:

> Act II, page 2, The mock priest must not wear a crucifix on his snorkel.

And then, later in Act II, quite bewilderingly:

> Omit 'the Duke of Edinburgh is a wow with Greek dishes . . .' Substitute 'Hark ye! Hark ye! the day of judgement is at hand.'

And in Act III:

> Omit 'the perversions of the rubber . . .' Substitute 'the kreurpels and blinges of the rubber'.

The next week, the BBC, with remarkable tolerance, reversed a ban on a Don Charles record called 'Angel of Love' after we had played part of it on the programme. The BBC spokesman said, 'It was a mistake on our part to ban the song in the first place and it was quite right of "That Was The Week That Was" to raise the matter.'

By now the already compendious list of writers on the credits at the end of the programme was being lengthened a little further by the addition of another name – Vernon Laxton. Vernon Laxton did not in fact exist, but when his inventors, Keith Waterhouse and Willis Hall, told us about their creation, Ned and I felt that the least we could do was to give Vernon a little additional street cred. Keith and Willis had invented Vernon Laxton in order to wreak havoc among their fellow writers. Knowing that there is nothing more infuriating to an author than someone who gets the name of his beloved characters or works of art slightly wrong, Keith and Willis set out to madden and infuriate, with great success. 'Vernon' wrote to Ted Willis, saying how much he would like to make a musical out of Ted Willis's character, Nixon of Dock Green. Ted Willis wrote back in fury that it was *D*ixon of Dock Green, not Nixon of Dock Green, and that in any case, if he wanted there to be a musical of Dixon, he would write it himself. Vernon was not finished. He wrote back to Ted Willis with his parting shot: 'Very well, I must warn you that in that case I shall go ahead with my plans for a musical of PC 49.'

Vernon Laxton wrote to Arnold Wesker shortly after *I'm Talking About Jerusalem* and *Roots* had been presented in the West End, asking if he could make a musical out of Arnold's play

'How About Jerusalem?' He added his congratulations on 'that marvellous send-up of all that socialist claptrap, "Boots"'.

Arnold Wesker wrote back denying Vernon the rights he sought in *I'm Talking About Jerusalem, not* 'How About Jerusalem?', and explaining that *Roots* (*not* 'Boots') was not intended as a send-up of socialist thought, but was in fact a passionate avowal of it.

Vernon Laxton and his inventors then turned their attention to the impresarios. They sent a page of execrable verse drama to twenty or thirty London theatre managements, with a covering letter reading: 'When I sent you a copy of my verse drama "Arise, Oh All Ye Phoenixes" last week, unfortunately I omitted page 47, which I now enclose. Please will you insert it into your copy, and let me know what you think as soon as possible.' Vernon had not, of course, sent the remaining pages to any of the theatre managements, but he received four critiques of the entire play within the next few weeks.

Throughout the winter of 1962–63 our feelings towards the Home Secretary, Mr Henry Brooke, were growing less and less sympathetic. More than any other individual, he personified for us everything that we rejected about authority, as it had been defined for us ever since we were old enough to care. One Labour MP, Marcus Lipton, had described him as 'the most hated man in Britain' – an epithet he had earned in a remarkably brief space of time.

In the second half of March Chris Booker and I decided to focus on Henry Brooke for the whole of our opening political sketch. Over the previous few weeks I had had the sublime pleasure of being Victor Sylvester, Peter Goodwright of 'Candid Camera', Edgar Lustgarten and Barry Bucknell, the arch-priest of do-it-yourself: now, however, it was time to be Eamonn Andrews and introduce 'This is Your Life – Henry Brooke', concentrating on some of his more notorious decisions.

I opened the red book: 'You were born Home Secretary a few short months ago . . . on Friday 13 July 1962 . . .'

We referred to the case of Carmen Bryan, a West Indian girl whom Brooke had proposed to deport for stealing goods worth two pounds from a supermarket. In particular, we quoted his own words on the subject: 'I think it would be a great act of injustice if I were to stand in the way of her returning to Jamaica.' Confronted by widespread incredulity at his attitude, Brooke had reversed his decision.

'Your word, Henry, isn't very eloquent, is it? Hardly worth keeping at all . . . Do you remember this voice?'

'Save me, save me.'

'Yes, you have a broad back, Henry, and you turned it on Robert Soblen. Unfortunately, Dr Soblen cannot be with us tonight . . .'

The late Dr Robert Soblen was a convicted American spy who had escaped to Britain from Israel. He wanted political asylum, but Brooke ordered that he be sent back to America even though no extradition proceedings had taken place, and despite the fact that Soblen should have been free to go elsewhere. We quoted Brooke's own words in the House of Commons: 'He is fit to travel and I must act as I have said I will.'

'Alas, Henry, Dr Soblen took an overdose of drugs and let you down.'

On a somewhat more farcical note there were the cases of George Lincoln Rockwell, the American Nazi leader, and Georges Bidault, the right-wing French political leader. We played a tape of Rockwell's voice recorded in Gloucestershire on 29 July. Two days after that, Brooke had announced that Rockwell would be officially banned from entering Britain. In the case of Georges Bidault, whom Brooke had forbidden from entering the UK, as Brooke was telling the House of Commons that he had no grounds for thinking that Bidault was in the country, the Frenchman appeared in a television interview filmed in Britain.

Now, in the same week as our 'This is Your Life', there was Brooke's treatment of the exiled Nigerian opposition leader, Chief Anthony Enahoro, who was sent back to his country to face at best imprisonment, and possibly execution, on political grounds. Brooke had assured the British courts that if Enaharo returned, he would be able to choose his defence counsel, even though he knew that Enahoro's counsel, Dingle Foot, would not be allowed into Nigeria.

'And so, Henry, to this week and the case of Chief Enahoro, the Nigerian opposition leader who has asked for asylum but whom you are sending back into danger. He got in without you noticing him – like Rockwell and Bidault. You've changed your mind – as you did with Carmen Bryan. And you have ignored the spirit of British tradition to please another government – like Soblen. Your policy, Mr Brooke, has been one of trial and error. Their trials. Your errors. On behalf of us all – particularly of Dr Soblen and Chief Enahoro – This is Your Life, Henry Brooke – and *was* theirs.'

Brooke: Just shows. If you are Home Secretary, you can get away with murder.

Henry Brooke was the embodiment of the Old Order as we saw it. We had always been led to believe that there was a decent ruling class who wisely guided our destinies. But *were* they decent? *Were* they wise? Forget about being wise, did they have the remotest idea about what was happening under their noses? Didn't they understand that Fifties discipline, order and authority were, in the England of the early Sixties, not only stifling, but discredited as well? And getting more discredited with every week that TW3 was on the air, because you cannot easily refute a laugh with an argument – even with a good argument, and certainly not with a specious one. Henry Brooke and TW3 were on different sides in the battle that was going on for the hearts and minds of middle Britain. And the Old Order was not winning.

If Henry Brooke was the embodiment of the Old Order, since the beginning of March we had been beginning to hear rumours about the man who was to become the symbol of that order, and its demise. John Profumo, the Conservative War Minister, was an unwilling – and, he would no doubt argue, undeserving – symbol. Certainly, when one writes about the Profumo affair today, one is writing about a phenomenon rather than an individual. The rumours were about his illicit liaison with a call-girl named Christine Keeler, whom he had been sharing with, among others, a Russian Naval Attaché, Eugene Ivanov. Up until

21 March the rumours could only be hinted at, then the Labour MP George Wigg had raised them openly in the House of Commons. On 22 March Mr Profumo formally denied them. The BBC lawyers therefore sought to eliminate innuendo about the matter – if they spotted it.

We managed to give Millicent Martin an updated version of 'She was Poor, but she was Honest'.

. . . See 'im in the House of Commons
Making laws to put the blame
While the object of his passion
Walks the streets to hide her shame . . .

We invented a spurious new Latin proverb, '*Pro patria sed non Profumo*'; and quoted a Lyons ad which was worthy of a mention in itself: 'Will make a pie for four people or twelve small tarts,' adding: 'Useful in the current scene . . .' And in our crystal-gazing for the summer, our predictions included: 'June: Christine Keeler appointed Conservative Party's chief PRO.'

All mischievous light-hearted stuff. We did not feel remotely as strongly about the Profumo affair as we did about Henry Brooke. The rumours were not so much shocking as fun, with more security high-jinks thrown in. Thanks to the mood of the nation – a mood in part engendered and in part reflected by TW3 – the Profumo affair was not a national disaster waiting to happen, it was more a national joke waiting to happen. And the waiting period between the denial in March and the dénouement which was to come in June simply encouraged the jokes, and the rumours, to multiply.

The other landmark event for me that March was only indirectly connected to 'That Was The Week That Was'. In the midst of idle chatter, someone happened to mention who was appearing on 'Juke Box Jury' – the only other live programme of the evening on BBC TV – that night. There was Chris Montez, Carole Carr, Spike Milligan and Janette Scott. *Janette Scott!* I had worshipped – nay, lusted after – Janette Scott since the age of fifteen when I watched her first screen kiss with Vernon Gray in *Now and Forever* from the stalls of the Carlton Cinema, Raunds.

I had never had either the time or the inclination to visit the 'Juke Box Jury' hospitality room on a Saturday evening since the previous November when TW3 began, and the show's host, David Jacobs, looked mildly surprised when I suddenly dropped in. But the mission was successful, gloriously successful. Jan and I both started saying, 'I've been so much wanting to meet you,' at the exact same moment, and then started to laugh. I invited her to stay on for the broadcast of TW3 and then have supper. She agreed immediately. We both excused ourselves for a few minutes and then returned to continue our conversation. (Later we found that we had excused ourselves for the same reason – to cancel the other arrangements we had both already made for that evening.)

Supper that night was enough for both of us. Although I was away in Ireland the next day, I was sure enough that we were going to be seeing much more of each other to alter completely one of my answers in mid-sentence during a recording of 'Desert Island Discs' on the Monday. Because our relationship might have become public by the time the programme was broadcast in April, I realised that a couple of apparently general answers might be construed as referring to Jan. I opened in cabaret that evening at Quaglino's and the Allegro with Jan providing moral support.

The edition of TW3 on Saturday 13 April was to cast a long shadow. Critics of the programme would usually speak either of 'undergraduate humour' or 'schoolboy smut'. The smut quotient – the 'naughty bits', as they might now be called – had never seemed very important to us. No doubt there had been the odd *double entendre* that we could have done without, but the liberating effect of TW3 had certainly not been primarily sexual.

However, the edition of 13 April was later to be seen as the one when the *double entendre*s quadrupled. It was a packed edition that ran more than an hour. It included a rousing 'What's My Line' on the subject of the eccentric Tory backbencher Sir Gerald Nabarro, and a heart-rending plea by Keith Waterhouse and Willis Hall for the return of the old *Sunday Pic*, rather than the new enlightened *Sunday Mirror*: 'How long ago now it seems to those happy days when I was reading about the religious sect that was nothing more than a cloak for sin . . . And of midnight orgies in the mansion home of a leading Cheshire industrialist . . .'

There was an Iris Murdoch parody, a visit from Edith Evans to read Caryl Brahms's poem 'Lay Waste the Lilies', and a splendid idea from Peter Lewis and Peter Dobereiner, set in 1993. The commentator, Richard Dimbleby: 'We are in Trafalgar Square once again for one of the great ceremonial occasions of the British calendar, the Aldermaston Drive . . .'

All good stuff. So where did the trouble start? It surely can't have been the exchange between two judges: 'What do you give these homosexual johnnies?' 'Half a crown and an apple, generally.' No, it was probably two pieces that we thought mocked suggestiveness. The less offending of the two was a piece called '*Tropic of Cancer*', which referred to the current controversy surrounding the banning of Henry Miller's novel. It culminated in the reading of a passage which John Albery had found in *Peter Pan*. If books were to be banned, then surely this had to go:

> 'It looked delightfully easy, and they tried it, first on the floor and then on the beds. 'I say, how do you do it?' asked John. He was quite a practical boy. 'You just think lovely wonderful thoughts,' Peter explained. He showed them again. 'You're so nippy at it,' John said. 'Couldn't you do it very slowly once?' Peter did it both slowly and quickly. 'I've got it now, Wendy!' cried John.'

It was the second piece that drew most of the flak. Denise Robbins of the Romantic Novelists' Association had complained about her members' lack of intellectual status. They wanted respect over a wider area. Maybe, we suggested, they should try expanding – into sport, for instance. There was soccer: 'He had done it twice in two minutes. Driven it between the uprights again.' There was cricket: 'As John's fingers stroked the ball, all the subtlety of his fingers attacking that impregnable fortress . . . curling in towards the leg . . . tired and triumphant, he had bowled his first maiden over.' There was boxing: 'He reached out and touched the leather gloves . . . in his mouth the salty taste of another's sweat.' And there was golf: 'She stood like a tigress, gazing down at the tempting turf. In her clasped hands she held the instrument of her happiest hours, long, strong and true, her number one.' It was certainly a wall-to-wall festival of *double entendres*, but it seemed fairly harmless – and fairly funny, though probably not quite funny enough in the circumstances. And in the sense that it gave a focus to a whole series of undirected – and, we thought, generally misguided – comments about sexual innuendo, it was clearly a mistake, though to us at that moment it was the proverbial cloud no larger than a man's hand. The trouble would come later.

The edition of 20 April made its mark in a different way. It was the week of the opening of the London Hilton, which had inspired Peter Lewis and Peter Dobereiner to produce a rendition of the works of the mighty Conrad in biblical language:

> And there was a great gushing of ic-ed water and a great puking of pip-ed music and a great charging of fifty guineas a night without breakfast. And Hilton said, 'Behold, I have given unto you the London Hilton containing everything meet for your needs; a view into the garden of your Queen, yea. And a library wherein you may read the Hilton Milton and 850 Hilton manservants and maidservants smiling Hilton smiles, which they smile not saying 'Cheese', as other men, but 'Hilton Stilton'.

However, the event which dominated the coverage of that particular programme was not of the scripted variety. It was Bernard Levin being punched by a member of the audience – and not just any member of the audience. During the previous week, in his role as theatre critic of the *Daily Mail*, Bernard had panned a one-woman show, *Savagery and Delights* with Agnes Bernelle, at the Duchess Theatre. He had written: 'She does not talk well, walk well or stand well, overlays everything with a horrid archness that makes one squirm, and when she reaches for a high note does so with a kind of throaty vibrato that made me think of a line by Mr H.F. Ellis to the effect, if memory serves, that the great white ox of Patagonia makes its peculiar hunting cry by banging its nostrils together.'

Miss Bernelle's husband, Desmond Leslie, had decided – perhaps understandably – that he must defend his wife's reputation. He obtained a ticket to the programme, and when Bernard was about to begin his discussion piece with, ironically enough, a group of pacifists, Mr Leslie strode from the audience. 'Excuse me, Mr Levin, but would you stand up a moment?' Bernard, looking surprised, stood and turned towards him. Mr Leslie said, 'Before you go on, Mr Levin, your review of *Savagery and Delights* was not a review, it was . . .' Bernard only had time to say, 'Yes, yes, but . . .' before Mr Leslie began to swing punches at him.

Peter Chafer, our floor manager, was first to the scene, and I was second. We pulled Mr Leslie away, and Bernard resumed his seat to considerable applause. He said smilingly to the CND group, 'Can we concentrate on non-violence, you and I?'

The last programme of the series, on 27 April, attracted 335 calls from viewers, of which a remarkable 288 were compliments. After the closing credits, we had fun with one recent row. A suburban couple sat staring at the television set. Although programmes had finished for the night, the set was still switched on.

Millie: I thought it was good.
Roy (Judiciously): On the whole. On the whole.
Millie: Well, it was something different.
Roy: Well, it was satire, wasn't it? What *we* call satire.
Millie: All jokes 'n' skits 'n' that.
Roy: Yes! Mucky jokes. Obscenities – it's all the go nowadays. By law, you see, you're allowed to do it. You can say 'bum', you can say 'po', you can say anything.
Millie: You dirty devil!
Roy: Well, he said it! The thin one! He said 'bum' one night. I heard him! Satire!

After discussing the matter further the couple decided to switch over.

Millie: We might get the last ten minutes of 'Whiplash'.

After that first series, an *Observer* editorial enumerated what it considered TW3's strong points:

> It has been brave; powerful interests have been affronted – organised religion, royal flummery, the CND leadership, Macmillan, Harold Wilson, Grimond and the press, including the tough tactics 'populars', have all been sent up with impartiality. It has not been self-important. Compared to *Private Eye* and the Establishment, it has not been very vicious; attacks on people's personality (as distinct from what they do) and grotesque injustice have not been the rule. And it has certainly discovered new talent.

Needless to say, not everybody agreed. 'Man of the People' worked out that as he had been told that 'at least twelve million' viewers had watched the last performance of 'That Was The Week That Was', then at least two million of them were readers of his column in the *People*. Under the headline 'Goodbye to a Gang of Low Schoolboys', he pronounced those two million of his readers 'bemused, deluded dolts'. 'Bemused and deluded by a bunch of juvenile clowns whose antics would not have got beyond a fifth form rag in any decent grammar school.' The Reverend John Culey declared in his parish magazine that Millicent Martin was 'a repulsive woman' with 'a grating voice', that Bernard Levin was 'a thick-lipped Jew boy', and that TW3's audience were a rabble who got their kicks out of 'an apparent victory of evil over good'.

For us the statistic that 'Man of the People' quoted – the twelve million – was thrilling, though, perhaps inevitably, the word 'satire' was being bandied about more than ever as the 'in' word for just about everything. Alan Brien recorded his nightmare – an invitation to the opening of London's first satirical laundrette. And I regularly received letters from proud parents saying, 'Dear David, When my son grows up, I want him to be a satirist. How should I go about it?'

For me it had been an extraordinary six months. I had been

'Stop laughing, you fool – they're taking the mickey out of people like us.'

through a heck of a transition, without feeling thrown by it. Apart from the stabilising effect of everything my parents had given me, there was the simple fact that we were just working too hard to have the time to get carried away. And it was a great help to be surrounded by people as wise and level-headed as Ned, Alasdair, Richard Armitage, Diana Crawfurd and now Jan.

Jan's experience in the public eye was invaluable. Thanks to the fact that her acting career had begun at the age of ten, she had had twelve years' more training than I had. And what training. At the age of fifteen she had been offered the lead role on Broadway in a new musical called *My Fair Lady*. She was not, however, a free agent. Because of her age she was contracted to the Associated British Picture Corporation, which had the right of veto over all her professional activities. This was in the days when the studios were still all-powerful. Nevertheless, on this occasion, she and her mother, the actress Thora Hird, were confident about getting an instant green light from C.J. Latta, then the head of ABPC. They arranged an appointment and told him the good news. Mr Latta listened, paused for a moment, and then uttered the immortal words, 'A musical of *Pygmalion*? Who on earth would want to go and see that? It could do your career immense damage – *no*.'

A few weeks after the last programme, when we were still on a high at the end of the series, a visit to the Montreux Festival provided Ned and me with something of a douche of cold water. At relatively short notice, and long after the official entries had been chosen, we were invited to bring a copy of the show everybody was talking about to be shown *hors de concours* at the festival, which was already established as the leading light-entertainment television festival in the world. The screening was a real anti-climax. With its attention to topical detail and its reliance on the news of that particular week in Britain, TW3 was scarcely ideal fare for an international festival like Montreux. Worse still, the soundtrack on the recording we had hand-carried from London was so blurred that even the British contingent could scarcely make out what was going on. Ned and I were left with the odd anecdote with which to console ourselves. In particular, one of the local officials had said to me in all seriousness, 'But Mr Frost, you must remember that we Swiss have lived through two world wars . . .'

As we left I vowed to myself that one day I was going to return to Montreux and make up for lost time. It was unlikely – only one BBC show could be entered each year – but it was definitely unfinished business.

When Donald Baverstock, Ned Sherrin and I climbed on board the plane back to London, our BBC tickets automatically took us into Economy. The refreshments were pretty sparse, but then a seventeen-year-old sound recordist with whom I had worked at Rediffusion very kindly brought us some champagne. ACTT rules insisted that the whole of the Rediffusion crew, returning from an overseas assignment, travel First Class.

Two weeks later I paid my first visit to what has ever since been my favourite hotel in Paris, the Hôtel Lancaster, with its old-fashioned comfort and understated elegance. The man responsible for introducing me to the Lancaster was an unlikely source for such information – it was not Egon Ronay, but Billy

Graham, with whom I was to conduct an interview for the *Daily Mail.*

Billy Graham was conducting a crusade in Paris at the Porte de Clignancourt. No one I asked in Paris had seemed to know quite where the meetings were being held, though, to be fair, this was not so much a reflection on Dr Graham's crusade as on my French. I was finally made aware of this fact by a very helpful lady who, convinced I was referring to Willy Brandt, told me very slowly, one syllable at a time, that I was in the wrong country and must catch a plane to Ger-man-y.

When the service began, the hymns were sung in French, but the 'sacred solos' by George Beverly Shea were in English, preceded by a translation. As Mr Shea's first song was 'He's Got the Whole World in His Hands' the interpreter's main task was to repeat the words 'dans ses mains, dans ses mains' approximately twenty-seven times.

Eventually, after all the preliminaries, came the message from Dr Graham. I was fascinated to discover that his impact was in no way diminished by having to speak through an interpreter. Though his critics in London had suggested darkly that he had developed an incantatory, indeed hypnotic, style of delivery, which lulled the unsuspecting listeners into making commitments they would not otherwise have made, it was clear that even when his words were interrupted every fifteen seconds or so for an interpreter, the power was still there.

'I was frightened. That's why I left England in 1954,' Billy Graham said the next morning in the lounge of the Lancaster. 'I don't want people pointing at me. I just want to point them to Jesus. And in 1954 I got frightened. I began to feel it was Billy Graham people were interested in, not Jesus Christ. I went to see the Archbishop of Canterbury – he was a good friend – and said that I could go anywhere in England and fill any stadium, but that I was worried.

'I explained why, and said that perhaps I should leave England. The Archbishop said that he thought that might be a good idea. But perhaps I was wrong. Perhaps if I'd gone all over England, there could have been a great revival . . . If I had known the right way to do it . . .'

In the *Daily Mail*, I fell to wondering what might have happened. 'Would we have become a nation as dull and narrow-minded as some of his followers? Or a nation as vibrantly alive and flagrantly Christian as Dr Graham himself? I wish he'd stayed.'

When I got back from Paris, I set off on a three-week variety tour with my TW3 colleague Kenneth Cope. We began at the Birmingham Hippodrome then went on to the Bristol Hippodrome and the Liverpool Empire, with a week at each. Ken and I greatly enjoyed our mini-tour, though two outside events, one political and one personal, tended to overshadow the second and third weeks.

During our second week, while we were in Bristol, the Profumo affair finally unravelled. However many rumours we had heard, there was still a degree of astonishment that Profumo, Macmillan's Government and the Establishment or whoever really had compromised themselves as much as we had, almost larkily, implied.

It was as if the Profumo affair had been the test case. Were the TW3 gang – and *Private Eye* and the rest – right or wrong? Was Britain in fact led by men of honour, and were we all just teenaged sneerers seeking to erode all that was fine and good in our green and pleasant land? The Profumo affair, however illogically, seemed to prove everything.

For years we had had a growing suspicion that the Old Order, while preaching stern Old Morality to its subjects, had been enjoying private passage-creeping on a basis that made even the New Morality look austere by comparison. Now the Establishment had been caught with its pants down and, unable to hide, was standing red-faced as everyone else fell about laughing. Game, set and match to satire!

Alfred O'Shaughnessy in *The Music Makers* wrote that each age is either an age that is dying or one that is coming to birth. The Profumo affair was the moment of passage. It was by no means the most significant event in the period 1956–63, but there is a moment in an earthquake when the pressure has built up and the tectonic plates start to shift. Something has to give. That moment was reached in the first week of June 1963.

And of course, if the Profumo rumours were true, what did that mean about all the others? The scene was set for a summer of Cabinet Ministers serving dinners naked except for a mask and noble lords who liked to strip naked after dinner in order for their guests to throw strawberry jam at them. The newspapers joined in gleefully. I picked up a *Daily Mirror* at Liverpool Street on my way to Beccles. Above the fold there was a huge headline: 'Prince Philip and the Profumo Affair'. When you bought the paper you were able to turn it over and read beneath the fold: 'No Connection Whatever'.

Ken's and my third week, at the Liverpool Empire, was overshadowed by the news of the death, of leukaemia, of Timothy Birdsall. He was just twenty-six. His friends had an inkling of what might be about to happen, but few of us were sure how much Tim knew. At the request of his wife Jot, Ned had produced a new contract for Tim, with much increased fees, so that he would worry less about the financial welfare of his children if he found out the truth about his condition during the series. Sadly, Jot was able to assure the BBC that the contract would never have to be honoured. Tim was the first artist to make drawing come alive on television. The impression was not just of a pen, but of a mind being transferred to paper. It speaks volumes for the taste of the British public that Tim's quiet, in some ways esoteric, throw-away humour caught on in the way it did. You used to strain to catch everything he said so as not to miss any of those almost incoherent little asides that used to spill out during our dialogues on the show.

In addition, his drawings in the *Spectator* and elsewhere had been growing in scope and stature every month. I found it difficult to come to terms with the fact that we would never know now what he would have gone on to do. 'He was too good to last,' Chris Booker said simply.

In June, Angus Wilson made a spirited attempt to explain TW3 and its impact in England to Americans through the magazine *Show*. 'The vogue for satire in England has come out of a general malaise, a sort of angry contemptuous disgust with the deadness of new affluence grafted on to old class-ridden

England; the discontent goes beyond political parties or even class loyalties.'

I was about to set off on my first trip to America myself. My love affair with the States began the moment I landed at Idlewild. I was well aware of what happened in the Fifties when Gilbert Harding, the legendary British broadcaster, had arrived in New York. In those days, apparently, the immigration forms still had a question to the effect, 'Is the reason for your visit to overthrow the Republic?' Gilbert had gazed at that disbelievingly and written, 'Not sole purpose of trip.' He was immediately arrested, albeit briefly. I was fortunate that my cab driver took me into New York by the Triborough Bridge route, so that on my very first visit I had that giddying view of the Manhattan skyline, at the time undoubtedly the greatest man-made view in the world. (Since 1973 it has been rivalled only by the view from Kirribilli of the Sydney Opera House and the Sydney Harbour Bridge.)

It had been a commonplace prediction that I would find the service in New York poor and New Yorkers rude. Quite the reverse. I was taken aback on my first visit to a shop where, having said, 'Thank you very much', a remark that would end a conversation in a shop in England, the assistant replied, 'You're welcome.' 'Oh, thank you very much,' I said in surprise. 'You're welcome,' she said. 'Thank you,' I said. 'You're welcome,' she said. The conversation could have gone on almost indefinitely if I hadn't been late for the theatre.

The theatre in question was the Golden, where *Beyond the Fringe* had been playing since October 1962. It was a great success, as was The Establishment, New York-style. I was staying at the Algonquin – and listening out for Round Table aphorisms everywhere – but at the weekend I went out to stay with Peter Cook, John Bird and the rest of the crew in Connecticut. It was there that Peter saved my life. Somehow I got out of my depth in the pool – a foolish move for anyone with my lack of swimming skills – and was rather lost for words, which tended to be replaced by gulps. At first Peter said that he thought, 'Ah, ho ho, David is making a satirical attack on drowning.' But then luckily he realised that matters might be getting out of hand

and fished me out. 'Thank God I did,' he said later. 'With all those stories at the time about our rivalry, no one would have believed I didn't do it on purpose.'

That was just about the only bad moment of my entire trip. The first-time visitor from London who was always being credited with a 'classless accent' back home loved the classlessness of New York. You did not need to be there for very long before you got a sense of the invigorating mobility of American society. Anybody could be President – and indeed, a couple of times in the intervening years, has been.

Among the publications, I was struck by the 'morbids' and by the Hollywood fan magazines. Both were new to me. The morbids like the *National Enquirer* and the *National Insider* had headlines like 'The Sunshine is Killing my Baby', 'Two Vicious Dogs Bit Boy 80 Times', '7m Sexless Giants Looking for a Steady Job' (eunuchs in India, not out-of-work civil servants) and 'Sues for Divorce, Wife Won't Sleep in Coffin'. I'd never seen anything quite like it. (You must remember this was some twenty-five years before the birth of *Sunday Sport*.)

The Hollywood fan magazines were past masters of the come-on sort of headline. Hayley Mills's 'Wicked, Wicked Ways' turned out to be her enjoyment of dressing-up and the fact that she was 'wild about shoes'. 'How Liz and Burton Make Love – 8 Pages of Pictures' turned out to be a set of stills from *Cleopatra*.

Impressions crowded in upon me. I was getting used to pavements being sidewalks, ground floors being the first floors; I learned that it wasn't lemon I wanted my drinks without, it was lime; and that the fact that a sign flashed at you with the message 'Don't Walk' didn't mean you had to run.

I left determined to return as soon as possible, and plunged straight back into English life at its most English – a summer season at the seaside, in this case Weston Super Mare. My co-star was Al Read, whom I regarded, whenever I heard him on radio, as a genius in his powers of observation. The show was called *Big Night Out*. In all conscience it was not a particularly big night out. The entire company, including Al and myself *and* the orchestra, numbered a total of thirteen. The Musical Campbells made up two, as did Allando and Babs, two very good dancers of the 'Five Feet in Harmony' variety. The Wedgewoods numbered three and the Don Riddell Four – who were the orchestra as well – completed the line-up. A cast of thousands it wasn't.

After Weston Super Mare (and a couple of Sunday concerts at Bournemouth) I made a quick talent-spotting trip to the Edinburgh Festival, then plunged full-time into preparing the next series of 'That Was The Week That Was'. It was at this stage that the BBC's Controller of Programmes, Stuart Hood, made a disastrous intervention. In the course of a press conference at Blackpool, he said of TW3: 'The programme was criticised towards the end of the run for smut, and this is something which we will be keeping a very sharp lookout for . . . We have seen what the mistakes on the last series were and it will be my hope that those mistakes will not be repeated.'

When this statement was reported to us, Ned and I were furious. It was such a gift to our enemies. You don't label yourself with a pejorative word like 'smut'. If you must make the point at all, you talk about the programme having 'possibly on some occasions been a little too outspoken on matters of sex'. You don't accuse yourself of smut any more than freedom fighters describe themselves as terrorists.

What's more, we didn't think the show had been guilty of smut anyway. Sure, there may have been a few too many *double entendres*. The Romantic Novelists item we did remember as an error. But smut? Nonsense, we thought. 'I don't think we have had smut in programme,' Ned told the *News of the World*. 'The fly buttons and knickers sketches were just good jokes,' he said to the *Mirror*. 'Smutty is the wrong word,' I added. 'We're bawdy, healthy and robust. We will go on being bawdy.' In other interviews we talked of 'honest vulgarity'. All this must put us on a collision course with Stuart Hood, suggested the *News of the World*. The *Daily Express*, still very much in the anti-TW3 camp at that time, said in an editorial headed 'No More Smut – What is Happening in the BBC?':

> First Mr Stuart Hood, the Television Programme Controller, says that the smut will be cut out of the programme 'That Was The Week That Was' when it returns on 28 September.

> Then the show's producer denies that there was ever any smut. The impression is given that the programme will continue as before. Mr Hood must tell the BBC's bright young men that they do not have a licence to behave as they please. He should say that either they mend their ways or else they do not return to the screen.

As far as TW3 was concerned, Stuart Hood had scored a spectacular own goal. Try as we might, we realised that we could not possibly succeed in turning the subject of the debate into 'honest vulgarity' when a juicy word like 'smut' had been introduced into the dialogue. We did not know at the time how much agonising there had been in the higher echelons of the BBC about 'That Was The Week That Was' while it had been off the air. However, there was one other straw in the wind. Stuart Hood had also announced: 'The programme will be fifty minutes long, and there will be a programme after it.' Instead of an open-ended TW3 closing the evening on BBC 1, it was now to be followed by a rerun of a truly forgettable series.

B.A. Young wrote despairingly in *Punch*:

> Why the BBC has so evidently decided to harass the opening of the second season of 'That Was The Week That Was', after having earned such adulation for having introduced it last year, is simply one of those minor mysteries about the Corporation that it may never be given us to understand . . . And so we see the programme planners robbing TWTWTW of the charm of its unpredictable duration and its basic requirement of being the last programme of the week and packing it into a firm schedule before – I can hardly believe it – 'The Third Man'.

I suggested a counter measure. Why didn't we get hold of the plots of 'The Third Man' and, at the end of the programme, why didn't I simply read them out, and give away the endings? Wouldn't that sabotage 'The Third Man'? Ned loved the idea, though both of us thought that all hell would break loose when we tried it.

We began the new series the way we had ended the last one, with Roy Kinnear and Millicent Martin discussing what was on television. They couldn't quite recall what 'That Was The Week That Was' had been. Then one of them remembered. 'You know, they had that young critic . . . he used to insult people . . . W.A. Darlington . . .' But it was when they remembered the phrases 'the bum and po show', and 'take your knickers off', that they started to get enthusiastic. The sketch was only intended as a throwaway but it summed up our feelings about the ludicrousness of the incipient Grundyism.

It was the week of the publication of the Denning Report on the Profumo affair. That was where the song began:

Macmillan's been reading Lord Denning in bed
He'd have found it might be livelier
With a Trollope instead

There were spoof reviews of the work. One from the drama critic of the *Sunday Times*, Harold Hobson: 'Whether Lord Denning knows it or not, he has written a very moral book.' Another from the Attorney General, Sir John Hobson, 'A masterpiece of suspense – in fact I thought I was going to be suspended myself.' Eddie Cantor, we reported, had recorded his comment in 1932.

Mandy, Mandy, there's a minister handy.
Everything's fine and dandy
If we can only make him pay . . .

As the main *oeuvre* of our coverage, there was one of Geoffrey Martin's memorable photomontages – the Denning Report animated to the lyrics of 'I Could Write a Book'.

The team excelled themselves in a Beatles number on the Liverpool Sound and then an item on the Sheffield Sound – a policeman with a rhino whip, following recent allegations against the constabulary of that particular city. 'Which once again raises the question,' I added, 'should people in police custody be armed?'

Sir Cyril Osborne MP, feeling, he said, like 'a puritan in

Babylon', had come to the studio to take on Bernard Levin. He was in a spirited mood. At one stage Bernard said resignedly to him, 'Make your silly point.' 'I'm trying to make a silly point to a silly person . . .' said Sir Cyril.

'You're gonna have these statistics whether you like it or not,' Sir Cyril said later. '"Whether you like it or not" seems to be your favourite phrase, Sir Cyril,' replied Levin. With battle cries of 'Don't nod your silly head,' and 'Take sex out of this show and you've nothing left,' Sir Cyril refused to bow before the Levin onslaught.

Later, he told the *Daily Telegraph*, 'I felt I would like to give the performers a good bath. It is fantastic that Millicent Martin should be getting £1800 a week, which is all some hospital matrons earn in a year.' It would indeed have been fantastic if Millicent Martin was getting £1800 a week. Since I was getting £225 a week, I would have had something to say about it myself. The figure was, in fact, £180 a week.

After all the talk of censorship and a return to morality with Sir Cyril, a number of Civil Defence units had provided me with a perfect postscript. It was a card which read: 'The man who hands you this is an air-raid warden. Lie down and do exactly as he tells you.' There was an item about the *Radio Times* done in the 'What the Papers Say' format which didn't quite work, and then a powerful song called 'Time to Choose' inspired by the first night of the play *The Representative*, about Pope Pius XII's alleged indifference to the Holocaust.

Then it was time for Irwin C. Watson, a black comedian Ned and I had spotted in the United States during the summer. 'What does the C. stand for, Irwin?' I asked. 'Caucasian,' he replied.

Irwin had a puzzled, low-key delivery: 'I went to this hotel in the South. They said they'd give me a room with running water. How was I to know that Running Water was an Iroquois Indian?'

We were almost at the end of the show. I mentioned to viewers that there was a programme following TW3 called 'The Third Man', but, realising that they might well be 'wanting to get off to bed now', I told them the plot. 'It's about the ex-president of an unnamed South American state. The plane which seems to have crashed – hasn't really . . . and Marta, the fascinating girl spy, is in fact working for the enemy. So why bother?' The audience greatly enjoyed this little piece of in-house sabotage, though Ned and I were convinced it would be a one-week phenomenon.

Then it was back to the main news of the week. 'When Mr Macmillan asked what Christine Keeler was going to do after this was all over, and was told "She's going to go back to modelling," Macmillan said, "Oh God, he's not in it too, is he?" And that was it for the first of the new series of 'That Was The Week That Was'.

It was a satisfactory start to the series, though nothing breathtaking. The second show was also a pretty workmanlike effort. There was a surprising headline from a newspaper in Stratford-upon-Avon: 'Denning Report Clears Profumo', an interpretation which had eluded most other commentators. And, to our delight, nobody had attempted to ban references to the plot of 'The Third Man', so I was able to tell viewers that this week's edition was called 'The Indispensable Man', and to inform them that 'Zoltan Elescu tries to get a plane to help Harry Lime transport air-conditioners to Calcutta.' Dr Fourtier, I warned viewers, was not to be trusted. The villain of the piece would turn out to be Vassily Gurevidivi, who tries to kill Harry Lime, but the police rescue him. Once again we had saved viewers from having to spend half an hour watching 'The Third Man' – public service broadcasting at its best. After a couple of weeks more, Ned told me that Alasdair Milne had told him that Stuart Hood had told him that Sir Hugh Greene had told him, 'Make "That Was The Week That Was" the last programme on Saturday night again.' Ned and I celebrated a highly improbable victory.

'The Third Man' apart, these first few weeks were not particularly victorious. There was a general feeling in the air that TW3 was not performing up to its previous standard. Whether or not this was true – and I think the evidence is about fifty-fifty – it was perceived to be true. There certainly had not been an unforgettable humdinger of a show in the first few weeks of the second series. But there had not been a new Profumo affair either. Perhaps people's anticipation had been built to a point where it was impossible to fulfil. Perhaps, as Ned has said, the love affair was simply too hot not to cool down. And TW3's critics now had the words of Stuart Hood to use in evidence.

On the subject of smut, prudery and censorship, we had a piece from Kenneth Tynan which was one of those bursts of inspiration that sums up a whole issue. It was called simply 'Dreams Bit'.

> Dear Sir,
> I hope I am not a prude, but I feel compelled to lodge a protest against the recent outbreak of violence and sexuality in dreams. Many of my friends have been as shocked and sickened as I have been by the filth poured out nightly as soon as our eyes are closed. It is certainly not my idea of 'home entertainment'.
>
> Night after night, the most disgraceful scenes of perversion and bestiality are perpetrated in the name of 'freedom of expression', though I would call it licensed smut peddling. In the past week, for instance, I counted six rapes, one of them involving a woman old enough to be my mother (indeed, I thought at the time she was my mother), and several sadistic orgies in which grotesque and appalling liberties were taken with members of the Royal Family.
>
> Things have come to a parlous state when a loyal citizen and lifelong supporter of the church cannot drop off for a few minutes without being forced to witness such unedifying spectacles as last night's episode, in which a senior Buckingham Palace official was seen ravishing the middle-aged lady I mentioned before – and wearing my old school blazer to do it.
>
> Yours sincerely,
> Aren't we all.

Though Alasdair Milne cocooned us superbly from the pressures, we were vaguely aware of increased political rumblings in high places. They all came to a head on Saturday 19 October, the week Lord Home became Prime Minister and Leader of the Conservative Party. We were angry. Most people of our age were angry. The Conservative Party appeared to have learned nothing from recent events. We asked Chris Booker to write an appropriate piece, and over a day or so the idea emerged of Benjamin Disraeli writing a letter to his latest successor, which I would deliver. Throughout the programme members of the team would ask, 'What about Lord Home?' and I would reply, 'Later.'

Chris had prepared a rousing and stylish piece of invective in the style of Disraeli:

> Just as you are the holder of an ancient earldom through no intention of your own, so stage by stage you have been raised up the ladder of our public life – again through no intention of your own – until at last you have been lifted above the heads of the multitude as a bloody and archaic sacrifice. Your bleak deathly smile is the smile today not of a victor – but of a victim. You are the dupe and unwitting tool of a conspiracy: the conspiracy of a tiny band of desperate men who have seen in you their last slippery chance of keeping the ladders of power and influence within their privileged circle. For the sake of that prize, which can at best be transitory, these men are prepared to dash all the hopes of the party they profess to love, and of the nation which they profess to serve – or rather the two nations, which by their actions they seek to perpetuate.
>
> . . . You have always drifted with the tide – the tide of appeasement, the tide of Suez, even the tide of growing rapprochement with the forces of Communism – you have drifted without understanding and that tide has eventually left you naked and exposed on the shore. The art of statesmanship, as my contemporary Mr Bright once observed, consists as much in foreseeing as in doing. You, my lord, in your sixty years have foreseen nothing . . . You are qualified only to accept one lesson from history: let it be this. That of all the men who have held your office in the past sixty years, there have been but two kinds. Such ministers as Mr Gladstone, my rival, Mr Lloyd George and Macmillan, your predecessor, who understood and mastered their office but grew jealous and held on too long. So that they

were eventually hustled out, more vilified than they deserved, their exercise of power turned sour by over-use. And on the other hand, such tiny men as Eden, Bonar Law and Chamberlain, who may have promised much but proved no better in their offices than would the meanest of their supporters. For these men, my lord, history has no gratitude, no honour and no mercy. Reflect for a moment, my lord, in this hour of your triumph, into which of these two categories your ministry is likely to fall.

At the end of the programme I summed up with a quick ad-lib: 'So that's the choice before the electorate. On the one side, Lord Home; on the other, Harold Wilson. Dull Alec versus Smart Alec. Good night.'

There were more than six hundred phone calls of complaint, and only sixty of congratulation. The *Daily Herald* managed to headline its story with the upbeat words 'TW3 Smashes Complaints Record', but in the corridors of power and on the sixth floor of Television Centre, the reaction was not discernibly positive. We knew our piece had been savage, but we thought it was more than justified. Others felt that we had 'gone too far'. In retrospect, that item was probably the death-knell of TW3, although for the next three Saturday nights it seemed to be business as usual.

Then, on Wednesday 13 November, came the stunner. The BBC announced that 'The present run of "That Was The Week That Was" will end on 28 December 1963 and not continue, as had originally been intended, until the spring.' The reason given was that 1964 would be an election year, and 'the political content of the programme, which has been one of its principal and successful constituents, will clearly be more and more difficult to maintain'. This time the new complaints record was on our side. 'Election year? Tell that to the Marines' wrote the most widely quoted viewer. Other newspapers ruminated on why the BBC had not realised several months earlier that an election was due in 1964. In the *Daily Mail* Peter Black called it 'a win for the crypto-idiots who think it vulgar to criticise their betters, and the crypto-fascists who cannot bear to see authority mocked'. Harold Wilson as Leader of the Opposition said, 'The Labour Party has enjoyed attacks made on itself with attacks made on others. We would very much deplore it if a popular programme were taken off as a result of political pressure.' Some cynics wondered if Harold would have enjoyed the programme *quite* as much if he had been in government, but in general the reaction was almost unanimous.

Sir Cyril Osborne, characteristically, had a minority view:

I'm damned pleased. It wasn't English at all. There are some things that English men and women hold as sacred, and they are against these Clever Dicks and their filth. I think I helped to kill the programme when I sent to the powers-that-be hundreds of letters I had received from ordinary people who saw me on the programme. Everyone was on my side, you know. They are sick of sneers against everything that is nice and decent. If I helped to get it off television, I'm delighted.

'The real reason it's off is that nothing we can think up nowadays can ever be funnier than the politicians themselves!'

Ned and I sat in the office on that Wednesday morning trying to work out what our reaction should be. We knew that Martin Jackson of the *Daily Express* was on his way to Lime Grove seeking an interview. Though our initial reaction was obviously to let rip, we quickly decided that an extreme response, or taking verbally to the streets, was out. It would be unproductive, and could look like a case of 'They've taken our ball away.' We asked David Nobbs and Peter Tinniswood, who worked as a team at that time, to start on a 'Cancellation News', and resolved that while Saturday night's proceedings would certainly not be muzzled in any way, for the time being we would try and make our points as clearly, but as lightly, as we could.

We rang the rest of the team to coordinate our approach, and then spoke to Martin Jackson. The BBC's actions were being seen as petty, but we tried to stay cool. I told Martin the same thing I told other journalists, in almost the same words: 'In a way, it's a compliment. I am delighted the show is being taken so seriously. Though, in a sense, I suppose election year is just when it's needed most.'

'TW3 Killed – BBC Faces Storm' said the front page of the *Daily Mirror*. Dee Wells in the *Daily Herald* chimed in with the headline, 'The BBC Goes Back to Beddy-Byes'.

Willie Rushton was quoted as saying, 'This shows there's still a healthy fear of satire.' Millicent Martin added, 'What a super way to go out. This is really the final acclaim. We have to stop because people might have done what we say.' By Saturday morning this approach seemed to have paid off. There, to our astonishment, in *The Times* was the BBC's Director of Television, Kenneth Adam, giving a 'Satire is dead, long live satire' speech on the Friday. He told his audience at the Friday Night Club in London that television satire would not end with the death of TW3. 'I do not believe we could stop this kind of programme for good even if we wanted to,' he said.

The 'most insidious' canard he wished to dispose of was that 'we do not mean what we say when we talk of returning to political satire after the election. To those who use inelegant or irresponsible phrases such as "the BBC returns to beddy-byes" I would say, "Wait and see." TW3 is the voice of dissent and it uses a different instrument, a plain and pointed pen with which it has pricked many a humbug and burst many a fraudulent balloon.' The audience it created 'will not be indefinitely denied, nor do we intend it should be. And that is not a pious hope, it is a promise.'

Having read these words with some astonishment, we got on with the show. David Nobbs and Peter Tinniswood had prepared a splendid draft of the 'Cancellation News':

> The BBC announced this afternoon that the present series of 'Andy Pandy' will end on 28 December. It is felt that in an election year the political content of this programme, which is one of its most successful ingredients, will be more and more difficult to maintain.
>
> Also under the axe is 'Dr Kildare'. I quote: 'In a recent episode a young woman was shown in labour pains.' To comply with BBC regulations she should also have been shown in Conservative pains, Independent pains and Nat-Lib pains.'

Al Mancini brought me a stop-press piece of paper: 'And it seems that "Compact" will end as well. But don't worry. The BBC assure us that "When they become viable again, badly written trivial programmes of this nature, with no political, humorous or social content whatsoever, will continue to be shown at peak viewing hours." "Panorama" and "Gallery", of course, will continue. They have no political significance in election year or any other year.'

There was also a reference in the programme to one of life's little ironies. 'The American version of "That Was The Week That Was" aired last Sunday. It seemed to go quite well, but of course they're going to be in trouble next year – they have an election coming up.'

The NBC pilot special had been hosted by Henry Fonda, described in one British paper as 'America's David Frost', which, if he ever saw it, must have bewildered him considerably after thirty years' highly distinguished service in films and television. At the time it just seemed like another news item to me. The realisation that the BBC's sudden decision might actually give *me* the chance to be 'America's David Frost' had not yet sunk in.

The *Spectator* summed up: 'Of course, TW3 isn't what it was, which simply means that we aren't what we were. The programme itself has changed our conception of television, made us greedier for shocks and new sensations. Now we blame it because we're less shockable. I suppose people soon turned against Columbus for not discovering America every week.'

The following Friday night Ned and I were due at the Dorchester Hotel, where the Guild of Television Producers were to honour the production team of 'That Was The Week That Was' with their special award. The early editions of the newspapers on Saturday 23 November were full of headlines like '"That Was The Week That Was" Wins an Oscar' (*Daily Express*) and 'TW3 Wins a Real Pat on the Back' (*Daily Mirror*). Alas, the later editions had a far more serious priority. As we arrived at the Dorchester, the news was just coming through from Dallas that President Kennedy had been shot, perhaps killed. Nothing else mattered for the rest of the evening. Ned and I took it in turns to find hotel phones in order to talk to our writers about how we could do justice to the news. At the end of the evening Ned went back to the BBC Television Centre while I went off to fulfil what had become a commitment for which I had no heart – the fifth of my six appearances at Quaglino's that week in cabaret. I have never been less in sympathy with the old maxim that 'the show must go on' than on that particular evening, but I got through it and went off to meet up with Ned. We reached no conclusions, and agreed to try again the following morning.

Next day we began trying to work out what we should do about the assassination before we dealt with the rest of the week. It rapidly became clear that there *was* no 'rest of the week'. That was it. We abandoned rehearsing material about Labour policies, Questions in the House and the South African national anthem, and sent the cast home for a few hours.

Chris Booker drafted some linking lines for the programme and for an ensemble reflection by the whole cast, which I edited. Herbert Kretzmer was at work on a song for Millicent Martin, with music composed by Dave Lee. We asked Bernard Levin for two pieces – one on his reflections on power and the other a throw-forward to the years of Lyndon Johnson. Ned asked Caryl Brahms to prepare a poem about Jackie Kennedy, and contacted Dame Sybil Thorndike to read it. Donald Baverstock was very clear on our priorities. TW3 had begun with the emphasis on words, the right words. The right words tonight would catch the mood of a funeral oration, an elegy, something which seemed to have been lacking in all the news coverage. Donald had one other inspired thought that day. Long before satellites could beam words and pictures live from continent to continent, he ordered that the programme be recorded on the American line standard as well as the British line standard, so that it could be flown immediately to the United States.

Somehow or other Herbert Kretzmer and Dave Lee managed to finish the song, and Millicent Martin had a chance to rehearse it – once. We thought Bernard Levin's piece on President Johnson might be a touch too long, but when we tried to edit it, we found it was so tightly structured and clearly argued that the most we could remove without spoiling it was five lines. Donald Baverstock had a last-minute thought for one of my pieces to camera. And following Bernard Levin's piece – it felt so right during camera rehearsal – we decided that all that was needed from me at the end was my concluding paragraph, and not the three paragraphs that led up to it.

Most weeks Ned and I conducted a warm-up before the show. On that particular evening, it had to be a freeze-up. I explained to the audience that there would be none of the usual diverse review of the week and no – absolutely no – jokes.

I spoke first:

> The reason why the shock was so great, why when one heard the news last night one felt suddenly so empty, was because it was the most unexpected piece of news one could possibly imagine. It was the least likely thing to happen in the world. If anyone else had died – Sir Winston Churchill, De Gaulle, Khrushchev – it would have been something we could understand and even perhaps accept. But that Kennedy should go – well, we just didn't believe in assassination any more. Not in the civilised world anyway.

Roy Kinnear spoke next:

> When Kennedy was elected three years ago, it was as if we'd all been given some gigantic, miraculous present. Suddenly, over there in Washington was this amazing man who seemed to be so utterly right for the job in every way that we took him completely for granted. Whenever we thought about the world, we had that warm image at the back of our minds of a man who would keep everything on the rails. And now that present has been taken away from us; when we thought we still had five more years before we need start worrying again.

Then David Kernan said, 'It's funny how people used to talk about Eisenhower as a father figure. Kennedy was far more of a father figure to most of us than Ike ever was.' Al Mancini talked about the bad luck that had dogged the Kennedy family. Kenneth Cope talked about the unprecedented reaction to the news of JFK's death around the world. Willie Rushton talked about the film-star image, the expectations we had of him. Lance Percival continued:

> But once Kennedy was in office the dream came true. When most statesmen die they have to be explained away with words like integrity and cunning and courage. But Kennedy did not need such apologies – for he was simply and superlatively a man of his age, who understood his age, who put all his own energy and the best brains of his country into solving its problems, and who ended up, in more cases than not, by doing the right thing at the right time because he had gone about it in the right way.

Then it was my turn to sum up the opening.

> Few people would have thought at the beginning of this year that, by its end, we would have lost the Leader of the Opposition in Britain, Pope John in Rome and the President of the United States. We've been very aware of death this

year. Even here in this studio we have lost someone we still miss. But with the murder of John Kennedy death has become immediate to people all over the world. For the first time, because of the stature of the man and the nature of a shrinking world, people everywhere feel they've lost someone they'll miss.

Yesterday one man died. Today, in America, sixty lost their lives in a fire. And yet, somehow, it is the one that matters. Even in death, it seems, we are not all equal. Death is not the great leveller. Death reveals the eminent.

Those last two sentences were Donald Baverstock's last-minute addition. Then we segued into Herbert Kretzmer's song, 'The Summer of His Years'. With its western flavour and its insistent Civil War beat, it remains moving to this day, as was demonstrated by viewers' reactions when we played it on TV-am on the twenty-fifth anniversary of JFK's death.

I linked into Bernard Levin's reflections on power, spoken by Robert Lang. Then Dame Sybil Thorndike read Caryl Brahms's words, 'To Jackie'. Bernard Levin then spoke the second piece we had asked him to write – about the prospects for the future under President Johnson. In the twenty-four hours since President Kennedy's assassination, many heart-broken commentators had understandably sought to underline his greatness by deprecating his successor. In the emotional atmosphere of the moment, that was very easy to do. Yet Bernard, in one of his many finest hours, resisted that. He saw through it.

I believe that this global responsibility has fallen into good hands. The contrasts between President Kennedy and his successor are more obvious than important. Johnson, unlike Kennedy, is not an intellectual; but neither was Truman. Johnson is provincial where Kennedy was metropolitan; but his years as leader of the Senate gave him a knowledge, understanding and control of the realities of power in politics almost as sophisticated as that of Roosevelt . . . Though a Southerner, his record on the colour question – the rock on which America's future must either

> be built or sink – is one of the best in the Democratic Party; it was he who steered through the Congress the only successful Civil Rights legislation of recent years, and during the 1960 elections he and his wife faced physical violence in their home state for his liberal stand . . . Nobody tonight can wish more fervently than President Johnson himself that this dreadful opportunity had not fallen on him. But since it has, we, citizens of the alliance he now leads, have the right to hope for much from his leadership, and the duty to wish him well with all our hearts. I think those hopes and wishes will not be disappointed. A poet hymned an earlier, narrower moment of crisis in the life of the United States; how much more bitterly relevant are those words today.
>
> *Sail on, oh ship of state,*
> *Sail on, oh Union strong and great,*
> *Humanity, with all its fears,*
> *With all the hopes of future years*
> *Is hanging breathless on thy fate.*

The programme, twenty-two minutes long rather than the usual fifty or fifty-five, was virtually over. I summed up: 'The tragedy of John Kennedy's death is not that the liberal movements of history that he led will cease: it is that their gathering momentum may be lost. That is the aftermath of Dallas, 22 November. It is a time for private thoughts. Good night.'

Thanks to Donald Baverstock, by Sunday night the programme was available to American viewers on NBC. At their request, it was repeated more than once on Monday. The Congressional Record of Wednesday 4 December includes the words of Hubert Humphrey:

> 'Art,' said the philosopher Santayana, 'is the trick of arresting the immediate.' This programme did indeed arrest the immediate. In all its ugly hardness but also in its searing tragedy, and in its depth of meaning in history, hope and duty. We have apparently been studied deeply – far more

than from Friday evening to Saturday night, the time it took to write and produce the program.

It is humbling to know what our friends think and hope. I wish to thank the British Broadcasting Corporation and through them the individuals who wrote and produced the program. I ask unanimous consent to have the BBC-copyright transcript printed in the Congressional Record.

Bernard's two pieces for the programme were a reminder of how often he had excelled in the series not only as an *agent provocateur* in ad-lib face-to-face combat, but also in prepared pieces. My own favourite was the piece he wrote for us on the subject of John Milton:

There is no such book as *Paradise Lost*. I begin thus *in media res* because the thesis I have to advance is so startling that there is no point in trying to break it gently. The simple truth is, there is no such book as *Paradise Lost*, and what is more there never has been . . . It is true that if you go into a library, say, or a bookshop that stocks the classics, you will find upon the shelves various editions of a book labelled *Paradise Lost* by John Milton. And it is equally true that if you open one of these volumes at the first page, you will find a work beginning:

Of man's first Disobedience and the Fruit
Of that Forbidden Tree . . .

You may read on, wondering what on earth I'm talking about. But about line 38 ('of rebel Angels by whose aid aspiring . . .') the reader will be struck, if he is quick-witted, by the realisation that he has not so far understood one word of the proceedings, that there have so far been only two full stops and the same number of main verbs, and that he would much rather be watching television. Certain tougher individuals may struggle on for a few more lines, perhaps getting as far as line 56 ('. . . round he throws his baleful eyes') before giving up. And I believe that one or two readers have managed to get as far as line 75 ('Oh, how unlike the place from whence they fell!') before collapsing into neurasthenia. There are, as it happens, a further thirty-four lines; the work ends on line 109 – a singularly meaningless line, reading 'and what is else not to be overcome?'

And that is all . . . The remaining pages of all the books labelled *Paradise Lost* consist of gibberish, words put down in any order to fill out the lines, excerpts from dictionaries, phone books, cookery books, manuals of instruction enclosed with electrical apparatus, the Bible (a very popular source, this last) and anything else that the particular editor can lay his hands on to disguise the fact that there is no such work as the one of which he is supposed to be producing yet another uncalled-for and unwanted edition . . . It is a rarely observed but undeniable fact that all the quotations from *Paradise Lost* are from the first eighty-one lines of Book One . . .

Bernard was also responsible for inventing the ultimate rebuff to the more intolerant letters from 'Disgusted of Droitwich'. His replies would conclude with the simple words, 'Dictated by Mr Levin and signed in his *presence* by . . .'

After the Kennedy programme, TW3 remained in high gear for the rest of its run. Maybe the thought of having 'only five weeks to live' concentrated our minds wonderfully; maybe TW3's imminent removal concentrated other people's.

Like the funeral of a man at the end of a long and happy life, the programme at the end of TW3's somewhat shorter happy life was more of a celebration than a wake. We reprised a lot of the sketches I have mentioned, and during the closing credits we dismantled the set – a task made easier by the fact that we didn't really have one – and the cast disappeared from view in a sports car.

TW3 had lasted for a span of thirteen months with a total of just thirty-seven editions. It had been a short run, but the memories lingered on. Its impact was probably two-fold – in television terms and in social terms. In television terms, Sir Hugh Carleton Greene's biographer, Michael Tracey, has written: 'TW3 blazed a trail; it opened the possibility of political humour on TV; it signalled new kinds of language, thought and wit.' The BBC certainly became 'us' against 'them' for the first time since the advent of ITV in 1955. The artificial barriers between current affairs and comedy, and between journalistic research and humour, had been breached. Other producers were already telling us how TW3 had liberated them to experiment in previously forbidden or uncharted territory.

In social terms, TW3 sprang to life at a time of rising dissatisfaction, in November 1962, untainted with the brush of the Fifties. Increasingly, as a country, we no longer trusted the people whose business was leadership, who were born to rule, and who were older and knew better than us. Indeed, some of those with the most self-righteous outward moral tone were already exhibiting the greatest inner moral corruption. In London there were some other vehicles for this protest, such as *Private Eye* or The Establishment, but out in the provinces for a mass audience there was only 'That Was The Week That Was'. Whether TW3 triggered the mood more than the mood triggered TW3 or vice versa is probably unanswerable. What is certain is the interaction between the two. TW3 was probably one step – or two or three – ahead of what people were thinking and feeling, but not yet saying. It was never seventeen steps ahead. That would not have caught on: there would have been no expectant or receptive mood to tap. TW3 was not some blinding light on the road to Damascus: it was a lens, focusing the light without absorbing it.

'But, Mr Frost, was it satire?' (And does it matter!) Juvenal defined satire as an outburst against a serious wrongdoing or folly in the social or political sphere, so I suppose the answer to the question is, 'Sometimes.' Sometimes it was satire, sometimes it was documentary; at other times it was sketches, jazz, confrontation, vaudeville, revue or just simply some bloody good writing from some bloody good writers.

At the end of 1963, the society-based dogma of the Fifties had been discredited; the individual-based Sixties were getting into full swing. 'Do your bit' was no longer the motto. Now it was 'Do your thing.' Of course, that was not the whole truth either. But it was the half of the truth needed at the moment.

FOUR

First-Time Commuter

WITH A REMARKABLY PRECISE sense of timing, I set off for a new adventure in the United States on the first day of a new year, 1964. Jan arrived three days later, having informed a posse of inquisitive reporters at London Airport that she was 'going to get a refill for my mother's pen'.

The producer of the American TW3, Leland Hayward, had approached me early in December to guest as 'our London correspondent' on the first three programmes of the American series. Both Richard Armitage and Diana Crawfurd had understandably counselled against accepting the offer. The money wasn't great, and it was not a hosting role, more a guesting one. Everybody I spoke to felt that I should wait for a better opportunity. I couldn't see what that better opportunity would be, and decided to make the best of this one. Besides, my trip to America the previous summer had whetted my appetite. It was time to have a go.

The first thing I noticed when I arrived was the age of almost everybody associated with the American TW3. Leland Hayward and his team were of a different generation to the TW3 team in London. They were not young people new to television, who reflected the trends in society and among their equally exasperated peers: they were older, more established figures trying to reflect a trend in entertainment which had been highly successful in its out-of-town try-out, and could hopefully now be equally successful on the Great White Way.

Leland himself was over sixty. Despite his youthful close-cropped hair, he was an unlikely choice for the role he was fulfilling. He was one of the aristocrats of the theatre, 'the man who brought you *The Sound of Music*', and Herman Rush of Herb

Siegel's GAC agency, who had negotiated the rights to the show with the BBC, had brought him in for a sound reason. He figured that before any of the very conservative American networks would consider taking on such a controversial project, they would need reassurance on the grounds of taste. Who better to provide it than Leland Hayward?

Leland had become a real American gent. He would probably never have understood a group of twenty-four-year-olds who wanted to tear down the American Establishment of which he had worked so hard to become a member, but he was a great character. Over a welcoming drink he told me the story of his visit to Baroness von Trapp, in order to get her permission to be portrayed in *The Sound of Music*. He found that there was a priest with whom she was sharing her house. And her life. She was also, Leland told me, somewhat less sympathetic than her later theatrical and screen portrayal. Leland had been as generous as possible: 'We are portraying you in the best possible way; with Mary Martin, and music by Rodgers and Hammerstein. It's obviously a privilege to be depicted in this way, but we do need your permission, of course, and I am prepared to make a very generous suggestion to you of ten per cent of the profits. *Ten per cent* of the profits.' Leland had expected an immediate, pleasantly surprised and deeply grateful acceptance. Instead the Baroness had replied, 'My dear Mr Hayward, I never make any decision like this without the help of the Holy Ghost, so if you will excuse me for a moment, I will go to the church to consult the Holy Ghost.' She rose, gathered up her live-in priest and went off to the church, leaving Leland and his wife sitting there for an hour. The Baroness finally returned, smiled a beatific smile, and said, 'My dear Mr Hayward, the Holy Ghost says fifteen per cent.'

Leland was a possible ally. He had seen the potential box-office value of the 'host and co-creator' of the original, but Marshall Jamieson, the line-producer, was, I suspect, slightly less convinced. Or at least mildly bewildered about how to integrate my contributions with those of the company he had already assembled. Of the two link-men of those early editions, Elliott Reid, a veteran of many light revues, was genial. His co-host,

Henry Morgan, could not always disguise the fact that he thought I was superfluous.

The atmosphere was perfectly pleasant, but for someone with only three weeks in which to make his mark, a touch fragile. The writers were led by Bob Emmett, a seasoned TV pro from more traditional variety shows, and Gerald Gardner, inventor of the best-selling *Who's in Charge?* political caption books. They seemed glad to have me around but, as I became aware that even the lines they wrote for me might be hijacked, I quickly realised that I had better supply as much material for myself as I could.

It was clear that TW3 in the United States was going to be a very different working experience. TW3 in the UK had been intensely communal, collegial, founded on teamwork. TW3 in the States was going to be lonelier and more competitive, with more fighting your own corner. Naturally I wished it was otherwise but, as the new boy on the block, I could scarcely rewrite the local ground rules. When in Little Italy . . .

In the midst of all this, AFTRA – the American Federation of Television and Radio Artists – stepped in. Two days before the first show they advised the US Immigration Service to deny me a working visa. Leland Hayward had applied for this on my behalf, and had assumed that events were taking their desired course, as they usually did in those days in the theatre. Now he went back into battle. He immediately announced that he considered me essential to the show. Needless to say, I was mortified by the development, but felt that publicly I must play it cool. 'There is nothing I can do about it,' I told British and American press alike. 'Perhaps the whole thing is a reprisal for our selling those buses to Cuba. If I don't get the permit then I shall just have to settle back and take pleasure in watching the first show.' That was OK as a public front, but it did not reflect how much I was holding my breath – 'Pacing up and down our apartment at the Shoreham,' Jan said later. Contrary to the advice I had received in London, I felt that an opportunity like this would not readily come again.

It was only on the morning of the first programme that I knew for sure that all was well. Late the night before, Mr P.A. Esperdy, the District Director of the US Immigration Service, had granted the visa. 'The evidence clearly established that he is a man of exceptional merit and ability, as contemplated by the Immigration Statute,' he was reported to have said. I had never met Mr Esperdy at the time, and I have never met him since, but I wish him to know here and now that if he or his family are ever in London, I hope they'll call me up and come round for a drink.

At 9.30 that evening, TW3 hit the air. Nancy Ames was America's TW3 girl, and the first comments within the opening number came from Elliott Reid and Henry Morgan. My first intervention was to the effect that 'German Chancellor Ludwig Erhard, after recently enjoying the bounteous hospitality of the LBJ Ranch, expressed his gratitude this week by re-naming one of Berlin's most beautiful thoroughfares.' Cut to caption: 'Unter den Lyndon'.

The sponsors included Clairol ('Only her hairdresser knows for sure'), Raleigh and Bel Air light menthol cigarettes, and Speidel Twistoflex. They were all regular supporters of the programme, although Speidel's motto always remained something of a mystery to me – 'The wristband so flexible you can even tie it in a knot.' If you wanted to . . .

There was a good item on the House Rules Committee, a blackout on anti-semitism in an Arab hotel, in which I took part, then a trio of predictions from yours truly. '25 June: Liz Taylor free to marry at last. "I shall let her go," says Richard Burton.' Then a hand ballet from Burr Tillstrom, the great puppeteer. Burt had created this especially for the show, in a week when the Berlin Wall was opened for the first time – then closed again – when one and a quarter million meetings became, a few short hours later, one and a quarter million farewells. Using just his two bare hands, Tillstrom caught magically the feeling of one such meeting and farewell.

There was an interview with 'one of the best-dressed women in the world', Mrs William Weinberger Haverstraw, played by Doro Merende 'with pyjamas designed by Frank Lloyd Wright': 'Furs make me nervous, I always wonder if they are dead.'

'Mrs Weinberger Haverstraw, why do you prefer American designers?'

'They're the only ones who give stamps.'

There was a good political blackout, and then I had a brief monologue which was nearly cut but which I managed to preserve. It included a reference to General De Gaulle speaking of 'My bomb, my France, my army, my Europe and even occasionally, *mon Dieu*'; and a reference to the fact that Lord Home was in bed with flu 'or if you prefer, Lord Home was in bed with Flo.' It also included, with a superstitious flourish, a joke I had included in the first programme of the English series: 'I'm old enough to be your Führer,' but this time attributed to Erhard rather than Adenauer. Highly topical!

After an announcement that TW3 would be pre-empted the following week for the 'Bob Hope Christmas Special', the titles rolled. 'Our London Correspondent' appeared 'by special arrangement with the British Broadcasting Corporation'. We saluted the flexibility of the wristband, and that was it.

I had done just about enough to get noticed. According to *Newsweek* I summed up TW3 this way: 'The show should speak for the personal against the public. It must attack what is currently ludicrous and pernicious. And it must have an attitude, a point of view, a basis of moral values. The basis may be as inconspicuous as the backside of the moon, but it must be there.' Over the next two shows, with the combination of new material and the best of British – like the Hilton Hotel monologue – the Frostian foothold on American satirical soil became a touch firmer. On 3 February Leland Hayward announced that he had asked me to stay on for three more appearances on the show before returning to England. I was quoted in the *New York Times* as saying, 'Since I am taping sequences for a new British TV programme, and have to be here for at least two weeks, I have agreed.' That was traditional English understatement for 'Yippee!'

It had been a curious experience fighting for a place in your own show, but it had been worth it. The *New York Times* report went on, 'The first half-hour TW3 on the National Broadcasting Company received a cool reception from some television critics.

In the last two weeks, however, critics have said that its satirical point has been sharpened. "The important thing," Mr Frost said, "is that it's getting tougher. And I'm sure it will get tougher in days to come."'

All press interviews about the American TW3 involved the same tightrope walk: wanting to support my new colleagues, without suggesting that I would have done the show exactly the same way if I had been in control from the outset myself. After a six-week stay, Jan had to fly back to London and was confronted by a similar – perhaps identical – posse of reporters. She achieved a neat double. Was she planning to marry David Frost? 'David was in America while I was there and I saw a great deal of him. I also saw a lot of other people, including the four Beatles, and I am not marrying them either.'

The New York sequences that I was taping for a new British TV programme to which I had alluded were with Mike Nichols and Elaine May, at that time a celebrated comedy duo, prior to their separate and continuing careers as directors. The programme for which they were intended had a working title of 'The David Frost Programme', a brilliantly original title, variations of which I have used ever since. Its eventual title when it was screened in May was 'A Degree of Frost'. It was a BBC Light Entertainment Department programme, and although Tom Sloan, by then Head of BBC Light Entertainment, had been one of TW3's most unbending adversaries within the BBC, it obviously made no sense to continue jungle warfare on a personal basis. A chance meeting had given me the opportunity to suggest what became 'A Degree of Frost', and Bill Cotton, Jr., then Head of Variety, had eagerly championed it. I planned to corral some of our TW3 writers, maintain the IQ level of the comedy, and intermingle some conversation and some top acts. Mike Nichols and Elaine May were the first to say yes.

Nichols and May albums had been borrowed and reborrowed at Cambridge. Now they had agreed to perform two of their best sketches for me, in what turned out to be almost their last joint television appearance. These were heady days: taping a 'Tonight Show' with its new host, Johnny Carson, then returning to

Studio 6H for our own rehearsals, where across the hall Johnny's predecessor, the legendary Jack Paar, was taping his Friday night show, which followed TW3. Jack Paar's own predecessor, Steve Allen, came and guested with us on TW3. He volunteered to help with the warm-up. 'Do they get this show in Des Moines?' shouted a member of the audience. 'They *see* this show in Des Moines,' said Steve, 'but they don't *get* it.'

P.J. Clarke's was the place to go on a Sunday night in those days. Arriving direct from their live show, Bennett Cerf, Arlene Francis and the rest of the 'What's My Line?' team would hold court. Meanwhile I got myself used to the idea that minced beef, when called a hamburger, became the 'in' thing to order. I have a patchwork quilt of recollections of that first sustained stay in New York. My first bacon and eggs garnished with strawberries. My first sight of a piece of bacon drowned in maple syrup. Bermuda shorts, drains that steam, and slowly but surely finding your way around the *New York Times*. The London *Times* just could not match its range. Somehow I have never been able to escape the suspicion that, hidden among the paper's catacombs or tucked away in its filing cabinets on 43rd Street, there is a Pulitzer Prize winner on almost any topic the reader could name just waiting to be called out for a brief emergence into the sunlight of the printed page.

I was amazed by the influence of what I regarded as perverse lobby groups like the National Rifle Association, whose power – inexplicably to me – had not been dented in any way by the tragic event in Dallas of 23 November. Then there were the game shows, particularly the reward shows, as we would call them now. Worst of all, undoubtedly was 'Queen for a Day'. Every day four ladies tried to top – or bottom – one another's accounts of the misfortunes, disasters and bereavements that had befallen them – preferably simultaneously. They were each shown a huge array of prizes that might alleviate a little of their suffering – if they won. And they won if the volume of applause they got from the audience was greater than that of the other contestants.

The compere spoke first. (He was in fact unspeakable.)

'And what's your story?'
'Well, I lost my husband with cancer.'
'Cancer, eh? Good . . .'
'And both my children are deformed . . .'
'Deformed? That's very good.'
'And I'm dying.'
'Wonderful!'

'Makes Hughie Green look like a vicarage tea party,' I noted at the time.

I had managed to live in London for two and a half years without really becoming conscious of a breed of men (and women) known as psychoanalysts. It was impossible to spend two months in New York without becoming very aware of them. Americans did not sweep problems under the carpet as we Brits were inclined to do: they seemed to concentrate fiercely, almost avidly, on them – or on the latest health fear. At the beginning of 1964 the focus was on smoking, following the Surgeon General's report. The reaction to this was immediate. One store in Fifth Avenue that had cigarette lighters in the window a week earlier had 'lighters' only on sale by the following week. And at eight dollars a time less. On Madison Avenue I saw a 'family charity chest' that looked suspiciously like the previous week's hundred dollar cigarette box. 'But Marvin,' said a lady at the next table to mine in the Persian Room, 'you promised you would give them up. You promised . . .' 'Yes, I know, honey,' said Marvin, back-pedalling desperately. 'But it's very cold in here. I'm only smoking to keep warm.'

Before I left for London at the beginning of March, Leland Hayward announced that I would be returning at the beginning of May for the last two months of the season, following the fulfilment of my commitments in England. The main commitment in London was the 'A Degree of Frost' special. I plunged straight into sessions with Joe McGrath, the producer, and with the writers I was hoping to use, like Frank Muir and Denis Norden, Barry Cryer, Christopher Booker and others. Over dinner at Ray Parkes with Paul McCartney and Jane Asher, I asked Paul if he would agree to a rare interview. He said he would.

However, before 'A Degree of Frost' I had an interview to tape for BBC 2. It was the first David Paradine Production. I had decided to call any companies I might need by my middle name – Paradine – rather than by my surname. It sounded more low-key, less of an ego trip. Producing a programme myself was very different from my experience on the American TW3, though not that dissimilar to the British TW3, where Ned Sherrin and I had worked so closely together on the content. However, booking studios – and watching the budget – was a new experience.

Appropriately enough, the subject of that first Paradine production was Billy Graham. 'It is also,' Kenneth Lamb, BBC Head of Religious Broadcasting, announced, 'the launch of religious broadcasting on BBC 2.'

I asked Billy if he was concerned about over-simplification: 'If something is complex, while it would be good if one could simplify, if it is complex, the only way one could honestly present it is as complex.'

'Yes,' he answered, 'but the first step is not . . . It's like a door. Here's a door. And over that door it says, "Whosoever will, let him come." That includes you, me, everyone. I take a step through that door, which is the step the evangelist is involved in. That's a very simple step.'

And what if he was 'off form'? In more earthly pursuits that would simply be a matter for chagrin – but where the immortal fate of human souls is at stake, how did it feel then?

Billy Graham responded, 'Well, you see, I believe when the Gospel is preached, however badly, and however many mistakes there may be, that the Holy Spirit is the communicating agent.

'The people are not really listening to me after about ten or fifteen minutes if I am really preaching the Gospel, because there is something inside the human heart when truth is preached that says, "Yes, that's it." Now I know that I may preach it rather poorly and I know that maybe some evening I may not be feeling up to par physically and all the rest of it, and I may leave out many things that I wanted to say. But God knows my motive and He knows my heart and God uses even that simple presentation that might have been poorly done and He applies it to the human heart because salvation, the Bible says, is of God.'

Billy said that Cecil B. de Mille, contrary to my impression, had been 'a great Bible student. I was very close friends with Mr de Mille because in 1950 he asked me if I would go into films and I said, "No, God has called me to preach."'

Billy Graham also spoke out against sex before marriage – fornication.

Graham: It hinders, I've talked to many psychologists on this point, it hinders real love within marriage.

DF: But not always does it destroy a real love, does it? Not always?

Graham: I don't know that it always destroys, but it always hurts and blunts real love. Yes, always.

Frost: Always?

Graham: Always.

This exchange – and its exquisite onomatopoeia – entered into Diana Crawfurd's and my private vocabulary. From then on, whenever we met, she was likely to gaze at me sternly, 'I hope, David,' she would say reprovingly, 'that you have not been blunting your love again.'

I began 'A Degree of Frost' by returning, *inter alia*, to my early love from Cambridge days, the *Reader's Digest*. I reported on some of its 'latest articles', including 'A New Nose Changed my Life – I Now Have Two', 'I Met my Wife on my Honeymoon', 'New Hope for the Dead', 'I Spent my Vacation in my Chimney' and 'How to Take a Group Photograph of Yugoslavia'. We played the first of the two Nichols and May sketches, 'Wrong House', as an *hors d'oeuvre*, and then it was time for a mock salute to 'Sportsview' on its tenth anniversary before introducing the Swingle Singers, whom we had brought over from Paris, and whose vocal interpretations of Bach had, to quote the *Radio Times*, 'caused a sensation in the music world'. Then it was time for Paul McCartney. I asked him, 'As we've been rehearsing today, I've been wondering whether you ever expected things to be as good for you as in fact they've been?' It was a question

I sometimes asked myself. 'When you started as a group, did you expect things to go like this?'

'No,' said Paul. 'We used to think of things in stages. Still do, I think. When we first started off, playing in The Cavern, I thought first of all, let's get a record contract. We all did. We got a record. Then we said, let's get a number one hit. Got one of them. Then we went on. We do it in stages . . .' It was an approach that sounded familiar: neither of us could lay claim to a five-year plan.

'When people ask you, "What's the best thing about being one of the Beatles at this stage?" you usually reply, "The money," as the first quip. But what after that is one of the good things?'

'Being able to do things that you enjoy doing,' said Paul. 'You get a bit of power when you reach a certain stage. In that you can suggest things to people that you want to do. We can turn around to Brian [Epstein] and say, "Could we do such and such a thing," like a film, and he can say, "I'll try and fix it, boy." And he does. He's good like that . . . We can now do more things that we'd like to . . .'

That was very much how I felt, too. In our very different ways, Paul and I were both very lucky to have that sort of independence.

In addition to the Nichols and May tape, I had also brought from America a tape of Burr Tillstrom and his memorable Berlin Wall sequence. Frank Muir and Denis Norden had written a splendid sketch on censorship, analysing the unacceptable meanings implicit in the old joke 'Who was that lady I saw you with last night?' 'That was no lady, that was my wife.' Geoffrey Martin had produced another one of his special films employing captions and bench camera work set to music. With Christopher Booker's help, we examined how life in Britain might appear if it was looked at in the same way that Russia had been in innumerable reports over the past year:

> Britain – godless tyranny or awakening monolith? Superficially there have been many changes in Britain in recent years. There is an air of greater prosperity – everywhere young girls chatter gaily in their cheap summer frocks, cos-

> metics and nylons are much more freely available than they were fifteen years ago, and Government decree has put an end to the traditional London sight of women working in the streets to all hours of day and night. But behind the façade, has it all changed that much? The crowds jostling one another in the airless Underground are grey-faced and depressed, the new buildings shooting up all over London are ugly and shoddily built. Workers find that their shoes fall to pieces after only a few months' wear. An overcoat may cost a worker as much as eight weeks' wages – if he insists on vicuna. Caviar is in short supply, and everywhere there are huge hoardings exhorting the workers to buy cheap food substitutes, like this synthetic butter, made from vegetable oils, and called margarine. Sales of Russian vodka have reached an all-time high, and everywhere groups of teenagers gather round short-wave radios and gramophones to listen to the pounding beat of Tchaikovsky and Shostakovich. How free is life in Britain today? Well, at Easter and other big festivals, many of the churches are full. But it is mainly the older people who go . . .

The Swingle Singers gave us an encore, and the show rounded off with the main Nichols and May sketch, 'Interview', and one of my favourite sketches, BBC-BC, the Old Testament newscast, by Bill Oddie and John Cleese. It was a joy to perform: 'At the weigh-in for the big fight tonight Goliath tipped the scales at fourteen stones four pounds and David at thirteen stones four pounds. David's manager said later, "The odd stone could make all the difference." And finally a theatre review: At the opening tonight of the Gaza Strip, Samson, this year's Mr Israel, brought the house down.'

We had planned to produce a show that was different from TW3, but consistent with it. The comedy still had to be irreverent, although it was less political. The music and comedy guests had to be the best of their kind, but it was important that their 'kind' was right too. From the reaction, we seemed to have got the mix right. Although Ned, Alasdair Milne and I had had many meetings over the months about the possible shape of 'satire in the autumn', it was probably no accident that the first BBC leak about the fact that the new three-times-a-weekend programme was to be hosted by D. Frost came just a week after the reaction to 'A Degree of Frost'.

By the time 'A Degree of Frost' was transmitted, I was back in New York for a sustained stint on TW3. I was particularly taken with the work of a writer called Dee Caruso, who wrote for me what over the years my friends have come to know and love – or feign to love – as the Ernst Finster joke. It was guaranteed to produce at least four or five laughs every time. 'We have just heard that at the Detroit Coliseum today Ernst Finster, the Finnish pole vaulter, pole-vaulted a height of 19 feet 8 inches. Unfortunately the roof of the Detroit Coliseum . . . is only 16 feet 3 inches high. So that in one jump Finster broke both the indoor and outdoor records . . . as well as two collarbones and one asbestos tile' (British version: 'one Marley tile'). I have used that joke in warm-ups all over the world, though at one stage I did desist for a while because it was simply too sure-fire, and therefore too accurate. If an audience did not seize the four or five opportunities they had to laugh at the Ernst Finster joke, they would not laugh at *anything*. The performers might as well go home – it was all too depressing a prospect. So I put the joke back into the show itself, where it no longer had the precognitive power to destroy everybody's confidence.

Dee's sense of humour was very New York – and very funny. For example, this little interview:

Interviewer: Tell me, Herr Hitler, if you had to do it all over again, would you do anything differently?

Hitler: Yes, I would change the moustache. It made people think of me as a villain.

Interviewer: But surely, Charlie Chaplin had a moustache and people didn't think of him as a villain.

Hitler: Let him open just one concentration camp . . .

There were more one-liners in the American TW3 than in the British.

This week Red China set off its first atomic bomb. The communiqué stated that a bomb was exploded in a lightly populated area. Or if the area wasn't lightly populated *before* the bomb went off, it is now.

One in every four people in the world today is a Chinese communist – so remember that the next time you see the Lennon Sisters . . .*

The Rhythm Method or, as it's more commonly known, Vatican Roulette.

There was a demonstration in Mississippi today to protest police brutality. But police quickly broke it up with clubs and teargas.

And there's good news for cigarette smokers. They're not fattening.

During those last weeks of the first American season of TW3, in my off-duty hours I was fascinated by the professional skill of Liberace, who was appearing in a Broadway hotel restaurant, the Royal Box at the Americana Hotel. The lovable self-deprecation as he glanced down at his glittering sequins: 'You know, sometimes when I look at this stuff, I can hardly believe it myself! But it's all real . . . I bet you'd like to see what's underneath! That's all real too!' The flattery of the audience after playing a snippet of something classical: 'I love playing that sort of music. I'm so glad *you love listening to it.*' And the ongoing obeisance to wealth. Throughout the show he paused to mutter, 'I'm almost ashamed to take the money. (PAUSE) But I will.' Or the endearing couplet:

My clothes may look funny,
But they're making me the money.

* For Britain, the figures had to be massaged – they became 'one in three' and 'the Beverley Sisters'.

Good old Lee. Whatever you thought of his act, you had to hand it to him – he knew how to make money.

For sheer artistry, there was nothing to match Barbra Streisand in *Funny Girl* at the Winter Garden. Her sense of comedy could hardly have been bettered. Neither could her acting. And, just as a bonus, her body carried with it an enormous sex appeal. As she arched her back, as her body almost pouted, she was the first all-Semitic Cleopatra. A totally unorthodox, oddly vulnerable beauty that made nonsense of those lines about the bridegroom being prettier than the bride, but who cared about that?

As I advised British radio listeners in one interview, 'If you have one free evening in New York, Miss Streisand is the person to see. If you have two, see her twice.'

Out in the streets, the summer humidity in New York was unlike anything I had ever experienced before, and unlike the theatres and restaurants, the cabs were not air-conditioned, though the drivers remained almost as Runyonesque as they were supposed to be. On one boiling day early in July, the cab in which I was travelling was stuck in a traffic jam. The minutes passed and we did not move. We just sat and sweltered. I bore it in silence, because there just seemed to be no words to express our misery. The driver found them: 'Better maybe we never *invented* the wheel, huh?' he said.

The TW3 season ended on Friday 10 July. That evening the *New York Post* reported:

> Leland Hayward, executive producer of the series, said Britain's David Frost had agreed to return to the show next fall with Phyllis Newman, Nancy Ames and Burr Tillstrom. Frost could become TV's first transatlantic commuter inasmuch as he is scheduled to start a new BBC show in the fall. He recently expressed some doubt over ocean-hopping between shows. 'A doctor friend of mine says he wants to examine me if I try it,' he said. The doctor apparently has a case. 'He's going to commute,' says Hayward.

The first season of TW3 in America had, on balance, been a success. It hadn't been quite as outspoken as the original, but it had probably been as forthright by the standards of American television as TW3 in Britain had been by the standards of British television. That fact is attested to by the fond memories of the series to this day in America. 'Remember,' I told one interviewer, Harold Stern, 'it's difficult to accomplish in twenty-five minutes what it took fifty minutes to do in England. We were able to do longer, more documentary looks at people. Here it would be insanity to devote eight minutes to any one person. There are other differences. It's different when you are actually the last show on the air on Saturday night, as we were in England during our first season. That makes you the last show of the week, and when you say, "That was the week that was," it has more meaning.'

The social dynamics were different. It had turned out to be as difficult as I had feared for a group of older people in America to reproduce the feelings that young people had in England about a regime which had been in power for twelve years. The conditions were ripe in the UK for that sort of demolition job. In America in January 1964, in the aftermath of the Kennedy assassination, people naturally wanted to build Johnson up rather than knock him down. Though the mild irreverence of the US TW3 still came as a breath of fresh air to the audience, the show was in part swimming against the tide. And American networks were a good deal more strait-laced than Hugh Carleton Greene's BBC.

Considering all that, Leland and his team deserved their renewal from NBC for another season. But the programme was moved to Tuesday nights at nine-thirty, which was both good news and bad news for me. Bad news in the sense that Tuesday nights made it yet more difficult to say 'That was the week that was,' rather than 'That was the last seven days that was.' And the competition was very tough – 'Peyton Place' and 'Petticoat Junction' in its heyday (that should probably be spelt hay-day).

Network television in the States was a much more rigidly competitive system than in the UK. We had one commercial channel competing with the BBC. In the States there were three commercial channels competing with each other, and shows needed a thirty per cent share of the audience if they were to survive. That meant there was much more of a 'sudden death' element about American television and, with the financial stakes so much higher than in Britain, the obstacles placed in the way of experimentation – and indeed non-mainstream programme forms like documentaries – were much greater. American television executives tended to play safe more than their British counterparts. That fact alone made TW3 something of a phenomenon.

The good news, in a personal sense, was that the Tuesday night slot enabled me to have the best of both worlds. If the original idea – that of a Monday to Friday show – had prevailed in the UK, obviously I could not have done both. If TW3 in America had stayed on a Friday, I could not have done both. Somebody up there must have liked me, or decided that BOAC needed the revenue.

As I prepared to leave New York to return to Europe to spend the summer with Jan, one interviewer asked me what I most enjoyed about America. Was it the fact that there was no class system, unlike the UK? The answer to that question, and to the assumptions that underpinned it, had to be a series of 'yeses and noes'. It was certainly true that class did not seem to permeate life in America to anything like the same extent. But there was surely a status system at work, nonetheless. There was the status of breeding – the old WASP families, the Boston Brahmins, the Southern aristocracy. There was the status of sheer wealth, which came not so much from centuries of barony but from a few generations of dealing, like the Vanderbilts and the Rockefellers. The significance of that kind of status was, I suspected, that it counted in the long run only if new money was translated into political clout. The Vanderbilts were decimated by Roosevelt; the Rockefellers survived and prospered by proving to be as astute politically as they were financially.

An extension of this law, the survival of the richest, seemed to be the unquenchable American faith in the ability to get rich. No matter how impoverished, no matter now far down the greasy pole the aspirant might be, in America he really seemed to *believe* in the attainability of riches. Unlike his British counterpart, he did not perceive a system which planted roadblocks in the path of ambition – whether the ideological roadblock of taxation so punitive that real capital could sometimes only be made by devious means, or the class-designed roadblock of privilege. The fact that two such inimical embargoes on ambition could co-exist was in itself a commentary on the flaws inherent in British society. I used the word 'ambition'. That seemed to me basic at the time in delineating a great contrast between American and British attitudes. In Britain 'ambition' could be, and frequently was, used in a pejorative sense. In America it was not only regarded as a compliment, but a deficiency of ambition was seen as being as serious as a deficiency of red blood cells; you were enfeebled without it.

And yet . . . and yet . . . while the class system in Britain may have prevented people from feeling that the sky was the limit, it also protected them from the worst of the rat race, and gave them something of an emotional safety net. One of my agents in the States had just almost bankrupted himself by buying a house he could not afford on the 'right' side of a block in Beverly Hills. He would not have had to succumb to that sort of pressure in the UK. As with so many of the new lifestyles I was encountering and contrasting, there had to be a 'better way' – probably halfway between the two.

The summer passed blissfully. In terms of work, Ned and I were planning with Alasdair the new series which became 'Not So Much a Programme, More a Way of Life', with the first pilot programmes planned for the end of August. At the beginning of that month Jan and I flew to Kauai, the garden island of Hawaii, for a holiday. We arrived at a delightfully isolated resort at the end of the island called the Hanalei Plantation, next to a valley which could only be reached by boat, the original valley 'on which no human eye had ever set foot'. In those days it was still considered protocol for unmarried couples to book into hotels in separate rooms, and to ruffle the unused bed dutifully in the morning. Here, at the end of the rainbow, where all that was available was individual bungalows, that seemed absurd. How do you ruffle a bungalow? And why on earth should you pay for it too? So, for the first time we registered as Mr and Mrs Frost, and went to our bungalow. Given the press's fascination with the minutiae of our relationship, we were a touch nervous about the arrangement, but knew that, with an eleven-hour time difference, we were about as far from Fleet Street as we could possibly be.

The manager showed us to our bungalow, and then urged us to follow him to the beach, where a barbecue was in progress. He led us towards the first couple we encountered. 'Mr and Mrs Frost, may I introduce Alex Faulkner, head of the *Daily Telegraph* Foreign Bureau.'

He then departed and left us to our fate. Jan responded manfully, or womanfully, or personfully. 'Just his little joke,' she said, and both of us attempted a hopelessly forced laugh. It was the best we could manage. Luckily, however, Alex Faulkner was more interested in foreign affairs than in domestic affairs, so we got away with it.

But we were nabbed by a group of reporters on our return to Heathrow. After we had been asked what seemed like seventy-eight times about the subject of marriage, it was mildly diverting to respond, as I did when a later arrival turned up and asked, 'What about marriage?' with the reply, 'Marriage? What's that?' The other reporters took the point. Alas, the new arrival did not. Instead of quoting me turning good-humouredly, with a David Niven-like lift of the left eyebrow, and saying, 'Marriage? What's that?' he filed a story that I had said with a shrug, 'What's marriage, anyway?' A quite different angle. Inevitably, that was the quote that accompanied the photo on the front page of the *Evening Standard* that evening. Indeed the report actually said, 'Frost cut in with a shrug of his shoulders.' No mean feat in terms of body language.

When we got home later, we switched on the television. It was one of those early-evening discussion programmes. The moderator said, 'Well, there's no doubt about the quote of the day. It was David Frost's fearless analysis of the state of modern marriage when he said, "What's marriage, anyway . . ." What *is* marriage, anyway? . . .' A discussion on my fearless non-assertion then followed. It was by no means over-critical, and ended with the summing-up: 'Well, say what you will, agree with him or disagree, I think there's none of us here that would deny to David Frost the courage it took to say what he did.' Or didn't, as the case may be.

Back in London we waited for the date of the General Election to be announced. For most of the year, we had assumed that this would result in a routine confirmation by the electorate of the changes that had taken place in British political life during 1963. Now the polls suggested that the voting public was more innately conservative than anyone had suspected. Face to face with the actual possibility of Labour rule, they were clearly in two minds about whether they really wanted to say 'Let's go with Labour'. Neither the presence of the 14th Earl of Home on the one side, nor the white heat of the technological revolution on the other had yet made up their minds for them.

In America the first 'That Was The Week That Was' of the new season was due to take place on Tuesday 22 September. Jan and I took the *Queen Mary* to New York – another childhood fantasy had come true – and met up with the new team.

Leland had brought in Herb Sargent as producer. Herb was one of the wittiest and certainly one of the most quietly-spoken people I have ever met. He said of Nancy Ames, whose husband was a hypnotist, 'Nancy's married to a hypnotist. Or at least she *thinks* she's married to a hypnotist.' At the Caravelle, a waiter brought us some more butter, and took away a full ashtray. 'And some more ashes, please,' Herb asked. In the middle of a traffic jam, we had sat in a cab for all of twenty-five minutes and moved just four blocks. Suddenly Herb peered out of the window and said: 'I think we're coming to a town.' Herb's girlfriend, Gloria Steinem, had also been signed up by Leland as a writer, as had someone else whose sense of humour I felt was just right for the show – the puckish, bespectacled figure of Mr Buck Henry. Despite all his writing and performing, Buck's main achievement to date was, I felt, his performance as G. Clifford Prout, Jr, President of SINA – the Society for Indecency to Naked Animals, a movement dedicated to clothing 'the vital areas of dogs, cats, horses, cows and other domestic animals that stand higher than four inches and are longer than six inches'.

To Buck's amazement, G. Clifford Prout, Jr's movement had been taken seriously. It had succeeded in having an unclothed model horse removed from a New York store window, organised pickets outside offending establishments, and recorded a daily telephone message that made the SINA phone number the most overloaded in town: 'This is G. Clifford Prout, Jr. I speak not as a thinking man, but as . . .'

For a time Prout concentrated his attack on zoos. He told the *Los Angeles Times* that they were 'the burlesque show of the animal world'. People gathered around the gorilla pit for 'a vicarious sensationalism at the expense of their moral sense'. When he visited San Francisco, Prout declared it 'a moral disaster area'. The *San Francisco Chronicle* – 'The Voice of the West' – decided that the two main headlines of the day were 'War on Naked Animals' and, second, 'Two Russians Orbiting Earth in Formation'. 'Have you ever considered,' Prout asked the *Chronicle*, 'that grazing animals with lowered heads may not be grazing at all? Did it ever occur to you that many of them are merely looking away, so that they won't have to gaze at the vital areas of their grazing comrades?'

In Central Park, New York, a meeting of SINA was interrupted by the arrival of a mounted policeman. Prout was about to be served with a warrant for holding an unlawful assembly, but instead he turned round and served the officer with a SINA summons for appearing in public riding a naked horse.

The faithful adherents of SINA had to be prepared for some pretty cavalier treatment from head office. Replies were likely to be in the form of an all-purpose letter from G. Clifford Prout, with the answer relevant to them ticked off in pen, whether it was number three ('Thank you and the same to you; your letter is being turned over to the police for proper handling') or number eleven ('I have auburn hair, brown eyes, stand 5'8", weigh 165 pounds, 31 years old, enjoy swimming, bowling, dancing, volleyball, reading and fencing').

Yet Prout was bombarded with mail. 'Several of the letters,' said Henry, 'suggested that my association with animals was a good deal closer than I was prepared to admit.' A large number, however, pledged wholehearted support. A sweet old lady wrote from Dayton, Ohio, that she thought the Bermuda shorts proposed for horses in the SINA magazine were a trifle 'cumbersome'. 'Surely,' she went on, 'a better idea would be some sort of adhesive covering for the genitals?' The newspapers faithfully recorded it all. To Henry, that was one of the continuing wonders of the whole project. 'They always printed it. Without a bit of checking up. The fact that SINA had fourteen emergency clothes-mobiles spotted around the US, ready to rush into any area where animal morality was low. And that fourteen thousand world leaders of SINA were about to attend our world congress.' The secret of his success? 'The vital thing in any scheme like this is making people take the first step. After that you can do anything with them. If I can convince you that that plate is invisible, sooner or later I can take the whole room from you.'

I felt almost guilty that Buck's commitment to TW3 was interfering with such vital work.

We prepared for the first show. Nancy Ames was back, Phyllis Newman, who had joined us towards the end of the previous season, was back, and to the extent that the show had one, I was to be the host. The NBC ad for the show listed 'David Frost, Nancy Ames, Phyllis Newman, Unpredictability!' Unfortunately for us, most of the unpredictability was provided by the Republican National Committee. In the run-up to the forthcoming Presidential Election, they had decided to pre-empt a random half-hour somewhere on the networks each week in order to present a programme of their own. In the third week of September, they chose Tuesday night at nine-thirty on NBC. So our premiere show had to be postponed for a week. In the first two weeks of October, their random choice was, lo and behold, once again Tuesday night at nine-thirty on NBC. Indeed, we wouldn't even have got our one bite at the cherry on Tuesday 29 September if the RNC had had anything to do with it. They placed an order for that night at nine-thirty as well, but NBC pointed out that the Democratic National Committee had a prior commitment to present a one-minute spot during the show that evening. According to the *New York Times*, 'A network spokesman said yesterday that political parties usually wanted a half-hour time during the week and that TW3, "Hazel" and "Jack Benny" were NBC's only thirty-minute weekday shows.'

In the words of that British viewer, 'Tell that to the Marines!'

'TW3 is a live programme,' the spokesman continued. 'Its future shows have not yet gone into rehearsal, so the time is not so expensive to buy.'

This was nonsense. Situation comedies, whether recorded or not, were timeless. The *New York Times* added, 'NBC is under no obligation to sell the Tuesday night slot, but its instinct is to co-operate.' *Variety*, the show business bible, in the course of welcoming the show back – 'The programme has a new set of muscles owing to some promising cast changes and format revisions' – had some cautionary words: 'Tuesday night is an awkward time for the Sunday papers, church services or any sort of weekly accounting. That's one strike against TW3 this year. The series has perhaps the season's least enviable time slot, opposite "Peyton Place" and "Petticoat Junction", and that's another. Call it a foul tip that the GOP has pre-empted three of its premiere season outings, and it does look as though TW3 is being given nothing but roundhouse curves.'

There were more such moments to come. We lost a total of six shows, five of them in consecutive weeks following our one-off premiere, so that the Republican National Committee successfully kept 'That Was The Week That Was' off the air until the election. So the British experience was repeated after all!

This was my first experience of an American Presidential campaign – and of its vigour. It was clearly no coincidence that in America they talk of 'running for office', while in Britain they talk of 'standing for office'. It was also my first experience of the smears that can crop up in a US Presidential campaign. One day I saw a poster with a simple message. It was a large picture of Joseph Stalin smiling and saying, 'Why not vote for Goldwater?' Trying to link the right-wing Republican candidate Barry Goldwater, of all people, with the Soviet Union seemed a bit out of left field – no pun intended.

For the Republicans, Goldwater's running mate, Representative William Miller – what, exactly, we all wondered, is he representative *of*? – was charged with taking the low road, which he seemed to do with relish. The Democrats also got into hot water in their attempt to portray Goldwater as a threat to children. One of their commercials showed a little girl picking daisies and counting. When she got to ten, there was a nuclear explosion, followed by the words 'Vote for President Johnson'. Whether the commercial ever won a single vote for LBJ is not known, but it was thought to have been responsible for a drastic reduction in the number of little girls picking daisies.

As Buck Henry pointed out over a drink, even if all a candidate had done was to speak out against disease, poverty and famine, he was still vulnerable to the charge: 'In his last three speeches my opponent has echoed the Communist line.' Even the fact that he saw action in Italy, France and Germany, could emerge as: 'My opponent toured Europe at Government expense.'

Each week we would wait for the news that the Republican National Committee had struck again, but the devil finds work for idle hands. The scene was the King Cole Bar of the St Regis on 8 October. Herb Sargent and I were having a drink when we had the idea for a book. If Labour won the upcoming election in Britain, that would be a great springboard, if not for the regeneration of our beloved nation, then at least for a new generation of jokes. By 2.30 in the morning we had a title – *How to Live Under Labour – or at Least have as Much Chance as Anybody Else* – and an outline. The next day Charles Pick, Managing Director of the publishers William Heinemann, accepted the idea over the phone from New York. By Tuesday 13 October, Chris Booker and Gerald Kaufman had agreed to collaborate, and we had worked out a schedule for most of the copy to be written by 22 October, seven days after the election – assuming, of course, that Labour won. At Lady Pamela Berry's party at the Savoy on the fifteenth, election night, I felt that Charles Pick was somewhat schizophrenic. I suspected that he was probably a Conservative supporter, but I knew he was excited by the idea of the book. By midnight, the television screens seemed to have resolved by the narrowest of margins whatever internal debate he might have been conducting. 'We're on,' he said.

Our foreword was, we alleged, reprinted by arrangement with the publishers of 'Insight' and the forthcoming book *The Making of the Prime Minister, or at Least the Authors* by Anthony Howard and Richard West.

It was 9 p.m. on the grey evening of that fateful October day. Within seconds, as the gold ormolu clock on the white, recently replastered Adam mantelpiece of the historic red-carpeted Cabinet Room in an unpretentious Queen Anne terrace house in south-west London, the room in which Pitt had presided and Disraeli doodled, the room from which Neville Chamberlain had sent out that fateful ultimatum to Berlin and from which Ramsey MacDonald had sent out for fish 'n' chips – within seconds, as the clock ticked on, it was 9.01.'

I met with Christopher and Gerald in London, and Herb in New York, and scribbled on the planes between, often on BOAC notepaper. Indeed, two pages of the galley proofs came back beginning with the line 'BOAC takes good care of you.' On 17 November I was able to hand over a copy of the finished book to Charles Pick, who was visiting New York. For nostalgic reasons – or maybe just for reasons of far-sighted autobiographical tidiness – that meeting took place in the King Cole Bar, too.

It was a larky little book. It proved statistically that what happened on 15 October 1964 was something that no one in the country really wanted, but it then tried to help its readers to face up to the facts. It was no good trying to think any longer that Harold Wilson's Cousins got his job the same way Harold Macmillan's cousins got theirs. It was no good trying to think that Mr Edward Short would ever be the sort of national figure that Martin Redmayne was. Life in Tory Britain had been 'everything on HP'. Life in Labour Britain would be 'HP on everything.'

Anthony Wedgwood Benn was given full credit as the architect of Labour victory – because without him Sir Alec would never have re-entered the Commons. Then an up-to-the-minute riddle:

Q: What is the difference between Mr Richard Crossman and Mr Fred Peart?
A: Mr Crossman, the Minister of Housing, is a farmer. And Mr Peart, the Minister of Agriculture, lives in a house.

Remarks likely to win favour at parties included, 'I always said Harold got a rough deal from that Bank Rate Tribunal,' and 'I must say, that hat of Mary Wilson's looks prettier every time she wears it.' The television programme to avoid in the new era was 'Not So Much a Programme, More a Way of Life'. 'There's no room for that kind of destructive malice any more.'

'That kind of destructive malice' began on Friday 13 November. The brief but eventful history of 'Not So Much a Programme, More a Way of Life' divides into three clear phases. One, the soggy start; two, the getting-the-formula-right; and then, just when most people were agreed that we had managed that, three, the Gadarene rush to self-destruction.

The first programme was a bit of a dog's dinner. Quite why, after six varied pilots, we had not got our act more together is a bit of a mystery. Maybe the six pilots were *too* varied. Maybe the nature of our experimentation this time was different. With TW3 we knew where we wanted to go, and were trying to work out how to get there. With 'Not So Much', maybe we were not too clear even about where we were going. We did know that we needed a more relaxed pace, that would accommodate conversation in a way TW3 did not. Both Ned and I had imbibed the rhetoric about trying to produce a more low-key service programme, trying to escape the 'hysteria' that was produced by TW3. But in all truth, just re-reading those words, they are a euphemism for anticlimax, produced by a nervous management.

I was to be joined by Willie Rushton and P.J. Kavanagh as co-hosts. Although I was always hugely entertained by the beloved Willie, and liked P.J. Kavanagh the moment I met him, I did think that this three-headed monster was a bit of a loony idea. But while Ned and I discussed everything else to the nth degree, that was the one point on which I was somewhat reticent, as I could have been seen to have, shall we say, a certain special interest in the outcome. Which is an interesting comment on – and probably a shattering indictment of – my Britishness.

Anyway, for whatever reason, the first edition of 'Not So Much' was a hit-and-miss affair. The chat was subdued and too straitjacketed by its linkage to sketches or set subject matter. Having three hosts did not help. However, there were some palpable hits as well. Among the talkers, in addition to Bernard Levin, there were two new faces. One was Harvey Orkin, an American agent living in London. Beneath his world-weary face, there was a superb turn of phrase. In that first show he told us about his career as a press agent in Hollywood. He was representing Harry Straddler (the name was changed to protect the guilty), a 'confirmed bachelor' who was somewhat concerned about his emphatically unmarried image. What could Harvey do to improve it? Harvey had had a brainwave. He invented the 'Male Magnetism Awards', and announced them on a slow news Sunday. Number one was Joe DiMaggio; number two, Dwight D. Eisenhower; number three, Harry Straddler; number four, John Wayne. The four photographs duly appeared together in newspapers all over the States.

Then there was Patrick Campbell, Lord Glenavy. In those days we gave a brief biography of guests when they appeared for the first time, so we were able to quote the words of Patrick's mother: 'Indeed one wondered when one first set eyes on him, what one had been playing at.' His headmaster at Rossall told him, 'Rossall will prepare you for every kind of privation in later years. There is nothing you will not be able to face with impunity; hail, blizzard, starvation, torture or war.' He had been a personal aide to another lord, Lord Beaverbrook who, it was said, had telephoned his newly-appointed assistant at 5.45 a.m. and remarked, 'Unless we can gather the crops more swiftly, my lord, we shall no longer find ourselves among the labourers in the field.'

It was Patrick Campbell's stammer – no, his stutter – that made him an unlikely television personality. Indeed, on his most recent television appearance his diffident speech pattern had prevented him from opening his mouth for the entire thirty minutes of the show, as he recounted to us. He had been stunned by the question, 'Does your editor think of your ideas or do you?' and had never recovered. But, as he retold the story, it was clear that a star was being born.

Our first fledgling ring-around worked well too. A recent correspondence in the *Daily Telegraph*, inspired by Graham Greene, had convinced one Mr P.M. Moyce that a new, unkind game of

Daily Telegraph reader-baiting was abroad in the land. We asked some of our part-time contributors to pursue the idea. Alan Simpson and Ray Galton suggested: 'Sir, re the colour problem, wouldn't it be a wonderful contribution to racial harmony if, when she was of age, Princess Anne was to marry one of our black brethren from . . .' David Nathan proposed: 'Sir, As a consenting male . . .' and Claud Cockburn: 'I wonder how many of your other readers noticed on the television the other night the deeply striking resemblance between Mr James Callaghan and Jesus Christ . . .'

The music worked – Millicent Martin was succeeded by three different singers, Barbara Evans on Fridays, Annie Ross on Saturdays and Cleo Laine on Sundays. In the sketch department, it was clear that we had struck gold with John Bird and Eleanor Bron – back from The Establishment in the States – and Roy Hudd. Eleanor introduced her political hostess, Lady Pamela Stitty, and John Bird gave us his Jomo Kenyatta, complete with fly whisk, who in one fell swoop propelled this allegedly low-key, headline-avoiding service programme back onto the front pages. Jomo announced his – relatively – peaceful plans for the takeover of Great Britain: 'Britain will be ours. No doubt there will be the occasional bloodbath. But, I always say, you can't make an omelette without layin' eggs. I myself will temporarily assume the office of Queen until a reliable native replacement can be found.' Next morning there was a complaint from the Kenya High Commission. We gave Mr Kenyatta a chance to reply. John Bird popped up again: 'Good Evenin'. Well I always say, as in the words of an old proverb, he who is without stones let him throw himself into the glass house . . .'

Peter Black's welcome back in principle in the *Daily Mail* was fairly typical of the bemused reaction to the first weekend's proceedings: 'The formula is not as good as the old inspired casualness of TW3 (Why does TV stick to this superstition of never repeating good ideas?) but will work well enough if it can find better jokes that can run from week to week, and more speakers like Kaufman and Patrick Campbell.'

Over the next few weeks we tried to polish the format. The sketches were in good shape. John Bird as Harold Wilson monitored the first hundred days of the Government from the Labour side, with Eleanor Bron doing the same as Lady Pamela Stitty from the Tory angle. They were often joined by John Fortune and John Wells, and on Sunday nights by Michael Crawford as Byron, Peter Lewis and Peter Dobereiner's street-smart teenage dropout on a motorcycle, whose ultimate rebuke for anything was 'turgid'. We expanded the principle of the ring-around. When it came to the subject of film clichés we called to our aid Denis Norden, Dilys Powell, Elspeth Grant, David Robinson, Kenneth Tynan, John Russell Taylor and others. They did not let us down.

From the medical film: 'Get some sleep, Doc. We can't have you cracking up.'

From the biblical film: 'There's something about that carpenter's son . . .'

And from the South Sea island epic: 'The white men are leaving us forever, Manura. Do not weep, little one. It is better so. They brought with them nothing but lust and greed. Now they have again set sail for their own land and the island of Puki Puki will once again return to its peaceful ways. The women will once more fish and make the mali mali and we shall once more dance and play under the shadow of Kracka-Pitta-Petta-Moa-Koa.'

But had our viewers ever stopped to think what would happen *without* the clichés? The films might have stopped dead in their tracks . . .

Doctor: I've got wonderful news for you, Mrs Kowalski. Your son will never play the violin again!

Or the biblical epic:

Arab: We have followed a star to this stable. Tell us of the child within.
Local: It's a girl.

Or romance:

Brenda, will you do something for me? Just take off those glasses for a moment. (SHE DOES) Oh, well, it was just an idea.

Or the historical film:

Friend: What's the matter with you, George Frederick Handel? You've composed nothing for months now! Why, if I had a God-given talent like yours, I'd rejoice in it. I'd praise the Lord for it! I'd cry 'Hallelujah, Hallelujah.'
Handel (SHARPLY): What? What did you say?
Friend: I said I'd praise the Lord. I'd cry 'Hallelujah, Hallelu–'
Handel: No, no – *before* that . . .

Most of all, we tried to liberate the talk and strike the right balance between talk and sketches. In this we were greatly assisted by the calibre of talkers. In addition to Patrick Campbell, Harvey Orkin, Bernard Levin and Gerald Kaufman, we had regular visits from Denis Norden, Jonathan Miller, Norman St John Stevas, Brigid Brophy, Malcolm Muggeridge, Clive Irving, Iain Macleod, Nicholas Tomalin and more. By the beginning of December the press comments were getting much more positive: '"Not So Much a Programme, More a Way of Life" left us all rather disappointed when it first began,' wrote Alma Jones in the *Western Mail*, 'but now it is revving up extraordinarily well.'

On 9 December the newspapers reported that the BBC had decided to extend the original six-week trial run through until April. This was just too much for our friends at the *Express*. On Sunday 13 December Douglas Clark wrote a full-page article in the *Sunday Express* headlined 'Not So Much a Programme – More a Great Big Flop' and subtitled 'It's Time the BBC Switched off this Rubbish'. He began: 'What is to be done when the BBC in its awful arrogance, peremptorily tells the television viewers: You don't like this programme? All right, you can go on having it forever and ever. The complacent faith of these people in young Mr Frost resembles that of the stockholders in the South Sea Company before the bubble burst.'

But this was just a warm-up for Monday, when Robert Pitman

began a new series called 'The Hate Makers' – 'A penetrating *Express* series on people who have dominated the citadels of opinion and power'. Pitman wrote:

> It is in its way a solemn moment – the close of an era. Why are the Hate Makers dying?
>
> There is an excellent maxim on big newspapers. It is: never pick on the little man. Today, however, I must break that maxim. For any obituary of the Hate Makers must begin with the short life and sad decline of David Frost.
>
> There is no doubt that David Frost is lumbered with some misfortunes. One of them is his friend, Mr Gerald Kaufman, who resembles Bernard Levin, but without the looks and the charm.

When he came to sum up, Mr Pitman wrote:

> Mr Frost (at least an affable young man) has served his turn as the batman of the blimps. He has directed a thin spray of hatred and scorn at anyone who dares to disagree with him – and in particular against the ordinary man in the suburbs or in the country marketplace.
>
> If the ordinary man is in favour of anything – whether it is patriotism or the Crown or controls on immigration – you can be absolutely certain that Mr Frost will be against them.

The Express Group at the time had still not understood that, whatever the public outcry from the more vocal protesters, the ordinary man tended to identify *with* TW3, etc., and with its irreverence. The whole thrust of viewers' letters had always been 'Thank God for your programme speaking up for us against them.' Indeed, in the midst of some of the more hysterical attacks, such letters had been a great source of solace.

Robert Pitman's article was only the first in the 'Hate Makers' series. At the close of the article, in caps, was a simple legend 'Next: Bertrand Russell.' Next: Bertrand Russell! Day three was

John Osborne. *Punch* commented: 'Actually, it would be a rather nice club to belong to, wouldn't it?'

By the time we reached the first 'Not So Much' of 1965, the combination of scripted spot and unscripted talk was really clicking. The talkers on that particular show were Henry Fairlie, Gerald Kaufman and Nick Tomalin. We reviewed 1964. What, I asked Gerald, was for him the biggest mystery of the year?

'Julian Amery retaining his seat in the General Election by such a large majority.'

'What was the majority?'

'Ten votes.'

The group discussed Harpo Marx and T.H. White, the two people who had died in 1964 that they would most miss, the Chinese Bomb, *Fanny Hill* and *The Naked Lunch*; and Nick Tomalin initiated a rousing discussion on the subject of youth in the Sixties, its deification versus its condemnation, and its emergence as a separate political group. Meanwhile our cadre of talkers was expanding all the time. Peter Hall, Claud Cockburn, Jim Mossman, Robert Shaw and even Robert Pitman all made their debuts. The general reaction was summed up by Peter Black: 'Recently, the talk has become much more directed . . .'

One had to feel a sneaking sympathy for poor Edward Ashford, Vicar of St Nicholas's, Kings Norton, Birmingham. He claimed that 'tens of thousands of people' had thought that at least one evil had been destroyed when the BBC took off 'That Was The Week That Was'. But he added, 'Now that same evil has raised its head three times more strongly.'

My regular routine at the time was to fly to the States on BA flight 501 at 11.15 every Monday morning. This prompted from one stewardess my favourite 'apology': 'I'm very sorry, Mr Frost, I'm afraid it's caviar again.' With the advantage of the five-hour time difference, I was able to get to the Shoreham, have a shower and change and reach the TW3 offices by 4 p.m. on Monday afternoon. While lunch and dinner in the United States are often at least an hour earlier than in Britain, it was still a bit daunting, knowing that one had another full day's work ahead, to see on Madison Avenue every Monday afternoon at 4 p.m. a bar with the sign in the window: 'RELAX! IT'S THE HAPPY HOUR'. Buck

Henry and I would work, particularly on my monologue, until about 10 p.m. We would try and deal with one subject a week, and once or twice, when we were absolutely desperate for a punch-line at about 10.30 in the evening, would – in the spirit of SINA and indeed my school history essays – invent a spoof one. 'For as Voltaire said, "The folly of wisdom is ignorance, but the ignorance of folly is wisdom." Good night.' Delivered with enough self-confidence, and with a fast enough sting from the band, we could be on to the next item before anyone had time to figure out what on earth I was talking about.

Tuesday mornings were for other business and calls to Ned in London about the next weekend's 'Not So Much'. Then over to Rockefeller Plaza and NBC studio 6A. Normally I would fly back to London on the Wednesday and be in our Lime Grove office by 7.30 on the Thursday morning.

In February I also had to add the odd trip to places round the States and Canada to oversee a 'That Was The Week That Was' tour of the United States. The team was captained by Willie Rushton, who like P.J. Kavanagh had moved on from 'Not So Much' at the turn of the year. One Wednesday on my way to visit them in Shreveport, Louisiana, the Delta plane stopped off at Montgomery, Meridian and Jackson, all familiar names in the struggle for civil rights. As the flight taxied prior to take-off from Jackson, the stewardess came on the intercom: 'Welcome back to your Delta tour of centres of racial intolerance . . .' I could only assume that she was due to retire the same day. Or, if she wasn't due to retire the same day *before* her announcement . . .

At this stage, 'Not So Much' seemed to be about as on course as a live, three-times-a-week show could ever hope to be. But it was the calm before the storm. The storm broke about our heads following the programme of 27 February. It was preceded two days earlier by the news that Donald Baverstock was no longer Chief of Programmes at the BBC, and that Huw Wheldon would be the new Controller of Programmes, with Michael Peacock taking over as Head of BBC 1. (Three weeks later, when Donald Baverstock resigned from the BBC completely, Alasdair Milne resigned in sympathy because of the way Donald had been treated.) These events were not linked in any way with our impending storm, but they gave us more of a feeling of being out on a limb over the next few weeks than we would otherwise have had.

The eruption of fury over Donald Webster's sketch on the programme of Saturday the twenty-seventh took us somewhat by surprise. Tongue-in-cheek, he called it 'Tell me, Nurse Drew'. It was certainly much more savage than the title makes it sound. Father O'Connor, played by Brian Murphy, is visiting Mrs O'Hara, played by Patricia Routledge.

Priest: And how's the children? How's young Sean?
Mrs O'Hara: All right, Father.
Priest: And Michael and Kevin?
Mrs O'Hara: Much better, Father.
Priest: How's your Deirdre? And Oliver? And Carmel, Siobhan and Patrick?

Father O'Connor goes on to enquire after the health of another fifteen or sixteen children. Then Mrs O'Hara offers him a drop of whiskey.

Priest: Thank you, Mrs O'Hara, I will. Gowran's better, I hope? And baby James? Thank you. Won't yous have one yourself?
Mrs O'Hara: I can't afford it, Father.
Priest: Now, talking on that subject, Mrs O'Hara . . .
Mrs O'Hara: Here you are, Father. Two pounds this week, bless you.

The priest says he has a rather delicate matter to raise.

Priest: How's your youngest, Doolan? He's fourteen months old now, is he not?
Mrs O'Hara: He is, Father.
Priest: Well, Mrs O'Hara – I see no signs of a future blessing on the way.
Mrs O'Hara: No, Father.
Priest: Have you sinned, Mrs O'Hara? Have you been using those dirty black Protestant pills?

Mrs O'Hara: I have not, Father . . . although it says in the newspapers that they don't do much harm.

Priest: You read the wrong newspapers, Mrs O'Hara. Now, these pills enable you to predict the time of ovulation. Have you been predicting the time of ovulation?

Mrs O'Hara: Bless you, no, Father. It is always just after closing time when himself has had his fill of Guinness.

Priest: Is he still . . . er . . . being a good Catholic, Mrs O'Hara?

Mrs O'Hara: Well . . . nowadays not *every* night, Father.

Priest: And why not?

Mrs O'Hara: Well, Father – it's hard to make a decent living in Liverpool unless yous play an electric ukulele, and he's too old now to join a group. You see, he doesn't get his porter every night, Father.

Priest: Now, Mrs O'Hara, it must be hard times for you, I know that. Look here now, here's ten shillings back – spend it wisely, won't yous?

Mrs O'Hara: God bless you, Father. I'll buy some little shoes for Michael.

Priest: You will not, Mrs O'Hara. You'll give it to himself for his porter. A working man needs it, you know that.

Mrs O'Hara: Very well, Father.

Priest (finishing drink): Well, now, I'll be off. Oh, and give my regards to Deelan and Terence and Eileen. (Turns and addresses camera) We'll catch the Chinese up yet . . .

It was satire of the broadsword variety, rather than the rapier. But it was a valid target, and came across with considerable power. It was followed – and we thought set in context – by a vigorous debate between Norman St John Stevas, putting the Catholic point of view, and Dee Wells, supporting the underlying argument of the sketch. She in turn was supported by the audience.

Merseyside MPs, led by Simon Mahon, Labour Member for Bootle, tabled a strongly worded motion in the House of Commons:

> That this House condemns the action of the BBC who have outraged the conscience of the people of Merseyside in particular and millions of television viewers in general, by transmitting a disgusting and grossly offensive sketch in their production of 'Not So Much a Programme, More a Way of Life' on Saturday and deplores this flagrant and nauseating attack on the dignity of family life, and calls for an immediate improvement in the standard of such transmissions and demands a public apology by the BBC.

'MPs Call for BBC Apology' roared the headlines. Rather too quickly, we felt, they got one, in a letter from the Director-General of the BBC, Sir Hugh Greene, to Simon Mahon:

> . . . I agree that this sketch was open to criticisms that it misrepresented Roman Catholic teaching about the family and also the manner in which priests go about their pastoral duties. I regret the offence to viewers which resulted from these misinterpretations . . . The ensuing discussion dealt with a subject of legitimate public interest and gave an opportunity for the presentation by Norman St John Stevas of the Roman Catholic position on the social and economic aspects of birth control.

But the MPs were not satisfied. James Dunn, representing Kirkdale, protested, 'Why did David Frost get off the hook? He was the man who gave the offence in the first place. I'm not satisfied to leave it there.' Mr Walter Alldritt, of the Scotland Division of Liverpool, said, 'Frost should apologise personally.' Now the headlines read 'David Frost Must Apologise – MPs'.

Hugh Greene's apology was not enough for the Leader of the House of Lords, the Earl of Longford, either. Speaking in a debate about youth, he 'startled the Lords by suddenly referring to what he called that revolting programme', according to the *Daily Express*. He went on: 'I need not dwell on that, because the BBC has apologised, although the apology could have been framed much more strongly. But it is a serious thing when the BBC should be convicted of something of this sort.'

'Convicted'?

He continued: 'It is really criminal that such a programme should have been put on. It simply could not have been put on simply by some producer merely in a fit of aberration . . . For the BBC to be associated with a programme such as this, dirty beyond belief, leaves me staggered.'

Ned and I felt this was all too much, and I decided to respond by means of a statement:

> It is a surprise that Lord Longford, whose name has always been rightly associated with liberalism and tolerance, should allow himself to become the spokesman for this sort of pressure group.
>
> It is not just that he and his friends are spokesmen for a minority. That we all accept. It is that they are quite possibly spokesmen for a minority of that minority. It is quite clear from the hundreds of letters I have received that, not only did the non-Catholic public welcome the treatment of the subject, but so did a great many of the Catholics, who said that they felt that their leaders have been trying to stifle public discussion for too long.

It was clear from all our correspondence that the Catholic establishment was completely out of step with its rank and file on this whole topic. And for Lord Longford to suggest otherwise was humbug. However, I felt it would be unfair not to mention Simon Mahon as well, and one of his quotes in particular: 'I was surprised by Mr Mahon's extraordinary observation that in some mysterious way the sketch portrayed the entire population of Liverpool as "sex-ridden horrors". If he really feels like this he should obviously go further and get "Z Cars" taken off at once for portraying the entire population as thieves and juvenile delinquents.'

The newspapers quickly contacted the BBC, who responded equally quickly with the stirring words: 'His views in no way represent the BBC.'

The hysteria even reached the leader columns of *The Times*: 'Public confidence has been shaken more than at any period in

'Never mind who we are . . . Is David Frost in . . . ?'

the history of British broadcasting . . . gross offence . . . unpardonable . . . exhibition of coarse taste . . . what is tolerated by patrons of a third rate nightclub . . . panic flight from decent values . . . nothing short of abject repudiation . . . the overdue spring cleaning must come from within . . . their hearts must be heavy today.'

On the same day Peter Black tried to summarise his thoughts in the *Daily Mail*:

> Let us discuss the current question: should David Frost and Ned Sherrin be whipped through the streets?
>
> I think not. I saw the item in 'Not So Much a Programme' that all the fuss is about. Nobody has yet pointed out that it presented in satirical terms points made in earnest by Catholic writers such as Dr Anne Biezanek. This is a treatment the programme exists to supply about everything . . . the studio audience was clearly not put out by the sketch and, like the overwhelming majority of the public, was vehemently on the Protestants' side in the argument that

> followed. So the claim that 'millions of viewers were offended' ought to be set in perspective . . . Britain is largely run by puritanical pressure groups, of one sort or another, and I don't accept their claim that nobody must make fun of them. They should be good-humouredly and steadily made fun of.
>
> I object to apologies offered to them.

And one quote from a Sunday newspaper symposium of views on whether 'Not So Much a Programme' should satirise religious matters observed, 'Religion is sacred to many people.'

Intellectually, we felt that we had had the best of the argument, and that the response of our opponents had been hysterical. Institutionally, however, within the BBC, we had probably only just weathered the storm, and had probably used up some of our dwindling capital with the sixth floor at the Television Centre and back at Broadcasting House into the bargain.

According to Patrick Skene Catling in *Punch*, the viewing figures were looking pretty good: 'There are now more than six million viewers each night it's on – twice as many viewers as the BBC has ever had before for a Friday series at that hour, and three times as many as before on Sunday evenings. The Saturday evening figure is the biggest since TW3.' However, for a new BBC hierarchy trying to play itself in after the departure of Donald Baverstock and Alasdair Milne, it was probably possible to envisage more peaceful ways of spending the weekend than waiting for the 'Not So Much a Programme' hotline to ring.

When the next bombshell arrived – indeed, two bombshells in one weekend – Sir Hugh Greene simply did not have the heart (or the support) to carry on the fight any more.

On the last Friday in March, the twenty-sixth, there was a discussion on the value of door-to-door canvassing by politicians. Bernard Levin said there might be an advantage in *not* canvassing, 'the obvious example' being Sir Alec Douglas Home. He went on: 'If potential electors have seen Sir Alec on television only, they may have even come to the conclusion he's a cretin. They really may – because of bad lighting and his spectacles. If they have him on the doorstep, they'll be damned sure he's a cretin.'

When Patrick Campbell commented, 'Absolute drivel,' Bernard said, 'Well, I withdraw the word cretin. Imbecile.' In the ensuing argument, Bernard was outnumbered two to one – by Patrick Campbell and Iain Macleod. In the course of that discussion, he did modify and indeed withdraw what he had said. But the damage was done. 'Sir Alec a Cretin Row on BBC-TV' was all over the next day's papers.

Perhaps the most surprising comment on the affair came in the leader column of the *Sunday Telegraph*. Headed 'Frosty Politeness', the piece said:

> One of the more useful functions of 'Not So Much a Programme' is to supply material for a comparative study of various types of rudeness. Is it, for example, more reprehensible to describe the Leader of the Opposition as a cretin, as Mr Bernard Levin did on Friday, or to address the Bishop of Woolwich as John, as Mr Frost did in an earlier performance?
>
> Paradoxically, the laurels should go to Mr Frost. Mr Levin merely perpetrated a commonplace breach of the rule that no criticism of anyone should be stated in language more offensive than is necessary to convey its meaning.
>
> Though there is no reason intrinsically why bishops should not be called by their Christian names in public (St Peter certainly was), the practice of addressing a bishop as Mr so-and-so, or at least as 'Bishop', happens to be one of the conventions by which society expresses its respect for a useful and honourable office.
>
> Defying that convention is a more insidious, though less obviously shocking, threat to the amenities of life than hurling puerile abuse at ex-Prime Ministers.

'Really tells you something about the times, doesn't it?' I said to Ned after we read it. 'I don't know about that,' he replied, 'but it certainly tells you something about the *Telegraph*.'

On Sunday night a filmed item about the Duke of Windsor, a mock-operatic treatment of the Abdication, caused another storm. I had never particularly liked the piece – not because it was offensive (indeed it was very mild), but because I thought it didn't work. But Ned was keener to use it than I was not to use it, and it had therefore made its way into that Sunday's script. Early that day, it had been announced that the Princess Royal* had died. In retrospect, that should have changed Ned's mind, or converted my reluctant acquiescence into outright opposition to the item's inclusion, but it did neither. It was a real miscalculation, not assisted I fear, at least in my case, by a regrettable lack of awareness about how close the relationship between the Princess Royal and the Duke of Windsor in fact was.

A BBC spokesman said: 'We would deplore any suggestion that it was unsympathetic to the Royal Family or lacked due respect.' But that was certainly the way the item was depicted in the press.

On Monday, Sir Hugh Greene made an announcement. The performance of 'Not So Much' on 11 April would not only be the last of the current series, but the last – period. Of the Abdication sketch he said: 'There was an error of judgement. It was a mistake to put it on when the Princess Royal had died a few hours earlier . . . The difficulty is to combine freedom of expression with responsibility. I still think there is room for satire, but I am not sure we have the form right.'

The ending of the programme was quite a shock for Ned and for me. Although we had been aware that 'Not So Much' was probably regarded as something of a mixed blessing within the rearranged BBC hierarchy, and we had no written guarantees of its future, Ned had still felt sufficiently relaxed to discuss the programme's return on BBC radio that very weekend. This time we were not together when the news of cancellation came through. Ned was in London, I was in New York.

Ned defended the Alec Douglas Home affair, but admitted that we were probably wrong to put out the sketch on the Duke of Windsor: 'People seem to have taken it the wrong way.' On Sir Hugh Greene's decision, he made no comment.

I heard the news when I got to the Shoreham in New York that Monday afternoon. After two or three calls from the press

* The Duke of Windsor's sister.

in London, I put the receiver down and thanked my lucky stars that I had learned a simple tenet for dealing with stop-press telephone calls: 'Only respond to what you *know* people said, not to what your callers *say* they said.' Did I want to respond to Sir Hugh's ruthless axing? Did I want to respond to his vicious personal attack on me? Did I want to clear the air/put the record straight – the two phrases are virtually interchangeable, and mean 'dig your own grave' – by saying what I really felt about him? Luckily, I replied that I could not respond until I got back to London and studied his remarks in full.

Reactions were varied, though, in the main, pretty supportive. Milton Shulman in the *Evening Standard* commented: 'If one reads the collected works of Bernard Levin – particularly his writings as Taper in the *Spectator* – one would discover that, compared to the abuse he has heaped upon Harold Wilson, the word "cretin" is practically a term of endearment.'

Dee Wells in the *Sun* thought that in a way it was our own fault:

> When Baverstock was beaten they must have sensed which way things were going.
>
> When the Corporation apologised for the birth control skit that Catholics found offensive, they must have realised they were on finite, if not borrowed, time.
>
> With both these lazy-dog type hints knife-edging at them down the corridors already ankle deep with Baverstock's blood, it might have been the time for 'Not So Much' to duck. To remember that discretion is the better part of valour. That he who runs away lives to fight another day.
>
> Instead, they dowsed themselves with petrol, struck a match – and became the Hari Kiri Show . . . To be outnumbered by these safe, conventional goodies in grey flannel suits is only a dreary part of the national condition. To be outmanoeuvred, outflanked and, finally, ousted by them is a tactical error.

Dee's words in part mirrored my own feelings. The writing had been on the wall. During that last weekend, in particular, we had indeed played into our enemies' hands. But then again, perhaps the pressure on Sir Hugh Greene had mounted to the point that he would have found another pretext to kill 'Not So Much' anyway. Indeed, maybe he had already planned to make the announcement on that Monday anyway.

There had always been a difference between what the raised voices of the self-styled defenders of the moral fabric of the nation found acceptable, and what the wider, quieter public found acceptable. When the gulf between the two grew, as over the birth control sketch, it became increasingly difficult to produce what the BBC found acceptable – namely, a compromise.

The last show, on 11 April, was a fairly subdued affair. Michael Crawford as the teenage rebel Byron summed up:

> What it boils down to is: if the show was going on, the party they're all going to afterwards would be on what the BBC glob calls Entertainment Scale A. As it is, it will probably be on Scale D – two half-bottles of South African sherry and six free Woodbines in a glass, and everyone going around saluting as the ship goes down and looking as if they've got this secret pain they're being brave about. That smashes me to fragments. I shan't be stopping myself. I don't fancy being there when they all line up to commit suicide with their throat microphones.

Just in case Byron was right about the Scale D hospitality, we went off for a farewell party at Annie Ross's own club, Annie's Room, in Covent Garden. Donald Baverstock's successor, Michael Peacock, came too, having gamely told the newspapers: 'It has been a remarkable achievement in television. Something will follow in the autumn – but don't ask me what.' But at the party some of the 'Not So Much' crowd harboured unkind doubts about whether he was there as the impresario or the undertaker.

Our most passionate obituary came from John Osborne in the *Sunday Times*:

> The BBC appears to have become as perilous a place to inhabit as any United States Embassy within a stone's throw

of a Students' Union. For observers of national character, it has been an unhappy spectacle to study from behind the safety of one's own barred front door.

As we all know, most of the stones have been hurled at Mr David Frost and Mr Ned Sherrin, two faces which seem to loom in the dreams of many, and can even be seen by some leering out of every window at the Television Centre. In spite of a great deal of simulated boredom expressed about these two figures, they have set more typewriters rattling in Fleet Street than anyone else who has broken and entered our homes from the little box of failed promises.

When Orwell said that the English were the gentlest people on earth he meant the people who were actually *on* the end of Wigan Pier. He didn't mean the people who run it. For the voice of English violence is the voice of threatened profit, of those who believe in the virtue of 'getting on', 'leaving things alone', yet are possessed of the greedy desire to order the lives of all, and especially of those who are young, sexually immoral or simply speak out of turn. And, most of all, of those who appear to be all three, and are paid large sums of money – the thing the bourgeoisie care most violently about – and become rich and famous for their transgressions. Then the voice of Jeremiah is heard loud and clear in the correspondence column of the *Daily Telegraph* and in the first-class carriages of trains to Lewes, where, as I have often discovered, more violence smoulders than ever exploded into decent parlours from TW3 or 'Not So Much' . . . The cry of the English bourgeoisie is desolate indeed when faced with the anarchic implications of freedom. The English bourgeois is violent because his intuition is faulty and his loyalties collusive. His objectives narrow down to a nagging, painful sore of human undernourishment, he is understandably inaccessible to the relaxations of wit, irony, tones of voice, range of gesture or the delicacy of affection or even love that often huddles beneath the most outrageous lampoon.

I was touched by, and grateful for, this unprecedented example of 'hate-maker' solidarity – and I hoped that Mr Cooksey, my old mentor at Wellingborough, was enjoying it too.

Back in New York, it was time for another wake. The American 'That Was The Week That Was', having served its two seasons, was not being renewed for a third. There was nothing particularly sinister about this – any plotting against the American TW3 had happened at the *beginning* of the second series rather than at the end. TW3 had just not prevailed in the ratings over the combined strength of 'Peyton Place' and 'Petticoat Junction'.

The final show was on 8 May. Brought to you by Bufferin, Revlon Glo-coat and Score spray deodorant. No cigarette sponsors, because we were returning to the subject of smoking. There were some highlights from past shows, including Burr Tillstrom's Berlin Wall. We ended with some predictions for the future, the last of which ran: '31 December. It is predicted that by 1968 we will have a man on the moon. But will we have a man on earth?' And thus into a rousing Tom Lehrer finale. Tom had written a number of original songs for the series, and we reprised his 'We'll All Go Together When We Go', which seemed fitting.

In social terms, the US TW3 never had the same impact as its English parent because, as we have seen, the same preconditions did not exist. But its television impact was considerable. Tom Lehrer, for instance, had been writing landmark lyrics since 'Fight Fiercely, Harvard' and 'I Wanna Go Back to Dixie' in the late Forties, but TW3 was the first network show to which he had been a regular contributor. The worlds of the cult, hip humour of a Lehrer or a Mort Sahl on the one hand, and of prime-time television on the other, had traditionally been mutual no-go areas prior to the US TW3. After it, George Schlatter, who co-produced 'Laugh-In' with Ed Friendly, the NBC Vice-President who had previously been responsible for overseeing TW3, often spoke of the 'enabling' role of 'That Was The Week That Was' in making 'Laugh-In' possible. Later, NBC was to continue and develop the tradition with 'Saturday Night Live'.

TW3 was over. That was a blow to my ambitions in the States, but far less of a blow than the very existence of the series had been a boost. And I was hooked on America, and the generosity of a nation of immigrants to a recent arrival. I loved New York, and was amazed to find wilderness so close – only two hundred miles or so north of the city, you could lose yourself in virgin forests and great rolling downlands. By comparison we in the UK really were 'huddled masses', on a compacted island with cities spilling into one another. It was this transformation of scale, from the oppression of the cities to the elemental America, that I found so majestic. It was easy to imagine the driving curiosity of those first settlers.

But it was not only the scale of America in geographical terms that I found so breathtaking. It was the scale of the power (symbolised by the political conventions), and of the problems too – like civil rights. And the scale of the leaders produced to wage those struggles – like Martin Luther King. One of the greatest peaceful grantings of rights by a majority to a minority – rewriting three hundred years of history – was under way, but still in the balance. You could not just return home to the UK, switch on the latest pirate radio station, and forget the dramas that were being played out on that great stage. My home was Britain, but I resolved to seize every chance I could to continue my life and activities in the States. Tony Jay had once defined luck as the moment when preparation meets opportunity. I would try to be prepared for the next transatlantic 'luck' that came my way.

It was very much a watershed time in my life. My two series had come to an end within a month. And the two-year idyll with Jan had run its course in the past couple of months as well. Jan had been ready to settle down and get married; I had not. And neither of us was about to change. Inevitably we had begun to drift apart, almost without realising it. In the end our timing was simply out of synch, and Jan was married within the year to Mel Torme. Maybe, I thought, if we had met later . . . but no, that wouldn't have worked either, because Jan would probably have been married to someone else by then. It was just not meant to be, although that was an idea that took a lot of getting used to.

The day after I got back to the UK on 13 May, there was another bombshell in the papers. A headline in the *Evening Standard* read 'David Frost in £5m Damages Case'. The story began:

> Britain's David Frost, the National Broadcasting Company and others are named as defendants today in a court action seeking damages totalling £5,357,142. The action was filed in the Federal Court in Cleveland, Ohio, by two Cleveland residents and by three hundred descendants of a woman who has recently died.
>
> The plaintiffs stated that on or about April 20th, 1965, approximately fourteen days after the death of the plaintiffs' mother, Katherine Young, the defendants had caused the following statement to be uttered: 'Katherine Young, aged 99, of Syracuse, New York, expired last week leaving 322 descendants, including 14 children, 67 grandchildren, 172 great grandchildren and 73 great great grandchildren. She wins the booby prize for the week for Birth Control.'
>
> The plaintiffs stated that due to this statement they were caused to suffer 'much humiliation, chagrin, insult, injury, embarrassment'. [How on earth did people recognise them?] It infers that their origins were the product of excessive sexual activity [an interesting legal concept, this] and is an insult inflicted on them which time cannot eradicate.

They wanted five million dollars for count one.

Under count two we had apparently accused the plaintiffs of 'socially unacceptable sexual appetites, habits and behaviour', and they wanted another five million dollars for that (the remark, not the sexual behaviour). Just for luck, they also wanted 'a further and additional sum of five million dollars as and for punitive damages'.

In its own bizarre way, the story was quite impressive. When people read that you are being sued for some vast sum, they tend to assume that you must actually possess it.

'Dear David,' read one letter, 'I would like to congratulate you on your success in America. You have only been there for a few months and already you are being sued for five million pounds. We are so proud of you . . .'

Alas, I had a somewhat more accurate fix on the current state of my financial resources than did my loyal correspondent. American-style legal bills would be decidedly unwelcome, and I knew that you almost never win costs from the other side in a legal case in America. Indeed, that fact, combined with and compounded by the fact that lawyers in America were allowed to take a percentage of the winnings and forgo their usual fees, was what had made America the world leader in nuisance actions of this kind. The suit may have sounded absurd, but it was not good news at all.

There was one more shoe to fall. On Monday 17 May, Ned and I had breakfast at the Ritz. We talked vaguely about the future, and I asked him whether he thought it was time for me to move on to something new. Ned told me he had a very good reason for answering 'yes'. At a high-powered session at the Television Centre, he had been told that the BBC would like to find a new Saturday night satirical programme for the autumn, but not with Sherrin and Frost – only with Sherrin. In general terms, that was not really a surprise. The BBC could scarcely seem to be accommodating its critics while retaining both of us, and I was the most visible. However, in personal terms, it was a shock. My earlier remarks to Ned at that breakfast had been completely genuine. I had been wondering whether it was time to move on – but it is certainly more pleasant to do that over the pleas and entreaties of your employers. Ned and I agreed that I would 'resign' from the as-yet non-existent programme – 'making way for an older man' – before there could be any suggestion that I had been sacked.

In retrospect, it was a blessing in disguise. It was time to move on, and if there had been no new late-night satirical show in prospect, that is what I would have done. But if there *had* been a late-night satirical show – and I had been offered it on a plate – would I really have had the vision to say no? I doubt it.

Ned has since summed up his feelings at the time of that breakfast: 'It was unfair, but I was excited by the challenge of being without him. I had done three winters with David, and now facing a third series without his support was both daunting and attractive.' If I had put my own rather jumbled thoughts down on paper, they would probably have been similar – except for the fact that I was not facing a third series of anything at the time! However, Ned and I had been beginning to outgrow each other. I had enjoyed making the transatlantic journey on my own. I had enjoyed developing 'A Degree of Frost' on my own. 'A Degree of Frost' . . . now that was a thought . . .

FIVE

'The Frost Report'

NOW FOR THE GOOD NEWS . . .

When I contacted NBC about the law suit – very casually and unconcernedly, of course – they quickly announced that they were going to assume all the costs of defending the case against the Cleveland 300.

Much more important than that, Carol Lynley now came into town and into my life. She had flown in from Hollywood to star in an Otto Preminger film, *Bunny Lake is Missing*, with Laurence Olivier and Noël Coward, and we began a relationship that would blossom several times over the next eighteen years when geography, careers – and our other commitments – allowed. Otto expected his young actresses to live like nuns and get bags of sleep during the period that they had the signal honour of being under his command, so we kept our assignations secret, particularly from Otto. But one morning on the set he questioned Carol about why the skin on her chin was peeling slightly. She replied quickly, 'Sunburn.' 'Looks more like Frostbite to me,' barked Otto. Carol blushed, and thus was spared one of Otto's legendary temper tantrums. Her open-mouthed amazement at his omniscience was sufficient reward for the great man.

As for the next television series, there were two clear possible paths – comedy, of course, or ad-lib interviewing, probably with an audience – which 'A Degree of Frost' and 'Not So Much' had brought into the forefront of my thoughts. Should I continue to combine the two, as 'Not So Much' had done, or should I choose to specialise in one? I decided to specialise in both.

My interest in ad-lib interviewing had been fuelled by what I had seen on American talk shows. Although I was intrigued by many of their techniques, I did not want to confine myself in a talk/interview programme to the same rather limited showbiz agenda. Whatever I did in terms of interviews, I wanted to be more broadly based than that, embracing rather than vetoing current affairs as a major ingredient. I had talked a lot about not underestimating the intelligence of the audience, and this was a case in point. Why assume that a talk show that deals with subjects that matter will automatically get a reduced audience? If it was done right, surely the reverse could be the case. However, my thoughts were still relatively unformed in 'talk' compared to 'comedy', and I realised it was a much tougher sale.

I resolved to tackle the idea of a comedy series first, while still pursuing the right format for the talk series. Following the warm response to 'A Degree of Frost', BBC Light Entertainment was obviously the best potential launching pad. I had two get-togethers with Tom Sloan within a month, and chatted at length to Bill Cotton, Jr.

Throughout the next few months of planning, two men were indispensable to my brain-storming – Clive Irving, formerly the editor of 'Insight' at the *Sunday Times*, and by now executive editor of IPC magazines, and Tony Jay, who had severed his full-time links with the BBC in favour of a freelance career, and was now in the process of founding a new consultancy firm, JBM, with Donald Baverstock and Alasdair Milne.

Tom and Bill were both very interested by the idea of a follow-up to 'A Degree of Frost', though that was not necessarily to be the title. I felt it should contain at least two of the three ingredients of the special. Its humour should be intelligent and irreverent, but contemporary rather than strictly topical as TW3 had been, and social rather than purely political. Pace was important, too – particularly as we were thinking of peak time rather than late night now. And we should aim for the best of guests, as we had on the special – like the Swingle Singers from Paris and Nichols and May from the States.

Once it became clear that there was positive interest in a new series, the tension started to disappear and I was able to relax and enjoy a salad days sort of summer. There was plenty of romance in the air. There were also some gloriously civilised visits to East Bergholt to visit that inimitable old chawbacon,

Randolph Churchill. (As a point of principle Randolph liked to befuddle his *Evening Standard* readers with at least one unfamiliar word per article. 'Chawbacon' had been a recent discovery.) Randolph loved to gossip into the small hours – on occasions, long after midnight, he would expand the conversational group beyond his fireside with the aid of his telephone and a list of the bedside phone numbers of a number of unfortunate senior Conservatives. 'Are you steady on parade, Selwyn?' he would bellow down the phone at two in the morning. The phrase 'steady on parade' was invoked by Randolph whenever there was some crisis in the Conservative Party in which there was even a smidgen of danger that R.A. Butler might prevail.

Back in London, Clive Irving and I met regularly to discuss the idea of a possible club at 107 King's Road (which later became the Aretusa), with Peter Evans of the Peter Evans Eating Houses, and a dashing publisher of scientific journals, by name Robert Maxwell. There were the purely entertaining lunches too, with Len Deighton, Robin Douglas-Home – a wistful figure in some ways, but such a graceful one – and Willie Donaldson, the impresario who had brought *Beyond the Fringe* to the West End. He and I lunched together at the Hilton Rooftop Restaurant. The menu was in English, with a French translation underneath. No problem with that, except when they got towards the end. Once they had put *petits fours* in the English section of the menu, how on earth were they going to translate it into French? Their solution: with the coffee, we were offered *les frivolités françaises*.

There was also a little something special in the air at a lunch party that Tony Lambton organised in South Audley Street. He had the characteristically mischievous idea of bringing together Sir Alec Douglas Home and David Frost in the same room. I can report that we both played a very straight bat. Indeed, cricket was about the only thing we had in common that we *could* talk about.

At the beginning of August, there was a trip to Le Touquet to interview Robert Morley for *King* magazine, at the request of a friend, Bryan Forbes, who as a hobby was taking a flutter on the magazine business.

'Are you going to do another of those horrible satire programmes?' asked Morley. 'Well, they're not terrible, actually.'

I said that I was not in fact going to do another.

'You see, satire was a wonderful sort of toy to give the young,' said Morley. 'When I go to Oxford I always tell them the story about an island entirely overrun with dragons and a very old man saying, "What shall we do with the dragons?" And the young people get very excited, and he says give them all a rattle to drive the dragons away and after about two minutes the dragons get used to the noise and they can all go to sleep again. It's only the old men that are kept awake.'

Then he got on to what turned out to be a real Morley *bête noire*. 'I have subjects like education, that I find myself constantly discussing with people.'

'Why education?'

'Because I hate schoolmasters. I think that the trouble with the world is that we have such a rotten class of schoolmaster. I think when they write reports about our children, that is the grossest impertinence. I hate schoolmasters because they always try to influence the people they are serving. I mean, a waiter doesn't come to you and say, "I'll make this man into a delicious eater before I have finished with him." None of the waiters here criticised our table manners . . . All education should be closed down in England for about five years and the whole question reconsidered by somebody, possibly myself, as to what we should teach the children.'

In mid-August Clive Irving and I flew to Ceylon. The trip was partially at the invitation of BOAC – to whom we had suggested an in-flight magazine which so far they were successfully resisting – and partly at the invitation of some locals who wanted advice on setting up a television station in Ceylon. For me the great value of the trip was as an extended ideas session, but it was memorable in other ways too.

Despite its beauty, Ceylon in those days had remarkably few tourists. One of the main restaurants in Colombo was however doing its best to cater to Western tastes. On a trip to London, somebody had obviously noted the habit on many British menus of putting 'Grills (20 minutes)', and had extended that principle to Ceylon. There on our menus was the helpful information, 'Ice cream (5 minutes)', 'Roll and Butter (2 minutes)'.

On our way up to the highest point on the island, Nuwara Eliya, after driving for miles through deserted paddy fields, we came upon a lonely old battered shack which bore the slightly peeling legend, 'The Gregory Peck Tailoring Emporium'. Many years later I was able to tell that incredibly elegant star – one of the world's best-dressed men – how his trip to Ceylon to film *The Purple Plain* had been immortalised.

Everything in Nuwara Eliya was reminiscent of the last days of the Raj, particularly the Hill Club, the traditional white man's club. Yellowing copies of two-month-old *Daily Telegraph*s lay open in the reading room at the obituaries page. It was the last bastion of white supremacy in Ceylon, the only club that still barred 'the natives'. The odd thing was that Cedric Senaratna, the Oxford-educated Government official who was accompanying us, clearly rather respected it for that.

One of the club officials took Clive and me to one side. He pointed towards Cedric, who was fortunately just out of earshot. 'The reason why we don't let *them* into the Club is that they worship dirt. They don't just like it, they *worship* it. Absolutely worship it.' It may have been the dying twitch of a regime with a nobler past, but that taste of the white settler mentality at its worst stayed with me.

There were better moments; a torch-lit parade of elephants through the old highland capital of Kandy, for one. And the enthusiasm of one particular zoologist who pressed on me a series of photographs of elephants engaged in foreplay, insisting that they would make a splendid television programme. More than a quarter of a century later, alas, I have still not quite found the right moment.

On the way back from Ceylon, we stopped for a couple of days in Beirut. Above the hotel there was a rather worrying neon sign which read 'BO C TAK GO D CAR OF YO'. Did the people who maintained the sign also maintain the planes, we wondered.

With the BBC series that I had proposed in mind, we made a trip to the Casino du Liban to see what sort of speciality acts were starring in the floor show. 'You were quite right to come to the Lebanon for your holiday, rather than to one of those other Arab countries,' our cab driver told us. 'They're all Islamic. Lebanon is still basically a Christian country – that's why you can get all the drink, drugs and women you want.'

This was not, I later found, a definition of Christianity with which my father was familiar.

Back in London, a lunch with Michael Peacock and Tom Sloan at the BBC Television Centre on 25 August almost clinched the new series, subject to negotiation. The summer came to an end in the most delightful possible way at Ingham in Norfolk on Sunday 12 September. The occasion was the annual Lord's Taverners match against the Edrich family. It was the first time I had played in it. The Edrich Family XI was packed with former county cricketers like Brian Edrich of Kent and Eric Edrich of Lancashire and, naturally, was captained by W.J. 'Bill' Edrich.

Meeting him was a childhood dream come true. I approached him excitedly, though with some trepidation. 'What are you doing these days, Bill?' I asked him. My childhood hero paused for a moment and then replied, 'I'm in sewage.' For a moment, it was a bit of a let-down. Somehow sewage and childhood heroes did not seem to go together. But then he explained that he was the managing director of a sewage firm, and that somehow seemed more appropriate. From then on, my encounters with Bill, either on the cricket field or at a Lord's Taverners dinner, were always a highlight. His sudden accidental death in 1986 at the age of seventy was a great shock, although Bill himself would probably have approved of the timing – just hours after a St George's Day lunch at which his courage and leadership had been saluted by Air Vice-Marshal Dowding, who had served under his command during the war.

On 22 September the new series was announced. By now it had been christened 'The Frost Report', and to my great delight James Gilbert had been confirmed as its producer. Jimmy's track record at the BBC was formidable. He was also the only person I knew who, as a teenager, had taken a girl away for an illicit weekend, and been found out by his parents *seven months* later. The weekend had been in May, and Jimmy faced the full weight of his parents' wrath on 23 December. A Christmas card arrived from the hotel addressed to Mr and Mrs James Gilbert.

A few days after the announcement, Jimmy and I met with Tony Jay for lunch at White City – not the BBC, but the dog track. The restaurant was not doing a particularly thriving trade. Indeed, we were the only patrons there. But we scarcely noticed. The show was really beginning to take shape. We discussed how the contemporary rather than topical, social as much as political, humour could also be thematic, and decided that we would focus on one subject per programme. We also talked about guests, and Jimmy and I decided to make a talent-spotting trip to the Continent.

We left for Paris on 13 October. The trip, which lasted for four days, was fun, but in creative terms it was a total wash-out. In Paris we went to the Crazy Horse, Le Sexy, La Grigniatière and the Music Hall de Marais. In Amsterdam we visited whatever revues we could find. In Brussels we visited the Ancien Belgique, and it was at dinner afterwards that the penny finally dropped.

There was nothing wrong with the artists we had seen. They were very good of their kind – but there were too many of their kind. Once they started performing, it could be almost any variety show. And they simply wouldn't meld with the sort of comedy that we were planning. We had to go for broke. The show would stand or fall on its comedy, and its thematic approach. The music had to play a part in that too – it must also be thematic. With that in mind, I mentioned Tom Lehrer, with whom I'd recently had a drink in London. Maybe he could make a regular contribution. By the time Jimmy and I got up from dinner we were exhilarated. We dutifully completed the rest of our mini-tour by going on to Copenhagen, where I developed a life-long antipathy to Aquavit, and then returned to London.

My first task was to get in touch with Tony Jay to talk about the theme script. Or maybe my second task, as I was opening in cabaret for a week at Quaglino's that Monday evening. More important, as it later turned out, was a one-night cabaret I did that October. I had been approached by a Mr Dick Pack of Group W Westinghouse Broadcasting, who asked me to provide the cabaret for a large group of Westinghouse reps and station executives who were in town. The cabaret went well, and I thought little more of it at the time, but it was the beginning of a relationship that was going to loom large in my life before the end of the Sixties.

Jimmy and I were able to assemble a marvellous team for 'The Frost Report'. Tony Jay set to work on the theme scripts which would provide the basis for our weekly script meetings during the series. I lunched and re-lunched with the writers who had served us so well on TW3 and 'Not So Much a Programme'. New writers were coming on board as well: the young and talented team of Michael Palin and Terry Jones, the sage of Hatch End, Barry Cryer; Dick Vosburgh, he of the great beard and even greater puns, became a valued member of the team; Marty Feldman became our Script Associate; and a minor piece of detective work brought us Neil Shand. I had heard a joke while watching 'On the Braden Beat' which ran something like: 'Following the recent naval cuts, this year's Spithead Review will take place on the Serpentine.' I liked the style, and immediately set out to find the name of the writer. The result was a working relationship with Neil which has continued ever since.

Within the BBC, John Law, who was a full-time script editor in the Light Entertainment Department, was excited by the concept of the show. The Film Editor Jimmy chose, Ray Millichope, was outstandingly creative, as was our Film Associate, Jim Franklin, who initiated many of the ideas for the ways we played with voices on film.

At the same time Jimmy and I set to work on the task of trying to assemble the on-camera team. Jimmy had worked with Ronnie Barker already, and thought that after a series of successful but relatively limited roles, Ronnie's talent was ready to flower. He had also worked with the South African comedy actress Sheila Steafel, and we soon put her at the top of our list of probables for the girl in our acting team. I had already suggested that Tom Lehrer might have a musical contribution to make, and then one day in the lift at King's Court North on the King's Road, where my flat was situated, I met a girl with a guitar. Her name was Julie Felix, and we started talking. I heard a couple of recordings she had made, and went to one of her gigs. A lot of Julie's material was of the Joan Baez protest variety – it was not exactly a barrel of laughs – but she cared about content, and then there was the skill, the style and the captivating smile. She did an audition for Jimmy and me at the Royal Garden Hotel, and another part of the mosaic fell into place.

I had been keeping in touch with John Cleese's activities since he left Cambridge. He had toured the world with *Cambridge Circus* – a show which had begun life as the Footlights Revue of 1963, 'A Change of Plinths' – and had done a somewhat unlikely stint at *Newsweek* in New York. Now I felt it was time for him to return home and begin to claim his comedy kingdom. He would be great as a performer, but I was equally keen to have his writing talent as well.

On my visits to Danny La Rue's Club and to Winston's I had been particularly struck by the appeal of two of the members of his team, and I followed up both of them. One was a very pretty and talented singer called Jenny Logan, and we soon became 'just good friends'. The other was a diminutive Scottish chappie, who had had a long apprenticeship for stardom without having yet made it. He was ready, I felt, and television particularly would capture that irresistible twinkle as he delivered a punch line. I invited Ronnie Corbett to tea at the Ritz, and we talked about his joining the series. I had no doubt that we were signing up another star. As we talked, perhaps the most constructive comment I made was on the subject of height. Jenny had mentioned to me that Ronnie at that time was very sensitive about his height, or lack of it. I tried to emphasise that he should relax into it – and make a point of using it. Far from being a drawback, it was an enormous plus – a short cut to recognisability or memorability with the audience. Over the years Ronnie has developed that strategy with unceasing inventiveness.

As I left that tea, I was very happy for us – and for Ronnie. He had waited for stardom longer than any of us, yet his faith in himself was about to be justified. And he would cope with it superbly. He had been studying for this moment ever since he first went on stage, and there would be no missed cues now – whether off-stage or on.

In the midst of all these preparations came Christmas and the

New Year. I did a New Year programme for ITV called 'Year In and Year Out', talking to a group of children aged between seven and twelve from Dr Barnardo's Homes about their ideas of the important events of 1965 and their hopes, dreams and aspirations for 1966. Then on Monday 3 January I had a simple (as I saw it), private (as I organised it), little (as I planned it) idea. The early days of January are often the dog days of the year. The weather is usually pretty depressing, and the bills coming in from Christmas make it even more so. Wouldn't it be a good time to give a party, mixing up some of the friends I had got to know from varying walks of life? Right now, this week? I settled on breakfast as the time for the party, most of all because of the short notice. I thought that everybody's diaries around lunchtime and in the evenings would probably be full.

If the party was going to be on Friday morning, the invitations would have to be made by telephone. I booked the Carlos Room at the Connaught – to which I had been introduced by Randolph Churchill – and gave Tom Benson at Ray Parkes' a call to ask if he would consider providing some of his ulanovas for consumption in a rival establishment. Tom's ulanovas were a mouthwatering mixture of sour cream and caviar on a thick but featherweight prawn cracker. The texture was as good as the taste, and vice versa. Everyone seemed to respond warmly to the idea on the telephone. In fact, Paul McCartney was the only person who couldn't make it at the last minute. I did not tell anyone who else was coming, with the exception of 10 Downing Street, who needed a list.

Nine-thirty on the Friday morning was the appointed hour. Lord Longford and Lord Chalfont were among the first to arrive, along with Sir Joseph Lockwood of EMI and David Astor of the *Observer*. Paddy Campbell soon joined us, along with Lord Soper, the Bishop of Woolwich and Professor Freddie Ayer.

Cecil King was there from IPC, Kenneth Adam from BBC Television, and Robert Maxwell, Donald Baverstock, Len Deighton, Clive Irving, Jimmy Gilbert, Peter Evans and Cyril Bennett. The Prime Minister, Harold Wilson, entered a few minutes after the first arrivals, and was in sparkling form throughout. He left for Downing Street at about ten-thirty, champagne was served a little later, and a very enjoyable party came to an end just before eleven.

That would have been that. Except for the fact that the get-together at the Carlos Room had been included in the Prime Minister's itinerary for the day. So that morning at the press briefing, the reporters were duly informed. The reaction was, by all accounts, quite startling – or startled. 'The Prime Minister this morning attended a breakfast party.' *'A what?'* 'Given by Mr David Frost.' *'By whom?'*

Next morning the breakfast got quite remarkable coverage in the newspapers. I confined myself to saying, 'It was really a private party and a chance for a few friends who don't always meet to get together and talk,' and added, 'I'm a great believer in breakfast as an institution.' By Sunday morning Kenneth Rose in the *Sunday Telegraph* had found a cautionary passage from Disraeli's *Sybil*:

Lady Firebrace: It shows a restless revolutionary mind that can settle to nothing but must be running after gossip the moment they are awake.

Lady St Julians: Yes. I think those men who breakfast out, or who give breakfasts, are generally dangerous characters; at least I would not trust them.

There were further stories all the following week, and on the Sunday, Patrick Campbell devoted his column in the *Sunday Times* to the subject, under the heading 'The Big Breakfast'. He was being harried mercilessly by a friend:

> His reserve cracked. 'For God's sake,' he cried, 'tell me what was going on! What about Harold?'
>
> 'Harold came in,' I said, 'smoking his pipe just as I dipped into the caviar and I was so surprised I dropped my lump on the floor. He engaged himself in some easy chat with the Lords and I had three more quick fruit cups. Then we all sat down to breakfast.'
>
> 'Just anywhere?' he asked. 'No place cards or anything?'
>
> 'Just anywhere,' I told him. 'I sat next to Harold with

Donald Baverstock on the other side. Harold said to me, without further ado, "What about a barber?" I hadn't had my hair cut for some time, but I was a little surprised that he should take exception to it. Then I discovered he must have said, "What about Barber?" having reference to the cricketer, because he went on to talk knowledgeably and at some very fair length about the Test Match. I couldn't take any part in this at all, and neither really could anyone else. Apart from Harold we were all in a state of deep shock. There were four tables, you see, of six people each and we all kept glancing at one another out of the corners of our eyes, wondering what in the name of Providence we were all supposed to be doing there.'

'And what,' he said, 'in the name of Providence, were you supposed to be doing?'

'I haven't the faintest idea,' I said. 'Just having breakfast, I suppose. We finished up with champagne, but Harold left before that. I asked him if he was off to do a bit of governing, and he said he was. That's really all.'

'He looked at me broodingly for some time. 'Hopeless,' he said eventually. 'Didn't you ask Frost what it was all about?'

'I'm sorry,' I said, 'I didn't. I was too shy.'

In *Punch*, Basil Boothroyd thought he discerned a developing trend: 'I hear that since his success at the Connaught, the Prime Minister has been increasingly in demand as a breakfast guest. He recently headed Cilla Black's guest list (others present: Dr Leavis, Viscount Montgomery, Manfred Mann and the picture editor of *Honey*).'

According to Boothroyd, wrestler Jackie Pallo had also held a breakfast with the Prime Minister. '"I was demonstrating the step-over leg lock on Lord Hill," Jackie told me, "and accidentally knocked a plover's egg into Wilson's knee. He just laughed, and went on chatting to Sidney Thompson and his Old Time Dance Orchestra."'

After the ulanovas, it was back to preparing 'The Frost Report'. The first edition was broadcast live from the BBC Television

'He's a real *VIP – gets a twelve-gun salute and breakfast with David Frost.'*

Theatre at 9.40 p.m. on Thursday 10 March. It had been due to be shown at 9.05, but it was pre-empted from that time slot by a General Election broadcast by the Prime Minister. If, for a moment, this seemed like Barry Goldwater all over again, we soon realised that it was in fact rather good news. Election Day was Thursday 31 March, and what would be the first programme on the air after the polls closed, when all those tiresome embargoes on comment were lifted? Yes, 'The Frost Report', which would obviously have to take elections as its subject that night.

On the opening programme, we had chosen to deal with the subject of authority in all its various manifestations, since we knew that purely political comment would be the target of pre-Election restrictions.

'Perhaps it's best to begin with some examples,' I said at the opening of the show.

> This is authority, from the *Sun*: 'Council workmen are to rip planks out of seats and make holes in the walls of bus shelters in an attempt to make the shelters too uncomfortable for hooligans. Councillor Harry Beale said, 'Something has got to be done to stop the wrecking of these shelters. So far as I can see, this is the only way.'

That's typical of authority. Out to preserve itself even if it means defeating its own ends. Or this is authority, from the *Newcastle Journal*: 'At Middlesbrough Police Court yesterday a solicitor asking for excuse from attendance of a client said, "In the first place he's a man of not very bright intellect, secondly he is employed on important Government work."'

Of course, there is one example of an authority figure that we all recognise . . .

And we were into our first quickie, written by John Cleese.

Policeman: Charles Edward Fuller, I arrest you for the murder of Gladys Biggs.
Man: But I'm Henry Robinson.
Policeman: Oh. Henry Robinson, I arrest you for the murder of –

Terry Jones had another policeman quickie:

Policeman: Excuse me, sir, but do you recognise this photograph?
Civilian: Yes, yes – I do.
Policeman: Rather good of me, I think, don't you? – This is one on the beach at Bognor . . .

Julie Felix sang 'What Did You Learn in School Today?' Authority, we said, or people in authority, act in a more beastly fashion than ordinary people ever would. We quoted examples. This from the *Guardian*: 'Peterborough Rural Council has demanded four weeks' rent in lieu of notice from the relatives of Mrs Minnie Day, who vacated an old folks' bungalow without giving the statutory four weeks' notice.' Mrs Day had in fact *died* without giving the statutory four weeks' notice.

Quoting Tony Jay's theme script, I defined the job of an authority figure as 'preventing disturbance, tidying things over, covering yourself at all costs. It's got nothing to do with principle. It's the force which destroyed Antigone and St Joan. And one authority figure with whom we all come face to face very early is the headmaster, whether of a large state school or a small private school . . .'

John Cleese's private school was the educational equivalent of Fawlty Towers:

> I would like to welcome four new members of the staff this term, but unfortunately I could only get two . . . In place of Mr Boircnault, our late French teacher, we have engaged Mr Mboko. This will be the first time our syllabus has included Swahili, but we hope to resume French again next term. You may be interested to know that Mr Mboko was until last week Prime Minister of Chad. On weekday mornings he will teach the Sixth Form Swahili; and on weekday afternoons the Sixth Form will teach *him* English . . .

We inaugurated a device we were to use regularly throughout the series – 'The Language of . . .'

> Authority tries to protect its position by the language it uses, which never says what it means: 'The matter is under consideration' means 'We've lost the file.' 'The matter is under active consideration' means 'We're trying to find the file.' 'This is an urgent problem and we are therefore setting up a Royal Commission' means 'We hope that in three years' time everyone will have forgotten about it.' 'In the fullness of time' means 'Never.' 'In the not too distant future' means 'Never.' 'Never' means 'As soon as we dare.' 'We have had a full, frank and far-ranging exchange of views and both sides look forward to meeting again at a later date' means 'We are at war.' 'We are moving forces back a little to a better-prepared position from which to launch a future offensive' means 'We have just lost Dorset.'

Even the front page of the Bible, we pointed out, announced that it was 'Published by Authority'.

'Of course, one way of keeping out of authority's clutches is to remember the letter of the law . . .' heralded one of Jimmy Gilbert's filmlets. Ronnie Corbett was a bowler-hatted man walking along a path who sees a notice saying 'Don't Walk on the Grass'. He finds this just too tempting. He puts one foot on the grass and jumps back. Park keepers and policemen whistle at him and beckon him off. They close in on him, but to their total frustration he hops, he skips, he jumps and he dances – in fact, he does everything except actually *walk* on the grass. And authority is stymied.

'There are people who are just simply authority figures,' I went on. 'They may know something about the subject or not. They're just authority figures – Lord Mackintosh, Chairman of the Advertisers' Association, dedicated to persuading people to spend, was at the same time head of the National Savings Movement, dedicated to persuading people to save. The whole point is that an authority figure must never be obviously provably wrong but he never has to be right either. Sir Thomas Padmore had learned his lesson well when he gave evidence to the Royal Commission on the Civil Service: "What I have said has demonstrated that it is very difficult to find an answer to that question, but if I were pressed for an answer, I would say that, so far as we can see, taking it rather by and large, taking one time with another and taking the average of departments, it is probable there would not be found to be very much in it either way."'

Tom Lehrer then sang his own rousing song, 'It Makes a Fella Proud to be a Soldier'. We applauded the man somewhere in England who was a *small* rebel against authority: 'He keeps his milk of magnesia in a hot place. When the radio says "Turn the lights down low, it's time for dancing," he turns the lights up high and goes to bed. When the notice flashes on the television screen, he always adjusts his set; on the other hand, he never adjusts his clothing before leaving. He buys instant coffee, then makes it slowly. During the second chorus, he doesn't join in. He writes in all the spaces marked "For official use." He sends money now, accepts substitutes, reads instructions carelessly, remembers his troubles, under-acts his age, thinks small, keeps his chin down and does his worst. Moreover, he does it later.'

Ronnie Barker conducted a police training session, written by John Cleese. Then I added, 'Perhaps most important of all though is to realise that, stripped of its anonymity and so on, so much of authority is a confidence trick. A trick of phrase or of voice . . . I mean, some very distinguished authority figures might fare very differently if their voices underwent some slight change . . .' There followed a bit of wizardry from Jim Franklin. The visual form of Malcolm Muggeridge, but with a Cockney accent dubbed onto the picture; Robert Dougall with a Birmingham accent; Archbishop Ramsay with a Cockney Jewish accent; President Johnson with a cissy Oxford accent; Robin Day as a girl and Ian Smith as a black African.

I summed up: 'That's authority, really. Authority is obeyed and sometimes questioned. I suppose authority should be questioned and sometimes obeyed. Because it is often so ludicrous. For many of us, authority is summed up by the sign that one of the team found on the Yorkshire moors which said simply, "It is forbidden to throw stones at this notice."

'Next week, "Holidays". Good night.'

It was my first series in the UK since 'Not So Much', and we held our breath for the reaction. It was all we could have hoped for. Kenneth Eastaugh in the *Daily Mirror* said that what the programme did was 'to separate what we believe is sensible and rational from what we actually do and say'. T.C. Worsley in the *Financial Times* came up with the sort of double-edged compliment that you have to read twice to make sure that it really is OK: 'It is interesting that David Frost, who was, I suppose, the most widely-detested of the original BBC satire team, is the only one who has made an unqualified success of a show of his own.' And Kitty Muggeridge made her well-known comment, 'Malcolm predicted that after "That Was The Week That Was" David Frost would sink without trace. Instead, he has risen without trace!'

Meanwhile, my driving skills – or lack of them – made it into a profile in the *Sunday Times*. 'He runs a big Mercedes and drives it in heavy traffic as though it were a Mini. Other motorists, scrambling for the footbrake, catch a sign in his rear window: "The safest car in the world".' I felt I must do something immediately for my fellow road users. I didn't actually change my driving style – but I did remove the sign.

John Cleese was rightly given a warm welcome by the *Daily Mail*, who described him as 'another ex-Cambridge Union satirist of the "Good heavens, no, I'm not going to go on doing this for a living" school.' John told the *Mail* in March 1966, 'I can't see myself still in show business in three years' time.' He said that his interest was international politics: 'I've always wanted to feel I could be completely at ease in a very wide variety of situations. The study of politics could give me that.' John has maintained the same ambivalent attitude to show business ever since, but thank goodness he is still managing to overcome his in-built reluctance, albeit not as often as his admirers would like.

We added another semi-regular feature – my interviews with children on the chosen subject. In the programme on education, when I asked one small boy what he thought of school, he replied, 'Well, it makes you brainy, and that makes you sadder.'

One programme included a sublime little conversation with two Cockney children, that I still do not understand to this day. 'What programme do you like to watch?' I asked. After dutiful consideration the first replied, 'Well, I like to watch the Japanese programmes.' 'And the Chinese,' added her friend. What was the difference, I asked. 'Well,' said the first little girl, 'the Japanese, their eyes go up like this – and the Chinese, their eyes go down like this.' What were their favourite words? 'Japanese,' said the first little girl without hesitation. 'And Chinese,' said the other. At this point, I simply gave up.

Viewers' 'pet peeves' also became a regular part of the show. On the subject of advertising, for example, Squadron Leader Berkeley wrote:

> Why do advertisers continually announce '17 per cent more' without adding 'than what'? A few months ago I wrote to a well-known tyre company whose advertisements announce 'Twice the grip, twice the mileage'. I asked, 'The grip and mileage of what?' and added that I

> had invented a rubber with 847 times the grip and 943 times the mileage, but as my basic test piece was a banana, I doubted whether I had a commercial proposition.

Howard Bentley chimed in:' Obeying the advertisement, I have fitted a new carburettor which gives 30 per cent better fuel economy, a silencer guaranteeing 35 per cent more miles to the gallon, and a petrol additive that gives 40 per cent more to the gallon. Why doesn't my petrol tank overflow every thirty-five miles?'

Mr R.J. Lennox was concerned about all those official forms that state imperiously 'Do not write in this space': 'I suggest a small blob of candle grease, on the very good theory that if *you* can't write in that space, no other beggar will either.'

As the series progressed, my mother came up with a terrifically good idea, though she didn't know it. 'People in Beccles,' she said in her usual code for 'I' or 'we', 'are wondering about the way you smile at Julie at the end of her songs. They think there might be something special between you.' There wasn't at the time, but it was a damned good idea, and I acted on it, while wondering at the same time why I hadn't thought of it already.

'The Frost Report' was broadcast live every Thursday evening. Jimmy would begin rehearsals in the morning, while I was at home completing a first draft of my links, or 'CDM', as we called it. CDM was short for the deliberately otiose 'Continuous Developing Monologue'. The reason for using that particular phrase was to underline to everybody working on the show the importance of the theme. I would arrive at the studio at about four o'clock in the afternoon and run through the CDM.

This was an essential part of the editorial process, because there are two stages to selecting material, particularly one-liners, that you think will work. First, you can make a selection on paper. In the case of 'The Frost Report' there was a mass of material from Tony Jay's weekly essay, lines from our writers, press clippings that I had unearthed and comments of my own. That was the first part of the process. But then there is the discipline of actually saying those same things out loud. Suddenly you realise which lines are the strongest of all the originally strong lines you selected. Some do not quite 'scan'. Others you slightly rush through, and realise that you are either unsure or ashamed of them. After that read-through Jimmy and I would retire to my dressing room and edit the CDM – just as we edited the rest of the show – together. The final version was usually on autocue with about twenty or twenty-five minutes to spare.

Meanwhile, although I didn't know it at the time, at the Convent of the Sacred Heart, Woldingham, a fourteen-year-old girl called Carina Fitzalan Howard was reserving a front-row seat in the television room every Thursday night at 9 p.m. to watch what she told all her friends was her favourite programme. But more of that in a later volume . . .

Fridays were almost as important as Thursdays. On Fridays we would gather with the writers for a meeting with a double purpose. First, we would try to repair any gaps that we foresaw in the next week's show, for which most of the material would by then have been submitted. Then we would go on to consider Tony Jay's theme script for the following week's show, and find out which paragraphs ignited which writers. They were usually great meetings. It was a more integrated approach than we had used on TW3 or 'Not So Much', where we never held writers' meetings as such. Working to a theme, as we were now, the meetings were essential.

The most important thing about such a collectivist get-together is a positive approach to the ideas that are put forward, looking for the germ that will work. Never step on an idea; welcome the tentative idea with acclamation, never with scorn. To quote Tony Jay, 'Never meet ideas with pursed lips' – accentuate the positive, after all even a stopped clock . . .

After the meetings were over, St Mary's Church Hall, Paddington, would resound to the thumps and bangs of a five-a-side football match with a tennis ball for the more soccer-mad amongst us. No prizes for the name of the instigator.

Jimmy and I would talk separately to Julie Felix about her song for the subject in question. Tom Lehrer was a different matter. His maths duties at Harvard meant he could only pay one flying visit to the UK, to record all the songs for the whole series. The audience that night got a wonderful concert. Actually, Tom performed two concerts on that trip. Randolph Churchill was one of his most ardent fans, and I took Tom down to Randolph's history-factory at East Bergholt. The duet of Tom and Randolph singing the Lehrer classic about Wernher von Braun,

What goes up must go down,
But that's not my department,
Said Wernher von Braun

in Randolph's library also ought to have been taped.

There was a consistent underlying pattern to 'The Frost Report'. We tried to focus on the absurdity of many of the things that the British took for granted or tolerated, but often did not articulate or completely think through. The show was about our illusions and pretensions, and our widespread assumptions. Many of these were rooted in the past, but increasingly new Sixties myths were growing up as well. If you took the words of pundits and commentators at face value, you could have believed that a new Britain was growing out of the ashes of the old system. Mr Edward Heath had taken over from the 14th Earl of Home as Leader of the Conservative Party; the Clubs of St James's were yielding to the coffee houses of Chelsea; Carnaby Street was usurping Savile Row; Liverpudlian pop stars were weekending at ducal castles; dukes were going out to work; and ancient universities were welcoming upstart sons of hobnailed workmen.

Our contention was that British society was not changing that much, either for better or for worse, and that the changes were in most cases superficial rather than fundamental, and merely added to or reinforced the long-established contradictions and paradoxes of British life. We tried to separate the apparent from the real, and to decode some of our customs, attitudes and behaviour.

Class, or the myth of classlessness, was obviously at the root of it all. In reality class was still everywhere. When the Labour candidate in the most recent General Election had called at Floors Castle to solicit the Duke of Roxburgh's vote, he had been told by the butler, 'You must use the tradesmen's entrance.' As the College of Arms had informed an anxious hostess who sought their advice over the seating arrangements for a dinner party: 'The Aga Khan is held to be a direct descendant of God . . . an English duke takes precedence.'

We quoted a newspaper report which read: 'Princess Margaret travelled last night to Balmoral as an ordinary first-class passenger in the Aberdonian night train out of Kings Cross.' Why, if nothing exceptional was happening, was this thought worth reporting at all? And, as a student of Britain might have asked, could you really talk about 'an ordinary first-class passenger' any more than you could talk about your average, common-or-garden, man-in-the-street Pope?

Also, of course, it was so comfortable to have a class system. It still is. Once you establish yourself in the upper class, trivial accidents like a drop in income cannot dislodge you, so long as you keep the right attitude. The system is a perfect let-out for failures in the lower class, too. Instead of being forced to try harder, they can tell themselves that their lack of success is due to the system. Card games have always been more popular in England than chess, for the simple reason that if you lose at cards, you can always say you were dealt a lousy hand. In short, the system is a powerful buttress to that great English quality, the uncompetitive spirit.

John Law found a memorable way to dramatise the issue of class in his 'Three Classes' sketches, featuring John Cleese (tall, representing the upper classes), Ronnie Barker (medium height, representing the middle classes) and Ronnie Corbett (short of stature, representing the lower classes):

Cleese: I look down on him [Barker] because I am Upper Class.

Barker: I look up to him [Cleese] because he is Upper Class, but

I look down on him [Corbett] because he is Lower Class. I am Middle Class.

Corbett: I know my place. I look up to them both. But I don't look up to him [Barker] as much as I look up to him [Cleese], because he has got innate breeding.

Cleese: I have got innate breeding, but I have not got any money. So sometimes I look up [bobbing down] to him [Barker].

Barker: I still look up to him [Cleese] because although I have money, I am vulgar. But I am not as vulgar as him [Corbett], so I still look down on him.

Corbett: I know my place. I look up to them both; but while I am poor, I am honest, industrious and trustworthy. Had I the inclination, I could look down on them. But I don't.

Barker: We all know our place, but what do we get out of it?

Cleese: I get a feeling of superiority over them.

Barker: I get a feeling of inferiority from him [Cleese], but a feeling of superiority over him [Corbett].

Corbett: I get a pain in the back of my neck.

Crime, we found, was a prime example of class in action. A broad definition of crime in Britain was that it was any lower-class activity which was displeasing to the upper classes. Crime was committed by the lower classes and punished by the upper classes, and the whole paraphernalia of the criminal law and the criminal courts was based on the need of the upper classes to keep the lower classes in their place. Hence the phrase 'the criminal class'. The upper classes were made wards of court. The lower classes were hauled before the juvenile courts in need of care and protection. The upper classes sued each other for libel. The lower classes smote each other in public houses and were charged with causing an affray. The upper classes got divorces. The lower classes got five years for bigamy. If a lower-class man pinned somebody against a brick wall and beat the living daylights out of him, it was called assault and battery. If an upper-class man did it, it was called the Eton Wall Game.

As an Essex magistrate had said when dismissing a charge

of assault brought by a woman against her husband: 'It is not unreasonable, in a certain class, for a woman to have her face smacked from time to time, and to be punched about. It is the normal wear and tear of their married life.'

Although England's laws were designed on the whole to protect and preserve the upper classes and to catch out the delinquent class, the mesh of the net was not so precise that it never caught anyone from the upper classes. But if a law caught members of the upper classes too often, it was changed. That was what had happened with homosexuality in the Sixties. And that was what happened with the motoring laws. Offenders were offered the option of paying a fine or going to prison. The upper class paid fines, which did not bother them at all; the lower classes either begged, borrowed or scraped the money together as best they could, or went to jail where they belonged. But nobody wanted literate people to go to prison – they had a distressing way of revealing what it was actually like and destroying our illusions about training and rehabilitation with nasty stories about sadism and futility and buckets of stale urine.

The alleged victory of honesty over hypocrisy was another Sixties myth. We talked about our vital links with the Commonwealth, then cut grants to Commonwealth students. We condemned the colour policies of South Africa, Rhodesia and America, who really did have a problem, and congratulated ourselves that by our graceful submission to a West Indian cricket team and the enrolment of one black policeman, we had solved ours. We talked about redeploying workers when we meant sacking them and leaving them to fend for themselves. We banned tobacco advertising on television, which could manage without it, but not in newspapers, which could not. In the mid-Sixties, there was also a growing preoccupation with the 'generation gap' – particularly with reference to sex. We tried to explain both sides. How could one blame the youngsters and their pop idols? They were contemplating a transition from the world of the pop song, which displayed sex without love, to the world of the television commercial, which displayed love without sex.

Convinced by television commercials that marriage was a terrible monasticism in which all a father could do was give presents, romp occasionally with the happy, milk-fed children, get rid of his lumbago in a Radox bath, and watch his personal freshness, and in which the preparation and consumption of proprietary brands of food was a substitute for making love, they, not surprisingly, concluded that they had better have one hell of an orgy while they still had time.

One could sympathise with the parents' position, too. They had grown up in a culture in which you started as a poor student or apprentice, started to earn a bit more after you got married, and finally entered into your inheritance when you were in your fifties and the children were off your hands. The last years were the affluent ones. Now they saw young people doing it all the other way round. They were understandably resentful and jealous.

We were forced to conclude: 'The whole business of the sexy young English has been grossly inflated to feed the greedy imagination of an envious older generation.' In any case, nobody had ever said that the English manage without sex; it had been their incapacity to flirt easily, their uneasiness in the presence of tenderness that had distinguished them from other nations. And that was unchanged. A sociological team watched, in various countries, how often couples touched each other during conversation. The English came easily at the bottom of the list, as usual. They still had no unit of erotic currency of lower denomination than the full clinch.

Over the years, whenever Tony and I have been asked to contemplate the findings of 'The Frost Report' and *To England with Love*, the book we wrote after the series, we have ruminated gloomily on how little has changed. Maybe the grip of puritanism has loosened a little. Back in the Sixties we wrote: 'Drinking is restricted to certain hours of the day, and just when things are just getting really jovial, everyone is thrown out of the nice warm pub and made to contemplate their wicked conviviality in the cold street.' Those restrictions have been lifted, though many pubs take little advantage of the fact.

We also wrote:

> Taking without his consent someone else's money is regarded in England, as elsewhere, as sinful, but even their own is thought by the English to be rather filthy and dangerous, so they tuck it away in banks which then refuse, by opening at ten and closing at three, to let them get at it at obviously convenient times, like just before work in the morning or just after work in the evening. Finally, such of their own money as they do lay their hands on is not easily spent, since the moment they leave their work in the evening and are free to fling it about, the shops bang down their shutters and only raise them again next morning when everyone is safely back at work.

Thanks to American twenty-four-hour hole-in-the-wall cash dispensers and Asian shopkeepers, there seems to be some progress here, though nothing has changed about this: 'Three thoroughly uncivilised practices have a special virtue about them in England, all of them puritanical: opening windows in cold weather, going for long walks in cold weather and bathing in cold water.' Indeed, the strongest argument the British could find at the time for entering the Common Market was that it would be like a *cold shower* to our industries! What could be nicer? We even found one English masochist who liked a cold shower every morning – so he had a hot one.

On the subject of Europe, we noted that surely the Europeans 'must have noticed that the word "European" when spoken by an Englishman does not include the English'. How much has that changed? Maybe ten per cent? But this hasn't changed at all: 'The immediate reaction of an Englishman confronted with a European who does not understand him is to speak very slowly in baby talk and shout very loud, exactly the way they deal with the infantile and the senile.'

Today we take it for granted that fundamental changes in British society happen slowly, at best. The difference in the mid-Sixties was that so many people were convinced that they were taking place everywhere about them. Certainly there were raging social debates, 'shocking' new ideas, increasing lifestyle and generation gaps, and even some seeds of change. But behind the turbulence, the citadels of entrenched power and influence were not really in any imminent danger of falling like dominoes to the insurgents.

SIX

'The Frost Programme'

ON THE LAST DAY of the first series of 'The Frost Report' in June 1966, the BBC announced that there would be a new series the following spring. Two weeks later, Cyril Bennett, the Controller of Programmes at Rediffusion, announced what I would be doing in the meantime – a new three-times-a-week series called 'The Frost Programme', which was to run for thirteen weeks starting at the end of September. We described it as 'a mixture of humour, people, comment and entertainment'. No satire, we added. Cyril and I had negotiated the deal once 'The Frost Report' was successfully launched, and I had cleared it with the BBC. But 'The Frost Programme' was more than three months of planning away.

A week later, BBC Radio announced 'David Frost at the Phonograph', which was to be produced by Angela Bond. The reporters asked how it felt being produced by a woman. 'Aren't we all?' seemed to be the only possible response. 'David Frost at the Phonograph' was to take over from Jack Jackson's 'Record Roundabout' on the Light Programme for eight weeks, later extended to sixteen. The programme ran from 12 noon until 1.30 every Saturday, and we tried to make it as anarchic as possible.

Dick Vosburgh, Neil Shand and Barry Cryer would join me in the studio ready to hand me a last-minute line or chime in with one themselves. Dick was the master of the atrocious pun. 'An Australian singer is to open a clinic to cater for people from North Africa. It will be called Ifield's Moor Hospital' – this would lead into a record by Frank Ifield. 'And now here she is, ladies and gentlemen, Britain's nineteenth lady of song . . .' 'And now a lovely little ballad entitled "You are too Beautiful for One Man

Alone – So I've Brought Along a Group".' 'To Mrs Harriet Stritch, who phoned in a request, I'm sorry but the Rondo Doloroso from Meyerbeer's Third Symphony, opus 12, doesn't seem to have been recorded by the Kinks. Instead, here's . . .' 'And now, with only two records to go, an apology to Mrs Esther Pearson of Leicester. I'm sorry we didn't have time to play your request, Honegger's Diatonic A Cappella Oratorio for countertenor and mezzo-soprano in C sharp minor – but you *can* hear it tomorrow on "Sing Something Simple".'

Each week guests like Denis Norden, Larry Gelbart, Paul McCartney and John Cleese would come along to the studios and join in the proceedings. John was very much into his ferret phase at this time, and his ferret recipes caused such a response that we printed a special leaflet of them. Among the recipes was Mock Ferret Soup: 'Put the ferret in a large barrel from which it cannot escape. Then mock it with such phrases as, "It is generally agreed that you could not chase a vole, let alone a rabbit," or, "Even by ferret standards you are unimpressive." When the ferret is mocked, simmer in the Bay of Biscay and serve with a writ for libel.'

The recipe for Ferret Crumble was somewhat simpler: 'Take a very old ferret and sit and wait . . . and wait . . . and wait . . .'

One aspect of BBC Radio in those days was sacred – the news. It was cocooned on either side with instrumental music, to avoid even the hint of any accidental embarrassments by means of juxtaposition. We determined to try and do something about this, and every week we would ring the newsroom in the hope that the bulletin would open with a story that was boring and did not involve fatalities or tragedy of any kind. Eventually our moment of opportunity came. The lead story was just what we had been waiting for. Accordingly, at 12.29 and twenty seconds, instead of going into some instrumental music, I made an announcement: 'And now we come to our new feature of news requests, in which you request certain items of news that you would like to hear read by our newsreader. We have a request here from Mrs R.J. of Kidderminster, who would like to hear a really boring news item about the Italian Prime Minister arriving in London on his way to lunch at Chequers. Well, Mrs R.J., for you – here it is.' Over in the newsroom the newsreader could not ad-lib; he had to read out his first item: 'The Italian Prime Minister arrived in London today on his way to lunch at Chequers.' He sounded as though he was spitting out every word.

We knew we would not be able to continue with this modest piece of anarchy for very long, since we were dealing in sacrilege here, but we did manage one more week before thunderclaps from on high threatened Angela Bond's entire future with the Corporation. The following Saturday, at 12.29 and twenty seconds I announced that we were holding auditions for new newsreaders, and called upon the first candidate to do his best. Barry Cryer stepped up to the microphone and did a splendid drunken attempt at a news item, ending with a loud hiccup. The time was now 12.29 and fifty-five seconds, 'Thank you,' I said. '*Next!*' This time the newsreader sounded close to apoplexy.

Two very different stage performances stayed with me from that summer. One was a week of *An Evening with David Frost* at the Palladium in Edinburgh, with an overflow show called *An Evening with David Frost at 3 O'Clock in the Afternoon*. The other was a concert which the Lord's Taverners put on at Parkhurst Prison on the Isle of Wight. The remark that stopped me in my tracks was made by a prisoner who said to me as I was leaving, 'Come back in 1988. I'll still be here.'

When I got back to London, I went through the files of The New Bridge, an organisation which existed – and still exists – to help ex-prisoners. The first five case histories I read told a sad tale about rehabilitation, or the lack of it.

One ex-prisoner found a good job, and was doing well until anonymous phone calls to the management led to his past leaking out. His employer forced him to resign. A second also found a job, but was then blocked by the union, who said he had not paid any dues for five years. He would have to pay them before he could start work. The union then added that it could not accept the five-year apprenticeship he had done while in gaol, as it was inadequate. Its own usual apprenticeship lasted six months.

A third man came out of prison to find that his wife had been forced to divorce him by well-meaning friends, and that the case was about to be taken to law. A fourth, previously an accountant, found it almost impossible to get a new job. Eventually he got one as a labourer. It was difficult and degrading for him, and his accent was mocked by the men, but it was something. Within eight weeks it was nothing. The foreman got him fired because he thought he was after his job. The fifth could not think of a way to explain a blank insurance card, could not find anyone to talk to, simply could not cope, and committed suicide.

The stories had a profound effect upon me, and I have remained a supporter of The New Bridge ever since. It is a Cinderella among charities, and still needs more help.

The summer of 1966 was a hectic one. There were trips to Rome to see Richard Burton and Elizabeth Taylor, and to try and work out a way in which Richard could narrate a series of programmes based on the biography of Winston Churchill, who had died the previous year, that Randolph was writing. There were lunches at the Carlton Club with the promising young editor of the *Spectator*, Nigel Lawson, who persuaded me to write a press column for a few weeks. There were meetings to try and get a new invention, paper dresses – yes, paper dresses! – off the ground. These were the brainchild of Ossie Clark and Celia Birtwell, and we managed to get the idea as far as an unfruitful meeting with Johnson & Johnson. (I was becoming increasingly intrigued with projects outside television, but only in the Sixties, I think, would one of them have been paper dresses!)

There was also a memorable weekend with the aforementioned Randolph Churchill at the old Beaverbrook villa, La Capponcina, in the south of France. The highlight was a trip to Villefranche for dinner. One ill-advised souvenir seller stayed at our table a second too long. Randolph suddenly erupted, the colour filling his cheeks. He glared at the man, 'Why don't you f— off? F— off, f— off, f— off, f— off!' It was a somewhat unsubtle technique, but at least it had the merit of transcending the language barrier. The hapless souvenir seller backed out of the restaurant at a speed which certainly exceeded the local limit.

Randolph often referred to himself as 'an acorn in the shadow of the great oak'. He had spent his life running away from this daunting inheritance. Ironically enough, it was only when he faced up to it as a fact of life and wrote the official biography of his father that he achieved the widespread acclaim on his own behalf that he had always sought.

London was very much the 'in' city that summer. In July *Esquire* hailed it as 'the most civilised great city in the world . . . the fun machine', but it was the *Time* magazine cover story in April, which bestowed its accolade of 'the swinging city', that had really brought joy to the hearts of the tourist industry. 'London has burst into bloom,' reported *Time*. 'It swings; it is the scene . . . From Carnaby Street, the new way-out fashion in young men's clothes is spreading around the globe, and so are the hair dos, the hair don'ts and the sound of beat; in Czechoslovakia alone, there are five hundred beat groups, all with English names.' Really? Was Prague now a swinging city too?

I wasn't sure about this paragraph either: 'London today is in many ways like the cheerful, violent, lusty town of William Shakespeare, one of whose happiest songs is about "a lover and his lass, that o'er the green cornfield did pass".' Well, maybe – though the Rolling Stones' lyrics were a touch more explicit than that.

There was much emphasis on the fashion of Swinging London: 'Clad in tightly fitted, wine-red flared Edwardian jacket over a wildly ruffled white lace blouse, skintight, black bell-bottomed trousers, silver-buckled patent leather shoes, ghost-white make-up and tons of eyelashes, she pops into a cocktail party, not unlike the one Julie Christie goes to in *Darling* at Robert Fraser's art gallery on Duke Street . . . In London, everyone parties with everyone.' Assuming they had any time left after they had finished dressing up.

'Youth is the word and the deed in London – and well it should be: nearly 30 per cent of its population is in the fifteen to thirty-four age bracket, far more than the rest of the country as a whole.' Even those of us fortunate enough to be in that fifteen to thirty-four age bracket did not recognise all the lingo. 'Talking the flip jargon that has become basic English for teenagers, jet-setters and indeed any knowledgeable adult striving to maintain the illusion that he is at least young in heart, the switched-on London bird or beatle calls his urb "super", "fab", "groovy", "gear', "close" or "with it".' The six adjectives were all pretty familiar, but was the masculine of 'bird' really 'beatle'? And what on earth was an 'urb'?

Although the 'widening orbit of discotheques' where 'slimly handsome men go gracefully through their explosive, hedonistic, totally individual dances' rather passed me by, I could not claim that the effects were not beneficial for me. Partly on the strength of all this media excitement, I had managed to sell to ABC's new prestige series of specials, 'Stage 67', a show entitled 'David Frost's Night Out in London'. I booked a number of singers and entertainers including Lulu, Danny La Rue and the pop group Dave, Dee, Dozy, Beaky, Mick and Titch. The introduction reflected the current London scene:

> Greetings from London, the city of trim, mod dollies with flowing hair, only a little make-up, outrageous cloche hats and ornamental handbags. And the girls look pretty good, too . . . Carnaby Street, the only place in the world where they take your inside leg measurement for a tie . . . Of course, London is all things to all people. To the city commuter, it is merely the vast, sprawling, noisy, crowded city where he works. But to the tourist it is transformed into the vast, sprawling, noisy, crowded city where he spends his holidays . . . Dr Johnson said, 'When a man is tired of London, he is tired of life.' And then he died.

That part of the show was under control. However, I had one slight problem. I had promised ABC that I would deliver three out of the following list of mega-names: Laurence Olivier, Peter O'Toole, Albert Finney, Peter Sellers, Sean Connery and Peter Ustinov. I got Peter Sellers, who kindly agreed to do a wine-tasting sketch with me, but Sean Connery, Peter Ustinov and Peter O'Toole were all unavailable. That left Laurence Olivier and Albert Finney, with whom I was making no great progress. It was a real headache. Then a tantalising glimpse of possible salvation . . . I heard that the George Devine Award was holding an evening of plays at the Old Vic which had had their first performances at the Royal Court. They hoped that this evening would endow scholarships in Devine's name, but they hadn't managed to get any television coverage at all. From my point of view, however, what they had was intensely interesting. They had Laurence Olivier doing two scenes from *The Entertainer*, and Albert Finney doing one from *Luther*. My problems could be over . . .

There was no time even to do a camera rehearsal. We installed the cameras in the theatre just in time to shoot the dress rehearsal. We could not shoot the actual performance because all the seats had been sold, including those where we would have needed to put the cameras.

Ned Sherrin, always a man for an ad-lib situation, came in to direct the George Devine Award performance for me. I guaranteed the charity £8000, and paid the costs of the taping. I guaranteed a further £8000 if I could find additional uses for the material.

At the last minute we rushed around desperately distributing typewritten tickets so that we would have a decent audience sound for the dress rehearsal, and we managed to tape the proceedings successfully. They included many unique moments – Lynn Redgrave in N.F. Simpson's *A Resounding Tinkle*, Noël Coward making an unlikely appearance in Arnold Wesker's *The Kitchen*, Alec Guinness in Ionesco's *Exit the King*, and Nicol Williamson in John Osborne's *Inadmissible Evidence*. I managed to get a separate one-hour programme out of the material, with appropriate recompense to the George Devine Award, but that would come later – at that particular moment all I cared about was that we had both Laurence Olivier doing the unforgettable last scene from *The Entertainer* and Albert Finney as Martin Luther safely in the bag for 'David Frost's Night Out in London'.

When the show aired in the United States, it provided some interesting insights into the differences between Britain and America. It was well-received, but one review was headed, '"David Frost's Night Out in London" – Slick, Schmaltzy and Ingratiating'. A headline like that in the UK would have indicated that a pan was to follow. But the reverse was the case in

Left: 1939, Tenterden, with Jean and Margaret. 'It was probably not a good start to my relationship with my sisters that I was the only one of the three of us to be born with blue eyes and curly blond hair . . .'

Right: 1948, aged nine. In the back garden at Gillingham demonstrating my classic Bill Edrich forward defensive stroke (though the great man would not, I fear, have approved of the gap between bat and pad).

Below: July 1955. In the front garden of the Raunds manse with Father, Mother and Jean, hiding her pregnancy behind the roses.

Above: 1961, flanked at a Cambridge Union debate by two future interviewees, Leon Brittan and John Gummer, and by Bernard Levin, with whom I would be working on 'That Was The Week That Was' in little over a year.

Left: Graduation, 1961. A source of some pride and even greater relief.

Opposite page, top: With Peter Cook (left) and Peter Bellwood in a Footlights cabaret gig at a Cambridge pub.

Right: Giving my Art Prelman, the Head of Adulterated Rediffusion, in the 1960 Footlights Revue, 'Pop Goes Mrs Jessop'.

The first 'That Was The Week That Was'. On any normal show, this would be described as a photograph taken on the set, but with TW3 there wasn't really a set as such.

'It's a dacron tetralax masturpene in the new non-iron histamine luxipac.' Roy Kinnear as Baz in conversation with Jim and Nige in 'Jim's Inn' on the first TW3.

Above: On a day trip to Tangier with Jan and an unnamed chaperon. (The chaperon is on the left.)

Right: Mounting a satirical assault on the Mother of Parliaments.

Below: Accepting the prestigious Christine Keeler Chair of Applied Gymnosophy, 1963.

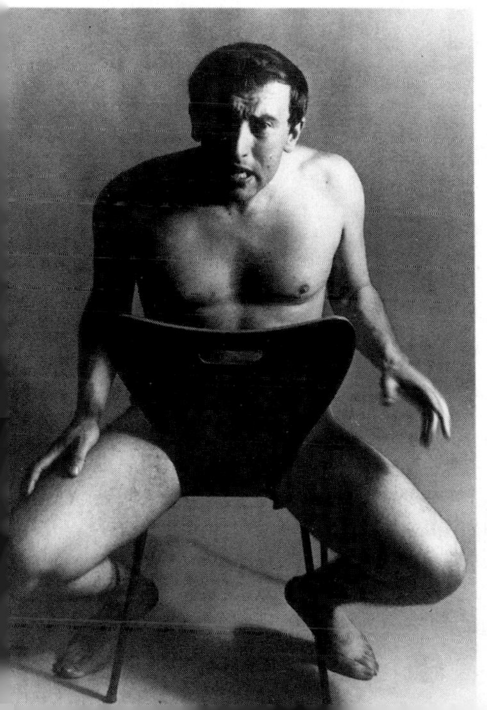

Right: On set in New York with Mike Nichols and Elaine May recording two of their classic sketches for 'A Degree of Frost'.

Below: With Paul McCartney for our interview on 'A Degree of Frost'. (As a novice interviewer, I soon abandoned this over-his-shoulder style for the more conventional face-to-face format.)

Below: 'I know my place.' Ronnie Corbett looking up to John Cleese and Ronnie Barker in one of John Law's classic 'Three Classes' sketches.

Left: 'Life in Tory Britain had been "everything on HP". Life in Labour Britain would be "HP on everything".' The author with a usually reliable sauce, 1964.

The surprise party in my garden at Egerton Crescent to celebrate winning the Golden Rose of Montreux.

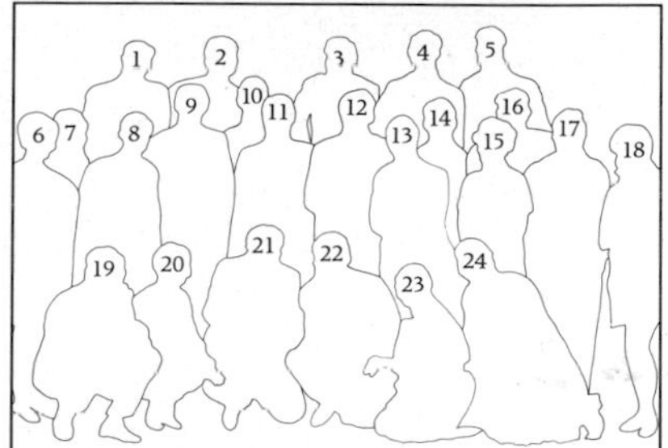

1 Ray Millichope (film editor)
2 Barry Cryer (scriptwriter)
3 Terry Jones (scriptwriter)
4 Michael Palin (scriptwriter)
5 Dick Vosburgh (scriptwriter)
6 Fiona Gilbert
7 Joy Barker
8 David McKellar (scriptwriter)
9 Graham Chapman (scriptwriter)
10 John Cleese (writer–actor)
11 Bernard Thompson (assistant director)
12 Tony Jay (theme scriptwriter and consultant)
13 Michael Wale (scriptwriter)
14 Eric Idle (scriptwriter)
15 Sally Adams (production assistant)
16 Neil Shand (scriptwriter)
17 Bill Wilson (production assistant)
18 Yvonne Sinclaire (assistant film editor)
19 Marty Feldman (script editor–writer)
20 Sheila Steafel (actress)
21 DF
22 James Gilbert (producer–director)
23 Julie Felix (singer)
24 Ronnie Barker (actor)

With the 'Frost Report' team outside the BBC Television Centre. Left to right: Julie Felix, Sheila Steafel, Ronnie Barker, John Cleese and Ronnie Corbett.

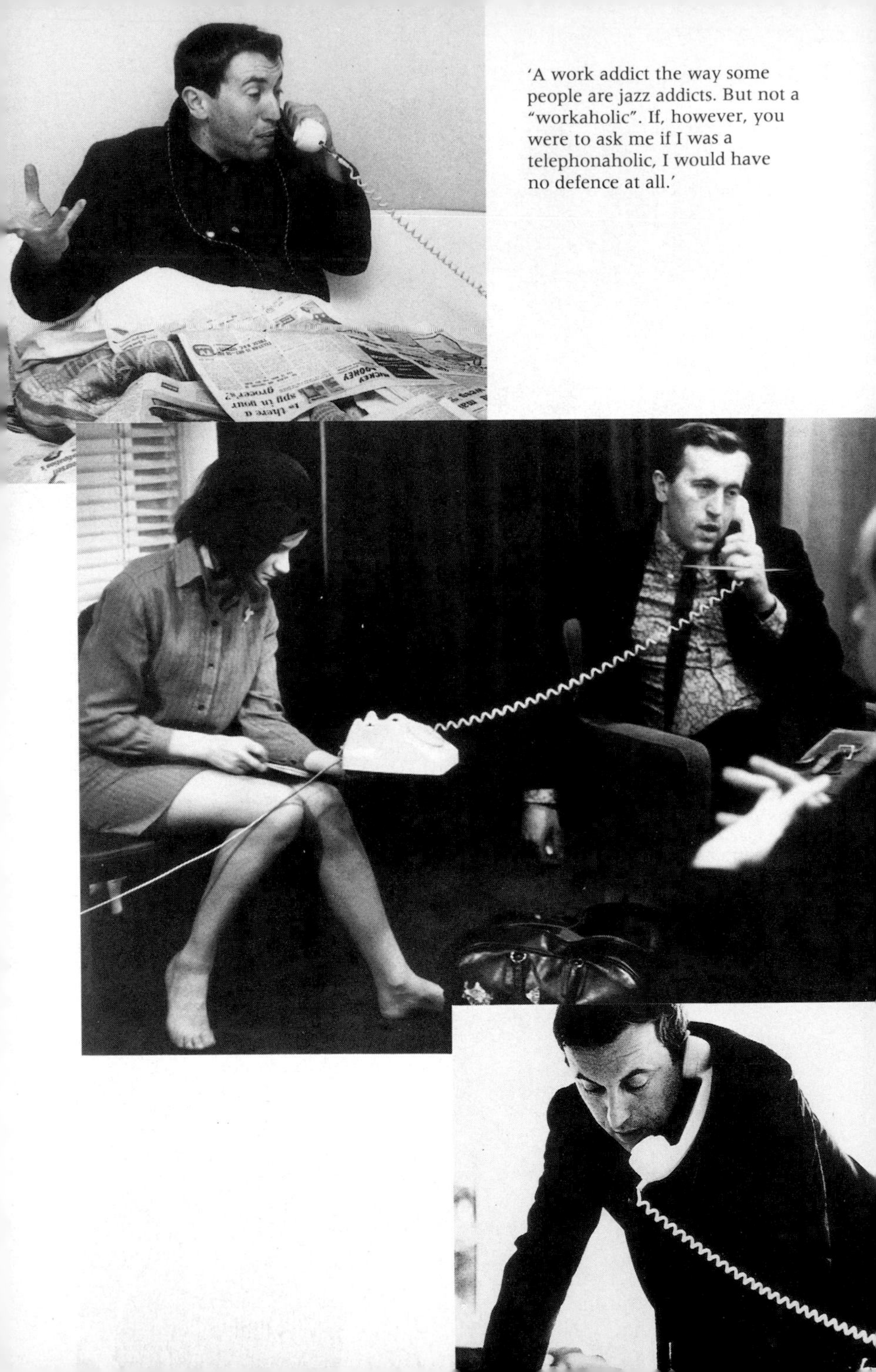

'A work addict the way some people are jazz addicts. But not a "workaholic". If, however, you were to ask me if I was a telephonaholic, I would have no defence at all.'

the United States. 'Slick' meant polished, not superficial. 'Schmaltzy' meant warm and human, not sickly sweet. And 'ingratiating' meant an admirable desire to please, not an exercise in sycophancy. Some American reviewers were just not ready for female impersonation, even when performed as harmlessly as by Danny La Rue. Frank Judge in the *Detroit News* described the programme as 'a strange mixture of brilliant entertainment, routine entertainment and disgusting entertainment'. He detailed the first two categories, then went on: 'and finally the disgusting entertainment; Danny La Rue is a British female impersonator. There is just one word for his performance, and you don't have to grope for it. The word is "vulgar". Some may argue that La Rue, who describes himself as a man, has the ability to look and act just like a woman. That may be a problem for him and his doctor to figure out.'

My main activity that summer was the planning of 'The Frost Programme'. While 'The Frost Report' was still running, I had been thinking more and more about a current affairs series. I had discussed it with only a few people – Tony Jay, Clive Irving and Cyril Bennett at Rediffusion, who wanted to experiment with an indigenous talk programme. He felt that London's drawing power for personalities was not exploited on television, that there ought to be a sophisticated and cosmopolitan catchment area for the right interviewer, doing the right interviews. Tony felt that current affairs programmes lacked a kind of animal contact with the real world. Clive thought that television followed newspapers too slavishly, and should seek out news for itself.

I believed there was a way of harnessing all these thoughts, and I was convinced that three things in particular needed demonstrating. Firstly, current affairs television was in danger of becoming too formula-bound and predictable. Secondly, the participants in the news needed pressing harder as people, to find out more of what made them tick. And thirdly, I thought television still persistently underrated its viewers and failed, quite often, to reflect them in its questioning process. It was Tony Jay who zeroed in on the catalyst for the various editorial instincts at play in this debate: the use of a studio audience not simply as a responsive backdrop, as it had been in 'The Frost Report', but as a key ingredient in the actual programme mix – to be brought into the proceedings according to need. It's a familiar enough idea now, but in the summer of 1966 it was thought revolutionary. What we most wanted was the interplay between the guests out front and a participating audience. We had always intended that the new series would be live: the audience would give it added electricity and unpredictability. And authenticity, too. The interviewees would be speaking at a specific moment in time, in front of witnesses. There were certain remarks that a politician could get away with in a one-on-one context, that would be impossible in the face of a two-hundred-voice groan. Two hundred was indeed the minimum figure we nominated for an audience 'quorum' – large enough for no one to be too self-conscious, small enough to give anyone a chance to be heard; the right size for a laugh not to sound like a giggle, nor a gasp like a hiccup.

Not everybody agreed. Cyril Bennett, for one, was very dubious. He was prepared to sanction a couple of pilot programmes using an audience, but said, 'I bet you a turkey dinner that you won't be using the audience by the time we go on the air.' Nothing concentrates the mind more than the imminence of a new series, and the great unknown in this case was the audience. Pilot programmes are invariably somewhat artificial, lacking the pressures of a real broadcast, but they do have the value of allowing experiments to be conducted in private. The two pilots for what became 'The Frost Programme' were very messy, with a lot of ideas trying to take flight. For topicality, the South African Prime Minister Dr Verwoerd having been assassinated, we asked James Cameron to argue before our audience that in some cases (and he felt that this was one) a political killing *might* be a blessing. Predictably, this became a very emotional argument. We examined the reality of an edict against premarital sex by the Reading Temperance Society. We had topical sketches.

All this didn't seem very coherent at the time, but somehow I had no fear of having to pay for the turkey dinner. The presence of the audience – fluid and varied – had broken the hermetic seal between the studio and the public. From the start, none of us assumed that our quorum of two hundred was remotely like a Gallup sample, and we avoided the implication that they could be in any sense an accurate reflection of all shades of public opinion. They were a random sample rather than a scientific one, a mixture of individuals and groups like, say, Women's Institutes and Working Men's Clubs who had applied to Rediffusion for tickets. At the outset they were simply people who had requested tickets for any programme that had seats available. Later, as the series became better known, they had often made a specific request for 'The Frost Programme'. Eileen Sands and her audience unit assembled them, and we did not know in advance who would be turning up. But they were engaged in our programme, not just mute wallpaper. We occasionally invited a particular group to augment a discussion, but this was the exception rather than the rule, and we always said so.

I could sense that this sort of participating audience would demand more of me and my guests than was the custom. The arena was suddenly that much bigger, and we were a little more naked in it, but the risks were well worth taking. We decided to dive in at the deep end – something I was a little better equipped for in a television studio than a swimming pool – and test our ideas from the very first programme. The result was the beginning of eighteen of the most experimental, and invigorating, weeks I can remember – with three programmes a week, on Wednesdays, Thursdays and Fridays.

Just before our first programme, a spokesman for the National Association of Schoolmasters, discussing their current pay claim, had been rash enough to state, 'People seem to forget that schoolmasters are probably the most valuable members of the community.' I remembered my conversation with Robert Morley in Le Touquet, and thought he would be the ideal *agent provocateur* for a group of schoolmasters and schoolmistresses. As he left his dressing room before the programme, Robert turned to me and said, 'I don't think we need any of that terrible clapping when I come on, do we? I mean I won't have done anything yet.' Respecting his wishes, I therefore asked the audience for a very warm silence please for Robert Morley. My guest was properly appreciative. 'Thank you,' he said. 'How nice and dignified. Just how I like to arrive. And actually if we can cut out the clapping I estimate we could get at least one more programme in each evening, and that would mean more work for the boys.'

We soon came to the nub of Morley's argument: 'Schoolmasters are always trying to change children. Somebody years ago told some schoolmaster, it may have been Plato for all I know, that his job was not only to teach, but to mould the character of children. I don't want them to alter my child, nor do I want them to go on this lunatic tack that every child must be an eager child, no child must be a lazy child, no child must be a fat child. I know that the lazy and the fat are the salt of the earth! And if you don't have children who run slowly, what fun is it for the children who run fast?'

After a few minutes of vintage Morley, I said, 'Now we've got some teachers in the audience . . .' He looked at me in mock dismay, his eyes popping like a startled walrus. 'Oh, that's a great mistake. I don't think you want anyone who knows about it! I thought the whole object of this programme was for people to talk, like you do, on a subject about which they know nothing whatever.'

The teachers had heard enough. They were eager to join in. One of them pointed out that seven out of ten children in this world do not go to school. 'They in fact follow the curriculum that you are advising. And where are these seven children? They're in Africa, they're in India, they're in South America. Look what's happened as a result of no education!'

Morley responded at once, 'I thought it was a result of their not having any money, not having any food. I thought it was the educated English who had rather spoiled the territories of India, for example.'

The teacher was disgusted. 'Well, that's enough. You need say no more if that is your view of what we English, or British, have done.'

Morley weighed in again. 'I mean, we were in India for many years. Why didn't we teach them?'

The teacher got in deeper. 'Educated Englishmen did it, you said it yourself.'

Morley nodded. 'I'm afraid so, yes.'

The teacher leant back with a bewilderingly self-satisfied air. 'Yes,' he said almost triumphantly.

Morley looked bewildered. 'Was that his point, old man, or mine?' I had to say that I thought it was thirty-love to Morley.

The debate continued. Morley told the teachers, 'I think the children of today are taught much as I was taught. I'm sure if I went into a classroom I would find the same dreary problems set, the same lunatic exercises. For instance, geography. I'm sure you teach them to learn twenty-four different cities in Australia. You ought to teach them sensible things. How to look up places in atlases, how to consult travel agencies and how to get somebody else to do the work for them. That's the secret of life! I only see the children after they've passed through your hands, and I know that the English child closes its desk and its mind simultaneously at eighteen.'

One of the schoolmistresses tried to regain some lost ground. 'What school did your children go to?' she asked. Morley favoured her with a smile.

'I educated mine abroad, my darling!'

Which was probably game, set and match to Morley. But more important to us, the sudden dissolution of formality and the new atmosphere of spontaneity was exactly what we had hoped for: after the first week Maurice Wiggin wrote in the *Sunday Times*, 'The programme . . . has a quality which has become the rarest thing in TV – you never know what's coming next.' Even more to the point, very often neither did we!

Frank Cousins was equally eloquent, in a very different way, during that first week. He had been the most powerful trades union leader in the country, was co-opted into the Labour Government of 1964, and then resigned on principle. I asked him what had angered him most.

'First of all, too easy an acceptance that we're only talking about 1.5 per cent unemployment or two per cent unemployment. But we're really talking about a man and his job! When a man's unemployed, he's out of work. He's one hundred per cent out of work . . . I was in a position that I had £5000 a year as a Minister; then they gave me another £3500 to make sure that I could talk eloquently about the need for the workers to control their demand for money!'

On our first programme day of the following week, the Wednesday, the front pages of the newspapers were full of the fact that the Home Secretary, Roy Jenkins, had decided not to confirm a sentence of birching imposed by magistrates on a man in Maidstone Prison. The Conservative MP Sir Cyril Osborne was fulminating about this decision. And Gore Vidal, we knew, was in town. It seemed the perfect opportunity to experiment with cut-and-thrust debate between two declared adversaries.

Sir Cyril Osborne was adamant that the Home Secretary's decision was 'a tragic blunder': 'We have a very serious problem in our country. Nearly as bad as you've got in yours. And we're trying to deal with this problem . . .'

'Through birching,' Vidal interjected.

Osborne: Do you talk in your sleep?
Vidal: No. I think that I'm awake.
Osborne: I wish I'd got you in my power. I'd keep you quiet.
Vidal: Now this is most interesting! They don't call it the English vice for nothing.

It seemed irresistible not to remind Sir Cyril that he had once been described as the only man who rang the speaking clock just for the pleasure of hearing the voice say, 'At the third stroke . . .'

After Sir Cyril had linked his arguments to a general support of the police, Vidal made his main riposte: 'It is difficult to conduct an argument with the nineteenth century. You used to hang people. I'm sure you're quite in favour of it. Hanging children for stealing a loaf of bread. I'm sure you would probably think that that would be good discipline, and that would be on the side of the police, and they would be in your power. But there's a liberalising movement in the world today. We have discovered that brutalising people physically does not make them any better, unless you believe that people are essentially animals, which is generally the conservative – I mean without the political connotation – the general reactionary point of view. Now if you hold that honestly, then there is nothing much to be said. However, if you treat people as animals, they will behave as animals. Like this young man in prison who's led these riots and so on. I was reading about his history today and I must say, any young man who has had the sort of life he's had, brutalising from the beginning, would behave that way.'

Sir Cyril responded, 'It doesn't brutalise them. You've had his sort of nitwit in both parties. In both countries they've had their way since the war. Instead of having stern discipline, we've had a soft psychiatric type of treatment. Well, what's the result? Crime has increased five times.'

The two adversaries were expressing the opposite poles of an argument that had come very much to the surface in the early Sixties. Sir Cyril represented the 'headlong lurch to destruction' school; Gore represented the 'dawning new age of enlightenment' school. To Sir Cyril, the imminent disappearance of birching (and indeed hanging) was taking away from decent folk one of the few weapons they had left to fight the rising forces of moral decay. For Gore, flogging was one of the last vestiges of an *ancien régime* which was rapidly being overrun by the new liberalism, and the new freedoms.

When I turned to the audience, I found that on this occasion the 'puritan in Babylon' was not alone. There was in fact a clear majority in favour of Sir Cyril's view that the birching should go ahead.

'You thought they would vote the other way, against it! Both of you did!' said Sir Cyril.

'Yes, well, I still think the other way,' said Vidal.

I felt an obligation to Sir Cyril to re-express the audience's view, 'That was a referendum in your favour, Sir Cyril. Let's say that quite clearly.'

Sir Cyril said that he was much obliged, and then launched into another speech about support of the police. I felt I had to disentangle the two arguments: 'Let's make this quite clear. We're all in favour of the protection of the police. But let me make this simple point. I don't wish to have bestial acts committed by the state on my behalf. It's as simple as that.'

The debate continued. Not only had it been extremely lively, but we had also demonstrated, I hoped, that we wanted the views and participation of our audience, whether they agreed with or confounded our own opinions. The strength of their support for Sir Cyril was just the first of many surprises audiences would give us in the weeks and years ahead. In the hospitality room after the programme Gore Vidal was kicking himself for having thought of one rejoinder ten minutes too late. 'Yes, I am in favour of birching,' he wished he had said, 'but only between consenting adults.'

The press and public reaction indicated that the programme was gathering momentum, though it was not yet a very fruitful exercise attempting to invite past, present or even aspiring Cabinet Ministers to appear on such an unpredictable hybrid as 'The Frost Programme'. The host had been a 'satirist', then an 'entertainer' – what on earth was he now? The price of having the freedom to switch from one activity to another is that you have to explain yourself at every turn. However, the advantages do usually outweigh the disadvantages.

Sometimes, when there is a particularly concerted attempt by the press to pigeonhole you, you almost get the feeling that versatility of any kind is regarded as a crime. 'But which are you really?' The truth of the matter is that when you are entertaining, you are an entertainer; when you are interviewing, you are an interviewer, trying to be the best you can. The same with satirist, journalist, talk-show host, public speaker or any other job description. You just have to make sure you keep track of your bearings and of the right approach to whatever happens to be your next assignment. It needs to be appropriate, and on target – which is a matter of instinct as well as preparation. Then you start to find that three hours working on one thing is a positive relaxation from three hours working on something else. But you do still need to keep explaining . . .

With this context in mind, you can imagine that we were particularly glad to learn that our explanations had persuaded a former Conservative Cabinet Minister, Ernest Marples, to appear on the programme. This was progress. John Cleese, who worked as an editor on the show as well as writing and appearing in some of the sketches, was in the hospitality room when Marples arrived. John was looking after another guest, Ernest

Baveystock, a veteran whom we felt would provide a change of pace. John reported that Marples arrived in the room looking distinctly fearful, like a Christian wondering if he should have actually volunteered for a guided tour of the lions' den. John tried manfully to keep Mr Marples and Mr Baveystock apart, reasoning that Marples was used to sharing a television programme with fellow politicians. However, years of political activity die hard, and Marples plunged across the room, his right hand extended to greet Mr Baveystock. 'What do you do?' enquired Marples. It was the question John had feared. 'I play the spoons,' said Mr Baveystock. Marples's face said it all. Luckily, other people were crowding into the hospitality room, and his line of escape was blocked.

As it happened, both Ernest Marples and Ernest Baveystock acquitted themselves well. Marples talked passionately about one of his pet causes, the need to change the top management in Government, and Ernest Baveystock gave a rousing performance on the spoons. Then he explained his technique. His left spoon was quite new, he said, but his right-hand spoon had been in his possession since the First World War. At this point our audience participated in a way that took me totally by surprise. They burst into a round of applause. I looked up, startled. 'You don't applaud *spoons*, do you?' I asked bewilderedly.

We were looking all the while for new stories that we could break or advance, or where we could take an approach that was more activist – not in the sense of advocating a particular policy, like an editorial, but in the sense of bringing matters to an audience as forcefully as possible, so that they would want to draw conclusions or take action as a result. There was an element of this in the Brabin Report. Mr Justice Brabin had just reported on his inquiry into the hanging of Timothy Evans in 1949 for the murder of his baby daughter at a time when he was sharing a house with John Halliday Christie, who had later been convicted of a series of murders. Ludovic Kennedy had brought the case to the public attention in his campaigning book *10 Rillington Place*. Now Brabin reported that the balance of probabilities was that it was Christie who had killed Evans's baby. We found Alexander Lovegrove, the prison warder who spent two months with Evans in the death cell. His simple and straightforward honesty in the face of his macabre duty were deeply affecting. I asked him whether Evans had continued to protest his innocence to the very end, right through that last long night before the hanging.

'Well, what he said, what he kept on saying, was it was Christie,' said Mr Lovegrove. 'All the weeks before the end, he said it was Christie. Every time he had a visit, he'd tell his mother and father it was Christie. But he seemed to give up hoping after his appeal. He went for his appeal and when he got back to the prison, I was there to receive him, and he said, "You can have my overcoat." Well, I knew then that the appeal had gone down.

'On the last night up to half past twelve we were playing cards, and he mentioned Christie once or twice, but he knew he had to go in the morning. Well, about half past twelve, one o'clock, he said, "I think I'll go to bed." He said, "Give me a call at half past three." Well, at half past three he was snoring. I went over and gave him a push, but I didn't wake him. I let him sleep. I left him alone till four o'clock. I had to shake him at four o'clock. He got up. He had a wash and I made him a cup of coffee. I brought some cakes in for him, which I wasn't supposed to do, but he didn't eat any cakes. He had a smoke and he started saying something about Christie, but I tried to take his mind off it. Then he just sat there waiting, looking round the cell. He was a pretty quiet sort of lad. The condemned cell is rather two cells in one: the bed is in the corner, there's a wash house in the other corner, and there is a door where you come in, and there's another door where he goes to the trap. He asked what that door was, but I told him it was to do with the engineers. And then at seven a.m. he shook hands with me with tears in his eyes. And I can tell you I was choked myself after being with him for two months. He wanted me to go in there with him, but the authorities didn't allow it. I would've gone, but it wasn't allowed.

'Well, about three years later, I looked at the paper one morning and right on the front page it had a story about a mass murderer – Christie. And I said to myself, "Where have I heard that name before?"'

At the end of the programme I added a postscript that had been discovered by one of our team, Peter Baker: 'At the official post mortem on Evans, after he was hanged, the doctor was puzzled by a number of small indentations on his knees. He couldn't think what had caused them. The explanation, he discovered, was that the Roman Catholic chaplain had kept him on his knees on a rubber mat for a very long time, exhorting him, if he was guilty of murder, to confess it before he died. What Evans said in his last confession, we don't know. But we do know that the priest said, some years later, that he did not, himself, think Evans was a murderer.'

Timothy Evans was officially pardoned by the Queen on 18 October 1966. But of course, with capital punishment, justice delayed is always justice denied.

We tried to vary the formula of the programme as much as possible. The next day we took our cameras to the foyer of the Aldwych Theatre for a live programme immediately following the first night of *US*, Peter Brook's crusading production about the Vietnam War. Mick Jagger was with us the following evening, and immediately demonstrated (as he was to do later in his career) the inaccuracies of the tabloid image which had been conferred on him. The humourless caveman was neither of those things. He discussed his power over audiences in an appealingly down-to-earth tone. 'There are certain things you do, movements you make, that you know will get a reaction, aren't there?' I asked him. 'Or are they completely unconscious?'

Jagger smiled slightly. 'They're not *completely* unconscious, but they're not entirely thought-out either. At one place in a song you might do something and everybody really likes it: you know, they all go mad. So when you get to the next town, you do the same thing – and there's no reaction.'

'Big in Torquay and nothing in Wigan! But is there anything that's surefire?' I asked.

'Rolling around on the stage always seems to work,' said Jagger matter-of-factly. 'But the daftest things you do, like that, you have to save till the end. If you really fancy going all over the floor, you have to save it up, you know, because your trousers get sort of dusty.'

John Cleese's contributions enabled us to vary the format further. At least once a week he would join me for a topical comment or sketch. That autumn, Parliament was discussing a much-trumpeted proposal that Harold Wilson had announced in August to appoint an Ombudsman, a public watchdog independent of Government, to investigate people's grievances against authority. 'So,' I said, 'soon you'll be able to send your complaints, on a postcard please, to the Ombudsman, or Parliamentary Commissioner, as he will be called.'

John, as a Government spokesman, intervened.

John: Excuse me, you won't actually be able to send your complaints to him. You'll have to send them to an MP, and he may then refer them to the Commissioner.

DF: Well, supposing he doesn't?

John: That's up to him. We don't want the Commissioner swamped with complaints. I think you forgot to mention that the Commissioner's name is Sir Edmund Compton.

DF: How has he been named, when his post hasn't yet actually been created by law?

John: That's just the sort of abuse that he will be investigating.

DF: I see. Well, anyway, we'll be able to get something done about some of those terrible local council decisions we are . . .

John: Actually, I'm afraid that as it stands at the moment he won't be able to touch anything to do with local government.

DF: But the majority of these kinds of complaints are about local government.

John: Well, as I've said, we don't want him swamped with complaints.

DF: Still, there's the police . . .

John: Sorry, no. The Commissioner can't investigate complaints against them – not the police or local government.

DF: That just leaves the hospitals.

John: Or hospitals. Not local government, the police or the health service. Those three.

DF: The Gas Board.

John: Those four. Not the nationalised industries. Those four.

DF: Oh dear, those four. Well, I suppose it's some consolation that at least the most underprivileged in Britain, the armed forces, will be able . . .

John: Ah, those five.

DF: Those five.

John: Those five.

DF: No others.

John: No. That's the lot.

DF: I see. So, if you've got complaints against anyone else you can send them on to Sir Edmund . . . or the MP.

John: Except if you could take action in the courts.

DF: What?

John: Except if you could take action in the courts.

DF: Now, let me get this absolutely clear. If I've got a complaint and it gets handed on by the MP, the Commissioner can investigate.

John: Yes, and I would like to point out here that the Commissioner has absolutely unrestricted access to all the files.

DF: I see. And then if he thinks I'm right, he can do something for me.

John: Yes, a report to the House of Commons.

DF: A full report.

John: Not quite full. A Minister can suppress anything that might be contrary to the public interest.

DF: But I'm a member of the public, and if I'm making a complaint it won't be contrary to my interest.

John: No, but the Minister's a member of the public, and it might be contrary to his.

DF: What happens when this thing is presented to the House of Commons?

John: Well, I suppose an MP can ask a question at Question Time.

DF: But he can do that already.

John: So he can . . . so he can . . .

DF: And anyway, how much is this going to cost?

John: About £200,000 a year, of which Sir Edmund will get £8600.

DF: But for a man in his position that doesn't seem much.
John: No, but he's not going to be doing much, is he?

Every point in that sketch had been taken straight from the record. Proof – if proof were needed – that fact is often not only stranger but dafter than fiction.

In the Britain of the Sixties, with so many established beliefs subject to question, there was a great deal of debate about sex and morality, and on the varying attitudes that people inside and outside the Church had towards organised religion's duty to provide a clear lead. On 16 October, a working party commissioned by the British Council of Churches reported on the subject. They had originally been asked to prepare 'a statement for the Christian case for abstinence from sexual intercourse before marriage, and faithfulness within marriage'. They found, however, that no such straightforward case could be made, and concluded, 'In the field of sexual relations, rules in themselves are not an adequate basis for morality . . . People sometimes matter more than rules.' They found that sex outside marriage was not automatically wrong, masturbation not necessarily wrong, and that the law on abortion should be liberalised forthwith.

Representing the two poles of Church opinion on the programme that night were the Bishop of Woolwich, the Right Reverend John Robinson, author of the bestselling *Honest to God*, in which he had questioned the necessity of believing in a personal God, and the Bishop of Willesden, the Right Reverend Graham Leonard, who had just sent a letter to his clergy expressing his opposition to all the principles of the report. I asked him to explain why.

'In the first place,' he said, 'I don't believe you can just pick and choose what you like from the New Testament. Why should you be prepared, as some people are, to agree there is pride, covetousness, deceit and sin, but say you'll accept adultery and fornication? You can't treat the New Testament in this way without making a nonsense of it.'

The Bishop of Woolwich did not agree. 'I don't think the report does pick and choose. Its virtue is that it goes to fundamentals, it doesn't go to isolated texts. Of course, I agree entirely that fornication, in the sense that the New Testament means it – which is irresponsible sex without any concern for the other – is basically destructive, and no one is defending this. I think the report is a balanced and conservative document.'

I rather doubted whether the authors of the New Testament had such a sophisticated view of the word 'fornication', but I wanted to move on to the basic issue. 'The key thing here, I think, is that almost everybody has thought until now that there was a firm, solid position,' I said. 'That relationships outside marriage were completely wrong in the eyes of the Church, and this rule was either a firm support for people not to indulge in them; or something that they knew they would have to conquer in their own minds before they could indulge themselves.'

The Bishop of Woolwich felt that the difference could be greatly exaggerated, because the report was really only giving expression to a very large body of opinion within the Church, which believed that rules are always guidelines, but never absolutes. 'You have rules about stealing or lying or killing, yet obviously there may be a conflict. You may have to tell lies to save a person's life, for example. Sex is the only field in which some churchmen have always said there are absolutes. Now this report is just bringing this field of morality into line with every other.'

But of course, as with so many Sixties debates, it was the disappearance of the old simple absolutes that many people found so threatening. The Bishop of Willesden was one of them. 'As I see it, law in fact sets you free until you have learned to do things spontaneously and generously by love. I know that as a human being I need the law, simply because I am still human . . . I try to go by the New Testament. It talks about the truth. It doesn't talk about ideas which people may or may not like.'

The novelist Edna O'Brien found all this conservatism laughable. 'I would give every girl, on her sixteenth birthday, a contraceptive intra-uterine coil. This seems to me to be what's important, not these obscure whys and wherefores.'

Author Alex Comfort, although an advocate of the new freedoms, did not agree. 'You'd put a girl off most terribly if you did that.'

Edna O'Brien responded, 'No I wouldn't. She has a choice to remove it if she likes.'

Comfort sounded almost despairing: 'We're talking about human beings! This kills me, because you sound as if you didn't have to deal with people, and I know you do. Both you and the bishops must have to deal with people extensively, and yet in an extraordinary way you're talking as if you never did have to deal with them.'

As the series progressed, we found ourselves wanting to give more and more attention to matters of morality and faith. Thus it was that at one of our breakfast meetings the idea of a humanist epilogue emerged. Many humanists had been pressing for more time on radio and television to put their point of view, and the Christians had an epilogue every night of the week. We decided that those who did not agree with them should have an opportunity to put their point of view as well, in epilogue form, and that Ludovic Kennedy was the man to do it. He certainly was. His five-minute humanist epilogue scarcely wasted a word or a comma.

Ludovic composed himself and gazed into the camera with clerical aplomb:

> These are some of the beliefs of the humanist. He does not know and he does not feel a need to know where we have come from, where we are going to, or what our purpose here is, if any. And he is as certain as he can be that nobody else knows either.
>
> As a rule of thumb to live by he believes that those actions that lead to human happiness are good, and those that lead to unhappiness are bad. He endeavours – and this is the core of his belief – to do to others as he himself would be done by. He is aware that there are many occasions on which he falls short of this ideal.
>
> He is not influenced in his actions either by hope of reward or fear of punishment in a world to come. He believes that Hell is a state of mind and that the Kingdom of Heaven is on earth. He believes that there are rational explanations for thunder, lightning and Mr Quintin Hogg.

To him there are in all human beings good impulses and bad ones. The good ones, such as bravery, unselfishness and love, are self-evident and indestructible. The bad ones, such as exploitation, greed and envy would cause chaos if left unchecked so societies everywhere have devised laws and institutions to check them. One such institution is marriage which was invented as a means of bridling man's unbridled lust. In this it has only been partly successful.

The humanist does not believe in any absolute standards of morality if the word absolute is intended to mean above and beyond man. His reason for this is that standards of morality are constantly changing. Two hundred years ago people thought it right to burn witches and hang boys. Today, with the possible exception of Lord Goddard, they no longer think so. The humanist therefore considers such crimes as murder, rape and stealing to be absolutely wrong only in the sense that most societies at most times, including his own, have disapproved of them absolutely. Because he does not believe in absolute standards, the humanist takes a more flexible attitude to such lesser shortcomings as adultery and lying. While the humanist recognises that if adultery and lying were practised on an indiscriminate and massive scale they would lead to much unhappiness and would therefore be deplorable, that does not mean that on occasions they are not permissible or even desirable. But the only judge as to when they are permissible must be man's own conscience.

The humanist believes that man's conscience can be shaped by self knowledge, and that therefore to know one's self is one of the highest aims of man. In search of self knowledge he draws inspiration from every source available to him, including the life and teachings of Jesus Christ.

He accepts nothing as revealed truth whether it be the tablets on Mount Sinai, the theories of Marx or Freud, or Mr Harold Wilson on the television. He prefers to make up his own mind for himself, accepting as true only what his conscience tells him is true. And when he acts according to his conscience he finds that he is in harmony with all other living things.

The humanist believes that when he dies his body will disintegrate into dust and that will be the end of that and about time too. And lastly, he does not believe that his beliefs make him any worse – or for that matter any better – than any other man. These are some of the beliefs of the humanist. God bless you all.

Needless to say, the first ever humanist epilogue unleashed a considerable flood of correspondence. But as Ludo spoke, I was aware of a considerable irony. Our recent guest, the Bishop of Woolwich, would have been happy to speak every word of it. It was a paradox to which we would have to return. But before that, we had another controversy to deal with.

In this case, it began with a re-reading of an invitation which I had received, and accepted, to appear in a concert for Medical Aid for victims of the war in Vietnam at the Royal Court Theatre on Sunday 13 November. The poster for the concert clearly featured the simple words, 'Medical Aid for Vietnam Celebrity Charity Show'. A leaflet added, 'When men, women and children lie bleeding, the political views of the victims are as irrelevant as those of the Good Samaritan.' A statement with which it was impossible to disagree.

However, when we checked with the committee, we found that the concert was funnelling all of its receipts via the North Vietnamese or Viet Cong groups in South Vietnam. When I informed my fellow performers of this, they were appalled. The organisers of the concert claimed that we should have understood what was happening. After all, one of their leaflets had stated that aid would go to the countryside of South Vietnam, wherever the casualties were highest and the need greatest. This, it seemed to me, fell somewhat short of full disclosure, and we gathered some of the other artists, including Larry Adler, Kenneth Haigh, Dudley Moore and Annie Ross, to discuss the matter on air with Dr Joan MacMichael, the Honorary Secretary of the Medical Aid for Vietnam Committee.

Once the programme got under way, it was clear that the

misunderstanding was widespread. Dudley Moore had assumed that the concert was for the South Vietnamese. Annie Ross thought it was for the whole of Vietnam. Larry Adler understood that the aim was 'to give medical aid to people in Vietnam who were casualties of the war. If it's true that the aid is going only to one side, I would prefer to withdraw my name rather than do the show.' Kenneth Haigh and others had believed that the funds would go through the International Red Cross. Cleo Laine and Johnny Dankworth thought the concert was for the children of Vietnam, whether of the North or South. Miriam Karlin had no idea that the aid was going to the North Vietnamese and the Viet Cong, and this would decide her against appearing.

When asked why the concert was going to benefit only the North Vietnamese and the Viet Cong areas of South Vietnam, Joan MacMichael repeated the incantation about the area where the need was greatest. I asked her why not the whole of South Vietnam: 'Well, we felt . . . we simply felt that the area under the Saigon Administration is very well supplied by the Americans. We donate aid where we feel there is real need. The Americans can supply the need for drugs and medical equipment in the areas controlled by them.'

The explanations were profoundly unsatisfactory, both on the reasons for the original decision and on the opaque way in which that decision was communicated – or not communicated – to those who were going to be involved. I said to the organisers, 'I feel the genuine critics of the way the war in Vietnam is conducted by the Americans are being ill-served when organisations like this, that are apparently independent, turn out not to be independent. That's doing a disservice to anyone who criticises the war. And you cannot deny that there are twelve people who believed that the money was going throughout Vietnam. We all thought it.' Mary Selway, also of the Committee, responded, 'We are concerned with the ordinary Vietnamese people who are caught in between two giants. We don't take sides politically. We merely want to help the people who are caught between the two. Why help a country which is pouring in millions and millions of dollars of aid?'

Larry Adler chimed in immediately, 'It's not a question of

giving aid to the Americans. Of course Americans don't need it. I thought we were doing a show for all civilians, regardless of which area they were in. That is why I wanted to do it.'

'Dr MacMichael,' I said, 'there's clearly been a misunderstanding here. Kenneth and Larry are witness to it. Will you agree, so that everybody can be happy, to donate the money to both sides, as we believed it would be? Can you give it to the International Red Cross?'

Dr MacMichael responded, 'Certainly I will take up the question and certainly I will give you an answer in as short as possible a time.'

It had been a dramatic half hour. We had all wanted to do the concert, but not under false pretences. Following the programme there was pandemonium. Several members of the Medical Aid for Vietnam Committee were as surprised as we had been. Neville Blond, Chairman of the English Stage Company, which was based at the Royal Court, decided that the concert could not go ahead if proceeds were going to Viet Cong and North Vietnamese casualties only. The Medical Aid Committee met in session two days later, on the Sunday night. After a five-hour meeting, broken off several times for phone calls to Mr Blond or to me, the Committee agreed that the profits should go to the International Red Cross for distribution to both sides, and the concert was able to go ahead.

It was no great victory, but it was certainly a modest advance for candour. It was also a lesson not only in the way in which language can be obfuscated to a point where it is downright misleading, but also in the selective use of language. I wondered if anyone would have dared to call a mission 'humanitarian' if it had been confined to the areas controlled by South Vietnam and the Americans. The fact that Larry Adler, with all his experience of being on the receiving end of blacklisting in America, had been one of the victims of the deception made the incident even more ironic.

The decision of the Committee was announced on Monday 7 November. By then we were already deep into preparing for that Wednesday's programme, on which the first guest was to be Colonel Mike Hoare, who had recently led an army of mer-

" It's all arranged . . . we get Barbara Murray and Annie Ross, Saigon get Roy Hudd and David Frost.'

cenaries in the Congo for eighteen months in the service of Moise Tshombe of Katanga. Tshombe was attempting to seize the whole of the divided and war-torn Belgian colony following the demise of the Lumumba regime. In the event, because of what he had to say, Hoare became the only guest. It soon became clear that the other items in the programme must be dropped, and I was loathe to interrupt the dialogue even for a commercial break. I recalled while I was on the air that the minimum permitted length for a segment on independent television at that time was four minutes. And that was how the programme came to run: a first half of twenty-nine minutes, and a second half of four minutes, all with Colonel Hoare.

War was again the issue. But war of a rather different kind. Not a matter of people fighting for their country, for a cause, but people who fought quite simply for money, for whom war was a trade. I described Colonel Hoare as 'one of the few men who have become legendary figures in their time – though the legend varies a little depending on whom you speak to about him'. He had led a band of mainly European mercenaries, sometimes numbering as many as a thousand. I found it a curious thing for him, and them, to have done. What had led this strange band of men to go to a country that was not their own, to fight for a cause that was not their own? Why had they done it?

Hoare responded crisply, 'Well, very plainly, there was only one good reason. Money! The money was extremely good.'

I asked him why he himself had gone there. 'Were you, like them, fighting for money?'

'No,' said Hoare. 'I'm a great believer in the doctrine of a man called Spencer Chapman. Spencer Chapman was a man who believed that to get the most out of life you must live dangerously. I've always believed this, and followed it to the best of my ability for the last thirteen years, and have enjoyed life as a result.'

I suggested that this was a rather strange way of enjoying life, if it meant killing people.

'No, not necessarily,' said Hoare. 'It means enjoying life while in danger of losing it.'

'And either losing yours or taking someone else's?'

'Yes, possibly.'

And what about this group of men who were all there for the money, how did he discipline them?

'At my level it was a question of personality and a grip on the men and perhaps, I hope, respect. A little farther down perhaps it could be Foreign Legion stuff: hard tactics, even fisticuffs. It could mean that a man would never come before me but there would be a trail of blood outside my office. Which probably meant that a non-commissioned officer had dealt with him.'

I marvelled at the military, almost English public-school, euphemisms. 'Fisticuffs'. 'Dealt with him'. But I let him carry on.

'There was one extraordinary case after we had taken Stanleyville. During the night some of my officers came and asked me to try a man for murder. Briefly the facts were that this man had found a young Congolese girl and raped her, which in itself, let's face it, is not an extraordinary occurrence. But what followed was. He took her down to the Congo River and made her walk along a little pier. This unfortunate kid walked along this pier and he was obviously going to shoot her. So, in a moment of revenge sparked with genius, she turned to him and said, 'You can't make love, you're too small.' Of course, everybody that was there laughed. He shot her. She fell into the water and was drowned. It was this chap they wanted me to try.

'They came to me in the middle of the night – a hell of a night with storm and rain and one thing and another, and I wasn't particularly good-tempered at that time. He broke down, and he said yes, he did do it, and in any case this was war and what do you expect and so forth. And he broke down and started to cry to one of my officers, a very soft type he immediately saw he could bring around to his viewpoint. He started in on him to intercede on his behalf and eventually I called a halt to the whole thing. It was a lot of nonsense. And we decided we would pass sentence on him, although we weren't a properly constituted court. It's the sort of thing that happens in a mercenary army. You can't avoid these things. I decided we would pass sentence, each one of us, and whoever's sentence was accepted by all would himself carry out the verdict. Well, I had a very tough captain there who decided the obvious thing to do was to take him down and to shoot him in the same way. Another said give him thirty-eight lashes. Another one said make him commit suicide. Well, in the course of the conversation we had discovered that this fellow was a professional footballer. So I decided the best thing to be done then was to pass a sentence that his big toes were to be blown off. So they agreed to that. So we took him down, and he was screaming and yelling, and we did it. I took out my Colt revolver and shot his big toe off each foot. We then threw him in a jeep and took him to the aerodrome where the hospital was and threw him in the hospital. And five days later he got an aeroplane that was going to Brussels and as the aeroplane went down the runway the wing touched a pile of drums and turned over and he was killed.'

The atmosphere in that North London studio was extraordinary. As Hoare's story sank in, I tried to come back to the point I had put earlier. How could people voluntarily put themselves into an atmosphere like that? Where such acts of savagery were going to take place, and where they were going to have to indulge in them too.

'Well, unfortunately, there is a tendency for one's standards to get lower and lower. Savagery begets savagery. My standards were dropping lower and lower.'

There must have been a difference between fighting for a cause and fighting for money.

'Well, basically, yes. But when you look at it in cold blood, when you're actually involved in action, action is the same everywhere.'

An African who happened to be in the audience spoke up: 'I would like to ask you a question. We accept that civilised societies have formulated civilised punishments for certain circumstances. But coming from a civilised society and saying what you say – that you knew that the man was a professional football player and it was your decision to carry out the punishment to blow off the man's toes . . . Now, if he was a singer, would you have cut his tongue out? If he was a painter, would you have cut his fingers off? Or if he did something with his eyes, would you have taken out his eyes? I mean, how far can these things be carried?'

Colonel Hoare responded, 'As an African, you should know extremely well how far they can be carried.'

The African was having none of it. 'Yes, but I can claim here I am uncivilised. I am a savage. I do not belong to the group of civilised . . .'

'Perhaps I can best answer your question,' said Hoare, 'by telling you this small incident which explains the great difference that exists between the African, mentally, and shall we say for this purpose, the European. On one occasion a soldier in the Congolese army picked up a live dove. There was a bed of coals in front of him which we were cooking our dinner on. He plucked out all the feathers from the live dove and threw it on the coals. He couldn't understand that we aren't made that way. We can't do those things.'

The African member of the audience was equal to the challenge. 'If you forgive me, sir, if you buy a lobster in any civilised restaurant in the world, it is thrown alive into boiling water.'

Hoare could only fall back on the argument that a large number of Africans are different from us in many basic matters. I asked him how they are different.

'Well, I've dealt with cruelty, haven't I? Cruelty is in them. This is the result of tribal warfare and so on. This is not a criticism of a fine people. I'm not necessarily saying this is bad. I'm saying it's different. To give you another example, take the matter of chivalry, or chivalry's offspring, sportsmanship. This is unknown in the African mind. There's no such thing as chivalry or sportsmanship.'

I could scarcely believe the juxtaposition of the word 'sportsmanship' with all that we had just heard. Neither could the African in the audience.

'May I interrupt again, please? Could we look at the history of Europe over the last thirty years – we don't have to get specific – and we think of certain atrocities committed in Europe . . . how does this justify your claim?'

Colonel Hoare had graphically demonstrated the falsity of those British newspapers who had sought to portray the Congo mercenaries as latter-day Boy's Own heroes saving civilisation from barbarians. That he had done so by his own words was more powerful than any third-party editorial could ever have been. I had gone into the interview hoping that something like that might happen – that Colonel Hoare could be lulled into digging his own grave, as it were. It was something of a high-risk strategy, in that I had to be prepared to switch tactics if Hoare's responses sounded too self-serving and sympathetic, but that was never necessary – even less so after the intervention of the African member of the audience. The notion of some form of white moral supremacy, still held by those who bitterly regretted the fact that Britain had divested itself of its Empire, was left pretty much in tatters.

In one of the following week's programmes a violent clash over the London Government Bill erupted between the

Chairman of the London Labour Party, Robert Mellish, and Quintin Hogg, who closed the debate on the subject for the Conservatives. As a debate, it was chiefly remarkable for the fact that Quintin Hogg managed to interject a ritual chant of 'Tell the truth!' at least eleven times during one ninety-second period. There was, I fear, more heat than light, though the sight of a Government Minister in the act of going ballistic had a certain awesome fascination.

Meanwhile, an invitation we had issued a couple of weeks earlier – with very little hope of success – was taking us back into the news again. Cyril Bennett had suggested an interview with Ian Smith, the Prime Minister of Rhodesia, and I had added the nuance of inviting him to come to London for it. Smith had made a unilateral declaration of independence (UDI) in November 1965, and not only was his regime unrecognised by any other nation (including South Africa), but it was technically in rebellion against Britain. The protocol problems a visit by Smith would present were mind-boggling, though unlikely to be tested. Now, however, to our astonishment, he had accepted our invitation. 'Smith on TV Risks Treason Charge', said one headline. 'Mr Smith Says Yes to TV Offer – But Risks Arrest' said another. The *Sun*'s lead story read:

> A pantomime situation arose last night in the Rhodesia crisis, following a television invitation to Mr Ian Smith, the rebel Premier, to come to London. Mr Smith has provisionally accepted an invitation to appear on Rediffusion's 'David Frost Programme'.
>
> In the programme he would discuss his rebel cabinet's proposal for settling the crisis. But in London last night it was believed that Mr Smith's acceptance of the TV invitation was a propaganda move, and that he would not come to Britain.
>
> If he did arrive at London Airport, without first obtaining the British Government's permission, he could be arrested on a charge of treason because he is technically in rebellion against the Queen.
>
> A Rediffusion spokesman said last night: 'We expect Mr

Smith to arrive here before Christmas providing, of course, his visit is acceptable to the British Government.'

There was no official comment from the Government, although 'unofficial sources' were busily at work, indicating official displeasure and generally pooh-poohing the idea of a visit by Smith. The Government clearly did not want to get in a position where it would appear to be muzzling free speech, and they were therefore in a rare quandary. The Independent Television Authority, which regulated television on the Independent Network in Britain, also did not want to intervene to stop such a programme. In Salisbury a Rhodesian Government spokesman confirmed that the Prime Minister had accepted the invitation, and added, 'Though naturally Mr Smith does not want to end up in the Tower.'

It was a splendid war of words. Whitehall talked off the record to *The Times*, who reported, 'Politicians would not, for instance, accept Mr Frost as an especially well-qualified chairman for a

'I thought I'd be staying at Claridge's!'

programme on the Rhodesian crisis, particularly after the naivete he and other entertainers first showed about a charity concert to succour injured and sick in the Viet Cong areas in South Vietnam.'

An editorial in the *Sunday Mirror* hit back: 'The pomposity of a woman of the bedchamber would have been coloured by more honesty. *The Times* manages entirely to overlook that it was Mr Frost who exposed the ruse to lure "entertainers" into doing this concert. Having watched two politicians behaving like backward urchins, having seen Quintin Hogg chanting the same phrase 140 times and Mellish gibbering back, many people would far rather entrust the nation's affairs to entertainers than to politicians.'

While the row continued, and we tried to nail down our scoop in Salisbury, the series of course went on. One appearance by John Allegro, talking about the implications of the recently-discovered Dead Sea Scrolls, led to another. Allegro summed up the significance of the scrolls as he saw them: 'The Dead Sea Scrolls are an extraordinary, wonderful collection of manuscripts, about four hundred different documents, found in caves in the north-western corner of the Dead Sea. They're about a type of Judaism of which also we'd only known, hitherto, second hand. But now we actually have original manuscripts. So we can now set this first-hand stuff against the second-, third- or fourth-hand stuff of the New Testament. I think they offer the possibility, at last, of getting underneath this rather crumbling story in the New Testament.'

When Allegro came to the question of the existence of Jesus as an historical figure, his own answer was negative: 'I can't see it. I think the Jesus of the New Testament is a sort of embodiment of the spirit of divination.'

Scarcely surprisingly, the vicar of the University Church in Cambridge, Canon Hugh Montefiore, who was my former dean at Caius, did not agree: 'The New Testament Gospels are about the only evidence we have for the life of Jesus. Now, it's a question of reading those and asking yourself, "Has this evolved? Is this legend? Or does the impact of the man break through the page?" This is a matter of judgement, which I think anyone can manage. You may think, when you read the New Testament, this man was mad; you may think he was bad; you may think he was the Son of God. All this is irrelevant. The point is do you think this was a man, or do you think it's a legend?'

This approach didn't sit well with Allegro. 'The thing cannot possibly be treated on this emotional basis. Is this a man? Does he shine through the page? That's rubbish. You are dealing with very, very complex documents and you've got to deal with them word by word.'

Canon Montefiore asked why. 'You see, you're a philologist. A student of words. And so, perhaps naturally, you think that one must examine these things word by word. But I think the words are there to express ideas. This is, I think, how we use words. And therefore I think we should look at the ideas and the facts which are represented by words.'

That's where the lines were drawn, and the reaction to the programme confirmed a belief I had held, that despite the growth in scepticism – or perhaps because of it – religion and everything that went with it was still a subject of consuming interest to the public, providing that the questions asked were those the public wanted to hear answered, and not imposed from above by dogma.

Indeed, the response to the various discussions in the series that impinged on religion convinced us that we should bring all these themes together – Allegro, the Bishop of Woolwich, humanism – and devote a whole programme to discussing the basic question, 'What *must* I believe to be a Christian?' Preferably with the Archbishop of Canterbury, Michael Ramsey, if he was willing to break with tradition and appear in a one-on-one conversation in front of an audience on something other than a religious programme. That was three precedents for the price of one, but I visited him at Lambeth Palace and explained what we wanted to do. Much to my delight, he agreed.

The programme that resulted was in some ways a statistical phenomenon. While the Archbishop held immense prestige and respect, I was told by everybody that we could not expect our usual level of ratings for such a programme. In fact, these fears proved unjustified because, I think, of the audience's deep concerns as well as the Archbishop's charismatic and lucid performance.

I began by putting John Allegro's opinion to him – that he felt there was no historical evidence for the existence of Jesus Christ. I quoted Canon Montefiore's reply about looking at the Gospels and seeing if He came through as a man. I said that I felt that wasn't altogether convincing, because King Lear, for example, comes through as a man, but that's because Shakespeare was a very good writer. What would the Archbishop say was the most important evidence for the existence of Jesus Christ?

He responded: 'Well, first of all, pagan secular historians with no religious axe to grind refer to Jesus Christ, His existence, His teaching, and His crucifixion. So I would say the existence of Jesus Christ was about as certain a fact as any in history. But coming to the specifically Christian evidence, what impresses me so much is that the records about Jesus are so widely diffused. You would expect exaggerations – there's no doubt we get them; you would expect discrepancies in details – no doubt we get them; but what impresses me so much is this consensus about the main facts in records existing in a number of localities where people who actually knew Jesus had spread. I call that very convincing historical evidence.'

I asked, 'Now, if I believe that Christ didn't exist historically, as Allegro alleges, can I be a Christian?'

'Well, you could be an adherent of Jesus Christ as a beautiful idea, or drama, or poem, or symbol, and I think that could be a real form of Christianity. But I think that Jesus really existed. Without His concrete existence I don't think there would've been any Christianity, though I think we could've had a sort of Christianity, just on the basis of what you're saying.'

'Would you say, for instance, that there was a virgin birth?'

'I think the evidence in St Luke's Gospel is very strong indeed that there was. Particularly as it's a narrative that seems to be quite unaffected by pagan ideas or pagan influences. I believe the historical evidence for it is very strong and convincing.'

'And do I have to believe that to be a Christian?'

'Well, I would say that it's possible to believe in the divinity of Jesus Christ and yet be doubtful about the virgin birth. I would never believe in the divinity of Christ *because* of the virgin birth. I believe in the divinity of Christ on the grounds of Christ's moral claims upon the disciples, and upon us, and then I would see a miraculous birth as congruous.'

We were beginning to define the lines of discussion. 'We've got the point, Archbishop, on the one hand, where one has to believe in Jesus Christ as an historical figure to be a Christian. On the other hand, one doesn't have to believe necessarily in the virgin birth. Do you, in order to be a Christian, have to believe that Christ was the Son of God?'

'I would say that the essence of Christianity is the belief that Jesus Christ was and is divine, so that we can worship Him as divine, which is more than to follow Him as a leader or a teacher. That's the essence of what distinguishes Christianity from other religions, the belief in His deity. I would rest the claim not on the particular words and sentences, but on the total impact of Jesus in His life, and His teaching, leading on to His death and His resurrection.'

Was the Archbishop referring to God, when he spoke of Him, as a personality, an outside personality, or as just a name for a concept?

'Well, I'm talking about God as the power, both beyond and within the universe, a power on which we all depend, a power with a purpose, a power that is good and righteous, and with whom we can have relations of a personal kind.'

'Relations of a personal kind?'

'Yes. So that the analogy of personality is the best analogy for describing our relation with God.'

'And so, in other words, to be a Christian I have to believe that I can have a personal relationship with God and that Jesus was the Son of God?'

'I think that that's the heart of Christianity.'

This led us straight to *Honest to God*. 'Now, what about the people in the Church, like the Bishop of Woolwich, who don't go along with that? How do you classify them?'

'The Bishop of Woolwich doesn't deny the divinity of Jesus Christ,' claimed the Archbishop. 'What the Bishop was doing was feeling after some new modes of expressing it and criticising the traditional image in which it is expressed. That's what he was doing. I think he got himself and a lot of other people into a frightful muddle in the process, because I think it's a muddled book and the argument is confused. But I don't doubt that he believes that Jesus is divine.'

'But if God is solely, as he seems to say, within us, it is very different to what you are saying of a separate being, isn't it?'

'Well, I agree that I think his language is confused and I think a reader could get the impression that he was so concentrating on God within that he was not letting us, or himself, think sufficiently about God beyond. I believe that God is both beyond and within. And I think indeed that it is this blending of beyondness and within-ness that is the most meaningful thing about God as I know Him . . . I'm more concerned with the reality itself than with the words by which we describe it. In fact I believe the old words and images are going to last, because we aren't improving them in our attempts to play about with them. But believe me, I am more concerned with the essence of the matter than with the words, because all the words and images are inadequate. It isn't a question that Woolwich's words or images are better than mine or yours or anyone else's. The real point is that all images are inadequate, and that's why we really have to employ a whole variety of images for our thoughts about God . . . I believe that any believer in God is again and again in real perplexity about the great weight of suffering in the world and only finds the answer to it in the fact of the cross of Christ and what we learn from the cross of Christ. That means that faith isn't an easy state of complacency. Faith is rather more like a sort of wheel that's always revolving round, going into perplexities and yet coming out serene and overcoming them.'

'In his book, the Bishop of Woolwich says that the personal conception of a God with a personal outside involvement is made morally intolerable by the question of suffering which he must therefore either cause or permit,' I said.

'Well, as a matter of fact, the problem of suffering is a terrible problem, whether you describe God in the more traditional way or whether you describe God in this alternative kind of way. I don't think that what you've just quoted really bears on it.'

'But how do you answer the problem of suffering that a personal involved God must either permit or cause?'

'I think of it like this. God doesn't cause suffering. God has made a world in which the great fact is human freedom. We human beings have free wills to love and serve God and one another, or to be selfish and sinful and make a mess of things. This genuine freedom of human choice is the condition of having a moral world at all, as distinct from an automatic kind of world. Very well then, we can, in our human freedom, make a mess of things. And it's our making a mess of things, as a human race, that has caused such terrible suffering. But meanwhile, we are shown through the cross of Christ the way of dealing with suffering by accepting it and turning it to creative uses in love and sympathy and sacrifice and heroism. It is indeed from scenes of suffering that the most stupendous human virtues and achievements have come. Considerations like that enable one to make the act of faith in God still.'

We moved on to the story of Adam and Eve, which the Archbishop described as 'a true parable . . . but truth of history, no'.

I asked, 'Now, if one had asked two hundred years ago, before Darwin and so on, probably someone would have said that it had to be believed as historically having happened. But now we're saying it's a true parable. Now as you look at the faith today, is it possible that in another hundred years people will say exactly what you've just said – about the resurrection?'

'Well, let's deal with that. In the last century, there was a big revolution in Christian thought, when Christians in this country generally gave up the literal Adam and Eve, but found that it didn't undermine belief in the divine creator. In fact, it rather enhances the picture of the divine creator if He creates the world and us through a glorious age-long creative evolutionary process.

'But now you ask specifically about the resurrection. I believe that without the resurrection there would've been, and can be, no Christianity at all. There are two reasons. Originally, the survival of Christianity happened because Jesus rose. Otherwise the whole thing would've collapsed. But now the essence of Christianity is that Jesus really does exist in the fullness of His personal being with an impact upon us. I would say that the resurrection really was the essence of the matter and, indeed, the primitive creed was that God raised Jesus from the dead and Jesus is Lord. That is to say I regard the resurrection as the absolute inner citadel that will remain. No resurrection, no Christianity. Then or now.'

'I don't have to believe the virgin birth, but I do have to believe the resurrection?'

'I don't see how, with the best will in the world, you're going to be a Christian without.'

'And, if by any chance evidence was ever adduced that there was no resurrection, there would be no Christianity, that's the cornerstone?'

'I don't like discussing such a hypothesis . . .'

'Ah, but a lot of people do feel that the resurrection itself is a hypothesis.'

'That is so completely remote.'

'But not remote from most people. Most people I think in this country believe that the resurrection anyway is a hypothesis.'

'Well, if the resurrection is a hypothesis, Jesus is a great dead ancient teacher of morals and religion and takes his place among a lot of other past figures who were teachers of morals and religion, and that's a good ethical system. But it's so different from what Christianity is and has been that I think I would call it a different religion.'

In the light of these very clear definitions, I asked the Archbishop to try and summarise the differences between Christianity and humanism, as he saw them.

'Christians and humanists both believe in the dignity of man and the supreme worth of man, and the conserving of human values and the betterment of man. But the divergence comes in that they have different views of what man's trouble is in depth and also what man's destiny is. Humanists believe that the human race is going to be put right by getting better and better through the spread of scientific knowledge and its application. We Christians believe that the spread of scientific knowledge and its application won't of itself deal with man's predicament, which is that he is estranged from God, his creator. So we diagnose the trouble differently in the same way we diagnose the goal differently. The humanist says that man's destiny is to be a competent moral citizen in this world. We say that man's destiny is eternal life in Heaven in fellowship with God, and that man's eternal worth rests upon that, the eternal destiny.'

The Archbishop had walked his personal tightrope superbly. An intellectual with sympathy for the perplexities of the doubter, but determined at the same time to try and soothe the distress and untangle the confusion in the hearts and minds of the faithful. 'The old words and images are going to last.' It was a message of certainty from a man with an open mind, and the Archbishop's distilled use of language made even the most complex thought come alive.

The next day we were dealing with the supernatural again, in a rather different form. It was just seven days since the Aberfan disaster in Wales, when a landslide engulfed a school and killed 174 children. In the aftermath there were several reports of people claiming to have had premonitions of just such a tragedy. One professor said that on the sheer law of averages it was not unusual in a case like this, with very clear and horrific images, that some people would have 'seen' it either simultaneously or beforehand, without knowing what their premonitions were based on. He advocated a computer centre, where people with premonitions could phone in and thus perhaps prevent a disaster from taking place.

Intellectually, the concept of whether it is possible to have premonitions which foretell something that can be prevented was fascinating, and worth exploring. Our research team arranged for people who had contacted the professor to come to the studio from all corners of the land. About an hour before the programme, the psychic zealots began to gather. I looked forward to the exploration of their theories, which was to be the main part of the programme, followed by a poetic epilogue from John Betjeman. Twenty minutes or so before we were to go on the air, Geoffrey Hughes, our unflappable producer, strolled into my office and said, 'David, I think you ought to come and talk to these people.' He was enigmatic about the reason for his suggestion. I seldom talked to participants before a programme, in order to avoid any sense of rehearsal, but in this case, like the rest of the team, I was expecting something exceptional and so decided to take Geoffrey's advice. It turned out to be exceptional, certainly, though not quite in the way I had expected.

I entered the hospitality room and went over to the first psychic forecaster. 'I understand that you had a premonition about the Aberfan disaster,' I said.

'Yes,' the intense-looking man replied. 'Aberfan was something black going down in Wales. My premonition was of something white going up in China. And so you see, I knew.'

I turned away, my confidence not quite as strong as it had been a few moments earlier. But I was not too concerned. After all, there were other people in the room who had had irrefutable premonitions. I spoke to the closest at hand, and asked him how he had learned in advance of Aberfan.

'Well, you see, I was out walking and I went to the top of this hillock and relieved myself, and then I knew . . .' There was a pause.

'Yes . . .' I said encouragingly.

'That's all,' he said.

I turned to a third guest. 'I understand you had a premonition about Aberfan.'

'Yes,' he said. 'I was driving along in my car, which is made of cavemen, of course, and suddenly I realised . . .'

He was about to go on, but I felt I had to seek clarification. 'In your what?' I asked.

'In my car, which is made of cavemen. You know, the cavemen lived on this earth many centuries ago, and when they died they turned to dust, and it is from their dust that my car is made . . .'

I got out of the room as fast as I could, and went into a huddle with Geoffrey. He was torn between horror and amusement at the look on my face. 'Well . . . ?' he said.

'Well, obviously, we can't possibly go ahead with this item. If it was something less tragic than Aberfan, or if we were doing this further away from a less serious event, it could be the funniest thing we've done. But to do this, about that, tonight – it would be awful. How many poems does Betjeman have memorised?'

Geoffrey and I took the only decision we could. The whole programme had to be Betjeman. We decided not to burden him with the news that he was now on for forty minutes rather than ten, and to apologise afterwards to our psychics for the unbearable way in which he had overrun. We had no time to consider what would happen if John and I dried up.

A few moments later, we were sitting in front of the audience as the signature tune played. John had seemed a little surprised that we had reversed the running order, but accepted this as one of the inexplicable vagaries of the electronic media. I began by asking him how poems came to him. 'Does the muse suddenly strike?'

His eyes opened wide with that look of wonderment with which, I always suspected, he even read a telephone book. 'But surely you've written a poem, David! Everybody we know has written a poem. You write a poem when you're deeply in love, or when you're very hurt by something, and you want to put it down memorably. It comes out like Hymns Ancient and Modern only too often, but it meant a lot to you, and you daren't show it to your friends, because they might laugh at you, and it's your child.'

'But these days, when people are in love, they just send flowers by Interflora.'

'Yes, but it isn't the same as talking about how you're mad about somebody; putting it down in words and sending it to them. Oh, it's wonderful. My first stuff was just rubbish. I mean it wasn't love, but at first I couldn't express myself, I was so mad about the person! Why should we be ashamed of the body and the delights of seeing how beautiful a person can be? I don't think it's a sentiment one ought to be ashamed of, do you? Even though I look absolutely hideous and frightfully old, we all go through these things, and it's silly to pretend they weren't there.'

John's words certainly appealed to the romantic in me. I hoped that the audience felt the same way, and prayed that they would join in. It was now or never. If they had nothing to say, there was a mere thirty-five minutes to go!

'I wonder how many people in the audience have actually written a poem when they've fallen in love. Anyone?'

A couple of hands went up. I chose one. 'I have. I don't think I can remember all of it though. Something like . . .

The orange rose faded, the orchid was too small,
So I planted a lily from the catalogue.
It grew faster than I expected, taller than I wanted,
But it's the most beautiful flower I've ever seen.
And it doesn't matter
That I've neglected the rest of the garden.'

The audience were captivated, and applauded. Over the applause I heard the man murmur something to the woman beside him, and her reply. 'That's marvellous,' I said. 'And the lady beside you says it was written for her. I'm sure I never thought to discover that . . . I imagined that poems just didn't get written any more like that. What made you write it? Why did you choose to do it in the form of a poem?'

'I just had something inside me that I wanted to express in some way, and I couldn't do it. And I tried writing and it just came, and I felt I'd achieved something from this – I'd put a feeling into words, which happened to be a poem, that I couldn't do in any other way.'

'Did you feel you could say more in a poem?'

'Absolutely! And it was something I didn't really want to say in prose. It was no good going to her and saying "I love you" or "I feel rather like this, it's a sort of ache here, or a tingle there." I just wrote it, and it made me feel better.'

I felt the programme had taken off. I turned to Betjeman. 'I wonder if you could get a better description of why people write poetry, John.'

'I agree. And it really was marvellous, David, to get someone in the audience to speak their poetry absolutely spontaneously like that, entirely unrehearsed. And it was real poetry. It was worth hearing and it came from the heart. It's in everybody; everybody writes poetry; they've got it deep in them. It was lovely to see it proved here in Wembley, or wherever we are. They all naturally write poetry and they daren't bring it out. English literature, examinations, things like that, they kill it. But it's alive.'

The programme too was alive. The rest of it seemed to go by in a flash. All thought of our psychics, still sitting upstairs in the Green Room, watching on a monitor, had passed.

For Philip Purser, writing in the *Sunday Telegraph*, this was the show in which 'The Frost Programme' had finally, 'to borrow an atomic metaphor, "gone critical"'. Naturally, he gave us the credit for having planned to do the whole programme with John Betjeman, as the air of spontaneous combustion would have been inescapable even for those who did not share in the secret of just *how* spontaneous everything had been.

After the programme, I walked back to the hospitality room to make my apologies. 'I'm terribly sorry,' I said to the first psychic I met. 'I hope you don't feel you've had too wasted a journey.'

'Not at all,' he said very generously, and then went on, 'As a matter of fact, on the way here I had a premonition that this might happen . . .'

During all this, the pace of the Rhodesian crisis had quickened. Ian Smith had met with Prime Minister Harold Wilson on HMS *Tiger*, moored off Gibraltar, from 2 to 4 December, and the British contingent had left the talks feeling they had a deal, only to discover that they hadn't. Smith had returned to Rhodesia and repudiated the so-called agreement. In terms of a Smith interview, days and hours mattered now.

There wasn't time for detailed arrangements for Smith to fly to London, even if we had been able to guarantee him Claridge's rather than the Tower of London. With three shows a week, it would be difficult for me to get to Rhodesia. And there were no satellite facilities at the time out of that part of Africa. So we had a problem. Then I recalled the technique of Ed Murrow's 'Small World', where the participants were linked by a sound circuit while separate film units recorded the visual proceedings. The various outputs were then flown to a central point and edited. We proposed interviewing Smith over the radio-telephone, filming him responding in Salisbury with me putting the questions in London, and then putting the two films together in London. The drawback was that this removed the valuable element of face-to-face interaction, but the pluses outweighed the minuses. So at ten o'clock on the morning of 8 December, from a small cubicle in the Rediffusion studios in Kingsway, we opened the line to Salisbury and to the rebel Prime Minister.

The interview was to have an effect greater than we had anticipated. In essence, it demonstrated what a difficult, indeed almost impossible, man Smith was to negotiate with. He began by trying to blur whether or not he had indicated that he would travel to HMS *Tiger* with 'power to settle'. Why had he signed a document, outlining the steps back to constitutional government, that his administration had since described as repellent?

'I quite frankly didn't see any reason for signing this document. But Mr Wilson was very keen to have a signed document to record this rather memorable meeting, with the signature of Sir Humphrey Gibbs. I didn't want to upset the little thoughts that he had in his mind, so providing it did not commit me, I agreed to sign.'

'So you think that Mr Wilson regarded it as a sort of souvenir of the memorable meeting?'

'I suppose an historic document to which he was very keen to have signatures appended.'

Mr Smith was creative, but not altogether convincing, in the factual area. 'We find at the moment that the African is not interested in our democratic system,' he said.

'But isn't it true that one or two of the leaders of the African people who've tried to turn to democracy have ended up in detention?'

'I don't think that this is so. They intimidated people to such an extent that these basic freedoms of democracy disappeared.'

'But how are they intimidating?'

'They are burning houses down, they are beating people. They have even murdered people.'

It all sounded wondrously vague. 'How many houses have been burned down in Rhodesia over the past year?'

'Oh, offhand this is asking rather much, isn't it, to ask me to give the exact figure? But we certainly have cases. We have cases of children, little babies who've burned.'

Even more vague. 'How many cases of little babies being burned?'

'Well, again, I'm afraid I haven't got the exact figure, but I can recall myself certain cases that come to mind immediately. You see, these people do live, the majority of them, in the country, in houses that have thatched roofs.'

While grateful for the local colour, I was intrigued that the 'certain cases' had not yet come to mind as 'immediately' as predicted.

'The Africans,' Smith told me, 'are highly suspicious, highly susceptible, for example, to witchcraft; easily intimidated. All along we have been asked to lower our standards to compromise, to get away from fair play.' (I half expected another lecture on chivalry and sportsmanship.)

Ian Smith had already demonstrated some of the techniques which I was to see again in later interviews. In particular, those vague quicksilver 'facts'. Sometimes he would resort to a form of sheer gobbledygook. At one point I reminded him that he was spending about six million pounds on white children's education, and the same amount on black children: 'And there are sixteen times as many blacks.'

'Well,' said Smith, 'one has to be practical. There's no use spending money to teach Africans if you haven't got the teachers, for example. This is an exercise that on paper might not seem to be quite in harmony, but in actual fact this is not the position.'

I have had cause to reread that transcript several times over the years, and I still cannot fathom the meaning of those words.

At the end of the interview I thanked Mr Smith and said goodbye. 'Much pleasure to me to accommodate you,' he said. 'And good luck.' He then turned to the technicians in the Rhodesian studio. 'Those chaps need it over there, don't they, more than I do.'

I was intrigued. 'Pardon? Who needs it?'

'You're supposed to have switched off by now,' responded Smith.

'All right,' I said, 'but you think we need the luck more, do you? I think that's the point probably that the two governments will never agree on.'

It was a revealing little vignette. On the surface, to wish Britain luck at that particular moment, and to feel that Britain needed it more than Rhodesia, was an absurd act of bravado. But I still think that when Smith said it, he had probably convinced himself that he really felt it. Self-deception may have been nine-tenths of his problem. That, and his unwillingness to stand up and be counted in his own cabinet, was in a sense his undoing. Although he may well have been outnumbered in cabinet by six to four, with his massive public support he could surely have railroaded the HMS *Tiger* solution through. The result, according to liberal constitutional experts (who had been delighted by the *Tiger* solution) would have been that majority rule would not have come to Rhodesia until 1999 – rather better terms than those Smith was to achieve thirteen years later. 'Always make concessions while you still have room to manoeuvre. Otherwise it will look like weakness rather than strength,' Henry Kissinger said to me many years later about Rhodesia. His words should be engraved in marble over the desk of the leader of any minority government. They were needed in Salisbury in the Sixties, just as they were needed in Tehran in the early Seventies.

As a footnote, I should add that there was one point on which the Smith bravado was more than justified. It was an exchange on the subject of oil.

DF: Isn't it true, for instance, that if there was a successful oil embargo, Rhodesia couldn't survive?

Smith: Well, you say if I flew to the moon I'd have no idea what it would be like there, and I've no idea what a successful oil embargo would be like.

DF: But you must have considered it, Mr Smith.

Smith: You want me to let you in on my plans now, do you?

DF: Well, it would be very kind, certainly.

Smith: Yes. But very foolish also, wouldn't it?

DF: It might be slightly unwise, yes.

Smith: (A chuckle)

DF: But you are confident you have plans to stop the successful oil embargo or to survive even if there is a successful oil embargo?

Smith: Yes, I have no worries as far as that is concerned.

DF: In which case? Surviving if there is a successful one, or stopping there being a successful one?

Smith: You can take your choice.

It was only years later that we learned that Smith was, in the event, able to rely on British companies and the British Government to evade their own oil sanctions.

The interview had a greater effect on the British people's opinion of Ian Smith than we had anticipated. The film of Smith answering the questions was mysteriously mislaid somewhere between Rhodesia, Johannesburg and London. At first, this seemed like a disaster, but in the end we decided to proceed with the soundtrack from the London end of the interview, television pictures of me, and stills of Ian Smith. When Philip Purser commented in the *Sunday Telegraph*, 'The Smith interview despite – or perhaps because of – the lack of pictures afforded the most illuminating and depressing glimpse yet of this hero shifting his ground,' he probably had a point.

By now the Christmas holidays were approaching, and with them the scheduled conclusion of the series. Cyril Bennett, however, had suggested a thirteen-week extension of the original thirteen-week run. That was getting a bit close to my other commitments – not to mention the breaking point of everyone involved – so we finally settled on a further five weeks in the New Year.

As our acknowledgement to the imminence of Christmas, we had an item on Christmas cards. I asked the audience what sort of card they would send to well-known people – Edward Heath, for instance. A man in the second row replied immediately, 'A group of young choirboys.' There was a slight titter from the audience. I was about to explain helpfully, 'You mean because he's interested in music,' but bit my tongue just in time, so as not to fall victim to the Sam Snead syndrome. (I refer to that moment in broadcasting legend when an interviewer was asking

Mrs Snead how the great golfer prepared for an important round. She had replied, 'Well, he always bangs his balls up against the living room wall.' The interviewer had added helpfully, 'His *golf* balls, you mean?')

We had certainly achieved our ambition of making news with what we did on the programme. Indeed, in January 1967 we even made news with what we did *not* do on the programme. There was a recurrent rumour that Frank Mitchell, the escaped Dartmoor 'axeman', was going to give himself up during a surprise live appearance on 'The Frost Programme'. It seemed an unlikely scenario to us, but police stationed themselves in strategic positions near the studio just in case.

We were rapidly approaching the end of the run, which would come at the beginning of February, but we felt that there was time for at least one more studio experiment. During the series there had been several occasions when adults told us what they believed children thought. We thought the children should have a chance to talk about the adults instead, or indeed anything else they wanted to talk about. I had conducted film interviews with children on 'The Frost Report', but an audience of two hundred children between the ages of six and ten would be a new experience for me, and hopefully for viewers as well.

Since the programme would not be on the air until after ten thirty, it was one of the rare occasions when we had to break our rule about live shows, and record the proceedings at five o'clock, thus hopefully avoiding the danger of a live audience who were fast asleep.

The children dying from hunger in the war-torn Congo, and other forms of suffering, were much on several of the children's minds, though not all of them were in agreement. Said one, 'If disasters weren't happening, what would our object be? If everything was perfect we would become selfish, we wouldn't have anything else to work for, apart from ourselves.'

This idea was offensive to the logical concepts of one eight-year-old. 'What that boy said just now about if everything was perfect then we would become selfish . . . well, if everything was perfect, we wouldn't be selfish – because everything would be perfect. And being selfish isn't perfect.'

At one point I asked our audience how many of them would like to have been a child of the Royal Family. Only about twelve hands out of two hundred went up. One of the twelve said, 'I wouldn't mind the money . . .' But a member of the majority summed up his feelings: 'They can never sit around a table and have a game of Scrabble.'

At the conclusion of the programme, I asked the children if they had any questions they wanted to ask me. One little girl was in like a flash. 'Why did you bite your fingernails during the break?' I had no excuses, and had to confess to setting a very bad example.

At this time our thoughts were very much on the Foreign Secretary, the Right Honourable George Brown, perhaps the most colourful and controversial figure in British politics of that era. I had been attempting to persuade him to appear on the programme for several weeks. He would be the first leading Cabinet Minister to make such an appearance. On 13 January I visited him in his cavernous office at the Foreign Office, to try and put his mind at ease. He was very much under attack from the newspapers, and the more he was attacked, the more he wanted a forum to express himself. On the other hand, the more he was attacked, the more fearful he became. After all, a lot was at stake for him. He was not only Foreign Secretary, he was Deputy Prime Minister as well. However under siege, he was at the peak of his political life. I was intrigued by the prospect of trying to explore this paradoxical man. Mercurial, irascible, sentimental, bombastic, charming, petulant, visionary – George Brown was able to switch in a moment from showing great warmth and intellectual range to appearing crude, or devastatingly rude. One senior Whitehall figure had said rather patronisingly that Brown had 'the best untrained mind' he had come across. I wanted to try and show the three-dimensional George Brown on television.

Although Brown provisionally accepted my invitation, we knew as the date of the interview approached that he had been in torment over the prospect for days, and that some of his Foreign Office colleagues had urged him to change his mind and cancel it. The problem was that the volatility of his nature was such that nobody, not least George himself, could be sure of the impression he would make. When he got to the studio he admitted that right up to the last roundabout before Wembley, he was still weighing the idea of turning back. (And this time there would have been no John Betjeman waiting in the wings!)

Before the programme he was agitated and tense – exactly the frame of mind that I feared could produce a disastrous interview. I had been mulling over the best way of putting him at his ease, and I knew that it was important, particularly at the beginning, to avoid the predictable questions about current policy and problems. I had thought of a number of possible alternatives. Seeing his agitation settled my mind for me. I decided to begin by talking about something which he was not normally asked to discuss – the sheer mechanics of being Foreign Secretary.

As he sat opposite me, with the signature tune playing in the background, the edginess was so apparent that I decided to add a brief interchange on one of his pet enthusiasms, football. I welcomed him and added, 'We must say how much we appreciate your presence, particularly in the week of this awful tragedy of West Ham, the team you've always followed, being knocked out of the FA Cup by Swindon . . .'

'Please!' said George. 'I imagine the referee came from the wrong place.' There was a chuckle from the audience, and the ice was beginning to be broken. I asked him to describe his activities over the previous twenty-four hours. He began with a flash of humour: 'Well, I came home last night, got home from Brussels, at ten thirty, took about an hour to get myself back on speaking terms with my wife, and then I started work on all the papers which I had to read – I don't mean newspapers, may I say – and I finished with that somewhere around three . . .'

As he expounded on his work schedule, the professional enthusiasm for his job took over, and the unease evaporated, to be replaced by a growing candour.

'You said a few weeks ago something about how, in the four months that you'd been there, we were back in the mainstream of events,' I said. 'What could you point to that you've changed or you've altered so far?'

'Well, I rather regret that statement, to tell you the honest truth. It was said, you know, rather loosely and friendlily as I often say many things. You know, a pleasant evening in a Labour Club, and I didn't expect, I literally didn't expect the news-hounds to pick it up and take it out of context and put it like that. It wasn't awfully kind to my predecessor.'

We talked about his near resignation over the Government's deflationary package the previous July, and his resultant move from the Department of Economic Affairs to the Foreign Office. 'I can see how attractive the Foreign Office was,' I said. 'And if the opportunity were to present itself, do you want to be Prime Minister, too?'

The reply was swift – and surprising. 'No. No. I tell you – I don't think I've ever said this before publicly – I ran very reluctantly in the race after Gaitskell died; very reluctantly indeed. I'll tell you a little story. On the night that Hugh Gaitskell died, I was dining with Herbert Morrison at his home, and I was there when I got the telephone call telling me that Hugh had died. And I said to Herbert, "This is going to present for me a terrible problem, because I don't want to run." And I didn't. I ran because it would have seemed odd not to run. My wife and all my close friends know how little my heart was in the race. And I have no intentions ever of running a second time round that course.'

That was a declaration that I knew many would doubt. 'You'd resist the opportunity that presented itself?'

'I'm not interested,' said Brown. 'I'm not interested. I think one of the things that one must do is to never make the same mistake twice. I don't believe I have what you need to be a Prime Minister. I think I've many other things to give and I'll give of them. But I never thought then, I don't think now, that that's anywhere on my menu.'

I could sense that the audience was agog at Harold Wilson's obvious successor taking himself out of the race, if and when it was to occur. 'Why do you feel the Prime Minister wouldn't be ideal for you?'

'Oh, for very many reasons. I'm much too – I don't know what the word is – you might say aggressive, you might say assertive. There are many different words you can use for it. I like to get things out, get them out quickly, get them done; whereas I think a Prime Minister needs – he's got to ride the team. He needs different qualities than the qualities I've got.'

George Brown was really speaking his mind. It was the moment to press on into other areas that were sensitive, indeed in other circumstances perhaps even forbidden. 'And do you think the Labour Party today would be different if the late Hugh Gaitskell was still with us?'

'Very different. Now here I'm really letting my hair down with you. He was a much closer friend to me than Harold Wilson, friendly as we now are, ever will be. I was very close to Hugh Gaitskell indeed. Yet it is absolutely true that Harold can get the party to do things that Hugh would have wished them to do, but could never have got. This is the same way, in a sense, that Johnson, in America, has been able to get the Democratic Congress to do things that Kennedy would have loved them to do but didn't really have the whatever it is, know-how.'

'Why is this? Is it just know-how?'

'Well it's partly know-how and it's partly understanding. It's partly being in touch with moods. Harold Wilson knows how far you can go, when you ought to move, how you ought to do it. Hugh Gaitskell never had that touch. And this is what makes a leader. The other man was a very distinguished man, I repeat. Much my closest friend. But he would never have made a successful Prime Minister of the Labour Party. It's a sad thing to say, but it is so. It's a question of knowing how to do it, and I haven't got this and I don't pretend to have. And you know, it's easier if one recognises it. Now, Hugh Gaitskell never recognised this, and I suspect if he'd been asked before he died, he would have said he was a very disappointed man. I, on the other hand, know I can't do it. So I'm not interested in that, whereas I know I can do other things. I can drive things through, issues through, and one makes one's own accommodation with life.'

The conversation turned to other current topics, but the tone remained the same. George Brown summed it up, in a sense, when he prefaced one answer by saying, 'It's very odd to be

"HOW WOULD YOU LIKE ME TO ARRANGE FOR YOU TO INTERVIEW CALLAGHAN, JENKINS, CROSSMAN, HEALEY, BOWDEN, BOTTOMLEY .....?"

discussing – it really is odd to be discussing things as frankly as this with you in front of an audience and cameras. It really is odd.'

The interview changed the then-current perception of George Brown more speedily than I could have imagined. The headlines zeroed in on the major news stories. For example, the *Daily Mail*: 'Brown: Why I'll Never be Premier'. One newspaper called it 'the frankest public interview ever given by a Government minister'. Another began its report, 'In a remarkable public confessional . . .'. By the following evening, both London evening papers were reporting what seemed to be a new established fact. Said the *Evening Standard*, 'Today everyone at Westminster hailed Mr Brown's performance as superb. Without doubt Mr Brown has now established himself as the warmest personality in the Government.'

The interview emboldened other journalists to weigh in with their own private perceptions of Brown. A columnist on the *Eastern Daily Press* said that it was the George Brown he knew extremely well, and that three-quarters of George Brown was like that. 'The other quarter is labelled "light the blue paper and retire hastily".' John Dickinson, the political correspondent of the *Evening News*, wrote, 'Mr George Brown in a single dream of a performance on the telly has now shown himself to millions as the captivating old charmer many of us on the inside have long known he can be – when he chooses.' He went on to predict that of course on Brown's next appearance he might return to being Vesuvius.

The portrait that had emerged from the programme may not have been the whole truth about George Brown, but it was certainly the aspect of the truth needed at that particular moment, when he was monotonously under fire. He had transformed the perception of himself, in a positive sense, as decisively and dramatically as Ian Smith had done in a negative sense. Whether the effect would be permanent or temporary depended of course in both cases on their future policies and conduct. In the meantime, however, George Brown had confounded the current stereotype.

While Friday's newspapers were examining Brown's performance the previous night, we were preoccupied with another very different encounter, due that same evening. A few days earlier we had run a sketch about the collapse of an insurance company, a fairly clear allusion to the then-notorious example of Fire, Auto and Marine, which had collapsed with more than £800,000 in forged assets, leaving many thousands of people with serious insurance claims unmet. Indeed, the total number of unsettled claims was later established to be as high as 45,000.

After the sketch had been transmitted, the founder and mastermind of Fire, Auto and Marine, Dr Emil Savundra, phoned the office to say how much he'd enjoyed it. The call was taken by a somewhat astonished Mike Gowers, one of our editorial team. Sensing the braggadocio in Savundra's nature,

'I only said we seem to be moving into a period of government by Frost – but let it pass.'

Mike – urged on by everyone else in the office – tried a long shot. 'Why don't you come on the programme?' There was a long pause, and then Savundra said, 'I don't think I could.' However, he would think about it. A few minutes later he called back. 'I'll do it,' he said. 'You polish your rapier, and I'll polish mine.'

So, the series which had begun with Robert Morley was to end with Emil Savundra. The eighteen weeks had shown how a live programme can really only develop on the air – by organic growth. We had started with three and four items in each programme, and we had ended with one or two. We had started with sketches, but as the series developed, they had become rarer. The lessons we had learned about audiences were invaluable, and there were more to come. One writer had hailed us for developing 'new normative dimensions of situational appropriateness'. I was grateful for the compliment, and vowed that, when I had time, I would also work out what it meant.

Whether Savundra had made his telephone call in order to receive the invitation, I will never know. For a long while, journalists had been pursuing him. Three newspapers, the *Sunday*

Mirror, the *Daily Mail* and the *Sunday Times*, had produced detailed and incriminating evidence of his swindle, but Savundra had evaded all efforts to have him reply to the charges. Now, here he was volunteering to face me. Right up to the time we went on the air we doubted whether he would go through with it – although once he was at the studio, it was clear that he had a towering self-confidence.

In preparing our research, we were greatly helped by the 'Insight' team of the *Sunday Times* who brought along their extensive files, and by conversations with Board of Trade Investigator Norman Nail. My first reaction on reading the material was sheer astonishment that the man was still free. But I was aware of how difficult it would be to bring all the material to bear in the interview. A complex case had to be marshalled on television both accurately and concisely for the lay audience. At the same time, I thought that the interview should drive towards one end in particular: Savundra's own sense of moral responsibility for the consequences of his actions. We needed first-person evidence of that, and we therefore asked along, as members of the audience, some ten or twelve victims of his swindles: people left without any settlement for life insurance claims.

Before we could reach this point I had to present, in some detail, the extent of the case against Savundra. I went back as far as 1950, to the first of a series of frauds, and led up to the embezzlements behind the collapse of Fire, Auto and Marine. Through this recital Savundra remained contemplative, even managing to insert a plug for his forthcoming memoirs, though when the sources of our material became clear, he began to lose his composure: 'The *Sunday Times* is the name of the rag which is now changing its name to the Sunday Swines . . .'

'You'll have to do better than that in the book,' I said.

When a member of the audience attempted to intervene, he turned on them. 'I'm not going to cross swords with the peasants. I came here to cross swords with England's bravest swordsman.'

'Nobody is a peasant,' I said somewhat grimly. 'They are the people who gave you money.'

'They have given me nothing at all,' said Savundra.

At this point the interrogation became detailed. Savundra did not fare well on the subject of the bank he had interposed in Liechtenstein, the interest-free loans he had received from this shell, or the forged share certificates discovered by the auditors. This he attempted to dismiss as 'one of the grossest misrepresentations by the family newspapers that made such a hoohah about this'.

I asked him why he didn't sue them on that specific point. Savundra replied that he had been away, but that the writs were ready. There was sheer disbelief in the audience.

'I have been away, I said. I've only just got back. The writs are ready. We will wait and finish your show.'

'To serve us with one, too?'

'Oh well,' said Savundra, 'why not?'

'Yes, it'll all be fun,' I said. 'That's what worries me about you. It is all fun to you, isn't it?'

'But of course,' said Dr Savundra. 'It's all fun.' At this point he accepted an invitation to face the audience. One woman alleged that when her solicitor tried to contact Fire, Auto and Marine after her husband had died in a car accident, there were constant delays, they kept 'messing us about' and instead of meeting the full claim, she was offered only £500, a fraction of what was rightfully due to her.

Savundra asked her when the accident had happened. It was nearly two years earlier. Savundra asked the woman why her solicitor had let the case hang around for that long. 'The only possibility is that there was a material undisclosure and that the company offered you a £500 *ex gratia*.'

The woman was passionate in her denial. Savundra delivered his reply as if he were scoring a debating point: 'You don't know about it, do you? I thought the poor gentleman was dead.'

He was challenged by two other women who had lost their husbands in car accidents and had failed to get any insurance money from Fire, Auto and Marine. Savundra listened, then gave an astonishing reply: 'The only thing I can say is this. All these and other heart-rending stories which I've heard recently have made me realise only too well that my selling out was the wisest thing I ever did.'

'How?' I said. 'How do you mean that?'

After all that had gone before, Dr Savundra then made the remark that ignited the audience and me. 'By selling out I have no legal responsibility and *no moral responsibility.*'

This made me angrier than I have ever been on television. 'You have *total* moral responsibility for all of these people.'

'I beg your pardon, Mr Frost,' said Savundra, 'I have not.'

'You say you are a Roman Catholic and it's the will of God. How do you get rid of moral responsibility? How do you sign a bit of paper that gets rid of past moral responsibility – tell me that, because we would all love to know.'

He launched into an attack on the whole concept of company law. I came back to the basic point. 'This is what horrifies me about you. Perhaps the Board of Trade aren't yet quick enough or clever enough to catch you on that. I hope they do, but how can you say that absolves you of moral responsibility?'

'By the simple, simple reason that you have forgotten, that the man who took over was the managing director of the company from the day it was formed.'

To give his so-called managing director such a build-up was totally unconvincing. Walker, the man in question, had been described by Savundra himself as 'purely a technical man'. With no experience of insurance, he had become managing director as a stopgap. To blame everything on him was pure Savundra.

'You're now saying that this man is responsible,' I said. 'You knew him for ten years. How on earth could you let him run this company? You have either to be stupid or dishonest.'

'Neither,' said Dr Savundra. 'You have surely delegated responsibility in your time.'

'But when you delegate, it assumes you're in authority, and if you're in authority, you take the responsibility. When a Cabinet Minister delegates to a civil servant, he carries the can.'

Dr Savundra did not respond directly, but suggested I get a few elementary books on the practice of management and study them. Time was running out. I just wanted to underline one more time what Savundra was saying.

'Let me just ask one last question. You can look at these people here – widows, widowers, whoever they are – and you can feel "I have no legal responsibility"?'

'Right,' said Dr Savundra.

'And you can say "I've signed a piece of paper and I have no moral responsibility either"?'

'Right,' said Dr Savundra.

The programme was over. As the signature tune played, it was normally the convention for me to sit with my guest for the closing thirty seconds, making polite conversation which was unheard at home. On this occasion, I felt I could not stand the hypocrisy of that. I did not want anyone to think that my feelings ceased when the programme ceased. I was still angry. On the spur of the moment, I simply strode off the set.

The programme may have been over, but the emotions it aroused echoed on. In the newspapers, headlines about Savundra and moral responsibility rubbed shoulders with cartoons of George Brown from the day before. A week later, Dr Savundra was arrested. The phrase 'trial by television' was invoked by some. During the interview I was of course aware of the danger of emotions taking over, of the feelings of the audience – however understandable – creating a climate of the pillory. The balance was well summed-up by Maurice Wiggin in the *Sunday Times*, who wrote, 'This was not just journalism, or theatre, or town meeting, or sport. It was all of them and it was instant, live. It was TV.' At the same time he rightly went on to warn that, taken too far, there could be a danger of demagoguery.

What few people understood at the time was the paralysis of the legal machinery which lay behind the Savundra case. It needs to be explained, not out of any special pleading for the Savundra interview, but because it makes a vital point about the investigative role of journalism as a whole.

In Britain, the press has no rights above those of the ordinary citizen. It is constrained by legal and official regulations more severe than in many other Western countries, particularly the United States – an exposé of the dimensions of the Pentagon Papers, Watergate or Irangate would be impossible. And television has a good deal less freedom than the press – it was, as one editor of *The Times* wrote, 'born in chains'.

'Little man! Take me to your leader!'

The problem raised in the instance of Savundra faces all television producers and all newspaper editors once in a while: if all the normal procedures for pursuing justice have failed, can journalism redress the wrong? Precisely because it is *not* institutionalised, journalism is flexible enough to play this 'long-stop' role, which it has done notably, for example, in the case of the Thalidomide children, where it created the pressure for reform, or the Don Bolles murder in Arizona.

In the case of Savundra, the journalistic role was complex. Successive newspaper campaigns had shown that Fire, Auto and Marine was a criminal operation, yet no prosecution had followed. The trouble was (as Savundra well knew) that both legal and Government action was constipated. The Board of Trade, which at that time regulated the insurance industry, had investigated Fire, Auto and Marine after the first press stories, but concluded that the relevant company law was weak and that prosecution was unsure of success. Clearly this was an extraordinary case in which not only did the regulatory arm of Government need encouragement, but the dedicated efforts of the press had also been unable to get action. Our programme produced no more evidence than had already been printed. Indeed, in volume it obviously contained far less. But what had been produced were two factors previously missing: the inability of

Savundra to give a satisfactory reply to the evidence already unearthed, and the visible impression of his character as he attempted to answer those charges. This was enough.

Some of the people watching the programme that night concluded that further delay in taking action against Savundra was intolerable. politically as well as legally. Only after seeing the interview did the Director of Public Prosecutions telephone the Fraud Squad to say that action must be taken straight away. Thus it was that a prosecution was initiated after the programme, not before, and Savundra was eventually convicted and sentenced to eight years' imprisonment. When he first appeared before the Ealing magistrate, his counsel, Mr Ian McCulloch, spoke about the possibility of contempt proceedings being brought against a prominent 'television personality'. He also criticised the *Sunday Times*, which had printed a transcript of the interview. No more was heard of this, but over a year later, when Savundra appealed against his sentence, the 'trial by television' issue came to a head.

Savundra's grounds for appeal were partially that the interview had prejudiced his trial. In dismissing the appeal, Lord Justice Salmon directly attacked the programme: 'This court hopes that no interview of this kind will ever again be televised . . . It was deplorable.' He said that it was not to be tolerated in a civilised country. This was strong stuff, and I found the grounds for it rather surprising. The interview had occurred 'at a time when it must have been obvious to anyone that Savundra was about to be arrested and tried on charges of gross fraud'. Lord Justice Salmon went on to add: 'It must not be supposed that proceedings to commit for contempt of court can be instituted only in respect to matters published after criminal proceedings have begun. No one should imagine themselves safe from committal for contempt of court if knowing or having good reason to believe that criminal proceedings are imminent he chooses to publish matters calculated to prejudice a fair trial.'

This raised another of the classic snares in the path of the British journalist. Coverage of any case classifiable as 'pending' or 'imminent' could be grounds for prosecution as a contempt of court – even though no action had been taken at the time. Obviously the definition of 'pending' or 'imminent' is impossible to quantify. The duration of the closed period between suspicion and prosecution has never been defined. The Appeal Court had said that it was 'obvious to anyone' that Savundra was about to be arrested, and that the Attorney General could successfully have prosecuted us for contempt. But none of the journalists who had worked for months on the story believed that a prosecution was in the wind. On the contrary, the Board of Trade had shown a peculiar lack of appetite for moving against Savundra.

As Norman Nail has since revealed, it was, in fact, only on the Monday following the programme that the Board of Trade and the Director of Public Prosecutions said that the Fraud Squad must act immediately and arrest Dr Savundra for something while the full charge sheet was being assembled. Otherwise the law would be a laughing-stock. As John Crosby wrote in the *Observer*, the programme was a case of 'lighting a bonfire of public opinion'.

I felt I had to respond to Lord Justice Salmon, and so I took the, for me, unusual step of writing to *The Times*:

> I have just had an opportunity to study Lord Justice Salmon's comments at the close of the Savundra Appeal.
>
> Of course everyone has a right to air their opinions about television, whatever their profession, but facts are a different matter and surely the first thing a Judge, of all people, should do is to check his facts.
>
> Had anyone on 'The Frost Programme' had any reason to think prosecution of Dr Savundra was imminent, we would not have dreamt of interviewing him about FAM. There had been no police action in the seven months following the initial newspaper coverage, and there was no official indication that there would be. Nevertheless, we checked privately with the Board of Trade and elsewhere and were informed, 'We have nothing on Dr Savundra. Go ahead.'
>
> At no point as far as I am aware did Lord Justice Salmon attempt to ascertain from anyone connected with the programme these events preceding the interview of eighteen months ago. One is reminded of Maitland's dictum that it is

sometimes difficult to remember that events now in the past were once in the future.

As it is we are left with a situation where, if the Judge's words were to be taken seriously, television programmes unearthing, say, a new Rachman would have to persuade a newspaper to print the fact before they could contemplate broadcasting it! And indeed even the newspaper would not necessarily be on safe ground.

We are all concerned about individual rights in Britain today but one of the most precious of the rights that the public has is the simple one of hearing the truth whenever and wherever it is available.

Television has shown that it has a real part to play in seeking the truth about matters of public concern, and to remove television from this role seems to be doing both public and individual a positive disservice.

'Trial by television' seems to be becoming more a slogan than an argument, but even those who employ the phrase most sternly would agree that it a rare, if not virtually non-existent, phenomenon. Would it now be unfair to suggest that tirade without trial by Judge is becoming a somewhat more prominent feature of our national life?

As a result of the Savundra case, company law was tightened up. The starting sum for insurance companies was raised from £50,000 to £250,000, and the Department of Trade was given greater powers to scrutinise company accounts. Any operator following the Savundra pattern now could not survive for long the kind of indictments published by investigative journalists then. There had been a blind spot, and we had provided just the pressure needed to overcome it.

'Trial by television' was a clever, emotive phrase. It had indeed become more of a slogan than an argument, and I do not believe that it accurately described either the Savundra programme or its motivation. Savundra was a singular, egregious experience. He offered himself, out of arrogance. The moth came to the flame, and was burned. Who could argue that he deserved less?

SEVEN

1967

AT THE BEGINNING OF 1967, there was one subject that tended to obsess television people whenever they met and talked. That subject was the Independent Television Authority's review of all the existing ITV contracts. The ITA had already announced that there would be some changes in the boundaries. Instead of one company, Granada, providing programmes for the north of England, Monday to Friday, and another, ABC, taking over at the weekend, there would now be two separate areas for the full seven days, one based on Lancashire and one on Yorkshire. It was generally assumed that Granada would be virtually unchallenged for the Lancashire area. In the Midlands there would also be a seven-day franchise, replacing the arrangement whereby ATV supplied programmes Monday to Friday, and ABC again did the honours at weekends. In London the weekend franchise, held by ATV, was to be extended to include Friday evenings, in an attempt to make London's two franchises (the other was held by Associated-Rediffusion) more equal. It was generally assumed that the ITA intended to give London weekdays to its current franchise holder, Associated-Rediffusion, London at the weekends to ABC, the Midlands to ATV and Lancashire to Granada, leaving Yorkshire as its preferred target for would-be new franchise holders. That had never been stated publicly, but it was taken as a 'given' by consortium-builders all over the country.

It was at an Associated-Rediffusion staff party on 9 January that the idea which became London Weekend Television was born. In drawing the raffle prizes, I had added that there would be a special extra prize – the contract for Yorkshire. Later in the evening, I suddenly had the very simple idea: why not go for

London? Why follow the pack and set your sights only on Yorkshire? London at the weekends could be vulnerable, and the talent needed for a winning bid might respond more readily to the idea of London. I knew I would.

And it was time for people with talent to get much more involved in the day-to-day programming decisions that ruled their lives. I'd been intrigued by the upcoming franchise round for some time, but now my thoughts really began to crystallise. What was needed was a new sort of animal – a television station where television people and their skills and expertise came first, and the money came second. It was well worth trying to make it happen. Although in many ways it would be very much a new challenge for me, it did not strike me for a moment as a departure from what I had been doing. It was a logical extension of everything that had happened to me over the past five years. I had been able to move from host to producer with a growing independence along the way: the new station would try to enshrine some of yesterday's 'exceptions' to the rules that I had been able to negotiate for myself in tomorrow's rules for everybody. But first we had to win a seat at the ITV table.

I decided to talk the plan through the next day with Clive Irving. Clive had pioneered the 'Insight' style of journalism in the *Sunday Times*, and was now Executive Editor of IPC Magazines. More relevant to this particular encounter, he was a first-rate ideas man. We met at the Kardomah Coffee House in Kingsway, and he confirmed that as far as he knew the London opportunity was not being considered by anyone else. He thought that going for London would be a brilliant tactic if it worked, a possible public relations disaster if it didn't. Other people to whom I mentioned the plan dismissed it as impossible, but Clive was a tremendous sounding-board and source of ideas. We were clearly running against the perceived wisdom: that on the ITA's past record the incumbent companies could rely on a preference for the status quo, regardless of the severe criticisms levelled at ITV programming standards a few years earlier by the Pilkington Committee, which had particularly attacked what it saw as the cynicism of ITV's prevailing 'give the public what it wants philosophy'. I was not so sure. I thought Pilkington had made a greater impact at ITA headquarters in Brompton Road than most people gave credit for, and that the Chairman of the ITA, Lord Hill, would be of a mind to seize his opportunity. Particularly since the main criterion apart from financial viability would be merit – as defined by the ITA.

Two nights after the Rediffusion party, the Director of the Royal Shakespeare Company, Peter Hall, was scheduled as a guest on 'The Frost Programme'. I decided to try out the idea on him after the show. Peter was enthusiastic. If I went ahead with the idea, I could count him in. His reaction had a profound effect on the course of the bid. There was no specific contractual negotiation that evening, but I felt that if one of our most distinguished and sought-after directors responded in that way, then maybe the impossible could be achieved. I made a list of other talent we ought to be seeking, and on the Friday of that week I met with Ray Galton and Alan Simpson, the brilliant scriptwriters of 'Steptoe and Son' as well as 'Hancock', at Chez Solange.

The following week I invited Humphrey Burton, then Head of Music and Arts at the BBC, to lunch at Wilton's. Among the perceived weaknesses of ITV, according to Pilkington, was arts programming, and there was nobody better to fill this gap than Humphrey. I thought he would need time to think about my proposition and its implications for him, but in the event he said yes before we left the table.

The next day a drink at the House of Lords with Lord 'Ted' Willis, the creator of 'Dixon of Dock Green', was a splendid chance to catch up on the latest gossip – all of it about Yorkshire. The front-running names were those of Lord Goodman and the *Yorkshire Post*. More of an outsider was a group led by the Conservative MP Aidan Crawley, a former Editor-in-Chief of ITN, and reputed to have Sir Jules Thorn, the founder and head of Thorn Electric, as one of its members. Ted Willis himself had a loose affiliation with this group.

The next morning, 20 January, in an attempt to interest the *Economist* in our bid for London, I had breakfast with Alastair Burnet, who was then its editor. Alastair was immediately intrigued, although the *Economist* was considering a bid for Scottish Television as well. I urged him to come with us for London, and he agreed to check the matter out with his colleagues.

That evening I had a date at the BBC Television Centre with the Head of BBC 1, Michael Peacock, to discuss, among other things, an upcoming special edition of 'The Frost Report' which was to be the BBC's entry for the Golden Rose of Montreux that year. After a few minutes' discussion I changed the subject, and asked Michael if he would be interested in my plans for London, which I then outlined. I could see that he was attracted by the idea of going for London, but he surprised me by saying that he had had discussions with one of the groups which was aiming for Yorkshire, namely Aidan Crawley's. He said that his mind was by no means settled on joining any bid, but that if he did, he felt a certain moral commitment to Crawley, as the man he had talked to first. No decisions were taken at that meeting, except one – that we would meet again for lunch the following week. Leaving the Television Centre that night, I thought that the odds were at least fifty-fifty that Michael Peacock would be joining us. Those were far, far shorter odds than any I would have envisaged on the way in.

At the same time, I suspected that I was the last person he would have chosen to make him an offer he could not refuse. I had always had the impression that Mike did not particularly like me, perhaps because of my support for Donald Baverstock. At that time in BBC Television you were either a Baverstock man or a Peacock man, and I had never hidden where I felt my loyalties lay. We were thus somewhat strange potential bedfellows, but we both had something to offer the other that neither of us could get anywhere else.

On Saturday morning I drove out to Dover Park Drive, just off the Common at Wimbledon, to meet Sir Geoffrey Crowther. As Chairman of the *Economist*, he would be an ideal candidate for us as Chairman. And one of his other interests, the British Printing Corporation, could possibly be an investor. The imposing figure of Sir Geoffrey greeted me at noon in his dressing gown, and we sat down to discuss my ideas. He was interested in the chairmanship, but feared it might clash with the *Economist*'s other interests. The British Printing Corporation had too much of an overdraft to be able to invest, he added. However, we returned to the subject of the chairmanship, and he undertook to think 'long and hard' about it.

Later that day I visited Max Rayne of London Merchant Securities in Hampstead to see if he was interested in investing. He thought that might be difficult, as he had a number of obligations elsewhere. I took this to be a reference to his close friendship with Lord Goodman. Perhaps the most constructive part of the day came in a conversation with Clive Irving. We were trying hard to think of other names who carried with them irresistible ability and irresistible cachet, and Clive came up with John Freeman, then the British High Commissioner in New Delhi. It was a masterstroke. John Freeman had been a junior Labour Minister before he resigned with Aneurin Bevan and Harold Wilson in 1951 over the principle of cuts in the National Health Service. He had been a highly respected editor of the *New Statesman*, and I had watched his landmark interview series, 'Face to Face', years before I knew that I might one day want to be an interviewer myself.

I called John the next day, and followed it up that evening with a letter typed on a borrowed typewriter on board my BOAC flight to New York. I outlined the current situation as far as I knew it, and then moved on to what was in effect my starting point:

> This whole current reallocation, and the resultant heart-searching, only makes sense if Lord Hill can get a better programming unit out of it. It is the first moment when the ITA are really on the search for people who care about television, and who will have the opportunity to do something about it. It is here that a top-heavy group like Lord Goodman's – full of moguls – suffers its greatest problem. There is very much a perception about the grouping that 'we', the money, shall have the bulk of the equity, and as for 'them' – the people who have the grubby responsibility of actually making television – well, lob ten per cent of the equity or less down into the galley. For the first time this attitude could be a liability.

This point was central to my philosophy. I went on:

> The groups that are not thinking of Scotland are all, at the moment, going for Yorkshire on the supposition that none of the big four will be fighting in that quarter. But there is one other alternative more attractive than this – going for London in competition with ABC. There is a great advantage here. While admittedly one is taking on an established force, at the same time one is not attempting to 'dislodge' them. They have to prove their credentials for moving from the Midlands and North, as much as we have to prove ours for coming on the scene. And when, as the ITA must, one looks at ABC's output in terms of its general suitability as half of the ITA masthead, culturally and intellectually or otherwise it is not reassuring. Even more, the introduction of Fridays into the weekend schedule gives the opening for a complete re-definition of what weekend programming is about.
>
> Should such an application as this succeed, ABC would not have to be rejected totally. They could still be awarded Yorkshire with an order to assimilate a *Yorkshire Post* shareholding; the ITA have shown in the past that they are prepared to shop around and switch around in order to get the best elements.

I was coming now to the subject of John himself.

> Of course the London weekend application depends on one thing – an unstoppable *television* team. A team that individually has a track record that can reassure the ITA that they can show what the newspapers would call 'courage' without taking what they themselves would call a 'risk'. It is this group of people that we are on the verge of achieving.

Since, as I wrote the letter, Sir Geoffrey Crowther was mulling over the possibility of becoming Chairman, and Michael Peacock was mulling over the possibility of becoming Managing Director, I did not begin by offering John either of these positions. I suggested instead the role of Controller of Programmes or Head of Current Affairs, News, Documentaries and Education, whichever he preferred.

I outlined the programme people who were coming aboard, and added, 'There is no one who could control and direct the whole programme output and quality of this group as well as you. From the company it should be possible to begin altering within a relatively short space of time the whole shape of ITV programming in general. Clearly any public mention of your involvement is unthinkable, until you have left the High Commission, or at least arranged to leave it.' The solution I most favoured was 'simply the announcement of your name in the confidential submission to the ITA, such as happened to one or two people last time. This presents no problems, and there is no barrier to complete discretion.' I concluded the letter, 'Naturally if the responsibility you envisage differs from the one I have suggested, I would be happy to hear what you would prefer, as this is something on which I very much hope we can work together. Indeed, by doing so, I think we can bring London weekends a great deal closer.'

I signed and sealed the letter, and sent it on its way. After forty-eight hours in New York I caught the overnight flight on Tuesday in order to be back in London in time for lunch with Michael Peacock on Wednesday. At lunch Michael indicated that the more he thought about the idea, the more he liked it. Over the next few days I had meetings planned with the legendary financier Charles Clore and the former ITN Chairman Sir Geoffrey Cox, as well as repeat sessions with Peter Hall, Alastair Burnet, Humphrey Burton and Ray Galton and Alan Simpson; but it occurred to me that even more important than these was a meeting with Lord Hill. The word was out that Lord Hill was prepared to give informal interviews to advise potential applicants on the qualities the Authority would be looking for. But more than that, I needed the assurance that new consortia who chose not to aim for Yorkshire would still be welcomed.

The meeting was fixed for Tuesday, 31 January at 10.30 a.m. The day before, Alastair Burnet called me after seeing Lord Hill on behalf of the *Economist*. He was about to go to Washington to interview the Secretary of State, Dean Rusk, but before he left he wanted me to know that Lord Hill had said that he was turning over several permutations in his mind, amongst them the idea of a 'shotgun marriage' between companies if there was a case for making room for new ones. This was good news. It bore out what I had said in my letter to John Freeman about ITA-inspired mergers, and confirmed me in my belief that the ITA were contemplating a larger-scale reconstruction than most of the pundits predicted.

When I was ushered in to see Lord Hill, I began by using a Methodist phrase to refer to the three-times-a-week 'Frost Programme' and thanked him 'for the use of the hall'. Lord Hill was very complimentary about the series, and singled out some specific programmes. The rest of the meeting was going to be crucial, but delicate. As the patron of what could be one of the most lucrative decisions in the gift of any public body, he could not actively court or guide the would-be applicants. What I needed to know was, simply, was I really wasting my time in putting together a bid for somewhere other than Yorkshire?

Lord Hill gave me the answer that I was hoping to hear. He welcomed challenges to any and all of the franchises. He went on to intimate that he was indeed contemplating a shake-up of ITV. 'I'm telling the Authority – this is the moment when we have the power; if it's not done now, it never will be. I intend to see that a decision is made by the Authority entirely independent of the pressures of the ITA establishment.' He repeated what he had said to Alastair about 'shotgun marriages', but he was careful not to point to any particular opening, nor to ask me about my own plans, which I certainly didn't volunteer.

He did say, however, that he felt that a lot of the criticism of ITV came from people who only watched it at weekends, and that this influential group might be appeased with more skill on the part of the companies. There should be, he said, 'new ways of attracting a mass audience'. His overall attitude was hugely encouraging to what we were attempting to do. And he certainly echoed my own sentiment that the ITV audience was more often underrated than overrated, that given the chance – as they had been with 'The Frost Programme' – they would vote with their switches. The reluctance of the other major ITV companies to share Rediffusion's risk with the series showed – to my admittedly partial mind – precisely the reliance on the proven formula over the unproven idea which Hill was now increasingly determined to test.

Buoyed up by this meeting, the next day I decided to call John Freeman. It was beginning to look increasingly as though the *Economist* would opt for Scotland, which would rule out Sir Geoffrey Crowther as Chairman, and add a further major post which John Freeman might prefer. When I called New Delhi, John told me that he was in fact on page three of his response to my first letter, and also to a second one I had sent him which had arrived only half an hour earlier. After we had talked for a few minutes I suggested that I came out to India in the next few days to talk to him about the idea. It might have to be a day-trip, but it was worth doing. John said he would consult his diary and try and work out a time, which he would include in his letter.

When the letter arrived it began, 'First let me say that I have the greatest interest in and sympathy with what you are attempting. It would be a wonderful achievement for the practitioners of television to seize part of the franchise from the moguls and I should like to be associated with it. Whether I can is a more difficult question.' He discussed the likely length of his posting in Delhi and the possibilities of what might happen next. 'If, for example, I were asked to move on to another diplomatic post of equivalent interest and importance to Delhi, I should have to think about it very seriously.' John thought he would probably be summoned to London for consultations in May or June, 'so I feel fairly confident that I can be in a position to give you a fairly straight answer – possibly hedged about a bit as to date – by around midsummer. Is this remotely helpful to you? I am not clear what are the pressures of time. I am indeed sorry I cannot now see my way to going further. But I am in an awkward position and you have given me very short notice. I much hope that I may have left the door just far enough ajar for you to keep your foot in it. We should be delighted to see you, and though this is a desperately busy time of year,

Saturday the 11th and Sunday the 12th of February are virtually free. I will keep them so until I hear from you. Your reaction to this letter, however, may make you decide not to come. You may feel – I hope not – that I have in effect turned your proposal down. Or, if you don't, you may feel that no useful purpose is served by a meeting quite so soon. I must leave this to you. In any case I am most appreciative of your writing as you did and I hope you will appreciate that I am seriously interested.'

That was enough of an encouragement for me to make the trip to New Delhi. John added a practical postscript: 'PS. If you do decide to come to Delhi, I should be grateful if you would make sure that the press didn't get wind of your intentions. If an airport reporter should notice *where* you are going, he should not be allowed to suppose whom you are going to see!'

The cloak-and-dagger element gave a certain added spice to the proceedings, but the key problem was going to be one of timing. We needed to be able to put John's name forward – albeit in confidence – when we submitted our application by 15 April. I crossed my fingers and booked the flights.

We had just two and a half months to build the consortium, and raise the £6 million the ITA demanded to know was absolutely secure. In an imperfect world, we would be very happy just to raise the money. But in a perfect world, as many of the investors as possible should add to the strength of the consortium either by virtue of their prestige or by virtue of whom they represented. Clive and I had been puzzling over how we could indicate the involvement of the region in the new television company, and I had suddenly thought of the London Cooperative Society. At first they were somewhat astonished to be approached, but very soon their Chief Executive Duncan McNab had them concentrating on the proposal and eventually saying 'yes'. In terms of prestige and reputation, there was no one more respected than Sir Donald Stokes, who ran British Leyland. I went to see him at his headquarters in Berkeley Square. He said that it would be an unusual investment for his company, but that he would put it to the board.

On Sunday 5 February I had lunch with Michael Peacock and his wife Daphne. By now Michael's mind was almost made up that he wanted to join the bid for London. He had not made any commitment to Aidan Crawley, but Aidan had been the first person to approach him. How would I feel about merging the two bids, with Aidan becoming Chairman? Merging the bids might not present a problem, except that I was adamant about going for London and not for Yorkshire. As for Aidan being Chairman, I would obviously be able to say more after I had met him, but I did agree that we needed someone to serve in the position. However determined the ITA might be about a radical reconstruction, I felt that the idea of a twenty-seven-year-old Chairman might be a bit more than they could take. (I was, in fact, not expecting to serve on the board of the new company in any capacity myself, because under the broadcasting legislation of the time a directorship would have precluded me from appearing in programmes for the consortium.)

On the night of 9 February Richard Armitage very kindly held a dinner for me on the *Queen Mary* at Southampton. Many of the guests were from the world of television, but I told none of them of my plans for the next day – to return to London via New Delhi. I set off on Qantas flight 758 at 3.30 p.m. and arrived in New Delhi at 8.30 the next morning. John had arranged a dinner for the evening – an opportunity to meet a cross-section of people including the legendary Indian diplomat Dr L.K. Jha, who John thought would interest me. But meeting John himself was more than enough for me. As an interviewer he had been a role-model and a seminal influence. In the flesh he had an immensely imposing physical presence that the single over-the-shoulder camera shot on 'Face to Face' could scarcely do justice to, as well as the same awesome surgical skill with words that had been communicated by television.

Apart from the dinner, the rest of the time was reserved for talking through the consortium and its plans. We went over the timetable again and again. John's posting to New Delhi would probably end about July 1968, but he wouldn't know for certain until May or June 1967. And then there was the possibility that the Prime Minister might wish him to serve somewhere else. What did 'another diplomatic post of equivalent interest and importance to Delhi' actually mean? John felt that he could not refuse to serve, if asked, in Washington or Moscow. The more we talked, the more it became clear that the only possible way to include John's name in the application was by finding a position that could be held open for him, and being quite frank about why it was not possible to specify exactly the date on which he would be joining. We decided that we had cracked it, and that was what indeed came to pass. John Freeman was named – confidentially – as Deputy Chairman, and the date on which he joined us would be the conclusion of his service in India, unless he was asked to serve in Washington or Moscow, in which case he would join us following his service there.

Despite the time problems, John's enthusiasm was obvious, and I climbed on the Air India jet bound for London much heartened by what we had arranged, and its potential effect on our prospects. But whatever role we could persuade John to play in the longer term, it was clear that he was not going to be an immediate controller of programmes. We needed the right man, and we needed him fast. I found the choice a relatively simple one. First, with all the strength in our ranks from the BBC, it seemed to me that we should choose an ITV controller. The ITA must be able to see that we were combining experience and expertise from the ITV system with our new ideas. That led us directly to the Controller of Programmes at Rediffusion, Cyril Bennett. He was immediately intrigued, and agreed that we also needed a sales controller from ITV. He suggested Guy Paine, who was performing that role at Rediffusion. We were all slightly concerned for a day or two about the legal implications for Cyril and Guy if they did not declare what they were considering to their employers. However, we were told that since it was the weekend franchise we were applying for, there was no direct conflict. Plenty of indirect conflict, but no direct conflict. We had some key BBC names – with more, I hoped, to come – and now we had two key ITV names.

Mike Peacock had arranged the meeting with Aidan Crawley for two days after I got back. It took place in a small room off the Simon Ward on the tenth floor of St Thomas's Hospital. The reason for this choice of setting was that Michael Peacock had just had an operation on his elbow. I arrived a few moments after Aidan. For a couple of minutes we made conversation. Not having noticed what a 'county' accent Aidan himself had, I talked about a rather stuffy meeting I had attended earlier. 'I can't stand these people who talk about "prorrfit" and "lorrss" accounts,' I said. 'Yes,' said Aidan, 'that makes me very crorrss.'

The meeting itself went very well, and although no firm decision to merge was taken there and then, it looked as though we would all be working together in a matter of a few days.

By now Tom Margerison, the science editor of the *Sunday Times*, renowned for his technical flair, had also joined us. He had been talking to Lord Goodman about Yorkshire, but shared my conviction that London was not as impossible as it had been made to sound. We were still waiting to hear from Donald Stokes, but I asked Tom what he thought about another industrialist I admired, Arnold Weinstock. Tom thought Weinstock would be a particularly valuable recruit – not only for his knowledge of the industry from a technical point of view, but also for his managerial and financial expertise. I called Arnold at GEC, explained what I would like to talk to him about, and we arranged to have lunch at GEC on 22 February.

In addition to financial strength, we wanted our group to have intellectual weight as well, and we determined to approach two publishers – William Collins through its Chairman Ian Chapman, and Weidenfeld and Nicolson through George Weidenfeld himself; and two colleges – Magdalen College, Oxford and University College, London. We also decided to try to enlist the support of the two main weeklies, the *Spectator* and the *New Statesman*. And so it was that on 20 February I was back at the House of Lords, this time to talk to Lord 'Jock' Campbell, the Chairman of the *New Statesman*. I was immediately taken with Jock, and asked him to become a member of the Board on the spot.

The next day I met with Tristram Jones of the *Observer* to see if they would be interested in joining us. Interested Tristram certainly was, but I felt as we talked that he regarded going for Scotland as a somewhat more rewarding exercise than going for London. That night we gathered at Michael Peacock's house for a brainstorming session. In addition to Michael and myself, Cyril Bennett, Humphrey Burton, Tom Margerison, Guy Paine and Clive Irving were there. Michael and I explained the thinking behind the talks with Aidan – that a merger would bring us Aidan as Chairman and any of his putative group that we wished to enlist. Aidan himself was happy with the idea of going for London. The idea received general assent, though the only member of Aidan's group who everyone specifically wanted to keep was Sir Jules Thorn. While we were on the subject of future planning, Michael explained that he had decided that he would have to resign from the BBC before our interview with the ITA, or before we went public, whichever came first. It was a courageous decision, and one that everybody admired. We were aware too of the immediate added credibility that this would bring to the consortium. If a man as senior as Michael, with so much at stake, took the consortium this seriously, so would others.

Lunch the next day with Arnold Weinstock was a delight. He warmed to the David and Goliath element in our project, and he warmed to its aims. As far as he was concerned, most television programmes he saw on the sets his company produced were pretty dull. Anything that produced better television or more programmes that got people talking, had to be good for his business as well. At the end of lunch he said he would give me a confirmatory telephone call, but as far as he was concerned, GEC were 'in'. I passed this good news on to Michael and Aidan when we met at three o'clock, and then went home to Egerton Crescent to meet Donald Stokes at 5.15. He had good news and bad news, but the good news outweighed the bad. The bad news was that the Board of British Leyland felt that this was too unusual and too unprecedented an investment for them, but the good news was that Donald would like to make a personal investment himself, and would be happy to serve on the Board.

In addition to arts programming – where we had Humphrey Burton – there were two other areas in which ITV was generally seen as inferior to the BBC, by the ITA as well as by the public. One was children's programming and the other was situation comedy. We determined to go for the best in both areas

– namely, Doreen Stephens who was head of BBC's children's programming at the time, and Frank Muir, who was in charge of their situation comedy. After a number of telephone calls I met with Doreen and Frank on the same day, 27 February. Doreen came on board at twelve, and Frank Muir joined us at five.

There was still one yawning gap in our provisions. We had not yet found a merchant bank to mastermind the financial side of the operation. We had some willing would-be investors, but we needed more, and they all needed some very detailed projections and paperwork before they could actually sign on the dotted line. Aidan said he had been discussing things with the Honourable David Montagu of Samuel Montagu. How about him? This was, as it turned out, an inspired suggestion. After pointing out that there were only six weeks to go – six weeks in which to get legally binding commitments for £6 million – and adding that the whole thing was quite mad, David set to work.

At the beginning of March, while David was concentrating on preparing the financial blueprint and marshalling further corporate backers, the rest of the group was working on ideas for the strategy and policy of the company and beginning to draft answers to some of the questions in the ITA's questionnaire. Tom Margerison was meanwhile spending most of his time with the architects Cecil Elsom and talking to Marconi about equipment. All these figures were being brought together by the accountants, Peat Marwick Mitchell. We had two deadlines to consider. The first was a meeting of all backers at Samuel Montagu at ten a.m. on Wednesday 5 April, to discuss and agree financial estimates, capital structure and shareholdings. Estimates of the preliminary expenses agreed by Peat Marwick Mitchell were to be presented as well. That would allow a final draft of our submission to the ITA to be ready for 15 April – the last date on which it could be handed in.

David Montagu was talking with those investors who had already promised to support us, like Arnold Weinstock, Donald Stokes and the London Co-operative Society. The Imperial Tobacco Pension Fund had expressed interest, and they came aboard too. In general, all investors were being kept to a maximum of ten per cent, except for a fifteen per cent stake for Thorn. I decided to see if the Greater London Council Pension Fund was interested in participating – as this would be particularly appropriate in a London bid – and went to County Hall to meet with the GLC Chairman, Sir William Fisk. Unfortunately, Sir William was unable to move fast enough financially, as the GLC elections were in full swing, but my other objective in seeing him – the hope that the GLC Planning Department might cooperate in our search for a studio site – was warmly agreed to.

Arnold Weinstock was a great source of enthusiasm throughout this period. He came to lunch at 46 Egerton Crescent with Cyril Bennett, Tom Margerison and Clive Irving, and then on 10 April he held a think-in at GEC headquarters at Stanhope Gate, which he chaired.

Oddly enough, this benevolent enthusiasm caused a problem. Jules Thorn heard about the meeting, and felt left out. From the vibes we were getting, I guessed I ought to sit down and talk it out with him.

'I hear you had a meeting at GEC,' said Jules.

'Yes, we did,' I said.

'I suppose that Arnold Weinstock talked all the while, did he?'

'Well, not *all* the while . . .' I smiled.

'If I had been there, he wouldn't have talked all the while,' said Jules, and paused for a moment. '*I'd* have talked all the while.'

By the end of our meal, Jules seemed mollified, and his shareholding still seemed to be in place. Indeed, he offered his Financial Director, Ronald Davis, to assist in any way we needed.

That was how a lot of time was spent, keeping in touch with our early backers and seeking new ones. David Montagu approached Sir Christopher Chancellor, the Chairman of the Bowater Paper Group, and got an encouraging response. In all his various encounters, David stressed one crucial point: that this would be a company in which the programme-makers played a central role in policy; that the programme philosophy should be supported by all the backers to the extent of not paring programme costs in order to maximise profits, and that the interests in the company should be relevant but diverse. This bridge between private enterprise and the public service concept of television was to prove one of the most decisive elements in our consortium's make-up, and the principle was carried right through the shaping of the company. Thirty per cent of the equity was reserved for the company's executives and creative staff. This was a revolution in terms of incentives for any independent television company.

Everybody worked right through Easter without a break, because by the first week of April all the backers would have to have cost and profit projections, company and management outlines and programme papers. Donald Stokes called from Melbourne and Auckland with ideas. Meanwhile, Lord Willis's loose affiliation with Aidan had come to an end. Said Lord Ted, 'Throwing in the towel over Yorkshire was a mistake, and so was the consortium's new target of a London contract.'

On the evening of 4 April, the day before the vital meeting with the backers, the research and financial deals had been completed and a command meeting was held over dinner at Aidan Crawley's house in Chester Square to plan final tactics – first with the backers and then with the ITA. We discussed the final drafts – one, in a blue folder, covering all programmes and policy, the other, in a brown folder, the Peat Marwick cost and profit figures and much of Guy Paine's and Michael Peacock's work. There had been moments when it seemed that the figures couldn't be made to add up. One reason was that they had to be calculated on the assumption of building a station completely from scratch, since it could not be taken for granted that existing studios would be available. But in under six weeks a company based on complex components, and embracing the new technology of colour studios, was guaranteed as viable.

Not that we were without last-minute alarums and excursions. The dinner meeting was due to begin at seven p.m., after a financial briefing at six-thirty from David Montagu. When David arrived he reported a setback – just half an hour earlier, Thorn's office had called him to say that Thorn had decided to drop out. Working with 'young Arnold' had proved too much to swallow for the old campaigner. Both men were strongly individualistic leaders, and maybe there would have been pressures as they tried to work together. As the younger man, Arnold had no misgivings about the partnership, but Jules's sensitivity could clearly not be overcome. As we discussed this blow, we decided that we had to find one new backer to take ten per cent, and replace the other five per cent we had just lost by increasing other stakes by a smaller amount. And that had to be done by ten o'clock the next morning. As David went on his way, he said he had one or two thoughts . . .

During the dinner that followed, everybody said that they felt that the application draft answered all the questions adequately, but that because they were composed under pressure by separate groups, there was no coherent style. Clive Irving was asked to rewrite the whole document, bringing out all the details and ideas, but paring down any effusive passages and giving it unity.

I arrived at Samuel Montagu early the next morning. David Montagu had terrific news. He had acted quickly to find a replacement by approaching Pearl Assurance, and after just forty-five minutes of talking to its Chairman, Sir Geoffrey Kitchen, Pearl had agreed to come in. At the meeting with the backers David, Aidan and I sat at one side of a green baize table, facing for the first time the representatives of all the interests which had agreed to support the consortium. Iain Macleod was there to represent Lombard Banking, a welcome recruit. Everyone had copies of the blue and brown folders, and apart from odd questions of detail, the meeting passed very smoothly. It now felt like a very tangible group. Arnold Weinstock had the last word: 'I think there's a real danger that this bid might be successful.'

Clive Irving's final draft of the application document was complete by the afternoon of Saturday 8 April. Clive and I went through it with Cyril Bennett, Tom Margerison, Michael Peacock and Aidan Crawley. Our review did not end until 9.30 p.m. Clive had done a splendid job. All the key material was there – what he and I had written on programme policy, what Michael and Tom had written on the management and technical side

– but it had all been sharpened by Clive's editorial skills. The manuscript was as uncompromising as we could make it.

> The first, and inherent, principle of the Company's programme philosophy is a respect for the creative talents – for those who, within sound and decent commercial disciplines, will conceive and make television programmes. The second is respect for those who watch them, the audience. This means quite simply the belief that no audience is either mass or minority but a changing formation of groups responding both to what is familiar and what is unknown, with differing interests and tastes, each with a right to be served by the public air.
>
> We believe that these interests and tastes aspire to new experiences and that they should find such experiences through television. This means we are concerned not only with the sheer numbers of the audience, but why people watch and who watches. We believe that the commercial viability is strengthened by evidence of an active, perceptive and participating audience.
>
> These programme-makers have been united by a common belief that the quality of mass entertainment can be improved while retaining commercial viability. Independent television has the capacity to be as complete a public service as the BBC, by being able to deploy the output of a variety of companies, each with its own character, to make a comprehensive and balanced whole.

That was what we felt. It was also what the Pilkington Committee had felt. We thought it was probably what the ITA felt, too.

Clive rewrote some of the sections again, working well into the night, and the next day the two of us stood by while two typists typed out the whole document again. Aidan and Michael arrived after lunch for a final refining session which lasted well into the evening.

The document was now complete – with some intriguing gaps, which were deliberate. Against the entry for the position of Managing Director were the words: 'A BBC Controller is committed to join us. His name will be given verbally to the Authority. He will appear in person when the Authority examines our application.' Against the entry for Programme Controller we wrote: 'The Programme Controller of one of the major companies (now on three months' contract) will join the consortium on a three-year contract if our bid is successful. His name will be given in confidence.'

In answer to the question about what experience the members of the group had, we continued to maintain confidentiality where necessary, although the entry for Head of Music, Arts and Drama would not have needed a Sherlock Holmes to unravel it: 'Our Head of Music, Arts and Drama has, we believe, the most impressive record in the production of arts programmes – both for artists and for the general public – of anyone in television in Britain, perhaps the world.'

We talked about the particular nature of weekends: 'The cardinal principle of our programme philosophy for weekend television is that no single group of viewers, even if it be the majority, should be served to the exclusion of all other groups; no single area or type of television programming, even if it be the most widely acceptable to the majority, should be permitted to predominate; no one aspect of our culture emphasised or over-emphasised while others are neglected; no one single standard prevail.'

There were to be 'Frost Programmes' on Friday, Saturday and Sunday evenings, and I agreed to become exclusive to ITV for the first time, for a period of three years. There had been some disagreement or misunderstanding between Michael Peacock and me over the details of the contract, but that Sunday evening, before we left, Aidan assured me that Michael had approved our compromise. Indeed, the summary was in Michael's own fair hand. I had been able to demonstrate that I was being paid at a marginally lower rate by the London Television Consortium (as we were starting to call ourselves) than by Associated-Rediffusion and the BBC, and so Michael had become reconciled – at least for the time being – to what Aidan once called 'the corrrst of Frorrrst'.

In our document we talked about our plans for one-hour plays, arts specials, children's programming and adult education. The Public Affairs Unit had in mind a programme called 'Seven Days', making the news make sense every Sunday afternoon. There were adult education programmes on fringe medicine, and regional programmes like 'The Treasure House', a series focusing on the fascinations of the British Museum, and 'Poor Father Thames', a crusading programme about the state of the river.

Everything had been carefully costed, including our guarantee to spend £2.2 million on new technical equipment, with special guarantees from Marconi, and £2.5 million on our new television centre in central London. We were able to report that 'Sir William Fisk and the GLC Chief Planning Officer, Mr Collins, have offered the Company their full support and cooperation including their good offices in finding a suitable site. We now have three very suitable sites in mind and we also have good reason to believe that planning consents, etc., would be granted without delay.'

There were echoes of my conversations with Lord Hill: 'It is at the weekend that most of the people who talk about independent television watch it, and the introduction of a three-day weekend creates the opportunity for a new company to produce – or attempt to produce – a whole new concept of weekend programming.'

A list at the end of the document showed voting share capital of £15,000, non-voting share capital of £1.5 million, and loan capital of £3 million. Thus, with our £2 million bank facility, we were in fact half a million pounds better funded than we were required to be.

Thirty per cent of the share capital, £450,000, was reserved for our group of active television participators. Aidan Crawley and I had five per cent each, which meant I had to find £75,000 at once – as potentially problematical a task as finding something like £750,000 immediately would be to a twenty-seven-year-old today. Needless to say, I didn't have it to hand, so I availed myself of a borrowing facility that Aidan Crawley, David Montagu and I had set up for all our colleagues with Barclays Bank (France).

The loan was secured on the LWT shares, so there was no personal guarantee, but nevertheless with my financial background as a Methodist minister's son, the moment you sign on for your first serious bank loan – and it's for £75,000, the maximum amount you could win on the pools at the time, and four or five times what your father earned in his life – well, you do pinch yourself once or twice just to make sure it's still you.

The document was as good as we could make it in the time. Next day it went off to the printers to be run off. On 14 April, a day early, twenty-five copies were sent by Aidan with a covering note to the ITA. There were eighty foolscap pages in a plain white folder headed 'The London Television Consortium, a group brought together by Aidan Crawley and David Frost'. Stage one of 'mission impossible' was complete.

Stage two would be the formal interview with the Authority; and six days after the closing date for franchise bids – there were thirty-six groups applying for the fifteen franchises – the ITA telephoned Aidan to set our interview for 5 May. We were told to present ourselves at the rear entrance of the ITA's headquarters, for security reasons.

The following week was the Montreux Festival, and the annual battle for the Golden Rose. Focused on light entertainment, it had become the premiere world television competition, so it was an entry in most television diaries. However, this year my interest was rather more personal. The BBC entry was 'Frost Over England', a special edition of 'The Frost Report' which had been broadcast in the UK a few weeks earlier as a curtain-raiser for the second series. As the week went by, the reports of the screenings in Montreux sounded more and more optimistic. By Tuesday evening James Green in the *Evening News* had the headline, 'David Frost Tipped for Golden Rose'. 'As the programme ended one German TV chief rushed to me with the comment "Britain has won the Golden Rose. That is easily the best show of them all."' Next morning Peter Black in the *Daily Mail* said that the screening had 'promoted that special buzz of talk which one hears only when a programme has set an audience alight'. All very exciting, but as Peter Black pointed out, there were two more days of entries.

I was delighted that our strategy for the programme seemed to be working: first, we had decided that even countries with no tradition of lampooning would be able to enjoy – even admire – the sight of the English prepared to laugh at themselves; second, we had decided to pay people in Montreux the compliment that we regarded them as capable of understanding the English language. We left the linking at the same length as in our British shows, the only change being that I deliberately cut down on puns (with the exception of one about 'Carnaby Street, better known as Mincing Lane,' which we found ourselves unable to resist).

By Thursday evening the omens were still looking pretty good, although the Dutch show had gone down well. A ticklish decision had to be taken. The only way to be in Montreux in time for the announcement of the result and then later for the evening's ceremonies was to take an early plane from London. But there was a danger of arriving at the Palace Hotel in Montreux, where the festival was taking place, only to find a large number of journalists eager to note that I had had a wasted journey, and then to report the fact gleefully. We decided that the risk was worth taking, and producer Jimmy Gilbert and I set out for Montreux on the Friday morning. Our flight was slightly delayed, and when we arrived at the Palace Hotel, Jack Bell of the *Daily Mirror* was standing at the reception desk. 'Congratulations,' he said, 'you've won both.'

'What? What do you mean, "both"?'

'You've won the Golden Rose,' said Jack. 'And you won the Critics' Prize, the press prize, as well.'

This was more than I had ever dreamt possible after my previous trip to Montreux.

Clearly, it had been quite a morning. According to James Green in the *Evening News*, 'There were twenty-four programmes from twenty-two countries in the contest. And so that there could be no possibility of the twenty-seven international judges being "got at" they were taken off in the ship *Henry Dunant* after breakfast today. The ship cruised around Lake Geneva while the jury eliminated entries one by one. Then the boat drew close to shore, fired her flags-of-all-nations fireworks and Mr Werner Hess, President of the Jury, broadcast the result.'

That afternoon telegrams started arriving at the Palace Hotel, including one which read, 'Hip Hip Hooray – Mike Peacock', and another, 'OK you can be Chairman stop Marvellous, Marvellous – Clive Irving, Cyril Bennett'.

That night at the presentation ceremonies I managed to say thank you in all the languages represented at the festival. Well, it wasn't actually quite as casual as that sounds. I had taken the precaution of doing a little research before I left London, just in case . . . But I had delayed committing them to memory until I was absolutely sure that it was necessary.

By the time Jimmy Gilbert and I got back to London on Saturday, Jenny had organised a marvellous surprise party at 46 Egerton Crescent. And on Monday the consortium got another boost – the announcement that Michael Peacock had resigned as Head of BBC 1 and was now Managing Director designate of the London Television Consortium, who were applying to the Independent Television Authority to run London's weekend programmes. The Londoner's Diary in the *Evening Standard* quite rightly observed that Michael's appointment 'much increases this group's chances of getting a London TV contract'.

As Michael cleared his desk, David Attenborough, the Controller of BBC 2, came in to give him a cigarette lighter. Knowing one of Mike's frailties was losing lighters and matches, he said, 'Have this – you'll have lost it by the time you ask to come back.'

There were still several names which we did *not* wish to announce, so we tried to keep the story confined to Michael joining a group led by Aidan and myself. All things considered, security had gone remarkably well, in view of the number of people involved with the consortium or with whom we had had to speak. Early on, apparently, the whole programme staff had been leaked to Donald Baverstock, under oath of confidence. He told Stephen Fay of the *Sunday Times* how to get Michael Peacock to admit he was with the group. But, like others who knew the outlines of the group, Donald had thought it was going for the weekday slot. That sort of mistaken idea we never discouraged. And Donald, who also thought that Aidan Crawley was going for Yorkshire, forgot his earlier scoop and became as confused as everyone else.

Each night of that particular week (except one) I was appearing in *An Evening with David Frost* at the Adeline Genee Theatre in East Grinstead – in aid of the Adeline Genee Theatre in East Grinstead. The one exception, Thursday, was for 'The Frost Report', which was live at 9 p.m. each week. On Thursdays I normally did nothing but work on the script and polish the show. That particular Thursday, however, there was also a lunch meeting at 19 Chester Square, Aidan's home, for a last-minute rehearsal of what we thought we might be asked and what we thought we might reply the next day at the ITA.

The next morning, 5 May, I met Aidan at nine o'clock, and we were joined at about ten by the other members of the consortium who were to attend. In addition to Aidan and myself, there was Michael Peacock, David Montagu, Tom Margerison, Clive Irving and Ian Bowie from Peat Marwick Mitchell. We all arrived at the rear entrance as instructed at 10.45 for eleven a.m. The rear entrance of the ITA doubled, we found, as a garage. From there a lift took us up to what appeared to one of the team to be a deserted ballroom. We were led through this back into carpeted civilisation, where we sat down and waited. And waited. The wait lasted seventy-five minutes, full of the sort of nervous, rather respectable jokes that people make when they have a vague feeling that their every movement may be being monitored by some force greater than themselves.

Finally, Lord Hill did appear. 'I'm sorry we kept you,' he said, 'but the delay was not of our making.' We had no idea to what he was referring. We knew that the previous interview had been with Associated-Rediffusion, but we did not learn until later what John Spencer Wills, the Chairman of Associated-Rediffusion, had done. Spencer Wills was also the Chairman of the holding company, British Electric Traction (BET), of which Associated-Rediffusion was a wholly-owned subsidiary. Clearly nothing in the group's history had prepared him for the sort of interview the ITA conducted. He had astonished, indeed appalled, his colleagues by launching into an attack on the whole basis of their accountability to the ITA, and hence an attack on the very interview that was taking place at the time. How could the Authority consider disenfranchising Spencer Wills's shareholders? The implication of his attack was that 'running public transport services' was sufficient proof of their suitability to run a public broadcasting service. Spencer Wills did not have this sort of trouble when he wanted to extend the contract of one of his bus companies. When he said that if Rediffusion were to lose its franchise, the BET shares would be damaged, Lord Hill cut him off with the cry, 'Then why, in damnation, raise it?'

The effect of the Rediffusion debacle, though we of course did not know it at the time, was suddenly to turn the ITA's mind to doing just what Spencer Wills had put into their heads – replacing the London *weekday* company. Several times during our examination, hints were dropped about the weekday alternative. 'Tell me,' asked Hill, 'why was it that you applied for this particular franchise? Was it because you thought it was easy to get?'

'We didn't think it was impossible,' I said.

Hill pressed the point. 'Are we to understand you would accept any other franchise?'

Aidan, a little off-guard, replied, 'Yes.'

Enjoying his little trap, Hill leapt in. 'Oh, I see – you'd consider Channel or Border?'

'Not exactly – we think they are particularly well equipped for their job,' I said.

The range of programming talent we had assembled could easily have coped with the London weekday opportunity – far more easily, as it turned out, than with the severely constricted weekend franchise. After our interview with the ITA I noted, 'We probably did not show sufficient response to the idea of moving to the weekday.' Our overwhelming joint inhibition was Cyril Bennett and Guy Paine, who would have been aligning themselves with a bid against their present employers. They had decided, unlike Michael Peacock, not to resign in advance. When we revealed verbally to the ITA at the interview that both Cyril and Guy were ready to join us, they were visibly shaken. It added to their feeling that Rediffusion was in a rocky position. I am sure that had we clearly volunteered to take on the weekday franchise at the interview, we would have won it. However, in addition to the Bennett–Paine factor, we were also concerned not to undercut all we had said about our excitement at tackling the weekend challenge.

After our interview, we retired to the Hyde Park Hotel for lunch. The mood was one of subdued celebration. We could not recall any major errors that we had made, and the Authority had certainly seemed sympathetic to what we were trying to achieve. All we could do now was wait.

The ITA was living up to its reputation for confidentiality. The only clue we had – and we could only hope it was an accurate one – was in a piece by Richard Wagner in *The Times* on 19 May. He wrote, 'The new contractor most likely to be appointed is increasingly expected to be the Aidan Crawley–David Frost consortium, who are seeking the London weekend slot. Michael Peacock resigned from the BBC to join them, and financial support is coming from one of Britain's largest electric groups. A member of the ITA described their planned programme presentation as the most original and interesting ever placed before him.'

As it happened, the wait was not too long. On Saturday 10 June we were summoned to present ourselves at the ITA at 11.15 the next day. Michael Peacock was away on holiday and could not be reached, but Aidan, Tom, David and I were duly on parade the next morning. It was in its way a quite extraordinary ritual; separate groups of men entering the building through a rear garage to be briskly interviewed by Lord Hill and then despatched out into the world again. It was supposed to be organised so that none of the groups should see one another. However, as we arrived, we saw Lord Derby departing, looking very downcast. We learned later that TWW, his company, had been disenfranchised by the ITA, and Harlech Television (later HTV) had been appointed to take over in Wales and the West.

Lord Hill gave us the good news, reading from a piece of paper in front of him. We had won the franchise for London at the weekend. The only condition of our appointment was that we were to accommodate as shareholders three newspaper groups who had been unsuccessful elsewhere – the *Observer*, the *Economist* and the *Telegraph* – because the ITA felt they had a contribution to make to ITV. Since I had asked the *Observer* and the

Economist to join the consortium early on, we were delighted to oblige.

We returned to Egerton Crescent to tell Clive, and then a little later Aidan's wife, Virginia, the thrilling news. We went to the Ritz for lunch, almost walking on air. The sense of euphoria was increased by the multitude of phone calls that began to pour in from newspapers and from friends. By the middle of the afternoon the first dizzy flush had dissipated, and gradually we became almost overawed by the scale of the undertaking. That was just as well. From that moment we had little more than a year in which to build, virtually from scratch, a company that would ultimately employ more than a thousand people, build one of Europe's most modern television complexes on the South Bank of the Thames, and endeavour to live up to its very ambitious plans.

'The Big Shake-up' dominated the Monday-morning headlines. And the news which we announced on Monday – that Frank Muir, Humphrey Burton and Doreen Stephens would be joining us from the BBC, as well as Cyril Bennett and Guy Paine from Associated-Rediffusion – dominated Tuesday's headlines. That Monday-night press conference was understandably a happy occasion for us. Even the crowd joined in: 'Will you buy the Wembley Studios?' 'We would look at it very closely,' said Michael Peacock. Back came a voice, 'So would I.'

Meanwhile, Tony Jay coined a new 'Language Of' in the style of 'The Frost Report'. 'He is a loyal BBC man' meant 'He joined the wrong consortium.' But whether they came from the BBC or from Associated-Rediffusion, all of our recruits had one thing in common – they were now homeless. It was Arnold Weinstock who came to the rescue, providing them all with temporary office accommodation at GEC headquarters in Stanhope Gate.

The refugees moved in. One of the first items of business was to decide on a name for the company. At first the favourite was 'Thames', but a majority for 'London Weekend Television' gradually emerged. But that was a fairly simple and straightforward decision. Most of those to be made over the forthcoming months were going to be a good deal more difficult, and a good deal more controversial, than that.

In one newspaper interview I was quoted as saying, 'A television bid is a bit like a political campaign. It takes organisation, stamina, secret diplomacy and funds.' Maintaining the political analogy, London Weekend Television now had to deliver on its manifesto.

According to Cyril, tensions soon began to emerge. Because he had felt so isolated at Rediffusion after Cyril's defection, Bill, Cyril's chauffeur, decided to leave with him. In the car one day Bill asked Cyril, 'What colour uniform would you like me to wear – blue or grey?' Cyril had not previously considered the matter. 'The car's blue,' added Bill. 'All right then,' said Cyril, 'by all means, wear blue.' A couple of days later Michael Peacock called Cyril into his room. (Closed doors among refugees already implied the arrival of formality.) 'I understand,' said Mike, 'that you have been discussing chauffeurs' uniforms with your driver.' 'Not as such,' said Cyril. 'All that happened was that Bill was wondering about whether to wear a blue suit or a grey suit.' 'That,' said Michael with finality, 'is a Managing Director's matter.' A story like that made it sound as if the honeymoon was coming to an end. The partners would have to start 'working at their marriage' if it was to be a happy one.

Obviously it had not been a long-held ambition to found a network company before the age of thirty. The opportunity was there, so I decided to take it. Was that audacious? With the benefit of hindsight, maybe. But at the time it just seemed like the logical thing to do.

I suppose I approached it with a sort of optimistic innocence and a youthful determination never to limit my horizons, or my options. And then there was the sheer excitement of the challenge and the chase. There were no age restrictions or other barriers in this particular race – unless they were self-imposed, or you allowed them to be imposed by school or society. If the odds appeared to be against you, you forgot the odds. In the words of Anton Rupert: 'He who does not believe in miracles is not a practical realist.'

When I attended (as a consultant to the Board) the first Board Meeting of LWT later that month, it was the first such meeting I had ever attended. 'Board Meetings,' one friend had said, 'always spend the most time discussing the least important item – like the colour of the bicycle sheds or something.' I was confident that our experienced and distinguished colleagues would never make the same mistake. Imagine my surprise therefore when the longest discussion at that first meeting was about the size of the directors' fees – which it had already been agreed were to be waived!

During the first few months of 1967, quite apart from 'The Frost Programme' and then 'The Frost Report', there was another project that took up a lot of time – and did so very enjoyably. That was 'At Last the 1948 Show'. It sprang from conversations I had had the previous summer after the first series of 'The Frost Report' had come to an end. I had suggested both to BBC and ITV executives that Ronnie Barker, Ronnie Corbett and John Cleese were all worthy of, and ready for, series of their own. I was surprised by the unenthusiastic response. 'Oh, they're very good as second bananas, but not for a series of their own,' was the sort of comment I heard several times. This seemed to me to be nonsense. They were clearly capable of being top bananas at once.

In the end I managed to persuade Cyril Bennett at Associated-Rediffusion to broadcast three series, one starring each of them, which he agreed to do providing that I produced and packaged them. In this way I would share the blame if anything went wrong, and the series would not have to be regulated through the normal, rather stereotyped, channels at Rediffusion. It was also the cue for my company, Paradine, to become a fully-fledged (or at least semi-fledged) independent production company.

Back in 1967, independent production companies were almost unheard of. There were no Government-inspired quotas stipulating that broadcasters had to reserve twenty-five per cent of their output for independents. Far from it. Broadcasters sought to stamp out independent production wherever it threatened to appear. Unless you had signed an irresistible star, or bought the rights to an irresistible book, your chances were minimal. And even if you satisfied those criteria, and got a series on the air, you could forget about an on-screen credit for your company. The existence of the independent production company remained a closely guarded secret shared only by the production company and the broadcaster.

Of course, as a freelance, I was also an 'independent' in terms of my own career as well. After my one-year traineeship at Associated-Rediffusion, I determined that I never wanted to be a member of anybody's staff ever again. There are advantages and disadvantages about being an independent, but for me there was no doubt that the advantages outweighed the disadvantages.

You certainly have to spend more time on setting up your projects as an independent, on finding the finance and/or the buyer. Some of my friends and colleagues would say that is time that could be spent more creatively, and I can understand their point of view. However, I enjoyed the selling and persuading – which sometimes had to be pretty creative too! – and I enjoyed even more the freedom that went with it.

If you are both producer and performer in a series, there is nowhere to hide when things go wrong – no organisation to cocoon you from blame – but in all conscience, unless you are prepared to walk that particular plank, you are probably in the wrong business anyway. There is less job security, certainly, in being an independent, and more financial risk – and for some that combination may well be anathema – but there are potentially greater rewards as well.

The most important of these I have already mentioned – the freedom. That is life-enhancing in itself: to be the master of your own time is a blessed state indeed. With freedom comes flexibility: the ability to do more than one project at a time, perhaps for more than one network at a time, or in more than one country at a time, or in more than one medium at a time. Not only that. You can usually retain more editorial and executive control. You are less encumbered by bureaucracy, you can move more quickly, and you can change direction when you sense an inbuilt obsolescence that no one else is yet aware of.

In practical terms, you can hope to end up with a bigger slice of the cake in terms of ownership. Perhaps you also learn more quickly and more directly from your mistakes – because you have to. They're not absorbed in anyone else's organisation – the only person they are costing is you. And the sheer diversity of switching from producer to fund-raiser to performer to executive to author to salesman to consultant to editor is a pretty healthy insurance against boredom setting in, or the adrenalin ceasing to pump.

However, all of that assumes success. And with Ronnie Corbett, Ronnie Barker and John Cleese, David Paradine Productions was just beginning. I felt that Ronnie Corbett would be superb as a Walter Mitty-like figure, downtrodden by the world about him. Rosemary Leach became his wife in 'No, That's Me Over Here', with Henry McGee as his best friend. The series was written by Graham Chapman and Barry Cryer and caught on at once. For Ronnie Barker we prepared a series called 'The Ronnie Barker Playhouse', so that we could capitalise on Ronnie's versatility by giving him six or seven half-hour playlets by various comedy writers, and then focus on the most successful character for a further series. The 'winner' of the first series was 'Lord Rustless', written by Alun Owen, and we immediately commissioned a series of that.

But in early 1967 I was concentrating on the John Cleese vehicle. Graham Chapman was an automatic choice as one of the on-screen team of four, both in his own right and also because of his role as John's script collaborator. Next we signed up another ex-Footlights man, Tim Brooke-Taylor. For the fourth member of the quartet, John had a highly original idea – the on-screen debut of Marty Feldman. Marty had been one of everybody's favourite writers for years, and was invaluable on the first series of 'The Frost Report', but nobody had seen him until that moment as an on-screen performer. This was of course because of his unusual appearance, though that was wildly unimportant compared with his comic genius. I remember having a drink in a bar with Marty two or three weeks into the series. A viewer came up to him: 'No, don't tell me. Wait a minute, don't tell me. Are you the one – are you the one with a big nose and boss eyes?' 'No,' said Marty, 'I'm the tall one with a Cambridge accent.'

How were we going to link the show? We decided to use a parody form of linking, with a beautiful – but very dumb – blonde who genuinely thought that it was her show. Thus the cult of the lovely Aimi MacDonald was born.

Aimi: Some people have complained that this show is not satirical. So the lovely Aimi MacDonald is going to be hard-hitting and outspoken and prick the sacred cows of British pomposity. Here goes – Mr Heath's got a glass leg! Next week – Mr Wilson's legs!

'Why did you call it "At Last The 1948 Show"?' asked the press. 'Because 1947 was such a bad year,' responded John. On other occasions he would give a longer explanation: 'The whole title was a joke about television executives,' he would explain. 'At Last the 1948 Show, arriving in 1967: the whole idea was that it had been on the shelf for nineteen years while TV executives decided whether to run it or not.'

Television executives around the country did in fact play havoc with 'At Last the 1948 Show'. It was a cult success in the London area, with terrific word of mouth and reviews, and good ratings as well. However, to viewers in most of the ITV regions, the reasons for this metropolitan hilarity remained a mystery. ATV did take the first series, but not the second; Granada took the second, but not the first.

The show had some of the best sketches that John and Graham and Tim and Marty have ever written. The first show, on 15 February, began, as several of the series did, with a mock trailer.

'Tempestuous Tim Brooke-Taylor in the role of a lifetime. You loved him in *Song of Budapest*. You rode with him in *Desert Tigers*. You fought with him in *Old Vienna*.'

Tim: Why can't you leave me alone?

'Vivacious John Cleese and his fire-eating penguin as the eminent power-seeking QC, Sir Habbakuk Vulture Pant.'

John as QC (to witness): Where were you on the night of the fourteenth?
Witness: Why?
John (camp): I waited up all night for you and you didn't come home.

'From the pages of Leo de Groot's great classic, *A Better Life Through Herbal Tobacco*, Rediffusion presents – "At Last the 1948 Show". And introducing your hostess tonight, Aimi MacDonald.'

Aimi: Hello, I'm your hostess for tonight, and I know we're going to have lots of fun. Well, that's quite enough of me, and now I'd like to introduce the first item. The first item.

In the first show John had two opportunities to play manic figures of authority. The first was a doctor.

John: Ah, come in Mr Potter, very nice to see you again, sir.
Marty: My name is Wilson and I have never seen you before.
John: Splendid, splendid. I do hope you haven't been waiting long.
Marty: I've been waiting for just over two days. My appointment was for Wednesday at twelve. It is now Friday evening.
John: Yes, well, I'm afraid the last patient did take rather a long time. And yesterday was such a lovely day – actually I was hoping to get away early this afternoon – are there many people still in the waiting room?
Marty: There are over 120 people in the waiting room and it's a very hot day.
John: Yes, isn't it?
Marty: Fifteen people have already fainted and the ambulances are running a shuttle service.
John: Well, well, well.
Marty: There's also a dead dog in the waiting room.

For the luckless patient it was downhill from there.

John: Mr Wilson, how's the eyesight? Can you read this card?
Marty: Yes.
John: Well?
Marty: It says 'R P M D F D 2 4 9 4 2 S L J S J T I J'.
John: Yes, it's from my aunt in Brighton. She must be out of her mind.

Graham Chapman gave us his classic one-man wrestling match, and John gave us a *tour de force* as the secret service recruiting officer interviewing Tim Brooke-Taylor. The first show ended with 'Treasure Troves', a beautifully choreographed sketch based on the simple premise that one of a television panel of four experts (Dr Alice Groinbalm of the Brownonian Institute, played by Marty) would, whenever handed a fragile and irreplaceable antique, take it, examine it and, without any expression, drop it on the ground, where it shattered into fragments.

The next week Graham Chapman explained DNA in a style reminiscent of the Regella Sketch from TW3: 'Now, DNA is the genetic unit, that is, a kind of code which controls the way in which each individual cell is formed. It's rather like having a lot of building sites linked together by a vast telephone exchange all controlled by an enormous invisible traffic policeman, which we scientists call PC Harris.'

The same programme also featured the Sidney Bottle courtroom case, which dated back to John's, Graham's and Tim's days in the Footlights at Cambridge, and contained John's cross-examination of Arnold Fitch.

John: You are Arnold Fitch, alias Arnold Fitch?
Graham: Yes.
John: Why is your alias the same as your real name?
Graham: Because it's easier to remember.
John: You are a company director?
Graham: Of course.
John: Did you throw the watering can?
Graham: No.
John: I suggest that you threw the watering can.
Graham: I did not.

John: I put it to you that you threw the watering can.

Graham: I didn't.

John: I submit that you threw the watering can.

Graham: No.

John: Did you or did you not throw the watering can?

Graham: I did not.

John: Yes or no. Did you throw the watering can?

Graham: No.

John: *Answer the question.*

Graham: I didn't throw it.

John: So . . . He denies it!! Very well, Mr Fitch . . . would you be surprised to hear that you had thrown the watering can?

Graham: Yes.

John: And do you deny not throwing the watering can?

Graham: Yes.

John: Aha!

Graham: No!!

John: Very well, Mr Fitch, would it be true to say that you were lying if you denied that it was false to affirm that it belied you to deny that it was untrue you were lying . . . You hesitate, Mr Fitch . . . An answer please, the Court is waiting. Aha. Ha ha ha ha ha.

Graham: Yes.

John (amazed): What?

Graham: Yes!

John (tries to work out the answer and fails): No further questions, M'lud.

The third show contained what became known as the 'Bookshop Sketch'.

Marty: Can you help me with *David Coperfield*?

Bookseller: Ah yes, Dickens . . .

Marty: No.

Bookseller: I beg your pardon.

Marty: No, Edmund Wells.

Bookseller: I think you'll find Charles Dickens wrote . . .

Marty: No, Dickens wrote *David Copperfield* with two *ps*; this is

David Coperfield with one *p* by Edmund Wells. I should have mentioned that.

Bookseller: Oh. Well, we don't have it.

Marty: Pity, it's more thorough than the Dickens.

That was just the beginning.

Not that Marty was averse to causing that sort of havoc in real life. After one taping, we all went for a drink. At the bar there stood a classic English Brigadier figure, with stiff upper lip and stiff upper moustache on the stiff upper lip. Marty suddenly broke away from our group, walked over to the Brigadier, gazed him straight in the eye – or as straight as he could manage – and said, 'What's a nice girl like you doing in a place like this?' The Brigadier looked stunned. He just could not take it in. Nobody would dare to say such a thing to him, so clearly it must not have happened. He must be imagining the whole thing. Marty left his dumbfounded victim and returned to the group, his mission accomplished.

There were the 'Mayhem Gradually Revealed' sketches. For example, the railway sketch.

Official: You know I don't have an easy job, Spriggs.

Spriggs: No sir, I know you don't, sir.

Official: I suppose each week I am forced to investigate about thirty serious complaints against the railways.

Spriggs: Yes, sir.

Official: In a bad week, perhaps fifty.

Spriggs: Yes, sir.

Official: And each complaint takes a great deal of time.

Spriggs: Yes, sir.

Official: Last week, Spriggs, I had to investigate several serious complaints against you personally. About forty thousand.

Spriggs: Sorry, sir.

Official: That's a lot of complaints, Spriggs.

Spriggs: It is, sir – lots.

Official: I haven't been able to leave this office for days, Spriggs, days. As a result my wife has gone off with an Arab, the dogs are dead and someone's opened a Chinese restaurant in my bedroom.

Spriggs: I'm sorry, sir. Can I go now?

Some of the sketches were surrealist, and very much the forerunner of 'Monty Python' – like the dentist who clambers into the mouth of his patient with his assistant and prepares to blast a bad tooth with dynamite. In the 'Siege Sketch' a singer was discovered on a high rostrum, wearing a widely billowing floor-length evening dress. As she was singing, three or four policemen arrived, and the first one directed a spotlight onto the lower half of the singer's dress. She carried on singing, blissfully unaware, while the policeman shouted, 'All right, all right, Bugsy Finsterwald – we know you're in there.' A window-shaped panel opened in the singer's dress and Bugsy's face appeared. He fired at the police. The inevitable Catholic priest appeared.

Priest: Bugsy! I'm coming in for you.

Bugsy: Get back, Father, this is no place for a priest.

The whole drama was played out and Bugsy shot as he tried to escape before the end of the song. The singer continued blithely to the end of her number, took her bow to routine applause and left the stage.

There was a John and Mary sketch which was set in Malaya.

Mary: Oh John, once we had something that was good and pure and wonderful. What's happened to it?

John: You spent it all.

And all the while there was Aimi there to introduce 'her' show. On one occasion she greeted her fans seated at the piano: 'Hello, everyone. Old ones, new ones, gay ones, blue ones, happy ones, sad ones, good ones and long ones with nails sticking in them. But first, a sketch.'

In the sketch John Cleese was sitting quietly in a railway

carriage. A little man, played by Marty, joins him and begins to destroy all his attempts at quiet reading.

Marty: I spy with my little eye something beginning with B or J.
John: Quiet.
Marty: It's easy.
John: Shut up.
Marty: B or J.
John: How can it begin with B *or* J?
Marty: For various reasons which become apparent when you know the answer.
John: What's the answer.
Marty: Ectoplasm.
John: Ectoplasm?
Marty: Mr B.J. Ectoplasm. He works in our office.
John: But you can't see him.
Marty: You can if you have an appointment.

There was the World War II RAF briefing:

> Just one word about the radios . . . We hope to have them in the planes for you by next week, but tonight you'll have to keep in touch by telephone, so take along plenty of loose change. I'm sorry the maps are not up to date, but you'll just have to do the best you can. You fly over Gaul, and drop the bombs just north of the Holy Roman Empire . . . just under the 'G' of Visigoths.

There was the town planner with his model spread out before him who suddenly collapses, dying, on the floor and just manages to get out the words, 'The cathedral . . . was poisoned.'

The series was full of bullying psychiatrists and cruel secret service bosses sending men on doomed missions. In other sketches the little men got their own back by paralysing the upstanding senior figures with boredom at bus stops, in railway carriages, or wherever they could find them. From beginning to end, 'At Last the 1948 Show' was determinedly insane. Or, as

Brian Sington of the *Northern Despatch* summed it up, 'Much of the humour – especially John Cleese's contribution – is based on the unbalance of the mind.'

Each of the two series we did in 1967 ended with one of John Cleese's epic songs, performed with appropriate solemnity and accompanied by a full brass band. The first series ended with the ferret song:

I've got a ferret sticking up my nose,
(Chorus: *He's got a ferret sticking up his nose)*
How it got there I can't tell,
But now it's there it hurts like hell,
And what is more it radically affects my sense of smell.
(Chorus: *His sense of smell)*
I can see a bare-bottom'd mandrill
Slyly eyeing my other nostril,
If he jumps inside there too,
I really won't know what to do,
I'll be the proud possessor of a kind of nasal zoo.
(Chorus: *A nasal zoo)*

This was believed to be the first time that the phrase 'nasal zoo' had ever been used in a musical composition.

While some of the more surrealist sketches in 'At Last the 1948 Show' were a precursor of 'Monty Python's Flying Circus', others provided a blueprint for the BBC's two series of 'Marty'. And just as Ronnie Corbett did in 'No, That's Me Over Here', and Ronnie Barker in 'The Ronnie Barker Playhouse', John Cleese had proved himself to be a very top banana indeed.

The second half of the year began at the same pace as the first half. In July I made a second trip to India. The purpose of this journey was not, first and foremost, to see John Freeman again, though that was a delightful by-product: it was to see the work of Oxfam in action prior to launching the Oxfam Christmas Appeal back in England. There were two ports of call – Bihar, which was suffering a second year of deadly drought, and Calcutta.

I saw old people living on Gaya Station in Bihar State, waiting for the daily delivery of sacks of corn in the hope that a few grains would fall out and enable them to scrape together a meal . . . even if it took three days. I saw a mother in Palamau appealing for more food as her child lay dying on her breast. As one Oxfam worker said, 'I honestly cannot believe when I look at their scarecrow arms and legs that any of them are still alive.'

I saw villages where the houses were crumbling back to the mud from which they were made. I saw women crouching in the fields from early morning through the heat of the day, digging for small shoots of grass for their cattle. I saw children crawling on the ground, looking for grass to eat themselves.

And I saw the daily sight of the vultures circling in the sky. Waiting . . .

Bihar had a population roughly the same as that of England, and the emergency feeding was saving millions of lives. Less than one pound kept one person alive for the whole of the famine. Ten shillings saved a life for almost a year.

The sight of children suffering from malnutrition was impossible to forget . . . scaly skin, pot bellies and thinning hair which ought to be jet black and was going white; many of them with eye and ear infections.

An Indian Government official told me that they estimated that eighty per cent of the children under five in India were suffering from 'malnutritional dwarfism'. That was bad enough in itself in its physical effects, but there was also increasing evidence to suggest that lack of food caused damage to the brain as well.

I found that even more frightening – that there was the possibility that all over the world, children were not only growing up deprived of food, but as a direct result they were also deprived of the very qualities they were going to need if they were to improve their country's situation. It was the most vicious of circles.

There were, however, some signs of hope. In one village an Oxfam well, combined with agricultural aid, had brought about a situation where a local man could say triumphantly, 'The land regularly yields ten times the previous yield and its existence can no longer be endangered by a drought year.'

If the situation in Bihar was bad, Calcutta was even worse. The density of the population meant that there was more misery and starvation to the square foot than perhaps anywhere else on earth. There was desperate drought, but if it rained, many of the lean-tos in which millions lived would suddenly be flooded. There seemed no escape. But there in Calcutta, I met a saint. His name was Major Dudley Gardiner.

He was now working with the Salvation Army. Previously he had been in the regular army. 'During my last few years in the service,' he said, 'I always wondered what I would do when I left it. And during those later years I was involved in many social problems in the military. So I thought it would be a good idea to slip into social work. I spent so many years in wars, and I realised the only people who prospered in wars were the warring parties; the people who suffered most were the civilians. So I thought I would try and work on the civilian side.

'When I came to Calcutta – I'd been here many times in the military – I met up with some Salvation Army friends, and we started this project looking after fifty-five starving people in the Social Service Centre, North Circular Road. From that we have built up our programme to what it is now – some 5800 people.'

Major Gardiner's day began with the feeding programme for those who lived within walking distance of the Centre. A ticket check at the gate separated the starving from the merely hungry. Every applicant was interviewed, preferably in his own room, and the ticket that the social worker signed would guarantee one meal a day for three months, which would give the applicant time to make plans. Meanwhile the ticket was his or her passport to survival. 'I'll always remember,' said Major Gardiner, 'what they said to me the day I began this programme. "Gardiner," they said, "you're going to start this programme. Remember it's seven days a week, because people eat seven days a week." So I said, "All right, I'll try." And God has been very good to us and kept me going eight years. I haven't so far missed a day.'

That fact became all the more amazing when I discovered that Dudley Gardiner's legs had become infected by a disease called philaria, which causes painful swelling and inflammation of the skin. I only learned about it when I saw his legs being bathed and new bandages and ointment being put on to bring a measure of relief in the middle of the day. And the most exhausting part of his day was only just about to begin – the food run.

More meals had been prepared in the kitchens. This time the brim-full dixies were loaded into a jeep. Within the next five or six hours people all over Calcutta would have meals delivered to within a short distance of where they lived. The greatest need, of course, was in the poorer areas of the city, in the back streets and the slums in what were known locally as the 'bustees'.

Said Major Gardiner, 'A bustee area is a conglomeration of buildings, all tightly packed together with a road going in between. Made of mud and bamboo, and slate roofs, they are packed together in alleyways. In these sheds whole families and groups of people live. Sometimes eight or nine people in a room ten foot by eight. There is no electricity, there is no water facility, and no sanitation whatsoever.'

Conditions like that meant that many of the people living there were just too ill even to go to the Salvation Army Centre. I had the chance of sharing one of the food runs with Major Gardiner. I saw the faces that he saw every day. The face of a seventeen-year-old, the third daughter of a widowed mother dying of leprosy. A daughter whose mother had lost both her feet, and walked around on her stumps. A daughter who whenever visitors were coming to their little hovel, went around with a wet cloth to wipe up the pus.

I saw the face of Sumil Sarkar, a ten-year-old boy with his leg in a cast who spent his life sitting on a refuse tip waiting for Major Gardiner's food lorry to arrive.

At each of Major Gardiner's stops there would be a group of people waiting, estimating the time of day from the arrival of the lorry, while listening to the hungry cries of their children. After eight years, the lorry was in a bad way. Major Gardiner had asked Oxfam for a new one, but their resources were under such pressure that they could not afford it.

The work that Dudley Gardiner was doing was clearly worthy of the epithet 'saintly' in its own right. But there was another reason why I felt that I had met a saint. Dudley Gardiner was not a religious zealot whose every sacrifice was bathed in the glow of an abiding faith in eternal life. He was probably more of an agnostic. He was not an unworldly, unrealistic dreamer. Most missionaries carrying out unbelievably exhausting, harrowing work have their faith to support them, but Major Gardiner said simply to me, 'You know the most difficult thing about this work? It's so boring. And so lonely. There is often no one to talk to, no one with whom to discuss books or music.' Then, in his darkest moments, he would remember the need, remember the faces, the hands outstretched that he had seen earlier in the day, and he would know again where his duty had to lie. I never saw Dudley Gardiner again, but I have never forgotten him. And I never will.

The new series of 'The Frost Programme' began in the last week of September. If the *leitmotif* of the first series had been a number of God-related programmes, that of the second series was a number of drug-related programmes. You could not go very far in 1967 without finding yourself in the middle of a debate about 'hard' and 'soft' drugs, and 'The Frost Programme' was no exception.

The summer of 1967 had been the Flower Power summer in London. With the release of the Beatles' 'Sergeant Pepper' album in June, popular music too had moved into the psychedelic mode. Kaftans, bells, candles and joss sticks were on sale all over Britain. The Beatles themselves, by this point, had dispensed with drugs (or they had become a more marginal concern), and had begun exploring the possibilities of Eastern mysticism. They had not been the first to experiment with hallucinogenic drugs, nor were they the first Westerners to become involved in Eastern mysticism, but in both cases they were role models. They had recently indicated their interest in Transcendental Meditation by joining the Maharishi Mahesh Yogi on a course at Bangor in Wales. Now the Maharishi was arriving in London on the Friday of our first week of 'Frost Programmes'. I arranged an interview with him at the airport, and invited John Lennon and George Harrison to come to the studio to talk about the impact that the

Maharishi and Transcendental Meditation were having on them. To my delight, they decided to make their first ever talk-show appearance on Friday 29 September.

When you first met the Maharishi, his high-pitched giggles were somewhat off-putting. Indeed, they remained that way throughout the conversation. The Maharishi said that TM was different from other meditative practices because it did not try to control the mind. Instead it 'uses the natural faculty of the mind to go to a field of greater happiness'. This was different to just sitting and thinking about life: 'Thinking is swimming on the surface of the mind. Thinking is like contemplation, but TM takes the mind deep into the thinking process . . . to the source of thought.'

When I asked how this was done, the Maharishi could only come up with a rather esoteric maritime analogy, which may well have left viewers less enlightened than before I had asked the question: 'See, a thought starts as an air bubble from the bottom of the sea, and coming up it becomes big enough to be appreciated.' But appreciated as what? And how?

I asked him whether he presupposed that every mind was naturally good: 'What about a mind that would naturally take a bad course? Or do you not think that any mind does that?' The Maharishi did not see it as a matter of good or bad, but of less and greater happiness, which he explained with a geomorphological analogy complicated by a musical metaphor: 'It is a positive experience, not an understanding. Something like this slope. If the slope is there what are floods? If the greater happiness is there, more better melody is there. The mind immediately shifts to that direction and experience.'

I was not much wiser at this point. This was not necessarily because I felt that all the Maharishi had to say was worthless, but the combination of his imperfect English and the different way that people from the East convey spiritual ideas rendered much of what he had to say esoteric at best. Towards the end of our interview another concern struck me: if the guru could not explain himself clearly, how would two of his newest disciples fare?

That evening the second half of the programme put my fears

to rest. John Lennon and George Harrison proved much better able to communicate the virtues of TM than their spiritual leader. Asked first what they had gained from TM, John and George both said that it had given them greater energy – or rather, as John said, 'I've got the same energy as before, but I know now how to tap it.'

I asked George about the technique of TM, and in particular the role of the mantra. 'Well, each person's individual life sort of pulsates in a sort of rhythm so they give you a word or a sound, known as a mantra, which pulsates with that rhythm, so by using the mantra rather than a thought – because the whole idea is to transcend to the subtlest level of thought – so you replace the thought with the mantra and the mantra becomes more subtle and more subtle until you've lost even the mantra and then you find yourself at that level of pure consciousness.'

The problem was trying to express what the experience was like. As John said, 'It's like trying to describe to somebody what chocolate tastes like.' I acknowledged that this was the perennial problem of explaining one's religious experiences – it was trying to 'express the inexpressible'.

Next I asked them about the relationship between TM and drugs, quoting Paul McCartney, who had said that the feeling meditation gave was a sort of permanent version of what drugs could give only temporarily.

George and John said that drugs could give you a glimpse of another level of consciousness: 'It can heighten your perception a little, but just to take the drug and hope it's going to bring that subtlety is a mistake, you know, it will never work.' I asked them whether this was why they had stopped experimenting with drugs. They said they had dropped them before meeting the Maharishi. 'We'd had enough acid, it had done all it could for us, you know, there was no going any further. It only does so much.' George said that you could not find your true self through drugs. This subtler level could only be achieved through meditation or from yoga.

I then turned the discussion towards the apparently exclusive emphasis of TM with the self. 'If you compare this with something like Christianity, which is concerned to try and find serenity to give energy through the Holy Spirit or whatever, at the same time a good fifty per cent of that is concerned with one's responsibility to other people. There doesn't seem to be any of that in this.'

John and George insisted that TM did not neglect the outgoing part, but their answers indicated that there was not much specific evidence of that. What they were really saying was that Christianity and all other religions were not very different.

'Everything you read about,' said John, 'or all the religions you know, they're all the same. You know, it's just a matter of people opening their minds up . . . Buddha was a groove, Jesus was all right . . .'

Leaving John's pantheistic theology for a moment, I asked how the Maharishi and TM could help the world's problems. George replied: 'It's the same thing that Jesus said about go and fix your own house, and everything's fixed up then. If you sort yourself out, if everyone was to go home and find out for themselves and fix up all their personal problems, then no other problems exist because they only cause the problems that exist in the world. It's all each person, individual, it's just up to him to do it.'

'But,' I asked, 'when each person goes deeper and deeper within himself, will he find good thoughts below?'

Lennon could only say that TM is 'for the good . . . and it's simple. So they're bound to be a bit better than they were, whatever they were before they did it.'

The press interest and the public interest generated by the interview led to our inviting John and George back to the next programme the following Wednesday.

I asked them whether TM and the Maharishi had changed their lives. They said it had not altered their attitude to money. They had already found out that money was not the answer. Said George, 'We managed to get lots of material things at quite an early age, and it was good really because we learned that it wasn't it; we still lacked something, and that something is the thing that religion is trying to give to people.'

George Harrison could have been speaking there on behalf of

an entire generation. The Beatles may have been Sixties heroes, Sixties icons, but they shared with their contemporaries the same sometimes frenzied search for inner peace. The young had lost faith in traditional authority (spiritual and secular), or, more to the point, they may not have had it in the first place. They had turned away from their cultural inheritance, leaving a vacuum, a need that had to be met. The young needed certainties, supportive beliefs to replace the ones they had either discarded or never had. Hence the search for gurus – although, ironically, most of the gurus proved far more ephemeral than the Beatles themselves.

After about twenty minutes I asked some specially invited members of the audience to join in the discussion, including another exponent of TM, John Allison, and the writer and barrister John Mortimer, who was very critical of the recent vogue for meditation. The discussion that followed focused on the assertion made by Mortimer that TM was inward-looking and did nothing to help others or solve the world's problems. What worried him was that TM seemed to be 'tremendously self-involved and finally tremendously selfish, and the idea of sitting very quietly perfecting yourself while everybody else goes to hell around you seems to be not really –'

John and George both interrupted to protest that TM need only take up twenty minutes each day.

'What I think one needs,' said Mortimer, 'is a little well-aimed loathing at things like President Johnson and Ronald Reagan and so on, and not sitting in San Francisco watching the flowers grow and letting Governor Reagan be elected perhaps as the President of the United States.'

John said that watching the flowers grow was not what they were talking about. The point of meditation was to 'expand the conscious capacity of the mind for right action'.

John Mortimer viewed the universe as 'a soulless biological thing, and it is for us to improve it, and we're not going to improve it if we're going to stay quite still enjoying peace and perfection'. His motivation was 'to do an imperfect best to improve the lot of other people'. He was attempting to re-assert the primacy of the group in the age of the individual.

I asked John and George if they thought that what John Mortimer was saying about meditation being selfish was fair. John Lennon replied, 'I don't see how it's selfish. We've no need to be here, you know, I mean we don't sort of dig doing TV for the fun of it. We're here just because we want, you know, we believe in meditation, so we're not being selfish.'

'Well,' said John Mortimer, 'we've got no need to be here either, really.'

'Well, look, let's all go home!' I suggested.

John Mortimer moved on to another point: 'Why should this abstract experience be any more valuable than any other experience? George Harrison talked about a "bliss experience". Well, you could have a bliss experience by drinking a hot bottle of whisky.'

'Yes, but a hell of a non-bliss experience the next morning,' I said. But what was the difference between the two experiences?

George replied, 'Because the bottle of whisky one is relative, could be relative bliss depending on how intoxicated you get, whereas with meditation you go beyond this ordinary experience that's on the relative level of experience; it's beyond that. This is why you can't tell the people about it, really.'

John Allison chimed in: 'It's just something that you have got to try. I cannot tell you what a strawberry tastes like. In the last resort, if you want to know what a strawberry is like, eat it. You may like it at the end of it, or you may not.'

'But it doesn't give the strawberry some translucent, mystical power . . .' said John Mortimer.

I concluded the programme by asking John Lennon, 'What is then the difference would you say between John Lennon before meditation and John Lennon after a few weeks?'

'Well, before I wouldn't have been here. I've got more energy and more happiness. I don't have an intelligence, though! I'm just happier, you know, I'm just a better person. And I wasn't bad before.'

'I'll second that,' said George.

The two programmes had told me something about meditation, and a lot about the two Beatles. They were however equally revealing about the Sixties. Indeed, it was a discussion that could probably only have taken place in the second half of 1967. The combination of drug-taking, idealistic politics, pacifism, hippie culture, getting back to nature, Eastern religion and 'finding oneself' made a unique cocktail.

On a superficial level the hippie phenomenon was a fashion cult like that of the Teds or the Mods, with its own distinctive clothes and music. At another level drugs were the predominant concern. This was about escapism, the search for fantasy, the unadulterated pursuit of pleasure. At a deeper and more serious level being a hippie was about 'finding oneself', the exploration of 'inner space'. Initially drugs were the vehicle for this exploration, but their possibilities and limitations led to an interest in Eastern mysticism, which seemed to offer a safer and more certain ride to self-knowledge. That's not to say that all hippies gave up drugs when they became interested in meditation, but hippie culture acquired a spiritual dimension. John's and George's personal odysseys reflected the search that was being undertaken by millions of their fans – to sort out what felt good from what merely sounded good.

The drug debate in 1967 was fuelled by two very different points of view. On the one hand there was the traditional view of the authorities – and probably of Middle England too – that the emerging drug culture was a cause for alarm. There had undoubtedly been a marked increase in the use of drugs in the Sixties. In the early Fifties cannabis use in Britain appeared to be mostly confined to the West Indian immigrant community and the jazz scene. Judged by the number of prosecutions, cannabis spread over that decade, but did not begin to increase rapidly until 1965. In 1967 prosecutions for cannabis doubled to 2393, and by 1970 the figure had risen to 7500.

Apart from the West Indian community, until the 1950s most drug dependants were middle-aged, and had become addicted as a consequence of medical treatment or, like doctors and nurses, because of their easy access to drugs. But in the late Fifties a new type of drug dependant had begun to emerge. They were the 'proselytising junkies', actively encouraging others to adopt their drug use and their lifestyle. There had also been a marked increase in the early Sixties in the use of amphetamines, the favourite drug of the Mods, and from 1965 in the use of the hallucinogenic drug LSD, which was not proscribed at first, but was included under the provisions of the Dangerous Drugs Act in 1967, by which time it was present in the country in significant amounts. The police and other authorities were greatly concerned about a drug problem that they feared could develop to North American proportions.

The other point of view – that of what was sometimes called the 'counter-culture' – flourished in the liberal, permissive atmosphere that pervaded most aspects of life in the Sixties (though not everybody's lives in the same proportion). It was a Sixties nostrum that repression caused greater problems than permissiveness, that there should be no taboo subjects. Most people were broadly in favour of more openness, but some wanted to push the boat out much further than the rest. They wanted to go beyond discussing the rights and wrongs of a matter, to remove all moral restrictions – making the question of whether or not to take drugs or have an abortion simply a matter of personal choice: 'Anything goes – as long as anybody wants it.' Such people were in a minority, probably even among the so-called intelligentsia or opinion-formers, but such was the mood of the times that they had an influence out of all proportion to their numbers. Quite often I felt out of sympathy with this intellectual pressure group. I certainly felt that it was irresponsible to advocate the legalisation of drugs, and wanted to see the advocates of this change properly challenged. Such an opportunity occurred on 25 October, on the eve of a new report by the pharmaceutical industry on drug addiction.

One of the key landmarks in the Sixties drug debate had been the recent full-page advertisement in *The Times* calling for the legalisation of marijuana. It began with the statement, 'The law against marijuana is immoral in principle and unworkable in practice,' then set out what it said was the contemporary medical view of the drug, and 'drew attention to the disproportionately heavy sentences available for those convicted of possessing the drug – ten years' imprisonment or a fine of £1,000'. The advertisement was paid for by the Beatles and was signed by sixty prominent names from the worlds of science, medicine, politics and the popular arts.

To discuss the subject on the programme were one of the key signatories of the advertisement, the Labour MP Brian Walden, and one of its strongest critics, Quintin Hogg. Quintin Hogg opened the discussion by emphatically stating that he thought it 'extremely irresponsible' of Walden as an MP 'to sign and compose an advertisement of that kind now on the subject'. Walden replied by accusing Hogg of attempting to capitalise on the fear, ignorance and prejudice surrounding drugs. He added that marijuana was not an addictive drug, that nobody had ever died from it, and that there was no evidence that it hooked you on any other drug.

There seemed to me to be one central point in this discussion. I asked Walden how he could prove that marijuana did not ever lead on to heroin. He replied that he did not say that marijuana did not ever lead on to heroin, but that it was false to claim that it is bound to lead or usually leads to it. Other things like alcohol could also lead to it, he added. It was a question of the addict's personality. That was not good enough, I felt. I said that if there was any chance that marijuana might lead to heroin addiction, then it was insane to propose this legislation. Walden protested that I was presupposing 'that there was a physiological line between the two drugs'. He said that at the heroin addiction unit in his Birmingham constituency (All Saints) marijuana was used as a non-addictive drug to wean addicts off heroin. I said that if there were close links between marijuana and getting off heroin, it was quite reasonable to be worried that there might be close links between marijuana and getting on heroin.

Quintin Hogg then said that 'almost everything that Walden has said is misleading. In the first place, what is dishonest about that is not to disclose the fact that we are bound to legislate in the form we do by the Single Convention on Narcotic Drugs [signed in 1961] which is ratified or acceded to in all the principal countries in the world . . . And the second fact that he did not disclose is that on reputable authority, that of existing heroin addicts, ninety-five per cent started on marijuana.'

At this point I asked a doctor sitting in the front row of the audience whether the young addicts he had treated 'passed through marijuana' or not. Citing a survey he had made of heroin addicts, he was of the opinion that 'the drug cannabis is a dangerous one, not necessarily in capital letters, because it does in an appreciable number of cases precede their addiction to heroin'.

I asked one of the organisers of the advertisement, Steve Abrams, an American and a prominent figure in the Sixties underground scene in London, who was also in the audience, to comment. Abrams said, 'Well, the first answer is that any correlation between the use of cannabis and the use of heroin would be due not to cannabis but to the condition of the prohibition of cannabis, which forces cannabis smokers to go into the black market, where heroin may also be available, to buy their cannabis.' I asked Abrams whether he smoked cannabis, and if so where he got it. Abrams said he took cannabis prescribed to him by a doctor: 'Anybody can get their doctor to prescribe Cannabis BPC.' I asked him why his doctor agreed to give it to him. Abrams replied casually, 'Well, you have to ask him about this, because that's obviously a professional matter, but perhaps he's prescribed it for paranoia.'

Hogg interrupted and, like a QC sitting in the High Court, said gleefully, 'That's a very considerable admission, isn't it? No more questions of this witness!'

I made the point to Abrams that 'the step from no drugs to heroin is an inconceivably large step, but the step from some drugs, even "soft" drugs – which is a subtle phrase to sound like "soft drinks" – the step from soft drugs to hard drugs is a *psychologically* easier step to take.' Abrams retreated from answering this point by returning to his assertion that marijuana was less harmful than alcohol.

All these comparisons between marijuana and alcohol seemed to me to miss the point. Even if we granted that marijuana was no more harmful than alcohol, society just could not cope with as many marijuanaholics as it already did with alcoholics. However, it was time to move on, so I merely contested the point, and said that his assertion would be very difficult to prove.

I then produced a photograph of a young boy. 'This is a picture of Peter Spackman at the age of seven or eight. This is another picture of Peter at the age of eighteen. And this is the headline about Peter this morning in the press: "Purple Heart Pills Led Boy to Heroin and Death at 20". Mr George Spackman is here with us now. Let me say straight away, George, I think it is very brave of you to want to talk about this.'

Spackman replied, 'It's not brave, it has to be done. I've got nothing to lose. People who sign petitions like that are irresponsible fools, with intellectual and irresponsible talk, and I say it with a dead boy, and I hope they want to go back to their cannabis and leave the country.' George Spackman then told us the story of his son's addiction, which began with purple hearts at the age of about seventeen, then other 'soft' drugs like amphetamines and marijuana, and finally heroin. He spoke of his son's compulsion for drugs despite the misery it caused him, his own sense of helplessness and of the fruitless efforts of 'doctors, psychiatrists, probation officers, policemen, friends, padres'. Spackman said that there were 'no soft drugs at all . . . Soft drugs, all drugs, at least in Peter's case, certainly killed him.'

Brian Walden said that his interest in the question arose out of his desire to assist hard-drug addicts. He felt desperately sorry for George Spackman, and would not say that you would not get similar cases. But Peter Spackman could probably, though not definitely, have been helped if he had attended a drug addiction centre like his in Birmingham. But he added, 'You won't get . . . addicts to come along and receive assistance if the whole thing is conducted in this kind of atmosphere, in which the subject is taboo, in which all the traditional values are going to be dragged up, in which there's going to be bitter prejudice against anybody who wants to help the addict, a feeling that the whole idea of discussing drugs rationally is somehow wrong and immoral and ought to lead to you being kicked out of the House of Commons, or kicked out of the country. That will do no good. I don't pretend, unlike Mr Hogg, that the medical evidence is definitely either way.'

I interjected, 'But if it is not definite either way, how can you propose that these laws be repealed, and how on earth is your treatment helped by the law making marijuana more available?'

Brian replied that his view on the matter was not the same as Steve Abrams'. 'Different people sign motions for different reasons. What I want, and still want, is a public discussion of what's involved. What that would reveal is an enormous conflict in medical testimony about its general effects. It would also show that there are some valuable uses for cannabis.' Pressed on the point, Walden said that personally he would not at that moment make marijuana legal. I said to him that 'signing that statement has given it added authority, and you've got to read between every line to realise that some people feel as you do. You have added power to the case of people you don't agree with, it seems.'

Walden denied that this was so. He agreed 'very substantially' with Abrams, who he was sure was not making a plea for general legalisation. (I was not so sure.) He reiterated that what he wanted was first a more rational discussion of the subject, and second, citing the case of a young West Indian immigrant who had received a five-year sentence for a first offence of taking marijuana, for the law to treat the taking of marijuana more leniently than the taking of heroin. I said, 'Everybody wants marijuana smoking to be legally treated very differently from heroin . . . But the point is that basically you're with us. You are saying that, until there is research and until we know, we can't dare repeal this law. But Mr Abrams was saying fifteen minutes ago, "Repeal it now and we'll find out, ask questions later."'

Shortly afterwards the discussion ended, with Hogg and Walden again at loggerheads. The whole discussion had been a reflection of how views on the drug issue had become sharply polarised. This was one subject on which I took the more traditional view. I thought that Walden was right to demand that drugs should not be treated as a taboo subject, but I felt that he was wrong to have signed the advertisement and thus associated himself with the trendy and ill-thought-out permissiveness of people like Abrams.

It was clear from the scores of telephone calls that were already jamming the Associated-Rediffusion switchboard that, out there in Middle England, a great many viewers felt that airing George Spackman's story and his observations upon it was a real public service. G.K. Chesterton's 'people of England who have not spoken yet' did not buy the arguments of the counter-culture. They felt that they did not often have the opportunity to make their thoughts known on television or in the other mass media, and that our programme was one of the few vehicles for doing that. In the midst of the liberal Sixties, it was a reminder that people could have views imposed upon them not just by Government or authority, but also by 'opinion-formers' who were all too often able to monopolise the media. In a sense we had identified a fault in the liberalism of the Sixties – its debates tended to be conducted by elites. I was all for a more liberal society, but you could not have a truly liberal one unless everybody was allowed to participate in it. 'The Frost Programme' was just one attempt to meet this deficiency. We hoped that LWT would be another.

The drug problem remained in the headlines, and later in the series we felt we had to return to it again. There had been reports in the press about a maverick doctor who prescribed drugs to addicts in London Underground stations and cafés. In view of strong evidence that the over-prescription of drugs by doctors was a major reason – indeed perhaps *the* major reason – for the alarming increase in heroin addiction in Britain, this was obviously a case that merited investigation. We invited the general practitioner, a Dr John Petro, on to the programme to comment on the press stories about him. After I had met with him to explain the format of the programme and what we had in mind, he consented to appear.

In introducing him I said that Petro (or simply 'the doctor', as I referred to him throughout the programme) had chosen this occasion to deny the allegations made against him in the press. The most important one was that he had over-prescribed heroin and cocaine. He said that he could only have done so 'unwittingly, on possibly very rare occasions'. I then referred to a report in the *Daily Mail* that he prescribed heroin and cocaine to a patient, a plumber, who was actually off those drugs and on the substitute withdrawal drug, Phyceptone, without a physical examination. Petro admitted that he had not carried out any sort of physical examination, but said that he had taken 'good care to find out all about him'. After I questioned him it transpired that taking 'good care to find out all about him' did not involve making even routine enquiries with the patient's other or former GPs or with the Home Office, who kept a register of addicts. This he felt was too time-consuming. He said that talking to the patient was 'more important than anything else'.

A doctor sitting in the audience said that it was the responsibility of every doctor to make enquiries before prescribing such dangerous drugs. He added that some of his own patients who were on Phyceptone had gone to Petro and been prescribed heroin and cocaine, even though they had been off them for a considerable period of time.

The doctor in the audience also said that because addicts went to Petro privately, they had to find money for their prescriptions and fees. As many of them were hard-up, they had to sell their drugs and their prescriptions. To back up this accusation he produced a statement from one of Petro's patients who had been forced to trade his drugs because his doctor's bill and prescription charge exceeded his weekly income from Social Security.

I then asked Dr Petro whether he had ever refused to give someone a prescription because they didn't have the money. The patient mentioned in the *Daily Mail* report had at first been sent away because he only had 12/6*d*. Petro replied, 'Yes, well, no, no.' In a rambling answer, he denied the charge.

We decided that we should continue with the subject the following night, and Dr Petro agreed to return. The patient whose case had been featured in the *Daily Mail* and in our first programme had also come forward. He told me that when he went to see Dr Petro, he was simply asked a few questions and then prescribed heroin and cocaine.

'What happened in your case about money?' I asked him.

'Well,' replied the patient, 'I only had 12/6*d* and, you know, he started to write out the prescription and when I told him I had 12/6*d*, he told me to go, you know. He refused to carry on writing at all.'

The patient had to go away and find the £3 for the prescription. 'He wouldn't give it to me until I had given him the money, the £3.'

Asked to comment on this, Petro claimed at first that he had not heard a word. I asked the audience if they had heard all right. They had. Dr Petro then said he was not sure the man had been a patient of his. I said that the *Daily Mail* had proof that the man was once his patient and that his account was true, but Petro insisted that he would not comment until he was certain of the man's identity. When I supplied the man's name (written on a piece of paper to protect his anonymity), Petro finally admitted this was the right person. All of this, I pointed out, was in the context of yesterday's discussion when, as I said to Dr Petro, 'you said with utter certainty, "I did not carry out a physical examination, but I took good care to find out all about him."' A doctor in the audience interjected, 'How do you distinguish patients from people who are using the Tube station, if you hold your surgery there? No wonder he's confused!'

Another man said he had also been given heroin and cocaine without a physical examination. A woman said that because Dr Petro did not keep records, she was able to obtain from him larger amounts of drugs than she needed or had received from him before. Next, the Head of the pioneering addiction unit at All Saints' Hospital, Birmingham, said that he had treated one of Petro's patients who had received prescriptions of fifty-six grammes of heroin a week. When the patient was given just one gramme of the drug by the specialist, he collapsed. It was subsequently discovered that he had been selling most of his prescription to pay Petro's fee. The specialist said that most of the addicts who came to Petro (or other doctors like him) would only be able to meet his fees in this way or by some other kind of criminal activity. He asserted that the only reason for the escalation in the number of narcotic users in Britain was over-prescription, citing the fact that in Birmingham the problem was being solved by rigidly controlling the supply and distribution of the drug.

There was just time for me to talk about the diagram another doctor had prepared which showed the spread of drug abuse: 'Dr Dalacron has shown a family tree of how one addict having a bit of heroin over has led another addict to be another sufferer and so on, so from that one addict who had too much heroin, there is now a family tree of thirty addicts.'

'What I am trying to say to you is this,' said Dr Petro, 'that knowingly I have only given what is necessary to the addicts. There may have been some instances when it has been misused.'

'But there seems to be so many in your case,' I said.

'Yes. I don't mind being a minority,' Dr Petro said, somewhat bewilderingly. 'I know what I'm talking about.'

The programme ended with Dr Petro again claiming that he did a lot of good with his work. 'Three-quarters of my patients are off cocaine and I have stopped their cocaine. I wonder whether you also have done so.'

A doctor in the audience replied, 'We have done this and we have a whole number of young addicts who at any time were able to go and see you because you don't check, and can get almost a limitless supply of heroin and cocaine.'

At the end of the programme, something happened that left us all quite speechless. Dr Petro was about to leave the studio, and was asking me if he could return to the show again to answer points made on the programme. I was saying, 'You will be given every opportunity to . . .' when Detective Sergeant David Patrick of the Scotland Yard Drug Squad confronted Dr Petro, took him aside and arrested him on a warrant issued by Marylebone Magistrates. He was charged with failing to keep records, and bailed the following day.

On the wider charges we had heard on the programme, there seemed to be only two possible interpretations. If Dr Petro had either deceived or was in collusion with the addicts he treated, he was worse than the common drug pusher, cynically making money out of drug addiction. If not, he was grossly irresponsible, unprofessional, misguided and naive.

In a lengthy postscript the next night, we described again the current situation and called for the Home Secretary to take up the powers given to him by the 1967 Dangerous Drugs Act and to prohibit GPs from prescribing heroin and similar drugs to addicts outside treatment centres. If, as we had been told, the treatment centres were going to take time to build and staff, that should not be allowed to stop others from tackling the urgent problem of over-prescribing.

Needless to say, it was the arrest of Dr Petro – and a related revival of the debate about 'trial by television' – rather than the procrastination of the Home Secretary that occupied the headlines. However, after our earlier theoretical discussions about the case for and against the legalisation of marijuana and the effect of hallucinogenic drugs, we had at least managed to dramatise the practical problem of over-prescription, which lay at the root of the heroin problem in 1967. If the curtailment of Dr Petro's activities – and of others like him – meant that there was just one less family tree for Dr Dalacron to document, the two programmes would have more than served their purpose.

In the autumn of 1967, Sir Oswald Mosley was attempting an intellectual comeback. This ersatz Führer had been something of a social menace in England in the 1930s, though fortunately never a serious political force. Had he faded gracefully from public view, nobody would have wanted to rake over his past history. But he didn't. He was trying to rewrite that history. In his newly-published memoirs he quite skilfully sought to rehabilitate himself and, in fact, got a surprisingly sympathetic hearing on both sides of the Atlantic. He was treated decorously on several interviews in America, but in London people had longer and more direct memories, particularly of what the Mosley thugs had done to Jews and Jewish property in London's East End before the war.

In the 1920s and early 1930s Mosley was regarded with high esteem; his reputation as an economist was high, and when he switched from socialism to his own invention, the New Party, it seemed for a moment that he had carved out a viable constituency. Then he caught the fascist bug. Impressed by both Mussolini and Hitler, he founded the British Union of Fascists and decked his men out in black shirts and boots. Psychopaths welcome. What interested me was the moment of transition, from being a politician able to win endorsements from such contrasting contemporaries as Aneurin Bevan and Harold Macmillan, to being a pocket Adolf. The hinge was anti-semitism.

Early in our interview, Mosley claimed that the word only came up after a rally at the Albert Hall in 1934. 'I contend and can prove that I have never been an anti-semite, whom I define as a man who is against Jews because they are born Jews. I, however, had a quarrel with certain Jewish interests, not all Jews, before the war for a perfectly specific reason. I rightly or wrongly thought they wanted a war with Germany, another world war.'

In response I quoted from three of his speeches of the time, including this: 'The great and powerful were afraid when our fascist movement opened its crusade against Jewry. Up to three years ago anti-semitism was unknown as a strong force in Great Britain. Today in any audience in Britain the strongest passion that can be aroused is the passion against the corruption of Jewish power. It is not we who perish in the struggle.'

Mosley again attempted to deny his anti-semitism. He tried to rationalise his words by saying that he had been driven to retaliation 'against Jewish rascals yelling at me and attacking my meetings with razors, bludgeons, weapons of every sort'. The Blackshirts, he said, had been created as an act of self protection – a deft inversion of history. 'But you say here,' I went on, '"up to three years ago anti-semitism was unknown as a strong force in Great Britain". It doesn't sound as though you disapprove of it very strongly.' Mosley was unable to explain away this approving reference to the growth of anti-semitism. All he could say was, 'It was unknown until they came out, as I thought, and as I still think, for good reasons from their point of view, to provoke a world war.'

We had invited to the studio some people who had lived in the East End at the time of Mosley's marches. One of them, a prominent East End communist called Solly Kaye, broke in. He waved a picture of Mosley taken in 1962 at a gathering of recrudescent neo-Nazis in Germany. Mosley claimed that none of them were anti-semites. Unfortunately, Mosley's opponents got too excited and tended to spoil their case by trying to shout him down, though I could understand their passion after Mosley delivered himself of this tribute to his Blackshirts: 'They were magnificent young men and I am proud to have led and organised them to put people like you out of meetings.'

In general, however, the excessive zeal of Mosley's opponents was playing into his hands, and he used this as well as he could: 'Now you see how we have to fight for free speech . . . Yes, you proved my case very well, thank you . . . He's proving my case up to the hilt . . .'

There was a tangible skeleton in my research file, and now was the time to produce it. In 1935 a speech of Mosley's was reported to Julius Streicher, one of Hitler's more odious henchmen. Streicher liked the speech so much that he sent a message of congratulation to England. Mosley sent a telegram back to Streicher, the text of which I now read out: 'I greatly esteem your message in the midst of our hard struggle. The forces of Jewish corruption must be overcome in all great countries before the future of Europe can be made secure in justice and peace. Our struggle is hard but our victory is certain.'

Mosley responded, 'As I have already told you, we were in a fight with those Jewish interests in this country in order to stop a war with Germany. And anyone in any country who supported us in that I would send a greetings telegram to.' But was Julius Streicher really 'anyone'?

After the exchange about the telegram, we had to take a commercial break. There was just time during this for Geoffrey Hughes to take a phone call in the control room from George Brown. George had been a trades union organiser in the East End in the 1930s, and said he had personally seen Mosley's Blackshirts beating up Jews. This message unfortunately did not reach me until after the programme went off the air. However, I was busy during the break too, mentally regrouping. I thought that the truth was coming through in my exchanges with Mosley, but I realised that I must not continue with too much more of the audience. With all their passion, Solly Kaye and his friends were helping the man they hated every time they interrupted him.

After the break there was immediately some progress. Mosley admitted that the murder of the Jews in the concentration camps was an outrageous and vile crime. Under pressure he also admitted that he had only changed his tune on this subject after the Nuremberg Trials.

'You are saying now that you in fact in the Thirties backed and imitated a man who turned out to be a monster.'

Mosley said, 'No. Imitation is completely untrue.'

I said, 'Let's just take a look at this piece of film. Can we see this piece of film?'

Mosley interjected. 'Can I answer that one?'

'Well, you can just watch the film first,' I said.

The film was a *coup de grâce*, a piece of newsreel of a Mosley speech which showed him with his arm raised in the Nazi salute before his men. As it ended I said to Mosley, 'That is one of two people speaking there. It is reminiscent either of Hitler or of Charlie Chaplin's Great Dictator. Which is it?'

'Yes, that's a very smart question,' said Mosley. 'Personally I think it's a very good speech about England's greatness to which we have all just listened. I am very –'

'But what about all that business?' I said, repeating the salute.

'Don't you know what that is?' said Mosley. 'What an incredible question: that was a salute two thousand years before Hitler was born.'

'But whose salute was it in the Thirties?' I said. 'Whose salute was it in the Thirties?'

'First Mussolini and then Hitler,' Mosley had to reply.

'And who is it reminiscent of there? Everyone in the audience –'

'Are you saying that Hitler imitated Mussolini?' asked Mosley.

'No,' I replied. 'I am saying that everyone in that audience is not going to think, "Oh, there's old Ossie imitating someone from two thousand years ago . . ."' As so often, the audience's response made its own point.

On balance, I asked him, did he think that it would have been better if Hitler had never existed?

'Certainly better that he should not ever have existed,' Mosley answered, 'because his existence led to twenty-five million Europeans being killed. And if I had my way those twenty-five million would be alive today, including six million Jews who never would have been killed if there hadn't been a war. They made the greatest mistake they ever made when they produced that war.'

In one paragraph Mosley was making the extraordinary claim that the Jews had 'produced' the war, and at the same time quoting the figure of six million Jewish dead when earlier he had said, 'I don't think nearly so many were killed as were supposed to be killed.'

'And today,' I said, 'you've nothing to show for it. And when your candidates stand in elections they try and choose in 1966 the three areas where they can capitalise most on racial unrest, and they end up with an average of just over three per cent of the votes. There's nothing left to show for your movement. What went wrong?'

'I polled 4.8 per cent, not three per cent. Four point eight,' said Mosley. 'And if you talked so much about Hitler, who doesn't interest me very much, we polled just about double what he did five years before he got power, so don't be too cocky about that.'

Did he think that one day he might still get power? 'Now there are two ways of getting power – one is by a consensus of the people of the nation, an agreement of everything vital in the country coming together, which I stood for before, and believe we can now possibly attain in the coming crisis. The other way is to build up a grassroots movement of the people. But never do it until the first method has failed. In life always try to do things gently, and only get tough when you have to get tough.'

'All right,' I said. 'And with Sir Oswald Mosley's message, "In life always try to do things gently," we'll say good night.'

I doubt if Oswald Mosley understood the laughter of the audience at that point. He saw everything through the distorting mirror of his own fantasies, and was irretrievably consumed by them. He would never see himself as others saw him. Indeed, how else could he have chosen as a title for his book such a *double entendre* as *My Life*?

Mosley had often been a metaphysical prophet of doom, and we were also visited one Friday by a very specific prophet of doom. Mr Anders Jensen from Copenhagen had predicted the end of the world on the following Sunday. His group had stocked their nuclear-proof shelter with tinned food and sterilised milk. After the war they expected rescue by flying saucers from a world that had otherwise been destroyed.

On the following Wednesday we invited Mr Jensen back to join us, thereby giving me the chance to begin the questioning: 'Tell me, Mr Jensen, what went right?' and to end with the words, 'Never mind, Mr Jensen, it's not the end of the world.'

During the autumn of 1967 there was a sea-change in the national political mood. As so often, it was flagged for us by our audience, and in two key instances not even when they were actively participating in a debate, which made their intervention all the more telling. In one discussion George Wigg, at the time the Paymaster General, was pressed to explain the economic problems of the Government. He remarked, as many Cabinet Ministers had before him, 'It's all due to the £800 million debt we inherited from the Conservatives, and –'. At that point the listening audience *interrupted* him with a groan. Instantly you knew, as you would never have known without an audience, that that particular alibi had outlived its usefulness.

The euphoria of 1966 had given Harold Wilson a decisive majority in March, but by now the sense that we had entered a period of inexorable progress was beginning to dissipate. When even as heavyweight a performer as Denis Healey, then Defence Secretary, could not get through a routine avowal of loyalty to the Prime Minister without provoking hilarity, that was an even stronger indication of a change in the public mood. Healey had said, 'There's nobody in the party who wants to replace Harold Wilson or thinks he can be replaced as Prime Minister. Infinitely the best Prime Minister we could have.'

'Pardon?' I said.

Healey repeated the words, 'He's infinitely the best Prime Minister we could have.'

'We must be hard up,' said a voice from the audience, to delighted laughter all round – more than the heckle would have garnered without the new mood in the country.

'That was interesting,' I said, 'that sort of reaction there. Why is it that when the question of the Government – like then – is mentioned, the whole audience interrupts us by groaning? This is a situation which seems to me extraordinary. It's such a potentially successful – it came in with such a wealth of goodwill in '64. What went wrong?'

Healey replied, 'Oh well, I can tell you what went wrong. What went wrong is that –'

'Labour got in,' said another voice in the audience. More decibels of laughter.

The audience were just two hundred people who obtained tickets at random – not a scientific sample of the population, as we were always at pains to point out – but if the politicians were listening, they were trying to tell them something.

In March 1966 the Labour Government had projected the image of a dynamic new approach to economic management: the confidence and optimism had remained high for much of that year. However, since the beginning of the decade the deep-seated decline in Britain's economic position had been indicated by serious balance of payments deficits. According to some economists, the best solution was devaluation. But in a time of fewer and fewer taboos, the word still had a taboo quality to it. It sounded defeatist and unpatriotic, and Harold Wilson was strongly against it. Instead of devaluing, he let the external debt grow while trying a series of policies to inhibit inflation: increased taxes, prices and incomes policy, wage freezes, etc. These policies failed. From 1965 inflation had begun to accelerate perceptibly. The Government had even antagonised the trade unions – the Seamen's Union took serious strike action in 1966, and the dockers in 1967.

Despite the warning signs, many were still complacent: the mood of expansion still made it seem as if Wilson's revolution was actually taking place. In 1967 Wilson was urged to devalue by some of the most influential members of his Cabinet and others, but he stubbornly refused until November, when a decision was virtually imposed on him as much by the pressure of his colleagues as by the worsening economic situation.

In our studio Peter Jay, then Economic Editor of *The Times*, said that a report by Harold Wilson's economic advisers had called for devaluation as early as mid-1965. In early 1966 a national strategy report by Labour's economic advisers and other experts had put devaluation as the cornerstone of future strategy. This report, Peter said, was suppressed by Wilson, who had the document destroyed and allowed no further discussion of the subject inside or outside Whitehall. Coming as late as it did, the 14.3 per cent devaluation was perceived as a defeat, a major blow to Labour's standing, despite the fact that the pound had effectively been losing its value for years. Wilson's 'pound in your pocket' speech proved a major miscalculation, and after devaluation Labour found that it could no longer maintain the same rhetoric of expansion and progress which had helped bring it to power. Harold Wilson had attached a symbolic importance to maintaining the exchange rate of the pound. Now that he had given in, it was inevitable that people would invest his devaluation of the pound with its own symbolic significance – of Labour's failure to deliver, to do better than the doddery old Tories of the bad old days. The general optimism and enthusiasm which had been built up over the preceding years did not collapse overnight in 1967 with devaluation. Many people were still optimistic and/or affluent, but the old excuses were becoming threadbare, and there was a new cynicism about the current government, as the Wigg and Healey audience vignettes showed.

The Healey interview was also notable for the fact that the Defence Secretary arrived looking and sounding very much like the proverbial bear with a sore head. He said later that he had had a raging toothache all day, but I suspected that the soreness was probably more attributable to his defeat by Harold Wilson over a ban on the sale of arms to South Africa. This ban had been introduced in 1964, and both Healey and George Brown had wanted to relax it, but had just been out-manoeuvred by Wilson, who later wrote that the dispute had caused 'strains' within the Parliamentary Labour Party and Cabinet 'more serious than any other in our six years of government'. The lobby correspondents had had a field day with the dispute, benefiting from leaked reports from both sides, but when I raised the subject with Denis Healey, he decided to brazen it out as if the row had never happened.

I asked, 'You were pictured as almost single-handedly sort of soldiering-on on the question of the sale of arms to South Africa. What to you were the principles at stake there?'

Healey replied, 'Oh, David, now you don't believe what you read in the newspapers, do you? That's obvious, and that's an awful mistake.' Then a transparent response: 'Some sections of the newspapers recently have tried to isolate individual Ministers as responsible for fighting a lonely and unsuccessful battle single-handed for an unpopular cause; it happened to poor George Brown and to me, it's happening to me on the F-111, but don't you believe all you read in the newspapers. In fact, as you saw, the Prime Minister took the trouble to deny these stories in Parliament only a short time ago.'

'Yes,' I said. 'I noticed Mr Brown sat there with a pretty black face while he was doing it.' There was laughter in the audience. They had obviously read the reports too.

Denis Healey decided not to contest that point, and said instead, 'Well, I'm waiting. Yes? Had you something to say?'

'No,' I said. 'I was waiting for you to say what did you feel was the principle at stake that made you in favour of the sale of arms to South Africa.'

Healey replied, 'I'm afraid I'm not prepared to discuss positions I did or didn't take in Cabinet discussion. You know that jolly well, David. That was rather an odd question for you to ask, wasn't it?'

The answer was pure humbug. I had only asked him about the principle at stake. So I replied, 'No, not at all an odd question.'

'Yes,' said Healey.

'Listen,' I said, 'if Number 10's publicity machine puts out the fact that you were in favour, you should surely reply. Are you happy about –'

Healey broke in to say, 'Well, if that were the case, I would be very surprised and shocked indeed because this would be a total breach of Cabinet security. Are you telling me and the audience that in fact the Number 10 publicity machine identified individual Ministers as responsible for holding particular views?'

I said, 'They never did it to me, certainly, but that is certainly what the journalists are saying, yes.'

Healey decided to get hot and heavy on this point. 'Well, I think that's a shocking allegation, if I may say so.'

'You think they're wrong to say that?' I asked.

Healey replied, 'I certainly do.' Then, somehow or other, he managed to keep a straight face while he said, 'I can't imagine that a publicity machine operated by any member of the Cabinet would ever be used for such a purpose. I suspect you may find you have to apologise for that remark tomorrow, but that's not my affair.'

But what about all the stories that had appeared on Saturday morning saying that he was in favour of the sale of arms to South Africa?

Healey responded, 'I read a lot of those reports, and the names of the Ministers who were said to hold one particular view differed in at least five of the newspapers.'

'They were all unanimous about you, though,' I said.

'No, they weren't,' said Healey. 'With respect, they were not.'

'Who wasn't?' I asked.

'Oh, I can't remember now,' admitted Healey, 'but I did go through it carefully and I noticed quite a number of Ministers referred to in some not referred to in others.' He came round yet again to the exemplary way he considered he had behaved as a 'loyal' member of the Government. 'One thing you should know, I think, is that no Cabinet Minister while he is a member of the Cabinet is prepared to discuss what happens in the Cabinet, and I am a member of the Cabinet and I intend to remain one so long as I'm wished to remain one, and I certainly don't propose to discuss the position taken by myself or any other Cabinet Minister in a private meeting of the Cabinet; if I were to do so organised government in this country would become impossible. Of course, I'm sure you wouldn't mind, but a lot of people would.'

'No,' I said, 'I'd love organised government; we're all yearning for it!'

The row over the 'Number 10 publicity machine' took most of the headlines the following morning. 'Whitehall Studies David Frost's Number Ten Remark' said the *Guardian*. 'Number Ten Staff Study Frost–Healey Row' said the *Financial Times*. 'Frost

Show: Legal Move Considered' said *The Times*. By Monday *The Times* was reporting that a copy of the transcript had been flown to Mr Wilson in the Scilly Isles by helicopter, while the *Financial Times* reported that the transcript was 'despatched from Number Ten Downing Street to the Scilly Isles on Friday by teleprinter'. It all sounded completely over the top to me, and of course it was. On this occasion the political antennae of the *People* proved more reliable. 'It now seems highly unlikely that any action will be taken by Mr Wilson or any other Number Ten officials. Politically such a move would be disastrous.'

After the programme three political correspondents had rung and agreed with my remark, and my attitude to the lobby system. I asked them to come on the programme themselves, but they declined the offer. 'It's my bread and butter . . . and my caviar,' said one.

Later accounts including the Crossman diaries documented both the activities of 'the Number 10 publicity machine' and also of a 'publicity machine operated by a member of the Cabinet' – the machine turned out to be that of Healey's ally, George Brown, and his press secretary, Bill Greig.

At the time some commentators said that if Healey wasn't ready or able or inclined even to discuss the South African issue, he shouldn't have consented to appear on the programme. This was the view of David Wood, the political correspondent of *The Times*. However, he supported it with the proposition that 'The Frost Programme' should, in any case, have been beneath Healey's dignity: 'Mr Frost is in business for laughs and for the theatrical *coup*. Within that framework he no doubt deserves his reputation.' It was the old canard about 'show biz'. However, a much more dubious strain in this argument was that serious issues were somehow too important for popular discussion: 'the point of such programmes must be the self-confident naivete of making difficult things seem easy . . . of taking a consensus of ignorance and treating it with the awed respect that was once given to knowledge'.

Nothing better encapsulates a view about the use of television that I will always contest. There is within it the classic elitist view of privileged comprehension, that only on some specialised and arcane plane can public issues properly be discussed. It follows from this that unless they are conducted on these terms, which automatically exclude most of the television audience, the arguments traduce the issues. It is obviously true that there are levels of complexity where issues cannot be pursued to their detailed technical conclusion in front of a television audience – the finer points of the SALT agreements, for example. But it is also true that on the level of public men being called to discuss their views and policies, they cannot really be accountable *without* being able to explain them in popular terms. And in this instance there was nothing particularly obscure at stake. Invocation of the Privy Council Oath of Secrecy was more humbug.

We would, according to Wood, 'inevitably debase the political subjects under discussion' because we would be inclined 'to pander to the prejudice and ignorance of the mass audience'. Carrying this argument to its logical conclusion, general elections would have to be abolished because they must 'inevitably debase the political subjects under discussion', because one man one vote means by definition 'to pander to the prejudice and ignorance of the mass audience', albeit temporarily renamed 'the electorate'. Surely their opinions could not be constitutionally binding once every five years, and yet totally worthless for the rest of the time?

In a personal and private sense, one event dwarfed all others in 1967. After 'The Frost Programme' of Friday 17 November, I made tracks for Beccles as fast as I could. My father, who had been ill for some time, had had a cerebral haemorrhage on the Thursday. The end was near. Indeed in an odd sort of way, we *hoped* the end was near. It was clear that he could never recover from the haemorrhage and be even remotely himself again. Nothing changed on the Saturday, then on Sunday morning, at 9.15, he had another haemorrhage and died. It was a merciful release, but that does not mean that it was not still a shock as well. Nothing quite prepares you for a moment like that.

I was supposed to be in London at lunchtime that Sunday to launch the Oxfam Christmas Appeal at the Charing Cross Hotel.

I asked my mother what she would like me to do. Mother said immediately that I must go. She wanted me to go, and equally important, she said that my father would have wanted me to go. It was just the sort of work he would have supported all the way.

With some misgivings I set off for London, having promised to be back as soon as I could. The food served at the reception was not a traditional Sunday lunch, but what would constitute a life-saving meal in India. A bowl of multi-protein wheat grain saturated with special milk was followed by small dark biscuits.

The theme of the campaign would be 'I'm staking a child's life on you this Christmas'. The main appeal for funds would be a facsimile airletter from India, which I signed, and which would be delivered by volunteers to more than six million homes. I explained that this appeal 'could save a million lives. An extra £180,000 would enable Oxfam to carry through its present schemes over Christmas and into the New Year.'

Was there anything else I wanted to say, asked one of the press. 'Yes, add that extra 14.3 per cent in all donations to Oxfam.'

We arranged my father's funeral for the Thursday. That morning I went to the funeral home to say goodbye, and the service took place at 12.15. Afterwards we invited family and friends to lunch at the Waveney House Hotel, and we had what was genuinely a wondrously celebratory occasion. There was so much in my father's life to celebrate. He had always been a trailblazer, and would not take no for an answer. His very entry into the Methodist ministry showed that. In 1928, everyone wishing to enter the ministry had to attend a theological college for two years and then serve as an unmarried probationer minister for three years, before becoming a full minister and being allowed to marry. Father had been the first to breach both of those conditions. When he heard the call to the ministry, he was already married with two children. He studied at home in his spare time. And at his first port of call in Horsham, instead of the usual Methodist probationer accommodation, which was hopelessly inadequate for a family of four, he had to buy a house and then sell it when he left.

Wherever he went he was asked to stay on after the traditional three years in that peripatetic ministry. Seven years at Tenterden, seven years at Kempston, seven years at Gillingham. He had been a true pastor, caring for his flock. That's why his sermons were so effective. They were always rooted in the everyday fears and problems of his congregation. He and Mother had made a wonderful team, both publicly in the life of the Church, and back home. And he had been a wonderful father to Jean, Margaret and me. His dash to Cambridge at the end of my first year had been typical of what he would do for his family, and for others too. I was so glad that he had been able to share five years of my career. He knew that both his daughters were happily married, and leading vigorous lives of their own, and he knew that things were going better than I could ever have hoped in London.

Maybe there were odd times in the long watches of the night when he thought wistfully 'if only' his son had followed in his footsteps and 'heard the call' to the Methodist ministry, but then again he had the satisfaction of knowing something that probably mattered to him as a father even more – that his son loved every moment of what he was doing and felt completely fulfilled by it.

Some of the obituaries particularly drew attention to his pioneering work in building – and raising the money for – new churches or extensions to existing churches, from a church on a new estate near Gillingham in Kent that cost £8000 back in the early Fifties right through to a £4500 extension that was about to be built in Beccles. The *Methodist Recorder* said that, 'The warm and radiant quality of his evangelistic preaching . . . continued undiminished to the very end of his distinguished circuit ministry.' His success as a circuit minister lay in 'saying the simple and fundamental things about the heart of God that find answer in the deepest hungers of the human heart'.

My father often quoted Tubby Clayton, the founder of a Christian organisation called TOC H: 'Service is the rent we pay for our room on earth.' And that was the philosophy on which he based his own life. He hoped and prayed that we would do the same, but that was always an unspoken message. He gave his children all the raw materials for living a decent, honourable life, but left the implementation to us. Like Billy Graham, he believed that faith in God was the path to a fuller life, not a more narrow-minded one.

And he believed that all of us had a duty to use to the full whatever time and talents we had been given. Nowadays when I talk about not liking to waste money but *hating* to waste time, I know the origin of that emotion. Money did not matter to my father. Time did.

He was such a good man. But never goody-goody. Just plain good.

EIGHT

'The Next President'

MY MAIN ASSIGNMENT in the United States in the first half of 1968 would not have happened without a lunch in London the previous October at the Royal Garden Hotel. Dick Pack and Chet Collier, two senior executives at Group W Westinghouse Broadcasting, had asked me to speak at a Westinghouse lunch. Group W had dominant television stations in major cities including Boston, Baltimore, Pittsburgh, Philadelphia and San Francisco. In addition they had a successful syndication division, which sold series like 'The Merv Griffin Show', a five-times-a-week ninety-minute talk show, throughout the rest of the country. On this particular occasion they were bringing 150 executives to London for a week's talks, addresses and functions, enabling them to look toward the future and see 'the world in perspective'.

Donald McGannon, the President of Group W, was at the hotel to welcome me for a speech which was, at my request, billed 'To England – and America – with Love' (which allowed me to speak about anything I felt like). I had also said I'd be happy to answer questions afterwards.

As I usually did, I began with some stories of air travel and my transatlantic commuting, like the pilot on a recent flight from Detroit to Los Angeles with an all-too irrepressible sense of humour who had announced over the intercom: 'Some people claim they're afraid of flying, but that's nonsense. It's *crashing* they're afraid of . . .'

After I'd told a number of anecdotes, I threw the session open to questions. One of the group asked me about techniques of interviewing. I underlined my point about how important it was to fit the technique to the occasion with my favourite Aesop's fable about the Sun and the Wind having a competition to get someone's coat off. 'The wind blew and blew, and the man drew his coat closer around him. The sun just shone, and the man took his coat off.' On some occasions – for example when the facts were really being done a disservice – you had to be firm, even tough, in order to get an answer, but there were many occasions when you achieved much more with a subtler approach.

After a few more questions I ended with my favourite quote from Ed Murrow, 'Television can entertain, and of course it must, and it can inform, and it must, and it can even inspire, but what television is or what it is going to become as a mass medium depends on the will of the humans who operate it; otherwise it is just coils and lights in a box.' I added, 'To me that is the challenge of television at the moment.'

The audience were very generous in their response, and before I left both Chet Collier and Dick Pack suggested that I should do more for Group W. On that visit to London they only had time to look at a few tapes, and talk generally about 'specials'. However, a dialogue was begun, and when Chet came back in December, he and I had lunch at Egerton Crescent, and over some of my housekeeper Luisa's irresistible lamb chops, we worked out the bare bones of a deal by which I would provide four specials a year for Group W. The series would be called 'David Frost Presents', and I said I wanted to introduce to American audiences some British stars whom I thought they would love if they got half a chance. I suggested Frankie Howerd and Tommy Cooper as examples. Both of those would be shows that I would introduce, and then step back and just produce.

They also wanted one or two of the specials each year to be 'Frost Specials', and so we tried to identify the right idea for the first one. Eventually we hit on a sixty-minute special in which I would interview all of the candidates for the Presidential race in 1968. Because I felt so strongly that an electorate needs to know more than mere policy statements, I wanted to talk with the candidates about their personal philosophies and what made them tick. After all, by definition none of them could spell out what he would do in an emergency, otherwise it would scarcely be an emergency. You just had to vote for the man you felt would respond to an emergency in the way you would wish your leader to respond. In a crisis, his personal qualities would be vital. I also wanted to ask all the candidates a number of the same questions, so that the viewers could make comparisons for themselves between their responses. Chet warmed to the idea, and 'The Next President' was soon to achieve inked rather than pencilled status.

Chet and I had lunch again on Friday 19 January 1968, and then I set off on a lightning trip to the States on the Sunday. There were two purposes for the trip. One was to promote the forthcoming publication of *To England with Love* – renamed *The English* in America – by doing the 'Today Show' on Monday morning and the 'Tonight Show' the same evening. After the 'Tonight Show' I flew to San Francisco to tape an interview with the longshoreman-turned-research-professor Eric Hoffer, for 'The Frost Programme'. 'I've lived all my life with idealists, and you know what the idealist here in this country has?' said Hoffer. 'They have left-wing principles and right-wing bank accounts.' Facilities had been arranged for me by Chet at the Group W station in San Francisco, KPIX, and we taped Eric Hoffer at nine in the morning on Tuesday so that I could catch the noon plane back to London in time for Wednesday's show.

When the series ended at the beginning of February, I planned to spend most of the rest of the month and March in the States. From 6 February to the twenty-eighth, I was committed to the book tour, and this was also a good opportunity to start setting up the interviews. In March my first priority would be the interviews.

Sol Stein, my New York publisher, did not believe in his authors wasting any time, and even had I been one of the Presidential hopefuls I was about to interview, I could scarcely have had a more packed schedule. My first full day in New York on 7 February started with a Mike Wallace interview for the CBS radio network, followed by a couple of telephone interviews and Channel 5's local lunchtime show. There were interviews with Helen Gurley Brown and Arlene Francis and then another appearance on 'The Merv Griffin Show', before late-night radio like Barry Gray took over. I managed to resist Sol Stein's advice about walking on to every television show clutching a copy of the book so close to my face that it would be impossible for the director to get a close-up without including it, as I thought this a trifle unsubtle. However, I had to hand it to him on the title. At first I had resisted his suggestion of changing it from *To England with Love* to *The English*.

'No, no, no, I know what I'm doing,' said Sol. 'It's a better title for this country, and it will remind people of Barzini's *The Italians* which was a big success.' He said he was hoping that somebody would compare the two books, and produce a quotable quote. And with the very first review that we received, he got it.

The English was book of the week in the *Saturday Review*'s advance book service for newspapers. In his review John Barkham actually said – that man Stein must have been psychic – 'I like it even better than Luigi Barzini's *The Italians* because of its sharper bite, its more epigrammatic sparkle. Besides, the Italians already have their *Decline and Fall*.' Sol Stein made sure that if you read the book pages of the newspapers, you would not be able to avoid seeing that quote at least once a week.

In Cleveland I met Paige Palmer at WEWS – it was the first time I had ever talked about a book on an exercise show – and got to know the redoubtable Dorothy Fuldheim, who loved books more than any interviewer I had ever met. In Chicago, authors obeyed an unwritten law that you simply had to talk to Bob Cromie for PBS, and then you had to do 'The Kup Show' with columnist Irv Kupcinet, and collect one of his souvenir coffee mugs.

All through the month Warren Wallace, my director, and I were busy trying to line up Presidential interviews for March. George Romney's candidature was looking increasingly shaky after his unwise admission that he might have been 'brainwashed' over Vietnam, and indeed on the day I left, 28 February, he withdrew from the race.

After a busy week back in London, concerned mainly with London Weekend Television, I set off for New York with Ian Davidson, a highly talented writer and performer from Oxford whom I had first spotted on the fringe at the Edinburgh Festival, and who was going to be my Associate Producer and researcher. We knew by then about our first two interviews.

They were going to take place in Manchester, New Hampshire, on the day of the primary, the candidates presumably feeling there was little more that they could do to affect that day's result, and that they should invest a little time in the future. Actually, there was only one real candidate we were interviewing that day, and that was Senator Eugene McCarthy. The other interview was with the perennial hopeful whose chances were always hopeless, Governor Harold Stassen. Why did we include him? Simply because under the equal time provisions governing this sort of programme, we had to. Furthermore, Harold Stassen had to have exactly as much time in the programme as Eugene McCarthy, Richard Nixon and anybody else.

We checked in at the Holiday Inn in Manchester. Our interview with Stassen was scheduled for the morning, and then the more serious business with Senator McCarthy took place at his hotel, the Sheraton Wayfarer, at 2 p.m. The session with Harold Stassen was not without interest by any means, but was in all conscience a pretty sad one.

'When one reads through, as I have done, the press clippings, one comes up all the while against phrases like "holding press conferences in hotel lobbies where the potted palms outnumber the reporters". Don't you feel sad when you read things like that?'

Harold Stassen did not agree. 'No, I recognise it as a part of a time in which your political influence is at a low ebb and you simply carry on.'

But didn't he feel now at this point that his political fortunes could only go to a lower ebb?

Stassen again chose to differ. 'No, as a matter of fact, they've turned up somewhat already, and no one knows what the future holds, of course.'

'Do you rule out the idea of the Presidency in '68?' I asked.

'No,' said Stassen. 'I've always said that I never close off future options of decision, but that I will endeavour to make the decisions on the basis of what will best advance peace.'

Alas, he did not seem to realise that they were decisions he would never have to make, that the electorate would make them all for him. We left the interview feeling sorry for Harold Stassen, but that, alas, is no prescription for success in politics.

When Senator McCarthy had entered the Presidential race on 30 November 1967, he had said he was offering himself on a single plank – peace. He would be entering several Democratic primaries in order to challenge the Johnson administration's policy of 'continued escalation and intensification of the war in Vietnam'. His announcement never really clarified whether he was seriously seeking the nomination, or just a change in policy. He had been reluctant to start his campaign in New Hampshire, a particularly patriotic and hawkish state. As late as 27 December 1967, he was saying that the New Hampshire primary was 'not particularly significant', and he still feared that it might be a trap set by Bobby Kennedy, who would seize on any failure by McCarthy and turn it to his own advantage. On 3 January, however, the reluctant formal announcement of his entry into the primary was made.

For the first month the McCarthy campaign had had little resonance, but the concern created by the Tet offensive in late January radically altered his importance. Although the Tet offensive was in fact quickly contained, it had a profound effect in shattering confidence in all-conquering American power. McCarthy had already become the leading critic of the war. The difference was that after Tet he had a national audience. In his November announcement McCarthy had said that he hoped his candidacy 'may alleviate the sense of political helplessness and restore to many people a belief in the processes of American politics and of American government. On college campuses especially . . . it may counter the growing sense of alienation from politics.' The students may not have fully registered his words back in November, but now, after Tet, thousands of them came to New Hampshire to help him.

In Manchester I noticed that a great deal of care had been taken in that conservative state by McCarthy's supporters to maintain a clean-cut wholesome appearance – beards, jeans and sweatshirts were proscribed. For the last three days before the primary, enough finances had been garnered for a major radio and television campaign. Exit polls were not yet as sophisticated as they have since become, but by the time I met Senator McCarthy at 2 p.m., there was something in his demeanour that suggested that good news was just around the corner.

Did the Senator generally recognise the picture of himself in the press, or did he sometimes feel it was of a different person?

The reply was vintage McCarthy. 'Well, some of them I think have read me pretty well, but they run in fads here, especially the columnists. I'm not sure that the column is a really good device – it calls for a kind of short-range, rash judgement – especially when they write three columns a week. Three rash judgements a week are really too much to expect of anybody. If one does it, the other is hard pressed and likely to pick up the same theme; so they go around in circles. Then they'll change the line, and we say it's like blackbirds on the telephone line here in the fall. If one flies away, they all fly away. If one comes back, they all come back down.'

McCarthy's religious beliefs were well known. Were there specific issues that he could point to where they had affected his political stance?

'In a limited sense of religious positions, I wouldn't say so,' he said. 'I think there have been four or five issues we've had in which the moral component has been quite high, and I don't know whether out of religion I was stronger for it than I otherwise would have been. Things like the early effort to do something about migratory farm labour in this country, which involved great injustice. The whole civil rights fight, the Test Ban Treaty, and I think, you know, as I went along by way of changing position or passing judgement on the war, as the war itself changed. This position to pass a moral judgement on an issue of this kind did have some bearing upon the action I have taken. I thought it reached a point where it was not morally justified, not just a question of being in the national interest – I think one can oppose the war on that basis alone – but it was not morally justified.'

When I asked him who he thought represented the best in American society, not surprisingly he chose 'the students and the young people of the country who have, for whatever the reasons may be, good or bad, broken out of the old mould, and are approaching the problem with a new kind of freedom of intellect, without the sense of guilt or the limitations of the old prejudices or the false conceptions which marked America'.

'If you were looking now at the political map of the world in ten years' time, in what main ways would it be different from today?' I asked.

'Oh, I don't think it would be very different from what it is now,' said McCarthy. 'I think you might have more stability in Africa. I think there will be some significant improvements in Latin America. I am hopeful that a country like Brazil will come along all right. As far as Asia is concerned, I think that there would be little change there unless we persist in making it. We're either in or out of Vietnam. I don't think it will make a significant difference in South-eastern Asia. I anticipate that the European countries will maintain their independence . . . If we could just work out something by which we could save England, why, we'd be all right.'

'The size of the British Empire might just continue to decline a little?' I asked.

'Well, it might, a little bit,' said McCarthy. 'But I think as long as the United States is as dependent on the pound as it is now, we'll have to save you somehow!'

By midnight it was becoming obvious that McCarthy would do much better than all the opinion polls had predicted, but nobody even then predicted how close the result would be. Of the Democratic vote President Johnson received 49.5 per cent (27,243) and McCarthy 42.4 per cent (23,280). When Republican write-ins were included, Johnson's margin of victory was only 230 votes (29,021 to 28,791). As the results became clear, McCarthy predicted nomination for himself for the first time.

Needless to say, McCarthy's achievement in the most unsympathetic of environments paved the way for an even greater effort in Wisconsin. It also paved the way for an announcement from Senator Robert Kennedy. On 16 March, Kennedy declared his intention to run for the Democratic Presidential nomination, so we began directing our phone calls in that direction, too.

Meanwhile we were back in New York at Gracie Mansion to interview Mayor John Lindsay. As it happened, our interview never made it into the final programme, because by then Lindsay was no longer a candidate, but I found his comments on leadership striking. When I asked him to define it, he replied, 'Well, leadership has a tone to it. There's a quality to it that must come through. I think that the person who will ultimately emerge as a leader of some power and direction is one that the people sense has within him an internal gyroscope that always brings him and therefore the institutions that he leads or commands back onto the course. What ultimately is needed is high quality, and if you have men who have character, then you are going to find leadership. It sounds very old-fashioned, doesn't it, to look for character, but that's ultimately what it comes down to, I think.'

His reference to character was far from being old-fashioned – it was in fact twenty years ahead of its time. When I did 'The Next President' again in 1988, 'character' had become the most sought-after quality in both the Democratic and the Republican races. But in 1968 Lindsay was the only candidate to mention the word, or give it any significance.

Our next firm date was with Governor Ronald Reagan of California in Sacramento on 21 March. In the meantime I went back to my New York base, which, thanks to his hospitality, was Clay Felker's duplex on the East Side. At that time Clay was the editor and creator of the recently-launched *New York* magazine, and his apartment reverberated with the voices and thoughts of contributors like columnist Jimmy Breslin, Peter Maas, author and confidant of Robert Kennedy, Joe Kraft, the political columnist from Washington, and many others. While waiting for Governor Reagan, I guest-hosted 'The Merv Griffin Show' on Monday 18 March. Allen Ginsberg was discussing a book on the subject of marijuana, which persuaded Susan Strasberg to talk about her experiences with psychiatry. I moved William Attwood of *Look* magazine on from talking about Prince Sihanouk, his reason for being there, to talking about Colonel Nasser, who interested me even more. The conversation took flight and the show was very well received within Westinghouse, although at the time none of us knew the significance of that fact.

We travelled out to San Francisco on the day before the Reagan interview, and I was able to ensure that I was in the right frame of mind by having dinner at Ernie's with Chet Collier. We got up at six the next morning and left for Sacramento at seven so that we would be ready to begin the interview with the Governor at the appointed hour, ten o'clock. At that stage of the race Ronald Reagan was a complete outsider, and the conventional wisdom was that he had no chance of ever becoming President. Throughout the interview he confirmed his reputation as a conservative. His conservatism was characterised by a strongly paternalistic view of society. 'I think sometimes in our own country, some of the rebellion on the part of youth is because we, their parents, they have seen us displaying a kind of hypocrisy. We are not, ourselves, following enough of the principles and standards that we try to teach them, so it isn't that they're rebelling against our standards, they're really crying out for someone to give them some standards. I believe that some of the disturbances on the campus are not the result of too much discipline. I think that they are like the small child stomping his feet and what he really wants is a parent to take him in hand and shake him and let him know where the guidelines are, and I think that our younger generation today would like to have someone, namely the older generation, set some guidelines and some rules and say, here, this is the framework. This is the pattern. You stay within that pattern. In this way, we can also give them a banner to follow, a cause to believe in, and I think people are looking for just such a cause.'

I wondered how many of the students I had seen in New Hampshire would recognise themselves in that portrait. The contrast with Senator McCarthy's view of young people could scarcely have been more marked. McCarthy applauded their desire to break out of the mould: Reagan wanted them to stay within the pattern.

'You talk about a sort of lessening of standards, a loosening of morals. What exactly does that phrase mean?'

This led Governor Reagan into one of those apocryphal homilies that were to become so familiar in later years. 'I think the decline of morality – well, let me explain. I have a man, a professor, on my staff here as liaison with our higher education institutions; and he told me of an example in his own campus experience of a young girl, one of the co-eds, and he was talking to her and she was deeply disturbed about things of this kind and about her own family. She loved them dearly, but her love stopped short of respect; and she told of an incident in which the girls had decided to have a slumber party and had chosen her home. She was to tell her mother that the girls had decided that chaperones were out this season. They'd have that slumber party without. Mother and father were going to have to find some place else to stay during the slumber party and the girl confessed to him that she was praying that her mother would stop her and would say, "Not on your life. We'll be here chaperoning." She said her mother got on the phone and started calling other mothers taking a public opinion poll of what she should do. The girl, as I say, admitted that she didn't believe this chaperone-less party was proper, and she wanted someone to give her a rule, to give her a guideline, so she could go back to the girls and even if she complained, be able to say, "I can't do it," instead of "I don't want to do it!"'

'This is really allied to what we have just been saying about rebellion and lawlessness,' I said, wanting the Governor to try and draw a line between different forms of violence in the streets. 'I mean, there's the mugger on the one hand, but there's the demonstrations and so on. To what are you really referring?'

Governor Reagan seemed not to differentiate. 'Well, it covers and is encompassed in this whole thing about the morality gap in our land . . .' He talked about crimes of violence, assaults on symbols of law and order, and demonstrations. 'Today, the demonstration precedes the negotiations. You don't know there's an issue until you suddenly look out the window and here comes the parade with the picket signs and they're ready to push the policemen out of the way. Here in this Capital, several weeks ago, a group with the bandoliers of ammunition and the weapons marched into this Capital and into the legislat-

Brainstorming for 'The Frost Programme' with (left to right) William G. Stewart, Tony Jay, Peter Baker, Geoffrey Hughes, Neil Shand and Bryan Fitz-Jones.

'The use of a studio audience not simply as a responsive backdrop, but as a key ingredient in the actual programme mix – to be brought into the proceedings according to need.' 'The Frost Programme'.

Above: Robert Morley on the first 'Frost Programme'.

Left: 'It really is odd to be discussing things as frankly as this with you in front of an audience and cameras.' George Brown on 'The Frost Programme', February 1967.

Below: 'The Frost Programme' on Transcendental Meditation: seeking enlightenment from George Harrison and John Lennon.

Right: Dr Savundra: 'By selling out I have no legal responsibility and *no moral responsibility* [illegible]' 'The Frost Programme', February 1967.

Below: Monday 12 June 1967. With Michael Peacock (left) and Aidan Crawley at a press conference twenty-four hours after Lord Hill, Chairman of the ITA, had given us the good news about our bid for the London weekend franchise.

'Bihar had a population roughly the same as that of England, and the emergency feeding was saving millions of lives.'

Charity cricket in Kent. Left to right: Ray Barratt, Graham Hill, DF, Nicholas Parsons, David Tomlinson, Ken Barrington, Colin Cowdrey and Leslie Crowther.

Saved! Charity football in Essex.

THE NEXT PRESIDENT, 1968

Above left: George Wallace at the Governor's mansion in Montgomery, Alabama.

Above right: Robert Kennedy at the Benson Hotel, Portland, Oregon.

Left: Eugene McCarthy at the Sheraton Wayfarer in Manchester, New Hampshire, on the day of the historic New Hampshire Primary.

Below: Hubert Humphrey in the Executive Office building of the White House.

Above left: Ross McWhirter and Mr Albert Cornelius, the 'Strongest Head in the World'. 'Frost on Saturday', September 1968.

Above right: Mick Jagger. 'Frost on Saturday', October 1968.

Left: Cardinal Heenan. 'Frost on Friday', December 1968.

Above: Muhammad Ali. 'Frost on Friday', December 1968.

Right: Noël Coward. 'Frost on Saturday', December 1968.

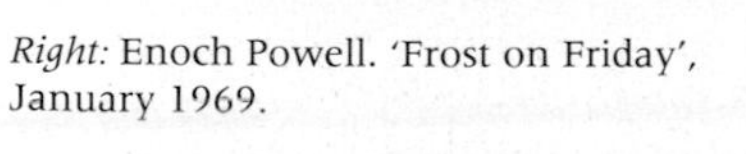

Right: Enoch Powell. 'Frost on Friday', January 1969.

Below: HRH Prince Charles on the eve of his investiture as Prince of Wales, May 1969.

Right: Rupert Murdoch. 'Frost on Friday', October 1969.

Below: Peter Ustinov. 'The David Frost Show', December 1969.

The first television tour of 10 Downing Street. Harold Wilson, July 1969.

ive halls, and it's a little shocking to Americans, even though we have quite a violent history . . . revolution is in the air.'

But in a country where everyone realised there might be riots or violence or whatever, guns were still very easily available, weren't they?

'Yes,' said Reagan. 'Although I'm not one who believes in overdoing the restriction on that, because the wrong person can always get the gun, so perhaps it's proper that the right person should have them at least available.' It was a wonderfully skilled reply, and 'not overdoing the restriction on that' became one of my favourite euphemisms.

The Governor returned to the paternalistic theme. 'Now, we have to assume that Government has access to much more information than the people, and that's particularly true under this administration, which has shown a reluctance to let the people have all the information; so Government has made a decision based on our national interest on the belief that in the defence of this country it is vital that we carry on this conflict in Vietnam. Some people without access to this same information are protesting vehemently and even to the point of now advocating literally help to the enemy and advocating that young men should refuse to fight for their country. What if these dissenters are wrong? And what if they succeed by their pressure in making this country withdraw from this position and then the course of history reveals that the Government was right?'

'I suppose they would say that their argument is: what if the Government is wrong?'

'Yes, but then we're asking for anarchy, aren't we? We have to assume that while Government does make mistakes, Government does have access to more information than anyone else, and therefore we have to assume that unless and until they can prove Government wrong and prove it legitimately in a legitimate debate, not in curbing these actions – it's like people arguing whether to put out a fire in the house while the house burns down.'

The Governor's words sounded like a rerun of one of those 'your elders know better' sentiments that had so upset us in Britain in the late Fifties. Later I asked him whether there was one historical character that he admired, felt more in sympathy with than any other?

'One historical character . . .' Reagan mused. 'Well, of course, the one above all is the man whose simple teachings in a three-year span between the ages of thirty and thirty-three set down rules which, if we had the courage to follow them, would solve all the problems of the world today. The Prince of Peace, the Man of Galilee.'

Ronald Reagan was the only candidate who brought up the subject of religion as such. Back in 1968 there was a feeling that John F. Kennedy's victory as a Roman Catholic had put the subject of religion to rest as a political issue. If anybody had told me at that moment that twenty years later in 1988 the race for the White House would include two ordained ministers and several born-again Christians, I would never have believed it.

Next day we had to fly back to New York, ready for our session with Richard Nixon, which his aide Len Garment had just confirmed. The interview took place at his new campaign headquarters at 450 Park Avenue, and we arrived just ahead of the furniture. We had managed to rustle up a couple of chairs by the time Nixon arrived. He looked rested, even tanned. He was also very much on a roll, having shed his old loser's image by winning more votes than any candidate had ever received in a New Hampshire primary. He had a seven to one margin over his write-in opponent, Nelson Rockefeller.

When I asked him what he would say was the one achievement he was most proud of thus far, Nixon picked what he did as Vice-President under Eisenhower, particularly in the international field. Was there any episode he would like to rewrite? He talked generally about the campaign of 1960, and the television debates with John Kennedy. But was there one remark that, looking back, he wished he hadn't said?

Nixon replied, 'Many people would say that the statement I should not have made was my criticism of the press when I lost for Governor of California,* and I would answer that question

* The notorious 'You won't have Richard Nixon to kick around any more' statement made in 1962.

now in this way. As a public man looking forward to the possibility of again running for office, to have made that statement was a very great mistake. When I first entered politics, a very wise old politician gave me some very good advice. He said, "Now, Dick, I want to tell you something. You're going to make many mistakes during the course of your political career, but remember this: never get into an argument with the press, 'cause they always have the last word." However, when I finished that campaign for Governor of California, I didn't have any idea that I would ever be sitting where I am today, being interviewed as a potential candidate for the Presidency of the United States. A private citizen has a right to express his views when he thinks he is being put upon.' Then came a pledge that turned out to be full of dramatic irony. 'However, as a public figure, I would say that that was a mistake, and I can also assure you that as far as getting in an argument with the press, it won't happen again as long as I'm a public figure.' He was speaking four years before Watergate.

But did he in fact recognise the picture of himself that he saw in the media? 'Is there one thing about you that you feel doesn't get enough play in the press?'

'Well now,' said Nixon, 'I'm not going to get in the business of criticising the press again!' He then proceeded to get into the business of criticising the press again – but indirectly and subtly. 'I suppose every political man feels that his critics in the press and otherwise make a mistake when they question the sincerity of his views . . . when they go to the point of saying, well, this man really isn't for peace because he stands for a firm line in Vietnam or in the Mid-East or some place else, then I say that's the kind of criticism that I think would well be left alone . . . Let's hit hard, but let's get away from these personal charges . . . I know Lyndon Johnson doesn't want to have any American boys killed, just as Senator McCarthy doesn't want to have them killed, but the larger question is not just ending the war in Vietnam. It's winning the peace. It's easy to end a war. The question is, do you win the peace for the next generation? I think we should debate that hard, but let's get away from questioning motives.' Then came the classic Nixonian disassociation, stressing his own immunity. 'Now, they can say what they want about me. I've been heckled by experts, so it doesn't make any difference what they say about me.'

I talked about Nixon's comeback, his fightback. Did he, in a purely personal sense, sometimes look back to 1962 and pinch himself to see if 1968 was true?

'I know that your people in Britain like to take a little wager, and I would say that in 1962, when I finished that campaign for Governor of California, I would have taken a bet of a million to one that I would never be running for public office again, although I'd always have an interest in public affairs; and as I look back on these last five and a half years, I marvel at what has happened. I don't mean by that that we're just little chips on the great stream of fate and that there's nothing we can do to change it. A man must be ready. He must be prepared. He must be willing. He just can't sit back and wait for that draft to occur, and I'm that kind of an activist. But unless the events are ready for the man at the time – both must come together – the man must be ready and the country and the events and the time must be ready. When they come together, then you have that chemical reaction which means success.'

How would he define political success?

When he first entered politics, Nixon said, he would have defined political success just as winning. But not any more. 'Success now would mean only being able to do something. Unless in the process of running for President I can contribute to the debate which will create a better chance for peace abroad and for peace and progress at home, my life will have been a failure.'

Nine years later, in 1977, Nixon returned to that theme at the climax of our interview about Watergate. 'Most of all, I let down an opportunity that I would have had for two and a half more years to proceed on great projects, programmes for building a lasting peace, which has been my dream, as you know from our first interview in 1968, before I had any thought I might even win that year. I didn't tell you I didn't think I might win, but I wasn't sure . . .'

Our interview with Governor George Wallace in Montgomery, Alabama, was fixed for the next day, so when we left the Nixon headquarters we headed straight for the airport. On the flight to Atlanta, we discussed Nixon's performance. In many ways it had been quite impressive. His answers had been clear and articulate. On the other hand, there had been a certain programmed quality to some of the responses. However, you still did not feel that he had totally conquered his obsession – later called paranoia – about his opponents and the press. You felt that it remained there just below the surface, but controlled much better than it had been on that unforgettable day in California five and a half years earlier.

At the time of our interview, Governor George Wallace was threatening to sweep the South as an independent or third party candidate. When he had formally announced on 8 February, he already had ten to twelve per cent of the national vote, according to the polls. The hard core of his following was of course in the Deep South, but he was getting an increasing amount of support from white, mainly blue-collar, voters in the North who responded not only to his long-standing rhetoric on race but to his newly reinforced rhetoric on their other fears and resentments, like rising taxes, bureaucracy and Washington.

The setting for our interview, the Governor's mansion in Montgomery, was by far the grandest we were to encounter during the series. Early on we talked, inevitably, about states' rights, and I made the point that the subject did not usually come up in connection with air pollution or oil depletion: 'It usually comes up in areas where a local state would like the Negro to have fewer rights.'

'Well, of course, your conclusion is erroneous,' said Wallace. 'When you say it comes up because people want the Negro to have less rights . . . The crux of the matter is that the people in our region of the country, the Southland, applied common sense and logic to the matter of race relations, and we had a slow evolutionary process in which we had peace and tranquillity unlike that existing any place in the world where there were people of opposite races.'

I noted that: *opposite* races – not different races.

'Let me then ask the age-old question that's asked on this race issue,' I said. 'Would you let your daughter marry a Negro?'

'I don't even want to get into a discussion of that business,' said Wallace. 'In fact, I don't even want to discuss the matter of race really, because the most important thing in our country is maintaining law and order. Race relations are going to work themselves out insofar as people are concerned. I'll put the question to you. Would you like for your daughter to marry someone of an opposite race? And I think that's a matter that will have to be left up – I don't believe in intermarriages of Negro and white – I'm candid and honest about it. I don't think it's good for either race. I think the races ought to remain intact. I think that God made one race, He made another race, and that it ought to be that way. But if anyone wants to intermarry, that's their own business.'

'But you think it's not good for either race?' I said.

'I think that it's not good for either race. That's right,' said Wallace.

'Because it does what?' I asked.

'Well, you see, that's one reason why I don't even like to discuss these matters with you folks. All you want to do is talk about race. Now, you come from England, where you folks passed a law over there where you don't even let Asians come into the country.'

'Oh, I know,' I said, 'we've got nothing to preach about.'

Wallace was by now warming to his theme. 'I just don't even want to talk about race. I'm not even going to talk about *bloodlines*.'

'Yes, but you made a point: you must explain it. You made the point you think it's not good for either race. Why is it?'

Wallace was getting angrier by the minute. 'I think, for obvious reasons, and I'm not going to discuss it any further. I'm not going to discuss it any further, that's all.'

Some of my crew, all of whom hailed from New York, had been decidedly nervous about this particular interview in the heart of the Deep South. The tension between George Wallace and myself did nothing to calm those fears. Indeed, I looked up to see the guy holding one of the lights waving desperately and giving me the signal to move on, to leave that particular line of questioning. I did not in fact do so, but it was probably the only time in my interviewing life that I have ever been directed by the electrician!

'But the reasons aren't obvious,' I said to Wallace.

'I'm not going to give you any. I don't have to give any reasons for it. I just don't think intermarriage among the black and white races is good. Now, that's – you've got what you want.'

'Well, no,' I said, 'I don't particularly want to –'

'Well,' said Wallace, 'I say I'm not going to discuss it any further.'

'Why, because it's irrational –'

'I just don't want to discuss it. I don't want to – *you* discuss it.'

'– or will come out as prejudiced?'

'I just don't want, because that's all you talk about is race –'

'No, let me make it clear,' I said. 'I want to talk about God and the country and a great many other things, but the point is, you're usually so explicit and good in your explanations that it makes one rather mystified why this is one point you can't explain.'

'Well,' said Wallace, 'I've mystified you now.'

'Ladies and gentlemen at home, you're all mystified,' I said. 'You once said, quoting your book, *Hear Me Out*, that if you had the choice and you had to choose, you'd rather be a fascist than a communist. Why is that?'

'Well, I don't know why I said that and I don't know whether I said that or not, frankly. I have seen many quotes in newspapers throughout the country that I never made. I saw them in *Time* magazine that I never made. I saw them in *Newsweek* magazine that I never made. So I don't know that I ever said that, because it would be a very poor choice to have to choose between communism and fascism. They're both evil systems in my judgement. If I had to choose between communism and fascism – I'll amend my statement – I wouldn't choose either. I'd just be a "non-chooser" if that's all I could choose. I'd just stand mute and not choose either.'

There had of course been two Senator McCarthys in the recent history of the United States. In addition to the liberal Senator Eugene there had also been Senator Joseph McCarthy, the leader of the notorious witch hunts against communists and communist sympathisers. I asked Governor Wallace, 'Which of the two would you say has made the greater contribution to American life?'

'Of course Senator Joseph McCarthy was in existence a pretty good while ago,' said Wallace. 'But Senator McCarthy was not far wrong in his attitude to the communist menace in this country. We see it every day today. We see even now Dean Rusk and the President saying there are communists involved in the demonstrations. We knew that five years ago. Dean Rusk now says the same thing that Mr McCarthy said some time ago. There were communists involved in movements of this sort. So Mr McCarthy may have been a little broad in some of his accusations, maybe, but in my judgement, the statement that communism is a serious threat to the internal security of our country is a fact.' Senator McCarthy being 'a little broad in some of his accusations' was immediately added to our list of favourite euphemisms.

Some of our crew remained nervous until we got on the plane at Montgomery airport. They had clearly been reading too many thrillers – they gazed out of the back window as if expecting us to be gunned out of town by a posse of beaten-up Buicks.

We caught a plane to Atlanta, where we changed flights in order to get to Portland, Oregon, in the middle of the night, ready for an interview with Senator Robert Kennedy at the end of his busy schedule the following day. The appointed time was 10 p.m., but we knew that could prove flexible.

Next evening we set up in a spare suite in the Benson Hotel, where we were staying in Portland. Considering what a busy schedule he had, Bobby Kennedy did pretty well and was with us by eleven o'clock. He said he was quite tired, but I soon noticed that fatigue in his case did not make him tetchy, but rather more relaxed. It was a good omen for the interview. My director Warren Wallace went over to the phone and rang the operator to say that we wanted no calls until further notice, and then we began.

We started with the so-called 'malaise' that so many American commentators talked about. 'I think it really comes down to the national purpose,' said Kennedy. 'What we are trying to accomplish and what is up at the top that's giving us some direction or some leadership. It's not that you're going to agree with the President on every issue. There's going to be tremendous disagreement, but the fact that he's giving the country some direction and there's somebody that you feel that's up there that's looking out for your own interest, not in a selfish way, and more beyond that, the interest of the country and the interest of the next generation. Though you might disagree with what he is doing, you can understand it and you rally to him and therefore to the country in time of crisis. For instance, President Kennedy's popularity was never higher than after the Bay of Pigs, when he said that we made a mistake but we've learned something from it. Although people thought that was a terrible disaster and a terrible mistake, and wasn't he stupid and foolish to do it, you still honour the fact that whoever it is, is part of you and part of your country and part of what you have such affection for.'

'That's what was exciting about the period '60 to '63,' I said. 'It seemed the first time that one person could set a style somehow, for a whole country.'

'It's what the people are, really,' said Kennedy. 'President Kennedy maybe stimulated it, but what made those days was not just – it wasn't him. He obviously played a role, but it was those young people who went and served, as I said. It was the young men and women who went and helped legislation. It was those who fought or struggled against discrimination, and it was people who were doing extra kind of things on behalf of their neighbour or their community, and felt that politics or political life was an honourable profession, as John Buchan, Lord Tweedsmuir said, and that you can make a difference.'

I asked him what he thought was his greatest achievement so far. He paused for a moment and then picked his role in the Cuban missile crisis by a narrow margin over his role in the election of 1960. 'It's interesting because you see, if the fourteen people who were involved – who were very, very significant, bright, able, dedicated people, all who had the greatest affection for the United States, probably the brightest kind of group that you could get together under those circumstances – if six of them had been President of the United States, I think that the world might have been blown up. That's the one side of it, and the fact is, the other side of it is, if Mr Khrushchev had been a different man at that time, the world would also have blown up . . . President Kennedy spent more time trying to give the Soviet Union time to calculate their position than to get the missiles out of Cuba. There was no question you could have brought it to a head at a much earlier time, and there were those involved in counselling President Kennedy who wanted to do it immediately. The idea of giving the other person time to understand what the consequences are is so important, to have some judgement about what he's going to do and will not do is so valuable. In the last analysis, if you ask me what the most important characteristic or what the most important qualification a person should have in that kind of position – it is judgement.'

I asked Senator Kennedy one of those questions I had also put to other candidates: 'As you read about yourself in the press, do you recognise the picture of yourself, or is there something that we should know about you, some quality that you reckon doesn't get full play in the press?'

Kennedy smiled. 'Kind, thoughtful, sweet – that kind of thing.'

'You think they miss a little . . .'

'Occasionally. I don't know. I think that they've had an opportunity to analyse me, so they can reach whatever conclusions perhaps much better than I can myself.'

That self-mocking quality was there again a few moments later. The quote I gave him was a gift really, but Robert Kennedy declined to take it. 'People sort of felt that you had to do the unpopular things. You quoted '60 as one of the things you're proud of. You had to do the unpopular things in '60.'

Another smile from Kennedy. 'Well, those people are my friends who excused me during those periods of time: "That's just because he has to do the unpopular things for his brother."'

How would he define leadership?

'I think to inspire people to exercise their best qualities . . . I was just thinking of that story about the French general who yelled out the window, "There go my people. I must follow them. I am their leader." I don't think that's it. I think it's the opposite of that.'

'You're often pictured in the open air. Some people write about you as if you're reckless and . . .'

Kennedy interrupted, in an attempt to assist me with my critique of him. 'Ruthless?' he said helpfully, to correct me.

'No, well – ruthless, too. We'll come to "ruthless", but I was only saying "reckless"! You just heard "ruthless".'

'Oh,' said Kennedy, smiling apologetically. 'That's what I hear so much.'

At this point the telephone rang. Warren Wallace picked it up. It was the operator calling to verify that we didn't want any phone calls. 'No, we don't – and that includes this one,' said Warren, and slammed down the receiver. Bobby Kennedy flashed that brilliant smile of his and said, '*He's* ruthless . . .'

I got back to the interview. 'No, reckless in the sense of all the physical things you do. Other people say you're very cautious. Which of the two portraits do you recognise more? Are you sometimes reckless?'

'No,' said Kennedy, 'I don't think I'm reckless.'

But he did like physical risk, didn't he?

'Well, I enjoy doing some of those kinds of things. Edith Hamilton wrote that men are not made for safe havens. That's part of a human being's life, or a man's life.'

'What about the other word you heard,' I asked. 'The ruthless – why do people say that?'

Kennedy smilingly declined another opportunity for self-promotion. 'I don't know. I'm sure you're going to get a lot of people to explain exactly why. I can't tell you. I think that's a difficult point for me to answer. I mean, why do you beat your wife?

'I suppose you'd rephrase it as decisive,' I said.

'No, I wouldn't try,' said Kennedy. 'They're entitled to what they think.'

Kennedy and Nixon clearly had diametrically different ways of dealing with criticism. I then asked Kennedy a question that

I had asked several of the candidates, only in his case it was, alas, soon to have an awesome dramatic irony. 'How would you like to be remembered? What would you like the first line of your obituary to say?'

'Something about the fact that I made some contribution to either my country or those who are less well off,' said Kennedy. 'I think again back to what Camus wrote about the fact that perhaps this world is a world in which children suffer, but we can lessen the number of suffering children.' He then added, in one of the simplest sentences I have ever heard from a politician, twelve words without a single two-syllable word in the sentence: 'And if you do not do this, then who will do this?' As those words sank in, he added, 'I'd like to feel that I had done something to lessen that suffering.'

Did he ever worry about how his children could ever feel that they had in any way topped what he had done?

'No, I think that they'll develop their own lives,' he said. 'I talked to one of my sons about it at one time. We were talking about what he was going to do and he said – he was twelve years old – he said, "I don't want to get involved in political life," and I said, "Well, what do you want to do?" He said, "I want to make a contribution." He loves animals and he knows all about them and he has read about them, and he said, "I want to make a contribution like Darwin and Audubon did." I think people work out their own lives. He wants to make that kind of contribution, and I think the other ones will do the same thing, just as long as they understand that in the last analysis, what is important is that they give something to others and not just turn in on themselves and decide that they are important. What they can contribute is the only thing that matters.'

'It would be quite difficult for them to find a higher office than, say, the Presidency of the United States, to move on to,' I said. 'But you think they're going to move on to separate fields?'

'Well, I suppose. But they're young, and I would hope that they would adjust.' He caught himself indulging in psychiatric jargon, 'Whatever that means!'

I asked Senator Kennedy to look at the United States in ten

years' time and say how it would look different and be different from what it was then.

'Areas in which I think we really have to accomplish something are that we've made a major contribution in trying to cut down on the reliance on nuclear weapons, that we've taken steps toward disarmament, that we've developed a system along with other nations of the world to help the underdeveloped nations of the world, and that we've established a system within our own country so that people can – even the very poor and the impoverished – educate their children so that they in turn could find decent jobs and live a decent life and not be hopeless and not be filled with despair. That's what I'd like to see.'

The fact that much of that still remains the agenda today is either a tribute to Kennedy's vision or a reflection on our shortcomings over the intervening twenty-five years. Maybe both.

After Kennedy had left, naturally we all talked about him. I could not remember an interview that had had such a positive impact on me. 'Charisma' is an over-used and ill-defined word, but when I am asked for my definition I am tempted to reply simply, 'Robert Kennedy.' Later I found that several of his phrases – like 'making a contribution' – had entered my own vocabulary, and none of the later revelations about his private life have dimmed for me the recollection of that late-night encounter in Portland, Oregon.

I flew back to London for thirty-six hours for a London Weekend Television board meeting, and was back in New York for the weekend. On Sunday night Clay Felker and I were in a group having drinks at Peter Maas's apartment, and the television was on for President Johnson's speech to the nation. The majority of the people in the room were probably opposed to his Vietnam policy, but the impact of his announcement did not produce any immediate cheers, only a stunned silence while the words sank in:'I shall not seek, and I will not accept, the nomination of my party for another term as your President.'

The rest of the evening was spent discussing what the consequences of Johnson's decision would be. I hope I played my part in the interchange of views about the national and international implications, but my own private thoughts were pitched at a much more mundane level – very soon we were going to have to fix up a date with the Vice-President, Hubert Humphrey, and there was no time to lose.

While we waited on news from the Humphrey camp, we were able to complete the rest of our jigsaw by talking with Governor Nelson Rockefeller, another of the Republican hopefuls. The Governor strode into the room where we were set up, and immediately exclaimed in that unforgettable gravelly voice, 'Hello, Dave!' Not since I was playing soccer for Raunds Town had anyone called me 'Dave'. For the rest of his life, Rockefeller continued to be the only person I knew who used that particular form of address.

'In an election year,' I began, 'everyone behaves a bit like a doctor, in the sense of trying to analyse what is wrong with the patient, as it were, America.'

'You need to be a psychiatrist now,' said Rockefeller.

'Everybody talks about the malaise,' I said, but if there was a malaise in America, what would he say it was?

'Well, I feel that the American people, perhaps for the first time, are beginning to lose confidence in themselves and in their country.' He said that he did not think this was justified, but that it was the effect of the three major problems of Vietnam, the cities and the ghettos, and fiscal problems.

I asked him whether there was any incident he would like to rewrite. What was his worst moment thus far?

'Well,' said Rockefeller, 'I would suppose that taking a stand on the subject of extremism at the Republican Convention four years ago and being roundly booed for fifteen minutes was a really interesting and valuable experience.'

'But as you stood there those fifteen minutes,' I said, 'you probably weren't thinking, "My, this is interesting and valuable!"'

'Oh, I did,' said Rockefeller, 'because I was given five minutes to make a speech. They postponed the time until it was three o'clock in the morning in the East, so that it wouldn't have too much impact on the East as far as television was concerned . . . I had been through an interesting campaign in California with bomb threats and calls, you know, something you really wouldn't sort of think in this country, and people who were supporting my campaign, women who were on committees run off the road at night, people breaking into their houses. It was a very interesting thing, so that I felt pretty strongly about taking this position on extremism . . .'

He could obviously hear the noise the audience was making, but were they demonstrating as well? Could he see them?

'Oh yes,' said the Governor. 'Shaking of fists, and they were pretty sore. I don't blame them in a way, because for quite a while, the conservative wing of the Republican Party had been frustrated in electing their candidates, and this was their chance, and I had been through some primaries in which I had just analysed the positions taken by Senator Goldwater. Now, I'm very fond of Senator Goldwater. He's an awfully nice person, but I think some of his positions were, let's say, not completely in tune with the times. By analysing these and discussing them, it did make it difficult, I think, for him, so that there was quite a strong reaction at the convention.' (Barry Goldwater being 'not completely in tune with the times' was another contender for the euphemism list.)

The Governor had a clear definition of leadership: 'The ability to determine through communications with people goals and objectives that are consistent with our heritage – in this country we've got a clear heritage – and then to find again in communications with people, a common means of achieving those goals. Lincoln once said that the thing that had bound the Federacy together was the common effort to lift the burdens from the shoulders of man, and this is a very interesting and a very exciting concept because, today, we really have that capacity in terms of modern society. To lift these burdens from the shoulders of man if we have the intelligence to use the forces which exist. I think we do, and this could be the factor that binds the world together, if we work together among nations to lift the burdens from the shoulders of man.'

At that first meeting I thought that Nelson Rockefeller wore his great wealth remarkably well. So often, a rich man trying to reach out to the common man talks down to his audience, or is unconvincing in other ways – you feel he does not really care. Nelson Rockefeller really did seem to care about lifting burdens from the shoulders of man.

On a flying visit back to London I was able to check on the progress with taping 'The Ronnie Barker Playhouse', and preparations for the second series of Ronnie Corbett's 'No, That's Me Over Here'. Back in New York again I spent a lot of time in the editing rooms with Warren Wallace and John McManus, our editor. It was there that we got the news that a date with Vice-President Humphrey had been fixed for 2.45 p.m. on 23 April.

We travelled down to Washington the day before, and checked in at the Mayflower Hotel. On the morning of the interview I had a brainstorming breakfast with one of the friends I had met through Clay, Walter Pincus of the *Washington Post*. After lunch we made our way to the White House. In a rushed first visit to one of the Vice-Presidential offices, there was not much time for anything other than the job in hand. It was an awe-inspiring experience to be in the White House at all, but I think that my abiding visual impression from that first visit was of the ever-present earpieces of all the Secret Service men. While the White House was not exactly cosy, nevertheless the nerve centre of the Western world was less forbidding than I had anticipated.

Hubert Humphrey had all the warmth we had expected. I began by asking him the question about the image of himself in the press. 'If there was someone who only knew you as a public figure, and got to know you privately, what would surprise them the most?' I asked.

The Vice-President's reply could have been construed as 'playing safe', but was probably just a result of his natural ebullience. 'Oh my, that's hard to say,' he said. 'Well, I guess most people know that I like a great variety of people. I really enjoy a wide variety of acquaintanceship, and I get a cultural enrichment, so to speak, out of it, at least a spiritual enrichment out of it. I like prize fighters, for example. As a group they're very interesting. People in the art world and in the theatrical world . . .' and so on. Then the Vice-President really went out on a limb. 'I like children. I like them very, very much . . . they're bright-eyed, and they make you feel good. It's sort of like tonic. I do tire at times of adults. I guess we all do.'

Looking back subjectively at his own career, what was the achievement that he was most proud of?

'I suppose it might be that day in 1948 when I stood before the Democratic Convention and asked my political party to take a stand on the basic issue of our time and the basic issue of all time: human rights.' Hubert Humphrey could certainly justly lay claim to that. 'I felt that the time had come when the Democratic Party had to take its stand, and I argued the case against the majority of the Resolutions Committee for a strong and effective and clear and unmistakable stand on the whole issue of civil rights.'

People in the South in the Democratic Party had taken their own direction in 1948, but now he was the choice of the Southern Governors as the next Democratic President. Did he sometimes pinch himself to see if it was true?

He said he did not. He felt that a man in public life ought to be an educator and a persuader. 'There has been a tremendous change taking place in America. It's come so fast that most people have even missed that it happened. All they see is the turbulence that's with it, but there is a basic change of attitude and a basic change of social institutions in America. It's been almost like a revolution. It's been a peaceful revolution in the main, and it's happened in the South just as it's happened in the North.'

Humphrey referred back to the events of 1948. 'In fact, that was just the opening of the door, and we haven't really marched out into the full sunlight of full opportunity and equal rights and human rights. We're beginning. That door is opening more and more. More sunshine is coming into American life, and I see it coming all across our country.'

Less than a month after the assassination of Martin Luther King, few people in America would have talked about sunshine. But you felt that Hubert Humphrey was not merely campaigning on behalf of the incumbent Administration, but that he really felt what he was saying. 'I believe with effort and determination and conviction and programme and courage, you can change these things. I believe in the capacity of the human being to shape history, to mould events, to create events and not just to be the victim of history or events.'

Hubert Humphrey was facing the problems faced by any Vice-President running for the Presidency while still in the shadow of the man who chose him as his running mate. As he learned throughout his campaign, it is hard to carve out an independent image while the boss is still in office.

After the Vice-President had talked of other great men that he had met, I asked him, 'Would you call President Johnson a great man?'

'Yes, I would,' said Humphrey. 'His greatness is in the knowledge and the techniques of government and understanding the big issues . . . I think that President Johnson's greatness also is in his tremendous dedication to the forward development of this country. He's not a radical, but he is a sincere and progressive, and he is a prudent, man.'

I said that there were rumours around about there being at some stage a sort of 'draft Johnson' movement. He would presumably have very mixed feelings about that?

'No, I wouldn't have any mixed feelings at all. If the Democratic Convention felt that the President wanted, or – I know he doesn't want it – that he should have the nomination, and if it was within the President's means to take on that responsibility again, I wouldn't have any mixed feelings.' Later press reviews of the interview were to concentrate on this pledge of loyalty. Mind you, they could have pointed out that the Vice-President set his President a pretty tough standard for re-admittance to the race: 'But I feel that if he can achieve what his goals are, namely an honourable and genuine peace in Southeast Asia and the unity of our country, or at least the reduction in the divisiveness that appears evident in our country . . . then that would merit any reward and any support that the Convention could give to him.' Since Humphrey was talking in late April, with less than four months to go to the Convention, such an achievement by August would also have merited several Nobel Prizes and a permanent place on Mount Rushmore.

If Humphrey became President, and his Vice-President disagreed on the grounds of conscience with one of his policies, would he expect the Vice-President to speak out?

'If it was a fundamental, basic cleavage,' said Humphrey, 'I would expect that that man would feel obligated to at least speak out.'

'Clearly,' I said, 'you haven't had one of those fundamental –'

'Not at all, not at all. To the contrary,' said the Vice-President. 'I believe that President Johnson will be known in history as having been responsible for some of the major breakthroughs in the social life and the social conditions of America, and breakthroughs for the better.'

The words of that particular endorsement were carefully chosen, but that did not alter their basic thrust – a vote for Hubert Humphrey would seem to many to be a vote for the record of the Johnson Administration. George Bush had some of the same problems in 1988, but with one vital difference – his boss, Ronald Reagan, was a popular President, unlike Johnson. Nevertheless, Bush handled his difficult position well. In an interview with me at Kennebunkport in September 1987, he made it crystal clear that he would not boost his own candidacy at the expense of a President he admired. Indeed, he managed to give a defiant, even macho, ring to his pledge of loyalty: 'If you said to me today, "I, in my infinite wisdom, can guarantee you'll be President if you'll give me three points critical of the President of the United States," I'll say to you, "Look, David, I don't want the job that much."'

My last question to Hubert Humphrey was the one about how he would like to be remembered. 'What would you like the first line of your obituary to say?'

'Well, as I think of it in these days,' said Humphrey, 'I'd like to be in a sense a sort of healer.'

As we heard those words, none of us doubted Hubert Humphrey's sincerity. He clearly wanted to do everything in his power to heal the divisions in America. What none of us knew was that sadly his nominating Convention in Chicago would turn out to be the most divisive in American history.

I had to fly back to London for our LWT press conference at the Savoy to launch the autumn schedule. Then it was back to

New York and the final editing. Fortunately I had managed to persuade Chet Collier, on the basis of the wealth of material that we had, to extend the sixty-minute special to ninety minutes, but quite honestly we could have used three hours. The eight candidates would still have only a maximum of nine minutes each.

As we edited, it was instructive to compare the candidates' answers to the 'communal' questions. 'Were there essentially any American characteristics?' Ronald Reagan felt that Americans had a certain innocence – 'I think Americans are kind of like puppy dogs. They love everybody, and they can't see why everybody doesn't love them, so when they go visiting some other country, they want to walk up, knock on the door and stick out their hand and say, "Hello, I'm Joe Smith from Arkansas."'

Richard Nixon said, 'One characteristic is what I would call a rather hopeless idealism. In view of the criticism around the world today of our activities in Vietnam, I suppose that sounds almost unbelievable . . .' It certainly would have done to Senator McCarthy: 'I think we had a kind of conception of America as a kind of the land of the innocent and the pre-ordained; this was a concept from which we had to escape, and I think we were escaping from it.' ('Were' implying until Vietnam.)

Some of the other questions sound almost antique by now. For example, I asked almost everyone, 'Do you believe in the principle "My country, right or wrong"?' Not a question that is part of the dialogue these days. Likewise, 'How do you define the word "communist"?' By 1988, it was card-carrying liberals that everybody was concerned about. In 1968 it did not occur to us to talk about the role of the First Lady. Despite the impact of Jacqueline Kennedy, the position had not yet grown to anywhere near its current prominence. There were also no questions in 1968 about abortion. It was not yet a litmus test. The famous (or infamous, depending on your point of view) Roe versus Wade Supreme Court decision was still five years away.

'The Next President' aired across the United States at different times during the last week of May. In New York it was transmitted on Channel 5 on Sunday 2 June. Three days later, just after he had claimed victory in the California primary, Robert Kennedy was assassinated. In Clay's apartment in New York, we gazed at the television screen in utter disbelief. No one had the words to encompass the grief that we all felt. It was announced a day or so later that Robert Kennedy's funeral would take place on Saturday at St Patrick's in New York. I called Larry Fraiberg, the head of Channel 5, to suggest that, as our inadequate tribute, we screened the whole tape of our interview under the title 'Robert Kennedy, the Man'. On Saturday night at eleven o'clock, the unedited film was aired, complete with clapper boards at the start of each reel. A week later, joined now by other stations, Channel 5 repeated it.

The 'what ifs' of history are often an unfruitful area of conjecture. But in the case of Robert Kennedy, they are almost impossible to avoid. Had he lived, he would almost certainly have won the Democratic nomination. Had he won the nomination, he would almost certainly have fared better against Richard Nixon, the Republican candidate, than did Hubert Humphrey. Humphrey's margin of defeat was so narrow that Kennedy in his stead would almost certainly have been elected, and the effect on American and world history would have been . . . ?

The horrifying end to Robert Kennedy's bid for the White House underlined once again the stark differences between British and American politics. Britain has no modern experience of political assassination changing the course of its electoral history as America had twice in the same decade. Britain's elections are never fought with a sense that the whole future of the society may be at stake: that there is a 'malaise' that may bring us down, a divisiveness that may tear us apart, a crisis that we simply may not survive.

Alongside the turbulence of America, and the sense of a generation rising up apparently intent on tearing down the whole fabric of society, the protests at Essex University, the London School of Economics and Hornsey Art School seemed trivial and positively staid.

The General Election of 1966 in Britain had been fought between three parties who shared a peaceful consensus about the way ahead. In 1968 America lay bleeding: in 1966 Britain was not even showing its bruises.

Vietnam was never a majority concern in Britain. It was a far-off war that involved us but peripherally. The fact that 'The Frost Programme's main coverage of Vietnam had been triggered by a theatrical evening devised by a world, rather than a British, citizen, Peter Brook, and by a domestic debate about dubious fund-raising underlined the insularity, albeit understandable, of British concern.

America in 1968 was profoundly pessimistic about its future: by comparison Britain in 1966 had been blithely optimistic. Even after the devaluation of November 1967, there was no navel gazing of remotely the same intensity as in America.

That to me was the underlying difference: the level of intensity. When America found a problem, they worried it to death. When Britain found a problem, they tried to laugh it away with self-deprecating humour. Each country's approach could have benefited from a forty per cent infusion from the other, but there was no mistaking the chasm between the two psyches.

While I had been keeping in touch with events in London through my flying visits during the first half of 1968, and by burning up the telephone lines, London was now calling much more insistently. After a brief holiday in the Bahamas, I had one more pressing commitment in New York before LWT went on the air. I had been asked to guest host the 'Tonight Show' on 4 and 5 July. With the help of Johnny Carson's production team, I set out to assemble two rosters of arresting talkers. The success of the two shows was naturally important to me personally, but I did not know then how important. Across town at 90 Park Avenue, the headquarters of Group W, Chet Collier was receiving a telephone call from Merv Griffin. Merv had a bombshell to drop. He was leaving Group W. He would complete his contract with Westinghouse, which had another eleven months to run, but then he would be joining the CBS network to take on Johnny Carson at 11.30 every night. Chet asked Merv to come and talk things over, but Merv replied that his mind was made up, and indeed the deal was already signed and sealed. Donald

McGannon, the President of Group W, called his principal aides together and appointed a four-man team headed by Chet to find Merv's successor. At least time was on their side . . .

Back in London, time was not particularly on the side of London Weekend Television. LWT had only been able to take over the Wembley studios three months before the first weekend's broadcasting. The schedule was as tight as it could possibly be. It was time to head for home.

NINE

On the Air with LWT

WHEN CYRIL BENNETT had announced the new LWT programme line-up at the beginning of May, the response had been positive. In fact, almost too positive. There were a few too many references to 'a revolution in television' for our liking. *Daily Mirror* readers, for example, were told that 'viewers are to get a programme format entirely different from anything yet seen on ITV or BBC'. Some situation comedies were being extended to forty-five minutes, admittedly, but that hardly justified the tag. How could you create a programme format that was *entirely* different?

In interviews we all tried to lower people's expectations rather than lift them to fever pitch. I told Aldo Nicolotti of the *Evening News*, 'We don't claim to have found the philosopher's stone as far as television is concerned. One can make no greater claim than to say we are trying to do something.' We even tried to carry the same theme across into the full-page ads announcing the coming of LWT. The first was headed: 'Flops we guarantee. Successes we only hope for.' We hoped this would lower the temperature a little. Then again, did full-page ads designed to lower the temperature merely raise it by their very prominence?

During the month before we went on the air, the company was able to announce that it would be acquiring a 2.5-acre site on the South Bank of the Thames, next to what is now the National Theatre. That was deliriously good news for the occupants of the top ten floors at Station House, Stonebridge Park, Wembley, the soulless building which had become the temporary home for all but the very few who were based at the Burlington Street headquarters. 'Wembley,' said Frank Muir, 'is the Florence of NW10.'

In one sense that last month before LWT got on the air was a frantic one. In another sense, although we did not know it at the time, it was the lull before the storm that was going to hit the company soon after it went on the air. Did any of the key players at London Weekend have an inkling of what was to come? Did anyone realise that the seeds of crisis had been sown? The true answer must be no – a countdown is not the moment for second thoughts. The adrenalin is working in the other direction, and there's no time for them anyway.

With the benefit of hindsight, the signs were there. Lord Hill had left the ITA when Harold Wilson offered him the Chairmanship of the BBC. Nothing automatically disastrous about that, but Michael Peacock had been relying on Hill's support in battles over networking. Michael's relationship with the Board was not as harmonious as it should have been. Several Board members found him arrogant. He had also alienated key figures in the network. And his remark to *The Times*, 'You won't have to be a moron to get something out of London Weekend Television,' was not guaranteed to ingratiate him with the previous weekend contractor, ATV, or its Managing Director, Lew Grade. The fact that ATV, Granada and the rest of the old guard had, under the watchful eye of the ITA, felt it prudent to admit a goodly number of LWT shows on to the initial schedule did not mean that they would not be waiting to pounce on anything that seemed less than an overnight hit. The BBC were concentrating even more of their firepower on Saturday nights; as a result there already seemed to be a reluctance around the network to risk their best shows when LWT most needed them – at the highly competitive weekend.

Such thoughts would have been out of place at the pre-launch party on the eve of LWT's first night. Crossed fingers gave way to optimism, and everybody wished everybody else good luck.

London Weekend's first night, on Friday 2 August 1968, was due to start at 7 p.m. with Frank Muir and 'We Have Ways of Making You Laugh'. At a recent press conference Frank had been asked what, if anything, made LWT different from other television companies. He had said it was 'The magic ingredient, Glee.' Alas, there was to be no glee for viewers from Frank on that opening night. Instead there was just a blank screen. ACTT had struck, in at least two senses of the word. The union had been greatly unsettled by the whole franchise row, and their threat of a national strike in August 1968 if new demands were not met was a by-product of that. It was no way to usher in a brave new world, and was a terrible letdown for everybody. So far, we gradually learned, the strike was not continuous, but selective. Recorded programmes were still getting on the air, but live programmes like 'We Have Ways of Making You Laugh' were not.

That did not seem a particularly good omen for my first show, which was due on the air at 9.15. The plan that had been worked out for my three shows a weekend (up until the end of the year) was that 'Frost on Friday' would be the more hard-hitting, current affairs sort of programme, and 'Frost on Saturday', while still an actuality programme, would be more on the lines of the more light-hearted 'Frost Programmes'. Sunday would be an amalgam of 'Frost Report'-type comedy and big-name variety. All three programmes were fully networked at the same time – quite a novelty! – with the exception of Granada, who felt that London Weekend's determination to play current affairs at 9.15 on a Friday was far too avant-garde, and scheduled the programme at 11 p.m. It was indeed in ITV terms quite a bold move to give the viewers current affairs at Friday night peak time, and differentiating the three shows helped Cyril to win them all good slots on the network. We did lose something in terms of total unpredictability, of course. With 'The Frost Programme' on Associated-Rediffusion, viewers never knew in advance whether they were going to get the Beatles or the Archbishop of Canterbury. Now we would have to ensure that there was still unpredictability within each of the three genres of programme.

It is a commonplace of current affairs programmes that whenever you start a new series, you vow that you will get Howard Hughes or the Pope for the first programme, and somehow it never works out that way. So it was with this, not just the first programme of a new series, but the first programme on a new station. None of the long shots came up (although one did for the second night), and in the last few days of our regular breakfast meetings we zeroed in on the 'conversion' of John Braine. John had been a socialist all his life, and one of the Labour Party's leading propagandists, in his own particular way. Now he had just announced in the *Spectator* that he had become a Conservative. The reason was freedom, he said. In some ways, however, he was a surrogate for all those Labour supporters or voters who were beginning to feel disillusioned and let down by the Government and its brave new world of white-hot technology. There is today a delicious irony about the identity of the man we chose as the passionate defender of socialism. Today he is one of the Tory right wing's greatest propagandists, and one of Labour's most outspoken critics, but then he was the editor of the *New Statesman*. One thing that hasn't changed is his name – Paul Johnson.

I began the programme with John Braine, who had been quoted as saying that he now regarded the left as representing 'what I would call in a very old-fashioned way the Forces of Evil'.

'John, thanks to the evil forces that we've been talking about, would you say overall that we're less free now than we were?'

John Braine did not mince his words. 'Oh, far less free – our freedom diminishes every day,' he replied, 'and life for the ordinary man gets worse and worse every day. The fact is, as far as this Government is concerned, if you're homosexual, or you're a long-term prisoner, if you're an immigrant, if you want an abortion, if you want a divorce, then the Government has something in its basket of goodies for you. But if you're a normal, law-abiding taxpayer, then life will get worse and worse.' There was strong applause at this point. 'The Government says it knows better than you how to educate your children, it knows better than you how to spend your money – what little you've got left after your taxes. And, of course, it knows how much money you should get, it says how much money you've got to get and in the case of some unfortunate people, it knows better than you what sort of a house you should live in, never mind whether you like the house you're living in or not, the Government knows better; the Government always knows better. And so your freedom every day and in every way diminishes and diminishes.' Just for good measure he added, 'The press on the whole in this country is left-dominated. *The Times* to begin with is left-dominated –'

This was news to me. 'How is *The Times* left-dominated? I hadn't noticed.'

John Braine described *The Times* as 'the English Pravda', and its proprietor Lord Thomson as 'the chief offender'.

'Now, in the front row listening to you there has been the editor of the *New Statesman*, Mr Paul Johnson. Would you exonerate him from this charge, or would you include him?'

John Braine had no doubts. 'I should say that in many ways he's the worst of the lot – in fact, I did say some time ago that when I was Pope, and as you should know any Catholic, whether married or not, is technically eligible to become Pope, he would be one of the first I should have burned at the stake.'

'Well, David,' Johnson began, 'I feel it a bit difficult to argue at this sort of intellectual level, frankly.'

John Braine interjected, 'He means it's a lower level than he's accustomed to.'

'No, I don't mean precisely that,' said Johnson. 'I mean, I find it difficult to argue when people are clearly thinking with their guts instead of with their brain, if I may put it that way.'

In debating terms, it sounded as though Johnson had won the point, but I suspect that in the late Sixties the growing disillusionment with the Wilson Government could be accurately described as a gut reaction, a Braine reaction. In politics it is vital to know what people feel as well as what they think. Even if they had never had it so good, if they did not *feel* that that was true, the Government could expect only ingratitude from the electorate. And by the second half of 1968, people were having a gut reaction to what seemed more and more like the empty promises Labour had made back in 1964.

When Kingsley Amis, who like John Braine started on the left and then moved over to the right, joined the discussion, I asked him whether he was also with Braine in this discussion.

'I thought a moment ago that I wasn't very much with him, but I think I am now . . . I think, though the Labour Party and many people in the Labour Party dare not admit it, they would dearly like to dismantle our freedom. And I say that because some of the people that they admire, or have a sneaking or unsneaking affection for, are enemies of freedom in other countries. Like Ho Chi Minh, like Castro, and the man who has really earned the title in all senses of the phrase to be the bloody fool of the twentieth century, that murdering moron Che Guevara.'

Another Sixties icon was being re-assessed!

The next night, on the somewhat lighter 'Frost on Saturday', we knew we had a coup from the world of show business – a whole show with Bob Hope. And since we had recorded it a couple of weeks earlier when he was in England, it also escaped the threat of union action.

Bob Hope's response when I asked him the 'Next President' question 'How would you like to be remembered?' said it all. 'As getting a laugh,' he said. 'I've got a couple of jokes for on the way to the cemetery.' And you knew that he had.

On Sunday, we were pitchforked right into the strike. The studio scheduled for the live transmission of 'Frost on Sunday' at 9.10 was nowhere near ready. What should we do? By lunchtime the decision had been made not to give in. We would move to the 'World of Sport' studio down the corridor and try to put together a management crew. Cyril Bennett became the producer, and he called Michael Peacock at the Old Burlington Street offices, where he was up to his elbows in talks over the dispute, and persuaded him to come out and take over as director. 'The Managing Director,' said Frank Muir later, 'is managing to direct.'

Frank himself was going to be the floor manager until it was 'pointed out' to him that, as a member of Equity, his activity would be an infringement of ACTT duties. Frank still did the warm-up, and Cyril Bennett took over as floor manager, the first floor manager I had ever seen smoking a Havana cigar, and certainly the first with whom I had worked who had absolutely no idea what he was supposed to be doing. We decided to tape the programme as soon as possible – which turned out to be 9.30 – and then if we ended up with a show, to put it on the air as quickly as possible – which turned out to be 10.40.

I welcomed the audience: 'You're sitting where they tot up

the sports results, and I hope it's not too uncomfortable. Talk about "trial by television" . . .'

I explained that another union, NATKE, the National Association of Theatrical and Kinema Employees, had said they could not change any props or scenery in the course of the programme, so the viewers were going to get a lot of shots of a drum kit, because we did want to use it at least once.

Peter Dunn of the *Sunday Times* watched the programme with a group of ACTT members who were busy noting down the names of members of staff who seemed to be collaborating with the management. 'At one point,' he wrote, 'ACTT members triumphantly noticed a man who came accidentally onto the screen and who appeared to be operating a camera . . . another name for the list. But he wasn't a TV man at all: he was Cyril Bennett's driver pulling cables across the studio floor.'

We had sketches from Ronnie Barker and Ronnie Corbett. We used the drum kit for our resident singer Julie Driscoll. Topping the bill in her first solo appearance without her brother Abi was the Israeli singer Esther Ofarim. And we had a chat session in the middle of the show on 'disasters I have known' with Ted Ray and Kenneth Williams.

We were very happy to have pulled it off. One man who was not so happy was the Assistant General Secretary of ACTT, Mr Alan Sapper. 'Not only is this action contrary to the ITA regulations,' he told the *Daily Sketch*, 'but this equipment can be quite dangerous if inexperienced technicians should handle it. They are walking on a knife edge and taking their lives in their hands.'

Someone stuck the quote on a notice board with the inscription 'Beware of killer cameras'. Though, to be fair to Mr Sapper – not everybody's first impulse – there was one moment during the show when I shouted, 'Help, I'm being garrotted!' as I was caught by the cable of a camera trundling past. (I was saved by Cyril Bennett's ever-resourceful driver.)

The reaction to that first weekend was distinctly encouraging. The headline on Julian Critchley's review in *The Times* was 'Honours go to London Weekend'. Peter Black in the *Mail* commented: 'Insofar as it got off the ground, London Weekend left slightly the deepest impression of the new start, though it had the advantage of inheriting the part of the week that was most obviously open to improvement.'

After the weekend, the strike intensified, and we were off the air for both our second and third weekends. Everyone at London Weekend felt in a state of suspended animation. It was maddening. We had been building up to this moment for fourteen months. And the *ad hoc* mixture of programmes that ITV was managing to transmit was a gift for the BBC, who were certainly not treating August as a holiday month. As far as the Frost shows themselves were concerned, there at least there was some good news. I got the message that one of our long shots had come to pass. General Moshe Dayan, the Israeli Minister of Defence, would be happy to give his first interview since the Six-Day War in 1967. He could not come to London, but we were welcome to travel to his home in Israel to record the conversation. On the Monday after our second blank weekend, we flew to Israel and checked in at the Dan Hotel in Tel Aviv. The interview had been set for 6 p.m. the following day.

The first impression you had on meeting Moshe Dayan was that he was nowhere near as tall as you imagined. The second and more abiding impression was the warmth of his smile. His home was full of archaeological artifacts, most of which he had dug up himself, and in private conversation that was the subject that really got him talking much more than any military topic.

In 1953 he had become his country's Chief of Staff, and he was acclaimed as a brilliant military commander after successfully planning and leading the invasion of the Sinai Peninsula in 1956. In 1958 he was elected as a Labour member to the Israeli Parliament, the Knesset. He had served as Minister of Agriculture under David Ben-Gurion until 1964. On 1 June 1967, with war against the Arabs imminent, he was appointed Minister of Defence by popular demand. Two days later he had publicly stated that 'diplomacy must be given every chance', but then on Monday 5 June he had launched a blistering attack against Arab forces from Egypt, Syria and Jordan.

I began by asking him about that remark that 'diplomacy must be given every chance'. 'Now, just before you said that, did you grin to yourself and think, "Well . . ."?'

'With everybody watching, I couldn't grin to myself,' said Dayan. 'No, you see, because I was appointed to be Minister of Defence, right away the first reaction in the Arab countries and probably outside was "That means war." I didn't like that . . . I thought that I should make such a move to abolish that . . . That doesn't mean that I had in mind at that time the next morning the war would start, but I didn't want the impression that, because I became the Minister of Defence, that meant the next day I am going for war. So I had to do that.'

I asked him what it felt like on the Wednesday (day three of the war) when he entered the gate of the old city of Jerusalem and went to the Wailing Wall. Said Dayan, 'I think I was really moved. You know probably not so much because of the Wailing Wall, but because of Jerusalem . . . You enter the gate and come into Old Jerusalem . . . and if you feel about Jerusalem the way we feel about it – I suppose almost every one of us feels that way about Jerusalem – then it is like going into a shrine. You feel there is something holy all around you.'

Dayan said he'd been concerned 'in the last minutes of the war, I mean, counting in minutes' whether his commander in the north on the Golan Heights 'would be able to do everything that he had to do within the time limit'.

I was intrigued by his mention of the time limit. 'You had a sort of timetable there because you had to do it before the cease-fire, didn't you?'

'Yes,' said Dayan. 'At that time, time was running out already. We had to stop the war. We had the Security Council already having their decision about it and I think that at that time the Syrians and the Egyptians and Jordanians already announced they were ready to cease fire, and it just had to become practice.'

I said that it was jolly good from his point of view that the Security Council took so long to get round to it, wasn't it?

Dayan's reply was remarkably specific about the way his mind had been working. 'No. I don't think that this machinery can work faster than that. I remember that before the Sinai campaign ten years or eleven years back, the Government asked me, "Can you do it? Take the entire Sinai within eight days?" and I said "I suppose I can, but why eight days?" And they said, "Now look here, the Security Council will be called on this day, it will take them two days to debate and then there will be one resolution, then we shall not obey, then there'll be another meeting, and the time that we have at our disposal will be more or less eight days." Now, this time, six days was the time that we had.'

In fact, Dayan had a little longer than he had expected. There was a gap between the time that the Syrians announced they were ready for a ceasefire, and the time that the United Nations observers managed to get to Damascus to confirm at what hour the ceasefire should take place. 'They couldn't find for six hours what time they wanted to stop the fight.'

'And you can do a lot in six hours . . .' I said.

'It was about enough, yes,' said Dayan.

I then asked General Dayan about war. 'Could it in fact be an exciting, exhilarating thing in a way, when you knew what you were fighting for?'

'It is the most exciting and dramatic thing in life, is war,' he said. 'It is probably the most hateful and unhuman thing, but war is the most exciting drama I think that can exist . . . I don't know anything else which gets people so excited. Not happy, of course, but really excited. Even when you try to follow the individual pilot going into the sky and waiting for the moment he would meet the other plane – is exciting. It is nervous, but it is exciting. The commander sitting . . . watching what is taking place, you are frightened, you are nervous, but you are excited. And I think that the most exciting event that can happen in life is war. I hope I am not sounding happy about war, but I think it is very exciting.'

Did he mean that although people talk about war corrupting, in fact it can bring the best out of people in a way?

'I think that war as such is probably the most unhuman act that people have invented . . . but within the framework of war you find individuals doing the most heroic acts and the most human acts, like trying to save the other fellow, though you know that you are risking your whole life, and probably you are losing your whole life.'

'Could it be almost a drug, really, because it is so exciting?'

'I haven't tried any drugs,' Dayan laughed. 'Never tried any drugs, never got drunk in my life. I don't know, I don't even play cards. I can't compare it.'

I said that the Six-Day War read like one of those Old Testament battles, because there was a lot of smiting going on.

'It depends what book,' said Dayan. 'You had better ask some of our religious people. They are sure that the army had nothing to do with it, nothing to do with winning the war. It was all the Almighty's act, nothing to do with our troops and planning.'

Had he felt the hand of the Almighty?

'I don't know,' said Dayan. 'I'm not Orthodox. I believe in the human spirit. I believe that.'

'You don't see it as simply that Jehovah was on the side of Israel?' I asked.

'No,' said Dayan. 'But I think that – I hope it will sound all right – that we were on the side of Jehovah.' The room filled with laughter.

Moshe Dayan said that he was very proud of the fact that the Jews never gave up their faith even when they were under very strong pressure to do so. 'But we didn't always fight back. Sometimes we just went on the fire, got burned or to the Inquisition. We sacrificed ourselves. I am not very proud of that. So I suppose that this generation of the Jews here now, they have both. They have the decision of the Jews in the past to stick to our own faith and believe. But also to fight back, not only to say, "All right, I will fight to my last drop of blood." No. "I will fight to *your* last drop of blood. I am going to win it. I am not going to just stick to my belief, but I want really to survive, to fight and to hit you back."'

'In a sense, do you feel that the Arabs have a case for feeling the way they do?'

Dayan answered the question straightforwardly. 'If I were an Arab, I probably would have thought the same way.'

If he were an Arab, he'd probably be a member of Al Fatah, I suggested.

'No, no, they're not very clever, no.' There was more laughter all round. But as for Arabs in general, 'I don't think that there is anything basic, personal, that would deny them living together with us in good and close friendship . . . I think that in daily contact the Jews and Arabs can live together.'

There was just about time for one more question. (Yes, you've guessed it.) 'How would you like to be remembered? What would you like to be the first line of your obituary? What would you like history to say about you?'

Dayan looked amazed. 'Do you ask it seriously?'

'Seriously. Really . . .'

'Then I will tell you serious,' said Dayan. 'What do you think I am dying for? To think what will happen later on? Taking all the trouble to die just to worry what is going to happen later on? I don't care a damn about what is going to happen after I die. Once I am dead – I am dead; and that is what I am dead *for* – not to worry about anything. You can say whatever you want after I am dead.'

His devil-may-care attitude to death fitted perfectly with his devil-may-care attitude to life. I thought as we drove back to the Dan Hotel that he would have agreed with Edith Hamilton. Men were not born for safe havens. Certainly he wasn't.

We flew back to London the next day, to be greeted with two more positive items. John Lennon and Yoko Ono had agreed to appear together on our Saturday programme; and Baldur von Schirach, the former head of the Hitler Youth and at one time the Reichführer of Vienna, had also agreed to an interview. Von Schirach had been released from Spandau Prison two years previously after serving a twenty-year sentence for war crimes. He was now living in Trossingen in Germany. A date had tentatively been fixed for the next day.

This would be his first interview since he had left Spandau, and we could not afford to give him time to change his mind. Next morning at 10.10 we set off for Zurich, the most convenient staging-point for Trossingen.

Fortunately I'd started my preparatory work on von Schirach when we made our first approach to him a few weeks earlier, but nevertheless overnight there was little time for sleep. In moments like that you have to strike a balance between sleep and homework. It is important to be properly briefed and prepared; but it is every bit as important not to arrive exhausted for an interview, particularly one like that which I was about to undertake. Its course was impossible to predict in advance: I had to be ready to seize whatever openings were provided.

On the flight to Zurich it was impossible not to feel a massive sense of culture shock from just two days earlier in Tel Aviv. Moshe Dayan had told me that of the Jews' two great enemies in the twentieth century, the Germans had been by far the worse. 'The Arabs are primitive. Probably now and again they act against us like they act against some other Arab people. Like the Egyptians fighting some of the Yemenites and using gas and whatnot. But with a modern and educated people like the Germans, the method that they used, no comparison whatsoever.' Now we were about to meet one of the few surviving leaders of that enemy.

Debriefing for history – or the first draft of it – both the architect of Israel's victories and one of Hitler's closest friends and colleagues carried with it a real responsibility. At the same time, it was a unique intellectual privilege, and for that I was profoundly grateful.

Von Schirach was living – with a lady friend – in some luxury in Trossingen. While the cameras were being set up, he suggested that we take a walk in the garden. 'At the age of twenty-three, you did your first programme on television. At the age of twenty-three, I was made head of the Hitler Youth. So you see, Mr Frost, we have a great deal in common . . .'

The thought almost stopped me dead in my tracks. I mumbled, 'Well, I don't know about that,' and changed the subject. As we talked it became clear to me that a routine prosecution of von Schirach would be fruitless. On questions like his direct involvement in the deportation of Jews from Vienna, even the combined efforts of the prosecutors at Nuremberg had not managed to nail him down for the court. In response to other accusations, it was likely that we would get only a brief, routine and spurious expression of regret. That, too, would get us no further. I decided that the most chilling programme could be achieved conversationally, and that the most telling point would be if viewers could see for themselves that Baldur von Schirach still did not understand the enormity of what his party had done, and had still not repented.

When von Schirach first met Hitler, what were the qualities that had immediately impressed him?

Von Schirach said that his father had been impressed by Hitler 'because he was so well informed about music'. His American mother had been deeply impressed by Hitler 'because she said, "At last, a patriotic German."'

'Was he a witty man?'

'Certainly, yes,' said von Schirach. 'In conversation he could be very witty, and he liked a joke at his table and would like to laugh about it.'

'What sort of jokes did he tell?'

'Well, he would like to make fun of certain people, and especially he liked to imitate the dialect of the Saxons, for instance. The dialect of Mr Ulbricht, yes? He couldn't do it well, but he enjoyed himself telling such jokes and tales in the dialect.'

'Those were the sort of jokes that he told, were they?' I asked, in search of further hilarity.

'Yes, there was a favourite joke he repeated again and again,' said von Schirach. 'When he heard that a Minister of the Cabinet or some important person belonging to the party was a hunter, he'd then start pulling his leg by asking him, "What is your favourite game?" and then the poor man, not knowing what was going to happen would say, "A stag" or "A roebuck" or something like that, and then he said, "How do you attack that poor little animal?" and he said, "Well, naturally with a gun." And then Hitler would say, "How is the animal armed? How can it defend itself?" And then that would go on and on and he would finally say, "There's really nothing to admire in a man who doesn't attack a wild animal with a spear or with a knife, but sits somewhere in the forest with a gun and then shoots it." And such conversation – it's just an example – would go on and on and on, and he could be very funny about these things, and very witty, although naturally the hunters were a bit sour when they heard such remarks. But that was his favourite topic.'

'He was against hunting?'

'Against hunting entirely,' said von Schirach. 'And against smoking and against drinking.'

'Did Eva Braun have any influence on Hitler, or was she just a decoration?'

'I think she was his pet,' said von Schirach. 'I wouldn't say there was an influence – Hitler wasn't the man to be influenced.'

'Did you ever see Hitler and Eva Braun have a row?' I asked.

'No,' said von Schirach.

'Why not, do you think?'

'Well, Mr Frost, you didn't have a row with Hitler,' said von Schirach.

'You certainly didn't have two, anyway,' I said.

Hitler had treated von Schirach like 'a political father'. He 'was very capable of friendship and very true to his friends'.

Was he mad?

'Certainly. Absolutely,' said von Schirach. 'And I should say we could almost fix the date. When he had declared war on Poland, I went to him and to the Chancellor and said, "This war will certainly involve also the United States. This war is going to become a world war like the last one."'

That was the moment when he thought that Hitler was starting to go mad?

'That was the moment when I thought now this man has no sense of reality. He has no feeling in his fingertips for the psychology of other nations.'

This was not, quite clearly, an argument about the morality of the decision, but about its practicality. And if the swift conquest of Poland in 1939 seemed to prove Hitler right and von Schirach wrong, there was a second revelation of madness to come. After Stalingrad, von Schirach claimed he had warned Hitler about the Foreign Minister, Ribbentrop. 'I said, "Now is the time to release, discharge, Mr Ribbentrop, one of the greatest fools in foreign policy, and get hold of Count Schellenberg, the great friend of Russia. And the man whom Stalin and Molotov knew as a true friend" . . . I mean, if that would have been carried out, it would have been disastrous for you, for your nation, yes?'

Did I notice a certain gleam in von Schirach's eye as he dwelt on that thought, or was I just imagining it?

'What did Hitler say?' continued von Schirach. '"Don't say a word against Ribbentrop, he is greater than Bismarck." After hearing that I knew the man is downright mad.'

I asked if there wasn't a bitter irony in something we had been discussing a little earlier on, when von Schirach quoted Hitler as loving to tell stories against hunting, 'and attack people who attack defenceless animals'. Because no man would ever attack as many defenceless human beings as Hitler had between 1939 and 1945.

'That's just the thing,' said von Schirach. 'He probably would never have killed a fly and a dog, but he probably just because of this was always ready to kill people.'

'What, of all the things he did,' I asked, 'do you think it's most important that people remember?'

There should have been only one answer to that question – the genocide of six million people – but von Schirach said, 'The most positive thing he did was to give work to the unemployed. During the whole Weimar Republic, no Government was successful in giving the unemployed their bread and butter. There was a great moral depression in Germany after the loss of World War I – not because we had lost the war, but because we had been humiliated in Versailles, deprived of honour, something that you cannot do to a great nation, and the Germans were, and are, and will be a great nation.'

Those last few words, and the way von Schirach said them seemed enough to put back the cause of German reunification by at least twenty-five years.

Von Schirach talked about his prison sentence: 'I must say now quite clearly, yes, there were many things that made this sentence in many ways ridiculous. I'll give you one example: I grew in one of the parts of the really great prison gardens, I grew tomatoes there, six hundred and about seventy or eighty plants, and when they were ripe I put them in a little carton, dumped them onto a dung heap because we were not allowed to eat them.' Von Schirach's aggrieved tone became more intense. 'And it was not permitted to give these tomatoes that the war criminals had grown to the hospital or a home for the old aged . . . It was destroyed – what we grew was destroyed . . .'

At that moment, von Schirach seemed almost unhinged. He was looking through the wrong end of a telescope.

Von Schirach had been sentenced to twenty years in Spandau 'for perverting a nation's youth'. I asked him if he had had as much influence over his youths as the Jesuits always said that they had over theirs.

'Yes,' said von Schirach. 'I loved the kids and the kids loved me.' The phrase hung in the air. It sounded more appropriate to a children's seaside entertainer than to the head of the Hitler Youth.

We then began to talk about the subject of the Jews. 'I asked Hitler between '32 and '33, "What are you really intending as far as the Jews go?" And he said, "They shall keep their shops, they shall keep their positions in the banks, in the commercial organisations and so on. I only do not want to have them in the Government." It is his quotation, not mine. I never had any objection to any Jew in the Government. My parents were friends of Jews, Jews were in the house of my parents, welcome guests.'

Von Schirach said that he only knew about the extermination of the Jews at the end of 1944. I pointed out that his wife had had a copy of *Life* magazine in 1943, so the family did see some foreign publications.

'But you see, during a war, all foreign publications are read with a certain inner resentment. You say propaganda and so on . . .'

So he had known about extermination, but had dismissed it as propaganda?

'Yes – and not only so. No. From Vienna Jews were being deported as I took over as the representative of the state in Austria, and I enquired about these deportations. And they said, "Well, yes, in Vienna they cannot live because the population would kill them, and it's much better for them to go into special Jewish camps where they are well treated."'

But he was also close to Hitler. 'It must have been very difficult not to know what was happening from his attitudes alone, mustn't it?'

Von Schirach admitted, 'He hated the Jews. That was the thing you heard almost every time you were there. But he would never tell you directly what he considered the final solution, that is now quoted so often.'

But there were so many things going on. There was what his wife had seen in Holland in 1943. The von Schirachs were reading about extermination in foreign publications which they dismissed as propaganda. There were the Jews leaving Vienna. 'It must have been very difficult for two and two not to add up to four, surely?'

Von Schirach replied, 'Mr Frost, we are human beings, and human beings are not always very brave. Also in these times, we close our eyes to many things that are happening. We do not accept them as facts because these facts are disagreeable. And, Mr Frost, something else. Now I do not want to excuse myself, I just want to – an old man has no other interest but the truth, the historical truth. I was there, I had a job, I was the Lord Mayor of Vienna. I was at the same time suddenly, forty-one, the man responsible for the evacuation in Germany. Mr Frost, I didn't have the damned time to think about anything else. From day to night I was working. My first rest was in a prison camp.'

'Now I understand,' I said. 'I couldn't believe that you absolutely knew nothing till the end of 1944, but what is humanly understandable is you sort of knew, but never admitted it to yourself, because people try not to admit things to themselves, don't they? . . . I mean, I suppose that when Hitler kept enquiring about the number of Jews in Austria – that was another time really when one just had to somehow not question the reason why he was asking, as it were. Was that so? I mean, what did you think?'

'Ours not to reason why. Ours just to do and die.' Von Schirach's choice of quotes was somewhat unsettling. 'But when

I took over this job in Austria I was called to the headquarters . . . and they told me, "Now, you have nothing to do with the deportation. That is the job of the SS. It's going on for quite a while, and it's not going to be discontinued." What could I do? . . . You know, the SS could be so very sweet about answering such questions. You always thought they were so nice and kindly.'

'You didn't really believe what they were saying totally, but it was easier to take it at face value, I suppose?' I asked.

'A politician never believes what he is told,' von Schirach admitted.

'If you had to pick one lesson, one conclusion that you'd like to draw, one concluding remark, what would it be?'

Von Schirach paused for a second and then said, 'May I quote *Alice in Wonderland*? "'If seven maids with seven mops swept it for half a year, do you suppose,' the walrus said, 'that they could sweep it clear?' 'I doubt it,' said the carpenter, and shed a bitter tear."'

That would take some working out. But it was time to conclude. I chose my closing words carefully. 'Herr von Schirach, what you've said has been most instructive. Thank you.'

I had found many of von Schirach's remarks even more chilling than I had expected, and I thought that viewers would feel the same way when they saw the programme.

Just to complete a schizophrenic week, when I arrived back at the office the next day it was time to view a rough cut of the Moshe Dayan interview, which we were broadcasting that Friday night. On Saturday night John Lennon and Yoko Ono were in marvellous, wacky form. Yoko produced her famous painting called 'Hammer a Nail In'. It was part of a board, and when you hammered the nail, you were supposed to get vibrations.

I asked some members of the audience to try hammering the nails in. One said, 'It gave me a feeling of satisfaction.' Another said, ecstatically, 'It's unbelievable.' I tried hammering in a nail as well, but when asked I had to admit, 'I just feel like a man hammering in a nail.'

On 'Frost on Sunday' that weekend our main guests were Peter Sellers, Sammy Davis, Jr., Danny La Rue and Ted Ray.

The show rose like a good soufflé. One of the best moments came when Sammy Davis, late getting to the studio, dashed on the stage during a sketch featuring Peter Sellers and me. He thought we had been ad-libbing waiting for him to appear: in fact, he shouldn't have been in the sketch at all. Getting out of that merely added to the entertainment, as Sammy did a quick impersonation of James Stewart and then fled.

On the following Sunday night, topping the bill we had the Beatles singing 'Hey Jude' in their first musical performance on television for ages. We had pencilled in the Baldur von Schirach interview for the following Friday night, and we were trying to line up Ian Smith for the following week. Then, quite suddenly, all hell broke loose. On Monday 9 September, Lew Grade chaired a network programme meeting. London Weekend had now had precisely three normal weekends since the strike. Ratings were only available for two weekends. But even with this flimsy evidence of what they claimed were unsatisfactory ratings, the old guard decided the moment had come to hit back. Faced with what the *Sunday Times* was to call a 'Palladium counter-attack', Cyril Bennett and Michael Peacock were unable to hold the line. 'Frost on Saturday' was moved from 6.45 p.m. to 10.55 p.m. Michael Parkinson's 'Sports Arena' was transferred from Friday evening to Sunday afternoon at 2.30, and Southern, Westward and ATV refused to have the Sunday play or the Saturday 'Frost' at all. Another report said that ATV would take 'Frost on Saturday' on Monday. (Maybe we should have offered to play 'Sunday Night at the London Palladium' on Fridays.)

Ironically enough, Tuesday's papers carried the latest ratings, which announced that 'Frost on Sunday' was number one in the London region. By Thursday, however, the newspapers had the schedule changes. Needless to say, the headlines concentrated on the 'Frost' shows. The Saturday show was to be dropped by ATV and Yorkshire, and retained at 10.55 by London Weekend and Granada. (Actually that was to prove a much more comfortable time, but that was not Thursday's story.) 'Frost on Sunday' would remain at 9.10 on London Weekend and Granada, and would play at 10.10 on ATV and Yorkshire.

For a day or two we were under siege from reporters on

the telephone and outside the building. That sort of scene is uncomfortable for everybody, to put it mildly, but it is particularly disconcerting for anyone who hasn't been through it before. I tried to reassure everybody that it was only a passing phase, and that those headlines would just be tomorrow's fish and chip paper.

Two questions were puzzling. First of all, why this panic after only two strike-free sets of ratings? Lew Grade and the rest had made great play with a BBC statistic claiming a sixty-one per cent audience share in August. That was hardly surprising with the strike anyway, but when the official figures came out – late – they showed the BBC still with a majority share, but only fifty-two per cent.

The second question was: Why the old guard hostility? Much of it could be traced to London Weekend's implicit – and in a few cases, explicit – criticism of what had gone on before. Writing about what he called 'an effective counter-attack by the old guard of television', Bruce Page in the *Sunday Times* stated, 'their resurgence was embodied in the rugged presence of Mr Lew Grade, of Associated Television, who has never been much impressed by talks of daring experiments in television'. That was probably true. Lew Grade certainly preferred a more traditional kind of television to that of the 'Frost' programmes. Maybe there was something personal in it too, although I could not think why. He was quoted as having said at the 9 September meeting, 'I got where I am by knowing what I hate, and I know I hate David Frost.'

I was rather shocked by this statement, which I vaguely assumed for two or three months to be true. It was only when the quote found its way into a later profile of Lew Grade by Nick Tomalin in the *Sunday Times* that Lew's immediate emphatic denial in a letter to the editor – 'I certainly do not hate David Frost and have never said so' – convinced me otherwise.

In the September article, one current affairs man told the *Sunday Times*, 'Nothing's changed. It's like the difference between the War of the Austrian Succession and the Seven Years' War. In between there was a certain amount of musical chairs among the powers, and a few new faces showed up. But in the end, it was much the same people again, fighting over much the same rewards.'

Howard Thomas, the Chairman of Thames, came up with some wise words on the ratings, which were now being assessed by a different company under a different acronym (JICTAR rather than TAM). 'The real pity is that the new methods of audience measurement are different. The new system takes a bigger sample and brings up results that are less "lenient" to ITV companies. The pity is that the new research started with the new franchises. That was a mistake. In the first place, it makes the comparisons odious because they are not relevant. In the second place, it confuses programme executives who have little against which to measure their successes or failures.'

'You and I are not on the network committees,' I said to Clive Irving that Thursday night, 'so there's only one way for us to get back at the old guard and this ridiculous panic, and that's with the shows we do between now and the end of the year.'

The next night the interview with Baldur von Schirach was our first counter-counter-attack to the Palladium counter-attack. What von Schirach had to say was quoted at considerable length in the newspapers the next morning, as were the comments of the World Jewish Congress, who were opposed to the screening of the programme. Alex Easterman, the Director of the National Affairs Department of the World Jewish Congress, had tried to persuade London Weekend not to broadcast it at all. He was reported as saying that he could not see 'any worthwhileness, topicality or justification for the interview'. Willi Frischauer, an author and journalist who felt personally involved with the subject because he believed that von Schirach was responsible for the deportation of his parents from Vienna during the War, and for their subsequent death, felt otherwise: 'One has to let these people talk,' he said, 'because they convict themselves out of their own mouths.'

That was before the programme was shown. After it Mr Easterman's comments seemed, albeit unintentionally, to agree with Frischauer's. He told the *Daily Telegraph* that he thought the programme was 'revolting' and went on, 'Anyone with any recollection of the horrors perpetrated by the Nazis must have been revolted by the picture von Schirach presented of himself.'

Exactly, we felt. Though I must say that I did agree with one letter writer who thought the programme would have been enhanced by a three-minute film at the beginning giving the main facts of von Schirach's record for anyone *without* any recollection of those horrors.

Although I did not realise it at the time, the next Saturday show was the beginning of a television association with *The Guinness Book of Records* that has gone on more or less ever since. On that programme we combined attempts on various records with short interviews with a selection of world record-holders in the audience. Both Ross and Norris McWhirter, the co-founders of *The Guinness Book of Records*, were there to verify the record attempts.

Two guests' achievements particularly stayed in the memory. One was a Mr Albert Cornelius, who was both the world sausage-eating champion and the possessor of the Strongest Head in the World. To prove the *bona fides* of this last title, Mr Cornelius placed a slab of concrete on his head and then persuaded Ross McWhirter – after I had declined – to break the said slab with a sixteen-pound sledgehammer. Equally unusual was the ex-scout master who had walked from Hartlepool to Hornsey vaulting pillar-boxes, a pursuit he called 'woggle-hopping'. We arranged for him to achieve his lifetime ambition of leaping over, or rather woggle-hopping, a double pillar-box.

The programme ignited my professional interest in *The Guinness Book of Records*. Some of the records were bizarre, others truly admirable. And there was always the fascination of somebody trying to be the best in the world at what they did – even if it happened to be something that scarcely anybody else would wish to do. As the McWhirters had rightly judged, we're all interested in superlatives – the biggest, the longest, the tallest, the shortest, the most and the least.

Over the years I have met an extraordinary cross-section of Guinness record-holders. Mr Mark Gottlieb was the first man in the world to play the violin underwater (Handel's Water Music, of course). Roy C. Johnston gained a place for having been struck by lightning five times. In the time it took us to get him on the air, he was struck a sixth time. He worked – rather unwisely, I thought – as a Park Ranger, and had to hide under his truck whenever a black cloud hove into view. In Brazil we found the living woman who had had the greatest number of children – thirty-three (and no multiple births – no cheating at all). When we interviewed her husband, he said that he was indeed married to her, and that he had indeed had thirty-three children with her. But, he went on, he had also had three outside romances, through which he had had a further ninety-two children. At which point Norris McWhirter almost fell off his chair. Then there have been record-breakers whose skill and daring simply take the breath away. I think immediately of Steve McPeak, completing the highest wire walk ever by balancing his way across a wire stretched between two German Alps at a height of nine thousand feet. And although these days *The Guinness Book of Records* no longer includes eating records, let us never forget Monsieur Mange Tout (born Michel Lotito), the man who ate an entire Cessna light aircraft. It took him six months, but he did it. He also ate several television sets and a wooden coffin. It was the first recorded case of a coffin ending up inside a man.

On 8 October I had lunch with Cardinal Heenan, the Archbishop of Westminster, whom I was hoping to persuade to appear on the programme. He agreed in principle. On the Saturday of the same week, we had an intriguing discussion of Sixties morality in our studio. The two main protagonists could scarcely have been better cast to represent traditional morality on the one side and contemporary permissiveness on the other. They were Mary Whitehouse, the leader of the Clean Up Television Campaign, and Mick Jagger, whose girlfriend Marianne Faithfull was expecting his child out of wedlock. He had recently said that he had no intention of marrying Marianne to make the child legitimate.

'Marriage is groovy,' Jagger said that night, 'but the lady I am with is already married, so I could be a bigamist. But then, I don't think it makes any difference. I think it is far better to love a baby than to have an abortion.'

Mick also said that he could provide 'a crazy but stable home for the child'. He said that 'some women need a legally signed

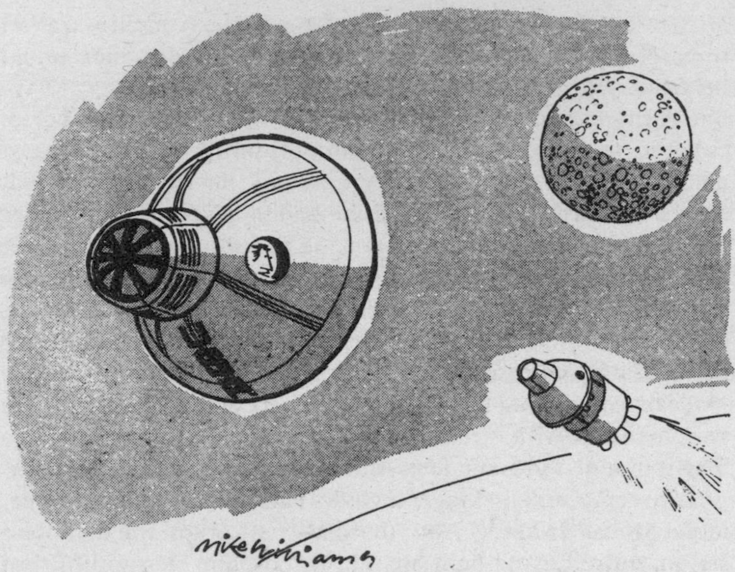

'It's either the Russians or a David Frost interview.'

piece of paper; they need security', but that was not for Marianne and him. Mary Whitehouse responded, 'I don't think you know a great deal about women. Women's security lies in a close and lasting relationship with a husband and family.'

She said that he ought to marry for the sake of the child, in case later in its life it was branded as illegitimate. Mick Jagger felt that it could be argued that a society which discriminates against an innocent child is not fit to pass judgement on anyone for acting according to his or her principles – out of the ordinary as they may be. 'The question one should ask before having a child is "What am I taking on?" To have a child is being committed for fifteen years. Some people just send a child to boarding school and that's the end of it.'

Mary Whitehouse was more tolerant than many people had expected her to be. She did not sit in judgement on Mick Jagger, but put her view this way: 'It is tremendously important that a child should be brought up within the marriage circle, and I think that bringing illegitimate children into the world is a kind of freedom which is not necessarily in the best interests of the child.'

Peter Black in the *Daily Mail* said that the interview was 'really a clash between the belief that mankind is inherently good and the belief that it is sinful and will mostly do the wrong thing unless restrained. In this I declare myself a Jaggerite.' I sensed however that the studio audience was giving Mary Whitehouse's views a somewhat more sympathetic hearing than they might have done a couple of years before.

On the weekend before the American Presidential Elections, we screened my interviews from 'The Next President' with the three candidates – Richard Nixon, Hubert Humphrey and George Wallace. On 6 November, the day after the vote, won overwhelmingly by Nixon for the Republicans, the Government issued a report that attracted our attention. The more we studied it, the more we realised that we had to do something about it immediately.

Back in the Fifties, the trend in housing policy had been to move families from inner-city slums either to the outskirts of towns or to new towns. One consequence was that the old slum areas were reduced to virtual wastelands. In the Sixties many local authorities, realising that in trying to solve one problem they had created another, decided to redevelop the old slum areas with estates of huge tower blocks. Politicians and planners alike saw the tower block as a solution to inner-city blight, not least because, with the latest construction methods, they could be built both quickly and cheaply. What concern there was – and there wasn't much – was of an aesthetic or sociological nature: the blocks' effect on the historical skylines of our towns and cities, and the difficulty of forging any sense of community among families isolated in high-rises. Very little attention was paid to the question of how safe they were until 16 May 1968, when a leaking gas main caused an explosion on the eighteenth floor of the twenty-three-storey Ronan Point block of flats in Canning Town, East London, bringing down a whole corner of the building and killing four people. The accident had caused anxiety about the method of construction – the Larsen-Nielsen

System – as an estimated 100,000 people lived in similarly-built blocks. The Government had announced an immediate and full inquiry into the accident.

The tribunal finished sitting on 2 August 1968. Four days later, before the report was ready, the inquiry's chairman, Hugh Griffiths, had warned the Housing Minister, Anthony Greenwood, of the risks faced by tenants living in these blocks. A week later, the Minister had advised local authorities that all gas supplies to the buildings should be cut off.

Nothing else happened until mid-October, when the tribunal's seventy-two-page report was handed to Greenwood. It took another three weeks before the report was published, a very long time considering the urgency of the matter. The Ministry said that it could not be published any quicker, but this contrasted unfavourably with the time taken to print Hansard, for instance.

The report concluded that a weakness in design led to progressive collapse of the flats. Initial structural damage could have been caused by a fire, or even by high winds. It estimated there was a one in fifty chance that all similar system-built constructions could collapse. The report was equally critical of the Government and the designers for not taking into account the possibility of a progressive collapse. The designers 'fell victim, along with others, to the belief that if a building complied with the existing building regulations and codes of practice, it must be deemed safe'. The report said that Ronan Point and similar blocks could and should be strengthened to guard against progressive collapse after explosion, fire or other accidental damage. Until this was carried out, all gas supplies to them should be cut off.

On the day of its publication, Anthony Greenwood made a statement on the report to the House of Commons. 'After consultation with the building industry and the local authority associations, we shall shortly give local authorities advice about the urgent reappraisal and where necessary strengthening of existing blocks.' The Government admitted that it had not appreciated the dangers of the Ronan Point system, and accepted the responsibility for ensuring that the regulations and codes of practice were kept up-to-date, but it said there was nothing wrong with the system which could not be put right.

Comparing the report with the Minister's statement, it seemed to us that Greenwood had left several important questions unanswered. We therefore mounted a special programme for 'Frost on Friday' on 8 November, two days after the publication of the report. Joining us on the programme would be two of the leading consultant engineers who had given evidence at the tribunal, Bernard Clark and Walter Frischmann, as well as Horace Cutler, Chairman of the Housing Committee of the Greater London Council, and Chris Hannington, Chairman of the Housing Committee of Haringey Council. Anthony Greenwood was invited, but declined to take part. A Ministry spokesman said later that he had a prior engagement.

We knew that we had to explain the flaws in the Larsen-Nielsen System as clearly as possible. Bernard Clark therefore used illustrations and a model to explain first how tower blocks like Ronan Point were built, and then how the collapse occurred. The essential weakness of these buildings was that they were 'composed of separate elements, as distinct from a building which has reinforcement going from one member to the other'. The large wall panels and floor slabs were just balanced up and bonded together with poured-in concrete, with 'no virtual link' between the two parts. 'So the key thing about a system like that,' I said, 'is because you don't have those things fully linked, something happening to one can have a domino effect?'

'Oh, entirely,' said Bernard Clark. Slowly and simply, he demonstrated with the help of his model. 'Now, the flat that caused the trouble was here and, of course, as soon as you get anything happening in that flat –' he paused for a second as the model collapsed '– that is precisely what goes on.'

I emphasised that we were dealing here not just with an engineering or a building matter, but essentially a human problem – it was about the 100,000 or so people living in blocks like Ronan Point.

I then asked Horace Cutler what he was going to do about their Ronan Point-style blocks, and what advice he was going to give to the people who lived in them. Mr Cutler said that they had taken off the gas and installed electric heating in all but one of the twenty-six blocks between eight and fourteen storeys high, and reinforced the structure in four newly constructed blocks, but he appeared to share Greenwood's complacency, and played down the chances of another progressive collapse occurring. 'This Nielsen-Larsen [sic] System has been operating for more than twenty years . . . and as far as I know there has only been one other, that is in Algiers, I believe, where something similar – there was an explosion, but not the progressive collapse.'

'No,' I said, 'but that was because certain steps have been taken in Algiers which hadn't been taken in the buildings in Britain.'

'This is perfectly true,' said Horace Cutler.

'I tend to feel in any case, anyway, that one is more than enough,' I said. 'I mean the fact that it hasn't happened for twenty years. It has happened now, and we don't want it to happen again.'

'I think we ought to keep this in perspective,' said Cutler, 'because there are a lot of people living in high blocks of flats who are getting a little bit nervy about them; and I from my position, I would assure them that I have looked at this thing – I am quite positive that they are safe – except in exceptional circumstances . . .'

I pointed out that back in February 1967 Mr Frischmann had warned about dangers associated with Larsen-Nielsen buildings, and perhaps the people of Ronan Point, if they had read what he had said, or if someone had told them about it, would have been accused by Mr Cutler of being 'nervy' then, 'and they would have been right to be nervy'.

Looking more directly at the Housing Minister's response to the report, I wondered how, in the light of all the expert opinion, the Minister could be so sure that 'In my provisional view, and that of my technical advisers, the risk will have been reduced to proportions that are negligible.' Frischmann said there was a contradiction between the tribunal's report and the Minister's statement. 'The Court of Inquiry said that "These blocks should be strengthened as soon as practicable," but the Ministry is saying that the wind is not a danger.' Frischmann was concerned that this might give the Ministry a way out of the problem of strengthening the blocks. He added, 'I very strongly object to the particular paragraph you mentioned, because I think if the Ministry is going to have expert advice – to say that this is not a danger – then the same experts should have given advice to the tribunal. The tribunal has found that these buildings have to be strengthened as soon as practicable, and I feel pressure should be put on the Minister to have this carried out as soon as practicable.'

'Well, exactly,' I said. 'If these buildings have to be strengthened because of danger, albeit a small danger, nevertheless they are dangerous every day until it is done, are they not?'

'Quite so,' said Mr Frischmann. 'This is vital.'

I turned back to Bernard Clark and quoted something he had told me earlier. 'If you were improving the buildings in which people live because of the dangers, then you would demand evacuation.'

'Yes, quite. Quite,' said Bernard Clark.

I turned to Horace Cutler. 'Now, would you handle evacuation of blocks? Could other councils handle evacuations?'

'I doubt if we could handle it on this scale, no,' said Mr Cutler.

We were almost at the end of our time. I summed up: 'Mr Hannington, you want a decision as fast as possible – right? Can we just simply say to the Ministry of Housing, why these unanswered questions, why these worrying facts? And this bland confidence? There must be a reason for the bland confidence. Well, let us know about it, but don't make us have bland confidence with no reasons and no facts to support them. And the floor of this programme is yours, Ministry of Housing, as soon as you want it.'

The follow-up to the programme on Monday was dramatic. GLC tenants from Stepney, living in blocks similar to Ronan Point, marched to County Hall to demand that the council took action. A representative of the marchers said, 'We had been told we were safe. We saw from the "Frost" programme we were not. It's terribly worrying.'

Anthony Greenwood responded by issuing a statement which

sharply criticised the programme (and also an edition of Thames Television's 'Today' programme) for creating 'serious fears among many tenants which are not justified'. He deplored statements 'liable to spread alarm'. The risk of gas explosion had been 'substantially' eliminated.

The Minister was still not answering the questions. I said in a statement that evening, 'What spreads alarm is not TV programmes, but unanswered Ministerial questions. In this case it was the absence of any answer from the Minister to the concern shown by two eminent structural engineers, Mr Bernard Clark and Mr Walter Frischmann, who appeared on the programme. Both were retained as expert witnesses during the Ronan Point inquiry. There are just as many unanswered questions now, but the basic one remains: Is the Minister able to say that these flats are perfectly safe for people to live in? If not, what degree of risk does he expect the people who are living in them to accept? The Minister still has an open invitation if he wishes to allay the fears of the tenants and these expert witnesses.'

The newspaper editorials were unimpressed with what Greenwood had had to say. The *Daily Mail* spoke for most of them:

> Mr Anthony Greenwood the Housing Minister has beaten all records for complacency over the Ronan Point Disaster.
>
> He took six months to find out exactly why the East London tower flats collapsed. He unhappily allowed his report to be issued on a day overshadowed by the American Elections. He was unable to go on television 'because of a previous engagement'.
>
> Now he has the gall to criticise as 'highly alarmist' the two eminent structural engineers who did talk to David Frost. He even tried yesterday to dismiss Mr Frost, who conducted a serious and important public discussion, as a 'professional entertainer'.
>
> Mr Greenwood clearly has no real understanding of the worries of the thousands of people who live in the two hundred similar tower blocks around the country. His prime concern seems to be to prevent not public confidence but his own job from collapsing. There is no use in him

> talking about 'complex technicalities'. The facts are plain. One block has fallen down because it was badly designed, and the Ministry's building standards were inadequate. It is time to turn off Mr Greenwood's gas. We have, quite simply, had enough of him.

The message now got through to Greenwood. On Tuesday 12 November he called a meeting of building and council representatives to ensure that any necessary strengthening of blocks was carried out quickly. This was progress.

At the beginning of the week Horace Cutler had also criticised the programme's treatment of the problem: 'The "Frost" programme should never have gone out until the full facts were known, or an expert witness from the Ministry was taking part. From what the two experts were saying, the most calm of people would have got worried. I'm not saying that the programme was highly alarmist – but Frost is like this.'

But that was at the beginning of the week. On Friday 15 November, without waiting for Ministerial advice, the GLC announced they were rehousing tenants from twenty-six blocks while remedial work was carried out. Mr Cutler and his colleagues had decided that they could 'handle it on this scale' after all.

Summing up the Ronan Point debate on the following Sunday, the *Observer* commented, 'The problem was still being considered in terms of units rather than people. The "Frost" programme on Friday 8 November changed that. Almost for the first time the continuing habitation of these flats became a human – and political – problem.' The *Observer* was able to add the good news that the new technical advice to be issued by the Ministry to local authorities which, only a week ago, the Ministry of Housing was forecasting would take 'two to three weeks' had been issued inside a week, and went on:

> Incredible though it may seem, it is only now – exactly six months after the Ronan Point collapse – that the national scale of the disaster is emerging. So complacent were councils after the tragedy that not only was work continued on

similar blocks, but tenants were moved into flats just as susceptible to collapse.

These are blocks which could be brought down by fire, relatively minor explosions, or exceptional high winds.

'Tenants are told that they are safe in winds up to sixty-five miles an hour,' said Mr Clark. 'But it's like an airline pilot telling his passengers, "Welcome aboard; I hope you have a pleasant journey; we will arrive safely unless there is severe turbulence, in which case the wings will fall off."'

For our follow-up programme, we had called Larsen-Nielsen themselves to ask them about the building technique. They told us that they never built higher than eight storeys, as the Danish Government would not allow it. Did the British Ministry of Housing not know that?

Although we did not know it at the time, 'Frost on Friday' and Greenwood's refusal to appear on the programme were discussed in a Cabinet meeting on 12 November, as an extract from the third volume of Richard Crossman's diaries reveals:

Cabinet today was chiefly about the report on Ronan Point which shows that the flats collapsed as a result of a structural fault permitted by our revised building regulations, so the Ministry is involved . . . Apparently the Ministry had got everything ready and the report clear in their minds when the experts suddenly said, 'Look, you must have new standards for the flats you build in the future but you can't impose it on existing flats. You will simply have to go along with two different standards.' Quite rightly Stevenson and Brown (the Ministry's Permanent Secretary and Press Officer, respectively) had said, 'That's impossible. We can't put that to the Minister, he can't survive on that.' And they have been fighting to get a satisfactory form of words. Then David Frost got hold of the report, said that people in the existing flats would be in danger, and summoned the Minister to go on his television programme. Tony had refused, all the press had attacked him for refusing, and he had then attacked television for irresponsibly inventing dangers. We started Cabinet with Harold [Wilson] saying, 'You see what happens, Tony is in a terrible difficulty because he has refused to go on television. But other ministers, Dick Marsh and Jim Callaghan, have been on the Frost programme. Oughtn't we to have some kind of rule?' Now two years ago we had a self-denying ordinance that we shouldn't go on David Frost's programme, until George Brown broke it and had an hour of Frost buttering him up with a most successful interview. Since then ministers have felt they could do well on it. Denis Healey had a bleeding row, but on the whole felt he had done satisfactorily. More recently we had Callaghan, and I'm told Dick Marsh was quite good, though I think poor Wedgie Benn was not . . .

(Mr Wedgwood Benn had suggested that I should give up one of my three weekly programmes to allow time for people who wanted more access to express their minority points of view. I had said that I would be happy to give up one of my programmes if the politicians would give up their Party Political Broadcasts. A generous offer that was, alas, never taken up.)

In the midst of all the controversy that week, the newspapers had also carried photographs of my wounded Bentley. At the junction of Brook Street and Bond Street I had swerved to avoid a taxi that went through a red light, and ended up ploughing through Fenwick's department store's front window. A few hours later I received a telegram from Bernard Levin which read, 'I have heard of shopping early for Christmas, but this is ridiculous.'

On that Saturday, 16 November, Enoch Powell, the Conservative MP for Wolverhampton South-West, made the second of his speeches on race relations and immigration. Now here was something that *really* justified the word 'alarmist'. That evening on the programme we took a look at one or two of Powell's statistics. He had contended that in Wolverhampton the immigrant population was six per cent of the total, but produced twenty-three per cent of the births. For the percentages to be accurate, they should have been taken from the total number of adults of child-bearing age in Wolverhampton, not the overall total. Calculated in this way, it emerged that immigrants in fact formed twenty-three per cent of the total, and produced about twenty-three per cent of the babies.

'In other words,' I said, 'instead of breeding like rabbits, which is what Mr Powell implies with his figures, they're behaving pretty much like the rest of us.'

As we worked on those figures, I said to our producer Geoffrey Hughes that we must try and get Enoch Powell on to the programme during the current series. Geoffrey thought so too. We had about seven weeks in which to set it up.

By now our television date with Cardinal Heenan was getting closer. We had arranged the interview in November, but the Cardinal had been taken ill with 'flu, and it was moved to 'Frost on Friday' on 6 December. Because of the Cardinal's commitments that evening, we taped the show at 4.15.

There had never been a time of greater turmoil in the modern history of the Catholic Church in Britain. Throughout the Sixties the development of new methods of contraception, in particular the Pill, and changing attitudes to sex and marriage and the role of women had finally forced the Roman Catholic Church to confront the question it had been avoiding for years – should it relax its strict view that all forms of artificial contraception were inherently sinful? In 1960 the new Pope, Pope Paul VI, had set up a Papal Commission (comprised of churchmen, leading laity and experts from the medical profession and other relevant fields) to enquire into the issue. The Commission came to the conclusion that the Church should change its teaching on birth control. On 25 July 1968 the Pope published an Encyclical on the subject, *Humanae Vitae* (Of Human Life). This was widely expected to endorse the Commission's advice. However, instead it reaffirmed the Church's traditional teaching – that 'every action which, either in anticipation of the conjugal act or in its accomplishment, or in the development of its natural consequences, proposes, whether as an end or as a means, to render procreation impossible' was contrary to God's Law, and therefore sinful.

The Encyclical caused a great storm throughout the Roman Catholic Church. It particularly disappointed and angered many

Catholics in Britain. Some felt that the Pope was completely out of touch with the practical problems of married life and modern society. Protests were made; a number of priests were suspended from their duties for voicing their opposition; fifty-five priests wrote to *The Times* saying that they were unable to accept the Pope's teaching in the Encyclical. After meeting to discuss the matter the English and Welsh Catholic bishops issued a statement on 24 September which acknowledged the Pope's authority as the Vicar of Christ, without (unlike their Scottish counterparts) giving an unequivocal endorsement of the Encyclical. Some priests and laymen were unhappy that the Bishops had failed to endorse the Encyclical unambiguously. Others were unhappy that the Pope's ruling had not been rejected. The majority of the Catholic laity remained confused and uncertain about the issue. That was the context in which I talked to Cardinal Heenan on 6 December.

The interview was largely, though not solely, concerned with the controversy over the Pill. It was also about Heenan himself: his faith, his ambitions, his regrets. He revealed himself as possessing an abundance of the essential Christian virtues of honesty and humility. But he also showed himself to be a man of great charm and not inconsiderable wit. When I asked him if he regretted never having had the opportunity of experiencing the love of a woman, he said, 'I hope I have experienced the love of many women – starting with my mother, of course.' The audience and I laughed with him.

After discussing the Papal Commission on Birth Control, I asked the Cardinal whether he thought 'the Pope, a Pope, would ever change the situation so that some means of artificial contraception is made acceptable'.

'I believe that in measurable time, five or ten years, everyone will accept what the Pope has said. I believe that. You see –'

'No, but – sorry – what do you mean?' I asked.

'I'll explain exactly what I mean. The whole scientific trend is towards natural rhythms for birth control, for family planning . . . Now, I believe the reason why people took to the Pill and have taken the Pill is because that is the most natural thing. It doesn't seem to interfere with the natural way of intercourse.

And I am quite sure that is the reason why the Pill has become so popular. I believe that in these days when we can transplant hearts and we can fly to the moon, it should be possible for the doctors, the scientists, to discover a very easy way of knowing precisely what is a safe period. I would guess, but it's only a guess, I would guess that within measurable time – five or six years – they will discover a simple way of deciding whether there is any danger of pregnancy. So that for certain, more or less for certain, a woman will know and her husband will know, that apart from five days when abstinence will be called for, that intercourse can take place without the likelihood of conception taking place.'

I said that if the safe period was really safe, then any couple who used it would be going against the Pope's ruling that 'each and every marriage act must remain open to the transmission of life'. The Cardinal insisted, 'Once a safe period is safe, provided the intercourse is natural, provided nothing is put to prevent birth, then it is open to life.'

I said there seemed to be little difference to me between the thermometer that would make that method safe, and the coil or the loop or the diaphragm that might make another method 100 per cent safe.

'I'm not suggesting you need an artificial aid to discover these safe periods,' said the Cardinal.

'Only calendars, and diagrams, and graphs, and thermometers . . .' I said.

We then moved back from the putative moment in future history to the present day, when the Cardinal had admitted that the safe period was not yet safe. 'What about all those people who are married, who must make love, and who can't trust the safe period? What's your advice to them?'

The Cardinal began to talk about some of the dangers of the Pill, which he felt had been insufficiently dealt with. I tried to put his remarks in perspective as quickly as I could, and then I asked him the same question again: 'We have this couple who want to make love because they're married and know that a pregnancy would be disastrous because of a stillbirth or because of a former cancer of the breast. What do you say to those people? The safe period, you know you've got to say, is not safe. What should they do?'

'Now, let's first of all talk about the safe period,' said the Cardinal. 'I agree with you, completely, that it would be dishonest, it would be impertinent for a person who is not concerned, who is not the father or mother of the family, to say, "Now look here, use the safe period. It may not work, but use it anyhow," because as you say, a pregnancy might occur and the mother might die. And then they could turn around to the priest and say, "And you told us to use this." Therefore it's quite clear that it's not for the priest to say use the safe period or not . . . Now what has not, I think, yet been sufficiently realised is – this Encyclical deals with the principles of moral life in marriage. The Pope does not at any point say that this is wrong or that is wrong in individual cases . . . For example, the English hierarchy's expression was "nothing in this Encyclical interferes with the primacy of conscience": that a person's conscience and ultimate decision depends upon himself.'

'Or in other words,' I said, 'if the Catholic couple take the decision on serious grounds of conscience to use a contraceptive, then the Church will not interfere with that?'

'The teaching of the Church is very clear,' said Cardinal Heenan. 'For the man is bound to follow his conscience, and this is true even if his conscience is in error, but this is a basic teaching of the Church, that every man, the Pope, you, I, everyone must follow conscience. Now, it's the duty of a Catholic to inform his conscience. But it could happen easily, particularly after this long period of dispute and doubt, it could happen that a couple might say conscientiously, "I'm quite sure that this is the right thing for me to do." And if that can be said conscientiously, "This is what I must do," then of course they must follow their conscience. There is no dispute about this.'

'They must,' I said.

'They must follow their conscience,' said the Cardinal.

'And if they go to their priest and say that they are doing precisely that, what should the priest say?'

There was a tense pause – everybody was holding their breath – and then Cardinal Heenan said, 'God bless you.' They were the words that Catholics everywhere had been waiting for, praying for, but probably not daring to hope for.

The Cardinal amplified his words. 'If they're really following their conscience, then in the sight of God, which is all that matters – the priest, the bishop, the Pope doesn't matter compared with God – if every person is really dealing with Almighty God.'

'But if a person is really following their conscience,' I said, 'and using some form of contraception, and goes to the priest and says so, then the priest should say, "God bless you," and not refuse them the sacraments.'

'Of course not, of course not,' said the Cardinal. 'If you – perhaps you don't know, but in the pastoral letter I wrote immediately the Encyclical was published, I insisted on this. I said, "Don't let this prevent you from receiving the sacraments" – remember?'

'Yes, I do,' I said. 'I read that. I read that, but you have never said it as clearly or as forthrightly as you did then. Thank you.'

Cardinal Heenan smiled. 'I didn't have Mr Frost to help me to express myself,' he said.

I laughed, and a little later, as a closing thought, I suggested that one day he might become Pope. The Cardinal replied, 'I hope not, but if so, I'll be very careful about writing Encyclicals!'

Cardinal Heenan's words were given great prominence in the national and world press and other news media. In his column in the *Catholic Herald*, under the headline 'Worldwide Impact of Cardinal's Broadcast', Norman St John Stevas reported that in St Louis, where he had been taking part in an international symposium on population, 'All radio and television programmes were interrupted with a news flash.' Elsewhere the *Catholic Herald* said that the interview had been well received by most Catholics, adding that the 'weight of his argument on conscience has relieved many priests'.

Cardinal Heenan had brought peace of mind to many Catholics all over the world. For non-Catholics and non-believers alike, he had also projected a living example of Christian caring and compassion while negotiating his way through what was for him a minefield of conflicting loyalties.

On 29 July 1969, the first anniversary of the Encyclical, an article in the *Guardian* ('How the Problem Pill Dissolved' by Alan Smith) said that the interview had been instrumental in preventing a serious split in the Catholic Church in Britain:

> The Church, it seemed, had cast itself off and was sinking fast. Words like 'ferment', 'turmoil' and 'rebellion' spiced the morning papers, and shortly afterwards the first reports appeared of dissenting priests being suspended. Curiously, it was David Frost who helped stop the rot.
>
> It is still Frost's interview with Cardinal Heenan – five months after the Encyclical was published – that provides the clearest guidance for Catholics who cannot accept the ban. Frost pressed Cardinal Heenan on ITV and was given the answer, 'If a couple say this is the right thing for us to do, and if it could be said conscientiously, then they must follow their consciences.' They must not abstain from the sacraments, and the priest must say 'God bless you.' A priest in one Northern city reported a 'staggering increase' in the number of communicants after that statement, in spite of some determined back-pedalling by the more hawkish Bishops. As far as guidance goes, there the matter rests.

Meanwhile, the Sunday shows were continuing to bubble along, and regularly won their place in the national top ten. At the beginning of December Caterina Valente, Tom Jones and Nina Simone all joined us on Sunday evenings, and the two Ronnies, Barker and Corbett, went from strength to strength. In addition, we had made a rare discovery – a new sketch-writer called Gerard Wiley, who seemed to have a ready-made ability not only to write consistently funny sketches, but also to provide what *Variety* would call 'boffo' punchlines.

One of his first sketches had been set in a doctor's waiting room, in which a group of silent and self-contained patients had gathered. Suddenly a breezy newcomer arrived in the shape of Ronnie Corbett. He tried to make conversation with his neighbours, a ploy that failed totally. He then started trying to tell jokes to the assembled gathering. These too fell flat. But he was not to be deterred, and slowly but surely he revved up the other patients to the point where they joined him in a song. Next he started a conga. When that was in full swing, he yelled, 'Everybody back to my place!' and the entire waiting room conga-ed their way out of the door. At this point the doctor and his nurse entered, and surveyed the empty room. Said the doctor, 'It's that bloody Dr Corbett, stealing all my private patients again . . .' It was a more or less perfect sketch. The theatre of embarrassment had been hilarious throughout, and then the punchline had provided a terrific surprise pay-off.

Naturally, we were anxious to contact this writer and encourage him to submit as much material as possible, but his agent, Peter Eade, explained to us that he was a very shy short-story writer – not used to script meetings and the like – and preferred to continue working quietly in whatever was the 1968 equivalent of a garret. Ronnie Corbett got in touch with Peter Eade and began negotiations for the rights to two of Gerard Wiley's sketches for use in the theatre, but he never got to meet the writer either.

For the next 'Frost on Friday' I travelled to New York to interview Muhammad Ali. We arranged to tape the show in front of an audience at the 'Merv Griffin Show' theatre, The Little Theater, on West 44th Street, next to Sardi's. At that time Muhammad Ali was in the middle of the most turbulent and controversial stage in his life. He had first come to the fore in 1960 when, as Cassius Clay, he won a gold medal at the Rome Olympics. Four years later, to great acclaim, he became World Heavyweight Champion when he defeated Sonny Liston. As much because of his flamboyant personality as his brilliant boxing, he was soon famous all over the world. Shortly after beating Liston, Clay joined the Nation of Islam, as much a black nationalist movement as a religious group, popularly – or unpopularly – known as the Black Muslims. As part of his conversion he changed his name to Muhammad Ali.

Members of the movement were told not to fight in Vietnam by their leader, Elijah Mohammed. Ali made it known that he was a conscientious objector on religious grounds, but he was denied exemption from conscription. In April 1967 he was called up. When he formally refused induction, the World Boxing Association stripped him of his title and boxing licence. Two months later a federal court in Houston found him guilty of violating the Selective Service Act, and imposed a $10,000 fine and a five-year jail sentence. At the time of our interview, Ali was out of jail pending an appeal.

For some Americans he was a coward, but to rebellious or alienated blacks and to the peace movement he was a hero. Encouraged by black activists, Ali became a spokesman for black solidarity. Taking an unabashedly anti-white and anti-establishment stand, he started lecturing on college campuses, and spoke at peace rallies and Black Muslim meetings. He still had the jail sentence hanging over him, but he had responded to the support he had received from his fellow blacks and others, and seemed to be enjoying his crusading role.

'One of the ironies,' I said, 'is that you've moved from fighting magnificently to, in the other area, not being willing to fight abroad and so on. What would you say was the vital moment of your conversion, as it were? I mean, there were various accounts of you attending a meeting on the corner of Lennox and 125th Avenue and so on – what was the moment? St Paul was going along that road to Damascus . . .'

'There never was a moment,' said Ali. 'This has been building up for four hundred years and it all started when the whites first brought us here in chains and slaved and castrated and killed and murdered us. Four hundred years. So this didn't just start, and I've always been prepared. Ever since I went back to Louisville, Kentucky, and was denied a beefburger downtown and I was the champion of the whole world, just fought for the great American flag, and in my own country, one-horse town, I couldn't get a beefburger. I didn't know what was wrong, but it wasn't right. I've been watching black people in demonstrations, black women kicked around, beat up and all unjustly treated, and this has always been building. But I'd like to say something – you mentioned that I fight in the ring but wasn't willing to go abroad to fight. See, boxing and the war cannot be considered in no way alike . . . The war is to kill, and boxing is not to kill. We have protective gloves . . .'

But could he ever imagine a situation in which there was such a moral battle going on that he would be prepared to fight for the United States?

'I fight for myself,' said Ali. 'We fought for the United States in Germany, we fought for the United States in Japan and died and – was it China, Korea – now we're in Vietnam, still we're not free. So I'm not so honoured to let you know I'll fight for the United States when I'm not free. My title was taken because of my religion – I'll be the last man to say this.'

'No, but if the Germans threatened, if 1939 and Hitler was today, or there was, which there won't be, a communist invasion, would you fight for the United States?' I asked.

'If I had been living then,' Ali answered, 'Uncle Tom and slow-thinking and slaving, like black people were then, I'd probably have thought it was an honour to go over there, you know. But as of now, with the truth that I've been taught by Elijah Mohammed and the history of my people, who are our real enemies? Not the Viet Cong, not the Chinese, not the Japanese. Our enemies, our oppressors, our opposers, are white Americans.'

But surely he did not think that white Americans were his total enemy. 'You said on one occasion, you were quoted as saying on one occasion, "All whites are devils," but that's not true, is it?'

'Elijah Mohammed teaches us that God told him that all whites are devils,' said Ali.

'Well, God was wrong on that occasion,' I said. But he didn't actually believe that all whites were devils?

'I really believe that all white people are devils. I'm not going to be no phoney. I didn't give up ten million dollars and fighting, I'd go to jail for five years, and now do you think I'm going to get on this TV show and deny what I believe? I believe every bit of it.'

I challenged him on the point, and Ali responded, 'The Christian Bible says all white people are devils.'

'The Christian Bible says all people are sinful,' I said.

'It says all white Gentiles and Jews are devils,' said Ali.

'No, the Christian Bible says all people are sinful,' I said. 'Now, if we say that the whole world, black and white –'

'Stop the show,' said Ali, 'and let me go and get my briefcase.'

'Yes, sure,' I said.

In less than a minute he was back with a copy of the Bible. 'I just found this the other day. It says here in the Romans – third chapter and ninth verse. "What then," it says, "are we better than they? No. In nowise, for we have before proved both Jews and Gentiles that they are all" . . . ummm . . . "as it is written there is none righteous, no, not one." Reading the Bible out loud did not come easily to Muhammad Ali, but the very laboriousness of his delivery gave it added poignancy. "There is none that understandeth, there is none that seeketh after good, they are all gone out of the way. They are together become unprofitable. There is none that doeth good, no not one. Their throat is an open" . . . what's that word?'

I took a look. 'Sepulchre,' I said.

'"Sepulchre. With their tongues they have used deceit." That's right. You all tricked . . . South Africa, tricked . . . South Africa. "The poison asp is under their lips. Whose mouth is full of curse and bitterness that they are swift to shed blood." We know this, us Negroes, for four hundred years we've been lynched and killed for just nothing. Martin Luther King, and all of us. "Destruction and misery are in their ways and the way of peace they have not known." That's right. "There is no fear of God before their eyes."'

'Well, that proves what I said, because that includes you and the black –'

'No, Jews and Gentiles,' said Ali.

'And the Greek word for Gentiles means non-Jews. Jews and non-Jews.'

'I'm talking about the Bible, what's in the Bible.'

'Now, if you say all blacks are devils as well as all whites –'

'No, no, the blacks not devils, no. Who've we lynched, who have we raped, who have we slayed?'

'Oh, thousands of people in the Congo and in Africa. I'm not against blacks, I'm saying blacks and whites, we're all awful, maybe.'

'No, everything black people do wrong come from you. Smoking, prostitution, homosexuality, lying, stealing, gambling, they all come from you.'

'Well, if you say that in the Bible it says that all people are sinful, I'd go along with that, and you've just read that long quote that proves that. It says all Jews and Gentiles. And in the Bible Gentiles means all people who are not Jews. Not whites, but blacks, greens, blues and everybody.'

'Well, you're teaching me something I don't know here.'

'Well, I thought I should tell you that, you see. A lot of the things you are fighting for are marvellous, but it's dangerous rubbish to suggest that all white people are devils and all black people are saints.'

'See, you're the Devil doing that kind of talking. I didn't say black people were saints, you lying just like the Devil.'

'You've got a marvellous case, and you're losing it by going too far.'

'I'm not going to let you prove I'm going too far. What I'm doing is right. We couldn't preach this every day if it wasn't right. Nobody challenges us, not even the white Government.'

'Yes, I challenge you. I challenged you and I was right.'

It was time to take a break, which we did. After it I asked Ali, 'If you had a class of white children and black children, small children, sitting in front of you, what would you tell them to help them to live together?'

He replied, 'There's nothing that I could tell them, nor would I try to convince them to try to live together . . . It's the two natures that will never get along. See, blacks and whites are two opposites. Opposites are something that's a hundred degrees different from another . . . So by nature, see, you're opposite, you're opposed. You opposes your opponent, if he's your opponent, he's your enemy. So by nature black and white have been enemies.'

'You were talking backstage before the programme to six people who all happen to be white,' I said. 'You got on fine.'

'Oh yes,' said Ali. 'We talked business together, but we'll never be able to live together. It's our natures.'

'But, I mean, you've got white blood in your veins, but you're fine –'

'I've got white blood in me because all slave masters used our women and raped them. Some of us look white because those slave masters raped our women.'

'Your great-grandfather was an Irishman,' I said. 'I mean, it hasn't spoiled you.'

'He's an Irishman. I don't want no mixed blood in me,' said Ali. 'I wish I was pretty and black all the way. Who'd want to get mixed up with other blood? No intelligent woman watching this show, black or white, want to introduce their grandchildren as half-brown, kinky Negroes. No black person or black man or woman watching this show want white boys and white girls coming to marry their children and in return introducing their grandchildren as little half-white, green-eyed, blond-haired white children. Every man like a son who look like him.'

Muhammad Ali's references to 'opposites' had echoes of a conversation earlier that year. 'But, I mean, you sound like Governor Wallace talking like that.'

'I'm with Wallace,' said Ali. 'If I had the vote, which I don't, I'd vote for Wallace because Wallace tells the truth, he talks the way white people feel.'

'Governor Wallace said to me – I asked him, "Would you let your daughter marry a black man?" And he got a good deal of criticism because he said he wouldn't want it to happen, and no – but would you want a daughter of yours to marry a white man?'

'Now you're just trying to start something,' said Ali. He delivered the line perfectly, and everybody roared with laughter. 'You're just trying to be funny. I'm not going to let you get me mad. We've been talking about this and you go and ask me a fool question like that.'

'You're saying it was wrong of people to criticise Governor Wallace, he was right?' I asked.

'No, I'm saying I like him because he tells the truth,' said Ali. 'He's not phoney . . . You have a Southern white man in America and you have a North one . . . And both of you look alike; you ain't that much different, you're just a two-hour jet flight, how do you change so quick? You haven't changed, but you's a little more educated, you's a little more educated, you's more scientific, you know how to smile. "I was raised with coloured people, oh, my mother had a coloured nurse." Well, I watch you more than I do the South, see, because when I get in the South, at least when I get out the plane they say, "Watch yourself, nigger." I say, "Thank you." I don't know what to do, you know, you're too nice.'

'But I mean to say, you think somewhere like South Africa's right, where they segregate the two?'

'Separation is good. Not segregation,' said Ali. 'Segregation is when you in power and you divide it unequally, you got your foot on the other man. Separation is equality.'

He returned to the Bible. 'I have another thing back there where God say when He come He's going to sit at the foot of the throne and He's going to bring all the nations together, like a shepherd gathers his flock, and He's going to separate them one from another as a shepherd separates the sheep from the goats. This is what God's going to do to the nations. That's now taking place.'

'But that's sheep and goats – ' I said.

'That was a symbolic gesture,' said Ali. 'The Bible speaks in parables. It didn't literally mean four-legged sheep. You are the goat and I am the sheep, see.'

'No, I'm the sheep, you're the goat,' I said.

'You have the characteristics of the goat, I have the characteristics of sheep,' said Ali. 'Check it out. Sheep's got oily skin, we have oily skin; sheep have woolly hair, we got woolly hair; sheep's nature's real humble, he don't fight back; that's black folks. And goat's got straight hair like you. He's got the eyes like yours. He's got the colour like you. He'll trick you, goat's real tricky, you all are tricky people. You are master tricksmen, the white race.'

'Sheep do what they're told,' I said. 'There's never been a sheep like you, has there?'

'I know what I'm told by my shepherd,' said Ali.

He returned to the subject of integration. 'We don't want to integrate with white, mess up ourselves . . .'

'Why?' I asked.

''Cause it's bad, it weakens us,' said Ali. 'See, a strong cup of coffee's black, to make it weak you pour white cream in it, you integrate it, you understand.'

'But it tastes better,' I said.

'No, no, it's stronger black. You want a rich dirt, you want the black dirt, you want the best bread, you want the wholewheat rye, you want the best sugar – it gives you less calories – is the brown sugar; they say the blackest berries bear the sweetest juice; your greatest world's boxers, football players, rock 'n' roll artists, jazz musicians, basketball players, we're the greatest on the planet. The black people in America are the best on the planet in everything they get a chance at.'

'Nobody in this world of ours today – nobody can do things on their own,' I said. 'Even your black coffee is composed on the one hand of black grain and on the other hand of uncoloured water. The black grains on their own make a horrible little mess in the bottom of the cup.'

'No, no,' said Ali.

'You need something else,' I said.

After the taping, I said goodbye to Muhammad Ali at the stage door. 'You know, Muhammad,' I said, 'at the moment you're behaving like a black George Wallace. But it's within you to become the black Bobby Kennedy.' Muhammad did not comment directly, but each time I met him over the years, I felt he was in fact moving in that direction. Some of the rhetoric was always there, but there was a basic warmth that the would-be militant could never disguise, even when he wanted to.

Two nights before we aired the Muhammad Ali interview, a new play had opened at the New Theatre in London – *Soldiers*, by Rolf Hochhuth. The play was about the ethics of war as expressed by the conduct of Winston Churchill and his colleagues in sanctioning the mass bombing of German cities, and, much more sensationally, by Churchill's alleged role in the assassination of his friend and ally General Sikorski, the leader of the Polish Government in exile, who died in a plane crash off Gibraltar on 4 July 1943.

At the time of an earlier programme we had done on the subject in October 1967, the play had just received its world premiere in Berlin, but plans by Kenneth Tynan, Laurence Olivier and others to put on a production in London had been thwarted by the Lord Chamberlain, who ruled that the play could not be staged in Britain without the approval of the families portrayed. Needless to say, the Churchill family, frustrated and angry at being unable under the law to bring a libel action against the author or producers of the play, were uncooperative, to say the least. They were particularly unimpressed by Hochhuth's claim that he kept in a Swiss bank vault a document containing the name of the person who had allegedly given him first-hand proof that Sikorski's plane had been sabotaged by the British. Without explaining why, Hochhuth said that he had sworn not to release the document for fifty years.

In that 1967 programme Randolph Churchill had mocked this claim: 'He says he has documentary proof, but he has it locked up, this Herr Hochmut.' Throughout the programme Randolph mispronounced the playwright's name, either deliberately or accidentally. (Given that '*Hochmut*' means 'cheek', and given Randolph's fascination with words, I have no doubt that the mispronunciation was intentional.) 'Of course, the only thing about these lies is that once they get started it is very difficult indeed to nail them down . . . You cannot kill a lie completely. I'm afraid that my father, careful though he was with his papers, did not leave a long, carefully typed-out list of Generals whom he did not assassinate. I could, of course, say that I have such a document in a strong vault in Switzerland *à la* Herr Hochmut, but I haven't anything like that.'

In conversation with the historian David Irving, who was backing the play, Randolph had had one more go at 'Herr Hochmut':

Churchill: Why doesn't he come here and defend himself?
Irving: Because he can't speak English.
Churchill: Well, he can have an interpreter.
Irving: I suggested that, and I was told that it would be stupid

on a popular programme like this to have someone who could only speak German.

Churchill: Well, put him on an *un*popular programme. (applause) Put him on '24 Hours'. He has less chance of being cut off that.

That had been back in October 1967. In September 1968 the Lord Chamberlain's power of censorship was removed. One of the Sixties' great targets had fallen. The removal of the Lord Chamberlain's power was heralded as a great, if by this time largely symbolic, victory for freedom of expression and artistic liberty. One side-effect was that there was nothing the Churchills or anyone else could do to stop Hochhuth's play from being performed in the West End. Kenneth Tynan (supported by David Irving) was still dedicated to staging the play, and on 12 December *Soldiers* opened at the New Theatre.

Since our first programme it had been discovered that the pilot and only survivor of the plane crash, Edward Prchal, a Czech, was alive and living in California (Hochhuth and Irving had been convinced that he had died in a fight in Chicago). In the play Prchal was given a key role in the conspiracy, and had deliberately ditched the Sikorski plane in the sea. This was the theory Irving wanted to prove – or believe. Clearly Prchal's reappearance was awkward for both the theatrical and historical wings of the Hochhuth camp. He was hardly likely to endorse the sabotage theory, and very likely to bring libel charges against Irving, Hochhuth and the producers of the play. Irving had reacted by working to discredit Prchal, claiming to have a wealth of evidence against him.

On Friday 20 December, eight days after *Soldiers* opened, we arranged for Edward Prchal to fly to London to discuss the Sikorski case and the allegations against him with, apart from Hochhuth, the main players in the Sikorski controversy – Irving, Tynan, and Churchill's grandson Winston, who had taken over the role of defending the family name after his father Randolph's death earlier in the year.

At the beginning of the programme I recounted the story so far, and then talked first to Prchal, the sole survivor of the crash.

He said that he was 'almost certain it was not sabotage'. However, he said that David Irving had claimed in a *Daily Telegraph* interview not only that it was sabotage, but that 'I have seventeen pounds of evidence on my desk.' 'But when I asked Mr Irving, "Can you give me half an ounce of that evidence?" Mr Irving had told me that he doesn't have any evidence.'

I said to Mr Prchal that Hochhuth had insinuated on more than one occasion that he was involved in some way in a plot.

'Yeah, I know. I know he does,' said Prchal, and then paused for a moment. 'How bluntly can I speak?'

'Say what you want to say,' I said.

Mr Prchal did precisely that. 'Mr Hochhuth is producing a slander of the century. But that's not his idea at all. He stole the show. He stole it from Goebbels, because it was Dr Goebbels, Reichminister of Propaganda, that after four hours, after the accident, he reported not only that simply British intelligence killed General Sikorski, but he also reported that £2000 of sterling had been deposited in Swiss banks on my account. Or it might be in the same bank where Hochhuth is hiding his evidence now . . .'

I asked Prchal if Hochhuth's claim that he was the son of the Czech General Prchala was true. Prchal said that this was a 'fantastic lie'. 'Does he know how to spell? His name is spelled altogether differently. That General had an *a* at the end of his name. I have *l*. My father died in 1936; he was a farmer.'

'And Herr Hochhuth also said that you were killed in Chicago. Is that true?'

The audience laughed, and Prchal responded in the same vein. 'Well, I don't know. Maybe actually what you see over here is my astral body.'

'But British intelligence hasn't substituted you?' I asked.

'No, I hope not,' said Prchal.

The credibility of the Hochhuth–Tynan–Irving case went from bad to worse. At one point, for example, Prchal introduced his ex-Flight Commander, Mr Llewellyn, who was in the audience. Llewellyn said that he did not think that sabotage had taken place. He had his own theory, that loose mailbags in the nose compartment might have jammed the controls. David

Irving called this 'a red herring'. 'The Court of Inquiry investigated this very point and found there were no mailbags in the nose compartment,' he said.

'Well,' said Prchal simply, 'it's not in the Court of Inquiry, in the findings.'

By the end of our allotted time, it was clear that we had not reviewed the whole case. I turned to the assembled company. 'May I ask everybody to come back, please, tomorrow night? Winston? Kenneth? Mr Prchal? David Irving? We will return to this subject and this huge question mark at the same – not at the same time – at whatever time it is in your region, tomorrow night.'

My thought was to continue with the discussion and pre-tape the next night's programme as soon as possible, while the adrenalin of the combatants was still flowing. First, however, we had to ask the crew if they would be prepared to stay on and work overtime. In those days in ITV this was by no means a foregone conclusion – indeed, quite the reverse. But in this case the crew were as excited by what was happening as the audience, and within ten minutes we had started again.

I began, 'We return to the subject of who or what killed Sikorski. At one point a theory was advanced by Mr Llewellyn that it was possibly because of mailbags in the nose. David Irving said that that was positively dismissed by the official report.' I turned to Peter Baker, our Associate Producer, to give evidence from his research.

'It is not true that the Court of Inquiry said that there were no mailbags in the nose,' said Peter. 'The Court of Inquiry never ever investigated this point at all. Never.'

'You said that they dismissed the principle of mailbags in the nose,' I said to Irving. 'That's what you said on the programme.'

'You dismissed it by saying that the Court of Inquiry investigated this possibility,' said Baker. 'That is not so. They simply didn't.'

Irving had no answer to this, and Flight Commander Llewellyn summed up, 'There was no discussion at the Court of Inquiry as to whether this sort of situation that I have described could have happened.'

The charges and counter-charges went back and forth in an atmosphere of tension and undisguised acrimony. Every so often there was a telling intervention from Mr Prchal.

'There is another thing, Mr Irving, may I interrupt?' he said at one point. 'Court of Inquiry, they are stating so and so, missing; so and so, wounded; and so on. You state in your book that my injuries were very light.'

'I quoted the Court of Inquiry,' said Irving.

'According to the Court of Inquiry? Read –' Prchal handed him the inquiry.

'I also traced the doctor that examined you,' said Irving.

'Read the first page,' said Prchal.

Irving did so. 'The first page of the Court of Inquiry which I have here says, "The first pilot: extent injured: seriously."'

'Thank you,' said Mr Prchal.

I said that I'd been to see the play the previous Saturday night and that there was no doubt that the audience 'all went out believing that the play had said that Churchill connived in the murder of Sikorski'. I said that it seemed to me that 'you can't, in the cause of good theatre, do that to the recent memory of a man. And that you've got to in the last resort say, "Well, let's fictionalise it, let's make it someone else, let's fictionalise it all."'

'If it was done to turn him into a villain,' said Tynan, 'I would agree with you. But it's done to turn him into a much greater hero . . . Many critics on right- and left-wing papers of all stances have reviewed it at great length. Not one of those reviews – not one – has said that it damages Winston Churchill's name.'

A voice chimed in from the audience. 'Mr Tynan, last Sunday in the *Sunday Times*, the reviewer dealt with your point very nicely. You say that this play enhances Winston Churchill's reputation by giving him the reputation of a private murderer.'

'Private?' asked Tynan.

'Yes, private. Political assassination is private, secret murder. And this is what you have accused Churchill of, and Hochhuth has, while you go along with it. And this reviewer said it would be as if to say you are helping a man's health by sticking a knife in his back. And yet you say all these reviewers are on your side.'

Winston Churchill returned to an unanswered question: 'A moment ago you said this was a libellous play on Churchill. You can't have it both ways. Does it libel him, or does it enhance his stature?'

'It li– it would have – it would have libelled him . . .' said Tynan. '. . . It would have libelled him, had he been alive. Since he's dead, it's not a libel.' He then mumbled a half-sentence of which only the word 'morality' was audible.

The closing music was fading in as a voice came from the audience: 'But surely, the truth comes into morality, doesn't it?'

The first of these two highly dramatic programmes had of course been broadcast live, but before the second could be shown, there was a little more drama in store. On the Saturday afternoon Kenneth Tynan, through his lawyer, Oscar Beuselinck, demanded a fee of £1000 for his appearance on the second show. If he failed to receive it, he would act to prevent the programme's transmission by obtaining a High Court injunction. The suggested fee was nonsense. All the participants in the first programme had received our normal fee of £50. By agreeing to take part in a second programme, they were obviously entitled to the same fee again. Talk of £1000 and High Court injunctions was obviously intended to frighten London Weekend into not broadcasting programme two. When I talked to the LWT lawyers about the demand, they were instantly and commendably dismissive. Tynan got an unvarnished 'no'. Just before the programme was due to go out, David Irving made a similar demand. That was summarily rejected too.

On top of everything else, the Hochhuth contingent were inefficient, too. I could not understand why Irving had not checked with Tynan to find out if his request for a fee had succeeded before exposing himself to a humiliating rebuke. It was instructive to see the way in which, when they felt that they had been bested, they moved to suppress the very freedom of expression they proclaimed to be their cause.

Although the Churchill family were unable to take libel action, Prchal, whom Hochhuth thought was dead when he wrote *Soldiers*, could do so. On 7 January 1969 he issued writs against Hochhuth and the publishers, producers, theatre owners and directors of the play. He was vindicated in court and damages were awarded.

Despite the Sixties' preoccupation with plots and conspiracy theories in general, from JFK to Dag Hammarskjöld, the two programmes, and the debate that followed them, seemed to put to rest in the public's mind any suggestion that Churchill had connived in the murder of General Sikorski. Which left us with only one small niggle. While establishing these facts, had we also given the play what would now be called 'the oxygen of publicity'?

The answer came with gratifying speed. On 6 March, the producers announced that the play would end its run.

For the first show after Christmas, we felt that our viewers deserved somewhat lighter fare. It seemed the perfect occasion to transmit an interview I had recorded earlier at the MayFair Theatre with Noël Coward. There are some people who not only live up to their legend, they are larger than their legend. Noël Coward was a perfect example. He was more like Noël Coward than even Noël Coward was supposed to be. Although – or maybe because – Noël Coward was certainly not a typical Sixties figure, his plays had been enjoying a revival of interest. Now *Star*, the film about the life of Gertrude Lawrence in which Coward was portrayed by his godson, Daniel Massey, had just opened.

I asked Coward, 'What is a star, would you say? You're a star. What is a star?'

'Oh, there are so many things that go to make a star,' said Coward. 'First of all, an indefinable quality. There are many, many fine actresses and actors who are not stars, and who can act quite a lot of the stars right off the stage. But if there is star quality there – and you can't define it, it's too difficult – but the stars have it and the non-stars don't.'

At what age did he know that he was a star?

'Two.'

It was just the sort of response that one expected from Coward.

'Did anything happen at two?' I asked.

'Yes,' he said. 'I was taken to church. The organ started and I was out in the aisle dancing, and was hauled back. And that was the start of it all.'

'What sort of a child were you, actually?' I asked.

'When paid constant attention, extremely lovable. When not, a pig.'

The man was speaking in aphorisms, and with that machine-gun delivery of his, dictating the punctuation as well! Having heard Coward's delivery of that last remark, I would be happy to lay odds that not even the most untrained of transcribers could possibly get it wrong, or hear it any other way.

I asked what had been his most poignant memory, his most precious, touching memory of childhood.

'That's dreadfully difficult,' said Coward. 'There were so many, I was constantly touched . . .'

'I'm waiting in the hope that you'll go on . . .' I said amidst the audience's laughter.

'Oh, that is a false hope,' said Coward.

If a film were to be made of his life, what would be the first scene?

'The first scene of my life? Oh, that's very difficult,' said Coward. 'I think the best scene in my earlier life was – I was sent to a kindergarten school kept by a rather angry lady called Miss Willington, and she queried my use of the English language. I was then seven, and said, "I am not going to stay in this school a moment longer." And she, unwisely, pursued me to try and drag me back, and I bit her through to the bone. And I can taste that taffeta blouse now.'

Did he still get a special feeling of anticipation as he sat in a theatre to watch a play and the lights went down?

'Always the thrill,' said Coward. 'It's never changed. When the lights go down in the auditorium and the footlights come into the glow on the bottom of the curtain, that to me is eternal magic. Sometimes it changes after the curtain's gone up . . .'

What was the most exciting night he'd ever experienced in the theatre?

'The opening night of *The Vortex* in New York City,' said Coward immediately, 'because we'd played a week in Washington and we'd not been received kindly. We'd played to less than $5000 on the week, and were ready for dead failure. And Lillian Braithwaite had already got a reservation on the *Aquitania*, and I came on and got a two-minute ovation, and gave the best performance I've ever given in my life. That was, I think, my greatest thrill because it was completely unexpected.'

Although *The Vortex*, with its treatment of drug addiction and adultery, shocked the London of its day, Coward said he did not write it to shock anybody. 'I wrote it, curiously enough, for the very strong moral impetus.'

'Do you feel that your moral impetus is as strong today as it was then?' I asked.

'I think it's stronger,' said Coward, 'but it doesn't necessarily mean that I am going to write about it. I was, after all, twenty-four when I wrote *The Vortex*.'

'What do you do with your moral impetus now, then?' I asked.

'Well, I give it groundsel, and feed it gently,' said Coward. 'It does all right.'

Inevitably, we talked of 'Mad Dogs and Englishmen'. 'The perfect thing about "Mad Dogs and Englishmen" is the rhyming, of course, isn't it, really?'

'Oh, I don't think it's the *only* perfect thing about it . . .' said Coward.

'What are the other perfect things about it?' I asked.

'Well, it's a bloody good tune.' He explained something about the song: 'I didn't say "a mad dog of an Englishman". I said "mad dogs and Englishmen go out in the midday sun". An Englishman would still go out in the midday sun. Mad dogs have learned better.'

What was the great dispute that Churchill and Roosevelt had over 'Mad Dogs and Englishmen'?

'Oh, I believe it was absolutely lovely,' said Coward. 'I had it later from both of them. I asked questions. They had a row because Winston Churchill said that "in Bangkok at twelve o'clock, they foam at the mouth and run" came at the end of the first refrain, and Roosevelt said on the contrary, it came at the end of the second refrain, and a very serious trouble took place. And later I went to Churchill and said, "Did you say that?" And he said, "Yes." And I said, "Well, you were wrong. Roosevelt was right." And he said, "England can take it."'

Noël Coward was so famous for his own remarks. Could he remember any occasions when somebody else's had stopped him in his tracks?

'Yes, I can. I came out of the stage door once with a glamorous crowd welcoming me with autograph books, and I was graciously signing them, and somebody said, "I'll give you three Noël Cowards for one Jessie Matthews."'

'You told Jessie?' I asked.

'Certainly I told Jessie. She never spoke to me for three weeks, she was so pleased with herself.'

Noël Coward talked and wrote a great deal about England. 'If I had to pick something that was really basic England,' I said, 'I would pick the funny little general stores cum tobacconists in the small towns of England.' What would he pick?

'I would pick those, and I would pick the greatest houses belonging to what used to be known as the landed gentry. I would pick the whole of England, not a little tiny bit. Because all the different portions of England contribute to what is England. You can't have only those dear lovable little creatures in their hovels, and you can't only have those grand duchesses in their great mansions. They've all got to mingle, as indeed they always have, and I shrewdly suspect always will.'

Did he ever wish that he had been a critic?

'Oh, good God, no. I also wish nobody else had ever been a critic.'

'Would you call it an honourable profession?' I asked.

'Oh, there are certain honourable critics. I can't remember any for the moment, but there certainly are some honourable critics. Hazlitt was an honourable critic.'

'He loved all your stuff, in fact?' I said.

'Mad about me,' said Coward.

Had there ever been moments when he had regretted his vast success, and wanted to give the whole thing up?

'Good heavens, no. Certainly not. There have been moments

when I have wished what I had done had been better, and other moments when I thought that it couldn't have been.'

What sort of beliefs had sustained him throughout his life? 'I mean, do you believe in God, for instance?' I asked.

'We've never been intimate,' said Coward.

'If you could choose an ideal life hereafter, what would it be? What would heaven be like?'

'*Tonight at 8.30,*' said Coward.

'Do you have a picture of a personal hell as well?' I asked.

'Oh yes, several,' said Coward, 'and they're all to do with overacting.'

Everyone thought of him as the most well-turned-out man imaginable. When did he become that?

'Oh, I don't think more than a few weeks ago,' he said. 'When I was young, I had a terrible feeling that socks and ties to match were the thing. Of course, they weren't. I've established a reputation for chic, which is really based on shifting sand. I'm not all that chic. I'm quite comfortable, and I have learned in later years that to wear what one is comfortable in is the best thing. And I remember my great teacher whom I loved very much, Charles Hawtrey, giving me a few tips, saying, "Don't worry about the handkerchief matching the socks, worry about never putting your hands in your pockets when a lady is in the room, because that is common." A funny bit of advice . . . As an actor, invaluable . . . I never have.'

'How would you define the word "common", actually?'

'"Common" I would define as people without that little extra bit of taste. Many common people can be absolutely sweet and lovable, and fond and friendly, but it has nothing to do with aristocracy either, as many of the aristocracy are extremely common. It is to do with taste. Taste is the thing. I think it must be acquired. You're not born with taste. A baby hasn't got taste, I don't think. Taste is not a question of personal appearance. It is a mental attitude.'

'Do you think it's important to be fashionable?' I asked.

'No, no, no, not at all. It's not important to be fashionable. I think it is very important to be clean.'

'One very good friend of yours said to me today, "I'd always go to Noël with my emotional problems and he'd sort them out. But he's absolutely frightful with his own." Is that fair?'

'Oh I say,' said Coward. 'He must have been a very close friend.'

'Would you care to elaborate?' I asked.

'No. I have gone in my life to very few people with my emotional problems, because I consider my emotional problems my own. Naturally my own private circle of friends, if there's an emotional problem, I go to and am helped by, but I do not go out roaring, and screaming and sobbing, when anything goes wrong, because I don't think it's anybody else's business.'

'I can't ever imagine you sobbing or being tearful,' I said. 'I can imagine you being in control whatever the situation.'

'No, my dear, I cry myself to sleep every night,' said Coward. 'No, I am not very given to emotional displays.'

'You're a hard man of granite, are you?' I asked.

'Not in the least,' said Coward. 'I'm a sort of chocolate milk sundae. But I have a tiny bit of vodka at the bottom of the milk sundae.'

I asked Coward when he had first met Laurence Olivier.

'I first met Laurence Olivier, I think it was in a play called *Paris Bound*, but when I really grew to know him was when I batted him on the head to make him play the bad part in *Private Lives*. And I did say to him, "This is the bad part. I've got all the answers. Why I am asking you to play it is that you're very attractive and I need a bit of competition." And he fell for it!'

When was Noël first called 'The Master'?

'I was called "The Master" as a joke, because my darling secretary, Lorne Lorraine, always called me "the master", and it sort of got around. And so help me God, I've been called "The Master" ever since.' A slight pause. 'Like Toscanini is called "The Maestro", you know.'

And how would he like to be remembered by future generations?

'Well, I would like to be remembered as somebody who has contributed a bit to the pleasures of other people. I would like to be remembered as a good friend, and rather an amusing character.'

I took the applause of the audience as a cue. 'I think you can reckon that your wish is going to be granted,' I said.

'Well,' said Coward, 'that's very nice of you. Thank you.'

It had been a memorably urbane and epigrammatic performance. I found Noël Coward much the same in private. We next met in New York at the Tony Awards (Broadway's Oscars). He and I, and Cary Grant, were among those presenting awards that night. Afterwards at the Pyrenees Restaurant nearby, there were drinks and an informal photo-call. Noël had been cornered in a booth by the paparazzi for at least twenty minutes when Cary and I were wheeled in one on either side of him to share the burden. As we sat down, without a flicker on the happy countenance he was presenting to the still-attentive photographers, Coward murmured pleadingly, 'Will somebody *please* take this smile off my face?'

Next day we had lunch in the Pool Room of the Four Seasons. After the head waiter had taken our order for drinks, Noël leaned forward. 'I do wish that water would keep still,' he said.

He was quite at ease telling stories that touched on his own homosexuality to a non-homosexual. As long as he sensed that you were in favour of sex in some shape or form, that was fine with him. 'I will never forget when I was being prepared for Confirmation, to receive the gift of the Holy Spirit – it was my mother's idea, I thought I had it already. The vicar put his hand on my crotch. I removed it and said, "Vicar, you are supposed to be preparing me for Confirmation. When I have received the gift of the Holy Spirit, if I'm in the mood, I'll telephone you."'

I never got to know Noël Coward well enough to be able to say for sure whether what lay beneath the surface was, as some suggested, simply more surface. Was he deep-down shallow, deep-down sad, or deep-down as upbeat as his conversation? I suspected that the light patina of incessant laughter was too brittle not to crack from time to time, but I did not know, and like millions contented myself with simply being grateful for the extraordinary entertainment it provided.

On the following Sunday, 29 December, there were two adjacent letters in the *Sunday Times*; the denial from Lew Grade that I quoted earlier this chapter, and another from Cyril

Bennett. Cyril had written specifically about ratings. 'The Network Programme Committee has never discussed London Weekend's Frost programmes – for one reason, because the programmes have never had the "lowly ratings" that Mr Tomalin imagines. On the contrary, "Frost on Friday" has had the majority of the audience against the opposition's entertainment since it began. "Frost on Saturday", likewise, has not only had the majority of the audience but, more significantly, has always pulled over the majority of the audience. "Frost on Sunday" remains ITV's highest-rated programme of the evening in all regions.'

I was glad that Cyril had taken up the cudgels on our behalf, though I didn't dwell on it, as I was already preparing for our next show. We achieved our target of having Enoch Powell on the programme by the narrowest of possible margins. He agreed to appear on Friday 3 January 1969, on the last 'Frost on Friday' of the series. Powell was undoubtedly the most controversial British politician of the late Sixties. From the early part of the decade he had moved steadily towards a more hard-line anti-immigration stance. From 1965 he had advocated the voluntary repatriation of 'unsuccessful or unassimilable' elements. By mid-1967 his views had hardened to the extent that he opposed letting the dependants of Commonwealth immigrants enter the country. And from the autumn of that year he was at the forefront of calls to control the expected flood of Kenyan Asians allowed into the country. But it was not until early 1968 that Powell really became publicly identified with the immigration issue. Before then his views, however extreme, had at least been put forward reasonably and soberly.

In February 1968, Powell made a speech on immigration at a Conservative dinner in Walsall. For the first time he attempted to identify with 'the sense of hopelessness and helplessness' felt by 'those of us living in the Midlands'. He told stories of schools with classes containing only one white boy. The outside world, he said, simply did not understand what he and his constituents were going through.

Five days after this speech, the Labour Government decided to introduce controls to limit the number of Kenyan Asians entering the country, despite the fact that they held full British citizenship under the 1962 Kenya Independence Act, and had been put under increasing pressure to leave the ex-colony by President Jomo Kenyatta. For the first time the right of all 'British citizens' to live in Britain was removed. It was widely believed that Powell had stampeded the Government into taking action. This was questionable, but whatever his influence, he would not have had any doubts about the potency of the immigration issue.

Two months later Powell was presented with another golden opportunity to exploit the immigration issue when the Government introduced a Race Relations Bill. The liberal left of the Conservative Party supported the legislation, but the right of the party, led by Powell and the former Colonial Secretary Duncan Sandys, was strongly against it. On 20 April in Birmingham, just a few days before the second reading of the Bill in the House of Commons, Enoch Powell delivered his major speech on immigration.

The speech was expected to be highly critical of the legislation, but few predicted how far – and how emotively – Powell would go in condemning it and the Government's immigration policy. He acknowledged that he would be criticised for what he was about to say, but he felt it was his duty to say it anyway. He talked of the fears and anxieties of his constituents and others ('ordinary, decent, sensible people') about the immigration problem, and repeated some of their stories of harassment at the hands of coloured immigrants – the 'decent, ordinary Englishman' who had told him that he would not be satisfied until all his children had emigrated, as 'in this country in fifteen or twenty years' time, the black man will have the whiphand over the white man'. Or the old lady – anonymous and suspiciously untraceable – who had had excrement pushed through her letterbox by coloured immigrants.

Powell juxtaposed these accounts with a virulent attack on the Race Relations Bill, which he argued would elevate the immigrant into a privileged class. 'The discrimination and the deprivation, the sense of alarm and of resentment, lies not with the immigrant population, but with those among whom they have come and who are still coming. This is why to enact legislation of the kind before Parliament at this moment is to risk throwing a match onto gunpowder.' The immigration situation, he said, had reached a critical point, but the flow of immigrants had not been stopped. 'We must be mad, literally mad, as a nation to be permitting the annual inflow of some fifty thousand dependants, who are for the most part the material of the future growth of the immigrant-descended population.' It was like 'watching a nation busily engaged in heaping up its own funeral pyre'. The speech ended on a highly dramatic note: 'As I look ahead I am filled with foreboding. Like the Roman, I seem to see the River Tiber foaming with much blood.'

The speech had a sensational impact, creating both intense excitement and anger. Edward Heath reacted immediately by sacking Powell from his Shadow Cabinet, telling him that he considered his speech to have been 'racialist in tone and liable to exacerbate racial tensions'. Although the speech was roundly condemned by the press, with the exception of the *Daily Express* and the *News of the World*, a majority of the public seemed to be behind Powell. Between sixty-seven and seventy-nine per cent of those asked in opinion polls said they agreed with him. The best-remembered expressions of pro-Powell feeling were the marches to Westminster between 23 and 26 April by London dockers and meat porters. Powell himself claimed to have received over 100,000 letters expressing approval of his speech, and only five hundred critical of it.

Although Powell's views on race were regarded with disgust and contempt by liberal opinion, there was no doubt that they had won him an astonishing level of popular support. This was likely to be one occasion on which the members of the audience were *not* going to be on my side. And although Ted Heath had banished Powell to the official political wilderness, the framers of policy for both parties were acutely aware of the popular response to his views.

As we sat down in our studio chairs just before the programme, Enoch Powell characteristically sprung a surprise. He produced two autograph books and asked me to sign them for members of his family.

I began the interview quietly, with questions about Powell's relationship with his colleagues, but the phoney truce was very soon over, as we turned to my suggestion that he was 'exaggerating the problem, and I think, in the long run, making it worse'. This was an area of ignorance and an area of fear, I said. He was dealing with dynamite. 'Don't you think . . . for instance, in that story about the woman who had excrement pushed through her letterbox and so on, that you had a duty to do more than merely put quotation marks around it? Didn't you have a duty to check that story, to find if it was true?'

A couple of exchanges will give a flavour of the debate. It was almost continual cut and thrust, as I had to persist in trying to get Powell to answer the question. In response to my suggestion that he should have checked the story to make sure it was true, the conversation went as follows:

Enoch Powell: I haven't the slightest doubt it was, but may I –
DF: But have you – did you check it at all?
Powell: I haven't the slightest doubt –
DF: Did you check it at all?
Powell: I haven't the slightest doubt, and I verified the source from which I had that information. Now –
DF: Did you verify the story?
Powell: I verified the source, and I haven't the slightest doubt that it is –
DF: But what do you mean, you verified the source?
Powell: – that it is true as it is typical.
DF: But it's not typical. I mean, I'm not saying it hasn't happened –
Powell: Ah, well now –
DF: I'm not saying – you say it's typical.
Powell: Yes, I do.
DF: You see, you keep using words like 'typical', as though there's millions of piles of excrement dropping through letterboxes up and down our green and pleasant land – and that's not happening. I said, 'Did you check the story?' and you said you verified the source.
Powell: Yes, indeed. And –

DF: But if I say, 'Did you check the story?' the answer to that question is 'No.' Not 'I verified the source.' Because –

Powell: I have answered your question. You asked me, and I –

DF: No. The answer was 'No,' and not 'Yes.'

Powell: I've answered the sense in which I verified that story.

DF: But this is dynamite . . . You might just as well, if you're going to use the word 'typical' like that, you might just as well say: 'The British Olympic Team are typical of British people; they're all being flown to Mexico to compete in throwing the hammer.'

Powell: But do you really disbelieve that in the areas where the immigrant population is taking over – and I use that word quite neutrally – one street, one area, after another, do you doubt that over and over and over again, experiences like these are suffered by women exactly like that person? If you don't, then go and ask the police. Go and make enquiries. You don't even need to do that. Read the Milner Holland Report of – what? four or five years ago – on housing in London, and you will find case after case similar, similar in its details, similar even in the excreta, to the one which I quoted, listed in that official report.

I wished that I had had a copy of the 1965 Milner Holland Report (The Report of the Committee on Housing in Greater London) about my person, but of course I did not. When I looked at it later – as did several commentators – I was intrigued to see how much the report went out of its way to emphasise that bad behaviour was not a racial matter, and when it came to the actual 'case after case', forty-seven cases in all, I could only find six which described bad behaviour by coloured immigrants towards white residents. Six out of forty-seven. It was another documented example of Powell being 'creative' with the facts.

DF: If you spread this sort of thing in this sort of incendiary atmosphere, you know that you are throwing the match . . .

Powell: You accuse me of throwing the match on to the heap. Now the heap of gunpowder in this case is the pent-up fear and anxiety for the future of the native population, which sees the extent of the numbers, the extending of the numbers and area of the immigrants. Now I want to ask you: What is the match which is most likely to ignite that combustible material? Not a politician who forces the whole of the country to see what is happening, who speaks what thousands of people in these areas concerned are saying to themselves, who answers their question: Why does nobody speak to us? Are we alone? Are we trapped?

DF: Listen, of course the politicians should pay attention to those people. But when you've got a situation in the country where there is a vast reservoir of fear and ignorance, justified because people don't know, people haven't met and so on, and when they do meet, there's always a period of adjustment. Then you can do two things with that fear: you can exploit it as, say, Hitler did it against a minority, or you can attempt to educate it. And it seems to me that you attempted to exploit it. You've quoted a constituent of yours as saying, 'In this country, in fifteen or twenty years, the black man will have the whiphand over the white man.'

Powell: Yes.

DF: But you don't think that, do you?

Powell: Well, I –

DF: I mean, you don't think the black man's going to have the whiphand in this country. I mean, it's nonsense –

Powell: In – in the areas concerned, unless something drastic is done, there will be a coloured majority in the foreseeable future over large areas, and there will be the whiphand over the white man held by the immigrant. This is – well, this is foreseeable.

We touched on some more statistics, and I made the point that when Powell had said that in the year 2000 there would be five to seven million immigrants, or one-eighth of the whole population, he was again guilty of misleading his listeners. In fact his figure was based on the alleged number of immigrants in the year 2000, but as a fraction of the population in 1968. The total population in the year 2000 would be much higher, and the fraction would therefore be much lower. His figure was exaggerated and misleading.

I asked him if he thought that his speech had led to any racialist showings of feelings in the streets. He said that he had no reason to think so. 'Let's take a look at the film that cropped up just afterwards outside the House of Commons,' I said. The film showed the dockers marching and shouting 'Enoch Powell!' There followed the booing of the black High Commissioner for Kenya.

Powell: And who was doing the booing?
DF: Your supporters.
Powell: How do you know?
DF: The people who just walked along with those placards.
Powell: I didn't see them doing it. Nor have I on any film been shown evidence that the booing of the High Commissioner was by the dockers who carried out that march. On the contrary, I have every reason to suppose that the men who marched up – and I had evidence from press photographers who had marched, as they said, backwards for six miles in front of them – not only were in the friendliest relations with the coloured people as they passed along in the dock area and otherwise, but were extremely anxious to avoid anything which could be even misinterpreted as being on their part directed against coloured people or immigrants as such.

Was it my imagination, or were there echoes of Oswald Mosley defending his Blackshirts in that tribute from Powell? However, his exoneration of the dockers was particularly novel.

'You've got evidence, of course, to support your amazing supposition,' I said. Powell did not have any evidence, but made his statement again.

DF: Until you've got some evidence on your side, I think that's fantastic. What about all those people who went around – to quote the case of the Indian student who was beaten up in Gospel Oak Road by thugs who were shouting 'We want Enoch,' or by the people who were shouting, 'Coloured people want burning. They're taking over. Enoch was right.' Would you like now to say something to those people, to dissociate yourself, and condemn that sort of thing?

Powell: I'm not going to start condemning the behaviour of people who are condemned by their behaviour anyhow. It is no business of a politician to set himself up as a preacher and –

But did he dissociate himself from them?

Powell: I'm not going to be put in the absurd position of dissociating myself from people with whom you know perfectly well I am in no way associated.

He tried to say that he was surprised by the impact of the speech, 'in which I said very much what I had been saying in many previous speeches . . . Very often a speech is first heard when it has been made ten times, and on the tenth occasion, people say, "Why didn't you say that before?" This happens to me over and over again –'

I could not accept this wide-eyed surprise.

DF: Well, how many times did you tell the excreta story before?
Powell: Well, clearly I haven't told that before.
DF: You haven't. How many times have you quoted the phrase 'grinning piccaninnies' before?
Powell: That was in the same letter, so don't double up, that doesn't count.
DF: How many times did you talk about the river Tiber and the blood and all that? How many times?
Powell: Because this was the –
DF: How many times before?
Powell: This was the first time that a Race Relations Bill –
DF: First time? First time?
Powell: No, no. This was the first time that a Race –
DF: You haven't mentioned those before –
Powell: – that a Race Relations Bill was in question.
DF: But you asked us to believe a lot with those dockers sud-

denly being replaced by stooges from the Whitehall set-up.

Powell: And now I'm asking you –

DF: But I mean, this is fantastic.

Powell: And now I'm asking you to believe that I was making –

DF: And you mention excreta, piccaninnies for the first time, and you are amazed by the response.

The first half of the programme had by now taken up almost forty minutes out of our total forty-five minutes, so I said, 'We've got to take a commercial break here. They've been waving at me for the last few minutes. I think we've probably broken every rule, because it's almost – anyway, let's take a commercial break now, can we?'

After the break, I said to my guest, 'We're trying to get some extra time, which I don't know if we will, Mr Powell.' If we got no extra time, there would be only four or five minutes remaining, so I asked him a basic question: 'A simple question, this, but I've never seen you say it: you do believe that racial discrimination's wrong, don't you?'

'If you mean – ' Powell began, only to be interrupted by shouts of 'Answer the question!' from the audience, which had generally been more on his side than mine, 'that people resident – sorry? Oh, no, no. One must define before one gives an answer, yes or no. Of course we discriminate racially and nationally in admitting to this country, so one must define what one means. If you mean that people resident in the country, equally citizens of the country, should be equal before the law and treated equally by the law and by all public authorities, yes.'

Powell agreed that it was wrong if a black man went into a bar and the barman said, 'We don't serve coloureds,' because it was a public place.

'Okay,' I said. 'If you advertise for a secretary and you add at the end, "No coloured person need apply," that would be wrong?'

'I wouldn't unconditionally say that that was wrong.'

In the moments that remained I tried to get him to say something positive about race relations, given that even he agreed there would always be some coloured people in this country.

'Say something to the white people and the coloured people: what's the most important thing in order to get – leaving aside how many you hope will leave or anything like that – what's the most important thing to make them live together happily?'

Enoch Powell was not about to say anything positive. 'The absence of fear that the number of coloured immigrants –'

I tried again: 'You've never, ever given a positive, warm bit of advice of the way that blacks and whites should behave together.'

'But I believe –' said Powell.

'Do it, please –' I said.

'I'm very much obliged to you, but I'll answer it my own way if you don't mind . . . I live in a constituency in which the behaviour of the white population towards the increasing number of immigrants has been tolerant beyond all praise, and beyond, I must confess, beyond all expectation. I would be ashamed of myself to go preaching to them about tolerance and how to behave. But if you ask me what is the essential thing for peace,' (Yes, you've guessed what's coming) 'it is the fear of a continuous and large increase in the numbers of the immigrants.' Appropriately enough we were cut off at the end of our time with Enoch back on one of his favourite slogans again.

What followed was instant activity. The time was now 10 p.m., and 'News at Ten' began its broadcast. Cyril Bennett called from home where he had been watching the programme, and spoke to Clive Irving. Clive felt that the programme should go on, and Cyril agreed one hundred per cent. He said that we should continue after the news at 10.30 for twenty minutes or so, and that the movie *Return to Glory* should be delayed until then. It was a typically flexible and quick-witted response from Cyril.

At the end of the news there was a commercial break, and then I said, 'Welcome back, for the first time, to part three of "Frost on Friday". And our thanks to Mr Enoch Powell for staying on, and our thanks to our audience, too, for staying on with us.' I then dealt with a postscript. The ITV reporter who filmed the demonstration that we had watched earlier had telephoned Nigel Ryan, the editor of ITN, who had then called us to say that the reporter was clear in his mind that the people he filmed in the demonstration were the people doing the booing. 'And he was there,' I said to Powell.

'He was clear in his mind,' said Powell, 'and I'll just put one point to you to remind you, and that is of the Notting Hill riots, and of the Dudley riots, which occurred years before my name was ever heard of in this connection. I think we ought to bear that in mind as a matter of proportion.'

A skilled debater's red herring. I brought him back to the point: 'I am saying the man who was actually there is clear in his mind –'

Powell: Is now clear in his mind that what?
DF: – as to what he filmed. Several of the dockers who booed.
Powell: Right. Okay. Well then, we're clear.
DF: All right. Do you accept that?
Powell: Yes. And you'll bear in mind about the Notting Hill riots, won't you?
DF: I will. I will.
Powell: So we're both clear again.
DF: I accept that. Marvellous. I'll bear in mind the riots in Tibet as long as you're clear about – thank you for accepting that point; I think it's a very valuable clarification of what we were trying to say earlier.

I hoped that that underlined sufficiently clearly the way Powell had moved his ground, but I knew that the emotional quotient in this particular argument was a high one.

DF: If we've got to live together, anything that inflames feelings between us all can wreck us, and you would say that a lot of the arrangements have. But if we've got to live together, it just seems to me you've got – however great your grievances – you've got to handle so carefully anything that may inflame the situation. Now, now you're going to say the numbers will inflame it, but anything one says may inflame the situation. It just seems to me terribly dangerous. That's all I'm saying.
Powell: Yes, indeed. But often not saying can inflame a situation.

DF: It's how you say it, isn't it?

Powell: No, not being heard. Often a failure to draw attention to something which can be dealt with now, but may be much more difficult – I will put it at its lowest – to deal with later. And so I agree with what you said. I agree with what you said about living together, and of course there will always be diverse races in this country living together. But the practicability of it depends ultimately on matters of number, and that is why effort now, policies now, which will limit the prospective numbers to what one judges – and this in the end is a matter of judgement – to be capable of being assimilated and lived with happily, that must be the prime duty of the politician, and it no way prejudices any of the other points which you put to me.

That was very nearly the end of the programme, apart from one interjection from the audience. A man shouted, 'Mr Powell, look at your language tonight. Look at some of the phrases you have been using tonight.'

'I'll willingly look at the phrases,' said Powell.

'Of how people are getting a whiphand, like a lot of people taking over a street, that was your very words. You said taking over a street,' said the member of the audience.

'No, no I didn't,' said Powell.

'Yes, "taking over a street". You said you were using it neutrally. Now that's not a neutral word: "taking over" is not a neutral word.'

'If they were Welsh or Scots,' said Powell, 'would you object to my saying that the Welsh or the Scots have taken over this street?'

The programme ended with Powell and me involved in another, albeit minor, verbal skirmish. After we were off the air, a number of members of the audience gathered around Mr Powell, many of them asking for his autograph. When one of the few black members of the audience attempted to question him, he said, 'Wait a minute, let the lady speak first. It's a custom in this country, you know.' The woman replied, 'It's a custom all over the world, Mr Powell.'

The LWT switchboard was besieged with callers, most of them

supporters of Enoch Powell. He had clearly won the popular vote, and his supporters thought he had carried all before him. What of the rest of the audience? According to the *New Statesman*, the programme demonstrated to the uncommitted 'what a deeply shifty arguer he is, refusing ever to give a straight answer to a straight question'.

Under the headline 'Come On, Enoch, Who Did Boo?' the *People* reported:

> It is seldom that the famous *People* team of investigators must admit they have failed on an assignment.
>
> Today, shamefaced, they confessed there is one question which they have drawn a blank . . . the search for the mysterious Boo-Men.
>
> The first important witness questioned was no help at all. Mr Powell had said on TV that he had met press photographers who agreed with him.
>
> Quote from Fleet Street photographer Harvey Mann: 'The dockers were doing the booing. They were yelling their heads off.'
>
> Several of the dockers seemed to agree.
>
> Quote from docker Fred Moore of Bermondsey: 'Once someone started booing, everyone did. That was the spirit of the thing. It wasn't a case of being disrespectful.'
>
> Quote also from docker Mike Maynard of Poplar: 'Some of the lads did boo and shout. I suppose it was because the man was coloured.'

And then they spoke to the one witness who should have had no doubt about the incident: the High Commissioner of Kenya himself.

> Quote from Dr Karanja: 'I have no doubt in my mind that the dockers booed me. I don't see how anyone can say it was anyone else.'

In the *TV Times* I summed up: 'The question that remains is not whether immigration should be limited or not, nor whether there is a problem or not. The question is: has the method of airing it chosen by Enoch Powell improved the situation or inflamed it?'

The debate about Powell's own motives would continue. Had he espoused the immigration issue for largely opportunistic reasons? With his path to conventional leadership already closed off by his dismal performance in the 1965 Conservative leadership race, had he searched for an issue to exploit which could enable him to appeal over the heads of both parties to the electorate? Or was he the ivory-tower intellectual sincerely pursuing his goals with an otherworldly disregard for the consequences? Of course, the numbers issue to which he perpetually returned was an important factor, but even that he ruthlessly exaggerated. In general his manipulation of statistics and of apocryphal anecdotes, and his refusal to say anything that would encourage a sense of community with the immigrant population, tended to place the casting vote with the cynics.

There were two separate festivities at the end of the series. After the final 'Frost on Sunday', which for the first time we pre-taped on the Thursday, we had all been invited to dinner at the Chinese restaurant opposite the studios by Gerard Wiley. This, needless to say, caused intense fascination. We were about to meet our mystery writer. Ronnie Corbett was particularly intrigued, not only because he and Ronnie Barker had played in so many of the Wiley sketches, but because Wiley had finally withdrawn his demands for a whopping fee for Ronnie to use his sketches, and had let him have them for free. A grateful Corbett had sent him half a dozen cut-glass goblets as a thank-you present.

Some possible candidates had already been ruled out by the *Evening Standard*. They had contacted Peter Shaffer, who had said no. Willis Hall? 'No, I know nothing about it.' Caryl Brahms had spoken for herself and her writing partner Ned Sherrin: 'Honestly, no, and it isn't Ned either.'

As everybody gathered in the restaurant the betting on Wiley's true identity reached a peak. Frank Muir was a favourite of many, and when he entered there was an immediate chorus of 'Aha! So it was you,' to greet him. Frank waved these cries aside with the embarrassed explanation that he was suffering from a touch of 'flu, and so would not be able to stay for the dinner. That made the favourite Tom Stoppard, but when everyone else had arrived, there was still no sign of him. The speculation was renewed.

At this point, Ronnie Barker stood up, and to everybody's complete astonishment announced: 'I am Gerard Wiley.' No one was more astonished than Ronnie Corbett. He recalled how, after a Christmas sketch had not quite worked, Ronnie Barker had muttered to him as they left the studio, 'Wiley really let us down with that one.' I remembered other occasions when Ronnie Barker had failed to understand a line in a Wiley sketch, and either Phil Casson, our director, or I had patiently explained to him what the writer was getting at. It had been a totally successful piece of sleight-of-hand, but what had given Ronnie the idea to do it?

'It's simple,' he said. 'When I started writing sketches, I wanted to make sure that they only made it into the show on merit. And I thought that the invention of Gerard Wiley might save everybody a lot of embarrassment into the bargain.'

The second festivity took place on the Sunday night, when I threw a party in the cavernous spaces of Alexandra Palace. I needed that amount of room because I had decided to create an indoor version of Battersea Fun Fair, and enlisted the help of Botton Bros to assist. Mr Botton was a great character, who not only dropped his aitches, but always found a place for them elsewhere in the same sentence: 'My heldest son, 'enery, used to work at the Hagricultural 'all . . .' he told me on one occasion. I invited what the newspapers referred to as two thousand of my closest friends to join in the merry-making. There was, I must confess, an ulterior motive this time. Most of my other parties at the end of series had merely been carefree celebrations. That was true this time, but in addition I wanted to deliver a good-natured 'up-yours' to those members of the ITV old guard and the media who had given us such a hard time back in September. I reckoned that nobody would spend £5000 on celebrating a flop, and that the subliminal message would get through.

The Great Hall looked terrific, filled with fairground attractions that included a helter skelter, a roundabout, dodgem cars, rifle ranges, hula hoops and all the fun of the fair. The food ranged from jellied eels, whelks and barbecued chickens to hot dogs, fish and chips (in paper bags) and rock made on the spot. The Bishop of Southwark, Dr Mervyn Stockwood, rode an ecumenical dodgem with Lord Longford, and then commented, 'Great fun. You can't be in the Church of England without being a good dodgem.' Mary Whitehouse tried the dodgems as well, and said afterwards, 'I knocked Stirling Moss for six.'

In the *Catholic Herald* Norman St John Stevas confessed:

> For the first time in five years I missed my weekly column. I was laid low, not by the Hierarchy but by the Caterpillar. Perhaps I should explain.
>
> On the Sunday evening I went to a party given by Mr David Frost at the Alexandra Palace to mark the end of his present television series. The party was an unusual one since Mr Frost had hired a fair and installed it in the palace. Inspired by the ecumenical sight of Lord Longford and the Bishop of Southwark in tandem in a dodgem car, I decided to try my luck on the Caterpillar, which looked innocent enough, but turned out to be a beast of the most ferocious disposition.
>
> It twisted, it turned, it bucked, it rolled, and above all it refused to stop. At the end of it as I tottered off I realised it had robbed me of all sense of balance. (Some, of course, would say that *Humanae Vitae* had already had this effect.)
>
> For four days I could not stand nor eat and the one New Year Resolution that I am quite sure that I will keep is that never, never, never will I mount the Caterpillar again. I only hope that others will profit vicariously from my grisly experience.

The *Glasgow Herald* summed up:

> Kingsley Amis was resplendent in a purple velvet dinner jacket, Cilla wore a black fun fur, and Marty Feldman, a

tartan poncho. But the sartorial honours were won outright by the Bishop of Southwark in his long plum-coloured cassock with a large Episcopal cross on a chain. Dr Emil Savundra was otherwise detained, and no one, I gather, spotted Mr Enoch Powell among the guests.

TEN

A New Show in New York

DURING THAT AUTUMN SEASON of 1968, thoughts of America in general – and the Westinghouse show in particular – were never far from my mind. When Ted Ashley, at that time the head of Ashley Famous Agency (who were my agents) came to London in October, he told me that he thought the Westinghouse decision was imminent. In early December Chet Collier called Richard Armitage, and negotiations began in earnest.

I began to get concerned about the way the LWT contract might look to Westinghouse, and the Westinghouse contract might look to LWT. Although I was confident that I could do five weekly shows in New York and three in London, I did realise that this was somewhat unorthodox. Talking to Richard Armitage in London, and to Jerry Leider and Gary Nardino at AFA in New York, we decided that the Westinghouse commitment had to come first. Only then could we integrate it with LWT. What we had to do with the Westinghouse contract was to budget for as much time in London at the weekends as possible.

While one American contract was being negotiated, another had been signed. I had had an idea for a film in which opinion polls were used to precipitate events, rather than merely comment on them. The idea had come from a recent by-election in Hull North, where a surprise eight per cent lead for one of the candidates in the polls on the morning of the vote had led to a twelve per cent victory by the evening, as opposing voters lost heart throughout the day. That was to be the starting point for the film – about a man who makes his way to 10 Downing Street by the expedient of manipulating opinion polls. I had asked John Cleese and Graham Chapman to write the script, which they had done, and Peter Cook was prepared to star in it, and worked with them on the final draft. Now Ken Hyman, who was running the studio at Warner-Seven Arts, had committed to finance the film, tentatively called *The Rise and Rise of Michael Rimmer*.

Actually I was involved in two films. The other was a shorter feature of about fifty minutes in length. It was called 'Futtock's End', and it was about a weekend of shenanigans at an English country house which made a superb vehicle for Ronnie Barker and Ronnie Corbett. But the number of people who wanted to back shorter-length films was minimal – where was I going to get the £50,000 to make it?

I decided to make it one of my Westinghouse Specials for the States, which brought in approximately £20,000, but the gap remained. At this point George Brightwell, my General Manager, came up with a brilliant suggestion. How about shooting the film entirely mute, and then using no dialogue – only sound effects? Would that make it more affordable? George, the director Bob Kellett and I went over the figures again. Sure enough, we were able to bring the budget down to close to £20,000, and I gave the go-ahead for the film to be made.

When the film was released (and thankfully it has been re-released ever since) the silent-film device was hailed as an artistic masterstroke. The fact that the inspiration owed more to my bank manager than to my creative muse remained a secret between George and myself.

While this was going on, I was also negotiating for the television rights to my childhood passion, the BBC radio serial 'Dick Barton, Special Agent'. I felt that a slightly tongue-in-cheek series, retaining all the slightly out of date 'stiff upper lip' approach of the original, could have a big following among both adults and children, each taking it on their own particular level. Dick, Jock and Snowy could follow in the footsteps of Batman and Robin.

By the middle of January 1969 the broad outlines of a deal with Westinghouse were becoming clear. The major stumbling block was my commitment to London Weekend. Don McGannon, the Group W President, and Chet Collier had to be in Fort Lauderdale, but realising that matters were becoming urgent, and not wanting to have to damp down press speculation with vague denials, they asked me to join them. I took the last flight to New York on Friday the seventeenth, and flew on to Fort Lauderdale the next day. Don, Chet and I met for dinner that night, and then spent the whole of the next day in session. By the time I flew back to New York at 5.15 in the afternoon, I had managed to convince them that I could do both shows. We had even worked out a tentative timetable, which divided up my week between London and New York, with five shows at the Little Theater in New York being taped in three days.

On the flight back to New York I was jubilant. There now seemed to be no obstacle to the deal, because I was sure that LWT would not need the persuasion that Westinghouse had. They would be delighted for me, I thought, and they would see that I had preserved half the week for the three LWT shows, and half the week for the five Group W shows, so the mathematics were in their favour. I asked Richard Armitage to go and talk to Michael Peacock, as his relationship with Michael was somewhat better than mine. Perhaps naively, I imagined that the conversation would be a formality. How wrong I was.

I arrived back in London at 9.30 on the morning of Friday 24 January. At ten o'clock I had a briefing meeting with Richard Armitage and John Stutter, my lawyer, and then Richard went off to see Michael Peacock.

It was soon clear that plain sailing was undoubtedly out. Michael said, and confirmed in writing, that he found my new schedule totally unacceptable. What if the planes were late, or delayed by fog? A contract the size of mine meant that I must be on first call to LWT throughout the week. All Saturday the argument raged back and forth. I did not regret delegating the negotiations to Richard, but I found the unavoidable delays between his bulletins almost interminable.

On Saturday night, in order to get my mind off the negotiations, I took Jenny to the movies. This proved to be a total disaster. The film was *Rosemary's Baby*, and being set in the States it merely reminded me continuously of the opportunity of a lifetime that seemed to be slipping away.

The following day, Richard went over to Michael Peacock's

house in Barnes, while I was busy on the phone. I had to call Chet in New York to tell him that there was a temporary hold-up with LWT, but that we hoped to have it sorted out within a day or two. We had given the ITA a pledge that I would be exclusive within the UK to LWT for three years. That didn't just mean not appearing on the BBC, it meant doing shows for LWT as well, and I was determined to fulfil that promise. At the same time, some of my colleagues at LWT were saying to Michael, 'You cannot block David on an opportunity like this and still expect to have his full-hearted involvement in his LWT shows.'

By Monday Richard was able to report cautiously that Michael was beginning to be convinced. The logjam was beginning to break. On Tuesday I was able to call Chet Collier with the good news that matters were resolved. I had intended to do 'Frost on Friday', 'Frost on Saturday' and 'Frost on Sunday' for thirteen weeks in the autumn. I could still do that, or alternatively I could do my thirteen weeks of 'Frost on Friday' and 'Saturday' in the autumn, and my thirteen weeks of 'Frost on Sunday' in the spring (that was the plan that was finally adopted).

In spite of all these provisions, in private Michael was still pessimistic. He thought that the press would portray my new contract as a defection. 'We had a terrible time dealing with that rumour that you were about to go off to *Harper's Bazaar*,' he said to Clive Irving, 'and you're a man of no public consequence.' Dear old Michael – he didn't mean it like that, but if there was an unfortunate way of putting something, he could be guaranteed to find it.

On Tuesday night, I took Jenny to the Mirabelle to celebrate. I thought something special was called for, so we had a bottle of 1890 Château Lafite. I was in a mood to celebrate, Jenny slightly less so. 'You've been a great source of strength during this weekend,' I said.

'Yes,' she said, with a touch of melancholy. 'I'm helping you towards something that is going to take you away from me.'

I could not argue very convincingly. I feared that might be true.

The next day I set off for New York to cross the *t*s and dot the *i*s with Westinghouse, armed with a warm telegram from Cyril congratulating me on my 'giant step': 'You have gone up to a different planet now,' he said, and wished me luck. The formalities of the contract in New York seemed almost endless, but Don McGannon and I finally shook hands at his house in Scarsdale at midnight on Saturday 1 February. Next day Group W announced the deal. Most of the headlines in New York were like that in the *Daily News*: 'Frost Gets Griffin Job'.

In London, in keeping with the British press's greater fascination with all things financial, the headlines concentrated on the 'million dollars a year' they said I would be earning. (In fact my guarantee was a great deal less than that. It was still very healthy – $350,000 a year – but the series would have to do ridiculously well if I were ever to increase the figure as far as a million.)

Despite his earlier reservations, in London Michael Peacock handled things expertly. He said that the contract was a 'unique compliment' to David Frost and to British television: 'The Americans will be introduced to that particular brand of exciting television which David has made his own over here. We have also entered into other arrangements with David for future programmes which ensure that he will continue to appear in this country for London Weekend.'

In the States, the announcement was the signal for a major sales battle to commence. None of the 140 stations who bought 'The Merv Griffin Show' had to take 'The David Frost Show'. In each and every case it required a separate decision, and not just a simple continuation. In New York, Los Angeles and Washington, 'The Merv Griffin Show' had aired on the independent Metromedia stations in the choice time-slot of 8.30 to 10 p.m. Now Metromedia were starting to produce their own five-times-a-week show, 'Allen Ludden's Gallery'. It was not yet clear whether Metromedia would buy 'The David Frost Show', and even if they did, it was by no means certain that it would win the 8.30 slot in competition with one of their own shows.

Westinghouse's salesmen went out on the road, planning as a first priority to nail down as many of the top fifty markets as they possibly could. Meanwhile Owen Simon, Group W's very gifted Head of Publicity, and Chet were preparing a promotional itinerary for me.

Simultaneously the latest of the Paradine specials for Westinghouse under the original contract was receiving good reviews in the States. The special, entitled 'How to Irritate People', was the brainchild of John Cleese, who wrote it with Graham Chapman and also hosted it, as well as appearing in the sketches. At the beginning of the show I identified John Cleese as 'the tall, cruel one', described the upcoming programme as an antidote to all that Dale Carnegie and *Reader's Digest* 'How to get along with people' propaganda, and left it to John. The show took the form of an illustrated lecture, with enactments.

How to cope with loud name-droppers at an adjacent table? 'Wait for a suitable pause, then applaud enthusiastically.'

How to cope with women who seek compliments by protesting that their homes are a mess? 'Reply amiably, "Not at all – I enjoy a little squalor."'

How to cope with an overbearing head waiter? 'Place the prongs of a fork about three-eighths of an inch inside his eyeball.'

John was particularly preoccupied with getting our own back from banks. 'Whenever you have an overdraft, the bank manager gives you a call to say that you owe some money and would you drop in and talk to him about it. Next time you have a positive credit balance at the bank, ring up the bank manager, say that he owes you money, and ask him to come round and talk to you about it.'

Summing up, John cautioned, 'If you want to irritate for pleasure, one fundamental rule must be observed: never push them too far. They'll explode, releasing all the tensions we've worked so hard to build up. And we don't want that, now do we?'

When I got back to London, I attended to the first and most important item of business regarding 'The David Frost Show', the selection of the producer or co-producers. Having worked with them on a regular basis for three years, I knew that I needed Peter Baker and Neil Shand to join me in New York. Peter agreed to come as Producer with Neil as 'Creative Consultant'; that in American terms was a new title, as it was in my experience, but

Neil thought it sounded better than the traditional 'Associate Producer' tag. He was probably right – it was certainly more noticeable.

We arranged for some offices to be booked at the Commodore Hotel in New York for April and May, since 'The Merv Griffin Show' would be in occupation at the Little Theater until early June, and I set off on a quick holiday before embarking on the pre-production. We went to East Africa for a break at the Mount Kenya Safari Club, then I decided to pay a surprise visit to my sister Jean and her husband Andrew at the Wesley Guild Hospital in Ilesha, near Ibadan in Nigeria. I loved the thought of giving them a surprise, so we did not let them know we were coming.

When our week's holiday in East Africa was over, we went to Nairobi airport to catch an Ethiopian Airlines flight to Lagos. That flight – or more particularly the airline – has stayed with me ever since. The first thing that happened after we got on board was an announcement that all the tourist passengers had entered by the wrong door, and they were to get off, go round and come in by the correct one. This took about ten minutes. Then, for reasons which remained a mystery to us, the pilot and the steward had a pitched battle in the front of the first-class section. The steward won, and the pilot retreated to the cabin clutching his left eye.

Next, the steps were taken away from the plane. All seemed momentarily normal, until the chief stewardess rushed over to the open doorway and yelled after a retreating airline official, 'Don't go! Don't go until you tell us how to operate the . . .' We never heard what the piece of equipment was that they did not know how to operate, and could only hope that it would not be required in flight, whatever it was.

Soon a voice announced that we were to have an opportunity of tasting the Ethiopian national dish – wot. 'Wot' turned out to bear a striking resemblance to one of those damp flannels without which most airlines feel a meal would be incomplete. This was however not a flannel – it was wot. That led to a real-life variant on the traditional Abbott and Costello 'Who's on first base' sketch, which surfaces in England from time to time as the 'I'd like a ticket to Ware' routine. A military-looking

Englishman in the seat in front of me summoned the stewardess. 'What is this food?' he demanded.

'Yes, wot is that food,' said the stewardess.

'What?' said the man.

'Wot,' nodded the stewardess.

'It's what?' said the man.

'Yes, it's wot,' said the stewardess.

'What?' said the man.

'Wot,' agreed the stewardess.

'What?'

'Wot.' The dialogue was unstoppable.

In order to serve the Ethiopian national dish, the stewardesses had changed from Western-style uniforms into a rather charming form of sari. Or it seemed charming for a few minutes. Then one of the stewardesses withdrew the end of her sari from where it was tucked in below her armpit, and proceeded to blow her nose on it. Although she tucked that piece of the sari away again under her arm – or perhaps because of that – the national dress lost a little of its earlier allure.

Back in London, I went over the scripts for the new Ronnie Barker series, based on the 'Lord Rustless' episode of 'The Ronnie Barker Playhouse'. I took Jenny by private jet for a lost weekend in Vienna, and then set off back to the United States for a visit to the National Association of Broadcasters' annual bash in Washington. The British Ambassador was John Freeman (Harold Wilson had indeed made him one of the two offers he felt he could not refuse after India), and he kindly threw a party for would-be buyers of 'The David Frost Show' at the Embassy – a first for syndication! Back at the Shoreham I hosted a show called *A Touch of Frost*, with the music coming from Gladys Knight and the Pips. Meanwhile in New York Neil and Peter settled in to the offices at the Commodore.

We were soon interviewing prospective candidates for a whole range of roles, including Musical Director. There were plenty of candidates, and plenty of clubs in which to listen to them. We also needed two or three writers for the humorous sections of the programme, and they had to be interviewed, though it is a perennial problem that some writers who cannot really write still 'give good interview'. Nevertheless, we ended up with a good team of Walter Kempley from 'The Tonight Show', Andy Smith and Ed Hiestand. We met directors and contenders for the roles of associate producers and bookers. The words 'researcher' and 'research' did not seem to exist in the then current American talk-show parlance. Indeed, most of the formats seemed to obviate the need for it anyway.

I owed it to Gary Nardino at AFA for solving the problem of who was to be my secretary/personal assistant. He recommended Cate Ryan, who was both pretty and bright. She had ambitions to become a playwright, but in the meantime was happy being a personal secretary, and had the sort of bubbling good humour I always like to have around.

Quite early on, we decided that we were not looking for a second banana. I felt it might get in the way of the sort of show we were planning to do. So although Johnny Carson had Ed McMahon, Merv Griffin had Arthur Treacher, and Joey Bishop had Regis Philbin, we decided there would be no equivalent on our show.

There was a more pressing problem – and that was the set. Being based in the Little Theater meant that I and my guests were placed on a stage above the audience in the stalls. That was the reverse of what I had always done in the UK – I liked to have the audience looking down at the proceedings, so that they felt more a part of them, more able to contribute than they would if they were seated in the body of a theatre, below my guests and myself. The theatre set-up in New York precluded that, but how could we minimise any sense of the audience being left out? And another problem: given that I was not always going to ask people to stay on stage for the rest of the show if a one-on-one interview with the next guest seemed preferable, how were we going to make the stage feel 'full' with just two people?

We were lucky to find, in Tom John, a designer with immense flair who could work to our difficult brief. He created a 'talk pit', a semi-circular platform lifted a few inches off the floor of the stage. Around the back of the semi-circle was a low wall, on which extra guests could sit if necessary. Within this area two chairs could be placed, which would make the talk pit seem fully occupied, while the talk pit in turn made the stage seem fully occupied.

As to the problem of access to the audience, and the audience's access to us, we decided to 'abolish' the edge of the stage. Instead of a straight drop down to audience level, we built in a step halfway down, so that not only was it easier for me to move out amongst the audience, but even more important, it was possible to sit on the edge of the stage and thus be much closer physically to them. When the show started, I found I used that downstage position in several different ways: sometimes we wanted someone to talk to a group in the audience; sometimes we felt that the audience needed to be closer to the guest; sometimes we simply wanted, say, a John Hartford to take us in a relaxed way through some of his hits on the guitar.

On 26 April, in a rare burst of domestic activity, I moved into a more permanent apartment at the Hotel Lombardy in the morning, and then went out to the Hamptons with Clay Felker in the afternoon to rent a house in Bridgehampton called 'Sail Away' for the summer.

The show's staff was coming together. To take charge of the show-business bookings, we had needed an Associate Producer who knew the field intimately. We were lucky enough to get hold of Bob Carman, who had performed the same role in California for Joey Bishop. He liked the idea of taking on a new, unproven show, though he made a cautious two-stage commitment to it. He would come East immediately, but he told his wife to stay out West for a while. He had heard that this syndication business could be pretty dicey in its way . . .

Clay recommended John Berendt, who joined us from *Esquire* to work on research. Jeanne Vanderbilt brought a welcome knowledge of who was who in New York. And Jonathan Reynolds, a bright young researcher who had worked for Eugene McCarthy, balanced the others' strengths. We knew we had to be strong in the area of show business, like the other shows, but we wanted to be strong in other areas which they normally did not touch.

Next we decided on our choice for Musical Director. Among the many people who had been suggested and whom we had met, including some of the biggest names in jazz, our favourite was Billy Taylor. Billy was – indeed still is – a superb jazz pianist, and was working as Program Director of Station WLIB as well as on his manifold community projects like the 'jazzmobile', his own musical attempt to bring peace to the streets of New York in summer.

On Monday 19 May we got the good news that Metromedia had decided to buy 'The David Frost Show'. What was still not decided was whether we would manage to retain the 8.30 slot. Channel 5 announced that during that week they would be trying out 'Allen Ludden's Gallery' in the 8.30 slot.

We kept our fingers crossed, and next day I set off for London on the way to Aberystwyth for an important assignment. I had been thinking that there could be no better way of starting a series in the United States, or indeed anywhere, than with an interview with Prince Charles, about to be invested as Prince of Wales. On television in Britain there was to be a joint BBC–ITV interview conducted by Cliff Michelmore and Brian Connell. For the cinema Martin Harris of Drummer Films was making an official film that was to be screened by the Rank Organisation. He asked me to conduct the interview section of the film and I agreed, said that I would of course donate my fee to charity, and asked whether I might be allowed to screen the resultant interview on television in the United States. This had, to my delight, been agreed.

I arrived in Aberystwyth, and met the Lord Lieutenant of Radnorshire, Brigadier Sir Michael Dillwyn-Venables-Llewellyn, at whose home the interview was to take place.

Prince Charles was only twenty, but the filming session with him the next day was a delight. It was the first time I had experienced the self-deprecating sense of humour that has since become his trade mark. As the first question, I asked him, 'Your Royal Highness, what would you like your first act as Prince of Wales to be?'

'Well,' said Prince Charles, 'it's very difficult to have any particular act, so to speak. I mean, I don't think I could sort of rush in and declare the whole place a republic or Home Rule for everybody, you know . . . I hope that my first act really will be to take, you know, a real interest in Wales.'

Had he found learning Welsh difficult?

'It is quite difficult, because it's very different from English. You pronounce the words differently. For instance, *u* is pronounced *e*, you know, and so this I have found is one of the most difficult things to do. And there's also that famous trouble with the double *l*s which is like "Llanelli". So all that happens is that I cover my poor tutor in saliva, you know, but on the whole it's a very good exercise in concentration and in hard work. I haven't worked so hard for a long time.'

'Going back now, can you recall your first memories?' I asked. 'I mean, when I was five I wanted very much to grow up to be a footballer for Newcastle United, but I think I would have liked the striped shirts, really.'

'You would have got clobbered on the head by a bottle, I should think, wouldn't you?' said the Prince. (A reminder that football hooliganism was already an issue back in 1969!)

But could he remember thinking, 'I'd like to grow up to be a – whatever it is?'

'Yes, you have the proverbial engine driver or something like that,' said Prince Charles. 'Of course, a sailor I wanted to be when I'd been on the yacht for the first time. Of course, a soldier, because I was always watching the Changing of the Guard, you know. And then when I came to start shooting, I thought perhaps it would be romantic to be a great gamekeeper, and take an interest in nature, and that sort of thing. But I found out, you know, I went from one to the other, until I realised that I was . . . rather stuck.' I thought that 'rather stuck' as a way of describing becoming King was a masterly piece of British understatement.

'When did you realise you were . . . "rather stuck" . . . at first?'

'That's another very difficult problem. I didn't sit up in my pram and suddenly realise that. But I think it sort of dawns on you because you are living in an environment in which everybody realises what they have to do. No, you slowly realise, you are meant to know, and that you oughtn't to do this because you're in such and such a position, you know.'

'Did, for instance, the Palace seem fantastically huge to play in?' I asked.

'Enormous, yes,' said Prince Charles. 'But, I mean, it was home, always. I mean, I didn't know really that there were any other houses, you know. For all I knew, everybody might have lived in a house like that!'

We talked about the Trinity revue at Cambridge, to which the Prince had contributed and in which he had taken part. I said that someone who was there had told me that one thing he did got the biggest laugh of the evening. What was that?

'Oh, that was a very silly thing that I suddenly thought of on the spur of the moment, and I asked the producer if I could do it. He wasn't very keen, but he let me in the end. All I did was just walk through the curtains, with an umbrella up, and just said, "I lead a sheltered life," and turned around and walked out again. I suppose it was so surprising to the audience that they all roared with laughter.'

We talked next about duty. 'Do you feel that duty is a different thing for a member of the Royal Family than it is for the rest of us?' I asked.

'I would probably define it as being something you have to do, something you feel you ought to do, without particularly wanting to do it,' said Prince Charles. 'I think perhaps this is what duty is, for most people . . . but I feel that the royal duty in a way is slightly more inbred, it has to be. I mean, it has to be trained in a way. I think in this sense it's slightly different. You have a wider and more permanent duty in the sense that you can't really relinquish it just, you know, when you want to. Whereas I think you might be able to if you were an ordinary person.'

'And you need special, as you say, training,' I said. 'When did you make your first public appearance with Her Majesty and Prince Philip – when you first saw all the vast cheering crowds and everything like that?'

'Actually, virtually my first appearance of all was public, because the news of it was pasted on the railings at Buckingham

Palace! But no, I suppose something like the Coronation was really the biggest one I can remember. I've never forgotten the appearance on the balcony, which was absolutely unbelievable with all the people milling, you know, down the Mall, which was very exciting indeed. And their terrific enthusiasm. And they went on, they were chanting all night long. I couldn't get to sleep at all.'

'You've got much more freedom than you would have had, say, fifty years ago,' I said, 'but nevertheless are there times when you feel you'd like to say, "Oh, I'd love to say so-and-so." I guess what I'm saying is – are there times when you feel confined?'

'There are many occasions when I do feel confined, because constantly, whenever you consider speaking publicly, you have to take account that what you say might be construed in other ways by people whose interests are affected by what you say,' said Prince Charles. 'This makes it difficult, because one continually has to go over everything you say, and think, "Now, have I said the right thing? Can I say this or can't I say this?" and there are certain causes and certain things like that that I should like to talk about. Whether it would have any effect or not is debatable. But, you know, you are confined in that sense that you might cause a political controversy.'

Although neither of us necessarily realised it at the time, we had talked about a number of themes that would recur throughout his life: the sheltered upbringing, the royal sense of duty and, most of all, the problem of finding ways to speak out publicly on the subjects about which he cared most passionately.

Before returning to the States, I had a meeting with Trevor Lloyd Hughes, Harold Wilson's Press Secretary, to make the final arrangements for a programme on which I had been working for some months. The Prime Minister and Mrs Wilson would give us the first-ever tour of 10 Downing Street for television. I knew that would be of interest in the UK, but I also thought it would make a splendid early programme for 'The David Frost Show' in the States.

After the weekend I flew back to New York and then on to Dallas for another one of our promotional shows for local television stations. This time the guest artists were Marilyn Maye and The Brothers and The Sisters, a group who gave the assembled audience a splendidly rousing patriotic medley. Cate Ryan came with me on the trip in order to get a taste of what was going on. However, even as a New Yorker, she was not prepared for the locals' inventiveness when it came to choosing names for the gents' and ladies' restrooms. Halfway through dinner she excused herself, and returned within thirty seconds. 'Excuse me, David,' she said, 'but am I a heifer or a steer?'

The following Monday, 2 June, saw our staff assembled for the first time. Three of the early suggestions for interviewees were Charles Lindbergh, Howard Hughes and Greta Garbo. Walter Kempley commented, 'On any new talk show, they always are.'

By Thursday there was no news on Lindbergh, Hughes or Garbo, but there was a 'yes' from Ed Sullivan. The only problem was that he was about to leave for an extended trip overseas, and would not be back before the first show aired. I felt that a big name like Ed's would be a plus, so we arranged a special taping on the Friday night at the Little Theater, after 'The Merv Griffin Show' was finished for that night.

Ed was a legendary figure in America at the time. His Sunday night show from eight to nine on CBS was a national institution. Quite why was not always clear. He was a good impresario, but the main appeal of his introductions was the mistakes he habitually made. All over America people collected them. I certainly did.

On one occasion I had seen him announce, 'And now, ladies and gentlemen, here they are – three young ladies from Detroit, the Supremes. Tell me, girls, where are you from?' He had once introduced 'the fierce Maori tribesmen from New England', which must have caused some head-scratching in Boston. Making a charitable appeal for funds to fight tuberculosis, he had said at the end of one programme, 'And remember, help stamp out TV.'

When Jack Jones had appeared on the show, on the rehearsal at 4 p.m., Ed beckoned him over at the end of his song. This was considered a great accolade.

'Wasn't Allan Jones your father?' asked Ed. 'He still is,' said Jack. The afternoon audience chuckled. At the end of the rehearsal Ed said to Jack that the exchange had gone very well, and he'd like to keep it in for the evening. Jack shrugged – whatever Ed wanted, it was his show. Sure enough, that evening, live at 8 p.m., Ed beckoned to Jack at the end of his song. Jack came over. Ed turned to him and said: 'Is Allan Jones still your father?'

In the months that lay ahead, there would be other guests joining us on a Monday night who arrived shell-shocked from their experience live on 'The Ed Sullivan Show' the night before. But on that Friday night Ed was in good form, and gave us just the sort of human interview we were looking for.

During that first week of June, we had prepared a special programme to commemorate the first anniversary of Robert Kennedy's death. It contained my whole interview with the Senator, together with some new commentary, and was called 'To Ask Why Not: Robert Kennedy and David Frost'. Feeling the way I did about him, I was delighted at how many stations chose to broadcast the programme.

On Monday 9 June 'The Merv Griffin Show' very obligingly taped a sequence with me for the last show of the series four days early, as I had to leave for London to pre-tape some of the big names who were currently in Britain in order to insert them in the first week or two of the series in New York. We were due to start taping, rather fearlessly, on Friday the thirteenth, so there was just time to squeeze in a press party for *The Rise and Rise of Michael Rimmer* on the Thursday evening at 5.30. Peter Cook was unfortunately abroad, but he more than made up for his absence with a cable which I read to the assembled gathering:

> Sorry not to be at press conference but I am a publicity-shy recluse known to my friends as the Greta Garbo of Hampstead. I once hired a public relations firm to stress how much I shun publicity, but unfortunately this failed to gain much coverage in the national press. I regard this film as a challenge, especially my underwater wrestling scene with eleven Tibetan lesbians, but Kevin Billington has assured

me that this is an integral part of the plot and is not being included for reasons of cheap sensationalism. And who am I to argue with the director of such tasteful and artistically shot films as *The Dutch Fanny Hill Meets the Giant Crab Monster*? As the film is a comedy set in the near future, I would rather say nothing about the scenario in case some of our more lunatic fantasies are seized upon by the Government and adopted as official policy. I must close as the cable has used up my holiday allowance. Wish you were here. Signed Peter.

Saturday night was a particularly hectic taping night, with two 'houses'. The first included Cleo Laine, Lulu, the two Ronnies, Frankie Howerd and Kenneth Williams. The second featured Charlton Heston, John Cassavetes, Peter Falk and Ben Gazzara, and John and Yoko, who brought with them a small white box which they presented to me on air. On the outside it said simply 'To David from John and Yoko', and then, in capital letters, 'A BOX OF SMILE'. I opened it, and there in the bottom of the box was a small mirror. I laughed at the neat thought, and of course I immediately had my box of smile. John was eager to talk mainly about pacifism, and universal love. I made the conventional objection to all-out pacifism by citing Adolf Hitler. What good would it have done if, when Adolf Hitler marched into a new country, people simply said to him, 'I love you,' I asked. 'Ah, yes,' said John. 'But what if they had been saying it to him all his life?'

Jerry Lewis, Lee Remick, Tommy Steele, Spike Milligan and the Rolling Stones were among the guests who joined us at the Mayfair Theatre on Sunday and Monday evening. During the day on Monday, we were at 10 Downing Street for the programme with Harold and Mary Wilson.

Mary Wilson guided me up the stairs, past the pictures of all our previous Prime Ministers. In a throwaway I called it 'the greatest rogues' gallery in the world'. Mrs Wilson immediately replied, 'Well, you can say that – my husband isn't in it yet.'

Mrs Wilson's favourite portrait was Disraeli. Her husband preferred Gladstone. 'Gladstone used to walk the streets of London trying to rescue fallen women,' said Mrs Wilson.

'Well, that was *his* story,' I said.

'If there's a crisis, you feel as if the whole building is seething,' said Mrs Wilson. 'You can feel it in the air, it's like electricity.'

Mary Wilson clearly took pleasure in the opportunity to rebut the image of her created by the *Private Eye* satirists in general, and 'Mrs Wilson's Diary' in particular. 'So many people have tried to present me as the little housewife who never went anywhere, and suddenly erupted into Number 10. Which is all nonsense. After all, my husband has been in Parliament since 1945, and, indeed, was a Minister in the Attlee Government.'

'But you don't drink Wincarnis?' (the decidedly non-U tonic drink that *Private Eye* alleged Mrs Wilson treated as if it were champagne).

'I've never tasted it in my life,' said Mrs Wilson firmly. 'And if I did, I don't think it would really matter. I'm sure it's very nice . . . and HP Sauce.'

'Do you subscribe to the theory that behind every great man there is a woman?'

'No, I don't. I think if a man is going to become successful, he would do that anyway. It's nice to have a woman to support him. But I think that men who have to have a woman to push them on are bound to fail later. Because they can't do it on their own.'

Monday had certainly been a packed day, and then some. About midnight I called Peter Baker in New York to see how the move from the Commodore into the Little Theater had gone. Pretty well, it seemed, but there were a few minor grievances. One of the staff refused to enter his office as it was across the hall from the ladies' room. Then the secretaries refused to enter the ladies' room as it was across the hall from his office. By the end of the day, however, both ladies' room and office were in use.

I flew back to New York late on Wednesday and went into the office on Thursday morning. I loved the atmosphere of the Little Theater, but the accommodation was by no means spacious. On the first floor (or the ground floor, as we would call it in England) there was just the elevator, which on that Thursday chose to celebrate my arrival by breaking down for the entire day. On the second floor were a lot of tiny offices, very few with windows, which had once been small, and clearly not 'star', dressing rooms. My office was on the third floor, and consisted of a room for me, another for Cate, and a dressing room and bathroom. The big staircase that led down from the second floor to the stage still bore the imprints of the feet of chorus girls through the ages when the Little Theater had been known as the Winthrop Ames Theater.

On the following Tuesday, six days before regular taping began, we had our first and only pilot taping. We hoped that some or all of the material would be usable on the series, but the main purpose was to iron out the bugs in the system. We had however counted without the power of women's liberation.

Prior to living on a regular basis in America, I had always understood that American women were the luckiest and happiest creatures on the face of the earth; that if any sex was put upon, it was the male sex, for the men worked morning, noon and moonlight to make their women, into whose hands the bulging pay packets were lovingly pressed, rich and prosperous and free of worry and ulcers and heart attacks and prematurely grey hair. Wrong! American women, I soon learned, were having a terrible time. I could not open a paper or magazine without reading a chilling despatch from the latest battle front in the sex war. America, the country which had seemed to me the least in need of women's liberation, was leading the way.

So for that first taping, we invited thirty or forty representatives of the Women's Liberation Movement to come and talk to me, and to confront Lionel Tiger, the author of a book called *Men in Groups*, of which they were highly critical. The result was mayhem, even before the show began. The women came in and at once began arguing – not with me, but among themselves – very angrily about whether they should sit *beside* me (which would show everyone they were equal to men), or *facing* me (which would show everyone they were opposed to men). They bickered and quarrelled on this point, presumably absolutely fundamental to women's rights, for forty minutes, and then most of them walked out in a huff, blaming 'male supremacist' me, who had scarcely got a word in edgeways!

'Why are you, a man, sitting on the stage while we were only in the audience?' one of them asked me in the lobby as they were leaving.

'Because it's my show,' I said simply.

'Why can't we be sitting on the stage like you?' asked someone else.

'Because there's not room for thirty or forty people on this stage,' I explained, somewhat more patiently.

'Why do they all call it "history"? It ought to be "herstory",' shouted someone else.

When Lionel Tiger finally made his entrance, and was allowed to sit on the stage, most of the remaining women departed. (They also complained that Mr Tiger had been introduced by name, whereas they had not.) The four members of the group who chose to remain went on to explain further their struggle for equality, as Mr Tiger discussed his book, which was based on the idea that men are basically and biologically bonded together.

After the taping was finally over, we repaired to Sardi's for a well-earned drink. The whole incident had been total chaos but, on the other hand, real emotion had been captured on tape. I had seen an extraordinary picture of a new popular protest movement in its early and extreme days. The item – much edited – was worth considering for our first week. In any case, the thought of trying to do it again was too much for any of us.

The show was scheduled for its premiere on Monday 7 July, which meant that we had to tape our opening show a week before, on 30 June. The reason for this was 'bicycling'. In those days you could not satellite a show all over the United States, as happens with syndicated shows today. Once the show was taped, the tape was flown to Pittsburgh, where copies were duplicated and forwarded to the main stations. That process took a week. In addition there were the smaller stations, to which it would be uneconomical to send a brand new tape. For those markets tapes were bicycled from the zero-delay stations to the one-week-delay stations, to the two-week-delay stations and, in a few exceptional cases, the three-week-delay stations.

All this, of course, had several direct consequences. A syndicated show could not follow a fast-moving news story. By the time the programme was broadcast, it would have looked hopelessly out of date. Thus, if we were going to make news on 'The David Frost Show', we would have to do it by initiating the story ourselves, or by introducing a new angle or a new speaker into an ongoing debate.

The stations who took the show on a delay also had an impact on seasonal shows, at times like Christmas. Jesus Christ was never actually born in syndication. There was no Christmas Day, only a vague holiday period which seemed to cover two or three weeks of undirected peace and goodwill, and party recipes.

We would be starting off with thirty-seven stations taking the show. The figure was much less than Merv Griffin's 140, but most of the thirty-seven were in the major cities, so Westinghouse regarded it as a sound, even promising, start. But none of us had any illusions about the task ahead. Building on that total – indeed, even retaining it – would depend entirely on how the show was received.

We spent the weekend before the taping of the first show in lengthy viewing sessions, deciding which pieces to put where. On the Monday night we put together the first show. I taped an opening and a closing segment, but the rest was what we felt was the strongest mixture we could put together of what we had already taped. There was the interview with Prince Charles from Aberystwyth, the conversation with Ed Sullivan from earlier in June, Mick Jagger and the Rolling Stones singing 'You Can't Always Get What You Want' from our taping in London, and the feminist confrontation from the previous Thursday.

Since there had been very little happening on stage, when we had completed the first show we went on to tape a further guest, the black Congressman Adam Clayton Powell.

Powell, an enigmatic and highly controversial figure in American politics, was a larger-than-life guest. He had succeeded his father as Minister of the Abyssinian Baptist Church in Harlem, and in 1945 he had been elected to Congress, where he became a leading spokesman against racial discrimination. As Chairman of the House Committee on Education and Labor from 1960, he helped pilot through the House some of the major anti-poverty and education aid legislation of the Kennedy and Johnson Administrations. However, he had undermined much of the respect he had won for this work by his frequent absenteeism and his increasingly scandalous private life. In 1967 he had been expelled from the House of Representatives for misusing public funds for his own travel and living expenses, after touring Europe, ostensibly to look at labour conditions, with two female members of staff, one an ex-beauty queen, at Government expense.

His supporters in Harlem had remained loyal to him, despite the fact that he was spending an increasing amount of time away, often on the island of Bimini in the Bahamas. Harlem had indeed re-elected him by an enormous majority, and he was permitted to resume his seat in January 1969.

I asked Powell what his definition of law and order would be. 'Law and order today is considered by many people a black boy running down the street mugging somebody, raping somebody, killing somebody. I want to know when this nation – that has no more customs guards today, mark you now, than when Calvin Coolidge was President – I want to know when this nation is going to get the big fat cats that run the narcotics and dope trade of the United States. When are they going to nail one of them? That's law and order.

'Law and order is: who killed Medgar Evers, the President of the NAACP of Mississippi? Who killed – and it will never come out in your lifetime – who killed my beloved friend Jack Kennedy? The truth has not come out yet. Who killed Martin Luther King? Where did Ray get the money from? *Time* magazine asked that two weeks in a row. Who killed Bobby Kennedy? That's law and order.'

'And on some of those things,' I asked, 'are you saying that you know the truth? Or that the truth should be found?'

'I know some of the truth,' said Powell. 'That's why they might get me next. They don't know where the truth is. I have about ten people that know it and have it in safe deposit boxes.'

But what truth did he know?

'All right,' said Powell. 'You go to the library tomorrow morning and get the Warren Commission Report. You'll get two volumes. You come to my office, and I'll tell my secretaries to let you see it. I've got twenty-five volumes.'

'The full ones that were published, you mean?' I asked.

'Jackie Kennedy's testimony. One half of her testimony was cut out of the Warren Commission Report.'

'What are you saying was cut out?' I asked.

'Go along, baby, go along baby, go along, sweetheart. Daddy loves you.' Powell said somewhat bewilderingly. 'The Deputy Sheriff of Dallas, sixteen points he made in his testimony: cut out . . .'

But what was Powell really saying? Did he have an alternative view of what occurred?

'I do not have the facts,' said Powell, 'but as a man of my age, sixty-one this year, forty-one years in the pulpit, a quarter of a century in Congress, I do now publicly say that there is a conspiracy in this nation. And who's financing it I do not know. But I think I'm on the right track.'

What sort of a conspiracy?

'Conspiracy to eradicate any man, black or white, whether it's the white man who supported Gene McCarthy in Chicago, or whether it's the blacks in North Carolina College – there's a conspiracy in this nation to eradicate or keep down in some way – doesn't matter how – the voice of protest, which made America great. We became great from protest. The *Mayflower* was a ship of protest . . .'

'If there is this conspiracy, then the people ought to know about it,' I said.

'They can't.'

'But at the same time you must go a little further with evidence, because it is very attractive to take three or four things that don't hang together properly and allege conspiracy. Because we all of us in a curious way want to believe that great men's deaths have a meaning. It is horrible to think that great men's deaths happened by chance, by a mad action, by a madman, or someone else. It is more attractive to us to believe there is a conspiracy. It is more attractive to us to believe we know about a conspiracy that somebody doesn't. So while I say that if there are facts that are not known, they ought to be known, at the same time it is terribly dangerous to spread thoughts of a conspiracy, I think, because it's so attractive to everybody. Unless you have facts to back it up.'

'I have facts, I have facts,' said Powell.

But although he said that he had facts, all Powell would repeatedly come up with was conjecture, or questions. He talked about the mystery of Martin Luther King's alleged killer James Earl Ray having money. I agreed that was a mystery. 'But what evidence do you have that that was part of a payment from those organising a conspiracy? Where did it come from?'

'I know where it came from,' said Powell, 'and I will not tell you. But when we leave here, I'll tell you.'

'No, no, no,' I said. 'Don't let's have private chats, let's talk to the people. They're . . .'

'No, no . . .' said Powell.

'You said they've got a right to know . . . can you name anybody who is to do with this conspiracy?' I asked.

'On that eye,' said Powell, indicating the camera, 'right there – no.'

'Because you don't know, or you can't say?' I asked.

'I know, and I can say,' said Powell, 'but I have paid my dues, baby, and I'm not going to go through this . . .'

'What is this "paid my dues"?' I asked. 'If the people have a right to know, you have a duty to tell them. Share what you know. If this is at the fount of American life, if this is a threat . . .'

Powell interjected, 'I haven't got any duty in life now except to live.'

'That's not the leader you started off talking about,' I said.

'No, that's my duty in life now,' said Powell. 'To survive and to live.'

'Now, that's not Adam Clayton Powell, leader,' I said. 'That's Adam Clayton Powell, dilettante.'

'I paid my dues,' repeated Powell. 'I've been out here forty-one years . . .'

'But how can you . . .'

'How old are you?' asked Powell.

'Thirty,' I said.

'All right. Ten years before you were born I was out in the streets . . .'

'Paying your wretched dues, yes,' I said. 'But if this is a terrible conspiracy . . .'

'Not wretched dues,' said Powell. 'Don't call them wretched.'

'Well, they're getting more and more wretched every time we talk about them. But the thing is, that if this is a great conspiracy, if it's rotting America, if it's an injustice, if it's what you're fighting, then you can't say, "I don't care, I've just got to live." If what you say is true, and you share what you know, you could change the course of current history. And you can't then just say, "I don't care."'

'How?' asked Powell.

'If you named a group of people that are the centre of the conspiracy you've alleged, and something was done about that conspiracy, and it prevented future assassinations, how dare you not say the name, if there is a name?'

There was a pause, but Powell did not agree. 'Who? Who? Who is going to enforce anything that anyone says, including you or myself?'

'They will check the facts,' I said, 'and if they're true, they will act.'

'Oh, they got the facts, man,' said Powell. 'You know that.'

'In a situation like this, the people's voice would be heard,' I said.

'The people's voice has been stilled in the land,' said Powell. 'The voice of the turtle cannot be heard.'

'Oh, no,' I said. 'Please, if this is important and you know, speak. Either that, or it's unimportant, or you don't know. Which is it?'

Powell said, 'I'll shut my mouth.'

'If you do know, and you're shutting your mouth, that's the most irresponsible thing you've ever done.'

'I got a conscience to live with, that's true,' said Powell. There were some groans from the audience.

'But you just said now you didn't care about conscience. You just said, "I've just got to live."'

'Well, that's part of living, is conscience,' said Powell. 'You can't live without a conscience.'

We were nearing the end of our time.

DF: Well, I can only draw the conclusion that you just do not have these facts, or you do not care.

Powell: Well, I would say at this stage of the game that I really don't care. I don't care.

DF: That is a tragic admission.

Powell: Yes, it is.

DF: And with that tragic admission . . .

Powell: I agree with you.

DF: . . . we take a break.

Powell: I agree with you.

DF: That's very sad words to hear.

Powell: I know it, sad for me.

DF: I hope you'll rewrite them. We're taking a break.

Powell: Bless your heart. Keep the faith, baby.

Neil Shand came over to me after the taping. 'Watching that just now, the staff were really exhilarated,' he said. 'I think they understand now what we've been talking about when we said we wanted to introduce some new ingredients into the talk-show formula.'

There really was a talk-show formula in those days. The guests were almost invariably from show business, or authors with a new book, and they were generally allowed about eight or nine minutes before a commercial break gave them an opportunity to move down the sofa to make way for the next guest. There were rarely, if ever, any confrontations.

Now we had had a real confrontation. And it had lasted for thirty-nine minutes. During the interviews I had been doing round the country for the past few months, I had often mentioned that on occasion I planned to talk to somebody for more than eight or nine minutes – maybe even for twenty minutes. At such moments I could feel the Westinghouse contingent willing me to stop, or figuratively slashing their corporate wrists.

What had they taken on with this guy? But now we had shown them one way that a longer interview could work.

There was another important factor in the flow of the Adam Clayton Powell interview. Before we started taping, I had explained that I would always decide when we went to a commercial break – not the Control Room, or a pre-arranged formula of ninety minutes minus eighteen minutes of commercials equals seventy-two divided by nine segments equals eight minutes a segment. Timing the breaks myself, as I had done with 'The Frost Programme' in London, was even more essential here, with more breaks to cater for. I had to take a break when the rhythm of the conversation allowed it, rather than risk a random interruption to a question or answer that I might have been building up to for three or four minutes.

After the Adam Clayton Powell taping, we once again repaired to Sardi's. This time the mood was not of exhaustion, as after our war of attrition with the feminists, but of exhilaration, as Neil had said.

We wanted to get the interview on the air as quickly as possible, so next day, when we assembled the second show, we made it the main ingredient, and added Tommy Steele and Cleo Laine from the London taping. On our first Monday night, 7 July, we switched on Channel 5 at 8.30 just to make sure that the show was really on, and then Clay Felker and Gail Sheehy joined us at the Oak Room for supper.

When the reactions started coming in on Tuesday morning, we realised that we had made one big mistake. We had become beguiled by the assorted highlights we had assembled, and the result was a show that seemed 'spliced together', as Kay Gardella of the New York *Daily News* put it. Jack Gould in the *New York Times* also had his reservations. He said that I was 'a visitor in search of a format', but added – fortunately for us – that he never judged a talk show on its debut, but would be returning to take another look in a few weeks' time.

Out at KTTV, the Metromedia station in Los Angeles, somebody had rather brilliantly anticipated this reaction, and made the Adam Clayton Powell programme the first one that they transmitted. The result was a resounding affirmation from Cecil

Smith in the *Los Angeles Times*, who began his review, 'Amid the torrents of trivia that flow from television's nightly talk shows, the new David Frost dialogues are like rare beefsteak in a marshmallow sundae world.'

The difference in the West Coast and East Coast reviews taught us an immediate lesson. In the search for highlights, we had been missing out on the continuity of a ninety-minute show. We resolved to change that immediately, although we knew that we had to sit back and live with what we had already programmed for the rest of the opening week.

The next 'David Frost Show' confrontation took place backstage, rather than onstage. The former Secretary of State Dean Acheson, and the senior Senator from Illinois, Chuck Percy, arrived to debate the Anti-Ballistic Missile System (ABM) issue. Since Acheson was a revered elder statesman who, as far as we could ascertain, had never previously appeared before an audience on a commercial television programme, I made an exception to my usual rule and came down to the Green Room to welcome him when he arrived. There was an immediate problem.

'I've prepared an opening statement which will last about forty minutes,' Acheson told me. I ventured that since the programme of ninety minutes had eight commercial breaks in it, his forty-minute opening might give us something of a problem. 'You mean people are going to come and stand in front of me and sell things?' he demanded.

'Well, not exactly that . . .' I went on to point out that obviously Senator Percy would want an opening statement as well, and he could scarcely get equal time if Mr Acheson was doing forty minutes. 'And then I shall want to ask you both questions, before we bring in the audience.'

'You mean that *you* are going to ask *us* questions?' said Acheson. 'But what do you know? That means we'll get off the subject entirely.'

We were getting nowhere fast. I decided that the moment had come to try and put my foot down, and hang the consequences. 'Mr Secretary, in all my years of television, that is probably the most insulting remark that has ever been made to me,' I said.

'But if there is anyone who has earned the right to insult whomever they please, it is yourself.'

There was a tense pause, and then Acheson said, 'I'm sorry. Tell me what you would like me to do.'

The ABM debate aired on the Tuesday of our second week. However, perhaps the most memorable moment of that week came in a conversation with the radio and television veteran Arthur Godfrey. As he was talking to me about the subject of overpopulation, he suddenly leaned forward and asked, 'Can I share a secret with you?' When I indicated that he could, he revealed for the first time that he had had a vasectomy. In the opinion of all the seasoned talk-show types who saw him say it, or reviewed the tape later, he had quite genuinely forgotten for a moment that he was on television. And that, of course, is an interviewer's dream come true.

On the Friday night of our second week on the air, Neil Shand and I took the overnight flight to London to work on ITV's 'Man on the Moon' project.

'Hello and good evening to the night of the great adventure,' I said as I welcomed viewers that Sunday night at 6 p.m. 'The night of drama. The end of an incredible voyage and the beginning of what may be a whole new world for all of us. Because tonight man lands on the moon and steps into the age of Flash Gordon and Dan Dare . . .'

We were planning a continuous programme running through until 1 a.m. Over at ITN there was Alastair Burnet, with Peter Fairley and Paul Haney. In the LWT studios, I had a revolving panel of guests. There were contributions from Sir Bernard Lovell, Ray Bradbury, Roger Bannister, A.J.P. Taylor, John Robinson, the Bishop of Woolwich, and Quintin Hogg. And forming another part of the constellation of stars, there was Sammy Davis, Jr., Cliff Richard, Lulu, Mary Hopkin, Ken Dodd, Cilla Black, Englebert Humperdinck and Peter Cook to provide the entertainment. The plan was six or seven hours without *longueurs*. Our studio at LWT would be on the air for the majority of the time, but the hard news call would always have primacy.

From the word go, the pace was right and the contributors on form. And throughout the evening the Head of ITN Nigel

Ryan's imaginative concept of uninterrupted coverage paid off. If ITV viewers were tempted to try the BBC, they were disconcerted by the sight of other programmes like 'The Black and White Minstrel Show' and 'Monitor'. Meanwhile our entertainers and talkers filled the gaps, but always within the moon context.

Even our telephone callers – an idea I had imported from New York – played their part. Mr Roberts of Eastbourne wanted to know if moon earth could help him grow bigger pumpkins. An unknown female voice greeted me breathily but somewhat inaudibly down the telephone line. 'But darling, I told you not to call me at the office,' I whispered back. As the night wore on, even Alastair Burnet could not resist calling up, disguising his voice as an ardent Scottish viewer.

We were due to go off the air at 1 a.m. while a Rita Hayworth film, *Down to Earth*, filled the screen until the moon walk took place. But, with hopes of an earlier time for that historic moment, the film was cancelled, and our seven-hour stint went on into the night until we were able to bring viewers the moon walk all within the same – by now – nine-hour programme.

A few days later the ratings underlined how right Nigel Ryan's hunch had been. On a worldwide news event, of the type on which the BBC usually creamed ITV, the average number of households viewing between 10 p.m. and midnight was BBC 1,900,000, ITV 5,450,000.

When I flew back to New York on the Monday, I was not alone. I was accompanied by my mother, who was then sixty-six. She adjusted to the experience of flying for the first time with the same nerveless aplomb with which she encountered any new challenge. That third week of 'The David Frost Show' began with Dr Benjamin Spock admitting that the swing towards permissiveness encouraged by his teachings might have gone too far.

No Frost series seemed to be complete without a visit from Billy Graham, and on the Tuesday – much to my mother's delight – we rectified that early omission. I asked him what he regarded as the most touching or moving demonstration of faith he had ever witnessed – which incident he would pick out and say, 'Now that is faith.'

'Well, I remember, for example, the opening night of our meetings in London in 1954, which you certainly remember,' said Billy. 'And the press was all against us, every newspaper. The Church leaders that had brought us there, many of them had deserted us. It had been brought up in Parliament as to whether I should even be allowed to land in Britain or not. And everything seemed against us.

'I had invited Senator Stuart Symington and another United States Senator to be my special guests there. And that afternoon Senator Symington called me on the phone and said the American Ambassador felt that because of all this bad publicity, that we should not come, and so we have decided not to come, we're going to have dinner this evening with Sir Anthony Eden – who was then the Foreign Secretary.

'And then I was called about a half an hour before the service in my little hotel, and they said, "The place is empty; there are four hundred newspaper people here taking pictures of the empty seats." And we'd rented this place for three months. And so my wife and I got on our knees and said, "Now, Lord, we're prepared for anything you want. It can be a total flop, or it can be a success. We leave it in your hands." I had great peace about it. It was an exercise in faith to even go out there.

'We went out there, we didn't see a person. We got out of the car and one of my associates came out of the door behind the arena and said, "Billy, the place is packed, and there's five thousand people on the other side trying to beat the doors down." And I said, "Where did they come from?" They said, "We don't know. God must have sent them." And we were there for three months, and not only did we not have empty seats, but we had two and three services a night on some nights to take care of the people. And ended up at Wembley Stadium with the press all for us, the Archbishop of Canterbury sitting by my side.'

Talking about his sermons, Billy said, 'First of all, I want the content to be accurate. I want it to be biblical, and I want it to be simple. I study to be simple.'

But what about those people who still said he made it all too simple?

'Well, now,' said Graham, 'for example, when Dr Karl Barth, the great Swiss theologian, the greatest theologian of his generation, was visiting America a couple of years ago, he was at one of our great seminaries, and a student asked him the question, "Dr Barth, what is the greatest single thought that ever crossed your mind?" And he bowed his head, and puffed on his pipe, and he slowly lifted his shaggy head, and they thought some tremendous statement was coming forth, and they were all on the edge of their seats, and he said,

> *"Jesus loves me, this I know,*
> *For the Bible tells me so."'*

The lines were familiar to me from Sunday school days some twenty years earlier. Karl Barth had chosen the words of a children's hymn to illustrate that there was no dichotomy between simplicity and profundity.

Religion had played a major role in many of my programmes during the Sixties. Sometimes the conversations with Billy Graham, the Archbishop of Canterbury, Cardinal Heenan and others had almost become interactive one-on-one sermons, shared with at least two congregations, one in the studio and another at home. The response of the audience, whether judged by their letters or the ratings, reinforced my belief that while many dogmatic programmes on religion were a turn-off to the public, the basic questions religion sought to answer about the meaning of life were still of abiding interest to most people. Indeed, I was one of those people.

In strict statistical terms, during the Sixties my church attendance record had slumped dramatically from its all-time high in the early Fifties. But I never entirely lost the faith that had crystallised for me at Harringay, though ever since Cambridge there had been parts of Methodist teaching – like its blanket teetotalism – that I could no longer begin to claim to observe.

More important, intellectually there were problems that perplexed me about the Christian faith – by which I meant the traditional Christian faith. Sincere as John Robinson undoubtedly was, I could not accept his definition of Christianity. If you were involved in a caring relationship, you were a Christian in his eyes. You could choose as much or as little as you wanted, from an *à la carte* menu. There had to be more of a *prix fixe* than that. Christianity had to be more demanding than that: otherwise it came perilously close to one of the clubs that Groucho Marx did not want to join because they were prepared to have him as a member.

Some of my concerns were, I know, shared by many, in particular the perennial question: how do you reconcile the concept of a loving God actively involved in day-to-day life with the pain and suffering distributed throughout the world in such an unfair and unequal fashion? Early in 1993 I had the opportunity to revisit this topic with Billy Graham himself. He had been battling Parkinson's Disease for three years or so. I asked him: 'Is God responsible for that?'

'I don't know,' said Graham. 'He allows it. And He allows it for a purpose that I may not know. I think everything that comes into our lives, if we are true believers, God has a purpose and a plan. And many of them are things that cause suffering or inconvenience or whatever. But it helps to mature me, because God is moulding and making me in the image of His son, Jesus Christ. Jesus Christ suffered more than any man that ever lived, because when He was on that cross, He was bearing the sins that you and I have committed. He was guilty of adultery. He was guilty of murder. He was guilty of everything you can think of. And He was guilty of our sins. He suffered in a way that we could never understand.'

'But, for instance,' I said, 'I thank God for having three healthy sons. But maybe that's not logical really, because if I am thanking God for three healthy sons, should the parents of a Down's Syndrome baby be blaming God?'

'No. I don't think they should ever blame God,' said Graham. 'I think God has allowed these things to happen in families throughout the years. A lady told me yesterday about all the troubles and difficulties in their family. She was from Colombia and she said, "I thank God for every bit of suffering I've had to go through, because it has made me a woman of God and a strong woman. I'm a better wife and a better mother as a result of the suffering I've had to go through."'

'But you can't really say that to the parents of a deformed child, can you?' I asked. 'How should they look at it?'

'You've asked me a question that would be very difficult for me,' said Graham, 'because I think there are some of these things that we'll never know until we get to Heaven. And I don't try to explain them, because I don't know the explanation, I don't know why. I only know the general principle is that God is a god of love and mercy. And God is working in your life to make you conform to the image of His son, and suffering is a part of life. We're told that we are going to suffer. Job said, "Man suffers as the sparks fly upward." And I think we are suffering constantly, and we are going to suffer all of our lives. I don't have all the answers. I just know that I trust God, who is a god of mercy.'

I still find Billy Graham's formulation difficult to take on board, but the fact that Billy Graham, once so roundly criticised as the apostle of an impossible certitude, could admit that there were questions to which he did not have an answer I found oddly reassuring: maybe the rest of us didn't need to feel so threatened by our doubts either.

I've asked many of my guests over the years the question: 'Do you believe there's a God, or do you know there's a God?' Certainly, at the end of the Sixties, I could give a positive answer only to the first half of that question, not to the second. However, I knew that many of my non-religious beliefs had been influenced by my Methodist childhood. My belief in the intelligence and integrity of members of the public, and their ability to make up their own minds when their democracy supplied them with the necessary raw materials, sprang directly from the attitude of the religious figure I knew best, my father. His appreciation of the value of each individual life and its propensity for good, and his total lack of condescension or pretension, made a subliminal impression and set an indelible example that was every bit as valuable in the studio as it would have been in a pulpit.

* * *

I have already observed that, at this time, there was very little confrontation, very little cut-and-thrust in most American talk shows. We took another step towards rectifying that deficiency on the Wednesday of the third week when we invited Miss Jacqueline Susann, author of *The Valley of the Dolls* and the then number one bestseller *The Love Machine*, to meet face-to-face with three of her critics.

Miss Susann said she wanted to be regarded as a 'storyteller'. After a few minutes, I turned to her three critics. Nora Ephron and Rex Reed both let her off quite lightly. 'I think women really kind of don't want to read very clinical descriptions of sex,' said Nora. 'What they want to read about are clothes being ripped madly off and thrown on the floor and people jumping out of their pants. I mean, that's what they want. Women, I am talking about. I think men prefer much more technical descriptions of the sex act. But women are very happy just kind of curling up and reading about – and of course, in Miss Susann's book, every six pages someone wants someone else, and they're staring across rooms and wanting each other and it's delicious if you're a woman, you know.'

Rex Reed said, 'My reaction to the book was not so much a literary reaction, because I think it's difficult to think of Miss Susann as the new Flaubert or the new Proust. I mean, I don't think of her as a writer so much as I think of her as a show-business tycoon.'

When it came to John Simon's turn to speak, the atmosphere changed. He asked Miss Susann, 'Are you writing a work of art, or are you just writing a piece of trash on which you can get rich quick, get famous quick, get known quick and make money?' His words were spoken with a staccato delivery, and overlaid with the German accent that he was born with. His question brought applause from the audience.

'What did you say your name was?' asked Miss Susann. 'Goebbels? Goering? Or Simon?'

'No, John Simon – names are immaterial.'

'No, you sound like a Storm Trooper,' said Miss Susann.

'But I'm asking you a question, Miss Susann. I'm asking you which of the two kinds of things you write.'

'I don't think that I have to answer you for one reason – I've heard of Neil Simon, Simple Simon . . .'

'In other words, you're incapable of answering me. Is that it?'

'I don't have to answer a statement,' said Miss Susann.

'Well, you are here to answer questions by critics. A critic has been asking you a question and you owe him an answer . . .'

'Well, I think the audience should answer you,' said Miss Susann.

'No, you are writing it – you have to answer it. I'm sorry. You cannot shunt the burden of answering the question.'

'All right, little man,' said Miss Susann. 'I was telling a story.'

'You were telling a story? Well, all right . . .'

'Why are you so uptight?' asked Miss Susann.

'I'm not uptight,' said Simon.

'You should go to your shrink and tell him that you've come to a show. Relax. It's fun.'

'I'll smile, I'll relax,' said Simon. 'I'll smile charmingly through my false teeth like you and I'll be fine . . .'

'Let me see you smile,' said Miss Susann.

'You're not answering questions,' said Simon, 'you're making stupid fun of me.'

'No, you just made fun of me. You said . . .'

'I'm not making fun,' said Simon, 'I'm asking you a question. I'm imploring you to give me an answer to one simple question.'

'Oh, lovely boy, I'm telling you a story – what do you want me to do? Shall I come and sit on your lap and tell you about three little pigs?'

'No, I'm asking you what kind of story you're telling. Let me explain . . .'

'A too-sophisticated story for you to understand, because it's dirty.'

'See, the trouble is, it's not dirty, Miss Susann. If it were honest to goodness pornography, it would be a thousand times better than what you've written. At least it would serve the simple purpose of turning people on . . .'

'Mr . . . what's your name? What's his – Simple Simon. Mr

Simon, what are you after? I have to try things out on people. I said to you . . .'

'I hope you realise that by calling me insulting names, you are making yourself ridiculous. I'm not calling you dumb Jackie Susann or swinish Jackie Susann – I'm calling you Miss Susann, and I'm asking you, do you think you're writing art, or do you think you are writing trash?'

'I'm writing a story by Jacqueline Susann.'

'But what category does that fall into? Is it the category of art or non-art?'

'I don't think a story has to fall into a category of either. I think a story should be a story.'

'You mean, there's something other than life or death, something in between the two? There's something that's neither of those two states? Would you define that, please?'

'I think that there are people who ask questions, and I think there are people that come on shows to try and gain a reputation at another person's expense by insulting them.'

'I assure you I don't need you for my reputation,' said Simon. 'I mean, the kind of reputation which would consist of putting you down would be so easily gotten and of such unlasting value, it would be of no interest to me whatsoever.'

At this point, Rex Reed interjected. 'If you are going to ask critics in New York to appear on the programme, you should have asked people who've read the book. Mr Simon admitted before we came on the show, he's only read thirty pages . . .'

'You've only read thirty pages,' said Miss Susann, 'and you're putting me through this inquisition.'

'I've read forty pages, actually . . . after which I couldn't stomach any more. I mean, how many swallows of a rotten stew do I have to swallow before I puke and know that this is inedible? Do I have to spoon out every last spoonful of that terrible brew in order to know that it is corrupt and putrid?'

'But I want to ask you one thing, Mr Simon. Have you been around television?'

'Yes, I have worked a lot . . .'

'Have you worked on television networks?'

'Well, I've been on shows, I mean, I haven't . . .'

'I mean, behind the scenes – have you ever worked on the network as a producer, director . . .'

'No, no . . .'

'Well, then, how would you – my husband has for twenty-five years. How would you know that what I am writing is wrong?'

'Since you think it is important whether one knew television people or not – I say it's unimportant – Dante never went to Hell, yet he wrote the best book about Hell ever written.'

I joined in for a moment. 'Why is it, do you think, that the book makes you so angry? Is it the book, or is it actually the success of the book?'

'No,' said Simon. 'If it's either of those, it's the book. It's because it's untrue.'

'But there are a million untrue books,' I said. 'This one makes you angry.'

'No. I think it is unimportant if an untrue book reaches two people, but I think if an untrue book reaches thousands of people who are not in the position to verify the untruthfulness of these statements, I think it is a kind of perversion, a kind of victimisation, a kind of stultification of the great American public. And I am against that in any form whatsoever.'

'Really, Mr Simon,' said Miss Susann, 'but I have nothing personal against you. I think you are a very attractive man. I really do. And you are – you've also . . .'

'If you are discussing looks, I mean, presumably we were discussing books . . .' said Simon.

'No, I think you are very attractive. You threw a little whammy at me. You said, "I'm not talking through my false teeth like you are." I'm not. They're capped, but they're not false. And that was kind of below the belt and nasty. But I think you're nice. At least we know you're not wearing a wig – because it couldn't be that colour and not be yours – but other than that, I think you've got kind of a nice smile and I think you could be very nice. And I think you've got a very attractive lady with you. And I'm sure you are very nice to her . . .'

'Will you cut off the soft soap. I mean, this is simply ridiculous – I mean, are we discussing me or . . .'

'I have said that I don't want . . .'

'Here – allow me – one more thing . . .'

'I will not allow you. You've read forty pages of my book . . .'

'Yes, but I want to talk about those forty pages . . .'

'It's not the whole book. It's as though I saw one of your ears and said what do you look like?'

'The point is, literature is not only a plot, obviously. The plot is almost the least important thing in a work of literature. What is important is character. What is important is style. What is important is command of language. What is important is control of atmosphere and situation and mood. And if you can't do that in forty pages, Miss Susann, you can't do it in forty million pages either.'

It will come as little surprise when I add that the participants in that particular discussion did *not* go next door to Sardi's and have a drink together afterwards. But the contretemps served to emphasise a couple of key points. First, the importance of good casting in a discussion – the most famous current author in America and the most cutting critic; and secondly, how important our commitment to flexibility was. I let the clash run for five segments, rather than the three we had planned. And I was able to choose when to go to a break without having to intervene at the wrong moment.

When you are orchestrating a discussion like the one between Jacqueline Susann and John Simon, it is important to know when to take a back seat. You are the catalyst, not the principal: you step in only when you feel that a line of argument is about to exhaust itself, and that it's time to move on. Ideally, that is a predictive role – you sense the declining fascination of the current topic a few seconds before the viewer does. But if it is going well, you just shut up.

Silence can be equally golden in a one-on-one interview. Again, the interviewer's role is predictive. You can be confronted with one of two kinds of silence. There is the fruitful silence, where you sense that if you allow the pause to continue, the guest could have something more to say, maybe something of a deeper nature. The other silence is the embarrassing silence, where the guest has quite simply clean forgotten what on earth he or she was about to say. That pause has to be filled as quickly as possible, because otherwise each second that passes will feel like an eternity. How do you know which silence is which? It's just instinct – you don't really know for sure, but you *feel* the nuance in the conversation that you should be responding to, and you go for it. If you are wrong more times than you are right, you are probably in the wrong business!

In the case of the Susann–Simon disputation, what had been remarkable was the level of raw hostility and distilled intellectual vitriol that it produced. I wondered what the reactions of the viewers would be. Would they feel that John Simon had gone too far? The answer was surprisingly clear-cut. Of the couple of hundred letters I read myself, only four were pro-Miss Susann.

During the fourth week of the show I met Madalyn Murray O'Hair. Known as America's most famous atheist, she must have made few converts that evening. Throughout the interview she ascribed only one reason to people's religious belief – a mixture of naivete and stupidity. This continual dismissal of the sincerely held beliefs of millions, who in her opinion were simply not as intelligent as she was, really began to get to me. 'Mrs O'Hair,' I said, 'for someone who does not believe in religion, you are incredibly holier than thou.'

The fifth week of the show began with something approaching euphoria. Jack Gould of the *New York Times* had been as good as his word, and had returned to the subject of 'The David Frost Show' after watching it for three or four weeks. His review began: 'In the few weeks that he has been on the air – his premiere clearly had been thrown together to meet a deadline and was obviously atypical –' (little did he know how carefully and deliberately we had laboured in order to make that mistake!) 'he has introduced the element of intuitive reportorial curiosity and has proved to be an agreeable and sophisticated alternative to Johnny Carson, Merv Griffin and Joey Bishop. Mr Frost is too experienced a hand in show business not to realise that he must offer his quota of pure entertainers, and he does. But this necessary ingredient of TV programming really becomes secondary to the attractive and alert way in which he can draw out celebrities, including performers, so that in the course of ninety minutes the quotient of interesting substance is remarkably high.'

My breakfast had never tasted better than it did that morning. Gould also had a comment to make on the way we formatted the show: 'Refreshingly, Mr Frost and Westinghouse do not buy the tedious nonsense that banal headliners must come on first and people with something to say should be squeezed into the closing minutes of a programme.' And there was more to follow. By the time I got into the office, Cate had a list of people who had called from Westinghouse head office, beginning with Chet. Mr Gould had set the seal on our first month's efforts.

Our guests during August ranged from James Mason, Dick Gregory and Burt Bacharach to William Buckley and Senator Edmund Muskie. Polly Bergen attempted to turn almost every question into a plug for her new perfume, 'Oil of the Turtle'. She built up to the point where she leaned provocatively towards me and said in an intimate whisper, 'Tell me, David, what does the smell remind you of?' That was easy. 'Garlic,' I said. (Mind you, to be fair to Oil of the Turtle, I can suss out the smell of garlic at twenty feet. But Miss Bergen was not to know that.)

On a programme about marriage, I met the Reverend Robert Truesdell, a man of the lightweight cloth from the Chapel of the Bells in Las Vegas, where he conducted an average of eighty marriages every Friday and Saturday night.

'We in the marriage industry –' he said.

'Industry?' I said.

'Industry. It brings seventy million dollars a year into the state of Nevada, and Las Vegas is truly now the marriage capital of the world.'

I asked him the reason for Nevada's popularity. 'No blood test,' he said romantically. 'In our chapel we have the beautiful red velvet backdrop and those wide chairs like you have in England. The couple can have real live organ music or they can have taped music of anything they like.

'For $28 upwards we can provide the chapel, the witnesses, a minister of their choosing – we have denominations on hand

– as well as veils and blue garters. We do not, however, supply guests. The couple have to do that themselves.'

We experimented with new formulae whenever we could think of them. When attorney F. Lee Bailey joined us we arranged for an argument to take place on stage. A few minutes later, Mr Bailey cross-examined members of the audience on what they thought they had seen. The divergences were even wider than we had predicted. We also had Mr Bailey demonstrate with the audience how he would go about selecting members of a jury.

On the next show one of the guests was the cartoonist Al Capp, whose views over the years had taken him to the right of Genghis Khan. 'I must be the rudest paid speaker on college platforms – and the highest-paid,' he said. When Capp took off on the manners, dress and body odours of students, a student in the audience, quite reasonably, began to object. Capp's response was unnecessarily savage, and misquoted the student. When Capp disputed this, I remembered the 'instant replay' facility of sports programmes, and called up the relevant moment. It had its effect. As James Gourgouras wrote, 'For the first time in our recollection, a non-sports programme utilised its instant replay facilities to prove a point under discussion. It proved at once that Capp was a fast talker, but not quite fast enough.'

Ted Sorensen, best known for his work as John F. Kennedy's speechwriter, joined us on 21 August, just over a month after Teddy Kennedy's unexplained accident at Chappaquiddick, in which his female passenger was killed. What he had to say on the subject was to surprise us all. I led into the subject gradually, and he began gently enough.

'It is possible, of course, that Edward Kennedy may one day be President of the United States. He is so young, and he will be eligible for the Presidency in a practical sort of way for so many years that anything is still possible. But he is certainly not going to be elected President in 1972.

'I don't know what will happen seven years from now, what people will think of Ted, how he, himself, will have reacted to this tragedy. When you consider all that's happened in American politics in the last year and a half, that nobody could have predicted, and all that's happened to the Kennedy family in the last six years, I don't think I want to predict what's going to happen seven years from now.'

Nevertheless, I suggested that if Edward Kennedy were overwhelmingly successful in the 1970 Senate elections, and the polls in 1971 showed him the strongest candidate, then surely he could still be the Democratic candidate in 1972.

Sorensen's reply was unequivocal: 'No. I don't think so. And to be very frank with you, I don't think he should be. I'm his friend, and when he called for me to help give legal counsel I responded to the call. But I think, as he said, his action at that time of pressure was indefensible. And I don't think that being so recent in the minds of the public and that being so clear an indication of his action under pressure at this stage in his life, that he should try for the presidency in 1972.'

Ted Sorensen's advice to his friend had been uncompromising – he had left no loopholes to allow himself to change his mind, or indeed to allow Ted Kennedy to change his. It was doubtless sound advice, but not the sort of advice that the audience had expected to hear from him publicly. That was what gave his words a particular resonance – even beyond their actual content.

By the end of August we had the big plus of an editorial accolade from *TV Guide*, the magazine with the largest circulation in the world. The article's last words were, 'It's a joy to watch.' Some of the phrases that people used about the show were memorable, even if I did not necessarily altogether understand them. Dwight Newton in the *San Francisco Examiner* wrote: 'He seldom fumbles a thought. He will chatter like a scrub jay gone high on gooseberry juice or discipline himself to total concentration on the most boring subject.' When you next see me talking like that, I'd like to be the first to know.

On 9 September I had an urgent call from Clive Irving in London. Chaos had broken out at London Weekend. The Board had decided that Michael Peacock had to go. Aidan Crawley had called him in, told him of the decision, and asked for his resignation. Michael had refused. Instead of saying, 'Well, you're out anyway,' Aidan had gone back to the Board for further instructions. That had given time for Michael to rally support among the senior programme people, several of whom threatened to resign in sympathy. A committee of the Board had then been set up to report back to a special Board Meeting that would decide Michael's fate.

Although I had known of the growing tensions about Michael's Managing Directorship, the Board's decision to act took me by surprise. I had played no part in that decision, although I immediately saw the need for it, and felt that, once taken, it had to be adhered to.

The company was clearly at a crossroads, and I determined to fly back to London as soon as I could. A commitment to host United Nations Staff Day for the Secretary General of the UN, U Thant, and a memorial service for Bishop James Pike meant that I could not leave until Saturday night, and had to be back to tape the next show on Monday evening. However, I would cram as much into a day and a half as I could.

I arrived on the Sunday morning and met with Tom Margerison, Guy Paine and Clive Irving from 10 until 12.15. At 12.45 I met with Aidan Crawley and at 2 o'clock with David Montagu. At 3.45 I spent an hour with Cyril Bennett and then went on to talk to Jock Campbell. The evening was taken up with Jimmy Hill, Guy Paine, Cyril, Tom and Clive, and we finally stopped talking at 3 a.m. On the Monday morning I met with David Montagu at 8, Aidan Crawley at 9.30, Arnold Weinstock at 10.30, Vic Gardiner at 12.45 and Frank Muir at 1.30, before catching the 3 p.m. flight back to New York.

I found a situation that was, to put it mildly, awful. It had not been a happy year for LWT. Michael's relationship with the Board had become a dialogue of the deaf. He regarded almost anything that members of the Board attempted to do – from asking questions to making suggestions – as unjustified interference. The Board in their turn looked in vain for any sign that Michael and his management team had the skill and experience to respond to changing circumstances. As someone who had recruited many of the members of the Board, I found this gulf particularly sad and, worse still, totally avoidable. They had come into London Weekend Television willing to help in any way they could. It was the total rejection of that desire to assist, coupled with a lack of diplomacy, that was at the root of their disillusionment.

That, of course, was not all. The doubtful portents which I mentioned earlier had become obstacles to success. The ITV old guard had not forgotten some of LWT's earlier pronouncements about their own previous output, and felt they still had scores to settle. Here again Michael's abrasiveness had not helped. The BBC were still concentrating their firepower on the weekends, which gave the rest of ITV an added reason to place their own favourite programmes with Thames, the weekday contractor in London, when the BBC opposition would be weaker.

Michael had also counted on support from Lord Hill in his battles with the rest of the network. He had understood that Hill intended to introduce a new system of networking, whereby programmes would be exchanged on a basis that reflected the actual costs of production. That would, of course, have assisted LWT with some of its more expensive programmes. However, Lord Hill had been plucked out of the ITA by Harold Wilson and sent off to the BBC before any of those reforms could be put into practice.

LWT's ratings over the first year showed a measurable drop from the previous twelve months' figures – from a fifty-five per cent share to forty-seven per cent. It also emerged that the ITA had miscalculated the revenue split between Thames and LWT. What was intended to be a 50–50 division of revenue was in fact 60–40 in favour of Thames, and would not have been 50–50 even if LWT's ratings had been better. During the first year Thames had a revenue of £16 million and LWT £11 million, but for the purpose of all inter-company transactions around the network, the basis of calculation was still 50–50.

The ratings mentioned above were now provided by a new system, which reported lower ratings for all ITV stations, so London Weekend's ratings problems may well have been exaggerated. Furthermore, in February 1969 the companies began to announce their revenue figures on a monthly, rather than a quarterly, basis. This increased the agencies' tactical room for manoeuvre against the weaker stations in general, and therefore

LWT in particular. Then, in April, the Chancellor of the Exchequer Roy Jenkins announced an increase in the advertising levy on ITV profits. And London Weekend also began to suffer from a fact of life that had dogged the latter days of Associated-Rediffusion – a London ITV station is Fleet Street's local station. No national newspaper was measuring Harlech's or Yorkshire's performance against its franchise document with the zeal that was being applied to monitoring London Weekend.

By February 1969, Humphrey Burton had been expressing his and others' dissatisfaction with the new Cyril Bennett schedule. 'Something has gone crucially wrong with our company,' he wrote in one memo. 'The central failure is to do with the mix on the screens. It is insufficiently different from what happened before.' To Cyril, this was just more pressure from the BBC faction. 'First let us make the programmes sufficiently better than they were before,' he wrote back. 'Then we might, just might, be able to make them different.'

In April, Michael Peacock and Cyril Bennett had scored a spectacular own goal. Having decided that the Public Affairs Unit was not performing to their satisfaction, they closed it down, without any attempt to underline the fact that public affairs programmes would still be produced by LWT. Needless to say, the press saw this as LWT reneging on one of its major pledges. And it would have been so easy to change the direction of the Public Affairs Unit, or to fine-tune its output, and reduce its staff, without ever going through the public obloquy that these actions made inevitable.

At a press conference on 3 July, Cyril Bennett made a statement which was, in a sense, the obverse of Lord Thomson's famous quote about an ITV franchise being 'a licence to print money'. 'The first duty of a commercial station,' Cyril announced, 'is to survive.' As an exercise in stating the obvious, this could scarcely be faulted. But its tone sounded markedly different from the franchise document, a copy of which had been leaked the month before.

A *Sunday Times* 'Insight' exposé in August did nothing to lift the state of siege, and by the beginning of September the Board had reached the conclusion that Michael Peacock was not the man to rectify the situation. Monday 8 September had been the appointed day for the Peacock resignation, but on Tuesday the ninth the Board had agreed to set up a sub-committee 'to consider the future management of the company', and to report on 18 September. That the Board had agreed to any delay at all seemed like an interim victory for Michael and 'the rebels', as they had come to be called, but now the next move rested with the sub-committee, which consisted of Lord Campbell, David Montagu and Aidan Crawley.

The Board had known how unpopular Michael was with the other ITV companies, and with the advertisers, whom he had never really convinced that he did not have an underlying aversion to the whole concept of selling. The sudden outpouring of support from the programme-makers had therefore taken them by surprise. Some of them were wavering, unsure of what was in the best interests of the company. I spent much of my day and a half in London listening, and catching up on details that had not reached me in New York.

However, nothing that I heard altered my initial reaction when I had heard the news the previous Tuesday. Indeed, it tended to strengthen it. When asked my opinion, it was simple and brief. First, none of the events of the past four or five days altered the diagnosis which the Board had gradually made over the past three months. And second, they could scarcely change what they had told everybody were their deeply-held convictions – developed over many months – in a matter of a few days, and hope to retain even a shred of credibility. If a referee ordered a footballer off the field, and then changed his mind when the player didn't want to go, he could scarcely hope to have much say over the conduct of the rest of the game.

What, I was asked, if the programme-makers who had threatened to leave carried out their threat? Emotionally, that was a tough one to answer. We had been through so much together in winning the franchise and getting the station on the air, that I hoped desperately that they would stay with LWT. However, tactically, there was no way that the Board could give in, and I hoped that in the event some at least would remain.

And what about the choice of Tom Margerison as Michael

Peacock's successor? That was fairly straightforward. It was not so much a question of whether Tom was the best candidate – in the circumstances, he was the only candidate. There was clearly no time for leisurely headhunting through the upper echelons of ITV and the BBC. The new Managing Director had to take over the moment that the 18 September Board Meeting made its decision.

As I flew back to New York that Monday afternoon, there was plenty of time to reflect on the situation at LWT. I thought that the sub-committee of the Board would probably stick to its guns, though it was too early to say for sure. They certainly did their job thoroughly, and talked to everyone who wanted to see them. For David Montagu, the clincher came in a meeting with Michael Peacock on the Wednesday evening, when he said he felt that Michael was threatening him personally.

On that Tuesday and Wednesday, my New York telephone bill reached epic proportions as I tried to keep in touch with the situation. On Thursday morning the Board met and announced its decision:

> The Board of London Weekend Television Ltd after the fullest consideration has decided to terminate the contract with Mr Michael Peacock as Managing Director. He has resigned from the Board. Dr Tom Margerison becomes Chief Executive of the company and Mr Guy Paine, Assistant Chief Executive . . . Lord Campbell has agreed to serve as Deputy Chairman of the company. There has never been any dispute between the Board and management about the programme objectives of London Weekend Television Ltd. The Board is confident that the new management will fulfil these objectives and that the company will discharge its responsibility to the public, the staff and its shareholders.

As it turned out, not all the members of the programming team who had threatened to resign did in fact do so. However, six did, and they included Frank Muir, Humphrey Burton and Doreen Stephens. The Board's statement went on to talk about them:

> 'We regret the decision of the six members of the programme staff who have asked to be released from their contracts and respect the sincerity of their convictions. They have undertaken to complete the projects on which they are working to ensure a smooth handover.

The next day, I was due to be starting my new series of 'Frost on Friday' and 'Frost on Saturday' for LWT, so I was back in London and already due to meet the press to discuss the forthcoming series. Needless to say, my programmes were scarcely at the top of the agenda that the press wished to discuss, so I made a brief statement: 'When talented people leave any company, of course it is news, but London Weekend is packed with talent and one thousand are staying . . . And of course it is rubbish to suggest Tom is going to water down the programme philosophy of London Weekend. In fact he will protect and reinforce it.'

The first sentence was a somewhat doomed attempt to be upbeat, but I meant every word of the last one. I knew that was indeed Tom's deeply felt intention, but I worried about whether the team was still strong enough to pull it off. How I longed for the leadership of John Freeman in an executive role at that moment. I said as much to John himself in Washington a few days later. His response was a bombshell.

He said that he had told Aidan and Michael that he might be prepared to join LWT after his stint in New Delhi, rather than going on to Washington, but that their response had discouraged him from taking the matter any further. He suspected that they had regarded him as a threat to their own positions. That was as may be – but he would have been a boon to the company, and the Foreign Service's gain was decidedly LWT's loss. On the shuttle plane back from Washington to New York, I made a mental note to do all in my power to make sure that LWT never missed out on such an opportunity again, if I knew about it at the time. (As it happened, the opportunity came much sooner than expected, in 1970, and *everybody* knew about it at the time!)

Shuttling back from Washington for a show in New York, commuting between New York and London, five shows a week here, two shows a week there – I received many comments from friends and acquaintances over the years that that sounded like a punishing schedule, with virtually no time off. All work and no play . . .

The truth is that it did not feel that way at all. First, the commuting. Although I suppose it would have been difficult to do any more flying than I was doing – over the maximum for pilots, I was told – it was not like spending seven and a half hours during the rush hour on the Southend–Fenchurch Street line, or strap-hanging for the same amount of time on the Tube.

A lot of the time was spent in the first-class cabins of BOAC VC10s in comfortable, albeit somewhat restricted, surroundings. And each time the destination – whether London or New York – brought with it a sense of excitement about challenges in store. Anticipation is arguably the best antidote to jet lag.

And, yes, I worked more hours than most, but that begs the question: what is the definition of work? I always found the work I was doing enjoyable – if I had not been enjoying it, I would not have done so much of it. Work was never toil, never

'I'll bet he finds it easier commuting between here and America than I do to town!'

boring, alienating or soul-destroying. In this I was, and am still, incredibly fortunate. R.G. Collingwood came closest to my own feelings when he wrote: 'Perfect freedom is reserved for the man who lives by his own work, and in that work does what he wants to do.'

That level of commitment to work also accorded very satisfactorily with my puritan Methodist inheritance, and the work itself had the added advantage of being financially rewarding to a degree beyond the dreams of most puritan Methodists. That was not essential, but it was very welcome, not only because of the lifestyle it gave me, but also because of the new ventures it helped me to pursue.

So was I a 'workaholic'? *Collins English Dictionary* defines a workaholic as 'a person obsessively addicted to work'. Well, not 'obsessively', I would say, but what about just being 'addicted to work'? The same dictionary defines addiction as, firstly, a state of being 'abnormally dependent upon something'. No, that's not it. Or secondly as 'devoted to something, e.g. a jazz addict'. Now, that's more like it. A work addict the way some people are jazz addicts. But not 'a workaholic'. If, however, you were to ask me if I was a telephonaholic, I would have no defence at all . . .

In the midst of all this, there was still time for some parties, sport, holidays, romance and relaxation – albeit sometimes in the same concentrated form as the work. And what of reflection and quiet contemplation? Yes, there has to be time for that. But reflection is a state of mind. You can reflect in the back of a taxi, you can contemplate on board a VC10, you can be alone with your thoughts in the middle of a football crowd.

In his highly literate screenplay for the film *The Slipper and the Rose*, a Paradine co-production of the Seventies, Bryan Forbes has Cinderella asking the Fairy Godmother how she performs her magic. 'That's a trade secret,' she replies, 'but it helps if you dream . . .'

You always have to find time to dream.

Back at the Little Theater in New York, we brought together a rather unlikely pairing, Clare Boothe Luce and Raquel Welch. Clare Boothe Luce was then in her mid-sixties, a prominent speaker on women's issues and the role of women in society. As a Catholic and a Republican, she was at the conservative end of the women's movement in America. Raquel Welch was at the height of her popularity as a sex goddess. Launched as America's answer to Ursula Andress in such films as *One Million Years BC*, she had become a major box-office attraction, despite the fact that most of her films had been low-budget productions which had been panned by the critics. The subject of the programme was to be women.

I asked Clare to elaborate on a speech she had recently made in Chicago on the psychological hang-ups of the modern woman. She explained that she felt that women had faced two revolutions which left them uncertain of their role in society.

'First, the control of her own destiny, in the form of being able to earn a living – that was her first breakthrough in the Industrial Revolution. And the second breakthrough is now that she has control of her own body. That is to say, contraceptive methods and the Pill.

'And the consequences of this revolution are being seen all over the world. We call it a revolution in morals, in the moral area.'

'When Clare said she has control over her own body,' I said, 'a beautiful smile spread over Raquel's face. What were you thinking about?'

'No, I was just thinking, I don't think we have control over our own bodies,' said Raquel. 'We have control over maybe childbirth to a certain degree, but I don't think we have control over our bodies. Because I feel that now that we are free of certain responsibilities for bearing children, and we can now express all the emotions that we do with our bodies sexually, that we are looking there for some incredible reward, which I wonder if it's going to be forthcoming. I wonder if we're not demanding too much of that, and of release totally, without responsibility. Maybe I'm not making myself clear, but it seems to me that we're not free at all by losing the responsibility of children. We're less free.'

'Why are you less free?' I asked.

'Because when you become free, then you really have to

discipline yourself somehow. Somehow then your brain has to – or your feelings of propriety have to govern you. It's no longer something from outside that you have no control. You have to have the self-control. You can't look to sex to be the answer, the escape from everything, the way to express everything. Because it isn't. But people are looking to it as that, and I think becoming disappointed.'

I reminded Clare that she had given her definition of love in the same speech. 'You said, "friendship with desire", didn't you?'

'Oh yes, oh yes,' said Clare. 'Yes, love in my view is friendship with, if you prefer, desire or lust or sex. But the durable component of love is friendship. Because obviously you can make love physically only if there is contact between bodies. You can love only if there is contact through love between hearts and minds. And bodies wear themselves out, and so does the desire. But what remains is the heart and the mind.

'And this is another reason I feel it's so important that women should stop thinking of themselves as the inferior sex, or the lesser sex. Because a true love is only possible between equals. It's always been that way. There is no love between master and slave. That's a fiction of Uncle Tom's days, that the slave can really love his master, or the master really love the slave. Because between equals there's always freedom. And so a man and a woman who truly love must each believe that the other as a person is important, and not inferior in any way.'

I asked Raquel if she agreed that desire could wear out and friendship go on.

'Yes, I think that's probably true. But I have an idea that without some kind of a friendship – or some kind of a thing more than physical – it's not nearly as good. The lust part of it's not nearly as good either. Because the brain, the mind, and all the things that happen inside it, it's a very erogenous zone.'

'The mind is a very erogenous zone' was a memorable phrase, and one that has rightly been credited to Raquel ever since. It was also a potent demonstration of how she had defied her stereotype throughout the discussion.

In the wake of the first wave of the Women's Liberation Movement, discussions like the one we had just had were taking place all over America. It had been a constant source of wonderment to me that America was the cradle of this movement, when you would have thought it ought to have been a country like Saudi Arabia or Iran. On second thoughts, I realised that revolutions always occur in countries where the rebels are closest to achieving their goals, not furthest away. You got demands for greater democratic expression, for example, in Britain or the United States, rather than in Russia – where they would not have been tolerated anyway.

Discussions of women's liberation in 1969 almost invariably included at least one woman who proceeded to alienate women viewers by linking the defence of women's rights in the workplace with a totally unnecessary attack on women who chose not to have a workplace, but to stay at home with their growing children.

The letters would flood in: 'Why make women ashamed of what is still for most of us our best hope of fulfilment – life as a wife and mother?' That, I figured, was just one of the natural excesses that occur in the first stage of any revolution, and would sooner or later pass. And indeed, eventually it was circumvented by the coining of new words like 'homemaker'.

In general American women, I felt, had been more successful than they intended to be. Sure, they competed at home with their men, who often made the mistake of thinking that their women wanted to win. Often they just wanted their men to show their mettle. Then they would have been delighted to lose. The male surrender took all the fun – and the respect – out of the contest. The battle of the sexes became a walkover.

It was in the third week of the London series that it really caught fire. The occasion was an interview with a new arrival on the London scene, a young Australian publisher, by name Rupert Murdoch. Six months earlier, Mr Murdoch had finally won his battle with Robert Maxwell for control of the *News of the World*, and he was now poised to take over the *Sun*. He had just started running a rehashed series of articles by Christine Keeler in the *News of the World*, and the negative response may well have taken him by surprise. There was outrage in many quarters that John Profumo, who had spent the past six years doing social work at Toynbee Hall in the East End, should be tried all over again, for what seemed to be no discernible purpose beyond circulation. Cardinal Heenan had withdrawn an article from the *News of the World* in protest. We had contacted him, and he had agreed to explain his point of view in a recorded interview.

As we sat discussing the programme over lunch at the steak house up the road from the Wembley studios, we decided that it would be wrong to spring such a potentially weighty contribution on Mr Murdoch live. I telephoned his office and spoke to Mr Murdoch himself, and told him of the Cardinal's recorded participation.

We then went back to the office to continue our discussion. Quite apart from the Christine Keeler issue, we had another major concern. Peter Baker, with his years of experience in Fleet Street, had put it very well back in New York. 'If I was Rupert Murdoch,' he had said, 'I would have realised that this Christine Keeler drivel is a no-win proposition. I would come on the show, admit that I had made a mistake during the transition period, and announce that I was cancelling the series forthwith. That way I would win massive sympathy from the audience as the sort of straight-speaking Australian who is prepared to admit his mistakes – "How refreshing, etc, etc." And I would leave you with thirty-nine minutes to promote me, because all you would have left is Murdoch's past career in Australia, his philosophy of publishing and whatever else. That's what I would do if I was him.'

We all agreed that Peter had made this sound like a very credible scenario, and certainly one that we had to be prepared for. After a few frantic calls to Adelaide in South Australia, and several to Fleet Street colleagues, we decided that we had enough of an insurance policy ready. We invited three or four interested parties, like Alexander Lyon, MP, to sit in the front row of the audience. In the event, they were joined by Mr Murdoch's PR man, John Addey.

'The Frost Programme' that night was already something of an event. As I said at the beginning, 'Welcome to the first ITV programme to go out live in colour. To our ITV viewers who are watching in colour tonight, we hope you will both like it very much indeed. For those of you who are looking at it in black and white, we hope you will find it colourful as well . . .' Little did I know how fully we were going to live up to that throwaway.

I began by asking the studio audience, 'How many of you think the *News of the World* is right to publish these Christine Keeler memoirs?' Nine or ten members of an audience of approximately 230 put their hands up. A majority indicated that they thought the *News of the World* was wrong, and 'a number about halfway between the nine or ten who supported and the majority who opposed' put their hands up to indicate that they didn't have a view either way. The attitudes of the audience seemed to mirror those expressed in other forums like the press. (This was not necessarily always the case.)

After some opening exchanges with Rupert Murdoch about newspaper publishing in general, I turned to the subject of the *News of the World*. 'Has there been anything in the last six months that you have kicked out of the *News of the World* on the grounds of taste or morality?'

'Yes,' he said. 'I wouldn't be specific on the stories, except in the case of the Keeler story. I certainly sub-edited a tremendous amount out of the book.'

'You have done that yourself?' I asked.

'Well, I had read the book first when I first made the decision, and I said that the greater part of the first part of the book should be left out. I did not think it was relevant or decent.'

In two short answers, Rupert Murdoch had rendered all the time we spent on the Peter Baker insurance line of questioning more or less superfluous. He had taken upon his own shoulders both the decision to publish the Keeler book in the *News of the World* and its condensation for that publication.

'You read the book?' I asked.

'Yes, I have.'

'Since we talked on the phone this afternoon, I spent four dismal hours reading through the manuscript. What did you think of it when you read it?'

'Well, the early part of it – when I got through the early part, I thought, "No we won't have this, it's not worth having, and it's unpleasant,"' said Mr Murdoch. 'Later, when I got into it, I got very interested in it. In the story of Stephen Ward. The telling by this girl of what happened when this society, when London was shaken by this incident. Not the incident of her having an affair with someone, but what follows, Parliament and so on. How different people reacted to that. The search for a scapegoat. The way that scapegoat was treated. I found it was very interesting. A story that had not been told before.'

'Had not been told before?' I asked.

'Not by her, at any rate,' said Mr Murdoch.

'The first episode, though, did not have a bit of scapegoat in it,' I said. 'It was all that early part you found so unpleasant. There was not a bit of scapegoat. You changed the phrases to having sex and so on from what is in the original text and so on, but there is none of that scapegoat social message and so on in the first episode, was there? It was pure early sexual encounters with . . .'

'This is the story of this girl, and what I am saying, all the earlier part that I said was . . . had been watered down or cut to pieces into one short episode.'

'And so the remaining . . . How many episodes are you thinking of doing at the moment?'

'I don't know. There may be five or six more,' said Mr Murdoch.

'And they are only going to deal with the subject of Stephen Ward . . .'

'Oh, no. Her going to jail, the Parliamentary side of it. The behaviour of the Labour Party in it. Very interesting indeed.'

'Not much of that even in the front-page editorial by Stafford Summerfield last Sunday. They listed things at the bottom. Perhaps someone could get that copy of last Sunday's paper. All the things listed were about "that great huggie bear of a man Ivanov" and so on. There was no reference to the great scapegoat issue. You are not selling it on that.'

'I'm not saying that it was sold . . . I'm not even too sure those plugs were as – right, if you want me to defend those plugs, I will. I will look at London Weekend commercials as to why you should be watching some entertainment. Whether this is really exactly what is on. I think that you could be searched pretty hard on that one. On the question of your advertising. That is no justification on my part, I agree. That editorial . . .'

'Some people say the trailers are better than the programmes, I suppose!' I said. 'But a lot of people have listed a number of the possible debits to this thing. The damage to a man, the raking up of something that is not inconvenient to the Establishment so much as unpleasant; the lowering of the level of Fleet Street. Now, against that, what do you put as the positive merit of this saga?'

'First of all, let me just cut that out, because this is like saying "When did you stop beating your wife?" You said about lowering the standards of Fleet Street. Are you assuming that I have lowered the standards of Fleet Street in the *News of the World*?'

'I am saying that those are three of the arguments used against,' I said. 'What is your argument of positive merit?'

'I am not accepting any of the arguments against,' said Mr Murdoch. 'Arguments of positive merit in this is that for the first time the whole story is being told through with the Ward thing, the later episodes in her life.'

'But it's not,' I said. 'All these books have come out. Wayland Young wrote a book. The end of this book is quotes mainly from the press and Wayland Young. The end of this book is proving the story has been told before because at the end we get into things that are mainly quotes from the court case, court reports, mainly reports from Wayland Young. I went through this.'

Mr Murdoch said that he saw nothing wrong 'in telling a story twice . . . You say that people should not write . . .'

'If you admit that the story has been told twice, then we are making progress. But, I mean, you started off by saying there were new things. I went through this. I combed this through very carefully and I could not find any new facts in it at all except a couple of minor personalities who were alleged to have offered more money than had been quoted before. But everything else was there. Everything else was either in Wayland Young, in the press or in the *News of the World*.'

'Yes, well, that may be my fault,' said Mr Murdoch. 'I have not read Wayland Young. I found the story interesting. A lot of it was new to me, and I certainly don't mind if it has been told before, some of it . . . Historians can only write one book? Once a historian has written a book of the 1960s, that's the end of it?'

'No, but once you say, it seems to me, one of the few arguments for the negative side of this would be the positive thing that there would be new facts, and you said it is the same story twice. I agree. I think Wayland Young deserves about a thousand pounds of the twenty-one thousand on the basis of looking through it. That seems to me to take away one of the possible reasons for publishing it. What other ones are there?'

'Would you say that again. You have taken away one reason?' asked Mr Murdoch.

'Yes. If it does damage to a human being, if it does do any of those things that people say, then you *could* come back and say, "But it prints new facts, the public must know the truth." But if it's telling the story a second time, as you have just . . .'

'. . . the first things that you have said about damage and so on,' said Mr Murdoch.

'You don't think it does damage?' I asked.

'I will come to that,' said Mr Murdoch. 'I'm just not letting you put words into my mouth.'

'No. But I'm trying to get you to propagandise. I'm trying to get you to say the positive reason that would outweigh any negative reason that I or someone else might bring out. And one positive reason that would, I think, compensate for damage that this had done is if there are any new facts, but I have combed through this and there is not a single significant new fact in the whole piece.'

'Well, I think that there would be a tremendous amount of new facts there that would not be known to everybody. Maybe they are known to you, but they are not known to the whole world or to our readers.'

'What sort of new facts?'

'Everyone has not read Mr Young's book or whatever it is. I don't know what you're referring to there. I think that the way that it's put to you, the story of Stephen Ward is new. Okay, it was covered in the newspapers at the time . . .'

'But what new facts?' I asked again. 'Like this? "Stephen brought Bill round and we spent a very amusing evening Bill running after us and trying to pinch our bottoms"?'

'Well, you are reading from there. I did not print it in the *News of the World*.'

'It may be in future weeks,' I said. 'And that is page forty-nine.'

After the break we had contributions from Cardinal Heenan on film, Alexander Lyon in the front row, and from John Addey the PR man, in the form of some ill-judged and counter-productive attempts to lead applause for his employer.

We then returned to the search for the positive merits of the story. 'It's not new facts, because we went into that earlier,' I said. 'You can't defend it on the grounds of new facts. What can you defend it on?'

'Well, I'm not sure of that,' said Murdoch. 'And secondly, you can certainly defend it as a cautionary tale. Whether it's a cautionary tale to young women, or a cautionary tale . . .'

'A cautionary tale about the best way to make £21,000?' I asked.

'You make that every week. Don't show horror about that,' said Mr Murdoch, unfortunately exaggerating my level of remuneration rather a lot. 'Come on, let's be grown-up about it . . .'

After a couple of members of the audience opposed to Mr Murdoch had chimed in, he said, 'It could well be that this feeling that has been whipped up – incidentally, whipped up by members of the sort of establishment that they don't want to be seen with Mr Profumo anywhere – but I grant you that the feeling here is very real . . .'

'That's an Australian view of England – it really is, you know. I mean, it doesn't work that way any more here, you know. It really doesn't. I mean, of course there's a lot of daft old school ties in this country and so on, but it doesn't work like that – the Establishment are not as well organised as that.'

'You reckon?' asked Mr Murdoch laconically. 'You keep saying that I am damaging this man. As long as John Profumo is alive – and long may he go on doing the good work he's doing and with the courage that he's got to face society as he's faced it – as long as he's John Profumo, everybody's going to know who he is and what happened. It goes with the name.'

'If everybody knows, then we don't have any value in the cautionary tale you were talking about earlier, because if everybody knows, you don't need to tell the story again, do you?'

'You're assuming I'm running every word of the book,' said Mr Murdoch. 'His name hasn't been mentioned in the story itself. It was on the plug on page one, I'm quite prepared to admit that.'

'Just one second – Rupert, one second,' I said. 'Here is the front page of the *News of the World*, where you were saying earlier on it's a social document and all of that. "Next week," and there are four things cited – four things are cited as actual instances. One is "First lessons in love", the first remarkable party with a huge sculptured symbol plus a little bit of censorship there, "The bathing party at . . ." and "A night with the Russian Huggie Bear". I mean, it's pathetic to say that that's a social document of our time.'

'Really?' said Mr Murdoch.

'Yes, pathetic.'

'If the Press Council does come down on you for printing this story,' asked Alexander Lyon, 'will you stop printing it?'

'I'll consider that then and the terms on which they come down,' said Mr Murdoch. 'So far there's been a great tendency to judge the story by people who haven't read it.'

'Your PR man's going mad again,' I said. 'Your PR man is the only person who's applauded – you must give him a rise. We've got to leave it there. Thank you very much indeed.'

I thought it had been a rousing debate, but Mr Murdoch emphatically did not feel the same way. He declined an after-show drink, and as he strode from the studio he told a reporter, 'London Weekend has made a powerful enemy tonight.' One of his party said later that that was the bowdlerised version. What he had said privately was 'I'm going to buy that blankety-blank company.'

With no new facts in the story on which to base a defence, if I had been Rupert Murdoch I would have taken the Peter Baker option. (Indeed, it was said later that he'd been contemplating that very approach in the car on the way to the studio, but had been argued out of it.) However, looking at it from his point of view, I could see why, in his first major row in Britain, he was damned if he was going to appear to climb down to an Establishment which he had convinced himself was both orchestrating the protests and out to get him. Much later, it was said that it was those same feelings about 'the Establishment' that led him to relocate his base of operations to New York. If that was indeed so, he owes it an enormous debt!

The word from the PR man's aides was that we had deliberately loaded the audience against his client, but that of course was nonsense – we had no more done this than deliberately loaded the audience against me for the Enoch Powell programme! Or for the interview with Christiaan Barnard, a week after the Murdoch confrontation, when my growing doubts about Barnard's methods with regard to donors found little echo from the audience.

Back in New York, 15 October was Moratorium Day, a massive day of predominantly peaceful protest by the anti-war movement. Our show that evening was devoted to the subject, with William Buckley – 'The youth of America are overwhelmingly on the side of heroism' – arguing against what he felt would be a precipitate withdrawal, and Adam Walinsky – 'Those facts are as fanciful as your casualty figures' – putting the anti-war case. However, the most emotional moment came from an unscheduled participant, Shelley Winters, who had come along to listen and was sitting in the front row of the audience. On the verge of tears, she interrupted the argument between Walinsky and Buckley and said, 'No matter what facts you gentlemen muster, you have to know that millions of boys and girls tonight, all over the country, are saying, "They made a goddamned mess of everything, and get us out."' The applause that greeted her statement indicated that she had spoken for much of the audience in the Little Theater. (It was abundantly clear that the Administration was attempting to obtain maximum publicity for anything that seemed to cater to that public mood, like troop withdrawals, while at the same time concealing, if it could, any escalation, like the illegal and tragic bombing of Cambodia.)

The young in America in the late Sixties still had some heroes they looked up to. They were certainly not the politicians who had led the nation into Vietnam or were keeping it there. They were the people who fought the system – like Ralph Nader. He was an indefatigable consumer safety campaigner, once described as a one-man lobby for the public. In the early 1960s he had taken on one of American enterprise's most powerful institutions, the automobile industry, and won. His campaign had led in 1966 to radical new legislation on car safety. Nader then turned his attention to other consumer and industrial safety issues. A pioneer and one-man band when he started, his work has in a sense been institutionalised in America's powerful consumer pressure groups.

In November 1965 he had published *Unsafe at any Speed: The Designed-in Dangers of the American Automobile Industry*. A swingeing attack on the industry for putting profits and styling above safety, the book became a bestseller. General Motors were concerned enough about his growing influence to put private detectives onto him. This move proved massively counter-productive when, on 6 March 1966, the newspapers published Nader's complaint that for the past month he had been under surveillance by detectives hired by the automobile industry, that he had received a number of intimidating phone calls, and that women had tried to lure him into potentially compromising situations.

General Motors had initially denied Nader's claim, but soon admitted that it had started a routine investigation of him. On 22 March, in a nationally televised hearing of the Congressional Sub-Committee investigating the automobile industry prior to initiating legislation, the President of General Motors had admitted that there had been some harassment, and publicly apologised to Nader. The Chairman of the Committee, after reading the text of the private detective's reports submitted by General Motors, concluded that most of the private investigation was designed to smear Nader's name.

I began my interview with Ralph Nader by asking him, if he

had to choose one thing that had come out of all his campaigning, what it would be.

'The uniform installation of seatbelts and shoulder harnesses. I think that's the one most important safety feature, if it's used. Even going to the point of protecting people in many collisions up to sixty miles an hour. That is pretty significant.'

It was indeed pretty significant for the motorist, and a pretty significant achievement for any individual to be able to point to. I asked him what he felt most passionately about at the moment. 'What change or reform in our society would you most like to see?'

'Well, it's something Englishmen also object to,' said Nader. 'The growing concentration of corporate power. Takeovers, mergers, stifling out the small businessman, controlling the market, abusing the consumer, violating the anti-trust laws, basically becoming more and more of a collectivist economy.'

As an example, he mentioned price fixing. 'Price fixing in this country is literally an epidemic. It's rampant. The Justice Department can't begin to have the lawyers to prosecute it successfully. That's one example of corporate looting, which far exceeds the looting in the streets, in terms of sheer dollars and numbers of people affected.'

'As you go into all these campaigns, what are the pressures on you?' I asked. 'Have people ever tried to buy you off?'

'Earlier in the campaign they would oftentimes make representations such as, "Why don't you come and join this so-called company and put some of your ideas to work?" It's done very subtly, you know. But it isn't being done any more.'

'What other ways do they do it?'

'Actually, no other ways any more,' said Nader. 'I think General Motors taught the rest of the companies of the country that lesson, at least. It just won't work now.'

'By putting a detective on to you. That was the biggest break you ever had, wasn't it? The fact that they put that detective on to you?'

'You may call it a break,' said Nader. 'It wasn't a very pleasant experience.'

'What was it like at the time? When you found out about it? Was it terrifying?'

'Friends would call me up and say, "Congratulations." I'd say, "For what?" They'd say, "I understand that you're being considered for a lucrative position in industry." I'd say, "Where did you get that idea?" They'd say, "Well somebody called me up and wanted to interview me, as a background." Of course the interview, which was basically an investigation by detectives, was engaged on the pretext that I was being considered by some unknown client for an executive position.'

'Is your phone ever tapped?'

'That's hard to say. It's difficult to have adequate detection facilities. I don't worry about it at all. As far as I'm concerned, anything I say over the phone is all right for the country to hear.'

'So you don't know,' I said. 'Obviously you haven't heard voices saying, "Ralph talkin' again, Frank," or anything like that?'

'I've heard a lot of voices,' said Nader, 'but it's due to bad telephone service!'

Ralph Nader's knowledge as a consumer advocate was as encyclopaedic as Norris McWhirter's on records. 'You get a more complete list of ingredients on dog and cat food than you do on food for human consumption. Literally.'

According to Nader, part of the problem was due to the consumers themselves. 'The consumers have a voice, they really have a part, if they would only speak up. You've got to develop a consumer power organised around things like the food industry, automobiles, insurance, telephone services, all these industries, in order to develop the voice of the consumer.'

He had been talking about consumer power. Over the years, as he'd been proved right again and again, he had gained more power himself. 'Power to influence, at least. Does it ever worry you that power will corrupt you in any way?'

'No,' said Ralph Nader. 'Because it doesn't amount to a whit. It just amounts to talking. You tell people their frankfurters are filled with fat, up to thirty-five or forty per cent; you tell them that their appliances are wearing out; tell them the cars are coming out with more average defects – thirty-two per car in tested cars by consumer reports last year. You tell them that –'

'Thirty-two defects per car?' I asked.

'Thirty-two defects per car. You tell them that there are illegal interest charges all over the country being charged, and they're concerned. But they don't do much about it. They're pretty complacent. They just sit and watch television.'

'Which has thirty-two defects per hour,' I said.

Luisa, my housekeeper in London, had had an eventful time that particular week while I was away. The reason was simple. John Cleese had included my telephone number in a sketch on 'Monty Python's Flying Circus'. John, playing an interviewer, had been speaking to a man who thought he was a mouse, and other people who had the same problem were invited to call 584 5313. Luisa told the *Daily Telegraph*, 'The telephone never stopped. One caller said, "Am I calling the mice? Can I have some cheese?"'

In his explanation to the *Telegraph*, John managed to blame the whole thing on the viewers! 'When we are doing scripts, we often use friends' numbers and addresses. I don't see why anybody should telephone the number. Perhaps they haven't got anything better to do.'

'Python' addicts in those days were clearly insomniacs. Luisa said the calls went on until four in the morning, when she managed to get the Post Office to start intercepting them.

When I interviewed Paul Newman in London the following weekend, I asked him if he was still hopeful about youth. 'You said on one occasion, "I began the Sixties with hope and end it with despair," rather poetically.'

'That came out of something that I was very privileged to be on – a 2½-hour programme on NBC evaluating the Sixties and predicting something about the Seventies – and before the show I said to Sandy Vanocur, who is a very bright man, "Well, you were in charge of the political area, how did you handle that?" "Well," he said, "I started the Sixties with hope and wound up with doubt." I said, "I wound up with despair," and he said, "Well, I can't document despair, I can document doubt," And I felt that was a rather interesting network way of handling it.'

By now life was getting quite complicated – interviewing American stars in London, and English stars in New York. It was an advanced case of the 'If it's Tuesday, it must be Belgium' syndrome. However, there were certain surefire clues. If you were eating soft-shell crabs, cheesecake or English muffins, you were almost certain to be in New York (English muffins had not yet made the journey to England). If you were eating potted shrimps or Twiglets, you were definitely in London. If the cab driver knew how to get to where you had asked him to go, you were in London. If you had to give him directions, you were in New York – although you did get an inspiring address on the thrill of being a new citizen as a compensation for the inconvenience.

Writers were an important ingredient in the show in New York, and next we welcomed to the studio Joe McGinniss, the author of a new book, *The Selling of the President – 1968*, and the Republican Majority Leader, Gerald Ford. Mr McGinniss's book was highly critical of the campaign that was used to 'sell' Richard Nixon to the American public. Gerald Ford was there to defend the President and his men's methods.

McGinniss's starting point had been his fascination with the way that Nixon had allowed his advertising men 'to make it appear as if he had changed his character simply through sophisticated technical uses of television'.

'A brief example. He projects a cold image. And this is the way people responded to him, so his advertising director said, "One thing we'll never do is put him all by himself in front of a TV camera, just sitting behind a desk talking. This is a very cold way to deal with people. Always have him in situations talking to other people so we can take pictures of him communicating. Having an interpersonal relationship. Giving and taking. Listening, nodding, patting on the arm, you know, responding with warmth, humanity." And the advertising director wrote in a memorandum to Nixon in November of 1967 that these situations should look unstaged even if they're not. And then they proceeded to go to New Hampshire and stage some very unstaged situations.'

As another example, McGinniss said that the advertising men

had 'talked about how he needed a sense of humour'. So they had hired Paul Keyes from 'Laugh-In' to provide him with one.

Gerald Ford did not agree. 'I'm not an expert in this business, but it's been my observation that television really reveals the personal qualities that a person has. Having known the President for twenty-one years, fairly intimately, I happen to think that basically he has a good sense of humour . . . What I'm trying to say is that all the technical expertise of the television industry can't make a person something that he isn't basically.'

'I think I'd like to draw one distinction,' said McGinniss. 'Television ultimately does reveal a man for what he is, if you are talking about this kind of television where the cameras aren't in your employ. Where you don't hire the cameramen and the technicians and stage the situation yourself. Here you come on and the cameras are neutral. They're simply transmitting. They're simply allowing you to communicate, but what I think Richard Nixon did with his television cameras was stage situations which were specifically designed to bring out personality qualities which even his own advisers believed he did not have . . . I really believe that all the people got to vote for or against last year was the televised image of Nixon. I think through the entire campaign he kept the whole country on the other side of the television screen. He would not allow himself to be questioned by professional questioners, only under circumstances where his own people would pay for an hour.

'They would pick the panel themselves, and then they would put him up live and say, "Here's Nixon answering Americans' questions." They were the questions of the Americans that his own television advisers picked. I don't think this is a very legitimate way to do business. They made a big deal the last night of the campaign with a two-hour telethon. "Call up and ask Richard Nixon a question," they said, but all of the questions asked Richard Nixon on the telethon were written by members of the Nixon staff.'

'I think you make a fundamental mistake assuming that the American people on the last night of a campaign are going to make a final decision,' said Gerald Ford. 'Maybe the propaganda people, putting on the television show, thought they were. But I have a lot more faith in the ultimate good judgement of the American people than to let them be sold by a propaganda operation the last night of an election. It just doesn't operate that way. If we ever get to the position in this country where through such techniques we're going to pick a President, then I think something's wrong with our system. I don't think it's going to degenerate to that position.'

'I think there is a lot of evidence to indicate it already has,' said Mr McGinniss quietly. According to him, our interview with Richard Nixon for 'The Next President' had been very much the exception that proved his rule, although of course Nixon's handlers would have known that the final edited interview ccould not be longer than nine minutes.

I found McGinniss's arguments very persuasive. The ability of political candidates to buy television time in the United States was a major weakness in the electoral system. It had two undesirable side-effects. The first was its manipulative power, both in the way that McGinniss had just outlined, and in thirty-second commercials which did scant justice to the complexities of the subjects being discussed. The second side-effect was equally serious. Buying television time was such an expensive business that it led to frantic and sometimes dubious fund-raising, and a feeling that successful candidates were not really their own man or woman because of their obligation to provide wealthy subscribers with a later *quid pro quo* for their support.

For both these reasons, I actually found myself recommending the British idea of free Party Political Broadcasts as the lesser of the available evils, on the thesis that it is preferable to bore the voters to death than to mislead them.

The kaleidoscope of guests at the Little Theater continued. In the first two weeks of November they included Cesar Chavez, Henry Fonda, Natalie Wood, Roberta Flack and Mahalia Jackson. On Friday 14 November, another Jackson strode onto our stage, the Reverend Jesse Jackson. This was, it transpired, his first national talk-show appearance. Jesse was twenty-eight years old at the time and, through Operation Breadbasket in Chicago, was attempting to end the economic exploitation of the black community in the United States. He was already adopting a strategy of trying to boycott businesses which discriminated against blacks.

Martin Luther King's widow, Coretta Scott King, had told me that she would like a fuller investigation into the person or persons responsible for the assassination of her husband. I asked Jesse, who had been with King when he was shot, 'Are you convinced it was one man, James Earl Ray?'

'It just couldn't have been one man,' said Jesse. 'But the reason I have not personally been so caught up in pursuing who did it, the real issue – and I think it's the way Dr King would perhaps have dealt with it – is not *who* killed Dr King. *What* killed Dr King? In terms of the atmosphere, it's obvious that the plan, the man being able to escape, where they found the man, and other bits and pieces of evidence indicate that far more people were involved. So it was a broader conspiracy, but there was a certain atmosphere – there is a certain atmosphere – in the nation that gives sanction to ambush and assassination of people who are not in the tide of agreeing with America yum-yum and some of her policies now that are in conflict with the best interests of mankind. I mean, we look at a nation of 200 million people, a nation that would come up nine years ago with two programmes – one to go to the moon and one to rid the nation of poverty – and nine years later $54 billion have been spent to get two men to the moon, to get two boxes of rocks of moon dust, and only $5.7 billion for forty million hungry people, twenty-eight million of whom are white . . . For the climate is set now that when you do speak out for the nation and against its sickness, you simply fall prey to those who are so sick that they want to be quiet in the face of this atrocity.

'You just don't say certain things in the South and live. You just don't say certain things and get a chance to work. You just don't do certain things and live to be twenty-one. When James Meredith started a march against fear in Mississippi and many people reacted by saying that it was a useless march, James Meredith was dealing with a very basic reality of black people in America living under that kind of tyranny where fear is instilled very early. And rather than coming to grips with that fear and using courage as an antidote, we live much of our lives escaping that fear.

'So when a black was asked while in the South, "Why don't you drink the water downtown?" he said, "Because I'm not thirsty." They said, "Why don't you eat downtown?" He said, "Well, I ate before I left home." "Why don't you go to the movies?" "I'm not interested." Which are lies that come in the face of the fear. That fear usually starts at a very early age, and you become so comfortable in the face of it until you walk by the water fountains and you aren't thirsty; and you walk by the food, and you really don't get hungry, because you've closed off that portion of your mind.'

'I read one quote of yours,' I said, 'where you were saying that instead of conflict between the poor black and the poor white, they should get together, and there should be a conflict between the haves and the have-nots. Can you see that happening? Can you see a sort of alliance of poor people, black and white?'

'Well, it's really happening by negation rather than affirmation. That is, we're backing into that relationship rather than going on into it because we see it clearly . . . We took this tour around Illinois last year and found these poor white mothers who were caught in the same bind that poor black mothers were caught in, and in that their drive to survive is stronger than their desire to be moral, ethical or white. The survival is really melting us into a new kind of relationship.'

Almost twenty years later, during the 1988 Presidential campaign, in which Jesse Jackson was a candidate for the Democratic nomination, I saw that 'melting' of which he spoke taking place. It was in that same state of Illinois, in Cicero, a town which had been a bastion of white prejudice. I joined Jesse at a rally outside a General Electric plant where there had been talk of lay-offs. As we were leaving, a white woman of about sixty came up to Jesse and, sobbing, laid her head on his chest and asked him if he could do something to save her husband's job. Jackson promised to do everything he could, and when he got back in the car he was quiet for a moment. Then he said, 'Did you see that? She approached me for help, something she probably never expected in her whole life she would do to a black man. She did it with trepidation, but she did it – and here in Cicero.'

It was white embracing black in the struggle for survival, just as Jesse Jackson had foreseen nineteen years earlier. But in the intervening years, his rainbow coalition has never become the political force he envisaged. His dream that a combination of all the have-nots could outnumber or overcome the haves has never become a reality. Indeed, statistically, as more and more poor blacks and poor whites desert the polling booths, it becomes more and more difficult.

However, one thing was clear at the end of that conversation in 1969: you needed no great prescience as you spoke to the Reverend Jesse Jackson to realise that you were talking to an emerging new national leader. And always there was that marvellous way with words.

'When we're unemployed, we're called lazy.' said Jesse. 'When the whites are unemployed, it's called a depression. Which is the psycholinguistics of racism.'

The following week, we were joined by Senator Eugene McCarthy, who, since losing the Democratic nomination to Hubert Humphrey in 1968, had also decided to give up his Senate seat. I asked him a question I had asked a number of political figures, without getting a definitive answer: 'Is it possible, in fact, for a politician to tell the truth, the whole truth, and nothing but the truth?'

'It depends on what you really mean by the whole truth,' said McCarthy. 'I think you can tell the whole truth. I don't know that you can tell all the truth.'

I reckoned I had my definitive answer.

Senator McCarthy's successor as the standard-bearer of the anti-war movement, Senator George McGovern, joined us two weeks later. His mood was troubled.

'I think President Nixon had an opportunity earlier this year when he was talking about bringing us together, and talking about lowering our voices, to accomplish some healing. I don't see where we've moved very far down that road. To talk about lowering voices and then to give us Mr Agnew as Vice-President, who calls people in the Peace Movement "impudent snobs" and "rotten apples" and that sort of thing, is very disturbing.

'It seems to me that what is under way in this country is a systematic attempt to broaden the divisions, to set what you referred to a while ago as middle America against the young people in this country. There is also the so-called Southern strategy, which seeks to exploit the prejudices of human beings, to set off blacks against whites, and an effort to play off the so-called intellectuals on one hand against the main body of people. All of those things seem to me to be divisive. They create a climate of fear and tension instead of healing.'

McGovern was documenting a crisis of faith in America. A country which, in late 1969, lacked confidence and morale in the face of a war that was bitterly dividing it. And there was no end in sight – to the war or to the divisions.

Back in London we had been wrestling with a different problem. The work of Professor Victor Wynn, Director of the Alexander Simpson Laboratory of St Mary's Hospital, had been brought to our attention. He was probably the world's leading doubter of the contraceptive pill. The Pill had been one of the major innovations of the 1960s, and by 1969 we were talking – incredulously – about the fact that one and a half million women in Britain were taking it. Once it had been introduced, there had very quickly grown to be a protective, almost conformist, shield around the Pill to guard it from its critics. Now Victor Wynn had come up with ten serious question marks about the Pill, and we had to decide whether to be the first to question – not attack, but question – this new conformity.

Our producer Geoffrey Hughes and I met with Professor Wynn, and we discussed his criticisms at length. It was a debate that often recurs in television – reconciling the conflict between fact-finding and asking the uncomfortable question with the danger of causing distress if the subject is an upsetting or inflammable one. In this case we decided that Professor Wynn deserved to be heard. We invited Dr Malcolm Potts, the Secretary of the International Planned Parenthood Federation, and a consultant gynaecologist, Mr Diggory, to debate with him.

The Professor outlined his ten reservations, which included

the metabolic effects of the Pill and 'clotting factors'; the risk of cancer; changes in the structure of certain organs; blood pressure; change of personality; fertility; ageing processes; genetic risk; and diverting attention from the development of 'really safe, simple and effective contraceptive methods'.

I turned first to Malcolm Potts, who said, 'Let me remind viewers that the commonest single cause of maternal mortality in Great Britain at the present time is death from abortion, so women have to face a number of risks, and you have to look at the Pill in this context.' Dr Potts said that he thought Professor Wynn had exaggerated the risks: 'The risk is of the order of tens in a million.'

Mr Diggory was particularly concerned about Professor Wynn's reference to the possibility of a link between the Pill and cancer. Dr Potts commented, 'Here Professor Wynn says that oestrogens cause cancer in animals, and this is quite true, but only in very high doses . . . The animal experiments all include levels of oestrogen that are ten or a hundred or a thousand times the level we are giving people, so this is an irrelevant and, if I may say so, a rather naughty remark, because it frightens women quite unnecessarily.'

Dr Potts and Mr Diggory accused Professor Wynn of quoting selectively from an American Food and Drug Administration report. 'Professor Wynn will, of course, agree that the end of that report says that there is no evidence against the Pill and recommends its continued usage.' A member of the audience intervened to point out that one of the FDA's recommendations was to 'increase the length of time in which it is possible to use the Pill in the US, to take away their two-year restriction'. Mr Diggory then had an important point to make: 'Now I do plead that we ask our viewers, all of them, that if they are worried about this, and I don't think they should be in the very least, but if they are worried by the programme or anything they hear, then I beg them not to stop taking the Pill now – I'm sure Professor Wynn will agree with this – but to go and see their doctors and discuss the matter with their doctors, and get some alternative contraceptive if they're going to change. But I should warn them the failure rate of all other contraceptives is at the very least ten or twenty times as high as that of the Pill, and unwanted pregnancies are going to occur.'

Both Dr Potts and Mr Diggory then pointed out that in the limited number of examples of a change of personality or fertility connected with the Pill, the changes were often for the better. As for the genetic risk point, Dr Potts said, 'Now, what we know is that some of the babies that are born to women who have had the Pill are abnormal. But the rate is no higher and no lower than in the population as a whole.'

It was vital that Dr Potts and Mr Diggory had all the time they needed to make their responses to Professor Wynn, and therefore we obtained an overrun for the programme into an additional Part Three, as we had previously done with Enoch Powell. At the end of the extended programme, I repeated Mr Diggory's warning. 'To those of you at home, obviously we will return to the issues raised by this next Friday. In the meantime, we can only emphasise: please check with your doctor if anything that has been said tonight worries you, or if you have a symptom that worries you. Thank you for being with us – please check with your doctor – thank you, good night.'

We discussed the programme amongst ourselves almost as much afterwards as we had before. Halfway through the programme, I had had second thoughts about whether we had got the structure right. Although we had decided to take Professor Wynn's ten points in a row, in the cause of clarity, I began to wonder if they made for too powerful an indictment when delivered continuously. However, after the over-run (and even before the follow-up programme), that seemed to have worked itself out. We had got responses from Dr Potts and Mr Diggory to all ten of Professor Wynn's points.

But had we been right to mount the programme at all? I reached one conclusion at the time: with the somewhat impractical benefit of hindsight, I think I would reach a different one now. After the programmes back in December 1969, I felt that the benefits of airing this debate when parts of it had seemed to be suppressed in the media outweighed the obvious risks of dealing with doubts about something so crucial to people's lives. At the time, some of Professor Wynn's points seemed well worth pursuing, although we would have been better off without his occasional juxtaposition of a mild fact with a much stronger assertion. On others of his points – like the suggestion regarding cancer – his opponents had probably put viewers' minds at rest about a rumour they may well have already heard about anyway. And all the debate that followed the programme could only underline the urgent need for more research, and might indeed trigger it off.

So, at the time, I felt on balance that we were right to have dealt with such an important topic. More than twenty years later, the Pill has been found resoundingly not guilty on those of Professor Wynn's points which have been finally decided, and I feel – though, as I say, only with the benefit of hindsight – that perhaps we did worry some viewers unnecessarily. Maybe it was the sort of subject that was too risky to deal with unless you had a written guarantee from every viewer that they would watch all of the programme – or none of it.

The deciding factor for me in coming to my conclusion is an exchange with Professor Wynn towards the end of the programme: 'What do you predict is the future of the Pill?' I asked him.

'That's a difficult question to answer, but I predict that its life is probably not more than two – or at the very most three – years.'

You can never conclusively refute a prediction at the moment it is made, but the fact that the Pill has now outlived Professor Wynn's scenario by more than twenty years indicates that in the perennial journalistic struggle to balance the responsibility not to alarm against the responsibility not to conceal, this was one that we got wrong.

As Christmas approached, Jane Fonda visited us at the Little Theater. I cannot think of anyone I have known for thirty years who has passed through more contrasting phases of life in that relatively short time. Her odyssey has reflected the moods of the times. As the star of *They Shoot Horses, Don't They?* in December 1969, she had not yet been dubbed 'Hanoi Jane' for her outspoken opposition to America's involvement in the Vietnam War, but she had already passed through her 'traditional

Hollywood daughter' phase and her *Barbarella* phase, and was now married to the director Roger Vadim, with a baby daughter, and was talking the 'finding yourself' language of the late Sixties. Although we did not know it, her odyssey had scarcely begun, but then as now, she was never boring. We began by reminiscing about our meeting in London seven years earlier, and then we turned to current topics.

'We hear a lot today about "the new morality" and so on. How would you define what is moral or immoral?' I asked.

'I think immorality is when you hurt physically or emotionally someone else. I try not to judge anybody, and the only thing I consider wrong is when you hurt someone. Otherwise, anything goes.'

It was a very Sixties definition – indeed, it could almost have been the Bishop of Woolwich talking.

I quoted a remark from Roger Vadim. 'He said on one occasion, "All marriage is science fiction. There's no contact between the world of a woman and the world of a man. Everybody knows that when they're born they're alone, and they're alone at death." Do you think people are that alone?'

'Yeah, I do,' said Jane. 'I think there are moments of contact. But I think essentially we all are. And that's fine. I mean, when we come to terms with that – I think people are unhappy when they try to pretend that they're not alone. We are alone. I can never know what's going on in your mind. I would love to. If you ask what's the one thing in the world I would like more than anything else, it's for even fifty seconds to be able to – Pow! – be in someone else's head and just see the world through their eyes. I mean, I really would like to know if anybody else looks at things the way I do. And I sometimes wonder.'

'Can you do it for fifty seconds into your husband's mind?'

'No, not to anybody. I have trouble doing it with myself. No, I can't do it with anybody, and you know, we are alone. I don't know what I am when I am removed from you or whoever I am with. I become somebody else; and I sometimes wonder if there's anybody there, if there's anybody home when I'm not reacting and bouncing off other people. And I do think it's what Vadim said. I think it's true. Men and women are like two planets – hopefully sovereign planets. And I think that's pretty exciting, you know. That's one of the reasons I like the fact that today physically you can't tell as much the difference between men and women. No, it's true. There's an island, and I wish I could remember the name of it, in the Pacific. There was some research done on it. It's an island where there are really no physical – I mean, no obvious differences between men and women. The men stay home and wash the dishes, the women go out and do the hunting or vice versa or whatever.'

The island sounded like a very Sixties discovery.

'There are none of the he-man, homebody-type images that we have in America, except for their natural physical differences, their sexes and their breasts and everything like that. All the rest is the same. And they're very happy. They're very happy.

"THERE WILL BE A LOT OF IMPORTANT PEOPLE HERE TONIGHT, SO TRY TO BE AS DAVID FROSTY AS POSSIBLE!"

There are no suicides. There's no insanity.'

'It's not natural, though, is it, do you think?' I asked.

'What is natural is what is basic. And I like to get down to basics. I like the fact that we forget all the trappings that we are taught. Men can't cry and women have to stay home and wash the dishes. Why can't men cry, and why can't women work?'

'Well, of course women can work,' I said, 'but in general a man is happier working than washing the dishes, isn't he?'

'Not necessarily,' said Jane. 'There are some men that are very good in the home, and some women that like to work. And it's amazing how many people try to make you feel guilty for that sort of thing. Reducing it to its simplest form, you realise that, trappings aside, it's true that they are two very different people. I mean, women are concrete and men are abstract. And I've never met an exception.'

'What do you mean?'

'I mean – I think it's one of the things, one of the reasons why art, music, sculpture, writing – it's mainly men that get it done. Men are capable – more capable, more gifted for abstract art, and women are essentially tangible, concrete, precise.'

'Well, I'm all for women being free to work and do whatever they want to do and so on, but nevertheless, for instance, with your husband, you wouldn't want to be the boss, would you?'

'No, I wouldn't,' said Jane. 'I mean, there's no chance of that anyway. No, I don't want to be the boss, but . . .'

'And you would want him to be.'

'He is. I mean, I wouldn't be married to him if he wasn't the boss. But his being the boss has nothing to do with whether I work, for example. There are times when I work. I'm an actress. I can make three or four movies a year. He's a director. He can make maybe one. And he needs more time. So he doesn't work for a couple of years. So I support us. Why not? He doesn't have anything to prove. It doesn't bother him. And yet the number of people that I know – I've read interviews, and they say, "Oh, you know, his wife is keeping him." What a lot of nonsense. You know, it's ridiculous.'

'But he decides when he wants to go and wash the dishes.'

'In fact, he doesn't wash the dishes. But it would be okay if he did. He's a great mother.'

'Are you a good father?'

'I think I probably would be.'

'We're getting metaphysical,' I said. 'You said on one occasion that you didn't really particularly want to get married, but you did. Why did you, if you didn't particularly want to?'

'Well, for several reasons,' said Jane. 'First of all, Vadim said to me one day, "Listen, it's just as boring to be an old unmarried couple as it is to be an old married couple." Then I have step-children and they were in school in America, and the teachers were beginning to look at me strangely. And then, you know, it's putting as much importance on marriage, if not more, to fight it than to do it.'

Again here, Jane's was a very Sixties, slightly shamefaced apologia for marriage. 'Do you expect it to be forever?' I asked her.

'I don't even think about forever. I think about now, maybe tomorrow. I think a little bit about tomorrow for my daughter more than for myself. But I don't know. Maybe it's just me. It scares me, it really does. It gives me claustrophobia.'

Jane's philosophy in 1969 distilled where a lot of the Sixties generation's 'head was at' at that time. They had influenced her and, as she fed her version of their creed back to them, she in turn influenced them.

The Sixties had been a pretty fruitful time for Jane – by 1969 she was well established in the first rank of American movie actresses. The Sixties had been a pretty good time for me, too – indeed, I don't know what I would have done without them.

For me, the timing had been perfect. It is difficult to imagine arriving in London in 1951, ten years earlier than I did, for a career in broadcasting and making progress at anything like the same speed. There would have been fewer opportunities to exploit, and less receptivity to talent – and fewer of the quantum leaps that were available by the Sixties. A different ethos had prevailed in the Fifties. By the beginning of the Sixties, the employee mentality was beginning to give way to the employer mentality. Also by the early Sixties, age, experience, one's elders, one's betters, one's superiors, institutions, authority, traditions, customs and conventions no longer seemed insuperable barriers. You could do your own thing. For some, that meant dropping out and doing nothing very much at all. But for many of us, it was a great spur to ambition. Energy and enthusiasm when met by opportunity generate both ambition and innovation. If the opportunity is there, you still need the will and the confidence to exploit it, but even that is made easier by an 'anything is possible' feeling in the air, like that which seemed to permeate London in the early Sixties. The heady atmosphere of optimism was decidedly contagious. It made the Fifties seem in retrospect even more bland, pedestrian and stifling than they had been at the time. Authority had scarcely been challenged in Britain since 1931, but now the time was ripe.

'The wind of change' to which Harold Macmillan had referred in an African context in February 1960 had certainly been apparent in my life during the intervening ten years. Commuting between London and New York in a VC10 had replaced commuting between Beccles and Cambridge in a 1935 Singer, and I was earning more in one night than my father had earned in a year (though my spending abilities were also growing effortlessly at roughly the same rate).

I recognised I had been on quite a steep learning curve in the Sixties too. My first television programme, 'Town and Gown' at Anglia, had been transmitted in the last few days of 1959. That had been the sum total of my TV CV prior to the Sixties. All the rest had developed during the decade: learning to talk naturally to a camera, and indeed an audience, and not at it; separating the sketch that will never work from the sketch that, with some judicious editing, just might; learning that you don't go to an audience for what you can get more succinctly from an expert, but for what they are uniquely expert about – their own feelings, their own opinions, their own emotions; developing the different ways to transform an interview into a conversation, whether by relaxing the diffident, ruffling the complacent, or just by altering the body language; understanding that there is no such thing as a self-standing brilliant question in its own right – that a question can only be judged by the response it evokes. That's because the interviewer/conductor/host in a topical television programme of the types we have been discussing is first and foremost a catalyst rather than a principal. He orchestrates, he makes things happen. His job is to make the various relationships work: interviewer and guest, guest and audience, studio audience and home audience.

If he is a producer as well, he should take time to do the same thing off-camera too. It only took one or two meetings when I first arrived in London for me to see how embryonic ideas can be killed stone dead at what is billed as an 'ideas meeting'. Whether the suggestions are for a sketch, a topical item or a possible interview guest, they're often made tentatively, even nervously: an abrupt brush-off can deny you ideas from the same source for the next six meetings, until he or she summons up the courage to have another go. We all know that warmth is the atmosphere in which most plants grow. Why try and challenge the natural law in a staff meeting? I am sure that the teams I worked with in the Sixties soon developed their own 'Language of Frost'. 'That's a terrific idea' meant 'That's not bad, but it needs work,' and 'That's not *quite* right yet' meant 'You must be joking – that's not right at all.'

Luckily, on 'The Frost Programme' the team worked out a silent system of assessing my reactions that removed the danger of any feelings of rejection. As someone was expounding an idea, Peter Baker or Neil Shand would be watching me out of the corner of their eye, and would suddenly murmur, 'He's glazing . . . he's glazing . . .'. Whoever was talking at the time would take the cue and segue painlessly into their next idea! The preparation of a topical television show is a collegial rather than a solitary pursuit. There are a few successful shows that people actually dread having to work on – not many, but a few – but even they would be immeasurably improved if the staff meetings had some fun to them, and some bouquets.

So, I had had a great time in the Sixties, and I loved – and needed – the freedom and the opportunities that the decade provided. Wordsworth had summed up the feeling very well in a different context: 'Bliss was it in that dawn to be alive, but to be young was very heaven.'

Despite all that, I never felt myself a real child of the Sixties. If I'd even tried to be a hippie – an unlikely scenario for someone with my work ethic! – I fear I would have been an awfully traditionally dressed one. I owned no kaftans, and even the groovy metropolitan garb that had so beguiled *Time* magazine left me cold. And the drug culture left me even colder. As for the Ad-Lib, the club that became the late-night temple of rock in the Sixties, I have to confess that I never actually visited it. And indeed the f-word, which even made it into the *Oxford English Dictionary* by 1972, has still not made it into this book in 1993.

Were the Sixties vital and dynamic, or flawed and phoney? Real and progressive, or superficial and self-destructive? Answer: all of the above. The society-based activities of the 1950s were being replaced by the individual-based activities of the 1960s. In fact, the more you examine the Sixties, the more you can see them as a re-enactment of the age-old contest between Classical and Romantic. That was the dichotomy in the early Sixties. The Fifties had been an essentially Classical decade: the Sixties came to life as a Romantic one. The Fifties concentrated on society and the group: the Sixties on the individual, the I-generation and the ego. The Fifties were intellectual where the Sixties were instinctive. The Fifties were rational and logical where the Sixties were passionate and emotional. Self-restraint and duty were the watchwords of the Fifties: self-expression and an absolute conviction that anything goes as long as somebody wants it were the watchwords of the Sixties. We were living in a sexual Golden Age – after the Pill and before herpes or AIDS – and all restrictions on individual freedom were to be summarily swept away. That might make sense when facilitating divorce or decriminalising homosexuality, but should the same apply to drugs, pornography or bringing unwanted children into the world?

Bertrand Russell had defined the battleground in his chapter on the Romantic Movement in one of the first books Mr Cooksey had prescribed for us at Wellingborough Grammar School, *A*

History of Western Philosophy. By Russell's definition, Rousseau was the original Sixties man. He had inherited a Fifties world, when the conditions had been ripe for change:

> By the time of Rousseau, many people had grown tired of safety, and had begun to desire excitement . . . from him the Romantics learned a contempt of the trammels of convention – first in dress and manners, in the minuet and the heroic couplet, then in art and love, and at last over the whole sphere of traditional morals.

The next step was inevitable.

> Revolt of solitary instincts against social bonds is the key to the philosophy, the politics and the sentiments not only of what is commonly called the Romantic Movement, but of its progeny down to the present day.

But, claimed Russell, in the end such a revolt cannot prevail.

> The Romantic Movement in its essence aimed at liberating human personality from the fetters of social convention and social morality. In part, these fetters were a mere useless hindrance to desirable forms of activity, for ancient community has developed rules of behaviour for which there is nothing to be said except that they are traditional. But egoistic passions, when once let loose are not easily brought again into subjection to the needs of society . . . by encouraging a new lawless Ego [the Romantic Movement] made social cooperation impossible . . . man is not a solitary animal, and so long as social life survives, self-realisation cannot be the supreme principle of ethics.

In the first half of the Sixties, the argument went all the Romantics' way. The focus was indeed on sweeping away the trammels of convention, the fetters of social convention and social morality, and the useless traditions. The tight rein of the Fifties was replaced by the free rein of the Sixties.

In the second half of the decade, the Classical arguments began to be heard again, as the Romantic vision of a regenerated Britain began to fade. Square society started to recover from its almost total loss of confidence. The investiture of the new Prince of Wales triggered a revival of interest in the monarchy; Neil Armstrong achieved a traditional societal goal when man walked on the moon; *Life* magazine pronounced that swinging London was dead; as the police seemed to stiffen their tactics against the protestors, they in turn complained about 'swingeing London'; the publisher John Calder felt it necessary to form a movement in 1968 to protect literature from what he saw as a growing danger of censorship; and Baroness Wootton's recommendations on the liberalisation of the drug laws were summarily rejected. Even John Lennon and Yoko Ono surrendered to the traditional institution of marriage at a wedding ceremony in Gibraltar in 1969.

In 1970 John Lennon acknowledged the limited nature of the progress to a new society: 'The people who are in control and in power and the class system and the whole bullshit bourgeois scene is exactly the same except there is a lot of middle-class kids with long hair walking around London in trendy clothes.'

The changes were not quite as skin-deep as that, but a new, somewhat expanded upper class had certainly survived – by reducing the size of its exclusion zone. Exclusion has always been the real motive for class antagonism. Remove the former, and you automatically reduce the latter. The new upper class was absorbing rebels and critics at a faster, somewhat less discriminating rate, but the old techniques of assimilation were still proving effective. American meritocratic values were not displacing the class system, they were being wedded to it, or welded on to it. In time that would make the class system less comfortable and put a higher premium on hard work and success, but it would not produce a classless society. That would remain an intermittent rallying cry and a distant dream for the rest of the century.

At the end of the Sixties the battle lines had been redrawn, but authority had only lost some of the battles, not the war. In politics both systems – thirteen years of Conservatism and six years of Labour – had failed to deliver: both forks in the political road turned out to be cul-de-sacs.

In the contest between Romantics and Classicists, the Romantics were probably still just ahead on points, but the gap was narrowing. All in all, not such a terrible balance. For the rest of the answers we would have to wait for the Seventies. What we did not know at the time was that we would wait in vain. The Sixties had been an epoch: the Seventies would only be at best a transition, at worst an intermission.

The thirteen weeks of 'Frost on Friday' and 'Frost on Saturday' in London had ended on 13 December. The new series of 'Frost on Sunday' would begin in January. Our last taping day of the year in New York was on 23 December. It turned out to be an important one.

Peter, Neil and I had been talking a lot about what the next move for 'The David Frost Show' ought to be. The show was well established by now, and the number of stations taking it had grown from thirty-seven to sixty-three. We felt it was time to move on to our next development. I was convinced that the area on which to focus was our longer interviews. We had discarded the traditional talk-show eight-minute ration right at the beginning with Adam Clayton Powell, and the longer interviews had gone on to become a regular feature. What about devoting the whole ninety minutes to one guest who merited it?

When we discussed that possibility with some of our production team and with the Westinghouse contingent, there were a lot of raised eyebrows, although relatively little outright opposition. I guess they were probably resigned to the fact that this was something I had to get out of my system before normal programming sanity was restored.

For us, the crucial question was who would give us the best shot. It was on that last taping day of 1969 that the opportunity presented itself. Peter Ustinov was in New York for the Radio City Music Hall opening of his new film *Viva Max*. Who better than Peter to launch our new experiment? I talked to him at his hotel, and was delighted to find that he was not just game, but raring to go.

When he joined me on stage, he saw his microphone in front of him, but did not notice the radio mike on my tie. 'Can they hear you?' he asked. As we talked, he demonstrated his skill with sound effects by doing a perfect impersonation of microphone feedback – 'howlaround', as the technicians called it. It took the audience and me several seconds before we realised where the noise was coming from.

'Two sound men downstairs have just had heart attacks,' I said. 'They were instantly fired, they've now been reinstated, and they're all right again.'

It was a mini-preview of the versatility and inventiveness that Peter was to demonstrate for the next ninety minutes. Since *Viva Max* was the story of a chaotic Mexican regiment retaking the Alamo, we began with the story of Peter's arrival in Texas.

'The Governor of Texas made a very moving speech when we were all sitting on a bench, in welcoming us, welcoming the film. "I am in favour of satire," he said. "There is no more healthy and wholesome thing than the ability to laugh at ourselves while never for a minute forgetting our greatness."

'Next was a very warm welcome from the Mayor of San Antonio, who again embarrassed me slightly by the effusiveness and warmth of his welcome. We're not used to that, you know. And he said, "I want to welcome these very wonderful . . . deluxe people." And I was very flattered to be a deluxe person. I'd never really thought of myself as comfortable and well-sprung.'

The military background of *Viva Max* led us on to Peter's four and a half years as a private during World War Two. His tales of life in the Royal Sussex Regiment were spot-on: towards the end of the war he had been ordered to write a film of the battle for Europe called *The True Glory*. A commission of five-star generals and admirals had been convened to consider the script. The chairman had announced, 'I have just been with General Eisenhower, and we've decided that since this film is not only for military consumption but also for the general public, we ought to limit our swear words to five, without in any way betraying that wonderful sense of humour. And it has been suggested that the swear words should be apportioned in the following way: two for the British forces, including, naturally, the dominions and the colonies; two for the United States; and one for France.'

This, said Peter, caused an immediate stir. 'A French general got up and said, "You're discriminating against France with the swear words, you will regret this. You are taking advantage of the fact that France is prostrate, occupied, that you are depriving us of the number of swear words we could have." And there was a tremendous scene. The civilian chairman eventually said, "I'm sure that when I talk to General Eisenhower tomorrow, we can reapportion those and make those six swear words instead of five: two for the British Commonwealth; two for the United States and dependent territories; and two, *mon général*, for *la France*."

'There was relative calm until an English admiral got up with the aid of a stick and said, "I want to put it on record that, in the course of a long and not particularly distinguished career, I have never heard such an asinine discussion between grown men. And if this is to be the tone of the conversation, I wish to claim both our swear words for the Royal Navy."'

After more tales of Mexican generals and Italian generals, we moved via a couple of airline anecdotes to another of Peter's great spheres of activity – music. He played the flute and the piano, didn't he?

'I play the flute better without the flute,' he said. 'You know, that's the real trouble. I was told there was a shortage of flutes in the school orchestra, but nature's given me a rather prominent upper lip, and whereas by the end I could usually get the right note, I always got the wrong octave. I was so embarrassed by this, especially in the quiet passages, that I just kept the flute slightly away from my mouth, and went . . .' Peter launched into a perfect thirty-second flute recital without a flute. 'I have a crack at a bassoon occasionally . . .' he added, and then became the perfect bassoon. Next he was a cello, and then 'a badly played cello by a very old man'. He ended his tour of the orchestra by giving us the reed section tuning up. It was quite literally a virtuoso performance.

After a brief sojourn with French opera singers in Algiers and ham actors in the West End of London, I moved Peter on to the subject of cars, another in his armoury of sound effects. Immediately there were the noises of a car that wouldn't start. 'It is much colder tonight, isn't it?' said Peter.

I asked him where the idea of using cars as such a rich source of material had come from.

'I fell in love with cars. I know psychiatrists will have a lot to say about this, but I was a car for a long time,' said Peter. 'I even remember the make – I was an Amil car, which was a small French runaround. That's when I was still of a size to be able to be a small French runaround, and I used to turn myself on in the morning and drive myself round all day long and eventually back into bed at night and switch off. It drove everybody absolutely mad, and I remember my mother having a bad toothache, and she suddenly lost her temper with me – not very often that happened – and she flared up. But her father was there, who was a dear old man, I vaguely remember him, he was the Chairman of the Russian Academy of Architecture. He was shuffling along and he stopped her when she flared up at me and said, "Sshhh, don't do that. It may be irritating, but it's his imagination developing." Rather nice for an old man. I never forgot it, and I stored it up.'

We moved on from cars to New York taxi drivers and then, at my instigation, Peter read an excerpt from one of his plays, *The Unknown Soldier and His Wife*.

After the reading, I mentioned that a tremendous amount of what he had written had been about war. Was it the subject that he felt most strongly about?

'No. I feel more strongly about peace, that's why I write so much about war.'

He had once said, 'We're all on this earth to experience a great adventure.' How would he summarise what his great adventure had been?

'Well, my great adventure is simply that I believe that education doesn't end when you leave school. I wouldn't be where

I am now if I wasn't learning more every day than I learnt at school. I think that we are united by our doubts and divided by our convictions. I think doubts are the most important thing in the world. I never like shutting a window onto any possibility, and therefore I mistrust people who have.'

He had also once said, 'Beware the middle-aged, beware experts, and beware politicians.'

'Oh, well, that I'm absolutely sure of, yes,' said Ustinov.

DF: Beware the middle aged?

Ustinov: Because they're further from the mysteries of birth and death than children or old people.

DF: Beware the experts?

Ustinov: Oh, because they know the subject so well, they don't know it at all – they no longer see it in its context.

DF: And beware politicians?

Ustinov: Oh, well, that's because people who reach the top of the tree are only those who haven't got the qualifications to detain them at the bottom. You can see that all around you.

Peter had once said that he was tempted by politics. Was that still true?

'Well, I think anybody that likes to talk on occasion is. I'm sure you were, too. I have that feeling. But then, I think it would be the wrong thing to do, because I think people like you and I have very, very important duties, simply because we have, perhaps, more freedom than most people. We have more freedom than politicians. We don't have to convince anybody, we don't have to kiss anybody's babies that we don't want to kiss. We don't have to dress up as miners in mining communities or pretend to play the ukulele in the South. We can be absolutely free and we can say more or less what we think. Once you have that capacity of saying what you think, you've got to think what you think, and that's an enormous responsibility, because you can quite easily go haywire with that. But I wouldn't like to forgo it.'

I nodded. I would have been happy to follow up on that, but there was just time to bring up something else he had just mentioned: 'You spoke just now about doubt being important. Another phrase that's very important to a lot of people that they would think conflicted with doubt is the phrase "peace of mind". Do you have peace of mind? Would you want peace of mind?'

'Well, I think doubt is an enormously important ingredient even in peace of mind. You've got to learn to live with it. It's when people talk about insecurity all the time – I wouldn't know how to live without insecurity, personally. I think security is absolute death. Think it over. If we didn't run any risks tonight we might have bored everybody, but I hope we haven't, but that's because we ran a risk. But if we knew we were not going to bore anybody, we wouldn't make any effort at all . . .'

Peter was so right. Taking a risk was sometimes crucial. The risk we had taken could scarcely be described as a death-defying one by motor-racing or mountaineering standards, but in its own modest terms it had still been a risk, and I knew, as I looked back at the decision to turn down a four-year deal at Rediffusion, go to New York for the US TW3, or go for London at the weekends rather than Yorkshire, that they'd all been risks well worth taking. And indeed, I had noticed that resisting challenges like that tended to have a calcifying effect on the individual who had turned them down. Mind you, there is no need to pretend to be a hero just for the sake of it. When you've decided to take the risk, you take out the best possible insurance you can find – like choosing Peter Ustinov for your first ninety-minute interview!

Afterwards, we went next door to Sardi's to celebrate. Thanks to Peter, our new 'product line' was well and truly launched. It would lead on to ninety minutes with Orson Welles, Vice-President Spiro Agnew, Jack Benny, Johnny Carson, Richard Burton and Elizabeth Taylor, and many more; and indeed eventually through the Seventies to 28¾ hours with Richard Nixon and twelve hours with the exiled Shah of Iran.

But that's another story . . .

INDEX

ABC 193, 254, 259
Aberfan 229–30
'About Anglia' 30
Abrams, Steve 306, 308
Acheson, Dean 467–8
ACTT 364, 367–8
Adam, Kenneth 33, 45, 102, 170
Adams, Jack 37
Addams, Dawn 30–1
Addey, John 494, 499
Adler, Larry 212–14
Albert, John 82
Ali, Muhammad 402–9
Allan, Elkan 40–1, 44, 47
Alldritt, Walter 147
Allegro, John 222–4
Allen, Steve 118
Allison, John 301–2
American Federation of Television & Radio Artists 114
Ames, Nancy 115, 131, 133
Amis, Kingsley 366, 438
Anglia Television 23, 30–1
Armitage, Richard 36–7, 86, 112, 264, 440, 442–3
Arts Theatre, Cambridge 29
Ashford, Edward 143
Ashley, Ted 440
Ashley Famous Agency 440, 448
Asquith, Anthony 73
Associated British Picture Corporation 86
Associated-Rediffusion 33, 36, 39–42, 44, 46–8, 87, 188, 195, 220, 254, 262, 265, 278–9, 283, 308, 364, 485
Associated Television 382
Astor, David 170
'At Last the 1948 Show' 283, 286–93
Attenborough, David 33, 277
Attwood, William 336
ATV 254, 286, 363, 381
Ayer, Prof. Freddie 170

Bacharach, Burt 480
Bailey, F. Lee 481
Baker, Peter 205, 413, 445, 447, 457, 494, 521
Bannister, Roger 468
Barclay, Humphrey 32
Barker, Ronnie 168, 177, 182–3, 283, 285, 293, 354, 368, 401, 436–7, 441, 447
Barkham, John 331
Barnard, Christiaan 501
Barnsole Road School 4
Barr, Charles 27
Bart, Lionel 59
Barth, Dr Karl 471
Baverstock, Donald 38–9, 43, 45–8, 50, 57, 74, 87, 105, 107–8, 144, 153, 162, 170, 257, 277
Baveystock, Ernest 202–3
BBC 31, 33, 38, 43, 45–6, 48, 50, 60, 73–4, 76, 94, 100, 102, 109, 117, 120, 124, 141, 147–8, 150, 152, 154, 159, 162, 188, 363, 382, 469, 484
BBC Radio 6, 188–9
Beatles 122, 297, 301–2, 304, 381
Beccles 19, 324, 326
Beccles & Bungay Journal 23, 66
Bell, Jack, 73, 276
Bellwood, Peter 23–5
Benn, Anthony Wedgwood 136, 395
Bennett, Cyril 39–40, 170, 188, 195–6, 220, 237, 265, 267, 269, 271, 277, 279, 281–3, 362, 367, 381, 423, 432, 483, 485
Benson, Tom 170
Berendt, John 449
Bergen, Polly 480
Bernelle, Agnes 83–4
'Best of TW3' 73
Betjeman, John 229, 231–2
Beuselinck, Oscar 415
Bevins, Reginald 61
Beyond the Fringe 37, 91, 163
Bidault, Georges 78
Big Night Out 92
Bird, John 25, 42–3, 91, 139

Birdsall, Timothy 21, 48, 53, 57–8, 90
Birtwell, Celia 191
Bishop, Joey 448
Black, Cilla 172, 438, 468
Black, Peter, 40, 55, 100, 139, 143, 149–50, 275, 368, 387
Blond, Anthony 26–7
Blond, Neville 214
Blue Angel 37–8, 42, 69
Bond, Angela 188, 190
Booker, Christopher 48, 51, 59–60, 63, 71–3, 77, 90, 99, 104, 119, 122, 135–6
Boothroyd, Basil 172
Brabin Report 203
Bradbury, Ray 468
Braham, Beatrice 38
Brahms, Caryl 48, 59, 82, 105, 107
Braine, John 365–6
Bramson, Neal 39
Breslin, Jimmy 336
Brien, Alan 85
Brightwell, George 441
British Council of Churches 208
British Printing Corporation 257
Brittan, Leon 32, 36
Broadsheet 34
Bron, Eleanor 139–40
Brook, Peter 205, 360
Brooke, Henry 49, 77–9
Brooke-Taylor, Tim 32, 285–6, 288
Brophy, Brigid 141
Brothers & The Sisters, The 454
Brown, George 239–44, 315, 320–1, 323, 395
Brown, Helen Gurley 330
Bryan, Carmen 77
Buckley, William 480, 501
Bull, Peter 44
Burnet, Alastair 256, 260–1, 468–9
Burton, Humphrey 256, 260, 267, 280, 485, 487
Burton, Richard 191
Bush, George 357

Cahiers du Cinema 27
Caian, The 35
Caine, Michael 41
Calder, John 524
Callaghan, Jim 395
Cambridge 14–15, 18–36
Caius College 14–15, 19
Cambridge Circus 169
Cambridge Review 31–2
Cameron, James 196
Campbell, Lord 'Jock' 266, 483, 486–7
Campbell, Patrick, Lord Glenavy 138–9, 141, 151, 170–1
Capp, Al 481
Carman, Bob 449
Carson, Johnny 117, 360, 448
Caruso, Dee 124
Casson, Phil 437
Catholic Herald 400, 438
Catling, Patrick Skene 150
Ceylon 163–4
Chafer, Peter 84
Chalfont, Lord 170
Chancellor, Sir Christopher 269
Chapman, Graham 32, 285–6, 288, 440, 445
Chapman, Ian 266
Charles, Don 76
Charles, Prince of Wales 450–3, 460
Chavez, Cesar 508
Cheese, George 14
Christie, John Halliday 203–4
Churchill, Randolph 163, 170, 181, 191–2, 410
Churchill, Winston 411–12
Clark, Bernard 389, 391–2, 394
Clark, Douglas 141
Clark, Ossie 191
Clarke, Kenneth 36
Clayton, Tubby 326
Cleese, John 32, 34, 57, 123, 169, 174–5, 177–8, 182–3, 189, 202–3, 206–7, 283, 285–8, 291, 293, 440, 445, 505
Clore, Charles 260
'Close Up' 44
Cockburn, Claud 139, 143
Collier, Chet 328–30, 337, 358, 360–1, 440–3, 445, 480
Comfort, Alex 209–10
Connell, Brian 40, 450
'Consumers' Guide to Religion' 63–5
Cook, Peter 20, 23–6, 29, 34, 36–7, 42, 53, 91, 440, 445–6, 468
Cooksey, Mr 10, 156, 522
Cooper, Tommy 329
Cope, Kenneth 48, 53, 89–90, 106
Corbett, Ronnie 169, 176, 182–3, 283, 285, 293, 354, 368, 401–2, 436–7, 441
Cordet, Helene 41
Coren, Alan 28
Corn Exchange, Cambridge 26
Cornelius, Albert 384–5
Cotton Jr, Bill 117, 162

Cousins, Frank 199
Coward, Noël 194, 416–22
Cox, Sir Geoffrey 260
Crawford, Michael 140, 154
Crawfurd, Diana 36–7, 86, 112, 121
Crawley, Aidan 256–7, 264–8, 270–1, 273–5, 277–8, 280, 482–3, 486, 488
Crescent & Froebel House School 4
Critchley, Julian 368
Cromie, Bob 331
Crosby, John 252
Crossman, Richard 394
Crowther, Sir Geoffrey 257, 259, 262
Cryer, Barry 119, 168, 188, 190, 285
Cutler, Horace 389–91, 393

Daily Express 11, 69, 93, 102, 104, 141–2, 147, 425
Daily Herald 55, 100, 102
Daily Mail 32, 37, 40, 55, 66–7, 83, 88–9, 100, 139, 149–50, 178, 243, 246, 275, 309–11, 368, 387, 392
Daily Mirror 73, 90, 93, 102, 104, 177, 276, 362
Daily News (New York) 466
Daily Sketch 55, 66–7, 368
Daily Telegraph 60, 66, 96, 130, 138–9, 383, 412, 505
Dankworth, Johnny 213
'David Frost at the Phonograph' 188
'David Frost Presents' 329
'David Frost Show, The' 73, 444–5, 447, 450, 453, 460, 467, 469–82, 525
'David Frost's Night Out in London' 193–5
Davidson, Ian 331
Davie, Donald 22–3
Davis, Ronald 269
Davis Jr, Sammy 380–1, 468
Dayan, Gen. Moshe 369–74, 380
Dead Sea Scrolls 222
'Degree of Frost, A' 117, 119, 121–4, 160, 162
Deighton, Len 163, 170
Denning Report 95, 97
Derby, Lord 280
'Desert Island Discs' 81
'Dick Barton, Special Agent' 441
Dickinson, John 244
Diggory, Mr 512–14
Dillwyn-Venables-Llewellyn, Sir Michael 450
Dobereiner, Peter 56–7, 82–3, 140
Donaldson, Willie 163
Douglas-Home, Robin 163
Driscoll, Julie 368
Drysdale, Bill 34
Duffield, Canon John 65
Dunn, James 147
Dunn, Peter 368

Eade, Peter 402
Eastaugh, Kenneth 177
Easterman, Alex 383
Eastern Daily Press 66, 244
Economist 256–7, 262, 280–1
'Ed Sullivan Show, The' 455
Edinburgh Festival 93, 332
Edrich, Bill 4, 166
Elsom, Cecil 268
Elvin, George 70
Emmett, Bob 114
Enahoro, Chief Anthony 78–9
English, The 330–1
Ephron, Nora 474
Esquire 192
Establishment, The 42–3, 91
Evans, Barbara 139
Evans, Edith 82
Evans, Peter 163, 170
Evans, Timothy 203–5
Evening News 244, 275–6, 362
Evening Standard 130, 153, 158, 163, 243, 277, 436
Evening with David Frost, An 190, 278

Fairley, Peter 468
Fairlie, Henry 143
Faulkner, Alex 130
Fay, Stephen 277
Feldman, Marty 168, 285–6, 288, 290, 292, 438
Felix, Julie 168–9, 174, 179, 180
Felker, Clay 336, 351, 449, 466
Fell, Barbara 58
Financial Times 177, 322–3
Finney, Albert 193–4
Fire, Auto & Marine 244, 246–7, 250
Firth, Tony 32
Fisk, Sir William 269, 274
Flack, Roberta 508
Fonda, Henry 103, 508
Fonda, Jane 44, 515–19
Footlights 19–21, 23, 25, 29, 32–4, 169
Forbes, Bryan 163, 490
Ford, Gerald 506–7
Forte, Charles 58
Fortune, John 34, 140

Foster, Peter 23
Fowler, Norman 36
Fraiberg, Larry 359
Francis, Arlene 330
Franklin, Jim 168, 177
Freeman, John 258–62, 264–5, 447, 488
Freud, Clement 37
Friendly, Ed 156
Frischauer, Willi 383
Frischmann, Walter 389–92
Frost, Jean 3, 6, 17, 446
Frost, Margaret 3, 22
Frost, Mrs Monna 3–4, 5, 17, 18, 179, 325, 326, 469
Frost, Rev. W. J. Paradine 3, 6, 18, 19, 22, 65–6, 324–7, 473
'Frost on Friday' 364–7, 389–94, 396, 402, 423–36, 443, 488, 525
'Frost on Saturday' 364, 367, 381, 384, 395–6, 423, 443, 488, 525
'Frost on Sunday' 367, 381, 401, 436, 443, 525
'Frost Over England' 275
'Frost Programme, The' 188, 195–253, 256, 261, 297–302, 304–24, 330, 360, 494, 521
'Frost, Report, The' 166, 168, 172–88, 195, 257, 278
Fuldheim, Dorothy 331
'Futtock's End' 441

Gaitskell, Hugh 63, 241–2
Galbraith, Thomas 70
Galton, Ray 139, 256, 260
Gardella, Kay 466
Gardiner, Major Dudley 295–7
Gardiner, Vic 483
Gardner, Gerald 114
Garment, Len 340
Gelbart, Larry 189
Gilbert, James 166–8, 170, 176, 180, 276
Gillespie, Robert 63
Gillingham 4, 7–8, 326
Gillingham Grammar School 7–8
Ginsberg, Allen 336
Glasgow Herald 438
Godfrey, Arthur 468
Goldie, Grace Wyndham 45
Goldwater, Barry 134, 353
Goodman, Lord 256, 258, 266
Gould, Jack 446, 479–80
Gourgouras, James 481
Gowers, Mike 244
Grade, Lew 363, 381–2, 422
Graham, Billy 8–9, 87–9, 120–1, 327, 469–73
Grainer, Ron 48
Granada 254, 286, 363–4, 382
Grant, Cary 422
Grant, Elspeth 140
Granta 19, 20–1, 26–8, 31–2
Green, James 275–6
Greene, Sir Hugh 97, 110, 147, 150, 152–4
Greenwood, Anthony 388–9, 391–5
Gregory, Dick 480
Greig, Bill 323
Griffin, Merv 360, 448, 460
Griffiths, Hugh 388
Guardian 68, 174, 322, 401
Guild of Television Producers 104
Guinness, Alec 194
Guinness Book of Records 384–5
Gummer, John 36
Gwynn, Michael 53

Haigh, Kenneth 212–13
Haines, Joe 74
Haley, Bill 12
Hall, Peter 143, 256, 260
Hall, Willis 61, 76, 81
Haney, Paul 468
Hannington, Chris 389, 391
Hansard 74–5
Harding, Gilbert 91
Harringay Arena 8–9
Harris, Martin 450
Harrison, George 297, 299–302
Hatch, David 35
Hayward, Leland 112–14, 116, 119, 126, 131
Healey, Denis 318, 320–3, 395
Heath, Edward 425
Heenan, Cardinal 385, 396–401, 494, 499
Henry, Buck 131–3, 135, 143–4
Hiestand, Ed 448
Higgins, Norman 29
Hill, Jimmy 14, 483
Hill, Lord 256, 258, 260–2, 274, 278–80, 363, 484
Hird, Thora 86
Hoare, Col. Mike 214–19
Hochhuth, Rolf: *Soldiers* 409–14
Hoffer, Eric 330
Hogg, Quintin 220, 222, 305–6, 308, 468
Holmes, Kenneth 16
Holt, Seth 44

Home, Alec Douglas, Lord 98–100, 150–2, 163
Hood, Stuart 50, 93–4, 97–8
Hope, Bob 367
'How to Irritate People' 445
How to Live Under Labour 135–6
Howard, Carina Fitzalan 180
Howard, Michael 36
Howell, David 20, 36
Howerd, Frankie 329
Hudd, Roy 139
Hughes, Geoffrey 229–30, 315, 396, 512
Hughes, Trevor Lloyd 453
Hulbert, Sir Norman 67–8
Humphrey, Hubert 108, 352, 354–7, 359, 387
Hutchison, Alan 34
Hyman, Ken 441

'I Thought I Saw it Move' 34
Idle, Eric 35
Independent Television Authority 221, 254, 261, 263, 265, 267–8, 272, 275, 278–80, 363, 443, 484
India 264–5, 293–7
Irthlingborough Secondary Modern School 15–16
Irving, Clive 141, 162–4, 170, 195, 255, 258, 263, 267, 269, 271–2, 277–8, 383, 432, 443, 482–3
Irving, David 410–15

Jackson, Rev. Jesse 508–11
Jackson, Mahalia 508
Jackson, Martin 102
Jacobi, Derek 32
Jagger, Mick 205, 385–6, 460
Jamieson, Marshall 113
Janner, Sir Barnett 75
Jay, Peter 319–20
Jay, Tony 39, 157, 162, 167–8, 174, 180–1, 195, 281
Jeans, Michael 23, 30
Jenkins, Roy 200, 485
Jensen, Anders 317–18
John, Tom 448
Johnson, Lyndon 107–8, 135, 335, 351, 356–7
Johnson, Paul 365–6
Joice, Dick 30
Jones, Alma 141
Jones, Jack 454–5
Jones, Terry 168, 174
Jones, Tom 401
Jones, Tristram 200
Judge, Frank 195
'Juke Box Jury' 80–1

Karlin, Miriam 213
Kaufman, Gerald 62, 67, 135–6, 139, 141–3
Kavanagh, P. J. 137, 144
Kaye, Solly 314
Keeler, Christine 79–80, 493–5
Kellett, Bob 441
Kempley, Walter 448, 454
Kempston 3–4
Kennedy, Edward 481–2
Kennedy, John F. 104–8, 340, 347–8
Kennedy, Ludovic 203, 210, 212
Kennedy, Robert 335, 346–51, 359, 455
Kernan, David 49, 53, 70, 106
King 163
King, Cecil 170
King, Coretta Scott 509
King, Martin Luther 509
Kinnear, Roy 48, 52, 58–9, 61, 95, 106
Kissinger, Henry 236
Kitchen, Sir Geoffrey 271
Knight, Rae 44
Kraft, Joe 336
Kretzmer, Herbert 67, 104, 107
Kupcinet, Irv 331

Laine, Cleo 139, 213, 466
Lamb, Kenneth 120
Lambton, Tony 163
Lamont, Norman 36
Lang, Harold 44
Lang, Ian 36, 69
Lang, Robert 107
Langdon, Donald 37
La Rue, Danny 195, 380
'Last Laugh' 25
Latta, C. J. 86–7
Law, John 168, 182
Lawson, Nigel 191
Laxton, Vernon 76–7
Lebanon 165–6
Lee, Dave 104, 105
Lehrer, Tom 156, 167–8, 176, 180–1
Leider, Jerry 440
Lennon, John 297, 299–302, 373, 380, 456, 524
Leonard, Rt. Rev. Graham 208–9
Leslie, Desmond 84
'Let's Twist' series 41–2

Levin, Bernard 32, 45, 49, 53, 55, 58, 70, 83, 85, 96, 104, 105, 107, 109–10, 138, 141, 150–1, 153
Lewis, Peter 56–7, 82–3, 139
Lewsen, Charles 63
Liberace 125
Lindsay, John 336
Linstead, Sir Hugh 74
Lipton, Marcus 77
Listener 60
Little Theater, New York 446, 448, 457–8, 490, 508, 515
Llewellyn, Mr 412–13
Lloyd, Selwyn 44
Lockwood, Sir Joseph 170
Logan, Jenny 169, 277, 443, 447
London Television Consortium 273, 275, 277, 280
'London Weekend' 39
London Weekend Television 254, 281–2, 331, 351, 357, 361–3, 368–9, 381–2, 384, 415, 440–3, 468, 482–8
Longford, Lord 147–8, 170, 438
Lord's Taverners 14, 166, 190
Los Angeles Times 467
Lovegrove, Alexander 203–4
Lovell, Sir Bernard 468
Luce, Clare Boothe 490–2
Lynley, Carol 161
Lynn, Jonathan 35
Lyon, Alexander 494, 499–500

Maas, Peter 336, 351
McCarthy, Eugene 332–5, 337, 358, 511
McCarthy, Joseph 345–6
McCartney, Paul 119, 121–2, 170, 189, 299
McCulloch, Ian 251
MacDonald, Aimi 286–7, 291
McGannon, Donald 328, 441–2, 444
McGinnis, Joe 506–8
McGovern, George 511–12
McGrath, Joe 119
McKellen, Ian 32–3
Mackintosh, Lord 176
Macleod, Iain 141, 151, 271
McManus, John 354
MacMichael, Dr Joan 212–14
Macmillan, Harold 61, 97
McMillan, John 46
McNab, Duncan 263
McPeak, Steve 385
McWhirter, Ross & Norris 384–5
Mahesh Yogi, Maharishi 297–300
Mahon, Simon 146–8
'Man on the Moon' 468–9
Mancini, Al 103, 106
Margerison, Tom 266–9, 271, 278, 483, 486–8
Marlborough, Douglas 66
Marples, Ernest 202–3
Marriott, Bryant 55
Marsh, Richard 395
Martin, Geoffrey 95, 122
Martin, George 40, 49, 69
Martin, Millicent 44, 49, 51, 53, 57, 59, 80, 85, 95–6, 102, 139
Maschwitz, Eric 33
Mason, James 480
Mathias, Tim 23
Maxwell, Peter 38
Maxwell, Robert 163, 170
May, Elaine 117, 121, 123
Maye, Marilyn 454
MCA 37
Medical Aid for Vietnam 212–14
Mellish, Robert 220, 222
Melly, George 44
Merende, Doro 115
'Merve Griffin Show, The' 330, 336, 360–1, 444, 446, 455
Methodist Recorder 326
Metromedia 444, 450, 466
Miall, Leonard 33
Michelmore, Cliff 450
Milinaire, Caterine 41
Miller, Henry 82
Miller, Jonathan 141
Miller, William 134
Millichope, Ray 168
Milligan, Spike 75
Milne, Alasdair 38, 45, 50, 56, 97–8, 123, 129, 144, 162
Mitchell, Frank 238
Mitchell, Ray 23
Monico, David 20
Montagu, Hon. David 268–71, 274, 278, 280, 483, 486–7
Montefiore, Canon Hugh 222–4
Montreux Festival 87, 257, 275–7
'Monty Python's Flying Circus' 505
Moore, Dudley 212
Morgan, Henry 114–15
Morley, Peter 40
Morley, Robert 164–4, 197–9
Mortimer, John 301–2
Mosley, Sir Oswald 313–17
Mossman, Jim 143

Muggeridge, Kitty 177
Muggeridge, Malcolm 141
Muir, Frank 119, 122, 268, 281, 363, 367, 436, 483, 487
Murdoch, Rupert 493–501
Murrow, Ed 233, 329
Muskie, Edmund 480

Nabarro, Sir Gerald 81
Nader, Ralph 502–4
Nail, Norman 245, 252
Nardino, Gary 440, 448
Nathan, David 139
National Association of Broadcasters 447
NATKE 368
NBC 103, 108, 116, 127, 133–4, 156, 158, 161
New Bridge, The 190–1
New Statesman 266, 365, 435
New York 91–2, 118, 124, 126
New York magazine 336
New York Post 126
New York Times 116, 118, 133–4, 466, 479
Newcastle Journal 174
Newman, Paul 505
Newman, Phyllis 133
News of the World 93, 425, 493–500
Newsweek 116, 169
Newton, Dwight 482
'Next President, The' 336, 358–9, 387, 508
Nichols, Mike 117, 121, 123
Nicoletti, Aldo 362
Nixon, Richard 340–3, 358, 387, 506–8
'No, That's Me Over Here' 285, 354
Nobbs, David 102–3
Noel Gay Artists 36–8
'Non-Reader's Digest' 21
Norden, Denis 119, 122, 140–1, 189
Norman, Michael 30
Northamptonshire Evening Telegraph 12–13
Northern Despatch 293
'Not So Much a Programme, More a Way of Life' 129, 137–54
Nott, John 36
Nottingham Forest 13–14
Nunn, Trevor 32

O'Brien, Edna 209–10
Observer 10, 35, 85, 252, 266, 280, 393
Oddie, Bill 35, 123
Ofarim, Esther 368
O'Hair, Madalyn Murray 170
Olivier, Laurence 193–4, 410, 421
Ono, Yoko 373, 380, 456, 524
Orkin, Harvey 138, 141
Osborne, Sir Cyril 95–6, 101, 200–2
Osborne, John 10, 154–5
O'Shaughnessy, Alfred 89
Owen, Alun 285
Oxfam 293–4, 296, 324–5
Oxford Opinion 28

Paar, Jack 118
Pack, Dick 167, 328–9
Padmore, Sir Thomas 176
Page, Bruce 382
Paine, Guy 39, 265, 267, 270, 279, 281, 483, 487
Palin, Michael 168
Pallo, Jackie 172
Palmer, Paige 331
Paradise Lost 109–10
Paramor, Norrie 49, 52–3
Parkhurst Prison 190
Parlophone 73
Patrick, Det. Sgt. David 312
Paul VI, Pope 396–7
Peacock, Michael 144, 154, 166, 257, 259–60, 263, 265–7, 270–3, 277–82, 363, 367, 381, 442–4, 482–8
Pearl Assurance 271
Peat Marwick Mitchell 268, 270, 278
People 85, 323, 435
Percival, Lance 44, 49, 52, 59, 70, 106
Percy, Chuck 467
Petro, Dr John 309–13
Pettigrew, James 68–9
Pick, Charles 135–6
Picturegoer 27–8
Pike, Bishop James 483
Pilkington Committee 255–6, 272
Pincus, Walter 334
Pitman, Robert 141–3
'Pop Goes Mrs Jessop' 29
Potter, Dennis 55
Potts, Dr Malcolm 512–14
Powell, Adam Clayton 460–6, 525
Powell, Dilys 140
Powell, Enoch 395–6, 423–6
Prchal, Edward 411–15
Preminger, Otto 161
Private Eye 457
'Profile of a Programme Company' 30
Profumo affair 79–80, 89–90, 95, 493–500

Punch 94, 143, 150, 172
Purser, Philip 233, 237

Queen 37, 50
'Queen for a Day' 118–19

Ramsey, Dr Michael 223–9
Raunds 9, 13, 16
Ray, Ted 368, 380
Rayfield, Tom 31
Rayne, Max 258
Read, Al 92
Reader's Digest 21, 121
Reagan, Ronald 336–40, 358
Redgrave, Corin 33
Redgrave, Lynn 194
Redhead, Brian 43
Rediffusion *see* Associated-Rediffusion
Reed, Rex 474, 476
Reid, David 33–4
Reid, Elliott 113, 115
Renfrew, Colin 32, 49
Reynolds, Jonathan 449
Rise and Rise of Michael Rimmer, The 441, 455
Robbins, Denise 82
Robinson, David 140
Robinson, Rt. Rev. John 208–9, 468, 472
Rockefeller, Nelson 352–4
Rockwell, George Lincoln 78
Romney, George 331
Ronan Point 387–90, 392–4
'Ronnie Barker Playhouse, The' 285, 354, 447
Rose, Kenneth 171
Ross, Annie 139, 154, 212–13
Ross, Charles 75
Roth, Andrew 74
Royal Court Theatre Club 37, 42
Rush, Herman 112
Rushton, Willie 51, 53, 102, 106, 137, 144
Russell, Bertrand 522–3
Ryan, Cate 448, 454, 458, 480
Ryan, Nigel 432, 468–9

Salmon, Lord Justice 251–2
Salter, Lionel 33
San Francisco Examiner 482
Sands, Eileen 197
Sandys, Duncan 424
Sapper, Alan 368
Sargent, Herb 131, 135–6
Saturday Review 331
Savundra, Dr Emil 244–53
Schirach, Baldur von 373–80, 383–4
Schlatter, George 156
Scott, Janette 80–1, 86, 112, 114, 117, 128–31, 157
'See You Inside' 75
Sellers, Peter 193, 380–1
Selway, Mary 213
Senaratna, Cedric 165
Setty, Max 38, 69
Shaffer, Peter 70
Shand, Neil 168, 188, 445–7, 465, 468, 521
Shapiro, Helen 52, 55
Shaw, Robert 143
Shea, George Beverly 88
Sheehy, Gail 466
Sherrin, Ned 38–9, 42–4, 46–51, 54–5, 66, 76, 87, 90, 93–4, 98, 104, 123, 129, 137, 148–9, 151–2, 155, 159–60, 194
Show 90
Shrapnel, Norman 68
Shulman, Milton 153
Sikorski, Gen. 409–14
Silverman, Sidney 68
Silvey, Robert 74
Simon, John 474–9
Simon, Owen 444
Simone, Nina 401
Simpson, Alan 139, 256, 260
Sington, Brian 293
Slade, Adrian 19
Slipper and the Rose, The 490
Sloane, Tom 117, 162, 166
Smith, Cecil 466–7
Smith, Ian 220–1, 233–7, 381
Smith's Trade News 26
Snead, Sam 237–8
Soblen, Dr Robert 78
Soper, Lord 170
Sorensen, Ted 481–2
Spackman, George 307
Spectator 90, 104, 153, 191, 266, 365
Spicer, Joanna 45
Spock, Dr Benjamin 469
Stage, The 38
Stamp, Terence 41
Stassen, Harold 332–3
Steafel, Sheila 168
Steele, Tommy 466
Stein, Sol 330–1
Steinem, Gloria 131
Stephens, Doreen 268, 281, 487
Stern, Harold 127

Stevas, Norman St John 49, 141, 146, 400, 438
Stockwood, Dr Mervyn 438–9
Stokes, Sir Donald 263, 266–70
Strand 37
Strasberg, Susan 336
Streisand, Barbra 126
Stutter, John 442
Sullivan, Ed 454–5, 460
Summerfield, Peter 496
Sun 46, 153, 173, 220
Sunday Express 32–3, 62–3, 141
Sunday Mirror 222, 245–6
Sunday Pictorial 8, 68, 81
Sunday Telegraph 54–5, 151, 171, 233, 237
Sunday Times 41, 95, 154–5, 171, 177, 199, 246, 251, 255, 266, 277, 368, 381–2, 414, 422, 485
Susann, Jacqueline 474–8
Swingle Singers 121, 123
Symington, Stuart 470

Tarbuck, Jimmy 14
Taylor, A. J. P. 468
Taylor, Billy 450
Taylor, John Russell 140
Tenterden 3
Thames Television 383, 484
'That Was The Week That Was' 43–50, 51–111, 144
  American version 103, 112–18, 124–7, 131, 133–4, 143, 156
'This is Your Life' 16
'This Week' 39–40
Thomas, Howard 383
Thorn, Sir Jules 256, 267, 269–70
Thorndike, Dame Sybil 105, 107
Tiger, Lionel 458–9
Tillstrom, Burr 115, 122, 156
Time 192
Time and Tide 30
Times, The 67, 102, 148, 221–2, 252, 280, 304, 319, 323, 363, 366, 368, 382, 397
Tinniswood, Peter 102–3
'To Ask Why Not . . .' 455
To England With Love 185, 330–1
'Today Show' 330
Tomalin, Nicholas 141, 143, 382, 423
'Tonight' 38–9, 48
'Tonight Show' 117, 330, 360
Torme, Mel 157
'Touch of Frost, A' 447
'Town & Gown' 33–5, 520
Tracey, Michael 110
Truesdell, Rev. Robert 480
Tshombe, Moise 215
Turner, Sue 33, 39
TV Guide 482
TV Times 435
Tynan, Kenneth 35, 98, 140, 410–11, 414–16

United States 91–2, 103, 112–18, 128–9, 134, 157, 328–61
Ustinov, Peter 525–30

Vadim, Roger 516, 518–19
Valente, Caterina 401
Vanderbilt, Jeanne 449
Vanocur, Sandy 505
Variety 134
Varsity 20–1, 32
Vassall, William 70
Vidal, Gore 200–2
Vinaver, Stephen 49, 53, 59
VIPs, The 73
Vosburgh, Dick 168, 188

Wade, Donald 75
Wagner, Richard 280
Walden, Brian 305, 307–8
Walinksy, Adam 501
Wallace, George 342–6, 387, 407
Wallace, Mike 330
Wallace, Warren 331, 346, 349, 354
Waterhouse, Keith 61, 76, 81
Watson, Irwin C. 96
Webster, Donald 145
Weidenfeld, George 266
Weinstock, Arnold 266–9, 271, 281, 483
Welch, Raquel 490–2
Welles, Orson 73
Wellingborough Grammar School 9–11, 13, 16, 522
Wells, Dee 102, 146, 153
Wells, John 140
Wesker, Arnold 76–7
Western Mail 141
Westinghouse Broadcasting 167, 328–30, 337, 360–1, 440–5, 460, 465
Weston Super Mare 92
'What the Public Wants' 46
Wheldon, Hugh 144
Whitehouse, Mary 385–7, 438
Wigg, George 80, 318
Wiggin, Maurice 199, 249

Wilcox, Desmond 40
'Wiley, Gerard' 401–2, 436–7
Willesden, Bishop of 208–9
Williams, Kenneth 368
Williams, Pat 54
Williams, S. G. 74
Williamson, Nicol 194
Willis, Ted 76, 256, 270
Wills, John Spencer 278–9
Wilson, Angus 50, 90
Wilson, Charles 32
Wilson, Dr Grady 8
Wilson, Harold 71, 101, 170, 172, 233–4, 242, 318–20, 323, 395, 453, 456, 484
Wilson, Mary 456–7
Winters, Shelley 501
Wood, David 323–4
Wood, John *see* Fortune, John
Wood, Natalie 508
Woolf, Robert 75
Woolwich, Bishop of 208–9, 212, 225–6
Wootton, Baroness 524
Worsley, T. C. 177
Wrenn, H. A. 22
Wynn, Prof. Victor 512–15

'Year In and Year Out' 170
Yorkshire Post 256, 259
Yorkshire Television 382
Young, B. A. 94
Young, Katherine 158

This is Orson Welles

Orson Welles and Peter Bogdanovich

This is the book that Welles ultimately considered his autobiography, but it's a memoir like no other. At once accessible, entertaining and revealing, Welles and Bogdanovich's collaboration is an unforgettable collection of penetrating, fascinating and often hilarious conversations undertaken over many years, on both sides of the Atlantic. With *This is Orson Welles* the master illusionist and self-confessed 'faker', in his own words, 'puts the record straight'.

'The Art of Bogdanovich's interrogation conceals itself in the ease of good friends talking, yet it elicits from Welles answers which show us his position and his character under the arc-light thrown upon them by his brilliant tongue . . . Such humorous charm is captivating' Philip Glazebrook, *Spectator*

'This is a book you must beg, borrow or steal . . . Welles pulls no punches: reading it is like being a privileged guest at his table, savouring that inimitable voice, as the pearls drop in abundance'
Bryan Forbes, *Mail on Sunday*

'Fascinating. A treasure-trove of insights' John Lahr

'Welles at his roaring best' *New York Times Book Review*

ISBN 0 00 638232 0

Laurence Olivier

A Biography

Donald Spoto

'Rivetingly interesting, admirably researched and exquisitely written – an altogether wonderful book' Sir John Gielgud

'A work of subtle critical insight, warm, human, and always highly readable' *New Statesman*

In the first biography of Laurence Olivier to appear since his death, Donald Spoto reveals the man behind the mask of the flamboyant, heroic actor. Based on meticulous research and many previously unpublished documents, this is the first full portrait of our greatest man of the theatre.